Curriculum

Alternative Approaches, Ongoing Issues

THIRD EDITION

Colin J. Marsh
CURTIN UNIVERSITY

George Willis
UNIVERSITY OF RHODE ISLAND

Merrill
Prentice Hall

Upper Saddle River, New Jersey
Columbus, Ohio

Library of Congress Cataloging-in-Publication Data

Marsh, Colin J.
   Curriculum : alternative approaches, ongoing issues / Colin J. Marsh, George Willis.—
   3rd ed.
      p.   cm.
   Includes bibliographical references and indexes.
   ISBN 0-13-094512-9 (casebound)
   1. Education—United States—Curricula. 2. Curriculum planning—United States.
   3. Curriculum evaluation–United States.   4. Curriculum change—United States.   I. Willis,
   George,   II. Title.

LB1570 .M3667   2003

                                                        2001058728

Vice President and Publisher: Jeffery W. Johnston
Executive Editor: Debra A. Stollenwerk
Editorial Assistant: Mary Morrill
Assistant Editor: Daniel J. Parker
Production Editor: Kimberly J. Lundy
Production Coordinator: Carlisle Publishers Services
Designer Coordinator: Diane C. Lorenzo
Cover Designer: Rod Harris
Production Manager: Pamela D. Bennett
Director of Marketing: Ann Castel Davis
Marketing Manager: Krista Groshong
Marketing Services Coordinator: Tyra Cooper

This book was set in New Baskerville by Carlisle Communications, Ltd., and was printed
and bound by R.R. Donnelley & Sons Company.

Pearson Education Ltd.
Pearson Education Australia PTY, Limited
Pearson Education Singapore Pte. Ltd.
Pearson Education North Asia Ltd.
Pearson Education Canada, Ltd.
Pearson Educaión de Mexico, S. A. de C.V.
Pearson Education—Japan
Pearson Education Malaysia, Pte. Ltd.
Pearson Education, *Upper Saddle River, New Jersey*

Preface

ABOUT THIS BOOK

Every educator has general ideas about what a curriculum is, for every educator understands that a good classroom is a place that systematically provides desirable activities that students otherwise might not undertake. But how do these activities come about? What should they be like? What kind of educational content should they entail? Why, from the virtually limitless number of possibilities, are some activities chosen while others are not? Who, in fact, does the choosing? On what basis? How can what is most valuable about these activities become internalized by students? Such questions are among the many fundamental curriculum questions that can and should be asked, for they deal with how planning takes place for education intended to enrich the lives of students, how those plans are translated into practical classroom realities, and how those realities are experienced at the deepest personal levels. Indeed, perhaps the most basic assumption we make throughout this book is that the curriculum is not well understood as a single thing. Rather, it is better understood as a composite of what is intended for the classroom (the planned curriculum), of what happens in the classroom (the enacted curriculum), and of how what happens in the classroom influences individuals (the experienced curriculum). One reason why we have written this book is to help readers uncover and clarify for themselves the complex nature of curriculum.

We make two other closely related assumptions as well. One is that the most desirable educational experiences tend to arise when there is flexibility in translating plans into actions. In other words, we believe that teachers need the ability to modify plans about what should take place in order to maximize the benefits of what does take place. Teachers find that, in any classroom, the specifics of the educational situation change minute by minute for all participants. What is good for one student at a particular time and in a particular place may not be equally good at a different time and place. Even when something is unequivocally good for one student, it is seldom equally good for all other students. (The ability of teachers to deal flexibly with such classroom complexities depends not only on their own deep understanding of fundamental curriculum questions, but also on the expectations of those to whom they are responsible [students, parents, other teachers, administrators, the public] that such flexibility is necessary for the highest quality education.) A second reason why we have written this book is to point out why such curricular flexibility is desirable.

Our other related assumption is that there are no single answers to fundamental curriculum questions. In fact, there are no easy answers at all. Our own approach in this book is, therefore, not to advocate the "best" or "most correct" answers to such questions but to identify and critically assess a full range of plausible answers that have been or can be offered.

A third reason why we have written this book is to help readers make their own informed choices about answering curriculum questions and thus to help them proceed with intelligent, well-grounded, and effective curriculum work. In writing a book that presents major theoretical and practical alternatives and invites readers to experience the dialectical tensions involved in choosing among them, we have attempted not to be advocates for any one alternative. In this sense, we think the book is consistent with perhaps the most important general trend in education (known by various names, such as constructivism, deconstructionism, and postmodernism), a trend toward not imposing definitive meanings on readers (or students) but toward encouraging them to find their own meanings and to develop their own carefully considered points of view in response to a book (or a curriculum). Nonetheless, readers should be aware that we hold our own point of view and, of course, have written from it. In general, we express that point of view increasingly directly and fully as we proceed through the book, and readers should find that it becomes increasingly clear.

■ THIS BOOK AND YOU

Although there are numerous ways to approach curriculum questions and issues, we have centered the book on the practical process of curriculum development. We have attempted to write a book that conventionally outlines the process but also addresses its underlying tensions from the perspective of those people who actually engage in making decisions about curriculum. Thus, we give considerable attention to questions about how the curriculum is experienced, but we have transposed them from the experience of students, refocusing them on the experience of curriculum developers themselves. In effect, we ask readers to become students of the broad process of curriculum development, learning about it in conventional ways but also considering it in terms of how it ultimately must be experienced, replete with all the underlying problems, tensions, ambiguities, and uncertainties unavoidable by those people—mostly teachers—who are fully engaged in it.

We hope the book works dialectically on two levels: the public level of directly providing information about, and analysis of, the process of curriculum development, and the private level of indirectly providing insight about personal experience with such work. We have intended the book primarily for teachers (and prospective teachers), the people who actually make (or will make) specific curriculum decisions for individual classrooms, but it should also be useful for teachers, administrators, and any other educational professionals who participate in making collective curriculum decisions for schools or school districts.

While attempting to engage readers in a personal dialogue in which they continuously weigh alternative approaches to curriculum and the ongoing issues that these alternatives entail, and through which they can carefully consider how choices can be made among alternatives, we have, nonetheless, attempted to be reasonably economical in the presentation of material. Beginning with Caswell and Campbell (1935) and ranging to Schubert (1986) and more recent books, a number of "synoptic texts" (to use the phrase coined by Schubert) have been written about curriculum. These are big, encyclopedic books that have endeavored to provide professional educators with comprehensive, state-of-the-art knowledge about virtually everything related to curriculum as both an area of practical work and an area of research and scholarship. Such books in themselves often constitute entire curriculum courses, particularly for aspiring specialists undertaking doctoral studies.

Our aim for this book is more modest; we have not attempted to provide everything. Instead, we have attempted to convey to readers what is most fundamental—perhaps even essential—about the broad process of curriculum development, including the alternative theoretical concerns and practical approaches that must be faced by people engaged in making curriculum decisions, and the basic issues that always surround such decisions. But we attempt to do so in a form that permits the book to be supplemented within a single course by additional readings or activities (many of which, we hope, the book suggests) appropriate for the specific students within that course. Therefore, we have also intended the book to be usable as a basic text within virtually any curriculum course but not to be a full course in and of itself. It deliberately leaves open to people who use it much of what planning, enacting, and experiencing a curriculum are about.

■ ORGANIZATION

Despite our emphasis throughout the book on the process of making practical curriculum decisions and on the dialectical tensions that underlie this process, we believe good practical decisions about curriculum are carefully grounded in clear and well-informed thought. Planning with precision while maintaining the flexibility to modify that plan in practice requires constantly weighing and then choosing among alternative courses of action, which, in turn, requires accurate understanding of what each alternative entails and what consequences flow from it. Our plan of organization for the book reflects this belief.

The first four chapters focus on the ideas and information that provide the background we think most basic to understanding the nature of curriculum itself and making decisions about it. This background provides a framework for readers to use in considering the alternative approaches and issues that the book presents and that educational professionals constantly deal with in practice. Chapter 1, "The Character of Curriculum," introduces readers to the underlying nature of curriculum. It does so primarily by identifying some alternative definitions of the term *curriculum* and different problems these alternatives entail. Chapter 2, "Curriculum History," describes how such problems and alternatives have been treated at different times within the history of curriculum within the United States. In particular, it describes nineteenth-century origins and twentieth-century conflicts among subject-centered, person-centered, and society-centered conceptions of curriculum, suggesting how these conflicts shape approaches to curriculum development today. Chapter 3, "Approaches to Curriculum," describes and analyzes three exemplary approaches to curriculum planning and development, pointing out similarities and differences. Chapter 4, "Curriculum Theorizing," focuses specifically on different approaches to curriculum that have become sufficiently refined since the 1960s so that they now represent organized bodies of thought about curriculum development supported by systematic research and scholarship. This chapter describes in detail three of these highly refined approaches, pointing out how such approaches have influenced curriculum decision making in recent decades.

The next four chapters are focused directly on the process of developing curricula. These chapters consider the process broadly and describe basic approaches to practical curriculum work itself. Chapter 5, "Curriculum Development and Change," examines the various individuals and groups participating in curriculum development, how they can function as cooperating or competing interests, and how and why changes in a curriculum can occur in schools. Chapter 6, "Curriculum Planning: Levels and Participants," differentiates among the planning of policies, programs, and lessons. It then explores how teachers, principals, parents, students, and external facilitators usually participate in planning. Chapter 7, "Curriculum Implementation," looks at what happens to a written curriculum as it is translated into classroom practices. This chapter considers what seems to be most critical in curriculum implementation, especially in light of what recent research both says and leaves unsaid about good strategies and tactics, and it describes some common approaches that have been used in schools to support the process of implementation. Chapter 8, "Curriculum Evaluation and Student Assessment," identifies how evaluation underlies ongoing curriculum development and change, explains how evaluating curricula and assessing student learning are related, describes some widely used techniques, and provides short illustrative case studies of four basic approaches to curriculum evaluation.

While the first eight chapters discuss the most basic issues underlying careful thought about curriculum, practical curriculum work, and the dialectical tensions involved, chapter 9, "Politics and Curriculum Decision Making," looks at curriculum directly in terms of the major issues that arise from the nature of curriculum decision making itself and from the external pressures exerted by society on such decisions. It describes what happens when disagreements arise about curriculum planning and development; discusses influences on curriculum decision makers from society and from political issues at local, state, and federal levels of government; and considers questions concerning who controls the curriculum, on what basis, and for what purposes, especially examining the implications of recent trends toward centralized decision making.

NEW TO THIS EDITION

For this, the third edition, we have modified the plan of the book, reversing the order of chapters 2 and 3 and thus placing our introductory examples of major approaches to curriculum after a description of the historical context in which they exist. Throughout the book, we have deleted some dated material and updated and added new material. Specifically, in chapter 1 we have added three new definitions of curriculum, and in chapter 4 we reorganized the categories under which various curriculum theorizers and their approaches are classified. Also in chapter 4 are new discussions of postmodernism, autobiographical methods, gender, and race. We now discuss comprehensive school reform in chapter 7 and charter schools in chapter 9. In many places throughout the book there is increased attention to constructivism, the use of new technology (such as computers and the Internet), and the influence of national and state standards on such things as accountability and high-stakes testing of students.

AN INTERNATIONAL COMMUNITY

Finally, readers might wish to bear in mind that although this book has been written for publication and distribution primarily in the United States—and thus the historical, social, and political contexts for schooling that it describes are specifically American—we believe we have still written it from an international perspective. Readers will note that references and citations are not only to practical and theoretical work in curriculum undertaken in the United States, but also in Australia, the United Kingdom, Canada, and—to a lesser extent—several other nations. There are limitations, of course, on our familiarity with curriculum work worldwide, but in this book, we have made a conscious effort to bring together the best and the most comprehensive thinking from an international community of curriculum scholars and researchers that is currently available in the English language. Despite the cultural differences that exist in schools in different nations, most of the work cited transcends national boundaries, we think, and has wide applicability to what is most basic about classrooms anywhere and about the process of curriculum development. We hope the international scope of the references cited will increase both the appeal of the book and its value for many readers.

ACKNOWLEDGMENTS

We gratefully acknowledge the following reviewers of this edition: David Adams, Cleveland State University; Bonnie M. Beyer, University of Michigan-Dearborn; Elizabeth Heilman, Purdue University; Daniel G. Mulcahy, Central Connecticut State University; Warren Schollaert, Armstrong Atlantic State University; and Kay W. Terry, Western Kentucky University.

Unfortunately, we cannot acknowledge all of the hundreds of professional colleagues who have made direct or indirect contributions to the creation of this book; however, our special gratitude goes to Paul Klohr, Ken Stafford, John S. Mann, and John B. Walton.

References

Caswell, H. L., & Campbell, D. S. (1935). *Curriculum development.* New York: American Book Company.

Schubert, W. H. (1986). *Curriculum: Perspective, paradigm, and possibility.* Upper Saddle River, NJ: Merrill/Prentice Hall.

Brief Contents

Contents

3   APPROACHES TO CURRICULUM   66

4   CURRICULUM THEORIZING   93

7 CURRICULUM IMPLEMENTATION   231

The Character of Curriculum

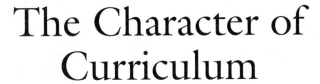

■ ABOUT THIS CHAPTER

Making decisions about curriculum includes considering what the curriculum should be, how it can be enacted in the classroom, and how students might experience it. There is no one correct way to do curriculum planning since making decisions about curriculum entails certain individuals or groups defining what is desirable and attempting to realize what is achievable in diverse human lives. Hence, planning the curriculum or making other decisions about it is always problematic; plans should be flexible enough to take advantage of the differences that inevitably arise between what is initially planned for enactment in the classroom and what actually happens there. This is even more the case with the growth of computer technology and the Internet.

In light of these ideas about the fundamental character of curriculum, this chapter will examine various definitions of the term *curriculum* and some implications that follow from them. We suggest, further, why most curriculum decisions include many different people with different points of view and why teachers normally occupy positions central to making such decisions.

The chapter concludes with a brief description of the topics discussed in subsequent chapters.

■ WHAT YOU SHOULD DO

1. Consider why it is or is not possible to create an eclectic and encompassing definition of the term *curriculum*.
2. Consider and carefully weigh alternative definitions of *curriculum* and the implications these definitions hold for schools, teachers, and students.
3. Build upon one or more of the definitions to develop a definition that encapsulates your own values and preferred approach to curriculum planning and development.

◼ SOME OPTIONAL APPROACHES

You may find it useful to consider this introduction to curriculum in terms of the following options.

Option A

1. Begin by considering the term *curriculum* and what people mean by it. What does the term mean to you? Why do you find your meaning of the term preferable to other meanings? What does your preference suggest about how you should conduct a classroom?
2. By suggesting that the curriculum is not a single thing but something multiple and continuously changing that includes the planned curriculum, the enacted curriculum, and the experienced curriculum, the chapter indirectly suggests numerous opportunities and numerous problems that present themselves to people, such as teachers, who make curriculum decisions. Carefully think through as many of these opportunities and problems as possible.
3. Ask yourself how much the curriculum varies among schools with which you are familiar. If there is much variance, why does it occur? How? How much variance is acceptable? Who decides?

Option B

1. Consider this chapter in light of the "hidden curriculum" (those parts of the environment that influence the experience of students but that either are not accounted for or cannot be accounted for in curriculum planning). Which is the more powerful influence on what students experience in schools: the planned curriculum or the hidden curriculum? Which hidden or unplanned parts of the environment seem to have the most powerful influence on students? Why?
2. What problems does the hidden curriculum pose for curriculum developers and for teachers? What opportunities does it present to teachers? How much flexibility should a curriculum plan have to permit a classroom teacher to take advantage of such opportunities? How would you take advantage of such opportunities?
3. Which of the alternative definitions of *curriculum* presented in the chapter permits a curriculum decision maker to consider the hidden curriculum? Which definitions do not? How do such differences influence your own preferred definition?

1.1   INTRODUCTION

The term *curriculum* (and its many synonyms) is used in numerous situations by people who believe they know its meaning. After all, even when used very loosely, the term seems to refer to whatever means are deliberately undertaken to achieve desirable ends, such as specific goals or standards. For example, the curriculum for a basketball team might include physical strength and endurance training, drills on specific skills, strategy sessions, and pep talks, all intended to increase the team's ability to win basketball games. Even when specific ends are not so easily defined, a curriculum may still be followed, as when parents undertake the care of their children, providing daily hygiene, food and shelter, and extended love, support, and discipline.

When the term *curriculum* is applied to what is done in schools, however, numerous difficulties may arise. On the one hand, everybody seems to know what schools should teach. In most of the developed nations of the world, there are few adults who have not experienced at least eight years of elementary and secondary schooling themselves, and many have experienced far more. On the other hand, there is almost never complete agreement about what the curriculum of the schools should be. This lack of agreement often results in confusion and frustration. In recent years the growth of the Internet has heightened such confusion. Now, with millions of Internet web pages and interactive educational sites available to students, the scope of the curriculum may vastly exceed what schools themselves can provide, and some authors predict that more and more of the curriculum will be studied by students in their own homes (Vine, Brown, & Clark, 2000).

Parents with children in school and who have strong views about what the curriculum should be may express those views directly to principals or teachers. Many other individuals from throughout society often make their own views known. From time to time, parents associations, the business community, trade unions, political parties, religious groups, and many other organizations firmly express collective views about the kind of learning children should obtain in schools. Whether individual or collective, these views inevitably vary depending upon the specific value orientations that underlie them. Should a curriculum emphasize the acquisition of factual knowledge, or the solving of societal problems, or the development and stimulation of individual talents? Which emphasis is the best? Should schools concentrate on the mastery of subject matter or the development of inquiry? Figure 1.1 lists just a few of the myriad basic questions commonly asked about the school curriculum.

1. What should count as knowledge? What types of knowledge are essential? Who decides what should count?
2. Who should control the selection and distribution of knowledge? What social and political forces influence curriculum?
3. Who should be involved in ensuring that a curriculum has a sense of unity, relevance, pertinence, and purpose? Are some of these attributes diametrically opposed?
4. How is the curriculum best organized? Can there be multiple forms of organization for the curriculum? Who is responsible for deciding? Who is responsible for doing the organizing?
5. Why do changes in curriculum take place? What influences from society lead to curriculum change? Who are the major change agents?
6. When has learning taken place? How can schools assess whether the goals of curriculum are being reached? Who should be responsible for evaluation? Who should be involved in collecting the information?

FIGURE 1.1
Some basic questions commonly asked about curriculum

But even when the people engaged in deciding on the curriculum of a specific school have similar value orientations, consensus usually remains difficult—if not impossible—to achieve. Why should this be the case? (This is perhaps the most elusive curriculum question of all!) The answer can be illustrated by a remark once made by a venerable and, we think, unusually wise educator of our acquaintance. What his long career, first as a teacher, then as a school administrator, and finally as a scholar of education had taught him about good classroom practice could be reduced, he said, to one central maxim: "precision in planning, flexibility in execution." He was not denigrating the other basic things that he insisted also go into good teaching, such as an intrinsic love of learning and the philanthropic desire to pass the superior aspects of culture on to succeeding generations. However, his remark captured the inescapable tension that underlies all classroom practice wherever classrooms exist and that is at the heart of making decisions about curriculum: a good classroom systematically provides desirable activities that students otherwise might not undertake, but in order to transform these activities into the highest-quality, most educative experiences for students, the classroom always needs to be able to take advantage of the not entirely foreseeable contingencies and opportunities that inevitably arise in human lives.

Such contingencies and opportunities might be the changing needs and interests of individual students, their different learning styles, the teacher's discovery of new ideas or materials, the community's growing insistence that the school educate students about emerging problems in society, or any number of far more pressing or far more mundane concerns. Inevitably, however, gaps arise among the curriculum that is planned for the classroom, the curriculum that is enacted in the classroom, and the curriculum that individuals experience in the classroom. Thus, the curriculum is never a single thing, and it never remains static. The answer to the puzzling and often frustrating question of why consensus about curriculum is so difficult to achieve follows from the hard truth that most people involved in curriculum deliberations fail to consider fully its essential, multiple, and dynamic character. Thus, each person may see only a small part (and not necessarily the same part) of the changing overall picture and insist that part is all there is to see.

Making decisions about curriculum, therefore, is understood better as an exercise in exploring and understanding alternative possibilities than as an exercise in reaching consensus by excluding alternatives. There is no single curriculum question upon which everyone must agree. Instead, at the most basic level there are three kinds of questions to be asked, and these deal, respectively, with the planned curriculum, the enacted curriculum, and the experienced curriculum. All three kinds should be considered carefully. The first kind of question focuses on what the planned curriculum should be in the first place and is, as originally stated in the nineteenth century by Herbert Spencer, What knowledge is of most worth? Some contemporary books on curriculum approach the subject as if this were the only question to be asked, suggesting that a correct answer (which they variously give) can be uncovered and that this answer becomes the planned curriculum that should be taught and learned in all classrooms.

The second kind of curriculum question focuses on the process of deciding what the curriculum should be. This process also deals with planning, but it is the planning of enactment. There is no one form this kind of question usually takes, but it can be stated as, How should the curriculum be developed? Considered broadly, the process of curriculum development includes not only planning what the curriculum should be but planning how it can be implemented, evaluated, and changed.

Most contemporary books approach curriculum in terms of this second question. Few of these books assume that there is a single curriculum that should be planned for enactment in all classrooms. Most such books suggest that the curriculum is subject to change as society changes, as the specific characteristics of the students for whom the curriculum is intended change, or as knowledge itself changes. In addition, most also assume that the comprehensive process of scrutinizing the nature of society, students, and subject matter—however complicated—should follow certain steps and is therefore fundamentally rational and knowable. Often the appeal of such books lies in the apparent objectivity of the methods they present. But these books, too, may misrepresent the fundamental character of curriculum in suggesting that, although the enacted curriculum is subject to change, decisions about it can be made in essentially nonproblematic ways. Atkinson (2000) argues that a postmodernist perspective requires participants in curriculum decision making to treat all planning as problematic, questioning what seems authoritative in order to obtain release from certainties.

The third kind of curriculum question focuses on the curriculum as it is experienced. When stated in the form of "how should the curriculum be experienced?," the question is amenable to answer by books (perhaps the most historically notable of which is Dewey's *Experience and Education,* 1938) that describe criteria for assessing the quality of student experiences. However, when stated in the form of "how is the curriculum experienced?," this kind of question is not amenable to a final answer at all. To be experienced, the curriculum must first be enacted, and this cannot be done in a book about curriculum, only in the classroom itself. Furthermore, in its fullest and deepest character, experience is individual, ongoing, and unpredictable. To be sure, the approach of some curriculum books includes presenting guidelines for surveying some of what students collectively or individually experience in classrooms, but few adequately account for the radical character of lived experience since lived experience defies complete description either before or after it happens.

In light of this introductory discussion of the most basic character of curriculum, we ask readers to consider engagement with it not as an attempt to provide closure on issues such as what the curriculum should be, how it should be developed, or how it will be experienced. We believe that single answers are neither desirable nor possible. While the broad process of curriculum development is not irrational or unknowable, neither is it ever nonproblematic, especially for those people engaged in it. There are too many alternatives in curriculum matters when it comes to "precision in planning, flexibility in execution." Not only do gaps arise, but gaps *should* arise among the planned, the enacted, and the experienced curriculum. This book is an attempt to help you explore alternative approaches to curriculum, consider the various consequences that flow from them, and develop your own thoughtful point of view to use in making practical curriculum decisions.

Although characterizing the field of curriculum can seem as difficult as attempting to nail Jell-O to a wall (Wright, 2000), we believe that the field is neither fundamentally chaotic and ill-defined (MacPherson, 1995) nor moribund (Schwab, 1970). Rather, it is possible to delineate "groups of curriculum workers who share persistent values and belief systems, consistently address some fundamental themes and issues in education, and identify similar tasks or decisions to be made and the appropriate people to make them" (Klein, 1990, p. 4). Thus, the question of who is to make decisions about the curriculum always arises. The position we take in this book is that the overall process of planning and developing the curriculum (including implementation, evaluation, and change) is usually best undertaken cooperatively by those people who have a perceived stake in the outcome, from educational officials, to students and parents, to members of the community, but that the persons most interested and best-equipped to do so are the professionals closest to classrooms: the teachers. They possess the expertise acquired by advanced studies extending over four or five years, and they have continual opportunities to analyze and reconsider their knowledge and beliefs in light of interaction with students in real classroom situations. Most important, teachers are the persons who enact the curriculum; therefore, their professional role is to span the gaps between the planned curriculum and the curriculum actually experienced by their students. They are the educational professionals who live closest to the underlying tensions involved in curriculum work and who have the most at stake in understanding what curriculum development actually entails and how it influences them and the students in their classrooms. This book attempts to speak directly to teachers (and prospective teachers) and help them make sense of the process of curriculum planning and development, a process that often feels chaotic and frustrating even to people experienced with it.

Despite the central role of teachers in curriculum development, their freedom to make professional judgments on curriculum is not without limits. They are constrained by things such as traditions, state laws, administrative directives, financial emergencies, and the immediate wishes of the community, and they are frequently confronted with the views of powerful groups within society that have vested interests in either preserving schools as they exist or changing them in some particular direction. Furthermore, evaluating the wisdom of teachers' curriculum decisions is made difficult by the very nature of the task, which is future oriented. Unlike the relationship between professional and client that exists in other professions, the teacher-student relationship does not have an immediately visible effect; in fact, teachers' influence on children entrusted to their care may not be felt for a long time, and the school itself is only one of several of society's agencies intended to influence children's lives. Additionally, a curriculum that is appropriate for one student may not be appropriate for another, and no two students necessarily experience the same curriculum in precisely the same way. Dealing with other human beings and the intangibles that are important parts of their lives is always problematic.

Within these limits, however, teachers still clearly have an obligation to participate in the process of curriculum planning and development. They can exercise significant influence either at the system level as delegates on various boards and committees or more generally through their professional associations, but the center of their influence on curriculum decisions is the place where they interact directly with their clients—that is, the school.

1.2 DEFINING CURRICULUM

Defining the word *curriculum* is no easy matter. Perhaps the most common definition derives from the word's Latin root, which means "racecourse." Indeed, for many students, the school curriculum is a race to be run, a series of obstacles or hurdles (subjects) to be passed. It is important to keep in mind that schools in Western civilization have been heavily influenced since the fourth century B.C. by the philosophies of Plato and Aristotle and that the word *curriculum* has been used historically to describe the subjects taught during the classical period of Greek civilization. The interpretation of the word *curriculum* broadened in the twentieth century to include subjects other than the classics. Today school documents, newspaper articles, committee reports, and many academic textbooks refer to any and all subjects offered or prescribed as "the curriculum of the school."

Many writers advocate their own preferred definitions of *curriculum,* which emphasize other meanings or connotations, particularly those the term has taken on recently. According to Portelli (1987), more than 120 definitions of the term appear in the professional literature devoted to curriculum, presumably because authors are concerned about either delimiting what the term means or establishing new meanings that have become associated with it.

Delimiting the term by the use of a preferred definition is a poor basis for constructive dialogue among curriculum workers (Walker, 1990). Hlebowitsh (1993) makes a similar point when criticizing commentators in the curriculum field who focus "only on certain facets of early curriculum thought while ignoring others" (p. 2).

We need to be watchful, therefore, about definitions that capture only a few of the various characteristics of curriculum (Toombs & Tierney, 1993), especially those that are partisan or biased. Portelli (1987), drawing on a metaphor developed by Soltis (1978), notes, "Those who look for the definition of curriculum are like a sincere but misguided centaur hunter who, even with a fully provisioned safari and a gun kept always at the ready, nonetheless will never require the services of a taxidermist" (p. 364).

The incompleteness of any definition notwithstanding, certain definitions of the term can provide insights about common emphases and characteristics within the general idea of curriculum. Consider, for example, the following definitions of *curriculum.*

DEFINITION 1

Curriculum is such "permanent" subjects as grammar, reading, logic, rhetoric, mathematics, and the greatest books of the Western world that best embody essential knowledge.

An example is the National Curriculum enacted in the United Kingdom in 1988, which prescribed the curriculum in terms of three core and seven foundational subjects, including specific content and specific goals for student achievement in each subject.

Problems posed by the definition.

This definition suggests that the curriculum is limited to only a few academic subjects. It assumes that what is studied is what is learned. It does not address questions such as, Does the state of knowledge change? If so, shouldn't the subjects making up the curriculum also change? What makes learning such subjects essential? Goodson and Marsh (1996) point out that the National Curriculum in the United Kingdom is simply a reconstitution of the subjects included in the Secondary Regulations of 1904, suggesting that "historical amnesia allows curriculum reconstruction to be presented as curriculum revolution" (p. 157). Griffith (2000) contends that a knowledge-based curriculum such as the National Curriculum does not exist independently of space and time. It should not be considered ahistorically, for it is neither neutral, factual, nor value free.

DEFINITION 2

Curriculum is those subjects that are most useful for living in contemporary society.

The subjects that make up this curriculum are usually chosen in terms of major present-day issues and problems within society, but the definition itself does not preclude individual students from making their own choices about which subjects are most useful.

Problems posed by the definition.

This definition seems to imply that what is contemporary has more value than what is long-lasting. It encourages schools and students to accommodate themselves to society as it exists instead of attempting to improve it. It leaves open questions such as, What accounts for stability in the curriculum? What is useful knowledge? If useful practical skills are increasingly emphasized, what becomes of intellectual development?

DEFINITION 3

Curriculum is all planned learnings for which the school is responsible.

"Planned learnings" can be long written documents specifying content, shorter lists of intended learning outcomes, or simply the general ideas of teachers about what students should know. Exponents of curriculum as a plan include Saylor, Alexander, and Lewis (1981), Beauchamp (1981), and Posner (1998).

Problems posed by the definition.

This definition seems to assume that what is studied is what is learned. It may limit "planned learnings" to those that are easiest to achieve, not those that are most desirable. It does not address questions such as, On what basis does the school select and take responsibility for certain learnings while excluding others? Is it possible for teachers to separate the ends of instruction from the means? Are unplanned, but actual, learnings excluded from the curriculum?

DEFINITION 4

Curriculum is all the experiences learners have under the guidance of the school.

To educators such as Dewey (1959), the curriculum is the sum of the meanings students experience as they engage in the activities of the school. Inevitably, it includes both planned experiences and unplanned ones. What is known as the "hidden curriculum" is the unplanned experiencing of things such as the taken-for-granted rules, rituals, and regulations of the school. Moore (2000) reiterates these points in saying, "Each individual child realizes its true self through its voyage of 'discovery' in the classroom or wider contexts of learning" (p. 20).

Problems posed by the definition.

This definition provides no basis for differentiating desirable and undesirable experiences. It encourages people to see activities and experiences as the same. It may make the tasks of the school impossibly broad. This approach leaves unanswered questions such as, Do all experiences (planned and unplanned) count as part of the curriculum? Which experiences are unique to the school? How can experiences (as opposed to activities) be guided? What is the relationship between subject matter and experience? Prawat (2000) contends that after 1933, Dewey increasingly emphasized the role of subject matter, stating "Teachers 'deposit' powerful ideas and make sure they are worked by the group" (p. 535).

DEFINITION 5

Curriculum is the totality of learning experiences provided to students so that they can attain general skills and knowledge at a variety of learning sites.

Emphasis is on learning rather than teaching, especially learning skills and knowledge at sites other than schools. The assumption is that all sites—including workplace sites—can be conducive to learning general knowledge. This approach to curriculum has been heavily publicized in a number of countries recently and is usually supported for economic reasons by business organizations, other vocationally oriented groups, and advocates of explicit competency standards.

Problems posed by the definition.

This definition usually leads to a narrow technical-functionalist approach to curriculum, requiring that unduly large numbers of outcomes and high levels of specificity be identified. Walker (1994) and Cairns (1992) are critical of the uniformity and the focus on minimum standards the definition encourages. Moore (2000) points out that the economic well-being of a nation depends on much besides vocational training.

DEFINITION 6

Curriculum is what the student constructs from working with the computer and its various networks, such as the Internet.

Obviously, this is a modern definition. It assumes that computers are everywhere—in the home, school, and office—and students, perceiving them as part of the natural landscape, are thriving. Although teachers have been slow in developing computer skills, many are now becoming involved. Advocates argue that the new computing technologies have created a culture for increasingly active learning; students can construct their own meanings as they locate sources on the Internet, explore issues, and communicate with others. Social skills are also developed through chat groups, conferences, and e-mail communications.

Problems posed by the definition.

Although some writers such as Vine, Brown, and Clark (2000) contend that schools in the near future will change drastically as students access more electronic resources from the home, others such as Reid (2000) and Westbury (2000) believe that schools will remain long-enduring institutions. Budin (1999) reminds us that technology is not a neutral tool. What is now available on the Internet, for example, is not necessarily what should be on it or what will be on it tomorrow. Furthermore, not all students have the same level of access to the Internet, and the learning it promotes may prove to be far more passive than now commonly believed. We should, therefore, be wary of excessive claims about active or constructivist learning made possible by computers.

DEFINITION 7

Curriculum is the questioning of authority and the searching for complex views of human situations.

This definition is consistent with the ancient Socratic maxim, "The unexamined life is not worth living." However, it may also overly encourage rejection of what is, making it a postmodernist definition. The term *postmodernist* implies opposition to widely used ("modern") values and practices. Hence, postmodernists are disparate in their own views, usually sharing only a desire to challenge what is modern, a readiness to accept the unexpected, and a willingness to conceptualize new ways of thinking.

Problems posed by the definition.

Postmodernism reduced simply to the process of questioning may not be helpful in identifying in practice how students should spend their time and energy. Although many authors are enthusiastic about the general potential of postmodernist thinking (Atkinson, 2000; Parker, 1997; Slattery, 1995), others (Barrow, 1999) contend that it is overly general, vague, and confused. It is subject to the charge of relativism. Moore (2000) contends there is a fatal, internal contradiction among those postmodernists who state that all truth is relative, when this statement itself would have to be nonrelative in order to be true!

DEFINITION 8

Curriculum is all the experiences that learners have in the course of living.

This definition places emphasis on the personal and social character of curriculum. *Currere,* a term developed by Pinar and Grumet (1976), is a variation of this approach (see chapter 4). Schubert (1986) suggests that this approach emphasizes the individual's own capacity to direct his or her life. Graham (1992) asserts that it takes into account how the individual is personally situated within society.

Problems posed by the definition.

This definition makes no distinction between what happens in school and what happens in life generally. It suggests that the school has no special responsibility for the curriculum. It leaves open questions such as, What is the relationship between academic experiences and life experiences? Are planned experiences as valuable as unplanned ones? Who decides the course of individual lives?

Many diverse values are implicit in these definitions of curriculum, and any particular definition gives rise to problems and questions. The definitions we have included are ordered to reflect a general broadening of what the curriculum is seen to include: from academic knowledge alone to more general knowledge, from unchanging knowledge to uncertain knowledge, from intellectual skills to practical skills, from emphasis on the course of studies to emphasis on the student, from planned activities to unplannable experience, from guidance by the school to choices made by individual learners.

Obviously, a definition that suggests that the curriculum is an unchanging body of academic knowledge to be learned in school implies far different things about curriculum development and the teacher's role in it than does a definition that suggests that the curriculum is how students experience life in general. At one end of the spectrum, planning is paramount yet relatively straightforward, for everything is seen as potentially fixed. At the other end, planning is difficult if not impossible, for everything is seen as potentially in flux. Indeed, at this end, what now has become widely known as the "hidden curriculum" often seems to take over; that is, parts of the environment that are unplanned or even unplannable (such as all the unacknowledged attitudes, beliefs, codes of conduct, and conventions for social relationships that form the overall, but constantly shifting, milieu of the school) seem to exert a more subtle but far greater influence over what students learn than does the official curriculum itself. Therefore, not only do writers of curriculum books have their preferred definitions, but so do specialists in curriculum work. Teachers have their own working definitions, even if only implicit in their actions. Our joint task is not to decide which definitions are the most appropriate but to clarify how different definitions and their related value orientations lead to different approaches to curriculum planning and development and to the different curricula that result. Figure 1.2 represents just a few of the many issues that must be considered in understanding the relationship between definitions of curriculum and the roles that schools and teachers play in curriculum development.

There is no one definition of curriculum that accommodates all perspectives and priorities in curriculum making. But . . .

. . . if a definition accounts for the role of the school, will the school of the future be found in:

- traditional classrooms?
- computer laboratories?
- community resource centers?
- workplaces?
- homes?

. . . if a definition provides a major role for the teacher, should that role be as a(n):

- information-giver?
- subject matter specialist?
- motivator?
- gatekeeper?
- resource person?
- counselor?
- mentor?

FIGURE 1.2
Definitions of curriculum and possible roles for schools and teachers

We wish to make three distinctions and then to acknowledge the working definition of curriculum that we ourselves adopt—but ask you to question—throughout this book. First, the term *curriculum* subsumes the terms *syllabus* and *course of studies*. A syllabus, such as one listed in a teacher guide, is typically a listing of content to be taught in a single course, although sometimes it is supplemented with a small number of general aims and objectives and some preferences for particular types of student activities. A course of studies is usually a similar listing but of a sequence of courses. In contrast, a curriculum is all of this and more. Many schools and school districts publish longer documents that they refer to as "the curriculum," but these documents are described more accurately as "curriculum guides." The guides typically include not only listings of content but also detailed analyses of basic concerns such as desirable aims and objectives, specific materials and activities, and possible experiences and forms of evaluation, along with explicit recommendations for interrelating them for optimal effect. In other words, a curriculum includes some notions of where the traveler is going, how the traveler might get there, and what life might be like not only on arrival but also along the way. These can be included in a written curriculum guide. Of course, the curriculum itself also includes making the trip.

Second, a curriculum necessarily involves some conscious planning, and this in turn will be reflected in what students actually learn. This is not to suggest that all plans will be achieved. Every teacher has to contend with the reality that many unexpected, unplanned events will occur in the classroom. Attempting to identify the hidden curriculum reminds us that students learn many things in school about social roles, attitudes, and values that are never part of any particular curriculum plan. The hidden curriculum for students includes more than the personal likes and dislikes of their teachers and the attitudes and values embedded in what their teachers do. It also includes the priorities of educational and political authorities about the power relationships between adults and students in schools, about controls over future employment opportunities, and about how such abstract concepts as justice and equity function concretely in society at large. If what is most worthwhile is to be reached in ways other than chance, curriculum planning is necessary; but, as we have suggested, for many reasons it is always problematic.

Third, it is unnecessary and, we believe, undesirable to separate curriculum from instruction. We are well aware that some authors contend that a curriculum consists of a structured series of intended learning outcomes and that instruction is the means by which these ends are realized. While separating ends and means is part of the logic employed in technical work, readers should clearly understand that *we do not regard the process of curriculum planning and development as inherently technical.* In fact, viewing it as technical has been historically (and currently) one of the greatest causes of confusion and frustration for people engaged in it. For instance, teachers know that their highest hopes for their students are never fully realized—that if they were, then teachers should raise their hopes still higher. Yet the technical view of curriculum as ends and instruction as means suggests something quite different. It suggests that unless hopes are completely realized, something is wrong with the curriculum, with instruction, or with both. What then? The usual result is that teachers uncomfortably attempt to gloss over the discrepancies that inevitably appear between hopes and realizations or unjustly take blame for them. Thus, the suggestion that teachers need to consciously separate ends from means seems to be a very dubious and unnatural dichotomy.

We hold an organic, holistic view of curriculum and instruction consistent with many recent trends that encourages teachers to be directly involved in making decisions about both curriculum and teaching by constantly monitoring and adjusting ends and means within unfolding classroom situations. This, we think, is what good teachers always do. Thus, a view of curriculum and instruction in which the two merge reflects a much more realistic view of what actually happens in good schools and classrooms than does an outlook that artificially dichotomizes the two. In this book, we have attempted to describe straightforwardly alternative approaches and issues in curriculum, but readers should be aware that our analyses are written from this organic, nontechnological perspective.

An Interrelated Set of Plans and Experiences

Consistent with this perspective, the working definition of the term *curriculum* we adopt in this book is "an interrelated set of plans and experiences that a student undertakes under the guidance of the school." This definition needs amplification. The phrase "an interrelated set of plans and experiences" refers to the fact that the curricula implemented in schools typically are determined in advance but, almost inevitably, include unplanned activities that also occur. Therefore, the curricula enacted consist of an amalgam of planned and unplanned activities; likewise, the experiences of students within this amalgam can be anticipated in some ways but not in others. Precisely how plans and experiences are interrelated can vary considerably.

The phrase also refers to the importance of both actors (teachers and students) and the resulting interactions that occur between them to produce the "lived" curriculum—what each individual personally experiences. The curriculum experienced in the classroom is often thought of as a one-way transmission of ideas and information from the teacher to a group of passive recipients, but in reality it consists of an ongoing series of communications, reactions, and exchanges among individuals.

This definition acknowledges the complexity of individual interactions while honoring the role of formal education as a collective attempt to enrich individual lives. It leaves primarily to the school the type of guidance to be provided (the planned curriculum), primarily to teachers how that guidance is provided (the enacted curriculum), and primarily to students how guidance ultimately is received (the experienced curriculum). However, it also leaves open many possibilities for students, teachers, school officials, and other interested persons to engage one another constructively at many points along the way.

Our definition of curriculum suggests that any curriculum includes both what is planned and what is unplanned. But this is a book about how curricula can be planned and developed. What, then, does our definition imply about curriculum planning?

The definition obviously presupposes that some conscious planning is possible and, indeed, desirable. Less obviously, however, it suggests ways in which any basic approach to curriculum planning must deal with the same fundamental concerns and questions common to all planning, regardless of the specific methods favored by different curriculum planners or their particular value orientations. For instance, our definition suggests that the learning activities experienced by students in classroom settings are managed and mediated by teachers so that intended outcomes can be adjusted to practical realities. A different definition might suggest that all practical realities should be accounted for first and that the curriculum, therefore, should be fixed in advance and teachers should do nothing whatsoever to mediate it in the classroom. Despite the very different approaches to curriculum planning that the two definitions would lead to, both still deal with the same series of common questions about the relative stability of the planned curriculum and the role teachers should play in maintaining or changing it.

Similarly, our phrase "that a student undertakes" emphasizes something much different about the temporal dimension of the curriculum than does the phrase "that a student completes." The latter suggests that curricula are created on the assumption that students will complete certain tasks and activities over a period of time. An even more open-ended definition than ours might suggest that there should be no time constraints whatsoever on the student's engagement with the planned curriculum.

Our phrase "under the guidance of the school" is intended to include all persons associated with the school who might provide some input into planning a curriculum, such as teachers, administrators, members of school boards, and even members of state departments of education who are employed as external specialists. Again, a different definition might lead to a more restrictive answer about who should participate in curriculum planning.

Not surprisingly, the most basic questions about curriculum deal with what the curriculum should be, who should engage in planning and implementing it, how it should proceed, and what its influence should be on students. Our definition suggests certain answers to such questions, but, for all practical purposes, there are no limits to the specific subquestions that can be posed or to the number and kind of answers that can be offered. We do not know precisely what the elements of curriculum planning are, nor do we think anyone else knows.

In subsequent chapters we revisit basic questions about curriculum as we engage in a detailed analysis of a number of curriculum processes.

1.3   WHAT COMES NEXT?

We have briefly explored in this chapter some of the many ideas about what curriculum is, how it can be defined, and who participates in it and how. We have promised that throughout the book we will identify and examine in detail what we have described as alternative approaches to curriculum planning, development, or decision making. However, since a process such as curriculum planning involves making judgments, either individually or collectively, and these judgments in turn depend upon value orientations, being familiar with several alternative approaches to planning is not enough. Also needed is an understanding of how various value orientations can lead to different curricula. We have introduced this issue in chapter 1, and we reconsider it in chapters 2, 3, and 4.

Chapter 2, "Curriculum History," explores the origins of different approaches that have been used over the decades to plan and implement curricula. For instance, some of the principles that can be used for determining the scope and sequence of curricula were in fact established by influential committees that met at the end of the nineteenth century. Yet many writers such as Kliebard (1974), Tanner (1982), and Hlebowitsh (1993) have commented on the inadequate understanding that contemporary educators have of past curriculum efforts. Newer curriculum reform efforts usually are uninformed about lessons that can be drawn from older ones. Chapter 2 describes the history of curricula in the United States, examining some of the lessons that can be applied to curriculum issues today.

Chapter 3, "Approaches to Curriculum," describes and analyzes three exemplary approaches to curriculum planning, pointing out similarities and differences. These examples introduce and flesh out what we mean by different approaches to curriculum and also introduce many of the ongoing issues of practical curriculum development that we discuss in later chapters.

Chapter 4, "Curriculum Theorizing," continues this investigation but focuses specifically on efforts undertaken since the 1960s to produce bodies of systematic thought, research, and scholarship that can be used directly to guide curriculum planning and development. In this chapter, we analyze a number of approaches to curriculum theorizing, especially in terms of their value orientations and their adequacy for guiding curriculum planning.

We shift emphasis away from planning and toward the more practical problems of curriculum development beginning with chapter 5, "Curriculum Development and Change." In practice, curriculum development varies enormously in scale, funding, use of specialized personnel, and many other ways. Efforts to change curricula (often called "curriculum innovation") occur continuously. Here we look at some strategies and methods that have been widely used for developing or changing curricula and why some have been successful and others have not.

Efforts by states to legislate for school reform rapidly gained momentum following the avalanche of national reports on education in the United States, especially between 1983 and 1985 (Seashore-Louis & Entler, 1988). Many states have moved toward statewide policies for curricula and statewide control, and this trend will probably continue well into the twenty-first century. There is some evidence that state reforms have led to more cohesive school programs, with increased time available for instruction; more formal graduation requirements; and tighter alignment of the objectives, scope, and sequence of curricula with standards measured by local and state testing (Odden & Marsh, 1987). However, some commentators denounce top-down centralization of education and its concomitant fiscal controls and regulations (Iannaccone, 1985). Although there is evidence that curriculum decisions made at the local level have been vastly reduced since the 1960s as federal and state constraints on local policymaking have increased (Boyd, 1987), local decisions are still important. The professional literature on curriculum implementation underscores the importance of "local capacity and will" (McLaughlin, 1987, p. 172). Individuals working together in local settings are still pivotal figures in curriculum development and are likely to remain so. Thus, both real and potential tensions between making curriculum decisions at federal and state levels or at the local level are increasing, and no end seems in sight. In light of these increasing tensions, chapter 6, "Curriculum Planning: Levels and Participants," discusses how different people and settings influence curriculum development, and chapter 7, "Curriculum Implementation," discusses how the planned curriculum is translated into the enacted curriculum by local schools and teachers.

But then there are such matters as accountability, assessment, and evaluation. People who make decisions about curricula may make mistakes, but, presumably, they should not go on making the same mistakes indefinitely. Why continue to use a curriculum unless there is some basis for believing it to be appropriate in the first place or for improving it over time? Usually the curricula implemented in schools must eventually be judged to be worthwhile in some way. Unless students seem to be making satisfactory progress, the length of time in which a new curriculum is tried out may be drastically curtailed or the curriculum may be dropped altogether. Evaluation applies, therefore, to curriculum developers as well as to students, and feedback about the suitability of a program may be just as important to teachers and administrators as grades and marks are to students. According to Clark (1988), public opinion polls indicate that many people hold negative opinions about how well schools are doing and are clamoring for reforms, especially for more national testing of students and more national examinations for the licensure of teachers. Evaluation is one of the most hotly debated topics in education in general and in curriculum in particular. Chapter 8, "Curriculum Evaluation and Student Assessment," analyzes basic issues within this topic and then examines four different approaches for evaluating curricula.

Chapter 9, "Politics and Curriculum Decision Making," looks at how curriculum decisions are influenced by pressures from society itself. Each school exists within a broad society. In some ways, each school curriculum must reflect the characteristics and the values of that society as it is, but in other ways, each curriculum implicitly carries within it the duty to attempt to improve society. This tension is inherent in the very nature of education, but it also manifests itself both as a professional tension influencing curriculum decisions in general and as an existential tension felt personally by people making such decisions. This final chapter considers conflicts that arise specifically from controversies concerning who controls the curriculum, on what basis, and for what purposes, focusing especially on ongoing issues that arise from current pressures for centralized curriculum decision making.

Clearly, not all decisions about curricula can be equally wise or equally defensible. Only rarely, in fact, can all alternatives be fully considered, seldom is the best of these alternatives clear, and inevitably the most controversial issues surrounding a decision for any particular alternative will remain. That is the nature of curriculum planning and development. We hope, however, that the approaches and issues we discuss throughout this book will help teachers and all others who make curriculum decisions to do so with increasing insight and increasing skill. If so, then readers should find that those decisions in which they participate will increasingly reflect their own values yet still honor the values of other participants and the best interests of both students and society.

■ QUESTIONS AND REFLECTIONS

1. The basic questions listed in Figure 1.1 are by no means exhaustive. What questions would you add or delete? How do you personally respond to each question?
2. Develop a definition of curriculum with which you can personally identify. Justify this definition.
3. "The struggle over the definition of curriculum is a matter of social and political priorities as well as intellectual discourse" (Goodson, 1988, p. 23). Reflect on the current social and political priorities of your country. Are these stronger than the current "intellectual discourse" of books (such as this one, or any other curriculum books with which you may be familiar) in influencing practical curriculum decisions? If so, why? What does this relationship between the political concerns of society and the concerns of curriculum academics bode for the future?
4. Examine a curriculum document used by your school district. Does it reflect one or more of the definitions included in this chapter? Explain which characteristics of the document are consistent with which definitions. What parts of the overall curriculum picture does the document seem to miss?

■ SUGGESTED READING

There are a number of excellent introductions to curriculum (see the chapter bibliography), including these:

Beane (1995)

Connelly & Clandinin (1988)

Hlebowitsh (1993)

Ornstein & Hunkins (1993)

Parker (1997)

Pinar, Reynolds, Slattery, & Taubman (1995)

Ross (2000)

Schubert (1986)

Slattery (1995)

Sowell (1996)

Walker & Soltis (1986)

■ BIBLIOGRAPHY

Atkinson, E. (2000). *What can postmodern thinking do for educational research?* Paper presented at the annual meeting of the American Educational Research Association, New Orleans.

Barrow, R. (1999). The need for philosophical analysis in a postmodern era. *Interchange, 30*(4), 415–432.

Beane, J. A. (Ed.). (1995). *Toward a coherent curriculum.* Alexandria, VA: Association for Supervision and Curriculum Development.

Beauchamp, G. A. (1981). *Curriculum theory* (4th ed.). Itasca, IL: Peacock.

Beyer, L. E., & Apple, M. W. (Eds.). (1988). *The curriculum: Problems, politics and possibilities.* Albany: State University of New York Press.

Boyd, W. L. (1987). Public education's last hurrah?: Schizophrenia, amnesia, and ignorance in school politics. *Educational Evaluation and Policy Analysis, 9*(2), 85–100.

Budin, H. (1999). The computer enters the classroom. *Teachers College Record, 100*(3), 656–670.

Cairns, L. (1992). Competency-based education: Nostradamus's nostrum. *Journal of Teaching Practice, (12)*1, 1–31.

Clark, D. L. (1988). *Education policy after Reagan-What next?* Paper presented at the annual meeting of the American Educational Research Association, New Orleans.

Connelly, F. M., & Clandinin, D. J. (1988). *Teachers as curriculum planners.* New York: Teachers College Press.

Dewey, J. (1910). *How we think.* New York: D. C. Heath.

Dewey, J. (1938). *Experience and education.* New York: Macmillan.

Dewey, J. (1959). The child and the curriculum. In M. S. Dworkin (Ed.), *Dewey on education.* New York: Teachers College Press.

Goodson, I. F. (1988). *The making of curriculum.* Lewes, England: Falmer.

Goodson, I. F., & Marsh, C. J. (1996). *Studying school subjects.* London: Falmer.

Graham, R. J. (1992). Currere and reconceptualism: The progress of the pilgrimage, 1975–1990. *Journal of Curriculum Studies, 24*(1), 27–42.

Griffith, R. (2000). *National curriculum: National disaster.* London: Routledge/Falmer.

Hlebowitsh, P. S. (1993). *Radical curriculum theory reconsidered.* New York: Teachers College Press.

Hlebowitsh, P. S. (1999). The burdens of the new curricularist. *Curriculum Inquiry, 29*(3), 343–355.

Iannaccone, L. (1985). Excellence: An emergent educational issue. *Politics of Education Bulletin, 12*(3), 4–15.

Klein, F. (1990). Approaches to curriculum theory and practice. In J. Sears & D. Marshall (Eds.), *Teaching and thinking about curriculum* (pp. 3–14). New York: Teachers College Press.

Kliebard, H. M. (1974). The development of certain key curriculum issues in the United States. In P. H. Taylor & M. Johnson (Eds.), *Curriculum development: A comparative study.* London: National Foundation for Educational Research.

MacPherson, E. D. (1995). Chaos in the curriculum. *Journal of Curriculum Studies, 27*(3), 263–280.

McLaughlin, M. W. (1987). Learning from experience: Lessons from policy implementation. *Educational Evaluation and Policy Analysis, 9*(2), 171–178.

Moore, R. (2000). For knowledge: Tradition, progressivism and progress in education—restructuring the curriculum debate. *Cambridge Journal of Education, 30*(1), 17–35.

Odden, A. R., & Marsh, D. D. (1987). *How state education reform can improve secondary schools.* Unpublished paper, University of Southern California, Los Angeles.

Ornstein, A. C., & Hunkins, F. (1993). *Curriculum foundations: Principles and theory* (2nd ed.). Boston: Allyn & Bacon.

Parker, S. (1997). *Reflective teaching in the postmodern world.* Buckingham: Open University Press.

Pinar, W., & Grumet, M. (1976). *Toward a poor curriculum.* Dubuque, IA: Kendall/Hunt.

Pinar, W. F., Reynolds, W. M., Slattery, P., & Taubman, P. M. (1995). *Understanding curriculum.* New York: Lang.

Portelli, J. P. (1987). Perspectives and imperatives on defining curriculum. *Journal of Curriculum and Supervision, 2*(4), 354–367.

Posner, G. F. (1998). Models of curriculum planning. In L. E. Beyer & M. W. Apple (Eds.), *The curriculum: Problems, politics and possibilities* (2nd ed., pp. 79–100). Albany: State University of New York Press.

Prawat, R. S. (2000). The two faces of Deweyan pragmatism: Inductionism versus social constructionism. *Teachers College Record, 102*(4), 805–840.

Reid, W. A. (2000). *Why globalization may cause fundamental curriculum change: A theoretical framework.* Paper presented at the annual meeting of the American Educational Research Association, New Orleans.

Ross, A. (2000). *Curriculum: Construction and critique.* London: Falmer.

Saylor, J. G., Alexander, W. M., & Lewis, A. J. (1981). *Curriculum planning for better teaching and learning* (4th ed.). New York: Holt, Rinehart, & Winston.

Schubert, W. H. (1986). *Curriculum: Perspective, paradigm, and possibility.* Upper Saddle River, NJ: Merrill/Prentice Hall.

Schwab, J. J. (1970). *The practical: A language for curriculum.* Washington, DC: National Education Association.

Seashore-Louis, K., & Entler, R. A. (1988). Knowledge use and school improvement. *Curriculum Inquiry, 18*(1), 33–62.

Slattery, P. (1995). *Curriculum development in the postmodern era.* New York: Garland.

Soltis, J. F. (1978). *An introduction to the analysis of educational concepts.* Reading, MA: Addison-Wesley.

Sowell, E. J. (1996). *Curriculum: An integrative introduction.* Upper Saddle River, NJ: Merrill/Prentice Hall.

Tanner, L. N. (1982). Curriculum history as usable knowledge. *Curriculum Inquiry, 12*(4), 17–26.

Toombs, W. E., & Tierney, W. G. (1993). Curriculum definitions and reference points. *Journal of Curriculum and Supervision, 8*(3), 175-195.

Vine, K., Brown, T., & Clark, G. (2000). Which way for information technology in our schools? *The School Principal's Handbook Series, 2000,* 5–8.

Walker, D. F. (1990). *Fundamentals of curriculum.* New York: Harcourt Brace Jovanovich.

Walker, D. F., & Soltis, J. (1986). *Curriculum and aims.* New York: Teachers College Press.

Walker, J. (1994). *Competency-based teacher education: Implications for quality in higher education, II.* Higher Education Research Conference, Canberra.

Westbury, I. (2000). *Why globalization will not cause fundamental curriculum change.* Paper presented at the annual meeting of the American Educational Research Association, New Orleans.

Wright, H. K. (2000). Nailing Jell-O to the wall: Pinpointing aspects of state-of-the-art curriculum theorizing. *Educational Researcher, 29*(5), 4–13.

Curriculum History

ABOUT THIS CHAPTER

This chapter traces the history of curricula in the United States. It points out how three different focal points for the choosing and implementing of curricula (subject matter, society, and individual) have predominated at different times and why each of these focal points must be considered and brought into some kind of appropriate balance with the other two. It does not suggest that one particular kind of balance is the most appropriate for use in developing all curricula at all times. Instead, in considering historical changes in American curricula, the chapter suggests how different assumptions concerning appropriate balance among focal points have been used in the past and how they may be used to inform curriculum decisions in the future.

WHAT YOU SHOULD DO

1. Become familiar with the different curricula that have predominated in the United States at different times and the influence of the changing social, political, and cultural context on these curricula.
2. Understand the three basic focal points around which curricula can be developed and the criteria for curricular choice associated with each.
3. Understand why these focal points must be brought into an appropriate balance.
4. Consider how historical evidence can be used to inform practical curriculum decisions.

SOME OPTIONAL APPROACHES

In undertaking what this chapter asks the reader to do, you may find the following options useful.

Option A

1. Consider the historical evolution of curricula in the United States in terms of the major social, political, and cultural forces that have influenced curriculum

change. Weigh the influence of each of these broad forces in light of the discussion in the chapter. Identify other forces that the chapter does not mention.

2. Using your general knowledge of American history as well as the information in this chapter, attempt to answer as fully as possible the following questions:
   - ❏ During the colonial period, what were the principal influences of European traditions on American curricula? What were the influences of the American frontier?
   - ❏ In the nineteenth century, what were the principal influences of American democracy? of immigration? of industrialization? of urbanization?
   - ❏ In the twentieth century, what were the principal influences of the emergence of the United States as a world power? of its social reform movements? of its participation in World War I and World War II? of the Great Depression?
3. Which of the three focal points for the curriculum (subject matter, society, the individual) has each of the historical influences served most to advance? Why?

Option B

1. Consider the historical evolution of curricula in the United States in terms of the major ideas of the people who have most influenced curriculum change. Weigh the influence of each of these people and their ideas as they are mentioned in the chapter. Identify the ideas of other influential people not mentioned in the chapter.
2. Using your general knowledge of American educational history, as well as the information in this chapter, attempt to answer as fully as possible the following questions:
   - ❏ During the colonial period, what were the principal European ideas about education that most influenced American curricula. Were these ideas modified by life on the American frontier? If so, how?
   - ❏ In the nineteenth century, what were the most influential ideas of advocates of the common school? of other educational reformers? of the major reports of the National Education Association?
   - ❏ In the twentieth century, what have been the most influential ideas of John Dewey? How have Dewey's ideas shaped American curricula? How have his ideas been distorted? What ideas (and whose) have arisen to counter Dewey's? How are Dewey's ideas germane today?
3. Which of the three focal points for the curriculum (subject matter, society, the individual) has each of the historical influences served most to advance? Why?

2.1 INTRODUCTION

The curriculum taught in a given classroom, school, community, state, or nation is never fixed in any final sense. Instead, any curriculum planned or enacted should be viewed as the end point of a series of human decisions, and, as such, it is subject to constant review and revision. New ideas about curriculum constantly supplant old ones, and thus curricula inevitably change. Nonetheless, there is usually a great deal of stability in curriculum, since changes are typically slow to be implemented.

Most curricula are end points of decisions made, or at least influenced, by a great number of people. Just as individuals are often slow to change their minds about how best to spend their own time, so, too, are whole societies usually slow to revise their collective thinking about how students can best spend their time in schools. The culture of a whole society changes slowly, even though specific social trends may come and go quickly. Changes in the broad social, political, and economic forces influencing schools are usually more evolutionary than rapid. The weight of tradition tends to take over, especially when the many complicated considerations that can and should go into curriculum decisions are misunderstood or only partially known, or when deliberations are brief or incomplete. People making curriculum decisions are often prisoners of tradition and their own unexamined beliefs; usually because they do not know what curricula have been, they fail to anticipate the many ways curricula can be.

This pattern of stability despite change has been the case in the United States. The curricula commonly taught in elementary, secondary, and higher education in the United States changed dramatically in some ways with the changing ideas and conditions of the twentieth century but in other ways did not actually move very far away from the traditional curriculum forms that prevailed in American schools throughout the nineteenth century—and even before. For instance, widespread calls in the 1980s and 1990s for basic curricula reiterated many nineteenth-century assumptions about what basic curricula should be. Indeed, many of the most widely proposed curriculum reforms of the 2000s are close reiterations of past practices, although their proposers are almost always unaware of any previous historical consequences. Both Hlebowitsh (1999) and Santora (2001) make clear the necessity of historical understanding for making informed and intelligent decisions about what future curricula should be.

This chapter considers the history of American curricula in terms of both stability and change, attempting to suggest how understanding of curriculum history can influence decisions relating to curriculum planning and development.

2.2   THREE FOCAL POINTS FOR CURRICULUM HISTORY

There are three basic focal points around which decisions about curricula can be made, although the variations in how these focal points can be viewed are virtually endless. For sound, practical decisions about curriculum, all three points should be carefully considered:

1. The first of these focal points is the nature of the subject matter itself. Does the subject matter being taught adequately represent to the student the reality of the surrounding world? Does the way the subject matter has been organized adequately reflect its own inherent logic?

2. The second focal point is the nature of society. Does the curriculum sufficiently reflect a broad range of the cultural, political, and economic characteristics of the social context in which it exists so that the student may both fit
into the society in the future yet also be able to change that society?

3. The third is the nature of the individual. Does the curriculum sufficiently
account for the interests and developmental needs of individual students so
that each individual may optimally benefit from it?

Despite the importance of all three focal points, at different times in the history
of American education, each of these points has prevailed over the other two in capturing the attention or imagination of educators and citizens. Thus, in different
eras, different—but often unduly narrow—approaches to them have dominated
deliberations and driven practical decisions about curriculum.

The Nature of Subject Matter

Subject matter is the content of the curriculum, and choices about what subject
matter to include within the curriculum are also choices about what to leave out.
The amount of time available for formal education—regardless of how extended
that education might be—is always less than the amount of time needed to teach students everything that might be learned about the world. Since subject matter must
be limited, some fundamental curriculum questions inevitably arise. Are some kinds
of subject matter more intrinsically worthwhile than others? On what basis can decisions be made about the inclusion in the curriculum of specific kinds of subject
matter? Answers to such questions deal with what we can consider as the external
and the internal characteristics of any subject matter.

External characteristics of subject matter deal with how accurately and how
broadly the chosen subject matter represents the reality of the world beyond the
student's immediate experience. Presumably, good subject matter should be rooted
in, and should accurately transmit, this greater reality. The rooting may be empirical. For instance, the subject matter of history must ultimately be based on events
that actually happened in the past, even as difficult as those events may be to reconstruct accurately and interpret reasonably in the present. However, the rooting
may be nonempirical. The subject matter of mathematics must ultimately reflect the
unchanging quantitative relationships that exist anywhere and everywhere, even
though knowledge of these relationships may actually be used to solve problems
dealing with specific empirical entities. Clearly, in the choice of subject matter for
inclusion within the curriculum, the accuracy of representation of external reality is
among the most important criteria to be considered.

Choices, however, may also be made in terms of the criterion of the breadth of
the external reality that different subject matters reflect, with the broader subject (or the broader principles within that subject) usually being preferred. For example, on the grounds of breadth of representation of the physical world, physics
would be preferred to mechanical engineering and mechanical engineering to automobile maintenance. The traditional defense of a liberal arts curriculum is that

such a curriculum includes the broadest and most accurate representation of both human experience and the natural world.

Internal characteristics of subject matter deal with the logic inherent in how the chosen subject matter is arranged. Any subject matter has its own organizing principles, or internal logic, that should not be violated. In history, the internal logic deals largely with the chronology of events; in mathematics, with the consistency of quantitative relationships; in the sciences, with causal relationships within the natural world; in grammar, with the consistency of linguistic representations; and in the arts, with the aesthetics of expressive representations in a variety of media. Since the time available to present a given subject matter is ordinarily far less than needed to present it in its entirety, those parts of the subject selected for presentation should be arranged consistently both with one another and with the inherent logic of the overall subject. This same principle applies to the internal characteristics of the overall curriculum, which is made up of many subjects, or subparts. It should retain a logical integrity. The traditional defense of a liberal arts curriculum also includes the idea that such a curriculum logically integrates all basic forms of human knowledge.

Such considerations about the accuracy, breadth, and consistency of knowledge itself dominated American assumptions about what the curriculum should be throughout the colonial era and much of the nineteenth century.

The Nature of Society

Another important criterion in choosing the subject matter to be included within the curriculum is usefulness. If the curriculum is to have utilitarian value, then it must lead the student not only to knowledge of the external world for its own sake, but also to knowledge that can be applied in the world. To determine usefulness, therefore, the nature of the external world—or the society in which the student exists—must be taken into account. Most directly, this means that the curriculum must acquaint students with knowledge and skills that are derived at least in part from the surrounding society and that can be applied instrumentally within that society to help obtain, at the very least, such universal, material necessities of life as food, shelter, and clothing. But what is useful at one time and under one set of circumstances may not be as useful as time passes or circumstances change. Therefore, as society itself changes, different practical pursuits will have potentially more or potentially less importance within the curriculum. Computer science, of course, had no utilitarian value within the curriculum before there were computers, but it has had increasing value as modern society has become increasingly dependent on computers. In a curriculum chosen for its immediate usefulness within society, therefore, automobile maintenance may under some circumstances be preferred to mechanical engineering and mechanical engineering to physics.

What constitutes usefulness within society, both immediately and in the long run, thus becomes an important question in curriculum planning. When material necessities are in short supply, society may consider a curriculum directed toward increasing them to be the most useful. However, when they are in abundance, society may decide that a curriculum directed to nonmaterial pursuits is at least as useful or perhaps even more so.

Criteria for selecting curriculum content based on utilitarian value also carry with them the problem of deciding how much the curriculum should reflect the society as it is in the present and how much it should reflect how the society should be in the future. For instance, vocational curricula may be considered useful because they train students to perform jobs that exist in the present, but such curricula may have little or no usefulness if future changes in society cause those jobs to cease to exist.

Furthermore, curricula that closely reflect the characteristics of the society that exists at the moment usually reflect both the desirable and the undesirable characteristics of that society. Currently on street corners, youths whose notions of utilitarian value are constrained by their limited vision of what life can be learn how to sell illegal drugs skillfully, but most societies ordinarily expect far better than this from the curricula taught in their schools.

Therefore, how much a curriculum promotes desirable future changes in society may in the long run prove to be a far better indicator of utilitarian value than how accurately the curriculum reflects, and thus maintains, the social status quo. For these reasons, inevitable tensions arise among different approaches to the issues of how and why curriculum content derived from the characteristics of society can best be useful.

Since these inevitable tensions may be resolved in numerous ways, criteria for selecting curriculum content derived from the nature of society may lead to decisions that are either consistent or inconsistent with those based on criteria derived from the nature of knowledge or from the nature of the individual. During the nineteenth century, when criteria derived from the nature of society began to challenge the preeminence of criteria derived from the nature of knowledge, the curricula of many American schools underwent some major changes.

The Nature of the Individual

The third basic focal point around which decisions about curricula can be made is the nature of the individual. While all persons in some ways are like all others, everyone is also unique. This consideration leads to the daunting realization that the same curriculum cannot be equally appropriate for all individuals.

Considered from the perspective of the individual, the purpose of the curriculum is not solely to teach subject matter derived externally to each individual's experience, nor is it solely to bring each individual into conformity with how society is now or should be in the future. Instead, the purpose of education includes fostering the developmental growth of each individual. In this view, were the curriculum to consist of eternally true knowledge and immediately useful skills, the curriculum would still never be an end in itself, for it is a medium through which the more important end of developmental growth is fostered. Since growth can never be quite the same for each individual, the same curriculum can never be equally appropriate for each student.

Furthermore, developmental growth in its broadest sense is neither solely physical, nor cognitive, nor affective. It is all of these combined. Hence, it proceeds in a wide variety of both tangible and intangible ways. In this view, the content of the curriculum must be chosen in light of not only what promotes growth for each individual in an immediate, public, and discernible sense, but in a long-range, private, and less easily discernible sense as well—in light of the dynamics of each individual's own experience. Put another way, as the individual interacts with the environment, the course of that person's experience is the curriculum, and the purpose of each interaction is to increase the quality of that experience (Dewey, 1938).

To take into account individual experience, the curriculum cannot be entirely determined in advance for any individual, let alone for any group. It must be based on the general patterns of developmental growth of all kinds, but it must also be a careful and appropriate response to what can be considered as individual interests and needs.

Interests can themselves be considered as motives or tendencies to action that constantly arise and are modified as individuals interact with their changing environments. These interests may be healthy or unhealthy, superficial or profound, of short or long duration, but they are always forcefully felt impulses toward activities that the curriculum can work in concert with or channel into more worthwhile directions.

Needs can be considered as those worthwhile directions in which the individual's impulses should flow, whether the individual is consciously aware of them or not. For instance, a young child may be interested in playing with blocks but not in reading. Whatever specific form a good curriculum could take, it might then provide opportunities for the teacher to encourage the child's continuing play with blocks in order to enhance the child's general aesthetic sensibilities and specific abilities to recognize spatial relationships; to increase the child's hand-eye coordination and other related skills, such as measuring and even mathematics; as well as a springboard from which to develop in the child new interests, such as reading books about constructing buildings. At the same time, the teacher might also read enjoyable stories to the child, pointing out that in the future the child himself or herself will be able to read stories and other materials that are enjoyable, interesting, and useful. In the example of playing with blocks, the purpose of the curriculum might be to channel a present interest consistently with a growing range of worthwhile needs; in the example of reading, the purpose might be to encourage the child to shape a worthwhile future need into a present interest.

Although within this view, considerations about subject matter and society enter into deciding what is worthwhile for the curriculum to contain, emphasis still falls on the developmental growth of the individual. Again, the same external curriculum will not be equally appropriate for each individual.

The curriculum, then, becomes a medium containing a potentially changing set of suggestions to the individual student, not a set of demands for all students. There are always other suggestions that may foster developmental growth as well as—if not better than—the curriculum immediately at hand. In this sense, the curriculum is also a set of suggestions to the teacher about how to take advantage of the present opportunities to promote worthwhile growth for each student in the long run.

At the turn of the twentieth century, these views began to be articulated for American educators, most clearly and most fully by John Dewey (1897, 1900, 1902), and the focal point of the individual began to be understood as a basis for curriculum choice. However, the time-honored focal point of subject matter still dominated the curricula of American schools, although gradually during the nineteenth century, educators had also come to recognize and understand the focal point of society. The history of the curricula of American schools during the twentieth century is, therefore, a history of how these three focal points for deciding on content and making other curriculum decisions have or have not been brought into appropriate balance.

2.3 THE COLONIAL ERA AND THE EARLY UNITED STATES

Balance among focal points of the curriculum was not an issue in colonial America and during the early years of the United States. Although the colonies along the Atlantic seaboard were mainly under British control during the seventeenth and eighteenth centuries, they were settled by immigrants from many European nations. Despite their differences, these settlers shared two common assumptions about education.

The first assumption was that only a few people needed much formal education. Mass education was still unheard of anywhere in the world, and in Europe at the time, the masses learned what they needed to get along in life in the home, in apprenticeships, and through the activities of daily living. There were some schools for the rising mercantile classes, but in general formal education was reserved for the very few, such as the clergy or the nobility, who might need to know how to read or to rule. In the harshness of the American wilderness, practical activities directed toward providing material necessities—not formal education—dominated daily life. In 1647 the colony of Massachusetts did pass a law requiring every township of fifty or more households to appoint a teacher of reading and writing and every township of one hundred or more households to establish a Latin grammar school, but enforcement of this law was uneven. Still, children in Massachusetts fared better than children in other colonies, most probably receiving at least some rudimentary instruction in reading and writing in what became known as "dame schools" (since in most towns, the teachers were women who conducted lessons in their homes). Throughout the colonies, however, most children received no formal education at all.

The second assumption shared by early settlers was that formal education should be directed at bringing people into conformity with some prevailing ideal of what an educated person should be. This ideal was not the same for all settlers, but despite their differences most settlers were Christians who saw the value of at least some religious training in order to make people more godly despite their inherently sinful natures. The most common model for the few formal schools that existed throughout the colonies thus became the Latin grammar school, for it provided the beginnings of a literary education necessary for males to enter the clergy. Members of the clergy needed to know the languages in which scriptures were written, so the curriculum of the Latin grammar school differed little from the curriculum of similar schools in Europe, centering on the study of Greek, Latin, and occasionally Hebrew. Some reading and writing of the vernacular language and some rudimentary mathematics were usually included also, and those few students who remained in school beyond the first few years might read classical Greek and Latin literature as well as scriptures, thus supplementing the predominantly religious purpose of education with exposure to the classical humanism that Europe had rediscovered during the Renaissance. Nonetheless, the curriculum of the Latin grammar school was presented predominantly as a vehicle of religious training and moral elevation. This curriculum was deemed suitable for all students, even the vast majority who were not destined for the clergy and who attended school only briefly. Of course, far fewer females than males received any formal schooling at all.

Given these assumptions about education and how they were worked out in the few schools of colonial America, the sole focal point of the curriculum was the nature of subject matter. The justification for all parts of the curriculum was that they were subjects that provided access to central and eternal truths. The Latin grammar school of Europe, designed to provide access to truths revealed in Holy Scriptures, prevailed as the model of what the American school should be. Since this kind of education was directed more at eternal life than at life in this world, it seemed unsuited to the necessities of coping with the harsh conditions and material privations in the colonies. One result was the development of the widespread belief that the activities of schooling, directed at cultivating the mind and the soul, were separate from the practical activities of life outside of schools.

The Harvard Curriculum

Figure 2.1 presents the course of studies of Harvard College in 1642. Harvard, the first institution of higher education in what was to become the United States, was founded in 1636, and its early curriculum provides a good indication of what elementary and secondary education in colonial America was meant to lead up to, at least for the very few members of the population who learned more than the rudiments of reading and writing. Although the Harvard curriculum does not list Latin as a subject of study, a reading knowledge of Latin was assumed and many of the oral exercises ("disputations" and "declamations") were carried out in Latin. Despite the heavy emphasis on ancient languages as vehicles for reading Christian scriptures, the curriculum had a humanistic and rational side. Some of the readings in Latin and Greek were of non-Christian, classical authors, and the curriculum specified some—usually brief—study of logic, physics, rhetoric, history, botany, ethics, politics, arithmetic, geometry, and astronomy. Still, the Harvard course of studies clearly illustrates how religious purpose and literary studies dominated colonial thinking about what the curriculum should be.

	8 A.M.	9 A.M.	10 A.M.	1 P.M.	2 P.M.	3 P.M.	4 P.M.
First Year							
Monday and Tuesday	Logic: physics				Disputations		
Wednesday	Greek etymology and syntax				Greek grammar, from literature		
Thursday	Hebrew grammar				Hebrew Bible readings		
Friday	Rhetoric	Declamations	Rhetoric		Rhetoric	Rhetoric	Rhetoric
Saturday	Catechetical divinity	Commonplaces		History; nature of plants			
Second Year							
Monday and Tuesday	Ethics; politics					Disputations	
Wednesday	Greek prosody and dialects					Greek poetry	
Thursday	"Chaldee" grammar					Practice in Chaldee: Ezra and Daniel	
Friday	Rhetoric	Declamations	Rhetoric		Rhetoric	Rhetoric	Rhetoric
Saturday	Catechetical divinity	Commonplaces		History; nature of plants			
Third Year							
Monday and Tuesday			Arithmetic; geometry; astronomy				Disputations
Wednesday		Theory of Greek [*style*]			Exercise in Greek style, both in prose and verse		
Thursday		Syriac grammar					Practice in Syriac: New Testament
Friday	Rhetoric	Declamations	Rhetoric		Rhetoric	Rhetoric	Rhetoric
Saturday	Catechetical divinity	Commonplaces		History; nature of plants			

FIGURE 2.1

The times and order of studies of Harvard College, 1642

Source: Copyright © 1970 by Lawrence A. Cremin. Reprinted by permission by Harper Collins Publishers Inc.

Franklin's Academy

One challenge to prevailing beliefs about education and the curriculum of American schools was made by Benjamin Franklin in 1749. Though unsuccessful at the time, Franklin proposed the creation of an academy that would emphasize training in practical subjects. The proposal reflected the influence on education of changes in society (for instance, the growing proportion of merchants and the middle class within the predominantly agrarian colonial society), thereby introducing to some Americans the idea that the nature of the society could also serve as a focal point for making decisions about the curriculum and foreshadowing educational developments of the nineteenth century.

Franklin found the curriculum and the educational assumptions of his day to be too narrow, and his proposal was designed to bring education into closer touch with the practical pursuits of colonial life. His solution to the problem of narrowness was not to abandon the curriculum of the Latin grammar school altogether, but to open it to a variety of other studies and purposes. In the academy he proposed, classical studies would still be taught but would not be required of everyone. Instead, students' prospective professions would determine which languages they studied: Latin and Greek for those preparing to be ministers, but only the modern languages French, German, and Spanish for those preparing to be merchants. Everyone would study English through reading, writing, and orating.

These ideas were not revolutionary in themselves; however, other suggestions were. Franklin's academy would include physical education, drawing, mechanical arts, mathematics, history, geography, civics, horticulture, science, religion, and other studies (though he did not use precisely these names). Instruction would not be exclusively through lectures and recitations, but would include active inquiry into the subjects studied and even field trips. About how these studies were to be prioritized Franklin was vague, merely saying of students, "It would be well if they could be taught everything that is useful, and everything that is ornamental: but art is long, and their time is short. It is therefore proposed that they learn those things that are likely to be most useful and most ornamental" (Willis, Schubert, Bullough, Kridel, & Holton, 1993, p. 21).

At the close of the colonial era and during the early days of the new republic of the United States, there were other proposals for providing formal education to increasing numbers of American children and for expanding curriculum choice. Some new schools and colleges were being established. Still, within American society at large, beliefs about the curriculum and its purposes had changed little, and the assumptions illustrated by the Harvard course of studies of 1642 still dominated thinking. It was not until the nineteenth century that the second focal point for making curriculum decisions—that is, society—became widely accepted, as presaged in Franklin's proposal.

2.4 THE NINETEENTH CENTURY

At the beginning of the nineteenth century, formal education in the United States was directed toward the training of the mind and was still limited to the small proportion of the population for whom such training was deemed suitable. The curriculum embodied the time-honored belief that a relatively few, well-ordered academic subjects were repositories of the highest knowledge and led to godliness, virtue, and understanding—the proper condition of cultivated human beings.

However, during the nineteenth century many Americans began to accept the then revolutionary idea that the masses could also become cultivated. Perhaps the single greatest influence on beliefs about education was the national experience with political democracy. At the beginning of the century, most Americans seemed to feel that governing was the province of only a relative few national leaders; those leaders needed to be well educated, but not the majority of people. By the end of the century, most Americans probably believed that democracy required broad political participation and thus everyone needed some formal education, not necessarily to be leaders themselves, but to be able to choose leaders wisely. Increasing proportions of the population obtained the right to vote, there was a growing impulse toward egalitarianism, and a distinct national identity began to develop. In these ways, especially, the religious purposes for education inherited from the colonial era gave way to secular purposes, and religion declined as a part of the curriculum of public schools.

In addition to the influence of the political life of the nation, major sociological changes during the nineteenth century gradually caused the curriculum of many American schools to become increasingly oriented toward practical subjects and social utility. Changes in society occurred as the United States became increasingly urbanized and industrialized, received massive waves of immigrants, and passed compulsory school attendance laws. By the end of the century, the elementary schools of large American cities were flooded with students for whom the curriculum inherited from the Latin grammar school seemed inappropriate. By the end of the century, that curriculum had been modified; however, to most Americans, it still seemed inappropriate to the new practical demands of American life.

The Common School Movement and the Expansion of the Curriculum

At the beginning of the nineteenth century, the same practical impulse that Franklin had captured in his proposal of 1749 had again manifested itself, this time resulting in the founding of numerous academies of the kind Franklin had envisioned. These academies were intended to open up education for a growing number of Americans, particularly the middle class, and they reflected a growing belief that America should provide opportunities for a natural aristocracy of virtue and talent to flourish, rather than to help maintain an aristocracy of wealth and birth. The new academies also were built on and extended a growing popular demand for universal elementary schooling.

Although, in general, the academies taught both academic and commercial subjects, they were private and charged tuition. Early in the century, therefore, educational leaders began to become aware of the incongruity of pushing for the development of a system of free and universal elementary education to be followed by secondary education provided privately. Thinking began to turn toward the idea of providing equal educational opportunities for all through a publicly controlled and financed system of elementary and secondary education (Butts & Cremin,

1953). Of course, this thinking did not become widely accepted by the general public until much later in the century, but it sowed the seeds of what became known as
"the common school movement," which paid considerable heed to the focal point
of society as a basis for making decisions about curricula.

Essentially, the common school movement was an effort to democratize
American education by making the same kind of schooling available to all. No
longer would differences in wealth or social status be abetted by differences in the
amount, kind, or quality of schooling available. Beginning in the 1830s, spokespersons such as Horace Mann and Henry Barnard argued vigorously that common
schools would provide great social benefits to the nation by increasing the general
wealth, decreasing crime and other social problems, and making all citizens able to
participate in a healthy political democracy. These arguments referred directly to
society as a focal point for curriculum decisions, but they also elevated the idea of
social utilitarianism to a moral plane considerably above what was immediately practical about the new commercial subjects (such as bookkeeping and surveying) that
were beginning to obtrude in earnest into the old academic curricula taught in
American secondary schools. Thus, in the way they espoused social utilitarianism,
the common school reformers were able to capture much of the moral fervor that
in the past had been associated with the religious purposes of the traditional curriculum. This moral fervor, combined with the practical benefits that education now
seemed to hold out to both individual students and the collective society, led directly
to increasing state control of public schools, increasing financial support for
schools, and the state-by-state passage of compulsory attendance laws (beginning
with the Massachusetts law of 1852).

By the middle of the century, local public schools were teaching not only the
usual staples of Latin, Greek, reading, spelling, grammar, writing, arithmetic, and
history, but also such subjects as French, geography, logic, citizenship, penmanship,
drawing, music, geometry, algebra, chemistry, natural philosophy (physics), botany,
astronomy, human physiology (including health and hygiene), bookkeeping, and
surveying. While the increasing variety of subjects taught in local schools seemed to
violate the idea of a common curriculum, which the reform movement had been
built on, the idea itself acted as a powerful catalyst for the expansion of the number
and the kinds of subjects that the public expected all public schools to teach. When
in 1862 Congress passed the Morrill Act, which provided support for the creation
of public colleges to be devoted to agriculture and mechanical arts, the idea of a
society-centered curriculum of practical subjects was formally extended to higher
education.

Reports of the National Education Association

The nineteenth-century transition from the traditional subject-centered curriculum
toward a society-centered curriculum was neither complete nor without controversy.
As the focal point of society came increasingly into prominence and more and more
practical subjects contended with traditional academic subjects for a place in the
curricula of American schools, the questions that Franklin had avoided a century

earlier in asserting that students should learn both what is useful and what is orna-mental could be avoided no longer. What knowledge is of most worth? Can the cur-riculum accommodate both knowledge that reflects the unchanging character of truth and that also reflects the changing character of society? How much of the cur-riculum should be devoted to which kind of knowledge? What principles guide the selection of the contents of a curriculum?

The latter half of the nineteenth century can, in fact, be described as a period of debate—sometimes quite contentious—between defenders of the traditional academic curriculum based on the nature of subject matter and advocates of a newer, more practical curriculum based on the nature of society. These debates took a variety of forms, there were many specific proposals for what the curricu-lum should be, different principles of selection were espoused, and, of course, the underlying issues remained unresolved. Among the most instructive examples from these debates are three reports issued by the National Education Association (NEA) in 1876, 1893, and 1895, the last two of which became both famous and in-fluential. All three reports were written from a traditional point of view and thus emphasized the importance of subject matter as a focal point of curriculum deci-sions. Yet in one way or another all were reactions to the growing influence of society as a focal point and helped prepare the way for a third focal point, the in-dividual student.

1876: A Course of Study from Primary School to University. Founded in 1857 as the National Teachers Association and changing its name to the National Education Association in 1870, the NEA had from its inception claimed to represent a unified profession of education. Its members included college and university leaders inter-ested in public schools, school administrators, and classroom teachers. During the nineteenth-century, the NEA remained small and was dominated by administrators, not teachers, but it achieved a powerful voice, particularly through the national re-ports it issued. Distinguished educators, such as Henry Barnard, Francis W. Parker, William Torrey Harris, Charles DeGarmo, Nicholas Murray Butler, Charles W. Eliot, William Rainey Harper, Charles McMurry, and Frank McMurry, put forward their ideas through the NEA during the last three decades of the century (Butts & Cremin, 1953).

In response to the national trend in the direction of society-centered curricula, the NEA in 1876 addressed the question of what the curriculum should be in a re-port titled "A Course of Study from Primary School to University." The report was presented by a three-member committee but was clearly the work of its chairman, William Torrey Harris, one of America's foremost Hegelian philosophers. Since 1868, Harris had been the superintendent of the St. Louis schools; he was later to be the United States Commissioner of Education from 1889 to 1906 and to exert considerable influence on the NEA reports of 1893 and 1895.

Based on his Hegelian views, Harris suggested that there could be a single, uni-fied curriculum linking elementary, secondary, and higher education and that the curriculum should reflect the unified nature of knowledge. The report, therefore, was very much a defense of subject-centered curricula. It relied on the criteria of accuracy, breadth, and consistency of knowledge as the justification for the specific subjects it recommended. While it admitted some social utilitarian claims and some curricular choice for teachers and students, it heavily emphasized the value of will and mental discipline, of rationality and the written word. At all levels of education, studies would fall into five coordinated groups that collectively represented how all of knowledge was organized. Important ideas introduced in elementary schools could be repeated in more advanced form in secondary schools and in higher education. The report described the five essential groups of knowledge as follows:

I. *Inorganic Nature,* treated in (a) Mathematics, the science of the general form of nature as existing in time and space, and hence as quantitative; (b) Physics, molar and molecular, including the science of the contents of nature in their quantitative aspect.

II. *Organic Nature or Cyclic Processes,* treated in Natural History and in all natural sciences which have for their object a cyclical process, whether that of life or not; hence, astronomy, meteorology, geology, botany, and zoology, and kindred science.

III. *Theoretical Man or Intellect,* treated indirectly in (a) Philology or the science of the instrument invented for the reception, preservation, and communication of thought; treated directly in (b) Philosophy which investigates the universal and necessary conditions of existence or the forms of the mind that appear in logic, psychology, ontology, and other spheres more concrete. The study of grammar is the propaedeutic to this field.

IV. *Practical Man or Will,* treated in (a) Civil History, which portrays man's progress in realizing forms of freedom by means of political organizations; (b) Social and Political Science, which investigates the evolution of institutions of civil society and their logical basis.

V. *Aesthetical Man, or Phantasy,* as developed in the Fine Arts, and especially in Literature as the symbolic portrayal of man to himself, the collisions of his real world with his ideal, and the reconciliation of the two. (Willis et al., 1993, p. 82)

The report then went on to identify the specific school subjects that should represent each of these groups at the elementary, secondary, and higher levels of education. Figure 2.2 outlines the curriculum recommended by Harris and the NEA in 1876.

The report can be considered as an attempt to create a grand synthesis of knowledge as the basis for a universal curriculum, and, in fact, its five groups of knowledge (usually with different names) are commonly used as divisions within a liberal arts curriculum. As the basis for a single curriculum for all American education, it was, however, ultimately doomed to failure for the simple reason that Harris's views, which thoroughly permeated it, so completely favored traditional academic subjects over modern utilitarian subjects as the repositories of knowledge. Hence, the report itself really represented only one side of the national debate. The curriculum it recommended was subject-centered; therefore, it failed to satisfy advocates of society-centered curricula. The issues raised by the changing nature of American society would not go away so easily.

DISTRICT OR COMMON SCHOOL.
TOPICS RELATING TO NATURE.
Inorganic.—Arithmetic, Oral Lessons in Natural Philosophy.
Organic or Cyclic.—Geography, Oral Lessons in Natural History.
TOPICS RELATING TO MAN; OR "THE HUMANITIES."
Theoretical (Intellect).—Grammar, (Reading, Writing, Parsing and Analyzing).
Practical (Will).—History. (Of United States.)
Æsthetical (Feeling and Phantasy).—Reading Selections from English and American Literature. Drawing.

HIGH SCHOOL PREPARATORY SCHOOL.
TOPICS RELATING TO NATURE.
Inorganic.—Algebra, Geometry, Plane Trigonometry, Analytical Geometry, Natural Philosophy, Chemistry.
Organic or Cyclic.—Physical Geography, Astronomy (Descriptive), Botany or Zoology, Physiology.
TOPICS RELATING TO MAN; OR "THE HUMANITIES."
Theoretical (Intellect).—Latin, Greek, French or German, Mental and Moral Philosophy.
Practical (Will).—History (Universal), Constitution of the United States.
Æsthetical (Feeling and Phantasy).—History of English Literature, Shakespeare or some standard author (one or more whole works read).
Rhetoricals (Declamation and Composition). Drawing.

COLLEGE OR UNIVERSITY.
TOPICS RELATING TO NATURE.
Inorganic.—Analytical Geometry, Spherical Trigonometry, Differential and Integral Calculus, Physics, Chemistry, Astronomy (etc., Elective).
Organic or Cyclic.—Anatomy and Physiology, Botany, Zoology, Meteorology, Geology, Ethnology (etc., Elective).
TOPICS RELATING TO MAN; OR "THE HUMANITIES."
Theoretical (Intellect).—Latin, Greek, French or German, Comparative Philology, Logic, History of Philosophy, Plato or Aristotle, Kant or Hegel, (or representative of ancient philosophy and also one of modern philosophy).
Practical (Will).—Philosophy of History, Political Economy and Sociology, Civil and Common Law, Constitutional History, Natural Theology and Philosophy of Religion.
Æsthetical (Feeling and Phantasy).—Philosophy of Art, History of Literature, Rhetoric. The Great Masters compared in some of their greatest works: Homer, Sophocles, Dante, Shakespeare, Goethe, Phidias, Praxiteles, Skopas, Michaelangelo, Raphael, Mozart, Beethoven, &c.

FIGURE 2.2
The NEA curriculum of 1876
Source: NEA (1876).

1893: The Committee of Ten. By the 1890s, immigration was at its peak and industrialization and urbanization were in full swing. Elementary school enrollment was growing rapidly, and the curriculum of most American elementary schools was far broader than it had been early in the century. This was also the case with the secondary school curriculum, but to a lesser extent. Whereas in the 1890s most children of elementary school age were obligated by law to attend school, most children of secondary school age were free to leave school, and many did so in order to go to work. As a result, only about 10 percent of the secondary school age population attended secondary schools, but of this group, about three-quarters went on to attend institutions of higher education. Given this situation, the secondary school curriculum was still dominated by the demand of preparing students for college admission.

Most colleges then required four years of Latin and three years of Greek for admission, but entrance requirements varied enormously (to the consternation of secondary school leaders) and were changing. Colleges were beginning to adopt the elective system, permitting students some choice within collegiate curricula, which themselves were expanding to include more utilitarian and professional subjects and to reflect the growing number of academic subjects now advocated by some forty professional associations (such as the National Geographic Society) representing different academic disciplines that emerged in the second half of the nineteenth century (Willis et al., 1993, p. 85).

Primarily to deal with the problem of college admissions, the NEA issued a report in 1893 titled *Report of the Committee of Ten on Secondary Schools*. This report generated intense interest and public debate. The NEA distributed 30,000 copies to educational leaders throughout the United States, and demand was so great that in 1894 the American Book Company published many more copies, along with a topical index. The committee urged the creation of four parallel programs (classical, Latin scientific, modern languages, and Greek) from those academic subjects that it recommended all high schools teach. Figure 2.3 represents the range of subjects (in terms of periods of instruction per week to be provided) that the Committee of Ten recommended.

Tanner and Tanner (1990) summarize the intent of the committee:

> The Classical and Latin Scientific programs required four years of Latin. The Modern Languages program required four years of French and German, whereas the English program called for four years of either Latin, German, or French. Commenting on the latter two programs, which did not require Latin, the committee stated: "The programs called respectively Modern Languages and English must in practice be distinctly inferior to the other two." . . . Thus the committee had created a track system, with two superior and two inferior tracks. Yet the committee intended all four programs to be equally acceptable for admission to college. (pp. 70–71)

Beyond this bias in favor of Latin, the committee did not distinguish between appropriate subject matter for college-bound and non-college-bound students, and even the classical curriculum included more modern subjects than were usually studied in American secondary schools at the time. Clearly, the four curricula the report recommended were subject-centered, not society-centered, as were most of the

First Secondary School Year

Latin (5 periods per week); English literature (2); English composition (2); German or French (5); algebra (4); history of Italy, Spain, and France (3); applied geography (European political-continental and oceanic flora and fauna) (4); **total** (25).

Second Secondary School Year

Latin (4 periods per week); Greek (5); English literature (2); English composition (2); German or French, continued (4); French or German, begun (5); algebra (option of bookkeeping and commercial arithmetic) (2); geometry (2); botany or zoology (4); English history to 1688 (3); **total** (33).

Third Secondary School Year

Latin (4 periods per week); Greek (4); English literature (2); English composition (1); rhetoric (1); German (4); French (4); algebra (option of bookkeeping and commercial arithmetic) (2); geometry (2); physics (4); history, English and American (3); astronomy (3, first half of year); meteorology (3, second half of year); **total** (31).

Fourth Secondary School Year

Latin (4 periods per week); Greek (4); English literature (2); English composition (1); English grammar (1); German (4); French (4); trigonometry and higher algebra (2); chemistry (4); history (intensive) and civil government (3); geology or physiography (4, first half year); anatomy, physiology, and hygiene (4, second half year); **total** (33).

FIGURE 2.3

Range of high school subjects proposed by the Committee of Ten
Source: After NEA (1893).

principles of selection that the committee used. However, some of the subjects (most obviously the optional subjects bookkeeping and commercial arithmetic) were society-centered, and some principles of selection employed the criterion of social usefulness. As a whole, the report was still traditionally oriented, yet it helped move high school curricula away from their traditional preoccupation with classical studies and toward greater emphasis on modern subjects, including the sciences.

The report, however, left no room for teachers to determine the curriculum to be taught, but it did leave room in the curriculum for subjects that could be justified in terms of their usefulness in society, not (as was the case with Latin and other academic subjects) in terms of their reputed usefulness in training the mind. It also permitted students to select their own general course of studies, even if not to select specific subjects within it. Another significant principle that emerged from the report was that any of the four courses of study should be regarded as a sound basis for college or for life. The committee attempted to minimize the distinction between preparation for college and for a terminal high school degree.

The report immediately agitated both traditionalists, who thought it went too far in promoting practical subjects, and nontraditionalists, who thought it did not go far enough. With a membership that included five college presidents, the committee long retained the reputation of helping to maintain college domination of high school curricula, although what the committee actually advocated was a college preparatory curriculum as the best preparation for both college and life in general.

1895: The Committee of Fifteen.   One group of educators particularly dissatisfied with the 1893 report was the Herbartians. Originally followers of the educational ideas of the German philosopher Johann Friedrich Herbart, the Herbartians began to exert considerable influence on American curricula in the 1890s. One commentator has called them the "pioneers in the curriculum field" (Seguel, 1966, p. 46).

Herbart, like Hegel, was a philosopher concerned with how knowledge is organized. His philosophy had direct implications for curriculum and teaching that had not been reflected in the 1893 report. For instance, Herbart advocated correlation and concentration as principles of curriculum organization; he believed that all knowledge could be centered around the core subjects of history and literature. He was also a forerunner of modern cognitive psychologists in suggesting that teaching should proceed through a five-step method of organizing and presenting subject matter so that students could relate it to what they already knew.

In addition to their concern that these principles had been left out of the 1893 report, many American Herbartians were particularly concerned with Herbart's cultural epoch theory. This theory suggested that subject matter should be selected on the basis of how the development of the child recapitulated that of the human race. Nine-year-olds, for instance, might be at a precivilized stage and therefore profit from the study of *Robinson Crusoe*. Still other, more enlightened, eclectic, and less doctrinaire Herbartians believed the curriculum should not be organized around cultural epochs, but around the development of the child within the social milieu. In this sense, the Herbartians were forerunners of the modern study of child development and foreshadowed many of John Dewey's ideas about individual-centered curricula.

Aside from the Herbartians, other educators were simply disappointed that the report of the Committee of Ten was confined to secondary education, and they clamored for a report of equal magnitude and influence for elementary education. Perhaps most educators of the day shared the belief that the Committee of Ten had moved in the right direction in recommending some subjects immediately useful in contemporary society and in providing curricular options. Most probably agreed that the influence of the classics was still too great. Therefore, many were disappointed when the NEA chose William Torrey Harris, then the U. S. Commissioner of Education, as chair of the Committee of Fifteen, and even more so when its report was issued in 1895, for this report bore the stamp of Harris.

The report provided no latitude for choices by teachers or students. Nor did it provide for any differences in abilities or interests of students. Not only did it spell out what subjects were to be taught to all students throughout an eight-year elementary school program, it prescribed the number, length, and—in some cases—type of lessons to be given in each subject. Figure 2.4 outlines the recommendations of the Committee of Fifteen.

The report did include in the elementary curriculum several subjects that could be justified in terms of their social usefulness (manual training, sewing, cookery, industrial drawing) and others that were not immediately academic (aesthetic drawing, vocal music, hygiene, physical culture), but only in limited amounts. The entire eight-year curriculum was devoted primarily to grammar, literature, arithmetic,

Branches	1st year	2nd year	3rd year	4th year	5th year	6th year	7th year	8th year
Reading	10 lessons a week		5 lessons a week					
Writing	10 lessons a week		5 lessons a week		3 lessons a week			
Spelling lists				4 lessons a week				
English grammar	Oral, with composition lessons				5 lessons a week with textbook			
Latin								5 lessons
Arithmetic	Oral, 60 minutes a week		5 lessons a week with textbook					
Algebra							5 lessons a week	
Geography	Oral, 60 minutes a week		*5 lessons a week with textbook				3 lessons a week	
Natural science and hygiene	60 minutes a week							
U.S. history							5 lessons a week	
U.S. Constitution								*5 lessons
General history	Oral, 60 minutes a week							
Physical culture	60 minutes a week							
Vocal music	60 minutes a week divided into 4 lessons							
Drawing	60 minutes a week							
Manual training or sewing and cookery							One-half day each	
Number of lessons	20 + 7 daily exercise	20 + 7 daily exercise	20 + 5 daily exercise	24 + 5 daily exercise	27 + 5 daily exercise	27 + 5 daily exercise	23 + 6 daily exercise	23 + 6 daily exercise
Total hours of recitations	12	12	11	13	$16\frac{1}{4}$	$16\frac{1}{4}$	$17\frac{1}{2}$	$17\frac{1}{2}$
Length of recitations	15 minutes	15 minutes	20 minutes	20 minutes	25 minutes	25 minutes	30 minutes	30 minutes

*Begins in second half year

FIGURE 2.4

The elementary school curriculum as proposed by the Committee of Fifteen, 1895

Source: After Tanner & Tanner (1990).

geography, and history, which the committee ranked in this order for their supposed value "for developing and training the faculties of the mind, and more especially for correlating the pupil with his spiritual and natural environment in the world in which he lives" and which, the committee claimed, "are the five branches upon which the disciplinary work of the elementary school is concentrated" (Willis et al., 1993, pp. 99–100).

This curriculum was, of course, a throwback to the elementary curriculum recommended in the report of 1876. The 1895 curriculum was almost entirely subject-centered; the Committee of Fifteen had not considered (or, perhaps, had considered but rejected) the focal point of society, which had increasingly come into prominence during the nineteenth century, and the focal point of the individual, which the Herbartians had begun to advocate and for which Dewey was soon to develop a comprehensive explanation. The report appealed to traditionalists but was denounced by other educators: "President Nicholas Murray Butler of Columbia University characterized it as 'an elaborate defense of the status quo' which faced backward rather than forward and which completely ignored individuality in education" (Butts & Cremin, 1953, p. 384).

The report was quickly challenged by the Herbartians and their allies. In fact, according to Kliebard, this challenge "became, in a sense, the Fort Sumter of a war that was to rage for most of the twentieth century . . . . The clash between Harris and the Herbartians marked the beginning of a realignment of the forces that were to battle for control of the American curriculum" (Kliebard, 1986, p. 20).

2.5   THE TWENTIETH CENTURY

Cremin describes the situation in the United States at the beginning of the twentieth century:

> Not surprisingly, sustained concern with the curriculum emerged in the United States during the early decades of the Progressive Era, when for good reason and bad the schools and colleges found themselves teaching an astonishing variety of subjects to an immensely heterogeneous clientele. Elementary schools had added nature study, drawing, music, manual training, and physical education to the traditional core of reading, writing, arithmetic, history, and geography; high schools were teaching natural sciences, social studies, and a host of trade and vocational subjects alongside the older fare of languages and mathematics; and the colleges were offering all manner of literary, scientific, and professional instruction under the twin banners of equal opportunity and public service. Inexorably expansionistic about the role and function of schooling, progressives of every persuasion pressed for including their favorite subjects in programs of study; relentlessly rationalistic about the nature and management of institutions, they pressed as vigorously for a rethinking of that program as a whole. The result was the modern curriculum movement, with all its infinite diversity and with all its prodigious influence. (Cremin, 1975, pp. 19–20)

Cremin makes plain that the Progressive Era refers to a worldwide social reform movement, not just to the development of progressive education in the United States during the first decades of the twentieth century. He explains that as part of progressivism in all phases of life, progressive education meant that schools should in many ways attempt to improve the lives of individuals:

> First, it meant broadening the program and the function of the school to include direct concern for health, vocation, and the quality of family and community life.
>
> Second, it meant applying in the classroom the pedagogical principles derived from new scientific research in psychology and the social sciences.
>
> Third, it meant tailoring instruction more and more to the different kinds and classes of children who were being brought within the purview of the school. . . .
>
> Finally, Progressivism implied the radical faith that culture could be democratized without being vulgarized, the faith that everyone could share not only in the benefits of the new sciences but in the pursuit of the arts as well. (Cremin, 1961, pp. vii–ix)

Thus, the forces influential in shaping American curricula during the twentieth century included traditionalists, who advocated subject-centered curricula, and two types of nontraditionalists: those who advocated society-centered curricula, and those who advocated individual-centered curricula. Both types of nontraditionalists were a part of progressive education in general, but they often formed a very uneasy alliance.

Early in the century, John Dewey became the guiding spirit of progressive education, but his ideas were by no means synonymous with progressive education. Besides, while Dewey's writings emphasized individual experience (see "The Nature of the Individual" in section 2.2), they also described how individual experience is influenced by society-as-it-is but can lead to social change and why subject matter can be used to increase the quality of experience. In actuality, therefore, the challenge that Dewey's ideas held for curriculum decision makers during the twentieth century was, first, to understand all three focal points for curricula and, second, to bring them into some appropriate balance in making practical decisions.

All defensible approaches to modern curriculum planning and development must meet the challenge of keeping the three focal points in appropriate balance; most issues in curriculum planning and development concern how to do so or arise from failure to do so. Unfortunately, Dewey's message was subject to misinterpretation, and reform-minded advocates both of society-centered curricula and individual-centered curricula often misinterpreted Dewey in their eagerness to expand the curriculum beyond the traditional academic subjects. For instance, many progressives placed undue reliance on the structure of society or on child nature as the principal consideration in deciding what the curriculum should be.

The Cardinal Principles of Secondary Education

Much of what transpired in the first decades of the twentieth century undercut the NEA reports of 1893 and 1895 as progressive education became a major influence on the changing curricula of American schools. Not only were more students attending school, but a greater proportion of the school-age population was remaining in school, thereby forcing school curricula to cope with the needs of the general public more fully than had been the case earlier. The shock to secondary schools was greater than to elementary schools, however, for elementary schools had begun facing the problem of expansion prior to the beginning of the century. But now, for instance, secondary schools in major cities were adding entire courses of instruction devoted to vocational training.

Responding to these new and rapidly changing circumstances, the NEA appointed the Commission on Reorganization of Secondary Education to consider what the curriculum of secondary schools should be. The report of this commission, *Cardinal Principles of Secondary Education,* was published in 1918 as a federal bulletin (U.S. Department of the Interior, Bureau of Education, 1918). Completely reversing the direction of the reports of the 1890s, the commission created a statement of principles intended to broaden the curriculum of American secondary schools to encompass virtually all of life's experiences, not merely academic subjects. This report became perhaps the most famous and influential national report on curriculum in the history of the United States and served to weaken the already loosening grip of traditional subject matter on school programs.

The commission first considered the need for reorganization in terms of changes in society, changes in the secondary school population, and changes in educational theory. It noted that society was changing politically and economically, commenting particularly on how vocational specialization was changing the character of family life. Not only did it note that the secondary school population was growing rapidly, it considered unsatisfactory that, of the students who entered the first year of elementary school, only one in three reached the first year of high school, and of the students who reached high school, only one in three graduated. It noted that changes in educational theory made plain the need for secondary schools to consider individual differences in students, to promote the continuity of developmental growth, and to reexamine how different subjects contributed to "general discipline" (the training of the mind) and how they could be applied in life outside of school. It next considered the place of education in a democracy, asserting that education should contribute to the development of each individual in order that each individual might contribute to the development of society "toward ever nobler ends." Finally, in light of all that it had noted, the commission deliberated over what the objectives of education should be, concluding that there were seven main objectives:

1. Health
2. Command of fundamental processes
3. Worthy home membership
4. Vocation
5. Citizenship
6. Worthy use of leisure
7. Ethical character

Aside from the breadth of these objectives, perhaps their most striking characteristic is how they shift the focus of the curriculum away from subject matter and toward the individual student. They suggest that what is important is what happens to the student within society, not merely within the school. While these objectives were not a curriculum in and of themselves, they defined the nature of any curriculum that followed from them.

The curriculum, then, became whatever contributed to the realization of these objectives. The commission pointed out that traditional subject matter could contribute to these objectives, particularly when taught as unified studies and not in isolation (for instance, reading, writing, and arithmetic could contribute to "command of fundamental processes"; geography and history could contribute to "citizenship"), but so, of course, could many activities of daily living. Therefore, under the impact of this report, the United States collectively moved closer to the progressive notion that a curriculum was not simply an arrangement of subject matter but could include any and all activities that promoted the development of the individual within society itself. Beyond shifting the focus of curriculum decisions away from subject matter, the report also called to the attention of educators some of the differences among the planned curriculum, the enacted curriculum, and the experienced curriculum.

Franklin Bobbitt and Activity Analysis

Even though the focal point of curriculum decisions shifted away from subject matter early in the century, differences among the planned curriculum, the enacted curriculum, and the experienced curriculum were not well understood at first, nor were their implications for making practical curriculum decisions well worked out. Therefore, the first half of the twentieth century can be considered a period of experimentation with new forms of curriculum organization and new principles for guiding curriculum decisions. One crude but influential attempt in the 1910s and 1920s to use society as the sole focal point for curriculum decisions and to put such decisions on a scientific basis was made by J. Franklin Bobbitt.

In 1918, Bobbitt's book *The Curriculum* appeared. Although Bobbitt's views did not run nearly as deep as Dewey's or those of certain other educational thinkers, *The Curriculum* was probably the first book to self-consciously focus on curriculum matters exclusively and to attempt the comprehensive task of providing both a full explanation of curriculum principles and a complete set of specific procedures for creating curricula. (In this sense, *The Curriculum* is the first attempt to create what we describe in chapter 4 as "curriculum theorizing.") These practical procedures, further elaborated in Bobbitt's 1924 book *How to Make a Curriculum* and W. W. Charters's 1923 book *Curriculum Construction,* came to be known as "activity analysis." The procedures emphasized efficiency, standardization, and specialization, and they gave a semblance of certainty to people struggling to find a formula to guide their selections of the many activities of daily living that could—and now seemingly should—be included in school programs in the aftermath of *Cardinal Principles of Secondary Education.*

Bobbitt's ideas for education were similar to the ideas about efficiency that were sweeping through American industry and other phases of American life at the time. Simply put, activity analysis meant that schools should no longer attempt to teach what might foster such intangible outcomes as "mental discipline." Instead, schools should teach what is immediately and tangibly useful as determined by surveying society itself. For example, a community could make decisions about a mathematics curriculum not by referring to the inherent organization of mathematics, as traditionalists had done (presumably leading to the same decisions for all communities), but by discovering the specific mathematical procedures and skills most used by bankers and merchants along Main Street. These could become the basis for the curriculum most useful to the students within that community. Furthermore, teaching could also contribute to the efficiency of this process by being directed at the same specific, tangible ends. If a goal of the curriculum were to teach the skills of bricklaying, then a master bricklayer could be photographed at work, the basic movements of efficient bricklaying identified and broken down into submovements, and students taught to replicate these movements. This process of identifying commonly used skills and fitting curricula and teaching to whatever was tangible and most common was deemed by Bobbitt to be "scientific."

In reality, what activity analysis did was to link both curriculum and teaching directly to society, particularly to those tangible characteristics of society that were most easily discerned by the curriculum planner or developer. The society as it existed at some particular place and point in time determined what the curriculum would be, not the society as it should exist or as it would exist in the future. Therefore, under activity analysis, the role of the school was not to initiate social change but to replicate the existing society and to fit the individual student into that society. Other considerations, such as debate about value orientations underlying the curriculum or even about the wisdom of activity analysis itself, seemed irrelevant to the search for this kind of practical efficiency and could easily be dismissed as nonscientific. In emphasizing the tangible characteristics of society, activity analysis anticipated the later development of behavioral objectives, and in emphasizing the selection of curricular content as a means of reaching previously selected ends, it anticipated Tyler's rational-linear approach to curriculum planning (see chapter 3). However, for all its influence in the 1910s and 1920s and for all its later influence on similar approaches to curriculum planning and development, activity analysis did not bring the focal points of subject matter, society, and individual into appropriate balance.

Child-Centered Pedagogy

Another approach to curriculum that at first seemed consistent with Dewey's ideas but that often led to another kind of imbalance was child-centered pedagogy. Dewey had, of course, emphasized child nature and developmental growth as important considerations in making decisions about curricula, but some educators misinterpreted him (if they interpreted him at all) as suggesting that the best curriculum was the curriculum that afforded children the most complete freedom to pursue their own impulses. This curriculum was, of course, no curriculum whatsoever, at least no curriculum apart from the inner experience of the child. Thus, some advocates of a child-centered curriculum assumed that child nature itself was intrinsically good and that above all else children were to be protected from all potentially inhibiting or corrupting influences from without. During the 1920s, "freedom" and "spontaneity" became watchwords of such advocates. Decisions about what the curriculum should be—if any were made—focused on the immediate desires of individual children and did not consider such criteria as the accuracy, breadth, and consistency of subject matter nor the usefulness in or for society of what children might learn.

In the hands of an accomplished teacher, pedagogy could be child-centered yet still honor all three focal points of the curriculum. For instance, a curriculum could follow the course of children's play, emphasizing first-hand experience, but the teacher could introduce a wide variety of instructional materials that embodied the three Rs and could make suggestions about how these materials were linked to the children's present interests and about how they might lead on to future interests. The curriculum might include field trips or projects that helped children see how their present interests and activities were connected to life in the general society. Life within the school itself could emulate life within a democratic community, as Dewey advocated (Dewey, 1900), with the curriculum evolving in response to the development of the children's own community. Unfortunately, this kind of balanced approach to individual-centered curricula was probably the exception and not the rule during the 1920s and 1930s among advocates of child-centered pedagogy, who collectively emphasized freeing children from restrictions.

The 1927 NSSE Yearbook

The opening decades of the twentieth century had brought complexity and confusion to serious-minded people who made decisions about curricula. Until the nineteenth century, the curriculum could be considered an arrangement of academic subject matter. Certain time-honored subjects held the center position, even if there were some slight disagreements about which less-important subjects should be included around the edges. During the nineteenth century, social utilitarian considerations became more prominent, and the curricula of American schools increasingly included practical and scientific subjects. In the twentieth century, however, ideas about equal educational opportunity, child development, individual differences, and healthy growth led to individual-centered curricula. Activity analysts and other progressive educators with similar but less extreme views staunchly advocated society-centered curricula. Traditionalists still strongly defended subject-centered curricula. American schools were seemingly being called upon to be all things to all people, but there was neither sufficient time nor sufficient opportunity for the curriculum to include everything. Perhaps above all else, there was no agreement on what principles—among the bewildering variety being advocated—should guide curriculum decisions.

Under these circumstances, the National Society for the Study of Education (NSSE) brought together in the mid-1920s a committee of the leading curriculum scholars of the time representing competing points of view about curriculum planning and development. Chaired by Harold Rugg, the committee labored for two years attempting to reach consensus on some common principles for guiding curriculum decisions. The committee eventually identified eighteen central questions (some with subquestions) as the principal foundations on which curriculum decisions are based, and it produced a short statement delineating the issues pertinent to answering the questions. These were published as the heart of part II of the two-volume 1927 NSSE Yearbook. Part II, which was titled *The Foundations of Curriculum-Making* and edited by Rugg (Rugg, 1927), also included a far longer section consisting of "minority reports," short statements by individual members of the committee indicating disagreement with the overall report, additions to it, or other positions on it. Part II was rounded out with a large set of quotations from Dewey and from prominent American Herbartians. Figure 2.5 is the list of eighteen questions on which the committee reached consensus.

LIST OF FUNDAMENTAL QUESTIONS ON CURRICULUM MAKING
Used as the Basis for the Preparation of the General Statement:
Foundations of Curriculum Making

1. What period of life does schooling primarily contemplate as its end?

2. How can the curriculum prepare for effective participation in adult life?

3. Are the curriculum makers of the schools obliged to formulate a point of view concerning the merits or deficiencies of American civilization?

4. Should the school be regarded as a conscious agency for social improvement?
   a. Should the school be planned on the assumption that it is to fit children to live in the current social order or to rise above and lift it after them? Are children merely to be adjusted to the institutions of current society or are they to be so educated that they will be impelled to modify it? Are they to accept it or to question it?

5. How shall the content of the curriculum be conceived and stated?

6. What is the place and function of subject matter in the educative process?
   a. Subject matter is primarily matter set out to be learned. It is the conscious and specific end of school activity (educative process), and the learning activity is exactly and precisely a means to this end.

   b. Subject matter and learnings are properly both subsequent and subordinate to some normal life activity or experience (the educative process) already under way from other considerations. Subject matter is called for when, and because, this life activity has been balked for lack of a certain way of behaving. This needed way of behaving, as it is sought, found, and acquired, is what we properly call subject matter. Its function is to enable the balked activity to proceed.

7. What portion of education should be classified as general and what portion as specialized or vocational or purely optional? To what extent is general education to run parallel with vocational education and to what extent is the latter to follow on the completion of the former?

8. Is the curriculum to be made in advance?

FIGURE 2.5
The fundamental questions of curriculum making

9. To what extent is the organization of the subject matter a matter of pupil thinking and construction of, or planning by, the professional curriculum maker as a result of experimentation?
10. From the point of view of the educator, when has learning taken place?
11. To what extent should traits be learned in their natural setting (i.e., in a life situation)?
12. To what degree should the curriculum provide for individual differences?
13. To what degree is the concept of minimal essentials to be used in curriculum construction?
14. What should be the form of organization of the curriculum? Shall it be one of the following, or will you adopt others?
    a. A flexibly graded series of suggestive activities with reference to subject matter that may be used in connection with the activities.
    b. A rigidly graded series of activities with subject matter included with each respective activity.
    c. A graded sequence of subject matter with suggestion for activities to which the subject matter is related.
    d. A statement of achievements expected for each grade, a list of suggestive activities, and an outline of related subject matter, through the use of which the grade object may be achieved.
    e. A statement of grade objectives in terms of subject matter without any specific reference to activities.
15. What, if any, use shall be made of the spontaneous interests of children?
16. For the determination of what types of material (activities, reading, discussion problems and topics, group projects, and so on) should the curriculum maker analyze the activities in which adults actually engage?
    a. For skills and factual material?
    b. For group activities?
    c. For problems and issues of contemporary life?
17. How far shall methods of learning be standardized? For example, is it probable that current principles of learning will favor the use of practice devices? For individuals? For groups? How is drill to be provided?
    a. By assignment, under penalty, of specially chosen drill material?
    b. By such personal practice as the felt connections call for?
18. What are the administrative questions of curriculum making?
    a. For what time units shall the curriculum be organized?
    b. For what geographic units shall the curriculum be made?
       1. In the United States
       2. Individual states
       3. A county
       4. An individual school
    c. Shall a curriculum be made especially for rural schools?
    d. What is the optimal form in which to publish the course of study?

FIGURE 2.5 *continued*

Source: After Rugg (1927).

The committee was careful to include some questions among the eighteen that were basic to each of the three focal points for the curriculum. For instance, the list included questions about the organization of subject matter, whether children should be educated to fit into the social order or to modify it, and whether the curriculum should be "made in advance" or take advantage of "the spontaneous interests of children." The short statement that followed delineating the issues that should be considered in answering the questions was also written broadly. It directed attention to such issues as "child growth," "effective social life," "the scientific study of society," "social improvement," "changing conceptions of learning and of the subject matter of the curriculum," and "the teacher's need for an outline of desirable experiences planned in advance." Despite the committee's efforts to accommodate all points of view, the minority reports made clear that most members were far from satisfied with what they had collectively agreed to. Many minority reports reiterated their authors' previous inclinations toward subject-centered, society-centered, or individual-centered curricula.

The consensus that Rugg had pulled together for *The Foundations of Curriculum-Making* proved too fragile to hold. No new, grand theory of the curriculum that balanced all three focal points and unified American approaches to curriculum planning and development emerged from the book. Despite its eclectic approach, the book was, in fact, heavily weighted toward the newer ideas being advocated by progressive educators; therefore, traditionalists were particularly disconcerted by much of what the book seemed to recommend. And among progressives of the day, there were too many partisan spokespersons for too many diverse approaches to curriculum for the consensus to win widespread allegiance.

In effect, *The Foundations of Curriculum-Making* was a noble attempt to eliminate confusion and to create a common approach to curriculum. It identified questions and issues with which curriculum decisions must deal and offered some practical suggestions. No doubt, it also achieved some of what Rugg hoped for it in giving definition to the then-emerging curriculum field and putting the work of early curriculum theorizers on a sounder intellectual and political footing than had previously been the case. But a lasting consensus proved too difficult. *The Foundations of Curriculum-Making* can be considered a forerunner of the illusory attempts to create a single curriculum theory, which began in earnest in the 1960s and which we discuss in chapter 4.

The Eight-Year Study

Despite the development of the new ideas about curricula, the curricula of most American schools remained subject-centered during the early twentieth century. Curricula were broadening in ways consistent with the *Cardinal Principles of Secondary Education,* and more and more practical and vocational subjects were being added. However, the new ideas themselves—especially those about individual-centered curricula—were difficult to understand, and the examples of individual-centered curricula that captured public attention (such as some extreme forms of child-centered pedagogy) seemed well outside the mainstream of American education.

Many educators who found the new ideas attractive still remained unconvinced about the workability of individual-centered curricula. Ironically, the largest, best-documented, and most compelling example of the workability of experimental, individual-centered curricula, the Eight-Year Study, remained relatively unknown in its own time, although over the years since the publication in 1942 of the first volume of a comprehensive five-volume report, it has taken on mythic proportions among historians of American curricula. The Eight-Year Study not only served to undermine many of the basic assumptions of the traditional subject-centered secondary school curriculum but also provided a forum and a training ground for many educators who ultimately became leaders in the field of curriculum (Willis et al., 1993, p. 285). Tanner and Tanner refer to it as "the most important and comprehensive curriculum experiment ever carried on in the United States" (1990, p. 227).

In 1930, the Progressive Education Association (PEA) appointed a Commission on the Relation of School and College. The problem that this commission reported on in 1931 was the same as the NEA's Committee of Ten had reported on in 1893: the inhibiting influence of college entrance requirements on secondary school curricula. Wilford Aikin, chair of the commission, later stated in *The Story of the Eight-Year Study* that during preliminary discussions every suggestion for changing the curricula of secondary schools was met by the same comment: "Yes, that should be done in our high schools, but it can't be done without risking students' chances of being admitted to college. If the student doesn't follow the pattern of subjects and units prescribed by the colleges, he probably will not be accepted" (Aikin, 1942, p. 1). The commission's report prodded the PEA into undertaking an experiment into whether curricula other than the standard sixteen Carnegie Units could serve as a satisfactory preparation for college study.

The commission formulated two basic purposes:

1. To establish a relationship between school and college that would permit and encourage reconstruction in the secondary school.
2. To find, through exploration and experimentation, how the high school in the United States can serve youth more effectively (Aikin, 1942, p. 116).

To fulfill the second purpose, the commission identified thirty secondary schools or school districts that would develop curricula in their own ways. The thirty schools themselves differed from each other, ranging from small, experimentally oriented private schools (for instance, the Dalton School in New York City) to the entire secondary school systems of major cities (Denver, Des Moines, and Tulsa). Their curricula also differed but, in general, were developed cooperatively by their teachers and students. To fulfill the first purpose, the commission arranged to have more than 300 colleges accept graduates of the thirty experimental schools and districts without regard to either course requirements or entrance examinations. The study got under way in September 1933 and followed a group of students through four years of secondary school and four years of college, concluding in 1941.

Ralph W. Tyler, then a professor of education at Ohio State University, was appointed to head the evaluation committee of the study and is widely credited with developing many of the innovative means that the study employed to learn what

happened to the students it followed. The students who graduated from the experimental schools were matched in 1,475 pairs with a similar group of students who
graduated from traditional secondary school programs. The matching was done by
the colleges, and each experimental/traditional pair of students was matched on the
basis of age, sex, race, scholastic aptitude scores, home and community background,
and interests. The students in each pair were then compared throughout their college careers not only in terms of scholastic achievement but in terms of personal
characteristics, such as curiosity, resourcefulness, systematic thinking, and participation in extracurricular activities. The general finding of the Eight-Year Study was
that the graduates of experimental secondary programs enjoyed a slight academic
advantage in college over the graduates of traditional programs but were decidedly
better off in terms of their personal lives. The conclusions of the Eight-Year Study
included the following:

> First, the graduates of the Thirty Schools were not handicapped in their college
> work. Second, departures from the prescribed pattern of subjects and units did not
> lessen the students' readiness for the responsibilities of college. Third, students
> from the participating schools which made most fundamental curriculum revision
> achieved in college distinctly higher standing than that of students of equal ability
> with whom they were compared. (Aikin, 1942, p. 117)

The Eight-Year Study seemed to demonstrate that individual-centered curricula
were at least as good a preparation for college as was the traditional subject-centered
curriculum and an even better preparation for life in general. In fact, the more
experimental and individually oriented the secondary curriculum was, the better
off students seemed to be.

Unfortunately, when the five-volume report of the Eight-Year Study was published in 1942, the United States and much of the rest of the world were in the
depths of World War II. Preoccupied with war and later with recovery from war,
the nation as a whole was little influenced by the report, which remained largely
unknown and unacclaimed except among a relatively small circle of curriculum
specialists and progressive educators. Although the Eight-Year Study led to no immediate transformation of the curricula in use in American schools, it nonetheless
demonstrated the workability and benefits of progressive curriculum practices
more or less consistent with Dewey's ideas about individual students, and it did
have some long-term impact on curriculum theory and development. Under the
leadership of Tyler, it originated in-service curriculum development workshops
and techniques of evaluation directed at ascertaining students' levels and qualities
of thinking, social sensitivity, appreciations, and personal and social adjustment. It
also brought Tyler himself into prominence among curriculum specialists and
served as a catalyst for the ideas about curriculum and evaluation that he would
form into the ends-means rationale (published in 1949 as *Basic Principles of
Curriculum and Instruction,* discussed in chapter 3), which became a highly influential approach to curriculum planning and development in the decades following World War II.

After World War II

By the 1920s, progressive education had significantly influenced curriculum principles and practices in the United States, and the focal points of society and the individual had begun to be used on a wide scale. There was, of course, considerable confusion about these new focal points and the challenges they offered to the traditional focal point of subject matter, but the nation was ready to experiment with new forms of education generally. This was particularly the case during the 1930s, when the economic hardships of the Great Depression created widespread dissatisfaction with the social status quo. But with America's entry into World War II, national attention turned toward training and preparedness. Individual-centered curricula seemed less important to most Americans; society-centered curricula seemed more important. Hence, during and after the war, as the national mood turned increasingly conservative, progressive educators tended to promote curricula once again intended to fit students into society. However, exacerbated by the Cold War and fueled by a growing belief in the power of science and technology to solve national problems, the conservative mood of the 1940s and 1950s turned more and more against progressive education generally and toward traditional academic education. The national mood was no longer conducive to educational experiments, and the public increasingly demanded that schools teach subject-centered curricula, which, it believed, would lead to academic excellence, something that, the public also believed, progressive educators had lost sight of.

Sputnik and the National Response

Given these circumstances, it is not surprising that Americans perceived the former Soviet Union's launch in October 1957 of *Sputnik* (the first human-made satellite to orbit the earth) as a threat to the nation's security. *Sputnik* seemed to represent Soviet superiority in science and military technology, which, if applied in a full-scale war, could lead to the destruction of the United States. One result of these fears was that for the first time the nation began to seriously entertain the idea that a single curriculum for all schools was not just desirable, but also feasible.

The difference between desirability and feasibility is critical, however. Most pre-twentieth century curriculum proposals assumed the desirability of a single curriculum. Their proposers may even have entertained some hope that the truth and wisdom of their specific curriculum would be universally recognized and, hence, that the curriculum would be adopted in every American school. Most, we think, were not really so naïve, for most probably understood the implications of the long tradition of local control of American schools extending back to the colonial era and the long-honored American values of independence and individual initiative. Historically, American education has been highly decentralized; it cannot be centrally controlled by the federal government without the passage of a constitutional amendment.

Prior to the twentieth century, therefore, most Americans may have believed in the desirability of a single curriculum, but they clearly understood why the universal adoption of such a curriculum was not feasible. Ironically, while the twentieth century brought a clear understanding to curriculum scholars of the pluralistic nature of curricula and, hence, of why a single curriculum is not necessarily desirable, during the second half of the century, Americans collectively seemed to have been moving toward the belief that the universal adoption of a single curriculum was—or should be made—feasible. This belief, of course, is in direct conflict with traditional American beliefs valuing independence and individual initiative. The underlying conflict is far from being resolved; it will likely influence trends in curriculum well into the twenty-first century.

America's response to *Sputnik* is a case in point. If *Sputnik* demonstrated the superiority of Soviet military technology, then, many people argued, that superiority must rest on a superior educational system—particularly in subjects on which technology rests, such as the sciences and mathematics. Based on this kind of reasoning, calls were quickly issued for American schools to train a new and better generation of scientists and mathematicians and to improve the teaching of other subjects as well. This emphasis fit neatly with the trend toward subject-centered curricula that had been building since World War II; only now national security, if not survival itself, seemed to demand nothing less.

There were, of course, numerous difficulties in this response. First, *Sputnik* was the product of a small and elite group of scientists, not of the entire educational system of the Soviet Union. Clearly, the creation of advanced military technology by the United States also depended on the work of elite scientists (as it had with the creation of the atom and the hydrogen bombs). Second, if American technology lagged behind Soviet technology, then attempting to overcome the gap by using schools to train a new generation of scientists and mathematicians would take at least another generation. Third, given the pluralistic, decentralized character of American education, there was little reason to believe that schools would collectively pull in the same direction, even in the face of what was a widely perceived threat. Fourth, even if schools were to pull together, orienting all students toward accomplishment and careers in science and mathematics might be beneficial for students who eventually undertook such careers, but the benefits (or potential detriments) for other students were unclear. There might be many but quite varied reasons for individual students to study science, mathematics, or any other subjects other than the reasons then dominating national thinking. In many ways, the national response was analogous to what might have occurred had the United States decided that national prestige depended on winning more Olympic gold medals than any other nation and the best way to do so was to have each school train its students for superior athletic performance in Olympic events.

Soon the national response to *Sputnik* became focused directly on the curriculum. Changing the schools in fundamental ways (such as hiring new, better-trained teachers more oriented toward subject-centered curricula) seemed too difficult and time consuming, but with sufficient amounts of persuasion and money perhaps most American schools could be enticed into quickly adopting rigorous academic curricula. Although the federal government could not prescribe curricula, it could and did provide money. The federal strategy was to create a series of curricular packages, which, if sufficiently attractive, many American schools might willingly adopt. These packages began with the sciences and mathematics and were later to be developed for other academic subjects. Some of the nation's leading academics (including Nobel Prize winners from prestigious institutions) participated in the deliberations that produced these packages. The thinking in federal agencies such as the National Science Foundation, which sponsored the development of these packages, was that the acknowledged experts in, say, the biological sciences best understood the nature of this subject matter and, therefore, should make the decisions about what the biological sciences curriculum should be, not the teachers who would eventually teach the curriculum.

The intellectual glue that held this approach together was provided by Jerome Bruner (Bruner, 1960), for most of the federal packages were based on Bruner's ideas about how the mind processes information. According to Bruner, everyone thinks in similar ways; therefore, a curriculum could be intellectual, academic, and much the same for everyone. Any curriculum should begin with what Bruner called "structure." The structure of an academic discipline is formed by the most fundamental ideas on which that discipline is based. When students learn these ideas prior to specific facts or peripheral information about the subject, the efficiency of learning is greatly enhanced and new information can be meaningfully related to what students already know. This effect can be further enhanced by what Bruner called "discovery"; that is, curricula should be designed so that students are not told what the structure of a particular subject is but are led to discover the principles for themselves. In this way, according to Bruner, students learn more, learn more quickly and meaningfully, forget less rapidly, find learning enjoyable, and are able to transfer what they learn to new situations. For instance, algebra is based on the principle of balance. Understanding this principle helps students understand how to balance equations. But balance is a principle that is so fundamental that it is transdisciplinary. Thus, what students learn about balance as fundamental in algebra also helps them learn about balance as fundamental in physics, chemistry, art, and other subjects.

The Curriculum Reform Movement

The entry of the federal government into curriculum development led to a series of well-designed curriculum packages in several areas of natural science and was termed the "curriculum reform movement," although it had little direct impact on other academic subjects. Bolstered by federally funded summer workshops that acquainted teachers with these packages, they were adopted by many American secondary schools (though far from a majority of such schools) during the 1960s. Perhaps the most notable feature of these packages was that many were designed to be teacherproof. Throughout the 1950s, critics had portrayed the schools as anti-intellectual, nonrigorous, and too much engaged in individual-centered curricula; *Sputnik* seemed to confirm those criticisms. Therefore, teachers were seen as being insufficiently knowledgeable about the subjects they were teaching. Certainly most teachers were less familiar with the structure of their subjects than were the Nobel laureates and other subject matter experts the federal government called upon.

Thus, there was considerable reluctance to entrust teachers with decisions about what Bruner indicated should be taught (structure) or how it should be taught (through discovery). Teacher proof curriculum packages typically contained explanations and directions for teachers and materials and directions for students that left little room for deviation from the curriculum that others had planned.

Such curricula were rejected by teachers for both bad reasons and good ones. As designers feared, some teachers did not understand the structure of the subjects they taught. Feeling threatened, many teachers attempted to avoid using the new curricula or to sabotage them when their use became unavoidable. Other teachers understandably felt that they should have a greater role in teaching a curriculum than simply passing out predetermined materials and directions at the beginning of a class period and collecting them at the end. Still other teachers, of course, welcomed the new curricula for the reasons Bruner had foreseen. Not surprisingly, especially where teachers learned how to modify these curricula to suit the specific purposes and students in their classrooms, these curricula were often used with considerable pleasure and success by both students and teachers.

Despite these first widespread efforts of the federal government to develop curricula for use in schools throughout the nation, the Curriculum Reform Movement had relatively little long-term impact on the schools. Adoption of the new curricula remained voluntary and sporadic. New curricula in subjects other than the sciences and mathematics proved even more difficult to design and to develop and for the most part did not materialize. But perhaps the most significant influence on the demise of the movement was that by the late 1960s, the general mood of the nation had dramatically changed once again. Skepticism about the wisdom of pursuing the Vietnam War was boiling over into outright defiance of the federal government, and the promises made at mid-decade by the Johnson administration to use education to end poverty, to promote social justice, and to create "the Great Society" in the United States were increasingly seen as unworkable and illusory. Education in general and subject-centered curricula in particular suddenly seemed to many Americans to have little power to deal with the many problems—mostly social in origin—that were dividing the nation. At the end of the decade, the attention of both educators and the American public itself was being captured (albeit briefly) by free schools, open classrooms, and how individual-centered and society-centered curricula could be worked out within them.

In retrospect, the curriculum reform movement of the 1960s seems to have been born of exaggerated criticisms of American schools and exaggerated fears about national security. Nonetheless, there was some measure of truth in both criticisms and fears, and the movement still seems an honest and straightforward effort to improve schools by improving curricula, much as some of the famous national reports of earlier eras had attempted. The depth of the fears themselves and the entry of the federal government into large-scale efforts to reform American schools seemed to change in some fundamental way how Americans thought about the curriculum. Education had gradually been assuming an increasingly important place in American life. For instance, by the 1960s, most Americans believed that without the benefit of an education, individuals had fewer opportunities for getting ahead in life socially or economically than had been the case in earlier eras, when hard work and individual initiative seemed sufficient by themselves. Since more now seemed at stake in education for both the nation and for individuals, Americans also seemed less willing to trust traditional state and local procedures for making curriculum decisions. More Americans than at any time in the past seemed to think that perhaps the nation would be better off if it could find a way of requiring everyone to study the same thing. Thus, the most lasting influence of the curriculum reform movement may have been to move many Americans to seriously consider not only the desirability but also the feasibility of a single curriculum.

A New Risk to the Nation

By the late 1960s, the belief in the desirability of a single curriculum was being reinforced by a pervasive and gradually deepening national malaise. This malaise was social, political, and economic. Problems that in previous decades seemed solvable now seemed intractable. The growing prosperity of the 1950s and early 1960s was giving way to recession and inflation. Above all, America was facing a crisis of confidence in its views and its ability to act on them. In the 1970s, national trends in education in general and curriculum in particular reflected this ebbing national confidence. Education no longer seemed to be the panacea it once was. Many people were unsure about what American schools should be doing in the first place and skeptical about how well they did anything.

In the 1970s, many pressures mounted on schools for what then became known as "accountability." On its surface, accountability seemed quite reasonable: it asked that teachers assume responsibility for what they do. Beneath its surface, however, it usually became the thoroughly unreasonable and unrealistic demand that teachers be held responsible for what their students learned. This position was taken despite the fact that teachers cannot control many significant influences on learning, such as the values a student's family holds about education or the adequacy of a school district's budget. Applied to curriculum, this kind of pressure led toward the narrowing of what was taught and how it was taught to small and nonproblematical units, especially those that could be most easily tested. This result was much like the result in the 1920s of the activity analysis advocated by Bobbitt and Charters.

Essentially, accountability was a popular but flawed way in which American society attempted to force schools to become more efficient. And when students did not seem to learn more, skepticism deepened further. More and more people came to believe that even greater efficiencies in what schools did would do little good if schools are not teaching the right things. Thus in the 1980s, the still deepening national malaise led to many efforts to reform school curricula. In that decade, at least 700 national reports on the state of American education were issued by various governmental agencies and private organizations. Most were highly critical of American schools. Yet despite the sheer volume of these many reports, one stood out far above all the rest in terms of its influence on curriculum nationally, and that influence has remained both pervasive and strong in the 2000s.

The National Commission on Excellence in Education

The report that so greatly influenced American education resulted directly from the political situation in the United States. Ronald Reagan, a Republican, was elected to the presidency in 1980, running against big government—especially against bureaucratic governmental regulations—and promising to reduce taxes. One of his campaign promises was to abolish the U.S. Department of Education, which had been established as a Cabinet-level department by his predecessor, Jimmy Carter, a Democrat. Reagan was displeased with the traditional support given by American teachers to Democrats, and the Department of Education was widely perceived as a bastion of teachers. Given the public mood of dissatisfaction with education in general and teachers in particular, the department was an easy political target. However, something went awry. Reagan's appointee as Secretary of Education, Terrel H. Bell, created the National Commission on Excellence in Education (NCEE) in August 1981, and when the NCEE in April 1983 released its report, *A Nation at Risk: The Imperative for Educational Reform,* the firestorm of public reaction was so great that Reagan found it more politically advantageous to embrace the report, portraying himself as an educational reformer, than to abolish the Department of Education, which had commissioned the report.

A Nation at Risk, apparently, told the United States exactly what it was ready to hear, for public approval was instantaneous and overwhelming. The report identified a crisis that it alleged the nation was facing; its proposed solution was largely through the reform of the curricula of American secondary schools. In the post-*Sputnik* years, most Americans had believed the greatest threat to national security was military, but in the 1980s, most Americans believed it to be economic. The opening paragraphs of *A Nation at Risk* played heavily on this fear. In overblown language and metaphors borrowed from athletic competition and the military, it began as follows:

> Our Nation is at risk. Our once unchallenged preeminence in commerce, industry, science, and technological innovation is being overtaken by competitors throughout the world. This report is concerned with only one of the many causes and dimensions of the problem, but it is the one that undergirds American prosperity, security, and civility. We report to the American people that while we can take justifiable pride in what our schools and colleges have historically accomplished and contributed to the United States and the well-being of its people, the educational foundations of our society are presently being eroded by a rising tide of mediocrity that threatens our very future as a Nation and a people. What was unimaginable a generation ago has begun to occur—others are matching and surpassing our educational attainments.
>
> If an unfriendly foreign power had attempted to impose on America the mediocre educational performance that exists today, we might well have viewed it as an act of war. As it stands, we have allowed this to happen to ourselves. We have even squandered the gains in achievement made in the wake of the Sputnik challenge. Moreover, we have dismantled essential support systems which helped make those gains possible. We have, in effect, been committing an act of unthinking, unilateral educational disarmament. (National Commission on Excellence in Education, 1983, p. 5)

The NCEE offered surprisingly little evidence to back up these assertions, and much of the evidence offered or the way the NCEE interpreted it was, in fact, highly suspect. Indeed, some of the evidence was contrary to the claim that the nation was being threatened by "a rising tide of mediocrity" in education. For example, it stated that

> [I]t is important, of course, to recognize that *the average citizen* today is better educated and more knowledgeable than the average citizen of a generation ago—more literate, and exposed to more mathematics, literature, and science. The positive impact of this fact on the well-being of our country and the lives of our people cannot be overstated. Nevertheless, *the average graduate* of our schools and colleges today is not as well-educated as the average graduate of 25 or 35 years ago, when a much smaller proportion of our population completed high school and college. The negative impact of this fact likewise cannot be overstated. (p. 11; italics in the original)

That the average citizen in 1983 was "better educated and more knowledgeable" than in the past can, as the NCEE suggests, be interpreted as an indicator of improving quality in education, since a higher proportion of citizens have been graduated from American schools in each generation. That the average graduate in 1983 was not as well educated as in the past, when, as the NCEE says, "a much smaller proportion of our population completed high school and college" cannot, as the NCEE claims, be interpreted as an indicator of declining quality (or rising mediocrity). Such an interpretation requires comparison of the educational attainments *of the same proportions of the overall population* who were graduates of American schools at different times, a comparison that the NCEE neglected to make. Perhaps the greatest irony of *A Nation at Risk* is that while it exhorts excellence, it is itself riddled with basic errors in logic and in the use of evidence.

Nor did it necessarily follow that the nation was threatened economically and its schools declining because the "unchallenged preeminence in commerce, industry, science, and technological innovation" that the United States had enjoyed since World War II was in question. In fact, the United States had pursued policies intended to help both friends and former military foes to democratize their political systems and to rebuild their economic systems. That other nations had made substantial gains economically and educationally could—and perhaps should, even in 1983—have been interpreted as being in the best interests of the United States. A more enlightened interpretation of the increasing prosperity and educational attainments of other nations was that such increases might represent the basis for a more prosperous and politically stable global community from which all nations could benefit. In such a community, the long-range prosperity of the United States would depend on cooperation and collaboration, not on hegemony. The xenophobic tone of large portions of *A Nation at Risk* was not only unseemly, but it probably helped further deepen the national malaise that gave rise to the report in the first place.

Recommendations. Given the kind of hysteria and atmosphere of crisis that the NCEE's rhetoric seemed intended to foster, its recommendations for reforming American education were remarkably prosaic. The NCEE made five general recommendations, but the first was the centerpiece of *A Nation at Risk*. Under the heading "Content," it recommended that high school graduation require the study of what it called the "Five New Basics," defined as four years of English, three years of mathematics, three years of science, three years of social studies, and one-half year of computer science. Additionally, for college-bound students it recommended two years of foreign language beyond studies begun in elementary school. Of course, with the exception of the one-half year of computer science, there was nothing at all new about these basic subjects or even the relative amounts of time devoted to each. This kind of organization of subjects had been the staple of the academic curriculum of American high schools since roughly the middle of the nineteenth century. In fact, with the additional exception of the demotion of the study of foreign languages from required for every student to recommended for only the college-bound, the high school curriculum recommended by the NCEE in 1983 bears an uncanny resemblance to the high school curriculum recommended by the NEA's Committee of Ten in 1893.

Completely apart from the wisdom or the lack thereof in its recommendations, the NCEE seemed nearly oblivious to the influences of the massive demographic and social changes that had swept the United States in the previous ninety years and resulted in the expansion of the high school curriculum to include many additional studies, such as vocational education. The NCEE made only passing mention of additional subjects that could supplement those it recommended. Yet the population of the United States had grown much larger and more diverse, and the high schools no longer served a small, elite group within the general population. In 1893, approximately 10 percent of the high school age population was actually attending high school (with most of those students going on to college); in 1983 nearly 90 percent of the high school age population attended. Nor did the NCEE seem at all concerned with the new developments in curriculum (such as individual-centered curricula) and pedagogy (such as the project method) that had been worked out in the twentieth century. Just as the Committee of Ten in 1893 had recommended that the same subject-centered curriculum that prepares for admission to college is also the best preparation for life, so, too, did the NCEE in 1983.

The remaining four recommendations were an anticlimax, for collectively they represented more of the same. Under the heading "Standards and Expectations," the NCEE recommended that "schools, colleges, and universities adopt more rigorous and measurable standards" (p. 27); under the heading "Time," that "significantly more time be devoted to learning the New Basics"(p. 29), including lengthening both the school day and the school year; under "Teaching," that salaries and working conditions be improved in order to attract and to retain better-quality teachers; and under "Leadership and Fiscal Support," that citizens "hold educators and elected officials responsible for providing the leadership necessary to achieve these reforms, and that citizens provide the fiscal support" (p. 32).

Amid the well-orchestrated media blitz that attended the release of *A Nation at Risk* in April 1983, President Reagan announced to the nation that any additional money that might be needed to support its recommendations would not be forthcoming from the federal government. The federal government had exercised its leadership in providing the report, he suggested; it was now up to the citizens of the United States to adopt its recommendations and to provide the fiscal support necessary for their implementation. In reality, President Reagan's tactic was much like the tactic adopted by the report itself. In announcing a new educational crisis and in making recommendations, *A Nation at Risk* played on some of the specific insecurities that accompanied the general national malaise, and in its concluding sections headed "America Can Do It," "A Word to Parents and Students," and "A Final Word," it exhorted all citizens to embrace its proposed solutions to the crisis, ending with this paragraph:

> It is their [students, parents, educators, and other groups] America, and the America of all of us, that is at risk; it is to each of us that this imperative is addressed. It is by our willingness to take up the challenge, and our resolve to see it through, that America's place in the world will be either secured or forfeited. Americans have succeeded before and so we shall again. (p. 36)

The contrast between the opening paragraphs of *A Nation at Risk* and its closing sections is striking. The NCEE had begun by portraying a national crisis in extreme terms: a rapidly declining economy caused by a crumbling educational system. Yet it concluded by suggesting that the crisis was actually quite simple to resolve: The educational system needed no extensive reforms in organization, personnel, or teaching practices; it only needed to get back to teaching a few basic academic subjects, to spend more time on this task, to test students more, and to measure the results more frequently. Without doubt, Americans would do this, the NCEE asserted, once they recognized what they had to do. The NCEE could give itself credit for both identifying the crisis and pointing the way toward its resolution.

A Legacy of Risk.   Amid the choruses of approval that greeted *A Nation at Risk,* some important points were lost. First, if the national crisis was economic, perhaps some examination and reform of the economic system was also called for. Perhaps the economic gains made by such countries as Japan, which the NCEE cited as signs of educational crisis in the United States, were due to differences in business practices and economic policies. For instance, if prior to the 1980s, major American industries had deliberately organized themselves in order to maximize profits by relying on cheap unskilled and semiskilled workers rather than on more expensive high-tech workers, then the decisions of industry leaders might be responsible for their difficulties in competing with high-tech Japanese industries, not the curricula of American schools. Furthermore, such decisions made by American industries might actually have reduced the incentives for prospective workers to achieve excellence in schooling. This kind of scrutiny of the American economic system, however, was incompatible with the laissez-faire economic doctrines of President Reagan, and it was much easier politically (as it had been in the post-*Sputnik* years) to blame a national crisis on the schools rather than seeking out and attempting to correct its real causes. Second, the educational crisis alleged by the NCEE may have been overblown. Certainly, the NCEE had difficulty in accurately interpreting the evidence it cited to justify this allegation, but was the evidence itself sound? And was the NCEE unbiased in its selection of evidence? Some thoughtful commentators believed the NCEE to be more than simply careless in its use of evidence:

> To build perception of 'mediocrity,' the NCEE turned to the SAT [Scholastic Aptitude Test] as one key index of several showing decline in achievement. The NCEE presentation of the SAT repeated earlier distortions. In a now familiar litany, the NCEE pointed to the long SAT decline from 1963–80, but it chose to ignore some key facts. The SAT *began* declining in the heyday of the post-Sputnik reforms. The SAT *stopped* declining the year before the NCEE reported. In 1982, black SAT scores *were rising faster* than white scores. This complicated picture of reality conveniently disappeared . . . [because these] facts in 1983 unfortunately contradicted some of the NCEE's claims, namely, that schools squandered gains made in the wake of Sputnik and the continuing decline still puts the country at risk. The NCEE was also mute on the positive NAEP [National Assessment of Educational Progress] scores from the 1970s. . . . (Shor, 1986, p. 109; italics in the original)

It is possible that the NCEE selected evidence in order to fit its own preconceived notions (and to persuade the nation of the correctness of these notions) rather than doing a careful analysis of the real strengths and weaknesses of American education.

Such suspicions about the motives and methods of the NCEE were later bolstered by Terrel H. Bell himself in 1988, when as the former U.S. Commissioner of Education, he published a book about his experiences as a member of the first Reagan administration (Bell, 1988). In this book, he suggested that among his purposes in establishing the NCEE were to save the Department of Education from abolition and to refocus the attention of the nation on the importance of education. If so, then these purposes were fulfilled, but perhaps at a highly significant cost to education and even to the nation itself. The greatest legacy of the NCEE and *A Nation at Risk* may have been to heighten and to perpetuate the stereotype that education is both the cause and the potential solution to virtually all national problems. Thus, the most influential and widely cited curriculum document of the 1980s appears to have reinforced this kind of stereotypical thinking, setting up educators to take the blame whenever the public might decide that the latest round of reforms had failed to solve national problems.

Implications for Curriculum.   In the last analysis, however, in order to have reservations about the implications of *A Nation at Risk* for curriculum decision making, it is not necessary to hold that the NCEE had a preconceived agenda nor that it deliberately exacerbated the existing national malaise. While excellence is a worthy general goal for American education, it does not follow that the best way of attempting to achieve excellence is through the same kind of curriculum (in this case, a subject-centered curriculum) being used in all American schools.

Although it is not surprising, it is certainly disappointing that the NCEE should recommend national curriculum reform while itself being so little acquainted with the major lessons of curriculum history in the twentieth century—particularly the need for balance among the focal points of subject, society, and individual in making any curriculum decision. Not only did *A Nation at Risk* tell the United States that a single, subject-centered curriculum was good for everyone, the example of the NCEE itself suggested that such a curriculum could be created and implemented top-down (that is, designed by a central group and widely adopted because of the wisdom, power, or persuasiveness of that group). Furthermore, the recommendations and the example of the NCEE left relatively little room for teachers to implement the curriculum flexibly. If the nation really were at risk because of poor education, it simply would not suffice, the NCEE strongly implied, for teachers to modify the best possible solution and to take it in many different directions. In effect, the planned curriculum was to be the enacted curriculum and the experienced curriculum as well. The NCEE was out of touch not only with the twentieth century curriculum history we have described in this chapter, but also with the development of curriculum theorizing during the 1970s and 1980s (which we describe at length in chapter 4). Its recommendations and example ignored the bottom-up, grassroots approaches to curriculum planning based on traditional American values of individual initiative.

2.6   PROSPECTS FOR THE TWENTY-FIRST CENTURY

Whatever its strengths and weaknesses, *A Nation at Risk* has set the tone for national debates about education since 1983. Certainly, throughout the 1990s and into the 2000s the American public seemed not to change its mind about what, in general, the NCEE had recommended. Talk about a national curriculum increased in both frequency and intensity, although little actually was done (such as amending the Constitution to create federal authority over education) to make such a curriculum feasible. Nonetheless, many politicians—including both Republican and Democratic presidential administrations—have advocated standardized goals for all schools, including the teaching of most of the "new basics" of the NCEE. For instance, throughout the 1990s the federal government promulgated a set of national goals (published as *America 2000,* 1991, and which we discuss in chapter 9) that explicitly mentions English, mathematics, science, and history and that reads like a spin-off from *A Nation at Risk.*

The current situation, however, is far from clear, since many contradictory expectations for American education now exist side-by-side, many of these bearing upon curriculum. On one hand, the nation collectively considers ideas that will help maintain its traditionally pluralistic educational system: site-based management (discussed in chapter 6), charter schools (discussed in chapter 9), and vouchers and tuition tax credits (two ways—perhaps unconstitutional—of providing public funds to expand private schooling). On the other hand, the nation considers ideas that will promote uniformity throughout its schools: curriculum alignment and high-stakes testing (both discussed in chapter 7) and accountability (discussed earlier in this chapter and again in chapter 9). The overall drift, however, is in the direction of uniformity. Precisely how this drift will influence curriculum decision making in the twenty-first century remains to be seen.

Still, not only does a single curriculum now seem desirable to many Americans, but many seem increasingly inclined to seek ways to make the widespread adoption of such a curriculum feasible, however unlikely it is that such a curriculum would adequately balance the focal points of subject matter, society, and the individual. The principal tensions over curriculum in the United States in the first decades of the twenty-first century are likely to be how to strike an appropriate balance among focal points despite the general drift toward uniformity and standardization.

2.7   CONCLUDING COMMENT

This chapter has briefly described not only different curricula that in the past have been used in or recommended for American schools, but also the different beliefs that Americans have held as a basis for these curricula. In effect, it also gives a brief history of changing conceptions of curriculum and changing approaches to curriculum planning and development. At some times to some people, criteria concerning the accuracy, breadth, or consistency of subject matter have seemed the most important in deciding what the curriculum should be. At other times to other people, criteria concerning the usefulness of the curriculum in maintaining or in changing the existing society have seemed more important. And at still other times other people have found criteria derived from the developmental growth of individuals to be the most important of all. Some approaches seem to place more emphasis than others on the planned curriculum, or the enacted curriculum, or the experienced curriculum and seem to lead to different roles for students, teachers, administrators, and other people involved in the process of creating curricula in use.

Not surprisingly, the curricula of contemporary schools are seldom pure types. Almost always, contemporary curricula have been created eclectically, through a variety of alternative approaches, whether the people most involved in their creation have understood that fact or not. This book is based on the assumption that anyone involved in contemporary curriculum planning and development should be aware of that fact and, indeed, of the possibilities of a well-reasoned eclecticism in their own curriculum work. That is the challenge Dewey identified at the beginning of the twentieth century, and yet, a century later, it is still not well understood. This chapter has been written, therefore, in the belief that familiarity with the changing approaches to curriculum in the past will help readers develop a critical awareness useful in selecting their own approaches and, particularly, in bringing the focal points of subject matter, society, and individual into appropriate balance in their own future decisions about what curricula should be.

■ QUESTIONS AND REFLECTIONS

1. Obtain the curriculum (or the curriculum guide) of a school or school district with which you are familiar. Is the curriculum primarily subject-centered, society-centered, or individual-centered? Does it explicitly acknowledge any of these three focal points? Does it make any provision for striking a balance among them? What historical approaches to curriculum seem to be implicit in it?

2. Interview administrators and teachers in your local school district. To what extent are they aware of the nineteenth- and twentieth-century history of curricula? What misconceptions do they seem to hold about what curricula were like 150 years ago, 100 years ago, and 50 years ago?

3. Attend sessions devoted to curriculum planning or development. Do the positions taken by any participants seem to reflect a knowledge of curriculum history? How might knowledge of curriculum history modify the positions of any of the participants? How might such knowledge modify the entire character of the deliberations?

4. Reconsider the entire history of the American curriculum, which you have read about in this chapter. Select two or three of the salient ideas, events, or trends that seem to you to have the most potential impact on curriculum decision making today. Consider how you might introduce them as evidence into some current curriculum deliberations.

5. Historically, have there been any connections between curricula centered on subject matter, or society, or the individual and curricula conceived as planned, or enacted, or experienced? If so, do these connections seem historical accidents or something inherent in the nature of curriculum itself?

6. Consider your own general value orientation. Does it predispose you toward one of the three focal points for making curriculum decisions more than the other two? If so, how do you propose to maintain a reasonable balance among the three focal points in your thinking and future deliberations about curricula?

7. This chapter has suggested that during the first half of the twentieth century, the three focal points for the curriculum often came into competition. Chapter 4 describes efforts since the 1960s (often referred to as "curriculum theorizing") to reduce competition among points of view. Attempt to anticipate the main ideas in chapter 4 in light of what you have learned in this chapter and of what you already know about curriculum trends since the 1960s.

8. This chapter describes a number of ironies, inconsistencies, and contradictions in how Americans approach education generally and curriculum issues specifically. Consider what the most significant of these are and how they affect curriculum planning and development today. Attempt to anticipate how they will do so in the future.

9. A curriculum can be based on perceived threats to a nation. List the pros and cons of attempting to create a curriculum on such a basis. Weigh each pro and con carefully until you arrive at your own opinion of the wisdom of this kind of approach to curriculum planning and development.

10. The social and educational history that this chapter describes is of the United States. The recent trends in curriculum that it describes are based largely on developments in the United States. Nonetheless, both history and trends have parallels in many other countries that can be applied relevantly to their own educational systems. If you are from the United States, consider how this chapter applies to curriculum issues in any other countries with which you are familiar. If you are from a country other than the United States, consider how the chapter applies to your own country.

■ SUGGESTED READING

Books on the history of the American curriculum (see Bibliography) include these:

Beyer & Apple (1988)

Doll (1993)

Franklin (1986)

Jackson (1992)

Kliebard (1986)

Kliebard (1992)

Seguel (1966)

Tanner & Tanner (1990)

Willis et al. (1993)

■ BIBLIOGRAPHY

Aikin, W. M. (1942). *The story of the Eight-Year Study.* New York: Harper & Brothers.

Bell, T. H. (1988). *The thirteenth man: A Reagan cabinet memoir.* New York: The Free Press.

Beyer, L. E., & Apple, M. W. (Eds.). (1998). *The curriculum: Problems, politics, and possibilities* (2nd ed.). Albany: State University of New York Press.

Bobbitt, J. F. (1918). *The curriculum.* Boston: Houghton Mifflin.

Bobbitt, J. F. (1924). *How to make a curriculum.* Boston: Houghton Mifflin.

Bruner, J. S. (1960). *The process of education.* New York: Vintage Books.

Butts, R. F., & Cremin, L. A. (1953). *A history of education in American culture.* New York: Henry Holt.

Charters, W. W. (1923). *Curriculum construction.* New York: Macmillan.

Cremin, L. A. (1961). *The transformation of the school: Progressivism in American education, 1876–1957.* New York: Vintage Books.

Cremin, L. A. (1970). *American education: The colonial experience, 1607-1783.* New York: Harper & Row.

Cremin, L. A. (1975). Curriculum making in the United States. In W. Pinar (Ed.), *Curriculum theorizing: The reconceptualists* (pp. 14–35). Berkeley, CA: McCutchan.

Dewey, J. (1897). My pedagogic creed. *The School Journal, 54*(3), 77–80.

Dewey, J. (1900). *The school and society.* Chicago: University of Chicago Press.

Dewey, J. (1902). *The child and the curriculum.* Chicago: University of Chicago Press.

Dewey, J. (1938). *Experience and education.* New York: Macmillan.

Doll, W. E., Jr. (1993). *A post-modern perspective on curriculum.* New York: Teachers College Press.

Franklin, B. M. (1986). *Building the American community: The school curriculum and the search for social control.* London: Falmer.

Hlebowitsh, P. S. (1999). The burdens of the new curricularist. *Curriculum Inquiry, 29*(3), 343–353.

Jackson, P. W. (Ed.). (1992). *Handbook of research on curriculum.* New York: Macmillan.

Kliebard, H. M. (1986). *The struggle for the American curriculum: 1893–1958.* Boston: Routledge & Kegan Paul.

Kliebard, H. M. (1992). *Forging the American curriculum: Essays on curriculum history and theory.* New York: Routledge.

National Commission on Excellence in Education. (1983). *A nation at risk: The imperative for educational reform.* Washington, DC: U.S. Government Printing Office.

National Education Association. (1876). A course of study from primary school to university. *Journal of Addresses and Proceedings.* Washington, DC: National Educational Association.

National Education Association. (1893). *Report of the Committee of Ten on secondary schools.* Washington, DC: U.S. Government Printing Office.

National Education Association. (1895). *Report of the Committee of Fifteen on elementary education.* New York: American Book Company.

Rugg, H. O. (Ed.). (1927). *The foundations of curriculum-making.* Twenty-Sixth Yearbook of the National Society for the Study of Education, Part II. Bloomington, IL: Public School Publishing Company.

Santora, E. D. (2001). Historiographic perspectives of context and progress during a half century of progressive educational reform. In L. M. Burlbaw (Ed.), *Curriculum history 2000* (73–85). College Station, TX: Society for the Study of Curriculum History.

Seguel, M. L. (1966). *The curriculum field: Its formative years.* New York: Teachers College Press.

Shor, I. (1986). *Culture wars: School and society in the conservative restoration, 1969–1984.* New York: Routledge & Kegan Paul.

Tanner, D., & Tanner, L. N. (1990). *History of the school curriculum.* New York: Macmillan.

U.S. Department of Education. (1991). *America 2000: An education strategy.* Sourcebook. Washington, DC: U.S. Department of Education.

U.S. Department of the Interior, Bureau of Education. (1918). *Cardinal principles of secondary education: A report of the Commission on the Reorganization of Secondary Education.* Washington, DC: U.S. Government Printing Office.

Willis, G., Schubert, W. H., Bullough, R. V., Kridel, C., & Holton, J. T. (Eds.). (1993). *The American curriculum: A documentary history.* Westport, CT: Greenwood Press.

Approaches to Curriculum

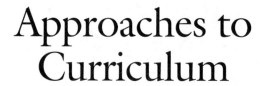

■ **ABOUT THIS CHAPTER**

Curriculum planning, curriculum decision making, and curriculum development are all forms of curriculum work; to be done well, all must be based on a clear and consistent understanding of what curriculum is. Thus, different approaches to curriculum work can be considered as different ways of thinking about curriculum and of connecting thought with practice, whether the many beliefs and ideas that constitute any particular curriculum approach are made explicit or remain implicit. In general, for any set of beliefs and ideas to be considered an approach, it must be sufficiently consistent and comprehensive to represent a reasonable guide for making coherent both thinking and acting. Different approaches can be characterized by the kinds of curriculum questions they focus on.

To exemplify these points, this chapter analyzes three well-known, highly influential approaches to curriculum: Tyler's rational-linear approach, Walker's deliberative approach, and Eisner's artistic approach. The analyses point out what different approaches do and do not have in common, the choices implicit within them, and the demands they make on people engaged in curriculum development.

■ **WHAT YOU SHOULD DO**

1. Critically compare the three approaches to curriculum planning of Tyler, Walker, and Eisner, especially considering what each suggests about how thought and practice are connected in curriculum work.
2. Reflect on the value orientations inherent within these approaches and what the approaches suggest about the work of curriculum developers and teachers.
3. Decide which approach or which parts of different approaches you would adopt in your own curriculum work.
4. Remain open to changing or modifying your preferred approach as you read subsequent chapters of this book.

■ SOME OPTIONAL APPROACHES

You may find it useful to read chapter 3 in terms of the following options.

Option A

1. Before reading this chapter, consider what seems to constitute adequate thinking about curriculum. Consider what seems to constitute adequate curriculum work. Finally, consider what seems to constitute the connection between thought and practice in curriculum. Then as you read the curriculum approaches of Tyler, Walker, and Eisner, identify and critically assess the implicit beliefs of each on this connection.
2. How useful do these approaches to curriculum planning seem to be? What different definitions of *curriculum* seem embedded in them? What different values and beliefs seem to underlie them? Compare these approaches with the postmodern approaches discussed in chapter 4.
3. With which of these approaches to curriculum do you most agree? With which do you most disagree? Reflect on why. What in each approach would you most change?

Option B

1. As in Option B for chapter 1, consider chapter 3 in light of the "hidden curriculum" (those parts of the environment that influence the experience of students but that are not accounted for or cannot be accounted for in curriculum planning). How fully must an approach to curriculum planning consider the hidden curriculum in order to provide a sound basis for making decisions about the planned curriculum? The enacted curriculum? The experienced curriculum?
2. Of the three approaches to curriculum planning described in this chapter (Tyler, Walker, and Eisner), which seems to cope most realistically with the problems posed by the hidden curriculum? Why? Which seems to be the most unrealistic? Why? Which seems likely to be the most widely used in the future?
3. Consider the schools in your community. How cognizant are they of their own approaches to curriculum planning? What ideas that can be drawn from the approaches of Tyler, Walker, and Eisner are likely to be of use to the schools in improving their curricula? How much resistance might any particular school offer to adopting these ideas? How might such resistance be overcome or at least minimized?

3.1 INTRODUCTION

In chapter 1 we pointed out why the essential character of curriculum is multiple and constantly changing and why efforts to precisely or finally define the term *curriculum* are fraught with peril. However, that does not mean that practical curriculum work is haphazard or that careful and well-informed thought does not go into it. On the contrary, because good curriculum work is so challenging, it may require more careful thinking than does almost any other practical enterprise. In many ways this entire book is about the connections between careful thought about the curriculum and worthwhile actions—particularly in schools, classrooms, and other learning environments that embody such thought.

Also in chapter 1 we used a number of terms to describe curriculum work without attempting to differentiate among them—in particular, *curriculum planning, curriculum decision making,* and *curriculum development.* While these terms are often used interchangeably and there is a great deal of overlap among them, they are not identical. The term *curriculum planning* carries with it the idea of carefully weighing various options for what is to be intentionally carried out in the classroom (the planned curriculum), sometimes for how it will be carried out (the enacted curriculum), and occasionally what some of its results might be (the experienced curriculum). The term *curriculum decision making* carries with it the suggestion of pushing beyond merely weighing alternatives to actually deciding which ones to carry out. Finally, the term *curriculum development* is the most comprehensive, for it carries with it not only the ideas of weighing and deciding but also of actually carrying out whatever options are decided upon, receiving feedback, and making constructive changes. Indeed, the word *development* itself suggests an unhurried, comprehensive, cyclical, and ongoing process in which careful thought and worthwhile actions constantly refine each other. Such topics as curriculum planning, implementation, evaluation, and change are often considered parts of the larger process of curriculum development. We discuss such topics in detail in chapters 5 through 8.

In this chapter we compare and contrast three alternative approaches to curriculum. Although different, each contains an implicit notion of what the curriculum is and exemplifies how thought and action can be connected in work such as curriculum planning, decision making, or development.

3.2 APPROACHES TO CURRICULUM

Since curriculum thought is elusive and curriculum work challenging, individuals and groups tend to develop particular approaches that do not necessarily make explicit their beliefs about curriculum. Their approaches, furthermore, reflect their own views of the world, their values and attitudes, and their priorities about knowledge, even though such underlying assumptions may not be consciously held. We use the term *approach* to indicate a set of beliefs, whether explicit or implicit, about curriculum and curriculum work, including underlying assumptions. To be considered an approach, this set of beliefs must be sufficiently consistent and comprehensive to represent a reasonable guide for coherent thinking and acting in curriculum. There is no specific line that designates a boundary between an inconsistent set of beliefs and a more consistent or comprehensive approach; the difference is always one of degree. Other terms sometimes used to describe what we mean by an approach are an *image,* an *orientation,* a *perspective,* or a *position.*

An approach to curriculum may be developed in detail by an individual or a group and can include copious papers and books on the subject, or it can be relatively undeveloped and little more than a speech or exhortation. Still, a reasonable curriculum approach should probably include the following:

- A discernible understanding of curriculum and the process of curriculum development.
- A value system sufficiently explicit to make clear the basis for specific decisions, such as preferred roles for participants in curriculum planning.
- A critical consciousness of the basic assumptions about the world, society, and morality on which understandings and value systems rest.

Not unexpectedly, a number of curriculum approaches have appeared over the decades. Some have been influential and remained little changed over long periods, while others have been ephemeral. Curriculum scholars who have analyzed approaches over the decades have categorized them. For example, Figure 3.1 summarizes the categorization of Posner (1998), who argues that the three most common categories of approaches to curriculum planning can be characterized by three different questions:

- *The procedural approach.* What steps should one follow?
- *The descriptive approach.* What do curriculum planners actually do?
- *The conceptual approach.* What are the elements of curriculum planning and how do they relate to one another?

Posner uses Tyler (1949) as the best representative of the procedural question. He labels Tyler's approach as "technical production" because it considers educational decisions objectively and because schooling is viewed as a means to produce learning. Taba's (1962) approach is also cited as a more elaborate version of this procedural approach. In this category Posner includes Schwab's (1970) approach as an

Approaches	Examples of Exponents
Procedural (technical production)	Tyler (1949), Taba (1962), Schwab (1970)
Descriptive (events and decision making)	Walker (1971)
Conceptual (levels of planning)	Goodlad & Richter (1977), Johnson (1977)
Critical (emancipation, critical reflection)	Freire (1970), Miller (1986), Grumet (1988), Pinar (1983), Lather (1987), Apple (1979), Giroux (1981), Eisner (1985), Vallance (1977), Barone (1987), Doll (1993), Slattery (1995), McLaren (1993)

FIGURE 3.1
Posner's categorization of approaches to curriculum
Source: After Posner (1998).

eclectic alternative, for Schwab accepts the need for technical expertise but rejects the means-ends orientation of Tyler and Taba.

Posner uses Walker (1971) to exemplify the descriptive question. Walker's approach concentrates on events that occur and decisions that are made by curriculum participants. It is sometimes termed a "naturalistic" approach since it does not attempt to suggest what should occur during curriculum deliberations; instead, it describes only what Walker has carefully observed as actually (or naturalistically) occurring.

For the conceptual question, Posner cites Goodlad and Richter (1977). Their approach postulates three different levels of curriculum planning: the instructional, the institutional, and the societal. He also cites Johnson (1977), whose approach stipulates that rational planning includes three distinct processes—planning, implementation, and evaluation—each of which, in turn, can itself be planned, implemented, and evaluated. The assumption of people who take a conceptual approach is that for curriculum planning, decision making, or development to be done most effectively, every point of decision along the way (such as the different levels of planning and the different processes that exist at each level) must be carefully identified and rationalized prior to taking action.

Posner claims that these three categories have much in common despite their differences and that the most widely accepted approaches to curriculum planning fall into them. He sees, however, a fourth category that he labels "critical," both because the various approaches within it are opposed to some or all of the basic assumptions implicit in more conventional approaches and because they are characterized by various ideological questions concerned with social equity and personal freedom, which, at the risk of oversimplification, we summarize as, Whose interests are being served? (see chapter 4). One example is Freire's (1970) "emancipatory" approach in which teachers and students become co-investigators undertaking critical reflection on political situations. Other examples include the gender-based approaches of Miller (1986), Grumet (1988), Pinar (1983), and Lather (1987); the social criticism approaches of Apple (1979) and Giroux (1981); the aesthetic approaches of Eisner (1985), Vallance (1977), and Barone (1987); and the postmodern approaches of Doll (1993), Slattery (1995), and McLaren (1993).

Despite the explanatory power of Posner's categories, some caveats need to be observed concerning curriculum approaches. For example, Jackson (1992) notes that no categories are mutually exclusive and that they should not be construed as representing conflicting allegiances. Therefore, it seems prudent to consider different approaches as neither fixed nor all-encompassing. Perhaps they are best considered as inclinations toward different ways of connecting thought and action within curriculum work based on the particular interests and experiences of those people who hold them.

Still, we maintain that carefully considering several of the most fully developed and most compelling curriculum approaches is instructive. Why have some individuals been drawn to a particular approach? What particular priorities and values have they opted for? What are the implications for curriculum thought and practice of their priorities and values? What are the alternatives? To these ends, we single out for analysis the approaches of three well-known and influential curriculum writers: Ralph Tyler, Decker Walker, and Elliot Eisner.

We note that, although each writer exemplifies one of Posner's categories (Tyler the procedural, Walker the descriptive, Eisner the critical) and presents persuasive ideas and arguments in support of his point of view, you should critically question each approach, developing your own interpretations and your own set of beliefs. There is no official or even stereotypical version of any approach.

Tyler's Rational-Linear Approach

Ralph W. Tyler began shaping theory and practice in education in the 1930s, when he came into prominence as the head of the evaluation committee of the Eight-Year Study (see chapter 2). During the 1940s, he worked out his approach to curriculum based upon a course on curriculum that he taught at the University of Chicago. An expanded version of the syllabus was published in 1949 as *Basic Principles of Curriculum and Instruction*. That book has been widely considered such a fine example of common sense and clarity that after more than half a century it is still in print and profoundly influences how curricula are planned and developed throughout the world. The principles that Tyler describes have come to be known collectively as "the Tyler rationale" despite his warning in the introduction to the book that it "is not a manual for curriculum construction since it does not describe and outline in detail the steps to be taken by a given school or college that seeks to build a curriculum" (p. 1). It is, Tyler contends, merely "one way of viewing an instructional program," and "the student is encouraged to examine other rationales and to develop his own conception of the elements and relationships involved in an effective curriculum" (p. 1). Nonetheless, the book does detail several steps Tyler thinks should be taken. Despite his warning, the book has often been treated as if it were precisely what he says it is not: a manual of the only right way to go about creating a curriculum (Hlebowitsh, 1999).

Tyler contends there are only four big questions that curriculum makers have to ask (see Figure 3.2). These questions are concerned with selecting objectives, selecting learning experiences, organizing learning experiences, and evaluating.

Objectives
What educational purposes should the school seek to attain?

Selecting learning experiences
How can learning experiences be selected that are likely to be useful in attaining these objectives?

Organizing learning experiences
How can learning experiences be organized for effective instruction?

Evaluation
How can the effectiveness of learning experiences be evaluated?

FIGURE 3.2
The Tyler rationale
Source: After Tyler (1949).

1. **What educational purposes should the school seek to attain?**
   Sources • Studies of the learners themselves
              • Studies of contemporary life outside the school
              • Suggestions about objectives from subject specialists
   The use of philosophy in selecting objectives
   The use of a psychology of learning in selecting objectives
   Stating objectives in a form to be helpful in selecting learning experiences and in guiding teaching

2. **How can learning experiences be selected that are likely to be useful in attaining these objectives?**
   General principles in selecting learning experiences

3. **How can learning experiences be organized for effective instruction?**
   Criteria for effective organization
   Elements to be organized
   Organizing principles
   The organizing structure

4. **How can the effectiveness of learning experiences be evaluated?**
   Basic notions regarding evaluation
   Evaluation procedures

FIGURE 3.3
Tyler's framework for answering the four basic curriculum questions
Source: After Tyler (1949).

These questions can be answered systematically but, Tyler believes, only if they are posed in this order, for answers to all latter questions logically presuppose answers to all prior questions (hence our characterization of Tyler's approach to curriculum as "rational-linear"). The questions form the four basic steps of Tyler's rationale; and putting his own warnings to readers aside, he devotes much of the book to explaining the specific framework he would use in systematically answering each question (see Figure 3.3).

Purposes.   Tyler identifies three sources of knowledge or information especially pertinent to answering the first question on the educational purposes of the school: learners, contemporary society, and subject specialists. He is quite eclectic about how these three sources can be used, stating: "No single source of information is adequate to provide a basis for wise and comprehensive decisions about the objectives of the school. Each of these sources has certain values to commend it. Each source should be given some consideration in planning any comprehensive curriculum program" (Tyler, 1949, p. 5).

These sources clearly represent the three basic focal points (individual, society, and subject matter) around which all comprehensive conceptions of curriculum are formed, but how is it possible in practice to combine all three sources? For instance, different sources could be seen as representing different epistemologies, ranging from existentialist views of the needs of students, to cultural transmission views of society, to essentialist or formalist views about the compartmentalized and ordered nature of knowledge. Is it possible to combine all three sources consistently, especially if they represent very different priorities? According to Tyler, this problem can be avoided by identifying a number of potentially usable objectives derived from each of these three sources and then passing them through the screens of philosophy and psychology to sieve out the most important objectives. Presumably, in this way, some objectives derived from each source will be used.

These three sources need to be studied more closely. For example, how do you go about finding out the needs of learners? It seems that Tyler is concerned not so much with finding out from individual students how they perceive their own needs as with doing studies of groups of students. Tyler suggests that we use scientific tests of students (such as norm-referenced tests on reading skills of 10-year-olds) to make decisions about whether students at a specific school need to receive instruction in particular reading skills or not. That is, his explanation of learners as a source of information is written from the point of view of scientific testing, and he clearly values data obtained in this way more highly than data obtained informally. Tyler accepts similar types of data as valid and reliable for deriving information about contemporary society and subject specialists.

Then again, consider the difficulties in trying to use contemporary society as a data source (Walker & Soltis, 1986). Tyler acknowledges the complexity of the problem, but he suggests that there are simply some aspects of society that are more important than others, such as societal needs regarding health, family, recreation, vocation, religion, consumption, and civic activities. This list, of course, while basic, is far from comprehensive. It is useful to note that Tyler omits many characteristics that other members of society might deem important. Not only has society itself changed since 1949, but so have the values that society collectively holds. Tyler's explanations of contemporary society as a source of data clearly reveal his own preferences, but they do not clearly reveal the extent of the problem we face in weighing values and then using them to choose among the aspects of a complex society in flux.

Further difficulties occur when Tyler considers subject specialists as a source of objectives. Kliebard (1970, p. 261) argues that learning subject matter is neither the only nor the highest purpose of education; therefore, the contributions of subject specialists would consist of defining how some purposes might be reached, but not what the highest purposes should be. That is, the subject matter content and the related methods to teach it serve to achieve some wider goal or aim. However, Tyler (1949, p. 26) seems to view subject specialists rather differently when he asks the question, "What can a particular subject contribute to the education of young people who are not going to be specialists in that field?" Here and elsewhere in his discussion, he seems to be looking for contributions from subject specialists that transcend the specifics of their particular subjects. Since any comprehensive curriculum covers more than one subject, the only real specialist in what the overall curriculum should finally be is the curriculum generalist, of course. Tyler's book is addressed to curriculum generalists, yet, ironically, he implies that many general decisions about curricula can be derived directly from the specific objectives of nongeneralists.

So far we have examined three possible sources for obtaining some tentative objectives for a curriculum. It is likely that the objectives will be diverse since they have been drawn from three very different sources. How, then, should we weigh the potential value of each objective? How, in fact, can we select some objectives for use in a curriculum while rejecting others? Anticipating such questions, Tyler (pp. 33–43) identifies two considerations that should be used to isolate the important objectives that will eventually become the instructional objectives. The two considerations are educational philosophy and psychology of learning. At first glance, these considerations look most helpful. If a particular philosophic stance is taken consistently in making decisions about a curriculum, that should eliminate certain objectives and retain others (Hlebowitsh, 1995). Similarly, if objectives that are not easily learned under classroom conditions are eliminated, then the curriculum plan is likely to be more successful in practice. However, Tyler's discussion provides no way of deciding which educational philosophy should be used (Kliebard, 1995). Will any philosophic screen do? Certainly not! Thus, we are still left with the dilemma. Then again, how can we be sure that certain objectives are or are not amenable to effective learning? Are some psychological principles of learning more appropriate than others, such as stimulus-response-reinforcement? How do we decide?

In Tyler's view, each school has its own values, stated or implied, about the nature of a good life and a good society, and in principle, it can discover and use these in its curriculum. But how can this task best be accomplished? Tyler (1949, p. 37) is vague on this issue, stating somewhat circularly: "For a statement of philosophy to serve most helpfully as a set of standards or a screen in selecting objectives it needs to be stated clearly, and for the main points the implications for education objectives may need to be spelled out. Those [objectives] in harmony with the philosophy will be identified as important objectives." He is more specific about how psychology might be used as a screen when he discusses certain principles in the psychology of learning, such as how maturation levels and environmental conditions affect learning. But here, too, he still throws the onus back upon the curriculum worker to make choices of objectives with very little guidance about how to undertake the task: "However, each curriculum worker will need to formulate a theory of learning in which he has some confidence and use it as a basis for checking his educational objectives to see that they are consistent with his theory of learning" (p. 57).

Tyler's ideas about the educational purposes of the school emphasize that we begin with well-defined objectives. Using current nomenclature, we might substitute the term *outcomes* for *objectives*. When objectives are specific and clear, subsequent decisions about what the curriculum should be and how it should be organized become less chaotic and more rational, Tyler believes. He is equally emphatic about the need to consider learners, contemporary society, and subject matter when defining objectives, but his explanations of how all this can best be done leave many questions open. This combination of specificity and openness makes many demands on us in attempting to follow Tyler's ideas about objectives. It can be considered as either a strength or a weakness of the Tyler rationale in general, depending on our point of view.

Selection of Learning Experiences.   A similar emphasis on a goal-directed, ends-means approach is equally evident in how Tyler answers the second, third, and fourth questions in his rationale. After selecting objectives, workers must then decide how to answer the second question about selecting what he calls "learning experiences." Learning experiences are actually activities that may be written into the curriculum plan and that provide opportunities for students to reach the objectives specified. For example, objectives might include the development of a student's skills in reading, and a learning experience might then involve the student's reading a particular story or book. The basic principle for selection that Tyler provides for us here is simply to select those learning experiences that are most likely to help students reach the objectives. Precisely how this is to be done is something that he again leaves vague, but the principle itself demonstrates how the objectives selected in the first step of the rationale control the selections made in subsequent steps.

Tyler does assert that learning experiences must be selected so that students have sufficient opportunity to experience and successfully complete the tasks required of them. He also asserts that learning experiences must enable students to gain satisfaction from carrying on particular kinds of behavior. Both assertions about designing learning experiences were quite advanced for the late 1940s, when *Basic Principles of Curriculum and Instruction* was published. The ideas are very relevant currently in terms of outcomes-based approaches and the use of authentic assessment tasks. Writing in the 1990s, Tyler (1992, p. 126) again asserted that "learning experiences of the curriculum should be on the activities that involve the children's aspirations and problems."

Organization of Learning Experiences.   In answering the third question, "How can learning experiences be organized for effective instruction?" Tyler introduces a range of helpful suggestions. Still, the ends-means character of his thinking is apparent here, for his use of the phrase "effective instruction" clearly carries within it the idea of efficiency. In other words, he suggests that a learning experience should be organized for precisely the same general reason that it was selected in the first place: as a means of helping students reach certain ends (the previously specified objectives). In this section of the book, Tyler uses many phrases that reflect this kind of rationale, phrases such as a "coherent program," "efficiency of instruction," and "effective organization."

Tyler also makes clear his belief that learning will be most efficient only if it is properly organized. Specifically, he suggests that each learning experience should be built upon earlier ones (vertical organization) and should be reinforced by activities in other subjects (horizontal organization). He incorporates the ideas of vertical and horizontal organization into three criteria: continuity, sequence, and integration. In his view, it is essential for us to identify the major concepts and skills to be taught; these concepts and skills are then introduced and reintroduced in successive teaching units. He stresses that continuity, sequence, and integration have to be experienced by the learners and are not merely tools for us to use. To experience the continuity of particular concepts, learners need to go into greater detail each time a concept is reintroduced within the sequenced curriculum; as they do so, they will be increasingly able to attain deeper levels of understanding of the concept by integrating new details.

Evaluation. In answering his fourth question, Tyler emphasizes the need for us to see how far the learning experiences that have been developed and organized actually produce the desired results. His notion of evaluation is determining the degree of fit between the results specified in the objectives and the results actually achieved. Ends-means notions of evaluation have, of course, been widely accepted and used in education, yet some ideas that Tyler described in 1949, a half-century ago, can still seem innovative, including the need to evaluate students throughout a unit and not just at the end. Indeed, Cronbach (1986) claims that Tyler invented formative evaluation by teachers.

Tyler emphasizes that evaluation involves getting evidence about changes in the behavior of students and that doing so is not confined merely to giving paper-and-pencil tests. For example, he advocates other techniques, such as observations, interviews, questionnaires, and samples of students' work—techniques that are now used both formally and informally, especially in evaluations that are not goal-driven. In the same chapter, however, he emphasizes the importance of developing appropriate instruments that can be demonstrated to be valid and reliable. Thus, in this part of the rationale, he further emphasizes scientific testing. This emphasis is understandable, considering that Tyler was writing in an era when traditional testing was much in vogue, but it also raises questions about whether Tyler was more interested in formal techniques of evaluation or in alternative means for obtaining data about students.

Conclusion. Despite certain ambiguities about how to select objectives and about how to use some sources of data, the Tyler rationale encompasses most of our basic concerns about curriculum (Hlebowitsh, 1992, 1999; Walker, 1990). Many other approaches have been based on Tyler. The excesses of some of these approaches have been criticized, but there has also been a tendency to criticize—perhaps fairly, perhaps unfairly—the Tyler rationale itself.

In reflecting on curriculum in 1975, nearly thirty years after the publication of his rationale, Tyler summed up what he thought his approach was about:

> [Curriculum planning is] a practical enterprise not a theoretical study. It endeavors to design a system to achieve an educational end and is not primarily attempting to explain an existential phenomenon. The system must be designed to operate effectively in a society where a number of constraints are present and with human beings who all have purposes, preferences, and dynamic mechanisms in operation. (Tyler, 1975, p. 18)

This quotation captures the basic reasons explaining why the Tyler rationale has proved so persuasive to curriculum workers over such a long period of time and also why it has left teachers to deal with the gaps that arise among the planned, the enacted, and the experienced curricula. As Tyler suggests, his rationale is primarily a way of simplifying complex situations sufficiently so that plans and procedures can be carried out rationally—that is, in ways that people engaged in the process can understand and, at least potentially, reach agreement about. For the purposes of communication and consensus building, it has had immense practical utility. It is not a way, however, of dealing with the underlying existential complexity that creates the lived character of the experienced curriculum or even with many of the characteristics of individual classrooms that teachers need to take into account in making their decisions about how to flexibly enact curricula that have been planned with precision.

In 1949, Tyler's rational-linear approach broke new ground in curriculum (see Figure 3.4). It had a relatively liberating effect at that time (Helsby & Saunders, 1993). Curriculum workers had for the first time an approach that appeared both comprehensive and workable. They were advised to concentrate on student behaviors in devising objectives for a unit and to emphasize appropriate learning experiences rather than simply identifying content to be covered. The guidelines for evaluating a curriculum were very different and far more comprehensive than were the summative tests used during the 1940s. So despite Tyler's warning that the procedures he was describing were not a series of steps to be followed, many educators have followed those steps, particularly in subjects with content that seems relatively easy to define and to sequence clearly (Milburn, 2000). In fact, a number of national curriculum projects of the 1960s and 1970s used procedural steps based on Tyler. In contrast, however, studies of teacher thinking and teacher planning (Bolin

	Before Tyler	Tyler
Purposes of instruction	General statements about what the teacher should do	Specific statements about students' behaviors to be used to bring about certain ends
Topics selected	Statements about content to be taught	Statements about learning experiences needed to achieve objectives
Organization of teaching	Support in general for teacher-directed, didactic methods	Support for teacher-directed methods but emphasis on concept development, vertical and horizontal integration of concepts, student awareness of the purpose of learning activities
Methods of assessment/evaluation	Use of content-based tests and standardized tests at the completion of a teaching unit	Tests to be based upon course objectives; informal and formal methods of evaluation to be used; evaluation to occur throughout the teaching of a unit

FIGURE 3.4
Advances made by Tyler's 1949 rationale

& McConnell Falk, 1987; Clandinin, 1986; Connelly & Clandinin, 1988) reveal that few teachers actually use objectives as their starting point in planning. Therefore, just as Tyler suggested, there are other forms of rationality and other approaches to curriculum that remain open for exploration.

Walker's Deliberative Approach

Decker Walker's contribution is through his deliberative approach (Walker, 1971, 1990). Whereas Tyler's starting point was identifying the linear logic of rational planning, Walker's was studying what people actually do in developing curricula. Tyler assumes that better curricula will result when those engaged in it follow the somewhat rarefied logic he identifies; Walker assumes that better curricula will result when those engaged in it understand the complexity of the process.

Of major interest to Walker is the question of how curriculum workers actually go about their task. In particular, in the late 1960s and early 1970s, he studied how personnel in national curriculum projects undertook planning. During three years as participant observer and evaluator with the Kettering Art Project (Walker, 1975), he meticulously recorded the actions, arguments, and decisions of the project team. By analyzing transcripts and other data, he was able to identify three basic phases, which he termed *platform, deliberation,* and *design.* Subsequently, he analyzed the documentary evidence of decision making of three other national curriculum project groups and was able to confirm his findings about the three phases. Walker then developed his findings into a framework for describing the process, which he described as a "naturalistic model" (1971). He used the term *naturalistic* because he wanted to portray how curriculum decision making actually occurred in practice, in contrast to other approaches that prescribe how curriculum development should occur. His three-step sequence of platform-deliberation-design has since been used at various levels of curriculum development, including small-scale projects with preservice teachers (Bonser & Grundy, 1988) and with in-service teachers (Holt, 1990; Kennedy, 1988; Ross, 1993), with students (Brice, 2000), as well as in large-scale programs (Ben-Peretz, 1990; Dev & Walker, 1999; Orpwood, 1985; Silberstein & Ben-Peretz, 1979). The model is depicted in Figure 3.5.

Platform.   Walker, building on the ideas of Schwab (1969), suggests that, whenever people come together as a group to engage in curriculum development, they always approach the task with their individual beliefs and values. They have their own perceptions of the task, ideas about what the chief problems are, assertions about what should be prescribed, and commitments that they are prepared to pursue and argue about. The preliminary phase is, therefore, to get everyone to join in, to talk, to discuss, and even to argue about their beliefs about what should be. Walker uses the term *platform* to describe any consensus that emerges because that term describes what future discussions, and eventually the resulting curriculum, will be built on. He concludes that a platform typically consists of various conceptions (beliefs about what exists and what is possible), theories (beliefs about relations held between existing entities), and aims (beliefs about courses of action that are desirable) that

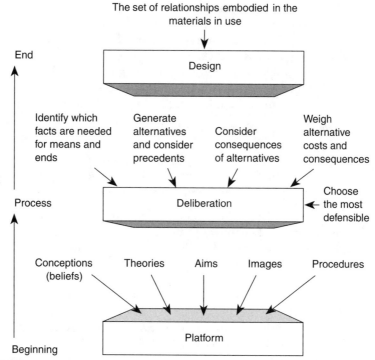

FIGURE 3.5
Walker's naturalistic model
Source: After Walker (1971).

ordinarily are relatively well formulated and thought out. But in addition, in the minds of planners, there exist less carefully thought out notions, which he calls images (beliefs that something is desirable without specifying what) and procedures (beliefs about courses of action thought desirable without specifying why). Presumably, the more that consensus—or at least clarity about beliefs—emerges during this phase, the more likely that subsequent phases will proceed expeditiously.

Deliberation. Whether a group achieves much or little consensus about the platform, it eventually moves into the second phase, *deliberation*. There is not necessarily a clear separation between these phases, for the process of deliberation is also concerned with consensus, but in deliberation, attention turns away from beliefs themselves and toward how they are used in assessing actual states of affairs and possible courses of action, toward what Schwab refers to as "the practical" (see chapter 4). In general, we should identify as far as possible what is problematic about the situation in which a curriculum is to be implemented and how the curriculum to be developed can mitigate problems. Walker's model specifies that the process of deliberation includes identifying relevant facts, generating alternative courses of action in light of precedents, considering the costs and consequences of all alternatives, and choosing the most defensible alternatives. According to Schwab, as reported in Reid (1999b, p. 391), such deliberations may involve "violent discussions and debate." As participants gradually grasp new meanings through the linking and extending of ideas, Barnes (1982) characterizes their talk as "rough draft."

Brice (2000) and Onosko (1996) argue that deliberative discussion is very complex and requires important communication skills and norms of behavior (which may be unfamiliar or at least little practiced by teachers), namely:

- Arguing coherently and fairly
- Considering relevant alternatives
- Capacity to question, examine, and reflect
- Willingness to question one's own assumptions and those of others
- Ability to identify competing arguments

Writers other than Walker who have built on the ideas of Schwab also elaborate on the practical character of deliberation. Pereira (1984) emphasizes that the purposes of deliberation are to clear away clashes between alternatives. Deliberation to him is "essentially a systematic method for formulating and entertaining an adequate variety of alternatives, alternative perceptions, alternative problems, and alternative solutions" (p. 5). Mulder (1991) perceives deliberation as a strongly context-bound and practical mode of curricular problem solving. Although the process of deliberation is seldom easy, without it the most fruitful alternatives may not be found. Reid (1988) remarks that deliberation "does not go in for ready-made solutions or axiomatic forms of reasoning. It suggests that good actions have to be discovered, and that the means for their discovering is the inventive behavior of people" (p. 2). Waks (2000) notes that curriculum problems are uncertain practical problems. For these writers, it is the ongoing searching that gives deliberation its unique qualities. Perhaps one may expect forthright discussion to lead directly to viable solutions, but that is seldom the case. Deliberation may seem very chaotic and frustrating for those people involved, as Walker (1990) admits when he notes that participants in deliberation usually enter holding different beliefs. Feelings run high. Common mistakes include failure to consider alternatives and oversimplification of what searching for solutions entails.

Design.   Deliberation finally leads to some decisions for action: we enter the third phase, *design*, when a group has achieved sufficient consensus about beliefs, problematic circumstances, and potential solutions so that particular courses of action can be taken more or less automatically, without further consideration of alternatives. That is, what the travails of the previous phases have made explicit for the group now forms the implicit basis for the group's actual curriculum design. Walker argues that the design phase of a curriculum development project typically contains both implicit and explicit considerations. Even though a project may have passed through the platform and deliberation phases, decisions may still be influenced as much by personal preferences as by rational discussion. The culminating activity for the design phase is the creation of the curriculum, which may include whatever specific subjects, instructions, teaching materials, or activities the group believes advisable.

Conclusion. Walker's deliberative approach attempts to portray accurately what actually happens during curriculum development. Because Walker based his approach on actual curriculum projects, he claims that it can be supported on empirical grounds. Subsequent studies, such as those undertaken by Ross (1993), support the accuracy of Walker's descriptions of the platform, deliberation, and design phases. Furthermore, it can be argued that Walker's approach is normative as well as descriptive. Donmoyer (1982, p. 3) suggests that, although the specifics within it are empirically based, it "resembles in a general way, if not in all important details, Schwab's normative model of how curriculums *ought* to be made."

Certainly Walker's approach is of considerable value to teachers. Knowing what typically happens during curriculum development—the assertions of personal beliefs in the struggle toward consensus, the use of deliberation in identifying problematic situations and weighing alternative solutions, and the interplay of the implicit and the explicit in designing a curriculum—can at least help identify potential pitfalls and frustrations in curriculum development. Walker's descriptions of what typically *does* happen certainly present a highly useful alternative to Tyler's prescriptions of what *should* happen. Tyler does not describe what happens when consensus cannot be reached in practice; Walker describes how curriculum development proceeds even when consensus is not reached. Walker's descriptions of the phases thus provide us with practical guidelines to follow, even if these guidelines are rather general.

Perhaps the two most telling criticisms of the usefulness of Walker's approach focus on what it does not consider. First, Walker studied only large-scale curriculum projects; therefore, the deliberative model that he describes may not apply as well to small-scale, school-based curriculum planning activities nor be as appropriate a guide for them. This criticism may be particularly valid since the curriculum development teams Walker studied included full-time educationists, many of whom were considered experts. In addition, funding for the projects was often substantial, and material resources and expert consultants were readily available. In contrast, lack of time, expertise, and funding, as well as political dictates (Reid, 1988), often bear down heavily upon school-based curriculum development. In individual schools, there may be little incentive for teachers to engage in full-scale deliberations.

Second, Walker's approach is directed almost exclusively to the designing of a curriculum. His descriptions do not tell what happens to people after a curriculum is designed. Do teachers and other curriculum developers still deliberate in the same ways about curriculum implementation, evaluation, and change? Individual teachers must decide, therefore, how helpful Walker's approach will be to them in enacting the planned curriculum and in assessing how the enacted curriculum is actually experienced by their students. In doing so, they may wish to refer to the chapter in Walker's own synoptic curriculum text (Walker, 1990), which further elaborates his ideas on deliberation nearly two decades after his model appeared initially.

Eisner's Artistic Approach

Elliot W. Eisner is a highly respected scholar who has published widely since the 1960s. His special interests are art education and curriculum. His earliest papers and books are memorable for their vigorous attacks on vogues of the 1960s, which, he believed, overemphasized behavioral objectives and traditional academic subjects within the school curriculum. His subsequent articles identified weaknesses in the empirical-analytic mode of educational research, which was virtually the only form of research accepted at that time by the American educational research community. Eisner pointed out the need to develop qualitative modes of research, and by the mid-1970s, he had combined his interests in art education and curriculum into his own qualitative mode. In a series of articles and books (for example, 1972, 1978, and 1992), he portrays social reality as negotiated, subjective, constructed, and multiple; he maintains that there are many ways in which individuals construct meaning. Hence, he considers individuals who make decisions about curricula similar to artists choosing among an almost limitless variety of ways of representing their views of reality, in response to which students choose how to modify their own views.

In a major book, *The Educational Imagination* (1979), Eisner worked out his artistic approach to education. (He has elaborated on this approach and provided additional details in later works.) He states, "I believe we need theory that unapologetically recognizes the artistry of teaching and that is useful in helping teachers develop those arts" (p. 18), and "I believe what the study of education needs is not a new orthodoxy but rather a variety of new assumptions and methods that will help us appreciate the richness of educational practice" (p. 19). In various chapters of this book, he maps out how this artistic approach can be used in curriculum development. Figure 3.6 is an outline of this approach.

---

1. **Goals and their priorities**
   - The need to consider less well-defined objectives (expressive objectives) as well as explicit ones
   - The need for deliberation in talking through priorities
2. **Content of the curriculum**
   - Options to consider in selecting curriculum
   - Caveats about the null curriculum
3. **Types of learning opportunities**
   - Emphasis on transforming goals and content into learning events that will be of significance to students
4. **Organization of learning opportunities**
   - Emphasis on a nonlinear approach in order to encourage diverse student outcomes
5. **Organization of content areas**
   - Emphasis on cross-curricula organization of content
6. **Mode of presentation and mode of response**
   - Use of a number of modes of communication to widen educational opportunities for students
7. **Types of evaluation procedures**
   - Use of a comprehensive range of procedures at different stages of the process of curriculum development

---

FIGURE 3.6
Outline of Eisner's artistic approach
Source: After Eisner (1979).

At first glance, the headings that Eisner uses seem very similar to the steps that Tyler advocates, but the underlying rationality and the practical emphases are quite different, especially the mode of presentation and the evaluation procedures that Eisner suggests. Whereas Tyler believes that his four steps sequentially cover every-thing elemental in curriculum development, Eisner takes pains to stress that his headings cover just some of the many dimensions of curriculum, which can be in-vestigated in virtually any order. Perhaps with Tyler in mind, Eisner suggests that "the process is far more convoluted, circuitous, and adventitious than one might be led to believe by reading the literature" (p. 116).

Goals and Their Priorities.   Eisner makes the typical distinctions between aims, goals, and objectives. He considers aims to provide the general direction of educa-tion and a set of values, goals to be more specific statements of intent, and objectives to be the most specific statements of all. However, he is quick to point out that it is not always possible—nor even desirable—to have highly specific objectives. This point is reminiscent of the seminal article in which he mounted strong arguments for the use of expressive objectives to complement behavioral objectives (Eisner, 1969). He argued then that some activities that may be included in a curriculum can-not have predetermined objectives and that in these situations it is quite legitimate for the objectives to be expressed in general terms and after teaching has taken place. In *The Educational Imagination,* Eisner similarly de-emphasizes the importance of explicit objectives and asserts that the formulation of objectives does not neces-sarily have to precede teaching. He cautions that subjects should not be given higher or lower status in the curriculum simply because of the specificity of the objectives to which they lend themselves.

Of special note are the suggestions Eisner makes about how curriculum devel-opers might cope with competing goals and objectives put forward by different in-terest groups. This is where skills and talents of artistry are particularly needed, for, as he observes, the ability to negotiate which strategies and trade-offs will be used is essential if curriculum developers are to get beyond the ordinary constraints im-posed by competing interests and to initiate new programs. Eisner maintains that the artful process of arriving at consensus about curricular priorities has to involve participants in considerable discussion (deliberation) of the kind advocated by Schwab (1970).

Content of the Curriculum.   Like Tyler and Walker, Eisner emphasizes the need for curriculum developers to consider the three basic sources from which content can be drawn (individual, society, and subject matter). Here his particular concern is that a wide variety of specific sources, such as student interests and community needs, be given equal consideration with traditional academic disciplines. He is ex-tremely unsympathetic toward curriculum workers who select content merely be-cause it is part of an academic tradition: "Traditions create expectations, they create predictability, and they sustain stability" (p. 90). He concludes that much important content (for example, images of popular culture as conveyed by the mass media and even well-established subjects such as law, anthropology, and the arts) has tradition-ally been excluded from schools. He calls what is not taught the "null curriculum."

Types of Learning Opportunities.   Eisner also strongly favors providing students with a wide variety of opportunities for learning. His central message is that "educational imagination must come into play in order to transform goals and content to the kinds of events that will have educational consequences for students" (p. 119). Here, of course, he is making a clear distinction between the planned curriculum and the enacted curriculum, implying that, although academic specialists may know their subject matter well, it is curriculum planners and teachers who have the responsibility of transforming the content into forms that are appropriate for students. His use of the terms *educational imagination* and *transformation* invokes the metaphor of artistry, which he uses throughout the book to convey how he believes teachers actually go about creating varied, meaningful, and satisfying learning opportunities for students.

Organization of Learning Opportunities.   In keeping with his emphasis on variety, Eisner also asserts that the curriculum developer-teacher should provide students with materials and activities that encourage a diverse range of outcomes and experiences. He argues that engagement in this process is more important than attempting to control its outcomes and that "it is the task of the teacher to facilitate the interests and goals that students develop as a result of such engagement" (p. 123). Since this kind of engagement requires the teacher to deal with many strands of the task simultaneously, Eisner likens the task to the creation of a spider web. A traditional, linear approach to the task has some benefits, he admits, but ultimately such an approach oversimplifies it. Eisner cites several statements from Dewey (1959) with which his own approach seems quite consistent.

Organization of Content Areas.   Not surprisingly, Eisner also contends that content should be organized and integrated in a variety of ways. While there are many social, political, and intellectual constraints discouraging the exploration of new forms of organization in most schools, he provides examples of schools that have successfully organized content in nontraditional ways.

Mode of Presentation and Mode of Response.   Eisner advances some of his strongest arguments in favor of an artistic approach when he describes what he terms *modes* of presenting and responding to the curriculum. He criticizes educators who "seem to operate on the belief that the written word is the only means through which one can legitimately demonstrate that one knows something" (1979, p. 130). Elsewhere he points out that the syntactical rules that apply to discursive statements (and especially to scientific statements) do not apply to poetic statements or to metaphors in general (Eisner, 2000). Metaphors have their own purposes, which they fulfill by deliberately bending ordinary logic, yet what they communicate through their mode can be more powerful than what can be communicated through the mode of ordinary language.

These ideas apply to communication in the classroom, and, as Eisner indicates, teachers who do not use diverse modes of communication in presenting the curriculum are, in effect, denying students educational opportunities to develop diverse modes of response. Students should not be restricted to a narrow range of communication; they should be given many options. This point is supported by the fact that, although some disciplines have specific modes inherently associated with them (for example, historians write prose, physicists express relationships in equations), they are not necessarily limited to these modes. Therefore, even curriculum workers who consider subject matter the most important source for the curriculum can still incorporate a variety of modes of presentation into their curricula and provide a variety of opportunities for students to respond in different modes. Eisner thinks curricula should include artistic forms of expression and understanding that "permit the visual and auditory form as well as discursive form—to create evocative forms whose meanings are embodied in the hope of what is expressed" (Eisner, 1980, p. 4).

His example of autumn makes the point very powerfully:

> [T]he forms through which knowledge and understanding are constructed, stored, and expressed are considerably wider than verbal or written discourse. What can be known, say, about autumn can take form in scientific propositions that deal with chemical changes in trees, in astronomical propositions about the location of our planet in relation to the sun, in poetic expression disclosing the smell of burning autumn leaves, in visual images that present to our consciousness the color of a Vermont landscape, in auditory forms that capture the crackle of leaves under our footsteps. Autumn, in short, is known in a variety of ways and the ways in which it can be known are expressible in a wide range of expressive forms. (1979, p. 128)

Types of Evaluation Procedures.   For Eisner, evaluation is not something that is done as a final step in curriculum development; it is something that pervades the entire process. In general, this idea is not new; it has been accepted by many educators over the years. Eisner, however, has developed a particularly sophisticated understanding of evaluation, which he describes incisively and advocates compellingly. He believes that evaluation is fundamentally the same natural process in which people constantly engage in attempting to make sense of the world around them and of their own lives (Eisner, 1999). Of course, some people do so better than others, primarily because they are more skillful at accurately or insightfully perceiving situations and at intelligently weighing their reasons for arriving at valuations. Some people are also more skillful than others at portraying their valuations and the reasons for them. This kind of public portrayal of valuing and reasoning is part of formal evaluation, but even in its absence, evaluation is always going on informally. Applied to education, these skills are what Eisner calls "educational connoisseurship" and "educational criticism." (In chapter 8, we analyze in some detail Eisner's explanation of educational connoisseurship and criticism.)

Eisner maintains that the skills of perceiving, valuing, and portraying are essentially artistic; they can be heightened through practice and experience, but they cannot be reduced to a specific method. Since perceptions and valuations are constantly being made throughout the entire process of curriculum development, and since the curriculum can itself be considered a means of portraying values, it makes little sense to insist that evaluation of a curriculum be undertaken only at the end of the process that creates it. Creating a curriculum is fundamentally an artistic process throughout, and Eisner advocates artistic means of evaluating both the process and the emerging curriculum.

More important, his view of evaluation reinforces his other views in *The Educational Imagination,* making clear that the planned curriculum, the enacted curriculum, and the experienced curriculum cannot be considered the same thing within an artistic approach to curriculum planning. This approach thus demands that many of the most important decisions about the curriculum be made in the classroom by the teacher who enacts it and who observes how the students experience it.

Conclusion.   Eisner's approach to curriculum differs from Tyler's and Walker's approaches in several basic ways. Both Tyler and Eisner suggest that the curriculum planner must attend to some similar things. Then they diverge: Tyler posits a sequence of invariant steps under a logic in which means (the curriculum) are valued only insofar as they contribute to ends (the objectives selected by the planner). Conversely, Eisner portrays an open-ended process in which steps may be taken and retaken in any order under a logic in which means (the process) are one with ends (the curriculum as planned, enacted, and experienced), all valued for their intrinsic qualities. Both Walker and Eisner see curriculum planning as problematic and proceeding through deliberation. However, Walker describes deliberation only as it has occurred in problematic situations to create the planned curriculum, whereas Eisner describes how artistry within deliberation can heighten the intrinsic values of the planned, the enacted, and the experienced curriculum. In contrast to both Tyler and Walker, Eisner holds the view that the social reality within which the curriculum planner and the teacher must make decisions does not simply exist by itself, but it is constantly constructed and reconstructed by those people who live it. He argues very convincingly that social reality is negotiated and can be constricted and limited by the symbols used to describe it (Andrews, 1989). Believing that traditional schooling does not make sufficient use of the range of symbols open to it, Eisner takes some common descriptors of what is essential in curriculum (for example, content or learning opportunities) and demonstrates how they can be used in selecting, organizing, and experiencing a curriculum that may satisfy the needs of individual students and teachers more meaningfully than does a curriculum traditionally arrived at.

Critics of Eisner have suggested he is at his best when reacting to the excesses of rationalistic approaches to curriculum but at his weakest when proposing alternatives (Oliver, 1987). Of course, this is a criticism that could be made of virtually any approach to curriculum. Many people have been able to identify weaknesses in existing approaches cogently, but few have been able to create new and viable approaches of their own. Still, is it possible that Eisner has overstated the metaphor of artistry? Levin (1980, p. 187) asks, "How are these artistic portrayals supposed to be used to stimulate reflection and discussion about important curricular issues?" One can ask even more basic questions, such as, To what extent is the process of creating a curriculum actually like art? What characteristics do this process and artistic endeavors have in common?

Regardless of how one answers these questions, Eisner's approach to curriculum development, far more than Tyler's or Walker's, insists that the process is inherently problematic: the teacher cannot avoid making choices that touch directly on the concerns of all those involved in creating a curriculum or potentially affected by it. Eisner's approach offers general guidelines, not specific steps, and therefore thrusts the teacher to the forefront of the process of deliberation and enactment. Perhaps reflection and discussion about the role of the teacher and what it implies are precisely what Eisner's portrayals are intended to stimulate.

3.3   IS ONE APPROACH PREFERABLE?

In this chapter we have presented three very different approaches to curriculum.

Tyler's approach appears to be prescriptive, despite his claim that it is simply one approach among many. Tyler insists that we proceed through a definite sequence of four steps, and he assumes an ends-means rationale. Simply put, ends must be selected first and all else follows from them. Therefore, there is little room for flexibly enacting the planned curriculum under the Tyler rationale. Tyler does leave open precisely how we can take the four steps, though the specifics he describes throughout *Basic Principles of Curriculum and Instruction* have proved historically to be persuasive examples. The examples have been so powerful, perhaps because Tyler is rather vague about criteria that can be used for choosing among various alternatives or perhaps simply because he describes no other examples. Thus, a whole range of very different value orientations can be used within the framework of the Tyler rationale, but Tyler's own approach still seems to be the one orientation that fits most comfortably within this framework.

Clearly, the approach does not describe how creating a curriculum actually occurs but how Tyler thinks it *ought* to occur. The general approach and Tyler's specific examples can be followed closely by curriculum workers. Doing so may lead to a precisely planned curriculum, but it will not account for the existential complexity that seems at the heart of the enacted curriculum and the experienced curriculum—that is, the day-to-day classroom.

Walker's approach tries to categorize the various activities that occur when groups are involved in curriculum development. Walker uses methodologies from the social sciences in order to produce an accurate description of what actually happens when people endeavor to develop a curriculum. But this is as far as the approach goes. There are no specific guidelines or criteria for us to use in making decisions about the curriculum itself. Such guidelines and criteria must be hammered out anew by each group through the process of deliberation. Walker clearly values the openness of deliberations that permit every interested party to have a voice in developing curriculum. Presumably, the curriculum that is developed in this way will reflect a balance between the diverse views with which the process begins and the consensus toward which it moves. Walker's rationality, therefore, is nontechnical; he is concerned primarily with practical reasoning and with how workable practical decisions actually get made within the complexity of real situations. The principal value of Walker's approach thus seems to be that it points out what is in store for curriculum developers when they deliberate.

Eisner's approach to curriculum at first glance seems similar to Tyler's, yet closer examination reveals profound differences. Eisner is extremely critical of the technical rationality inherent in Tyler's ends-means framework. Instead, he emphasizes the many choices that must be made by planners, teachers, and students alike in creating and experiencing a curriculum. He suggests that the entire process proceeds through a variety of modes of presentation and response. Eisner's approach is artistic; his values are those of the creative artist and the appreciative audience. The guidelines and criteria he offers are similar to those of any creative process. Thus, Eisner's approach is like Walker's in dealing with the complexities of specific situations. However, unlike Walker's, which deals primarily with procedural complexities, Eisner's deals with the personal, existential complexities that individuals bring to their decisions. Eisner is descriptive in offering a general approach that can be followed by curriculum workers, yet he is prescriptive in offering suggestions about what should happen when the approach is followed well. The approach itself provides us with considerable flexibility in making choices; it is applicable to the planned curriculum and, especially, to the lived qualities of the enacted curriculum and the experienced curriculum.

We have presented these three approaches for several reasons. First, they focus on some of the most basic questions that can be raised about curricula (hence raising some of the essential concerns of the curriculum planner and developer). Second, each is a well-known approach to curriculum. Finally, collectively they illustrate a range of value orientations nearly as great as the range illustrated by the eight definitions of the term *curriculum* we discussed in chapter 1. Readers should carefully consider how each of these approaches applies to their own preferred definitions.

When, now, we raise the question "Is one approach preferable?" you should be fully aware that we believe that no one approach provides the only possible—or even desirable—way of developing curricula (Milburn, 1992). One approach may indeed be preferable, but only to particular persons, for particular reasons, and at particular times—not to all persons, for all reasons, and at all times. For instance, our own definition of curriculum as "an interrelated set of plans and experiences that a student undertakes under the guidance of the school" carries within it certain values that seem to us more compatible with one of the approaches to planning that we have described than with the other two. However, the other two also offer practical help in thinking about and making choices about curriculum. In fact, when we have planned and developed curricula, we have used more than one approach. We have often borrowed from many approaches. Furthermore, we do not think we are unusual. The truth of the matter is that people engaged in curriculum planning and development are constantly faced with making choices about what often seems like a bewildering variety of alternatives. Yet somehow they do make choices—sometimes wisely, sometimes unwisely.

The purpose of this book is not to provide prescriptions and formulas for how to make choices or for what those choices should be. Our purpose is to give readers the information and insight that we believe will be most valuable to them in making their own choices in the most fruitful possible ways. Such choices can be rational, comprehensive, practical, defensible, yet personal.

■ QUESTIONS AND REFLECTIONS

1. Approaches to curriculum typically focus on procedures (what to do), descriptions (what happens), or concepts (what must be considered). Reexamine the exemplary approaches of Tyler, Walker, or Eisner specifically in terms of these three foci. Do each of these approaches have one focus only? Or do they actually have more than one?

2. What do you consider the characteristics of a good curriculum approach? What priorities would you give to matters such as the following:
   - Comprehensive goals and objectives?
   - Student participation in planning?
   - Flexibility built into the plan?
   - Sequenced learning experiences?
   - Adequate forms of evaluation?

3. Specific approaches to curriculum that have been passionately argued by some writers may remain very limited in their applications (Jackson, 1992). For any of the exemplary approaches included in this chapter, discuss this weakness.

4. There is a "misguided human tendency—an almost universal belief that objectives are an indispensable ingredient in the curriculum planning process. Tyler's Rationale is merely the most visible manifestation of that popular delusion" (Kliebard, 1995, p. 87). How important are objectives in a curriculum approach? Establish some key arguments for and against Kliebard's quotation.

5. Locate and read an existing school curriculum. Does this document include all the characteristics of a curriculum identified in section 3.2 of this chapter? If not, is the curriculum too narrow or are the characteristics too numerous?

■ SUGGESTED READING

There are a number of excellent books on approaches to curriculum (see the chapter bibliography), including the following:

Erickson (1995)

Glanz & Behar-Horenstein (2000)

Hlebowitsh (1993)

Jackson (1992)

Pinar, Reynolds, Slattery, & Taubman (1995)

Reid (1999a)

Schubert (1986)

Tyler (1949)

Walker (1990)

■ BIBLIOGRAPHY

Andrews, S. V. (1989). Changing research perspectives: A critical study of Elliot Eisner. *Journal of Curriculum and Supervision, 4*(2), 106–125.

Apple, M. (1979). Curriculum and reproduction. *Curriculum Inquiry, 9*(3), 231–252.

Barnes, D. (1982). *Practical curriculum study.* London: Routledge & Kegan Paul.

Barone, T. (1987). On equality, visibility, and the fine arts program in a black elementary school: An example of educational criticism. *Curriculum Inquiry, 17*(4), 421–446.

Ben-Peretz, M. (1990). *The teacher-curriculum encounter.* Albany: State University of New York Press.

Bolin, F. S., & McConnell Falk, J. (Eds.). (1987). *Teacher renewal: Professional issues, personal choices.* New York: Teachers College Press.

Bonser, S. A., & Grundy, S. J. (1988). Reflective deliberation in the formulation of a school curriculum policy. *Journal of Curriculum Studies, 20*(3), 35–45.

Brice, L. (2000). *Deliberative discourse enacted: Task, text and talk.* Paper presented at the annual meeting of the American Educational Research Association, New Orleans.

Clandinin, D. J. (1986). *Classroom practice: Teacher images in action.* London: Falmer.

Connelly, F. M., & Clandinin, D. J. (1988). *Teachers as curriculum planners.* New York: Teachers College Press.

Cronbach, L. (1986). Tyler's contribution to measurement and evaluation. *Journal of Thought, 21*(1), 47–51.

Dev, P., & Walker, D. F. (1999). From virtual frog to frog island: Design studies in a development project. *Journal of Curriculum Studies, 31*(6) 635–659.

Dewey, J. (1959). The child and the curriculum. In M. S. Dworkin (Ed.), *Dewey on education.* New York: Teachers College Press.

Doll, W. (1993). *A post-modern perspective on curriculum.* New York: Teachers College Press.

Donmoyer, R. (1982). *Curriculum and the common good.* Paper presented at the annual meeting of the American Educational Research Association, New York.

Eisner, E. W. (1969). Instructional and expressive objectives: Their formulation and use in curriculum. In W. J. Popham (Ed.), *AERA monograph on curriculum evaluation: Instructional objectives.* Chicago: Rand McNally.

Eisner, E. W. (1972). *Educating artistic vision.* New York: Macmillan.

Eisner, E. W. (Ed.). (1978). *Reading, the arts, and the creation of meaning.* Reston, VA: National Art Education Association.

Eisner, E. W. (1979). *The educational imagination.* Upper Saddle River, NJ: Merrill/Prentice Hall.

Eisner, E. W. (1980). *On the differences between scientific and artistic approaches to qualitative research.* Paper presented at the annual meeting of the American Educational Research Association, Boston.

Eisner, E. W. (1985). *The art of educational evaluation: A personal view.* London: Falmer.

Eisner, E. W. (1991). *The enlightened eye.* Upper Saddle River, NJ: Prentice Hall.

Eisner, E. W. (1992). Curriculum ideologies. In P. W. Jackson (Ed.), *Handbook of research on curriculum.* New York: Macmillan.

Eisner, E. W. (1999). The uses and limits of performance assessment. *Phi Delta Kappan, 80*(9), 658–661.

Eisner, E. W. (2000). Those who ignore the past . . . : 12 "easy" lessons for the next millennium. *Journal of Curriculum Studies, 32*(2), 343–357.

Erickson, H. L. (1995). *Stirring the head, heart, and soul.* Thousand Oaks, CA: Corvin.

Freire, P. (1970). *Pedagogy of the oppressed.* New York: Seabury.

Giroux, H. (1981). *Ideology, culture, and the process of schooling.* Philadelphia: Temple University Press.

Glanz, J., & Behar-Horenstein, L. (Eds.). (2000). *Paradigm debates in curriculum and supervision: Modern and postmodern perspectives.* Westport, CT: Bergin & Garvey.

Goodlad, J. I., & Richter, M. N. (1977). Decisions and levels of decision making: Process and data sources. In A. A. Bellack & H. M. Kliebard (Eds.), *Curriculum and evaluation.* Berkeley, CA: McCutchan.

Grumet, M. (1988). *Bitter milk: Women and teaching.* Amherst: University of Massachusetts Press.

Helsby, G., & Saunders, M. (1993). Taylorism, Tylerism and performance indicators: Defending the indefensible? *Educational Studies, 19*(1), 55–77.

Hlebowitsh, P. S. (1992). Amid behavioral and behavioristic objectives: Reappraising appraisals of the Tyler rationale. *Journal of Curriculum Studies, 24*(6), 533–547.

Hlebowitsh, P. S. (1993). *Radical curriculum theory reconsidered.* New York: Teachers College Press.

Hlebowitsh, P. S. (1995). Interpretations of the Tyler rationale: A reply to Kliebard. *Journal of Curriculum Studies, 27*(1), 89–94.

Hlebowitsh, P. S. (1999). The burdens of the New Curricularist. *Curriculum Inquiry, 29*(3), 343–353.

Holt, M. (1990). Managing curriculum change in a comprehensive school: Conflict, compromise, and deliberation. *Journal of Curriculum Studies, 22*(2), 137–148.

Jackson, P. W. (Ed.). (1992). *Handbook of research on curriculum.* New York: Macmillan.

Johnson, M. (1977). *Intentionality in education: A conceptual model of curricular and instructional planning and evaluation.* Albany, NY: Center for Curriculum Research and Services.

Kennedy, K. J. (1988). *Creating a context for curriculum deliberation by teachers.* Paper presented at the annual meeting of the American Educational Research Association, New Orleans.

Kliebard, H. M. (1970). The Tyler rationale. *School Review, 78*(2), 259–272.

Kliebard, H. M. (1995). The Tyler rationale revisited. *Journal of Curriculum Studies, 27*(1), 81–88.

Lather, P. (1987). The absent presence: Patriarchy, capitalism and the nature of teacher work. *Teacher Education Quarterly, 14*(2), 25–38.

Levin, M. A. (1980). Can art stimulate program development? *Journal of Curriculum Theorizing, 2*(2), 10–14.

McLaren, P. (1993). Multiculturalism and the postmodern critique: Towards a pedagogy of resistance and transformation. *Cultural Studies, 7*(1), 118–146.

Milburn, G. (1992). Do curriculum studies have a future? *Journal of Curriculum and Supervision, 7*(3), 302–318.

Milburn, G. (2000). Understanding curriculum. *Journal of Curriculum Studies, 32*(3), 445–452.

Miller, J. L. (1986). Women as teachers: Enlarging conversations on issues of gender and self concept. *Journal of Curriculum and Supervision, 1*(2), 111–121.

Mulder, M. (1991). Deliberation in curriculum conferences. *Journal of Curriculum and Supervision, 6*(4), 325–339.

Oliver, J. (1987). *Educational connoisseurship and educational criticism: A critique.* Unpublished paper, Murdoch University, Perth, Western Australia.

Onosko, J. (1996). Exploring issues with students despite the barriers. *Social Education, 60*(1), 22–28.

Orpwood, W. F. (1985). The reflective deliberator: A case study of curriculum policy making. *Journal of Curriculum Studies, 17*(1), 293–304.

Pereira, P. (1984). Deliberation and the arts of perception. *Journal of Curriculum Studies, 16*(2), 347–366.

Pinar, W. (1983). Curriculum as gender text: Notes on reproduction, resistance, and male-male relations. *Journal of Curriculum Theorizing, 5*(1), 26–52.

Pinar, W. F., Reynolds, W. M., Slattery, P., & Taubman, P. M. (1995). *Understanding curriculum.* New York: Lang.

Posner, G. J. (1998). Models of curriculum planning. In L. E. Beyer & M. W. Apple (Eds.), *The curriculum: Problems, politics, and possibilities* (2nd ed., pp. 79–100). Albany: State University of New York Press.

Reid, W. A. (1988). The institutional context of curriculum deliberation. *Journal of Curriculum and Supervision, 4*(1), 3–16.

Reid, W. A. (1999a). *Curriculum as institution and practice.* Mahwah, NJ: Lawrence Erlbaum.

Reid, W. A. (1999b). The voice of "the Practical": Schwab as correspondent. *Journal of Curriculum Studies, 31*(4), 385–398.

Ross, E. W. (1993). Institutional constraints on curriculum deliberation. *Journal of Curriculum and Supervision, 8*(2), 95–111.

Schubert, W. H. (1986). *Curriculum: Perspective, paradigm, and possibility.* Upper Saddle River, NJ: Merrill/Prentice Hall.

Schwab, J. J. (1969). The practical: A language for curriculum. *School Review, 78*(1), 1–23.

Schwab, J. J. (1970). *The practical: A language for curriculum.* Washington, DC: National Education Association.

Silberstein, M., & Ben-Peretz, M. (1979). *The process of curriculum development: Two levels of interpretation.* Paper presented at the annual meeting of the American Educational Research Association, San Francisco.

Slattery, P. (1995). *Curriculum development in the postmodern era.* New York: Garland.

Taba, H. (1962). *Curriculum development: Theory and practice.* New York: Harcourt, Brace, & World.

Tyler, R. W. (1949). *Basic principles of curriculum and instruction.* Chicago: University of Chicago Press.

Tyler, R. W. (1975). Specific approaches to curriculum development. In J. Schaffarzick & D. H. Hampson (Eds.), *Strategies for curriculum development.* Berkeley, CA: McCutchan.

Tyler, R. W. (1992). The long-term impact of the Dewey school. *Curriculum Journal, 3*(2), 125–129.

Vallance, E. (1977). The landscape of the "Great Plains Experience": An application of curriculum criticism. *Curriculum Inquiry, 7*(2), 87–105.

Waks, L. J. (2000). Reid's theory of curriculum as institutionalized practice. *Journal of Curriculum Studies, 32*(4), 589–598.

Walker, D. F. (1971). A naturalistic model for curriculum development. *School Review, 80*(1), 51–65.

Walker, D. F. (1975). Curriculum development in an art project. In W. A. Reid & D. F. Walker (Eds.), *Case studies in curriculum change.* London: Routledge & Kegan Paul.

Walker, D. F. (1990). *Fundamentals of curriculum.* New York: Harcourt Brace Jovanovich.

Walker, D. F., & Soltis, J. (1986). *Curriculum and aims.* New York: Teachers College Press.

Curriculum Theorizing

ABOUT THIS CHAPTER

This chapter continues the historical investigation begun in chapter 2, which suggested that education in the United States throughout the twentieth century reflected a competition among subject-centered, person-centered, and society-centered concepts of curriculum. Beginning in the 1960s, efforts to end this competition began to emerge in the United States and in other countries under the general name of "curriculum theory." These and other recent efforts have significantly influenced current approaches to curriculum planning and development. This chapter considers what is meant by curriculum theorizing and categorizes a broad range of approaches. It describes in detail three influential forms of theorizing and points out their implications for the classroom.

WHAT YOU SHOULD DO

1. Consider and carefully weigh alternative ideas about curriculum theory and theorizing, how they lead to alternative approaches to curriculum planning and development, and how they follow from the historical antecedents described in chapter 2.
2. Critically compare the theorizing of Taba, Schwab, and Pinar.
3. Discover the different value orientations implicit in their approaches.
4. Consider the different implications that these approaches have for classrooms.
5. Learn how curriculum planning and development in the United States have been influenced by different kinds of theorizing.
6. Decide which parts of different theorizing you would use to guide your own curriculum work.

SOME OPTIONAL APPROACHES

In undertaking what this chapter asks you to do, you may find the following options useful.

93

Option A

1. Reflect on recent lessons you have taught. Try to justify your teaching in terms of the following questions: Why did you teach X? What were the underlying principles on which you based your decision to teach X and not Y or Z? How did these principles relate to
   a. Your personal philosophy?
   b. Your students' interests?
2. Having completed this act of self-analysis, carefully read about the examples of curriculum theorizing described in detail in this chapter. How do these approaches relate to the theoretical principles that you noted were the basis of your recent teaching? What parts of these approaches do you find unacceptable or weak? How would you change them?
3. Then read section 4.3 on the categories of curriculum theorizing in its entirety. How would you categorize your own decisions about what to teach?

Option B

1. Consider the history of curricula in the United States prior to the 1960s. (Review chapter 2, if necessary.)
2. Reflect upon how this history led up to efforts beginning in the 1960s to create curriculum theories.
3. Undertake a critical analysis of the approaches of Taba, Schwab, and Pinar. What historical precedents or antecedents does each reflect?

Option C

1. Examine the major categories of curriculum theorizing described in section 4.3.
2. Next, examine the various issues in, and ideas about, curriculum theory and curriculum theorizing (sections 4.1 through 4.4) that this chapter presents.
3. Ask yourself how your reactions to any of these examples of theorizing are related to differences among the planned curriculum, the enacted curriculum, and the experienced curriculum. Ask yourself how your answers are related to the maxim "precision in planning, flexibility in execution."

4.1   INTRODUCTION

In chapter 2 we outlined the history of curricula in use in schools in the United States and of various principles suggested at different times for making decisions about what school curricula should be. Thus far we have suggested that there is no one approach to curriculum development that should be followed in all places at all times since making decisions about how people should use their time and energy involves too many complexities to be reduced to a formula. We have suggested that readers (particularly teachers and prospective teachers) should be alert to the different value orientations and the different implications for classrooms that underlie different approaches. In addition, their own curriculum decisions can be informed by knowing something of both past and present approaches and understanding why and how people have made different decisions about curricula at various times and under various circumstances. Alert and so informed, individual decision makers can work out their own reasonable approaches to curriculum development that best fit their own beliefs and specific circumstances. In chapter 3 we analyzed three examples of well-known but different approaches to curriculum.

However, what if our suggestions are wrong? What if making decisions about what the curriculum should be is not inherently a problematic, open-ended process? Then there must be a certain set of principles—some theory—that can be used directly to guide curriculum decisions. Doubtless, many readers began this book with the expectation that it would clearly identify and articulate such principles; and as we ourselves have indicated in chapter 2, the history of curricula in the United States reveals that many—if not most—decision makers, regardless of the eras in which they lived, have looked for the single best way to go about their task. Many, in fact, have believed that the single best approach would lead to the single best curriculum. Recent efforts to develop national standards comprise yet another present-day attempt at delineating the preferred curriculum for all Americans (Clune, 1998). To be sure, history also reveals that there often has been competition among different approaches. It was not until well into the twentieth century (when investigation of underlying principles for curriculum development emerged as a separate academic field, as reflected by university departments devoted wholly or in part to the study of curriculum) that any real sense of problem about open-endedness versus closed-endedness began to enter in earnest into the consciousness of people who made, advised on, or studied curriculum decisions.

If our suggestions are wrong, however, then it should indeed be possible to search out and uncover a general set of principles or some definitive methods for guiding curriculum planning and development. In fact, during the 1960s the search for such principles in an attempt to end competition among different approaches to curriculum came to be known among many of the searchers themselves as the discovery, the creation, or even the building of curriculum theory. This attempt began largely as an effort to create scientific theory but soon became transformed into the pluralistic approaches to theorizing that guide curriculum planning and development today.

As part of their professional training, virtually all curriculum specialists and many prospective teachers now become familiar with contemporary curriculum theorizing. In this chapter we describe the many different forms that curriculum theorizing can take and raise questions about their adequacy, suggesting that readers choose carefully among the many different approaches advocated in recent decades. But further questions can always be raised about the actual influence of curriculum specialists themselves. In reality, the curricula in use in schools in the United States have probably always been influenced as much, if not more, by the opinions of society itself than by the opinions of professional educators. (Famous and reputedly influential national reports such as the Committee of Ten report of 1893 and *The Cardinal Principals of Secondary Education* of 1918 may represent exceptions, although it can be argued that their influence was less than their reputations would suggest and that the opinions of the educators who wrote these reports really reflected the opinions held by society at large.) During the second half of the twentieth-century, the development of pluralistic curriculum theorizing did not affect popular beliefs about what curricula should be. Contemporary theorizing suggests that curricula can be planned, enacted, and experienced in many different ways appropriate to many different circumstances and people, yet American society collectively still seems to be searching for a single best curriculum for all circumstances and all people. Numerous tensions arising from this situation seem likely to continue well into the twenty-first century.

This chapter examines the development of curriculum theorizing, concentrating on the period beginning in the 1960s—a time when many theorizers became conscious of the development of theory and when theorizing in the United States began to merge with theorizing in several other countries to create a truly international perspective on the approaches and issues involved. Did these trends lead toward an open-ended or closed-ended approach to curriculum? What does this recent history say specifically to people who make curriculum decisions for schools and classrooms today or who will do so in the future? These questions are among the foci of our investigation.

In the United States, as in other countries, curriculum theorizing has not advanced steadily. Over the last decades of the twentieth century, scholars grappled with vexing questions such as: What is curriculum theory? How might we obtain one? What is one good for, (McCutcheon, 1982)? Can an example be found (Kliebard, 1977)? The answers to these questions have been many and varied, and they have revealed differences in basic assumptions about what counts as valid curriculum purposes and content. On one hand, Westbury (1999) contends that these are not relevant questions at all, since the day-to-day reality of schools revolves around much less lofty and idealistic questions, such as, "What might we want to do in this here-and-now world?" and "How can or might we begin to do it?" (p. 357). However, curriculum specialists such as Giroux (1991) and Ornstein and Hunkins (1993) contend that we have to construct new vocabulary and new terms or metaphors if we are to make any advances.

Certainly new approaches with new terms and metaphors began developing during the 1970s. Whether they offer increasingly promising insights and directions is problematic. John Dewey's remark in the 1920s that we are still "groping" in curriculum matters may be equally pertinent today. Jackson (1992) has observed that the curriculum field remains "confusing." Wright (2000) contends that at the beginning of the twenty-first century, curriculum theorizing is still highly contested and in a state of flux.

Our investigation in this chapter reveals some of the reasons for the fractured and contested nature of curriculum theorizing.

4.2 WHAT IS CURRICULUM THEORIZING?

What is a theory? As noted by Vallance (1982), theories are typically defined in dictionaries and glossaries as one of the following:

1. A coherent group of general propositions used as principles of explanation for a class of phenomena
2. A proposed explanation, the status of which is still conjectural
3. A body of principles, theorems about a subject
4. That branch of a science or art that deals with principles and methods
5. Guess or conjecture

By the use of terms such as "coherent group of general propositions," "explanation," and "theorems," the first three definitions strongly imply that theories are created scientifically. Scientific theories are derived from the study of existing phenomena and lead to general explanations of those phenomena. They attempt to systematize or unify seemingly unrelated observations, to generate research hypotheses, to provide explanations, and to make predictions. They proceed by testing facts empirically and, therefore, are often considered to be objective (that is, derived directly from the objects of study) rather than subjective (derived from what is in the mind of the subject who does the studying). However, some scientific theories do change quite drastically, as was the case, for example, with conflicting theories about light. Also, in actuality, any particular scientific theory always involves value judgments by scientists about what to observe in the first place, what to leave out, and how to unify divergent explanations.

Critics of published curriculum theories might consider them all to represent the fifth definition, "guesses or conjectures." In some ways this would be a fair assessment, for no curriculum theory existing to date is either general enough to be scientific (as the first three definitions suggest) or specific enough about the "principles and methods" (which the fourth definition calls for) to be considered the single best guide to curriculum development. We are left with the idea that a curriculum theory somehow deals with principles and methods for creating curricula, but precisely how it leads to specific curricula we still do not know. There are several reasons for such unimpressive advances in the development of curriculum theories, the major one being that the experienced curriculum—particularly what we have referred to as its "lived" qualities—is never sufficiently regular, orderly, and periodic to enable principles and explanations to be developed. The curriculum in use in classrooms is so idiosyncratic that it is extremely difficult, if not impossible, to come up with anything close to universal generalizations (McCutcheon, 1982, 1985; Molnar, 1992). Miller (2000) refers to the "riotous array" of theoretical approaches in curriculum.

Yet there are various curriculum writers who maintain that a curriculum theory should aspire to universalness. For example, Beauchamp (1982) argued that a curriculum theory must provide an organized explanation—a set of related statements or propositions that gives meaning to the phenomena. In Ornstein and Hunkins's (1993) view, the purpose of a curriculum theory is describing, predicting, and explaining curricula phenomena in ways that serve as policy for guiding practical curriculum activities. Other writers are far less optimistic about the purposes of a curriculum theory. McCutcheon (1982) perceived a curriculum theory as simply an integrated cluster of sorts of analyses, interpretations, and understandings of curriculum phenomena, and Kliebard (1977) suggested that a curriculum theory is a more or less systematic analysis of a set of related concepts. Macdonald (1982) did not attempt to define what a curriculum theory is, but the following observation makes evident that he saw theory as underlying all our thinking and action:

> Curriculum theory is what speaks to us "through it" and what we do is informed by theory; but neither the specific words of theory nor the specific pedagogical acts of educators are the reality of education. What defines each is the spirit and vision that shines through the surface manifestations. (p. 56)

The frustration for curriculum writers is that, although the conceptualizing of curriculum theories still eludes us, the potential use of curriculum theories is very clear. Appropriate curriculum theories (if we had them) could guide the work of teachers, policymakers, administrators, and anyone else involved in curriculum planning and development. They would help researchers analyze data and provide a much needed impetus and direction for curriculum research, with the benefits flowing on to classroom teachers. The various ideas we have cited make obvious that there are many divergent directions still being explored in curriculum theory and that the situation today is just as "gritty and ragged" (Klohr, 1980) as ever. Few definite decisions can be made while the nature of curriculum theory itself remains so ragged around the edges. Today some directions in curriculum theory are being followed and, in some instances, appear to lead to advances, while other directions now appear to be dead ends.

One dead end is to consider curriculum as an institutionalized academic discipline (Johnson & Reid, 1999). As some scholars see it, a discipline must have two attributes: delineated areas of knowledge and particular forms of inquiry. If curriculum is to be considered an academic discipline, then one might argue that perseverance and insight is all that is required from curriculum theorists to uncover the areas of knowledge and forms of inquiry (Mann, 1968). But curriculum seems dependent on other disciplines. Traditional writings on curriculum refer especially to the disciplines of philosophy, psychology, and sociology (Ross, 2000). Pinar et al. (1995) and Wright (2000) include many other disciplines and fields, such as psychoanalysis, theology, political science, aesthetics, multiculturalism, phenomenology, and postmodernism.

Another approach is to attempt to establish the key questions that need to be answered by a curriculum theory. For example, Kliebard (1977) suggested that the fundamental question for any curriculum theory is, What should we teach? This question then leads us to consider other questions, such as:

> Why should we teach this rather than that?
> Who should have access to what knowledge?

What rules should govern the teaching of what has been selected?

How should various parts of the curriculum be interrelated in order to create a coherent whole?

Beyer and Apple (1998), Posner (1998), and Ross (2000) extend this list to include broader, more politically sensitive questions:

What should count as knowledge? As knowing? What does not count as legitimate knowledge?

Who defines what counts as legitimate knowledge?

Who shall control the selection and distribution of knowledge?

Who has the greatest access to high-status and high-prestige knowledge?

How shall curricular knowledge be made accessible to students?

How do we link the curriculum knowledge to the biographies and personal meanings of students?

However, it is doubtful that a curriculum theory can be uncovered simply by posing questions. Can empirical evidence be obtained or normative arguments worked out that provide definite answers? If not, what priorities should be adopted and on what basis? Again it seems that the diverse classroom settings and circumstances that curriculum decisions need to take into account defy any attempt to provide straightforward answers to these questions. Even the most fundamental question about curriculum seems, therefore, to lead to an infinite regress of subquestions.

Curriculum Models

One possible approach to curriculum theory is to abandon ambitious plans for producing all-embracing curriculum theories and to concentrate on models of curriculum. Vallance (1982) and Posner (1998) advocate the development of models of curriculum and suggest that models, although they may lack statements of rules and principles that theories include, can identify the basic considerations that must be accounted for in curriculum decisions and can show their interrelationships.

Curriculum scholars have made some notable advances in creating models, as is evident in later chapters of this book, in which we give considerable space to discussions of change models (chapter 5), planning models (chapter 6), and evaluation models (chapter 8).

Models can provide useful, detailed perspectives on some particulars of the curriculum in action, but not the total picture. To the extent to which they fail to account for the complexities of the planned curriculum, the enacted curriculum, and the experienced curriculum, they are not entirely satisfactory solutions to the problem of creating curriculum theories.

Curriculum Theorizing

Yet another solution, and one that has been proposed by many recent curriculum writers, is "to shift focus from the end product (the curriculum theory) to the process by which a theory is sought (the process of theorizing)" (Vallance, 1982, p. 8). Although theorizers are apparently involved in activities, the outcome of which is the completion of a theory, their real involvement is actually with the processes of arriving at such an outcome. Theorizing is thus a general process involving individuals in three distinct activities:

- Being sensitive to emerging patterns in phenomena
- Attempting to identify common patterns and issues
- Relating patterns to one's own teaching context

If theorizing is defined in this way, then it can—and should—be undertaken by all persons with an interest in curriculum, including teachers, academics, and members of the community (Brady, 1984). Teachers in their daily work attempt to become increasingly sensitive to what is significant in their own classrooms and to establish some appropriate framework or orientation to guide what they do (Schubert, 1992). Academics, even though their primary motive may be to theorize in general rather than to guide teaching specifically, still interpret their experience with specific examples or episodes of teaching and attempt to identify patterns that may prove useful in orienting actions. In this way, the traditional dichotomy of theory-practice disappears since all now become practitioners who theorize about their teaching-learning experiences.

This approach is, we believe, the most fruitful approach to the problem. Emphasizing the process of theorizing rather than specific theories is, in fact, what many recent curriculum writers have done, although considerable confusion still exists and many different, more narrow approaches to curriculum much closer to scientific theorizing have their advocates. The terms *curriculum theory* and *curriculum theorizing* are often used interchangeably, but one underlying difference is critical. As we maintain throughout this book, the basic problem inherent in making the best possible decisions about curricula is not one that can be solved by discovering universal generalizations (even if this could be done) or by concentrating on models (even though doing so has some practical applications). This is what curriculum "theory" (in the narrow sense) attempts to do. The basic problem is how to think carefully about real people in specific situations and to arrive at the most desirable courses of action that can be carried out under prevailing circumstances, all subject to further change and improvement through further thought about what has been experienced. This is what curriculum "theorizing" (in the broad sense) does. Emphasis falls on the ongoing process, not on any particular result, and the ongoing process links thought with action—and the planned curriculum with the enacted curriculum and both with the experienced curriculum.

Seen in this light, the basic problem, then, is not one amenable to solution by "theory," but it is one amenable to amelioration by "theorizing," in which sensitivity to general patterns and to specific situations both play a part. The explanations conveyed through theorizing can also be in terms of specific examples, not merely in terms of generalizations alone. Attention to the specific keeps the general from becoming too ethereal and abstract; attention to the general lifts the specific above the particular and anecdotal.

Seen in this light, efforts that began in earnest in the 1960s to end competition among different conceptions of curriculum by creating general "theory" have been misguided and are destined to fail. Nonetheless, these efforts have contributed to the broader ones of today in "theorizing" and thus have left a valuable legacy. Clearly, curriculum theorizing can be done well in many specific ways, and variety in theorizing is itself a positive value. People inquiring into how to approach curriculum development constantly invent new ways of identifying common patterns and issues and of applying their perceptions to the specific situations in which teaching occurs. As Smith (1984) reminds us, what we should be doing is not extolling the virtues of a particular type of theorizing, but attempting to answer the question, Whose interests are being served and whose are not?

In the next section, we classify a number of alternative approaches to curriculum, particularly those undertaken since the 1960s. We describe in detail the theorizing of Hilda Taba, Joseph Schwab, and William Pinar (which parallel the approaches to curriculum planning of Tyler, Walker, and Eisner described in chapter 3), all of which have significantly influenced current theorizing. Our examination demonstrates the diversity of approaches available and the opportunities and dilemmas they pose for anyone inquiring into how to go about curriculum planning and development.

4.3   MAJOR CATEGORIES OF CURRICULUM THEORIZING

Since approaches to curriculum theorizing are so diverse and so many, forming a system of categories in which to assign individual writers is difficult, but doing so highlights the salient features of categories and writers as well as the differences among them. The difficulty in categorizing, of course, is that judgments have to be made about unique efforts at theorizing that often defy simple classification. The very act of creating categories results in labels that may only be relevant at one point in time or, worse, are deliberately biased to promote a particular point of view.

Some textbook writers on curriculum (Eisner & Vallance, 1974; McNeil, 1977) attempt to classify theories and theorizing in order to explain to their readers the relationships between different theoretical principles and the resulting school practices. For example, McNeil suggests that theories can be grouped into four categories, which he labels "humanistic," "social reconstructionist," "technological," and "academic" (see also chapter 3). He argues that holders of each of these views have different ideas about what should be taught, to whom, when, and how. Thus, humanists maintain that the curriculum should consist of experiences for learners that are personally satisfying; social reconstructionists assert that the major task of the curriculum is to bring about social reform and a better society; technologists have a commitment to providing efficient means to achieve any ends designated by policymakers as being important in a curriculum; and academicians consider subject matter content as the basis of any curriculum, knowledge of which is an end in itself, not a means to some other end such as solving social problems.

Eisner & Vallance (1974) list five orientations or categories: cognitive process, technological, self-actualization, social reconstructionist, and academic rationalist. These represent very different perspectives; hence, the inclusion of the phrase "conflicting conceptions" in the title of their book. Yet, they follow quite closely the categories listed by McNeil (1977). It is interesting to note that Vallance (1986) modified these orientations twelve years later by deleting "self-actualization" and adding "personal success" (pursuing a specific, practical end) and a "curriculum for personal commitment" (pursuing learning for its inherent rewards).

Still another example is Kliebard (1986), who identifies four orientations to curriculum theorizing that are similar to those of McNeil, as well as Eisner and Vallance. He includes humanists (who see themselves as guardians of the cultural heritage), developmentalists (who formulate schooling around the norms of child development), social efficiency educators (who advocate techniques of industry and business to increase student learning), and social meliorists (who hold the improvement of society as their major goal).

In the United Kingdom, Ross (2000) has more recently referred to content-driven, objectives-driven, and process-driven curricula, yet Reid (2000), in his review of Ross, bemoans the apparent coyness of English educators in grappling with curriculum theory.

While different categorizations help us to delineate and clarify different approaches among curriculum theorizers, we must eventually settle on one, and the categorization that we have adopted in this book is derived mostly from Macdonald (1971), who suggested that all curriculum theorizers seem to have one of three possible predominate purposes. The first is an immediately practical purpose. Here the interest is primarily on creating theory that identifies and solves practical problems of schooling. This purpose can be labeled "prescriptive" and has sometimes been called "curriculum trouble-shooting." The second is an empirical purpose that is also practical, but more indirectly so. Here the interest is primarily on creating theory that identifies and validates salient features of curriculum development and the relationships among them. This purpose can be labeled "descriptive." The third is an exploratory purpose. Here the interest is primarily on creating theory that is comprehensive, both in terms of understanding deficiencies in other forms of theorizing and in terms of overcoming such deficiencies. At first glance this purpose seems the farthest removed of the three from practical school problems, but it may prove the most useful in the long run. This purpose can be labeled "critical."

Similarly, Jackson (1992) provides confirmation that the field can be mapped in terms of the interests of curriculum theorizers. He identifies two groups. The first encompasses the immediately practical concerns of Macdonald's first two categories and includes those theorizers who serve the daily technical needs of personnel who work in schools. This group includes those who use a deliberation-based approach derived from Schwab (1970). Jackson's second group corresponds to those theorizers who hold Macdonald's exploratory purpose; it includes contemporary theorizers who are critical of traditions associated with the Tyler Rationale and who use eclectic sources to explore curriculum.

On this basis, we adopt the following three categories for classifying curriculum theorizers and their approaches:

1. *Prescriptive Theorizers.* This group attempts to create models or frameworks for curriculum development that improve school practices. Many members of this group have, in fact, held the belief that finding the best way of designing curricula will lead to the best possible curricula for schools. Ralph Tyler and Hilda Taba are members of this group.

2. *Descriptive Theorizers.* This group attempts to identify how curriculum development actually takes place, especially in school settings. The idea is to understand the various steps and procedures in curriculum development and the relationships among them. Decker Walker and Joseph Schwab are members of this group.

3. *Critical-Exploratory Theorizers.* This group attempts to understand deficiencies in past practices of curriculum development and to replace them with more adequate practices, particularly by considering curriculum in the broadest possible intellectual and social contexts. This group looks at curriculum in terms of its diversities and continuities, emphasizing what curriculum has been, is, and might be. Elliot Eisner and William Pinar are members of this group.

Prescriptive Theorizers: Creating the Best Curricula Possible

Not surprisingly, as school districts became larger and more bureaucratized at the beginning of the twentieth century, early efforts at curriculum theorizing were undertaken by specialists who attempted to provide assistance to practitioners working in schools. Dewey (1900, 1902) had begun to elaborate a new way of understanding education and a new set of practical yet nonprescriptive pedagogical principles, and various frameworks for curriculum development were proposed by influential figures such as Bobbitt (1918) and, later, Tyler (1949). Some of these frameworks were consistent with Dewey's ideas; some were not. Up until the 1960s, nearly all theorizing about curriculum development focused on ways to improve practices in schools. The major problem with most of these prescriptive approaches was that they assumed the characteristics of traditional, bureaucratized schools to be givens. Therefore, they rarely questioned—and thus frequently served to support—existing educational, social, and political systems.

Although the best known of these specialists became major "canonical figures" (Wright, 2000), there are many diverse prescriptive approaches, as depicted in Figure 4.1. Some specialists worked closely with laboratory schools located on university campuses. Others were involved in major studies of schools or with major curriculum development projects. As a consequence, they wrote directly out of their experiences with specific schools. Hlebowitsh (1999) describes the common concern of these specialists for the improvement of school systems as "dedicated to offering curriculum development frameworks centered on using the school for the maintenance and improvement of the public interest." Yet, other commentators have seen these endeavors much less positively, describing them as "control mechanisms" (Perkinson, 1993), "traditionalist" (Pinar, 1978), and "quasi-scientific" (Apple, 1979).

Social needs-child-centered
Dewey (1900, 1902, U.S.)
Kilpatrick (1918, U.S.)
Rugg (1927, U.S.)

Social efficiency
Bobbitt (1918, 1924, U.S.)
Charters (1923, U.S.)

Social needs-rational/technical
Tyler (1949, U.S.)
Herrick & Tyler (1950, U.S.)
Taba (1962, U.S.)
Goodlad (1984, U.S.)
Klein (1992, U.S.)
Tanner & Tanner (1995, U.S.)

Social needs-reconstructionist
Hughes (1972, Australia)
Skilbeck (1976, Australia)

Philosophical-academic rational
Phenix (1964, U.S.)
Hirst (1965, U.K.)
Peters (1966, U.K.)
Hutchins (1968, U.S.)

FIGURE 4.1
Prescriptive theorizers
Source: After Reid (1981).

Readers should note that there are numerous theorizers who are not listed in Figure 4.1 nor discussed below. Those who are listed are illustrative of major approaches within this category. The list in Figure 4.1 focuses on theorizing that arose mainly during the 1960s and 1970s and that may still dominate theorizing today, although Jackson (1992) and Wright (2000) contend that this group has lost some of its "space" in more recent decades.

Social Needs-Child-Centered.   The individuals involved in the social needs-child-centered approach begin with Dewey (whose ideas and influence we have considered in chapter 2). His numerous books, including *The School and Society* (1900) and *The Child and the Curriculum* (1902), describe his belief that the curriculum of the individual child is related to the role of the school within society. To Dewey, the social experiences of the child are the starting point for developing a curriculum and are at least as important as organized disciplines of knowledge. At the laboratory school on the University of Chicago campus, he involved students in household occupations such as weaving, cooking, and working in wood and metal as general methods of living and learning in society, not as specific, school-based studies (Dewey, 1902). Such activities illustrate that needs arise out of the nature of society, and the curriculum can reflect such general needs (Prawat, 2000) yet be individualized around what each child needs specifically.

The thrust of Dewey's earliest books is to use such ideas to improve schools; hence, he has been included in the first category. However, much of his later writing emphasizes the value of open-ended deliberation and its use in curriculum work. The difficulty in classifying Dewey in just one way points out the general difficulty of using any classificatory system with individuals whose theorizing does not fit neatly into its categories or who, over the course of a long career, might propose a number of theories (Chung & Walsh, 2000).

Also included under the subheading social needs-child-centered is Kilpatrick (1918), whose project method can be considered a continuation of Dewey's teaching about the need for children to engage in activities related to present living. In his writings, Kilpatrick proposes that units of work ("hearty purposeful acts") should replace subjects in order to enable children to focus on topics of interest and to become involved in problem-solving activities.

Social Efficiency. The distinct lack of homogeneity in this category becomes evident when examining other theorizers listed in Figure 4.1. Bobbitt's ideas about curriculum, for instance, are much different from Dewey's, for Bobbitt saw the curriculum as being determined solely by the characteristics of the existing society and not at all by the nature of the child (see chapter 2). In his two influential curriculum books, *The Curriculum* (1918) and *How to Make a Curriculum* (1924), Bobbitt argues that the metaphor of the factory and industrial production should be the basis for curriculum development. In his view, education is primarily for adult life, not for life as a child, and it is necessary to analyze the activities of adults to provide the long lists of objectives that he sees as determining the curriculum. The curriculum thus consists of knowledge and skills required in adult pursuits, and its purpose, therefore, is to fit the individual efficiently into the society as it is. Bobbitt's ideas about applying industrial efficiency to society and the schools were widely accepted by American educators during the 1910s and 1920s. Other authors followed with their own books on curriculum that emphasized the importance of specifying objectives using procedures of scientific analysis. While Bobbitt, Charters, Morrison, and others were hailed as progressive during the 1920s and 1930s (Gwynn & Chase, 1969), contemporary writers tend to criticize them for their pseudo-scientific, socially conservative approaches to curriculum.

Social Needs-Rational/Technical. The curriculum field clearly owes a huge debt to Ralph Tyler. His foremost publication, *Basic Principles of Curriculum and Instruction* (1949), is a very readable account of a set of ways to create a curriculum and the basis for Tyler's approach to curriculum planning, which we discussed in chapter 3. His approach, however, with its emphasis on a scientific derivation of ends and means, can be considered an extension of the principles expounded by Bobbitt. Tyler, like Bobbitt, emphasizes social needs as a starting point for the curriculum, but, unlike Bobbitt, he remains open to a variety of rational and technical ways of determining social needs and balancing them against other kinds of needs.

In *Basic Principles of Curriculum and Instruction,* Tyler considers what is required for developing a curriculum and then produces his four basic questions about purposes, selecting learning experiences, organizing learning experiences, and evaluation. He is not concerned about a number of other important curriculum matters, such as the effects of particular value orientations or how to make political decisions about competing claims, so Tyler's book should not be seen as an attempt to create a complete curriculum theory. However, his theorizing about issues such as objectives, selecting learning experiences, sequencing and organizing learning experiences, and using appropriate means of evaluation has also been considered as the basic framework for any overall theory that attempts to guide all curriculum work.

Thus, Tyler's theorizing has proved to be a powerful stimulus for many other scholars seeking to build on his ideas (Helsby & Saunders, 1993; Hlebowitsh, 1999). For example, Taba applied Tyler's principles to an approach to planning that emphasizes students' inductive thinking. In her book *Curriculum Development: Theory and Practice* (1962), she considers the nature of thinking and proposes ways for how thinking might be developed by the use of particular questioning strategies. She also widens the scope of Tyler's basic principles by considering learning experiences in terms of how they promote both cognitive and affective development. We discuss her theorizing later in the chapter.

Social Needs-Reconstructionist.   Some theorizers who take social needs as the starting point for curriculum planning and development see society as it is as neither desirable nor a given. In fact, they see society as so riddled with undesirable features that a primary role of the school is to reconstruct it for the better (Ornstein & Hunkins, 1993). Therefore, their approach to social needs is not to identify what is wrong with the student in comparison with the way society is but to identify what is wrong with society in comparison with the way it should be. Once this analysis has been undertaken, the curriculum can be developed as a means to correct what is wrong with society. Two Australian theorizers, Hughes (1972) and Skilbeck (1976), represent this point of view among prescriptive theorizers. Other theorizers who hold similar views about the wrongs of society but who have more pessimistic views about the ability of schools to distance themselves from these wrongs and become directly engaged in constructive social change are categorized as critical-exploratory theorizers.

Philosophical-Academic Rational.   Advocates about what knowledge is and what should be taught in schools dominated philosophies of Western education prior to the twentieth century. Many writers have argued that the purpose of the curriculum is to help children "acquire the tools to participate in the Western cultural tradition . . . [and obtain] access to the greatest ideas and objects that man has created" (Eisner & Vallance, 1974, p. 12).

A number of theorizers have held similar points of view about looking carefully at the nature of knowledge as the starting point for curriculum development and as the basis for a common curriculum (Ross, 2000). For example, Hirst (1965) identifies forms of knowledge based on academic disciplines. He claims that students must become familiar with the distinctive insights gained from studying enduring fields of knowledge. Phenix (1964) identifies somewhat different patterns of knowledge but argues that, through such patterns, knowledge reveals itself in its most teachable forms. In centering the curriculum on the nature of knowledge itself, philosophical rationalists de-emphasize the nature of the society and the nature of the individual as determiners of what the curriculum should be (Coulby, 2000).

Review of the Category.   These examples of theorizing are just a few of the many that have been proposed by prescriptive theorizers during the twentieth century. Several examples of rational/technical approaches tried in the 1960s and 1970s represent efforts to create scientific curriculum theories, but most examples listed in Figure 4.1 come much closer to theorizing in a less-technical sense, particularly those that in some ways acknowledge the lived qualities of the experienced curriculum. Kliebard (1974) points out that many of the efforts in this category of theorizing are incomplete because they tend to emphasize a particular interest of the theorizer, such as educational measurement or psychology. He criticizes Tyler on the grounds that his approach encourages the development of curricula in which the outcomes can be precisely and easily measured and so discourages curricula that do not emphasize measurable ends.

It is difficult to think of theories—whether by prescriptive theorizers or others—that are so comprehensive that they can accommodate a full range of different emphases, although over the decades serious efforts have occasionally been made by curriculum specialists in the United States to reconcile different theoretical approaches. The most notable effort was probably by the committee chaired by Rugg (1927), which in *The Foundations of Curriculum-Making* attempted to reconcile subject-centered, society-centered, and individual-centered approaches to curriculum (see chapter 2). The list of eighteen questions that the committee collectively proposed presumably presented a unified approach to creating curricula, but most members of the committee still felt compelled to provide supplementary statements of their own "to preserve the integrity of their own orientations" (Beauchamp, 1975, p. 66).

Despite the considerable differences among prescriptive theorizers and criticisms that their efforts have been incomplete, this group has dominated thought and practice in curriculum planning and development in the United States since the beginning of the twentieth century. Various educators involved in reviewing approaches used in curriculum (for example, Cornbleth, 1988; Goodlad & Richter, 1977; Kemmis, 1986; Marsh, 1987; and Olson, 1989) have expressed concern about the dominance of this particular theoretical orientation—especially Tyler's influence—since other, potentially more fruitful approaches to curriculum have yet to be tried out on nearly so broad a scale.

AN EXAMPLE: HILDA TABA'S APPROACH

Most efforts to create a single theory for guiding curriculum planning and development have come from curriculum development proponents, and within this group, Hilda Taba has perhaps come as close as anyone to describing a complete theory. As we have noted, Taba's approach is based on Tyler's work. It reflects the same kind of technical, ends-means rationality, but it is both descriptive and prescriptive. It emphasizes students' inductive thinking, and curriculum development projects based on it have incorporated a solid disciplinary emphasis (for instance, Durkin, McNaughton, Myers, & Wallen, 1974).

As a graduate student, Hilda Taba studied under Ralph Tyler at the University of Chicago and later worked with him in some major evaluation studies, including the Eight-Year Study. For many years she taught at San Francisco State University, and in her capacity as lecturer and teacher-trainer she was heavily involved in inservice activities with teachers in the Contra Costa County School District of San Francisco. Her theorizing reflects the practical experiences she acquired while working with teachers, the techniques that emerged from these experiences, and some specific tenets about thinking processes that she derived from contemporary learning theorists and developmental psychologists. Her curriculum approach was first published in a comprehensive volume *Curriculum Development: Theory and Practice* (1962) and further refined in two posthumous publications, *Teaching Strategies and Cognitive Functioning in Elementary School Children* (1966) and *Teachers' Handbook for Elementary Social Studies* (1967).

Basic Assumptions and Goals

Taba identifies three major postulates about thinking:

1. Thinking can be taught.
2. Thinking is an active transaction between the individual and the data.
3. The processes of thought evolve by a sequence that is "lawful."

Taken collectively, these postulates assume that individual students have to engage actively with classroom materials (organizing facts, generalizing, making inferences) if they are to learn and that there is an optimal sequence of learning activities. Thus, these assumptions lead directly to Taba's emphasis on inductive rea-

---

1. **Diagnosis of needs**
2. **Formulation of objectives**
   Basic knowledge (concepts and generalizations)
   Thinking (concept formation, inductive development of generalizations, application of principles)
   Attitudes, feelings, and sensitivities
   Academic and social skills
3. **Selection and organization of content**
   Basic concepts
   Main ideas
   Specific facts
   Patterns for organizing content
4. **Selection and organization of learning experiences**
   Sequence of learning experiences for cognitive development
   Sequence of learning experiences for affective development
5. **Evaluation**
   Diagnosis
   A range of instruments to evaluate whether objectives have been achieved

---

FIGURE 4.2
Steps in Taba's approach
Source: After Taba (1962).

soning in which students develop generalizations from collected data, and for Taba the goals of inductive reasoning are found in the processes of thinking as students go about the task of making observations about data and forming differing types of inferences from their observations. According to Taba, children will be required to think clearly if they are asked the right questions, and they will develop skills of inferential thinking and critical thinking if they are exposed to appropriately sequenced activities.

Steps and Stages

Although Taba's approach is based on the four steps of the Tyler rationale, it adds a fifth step, as shown in Figure 4.2.

Of particular importance is her first step, diagnosis of needs, which occurs prior to establishing objectives, the first step in the Tyler rationale. She also subdivides the four steps that parallel Tyler's, specifying that they include items such as the sequencing of learning experiences to promote both cognitive and affective development of students and the use of a variety of approaches to evaluate the growth of students' thinking skills. Taba also incorporates the idea of organizing activities in accordance with stages of a student's cognitive development and affective development, and she identifies separate stages for elementary and secondary levels of education for both areas of development. Figure 4.3 is one interpretation of Taba's approach in terms of classroom activities appropriate to the stages of cognitive development at the elementary level.

Teacher's Role

In Taba's approach, the teacher's role is to provide a supportive environment to foster students' use of inductive thinking and to initiate this kind of thinking by asking questions. The teacher begins by asking questions that either are focused on important generalizations to which the students' thinking will lead or are about specific topics or content areas from which generalizations will arise naturally. Early questions are diagnostic; they elicit information about whether students have sufficient background to make generalizations on the topics. When background is insufficient, the teacher should provide students with further sensory experiences with the topics (for example, readings, audiotapes, videotapes, field trips). Once students are able to begin thinking inductively, the teacher's task is to ask further questions and to provide activities that help students develop and refine their thinking skills (Erickson, 1995).

Use of a data retrieval chart (as shown in Figure 4.3) may be of particular help to the teacher because "it displays materials in a way that promotes generalizing and making comparisons, explanations and predictions" (Eggen, Kauchak, & Harder, 1988, p. 202). It is important that only raw factual data be recorded on the data retrieval chart so that students can link data together themselves to form generalizations. The teacher controls the pace at which the various stages of thinking are introduced in accordance with the abilities of the students.

Classroom Climate

Taba's approach requires a supportive, cooperative classroom in which students and the teacher are able to express their ideas and opinions without fear of ridicule or

---

Main Idea: Different crops and animals are all important to the farmer and have special uses.

Stage 1
1. Ask students to recall their observations about a recent excursion to the farm.
2. List some of the responses on a blackboard or chart.

"Think about your excursion to the farm. What are some of the things you saw?"

Stage 2
1. Ask students to identify the common properties in their listings.
2. Ask students to suggest how they might be grouped.

"From the items you have listed for me, which ones do you think might be grouped together?"

Stage 3
1. Ask students to suggest labels for their grouping.
2. Suggest to students that some regroupings may be necessary.

"Can you suggest a name for this group of . . .?"

Stage 4
Using butcher paper or an overhead projector transparency, construct a *data retrieval chart* (or students in groups might construct their own).

"From the groups we decided upon yesterday, I have made up this chart. It should help us collect more of the information we need."

Names	*Location on Farm*	*Uses*
Crops	_____	_____
Fruit trees	_____	_____
Vegetables	_____	_____
Animals	_____	_____

FIGURE 4.3
A sample series of stages for cognitive development in a third-grade elementary school class

reprimand. Under these conditions, the teacher may still initiate questions and activities to stimulate students to inductive thinking, but students, either individually or working in small groups, can often continue with the process without constant direction by the teacher.

Curriculum Development Exemplars

Taba's approach has been used extensively in both large and small curriculum projects. In the 1960s, she began a major social studies curriculum, which was continued into the 1970s by her associates as the Taba Program in Social Science, Grades 1–7. The program incorporates eleven major concepts selected from the social science disciplines, although the emphasis throughout is on thinking skills rather than on content. It has been used extensively in elementary and secondary schools in several regions of the United States. Other adaptations based on Taba's approach were incorporated into national curriculum projects of the 1970s, including the High School Geography Project (HSGP) and Man: A Course of Study (MACOS). In addition, the teaching strategies employed in Taba's

Stage 5

1. Ask students about each cell in the matrix chart.
2. Agree upon who will collect the information and where they should go to get it.
3. Ask students to suggest possible generalizations about their groupings.

"Let's start looking at the information we have so far by filling in the details in each square. What extra information do we need about . . .?"

Stage 6

1. Ask students to add the extra information they have collected.
2. Ask students to state some new generalization across several cells.

"What things are the same across the first two cells?"
"What things are different?"

Stage 7

Request students to explain the generalizations they have formed.

"Do you really agree with that point? Why is it correct? Are there any exceptions?"

Stage 8

Apply the generalizations developed to earlier work done in class.

"How do these points help us to understand what we did on . . . last week?"

Stage 9

Attempt to summarize the major generalizations developed during the previous activities.

"Let's go over the main points we have agreed upon."

Student Evaluation

Student's *comprehension* of the previous activities should be demonstrated by use of related written passages or of pictures.

"Read the following paragraphs and underline each time . . . is present."
"Look at the pictures of . . . and write down what things are the same."

Students' *application* could be evaluated by using if-then questions (orally or in written form).

"What would happen if . . .?"

FIGURE 4.3 *continued*

Source: After Eggen, Kauchak, & Harder (1979)

theory have been used frequently in preservice and in-service training programs (Anderson, 1981; Fraenkel 1992; Hall & Myers, 1977).

Evaluation of the Approach

Taba's approach is an elaboration of the Tyler rationale, emphasizing the development of thinking skills in students. Although the approach was elaborated by working with social studies teachers and social studies curricula, her sequential stages of thinking and the corresponding classroom strategies have application to other school subjects. Teachers can use the approach as a model for curriculum development simply by patterning their own curricula on the stages and strategies Taba worked out. Because the approach suggests flexible means for teaching thinking skills, it accounts for differences among the planned curriculum, the enacted curriculum, and the experienced curriculum; however, the ways in which it does so are not at all sophisticated. Nonetheless, it can and has been criticized for many of the same reasons that Tyler's approach to curriculum planning has been criticized, as well as for other reasons.

Kirst and Walker (1971, pp. 540–541) criticize Taba's approach on the grounds that it avoids any consideration of political conflicts—conflicts among ideas, individuals, and interest groups. They argue that curriculum development is neither rational nor scientific, as assumed by Taba, and that political considerations have to be built into any curriculum theorizing for it to be credible. McKenzie (1979) criticizes Taba's approach on the grounds that her inductive approach to teaching thinking skills provides too little information to enable a child to discover the ideas that are supposed to be learned. He maintains that students become bored with grouping data and making generalizations unless they are given many examples and counterexamples by their teacher. Anderson (1981), in his study of preservice teachers, found that student teachers using Taba's inductive teaching strategies were able to develop high levels of competency in students' thinking but that these levels were achieved even more effectively by using self-instructional modules. Joyce, Murphy, Showers, and Murphy (1989), in their review of research on information-processing models (including the Taba model), concluded that students can be taught thinking strategies and that "adding them to the instructional program has consistent, though modest, effects on the learning and retention of information" (p. 19).

Despite the many arguments that can be made both in favor and against the use of Taba's approach in curriculum planning and development, it has proved influential, probably for many of the same reasons that the Tyler rationale has proved influential: it is straightforward, understandable, and usable.

Descriptive Theorizers: Mapping the Procedures of Curriculum Development

Descriptive theorizers are not concerned—at least not directly—with providing specific answers to questions concerning what a curriculum should be. Rather, they are concerned with how such answers can be arrived at. To use an analogy, they are concerned with creating a map of the terrain on which curriculum decision making takes place, not with excavating specific plots of earth involved in school construction projects. An accurate map may be essential to a good construction project, but where roads and structures specifically are built depends on the beliefs and values of the designers of the project, on budgets and the availability of building materials, and on numerous other practical matters that vary from project to project.

Descriptive theorizers are similar to the prescriptive theorizers of our first category, however, to the extent that both groups view curriculum decision making as taking place primarily in schools or in large curriculum development projects that see schools as givens, thus supporting existing educational, social, and political systems. Nonetheless, descriptive theorizers do tend to have a broader vision primarily because they perceive curriculum problems as being largely indeterminate and open-ended. They understand there are no curriculum development procedures that ensure practical success. They argue that it is futile to search for a single best curriculum because of the diversity of curriculum problems and possible solutions. Therefore, most descriptive theorizers actually hold a wide vision about the organization of schools and the interaction of diverse individuals and groups. Technical, operational procedures are seen to be of less importance than deliberative processes (Reid, 1999a).

Because they view curriculum decision making broadly, as taking place in the same multiple and complex ways in which people make practical decisions within their own lives, they stress that the procedures of curriculum development also take place through what Schwab (1969, 1970), in working out Dewey's line of reasoning, has termed "practical inquiry." Schubert (1986) notes that the practical inquiry approach to curriculum theorizing can be characterized as follows:

- It involves everyday problem solving.
- It assumes that every teaching situation is unique.
- It focuses more on questions to be asked than on finding answers.
- It proceeds through the process of deliberation.
- It does not provide general solutions to problems, for each specific situation must be considered separately.

Walker's naturalistic model of the processes of curriculum deliberation (discussed in chapter 3) is one example of a mapping of how practical inquiry takes place. Other examples are listed in Figure 4.4.

While there are some descriptive theorizers who are concerned more with building scientific theory than with investigating practical inquiry, they have not been prominent since the 1970s. Still other theorizers concerned with identifying models of curriculum development, planning, and implementation (some of whom we discuss separately in chapters 5–7) also are unconcerned with practical reasoning. Therefore, for our purposes Figure 4.4 includes only one subheading, "deliberative."

Deliberative
Schwab (1969, 1973, 1983, U.S.)
Walker (1971, U.S.)
Westbury (1972, U.S.)
Connelly (1978, Canada)
Reid (1978, U.K.)
Roby (1983, U.S.)
Gough (1984, Australia)
Smith (1984, Australia)
Tripp (1984, Australia)

FIGURE 4.4
Descriptive theorizers
Source: After Reid (1981).

Deliberative.   Most scholars included under this subheading are concerned with meanings and choices, as are the critical-exploratory theorizers whom we discuss later in this chapter, but as descriptive theorizers they focus on how choices can be made well, not on what the consequences of such choices should be. Their concern has been described as "practical reasoning", "practical inquiry", or "deliberation," in which emphasis falls on considering the complexities and uncertainties of specific situations and working toward consensus about actions to be followed (Reid, 1994). Although the origins of practical reasoning are often attributed to Aristotle and Dewey (England, 2000), considerable attention has been given to the more recent writings of Schwab (1969, 1971, 1973, 1983), some of which point out how practical reasoning applies directly to curriculum planning and development. Schwab's writings, therefore, can be considered collectively as a prominent example of curriculum theorizing. Authors who have based their own work on Schwab include Walker (1971) and Westbury (1972) in the United States, Connelly (1978) in Canada, and Reid (1978) in the United Kingdom.

The use of deliberation or practical reasoning as an approach to curriculum theorizing begins with the premise that each situation that students find themselves in is unique and problematic (Dev & Walker, 1999; Waks, 2000). Therefore, each situation requires an interactive consideration of means and ends before the best solution or the best course of action can be found (Schwab, 1969). Reid (1979) agrees that curriculum problems are open-ended and solutions are unpredictable. He provides some insights into the matter by suggesting that curriculum problems have the following characteristics:

1. They pose questions that have to be answered. (By contrast, some academic questions do not demand an answer at any particular time.)
2. The grounds on which we have to make decisions are unsure. (In some fields of science, it may be possible to provide unequivocal justifications for a certain decision.)
3. We already teach something, and that something is a necessary point of departure for any fresh process of decision making. (Existing resources and interests of the students and community have to be taken into account.)
4. We have to make our decisions relative to a unique context. (Each problem is unique to a specific time and setting.)
5. We often have conflicting aims and, therefore, have to adjudicate between them. (The solution we choose will realize some aims but reduce the importance of others.)
6. We know that whatever we decide to do, the outcome will be, to a degree, unpredictable. (Hence, curriculum plans based upon fixed outcomes will always fall short of expectations.)
7. The justification of an act of teaching lies not in the act itself but in the desired ends we intend to achieve by it. (Each event only has meaning in terms of ultimate student learning.)

Given the uncertainties of curriculum problems, how, then, does the process of deliberation lead toward practical decisions about what the curriculum should be?

Building on Scheffler (1973), Reid (1979) maintains that within the process of deliberation there are three levels of justification that can be used in arguing for a point of view:

1. Teachers who believe they do not control curriculum decisions but must still give some reasons for what they teach often resort to "forced" justification.
2. Administrators who maintain that their decisions are consistent with general school policies are using "relative" justification.
3. Anyone who offers explanations in terms of fundamental purposes, rules, or laws is using "general" justification.

Many curriculum deliberations begin with forced justifications before moving into relative, and then general, justifications. Deliberation does not necessarily lead to a single best course of action (or curriculum), but it is an effort to identify courses of action for which there are the most compelling justifications, given the uncertainties of specific situations (Brice, 2000).

This form of curriculum theorizing probably underlies the informal deliberations of many groups that have made curriculum decisions, but its formal use in curriculum projects appears thus far to be limited. Walker used practical reasoning as the basis for his approach (or, in his terminology, as the basis for his naturalistic model; see chapter 3) for studying how curriculum developers came to decisions in an art project. He reports that curriculum deliberation, as practiced by developers in the project, was indeed structured and directly affected by the specifics of the situation they considered. There have been no other similarly detailed accounts of large projects, although small-scale studies have been undertaken by Fisher and Ellis (1990) and Brice (2000). Reid (1999a) is rather pessimistic about the use of this form of theorizing, even though he is a staunch advocate of the approach. He suggests that the skills of deliberation, if anything, are declining, possibly due to a belief that the time spent in exploring issues in depth is not a good investment. His view is that efforts to achieve greater efficiency and to use scientific procedures to solve curriculum problems will remain strong.

Deliberation or practical reasoning appears, therefore, to be an approach to curriculum theorizing that has tremendous potential, but this potential has thus far remained largely unexplored.

AN EXAMPLE: JOSEPH SCHWAB'S APPROACH

Joseph Schwab, a distinguished academic at the University of Chicago who originally trained as a natural scientist, published a number of influential papers on education and curriculum over more than four decades. Of these papers written from a non-scientific point of view, the four best-known and most seminal are "The Practical: A Language for Curriculum" (1969), "The Practical: Arts of the Eclectic" (1971), "The Practical 3: Translation into Curriculum" (1973), and "The Practical 4: Something for Curriculum Professors to Do" (1983). These papers collectively embody his approach. He also published a number of lesser-known papers (for example, 1950, 1954, 1960) that provide important insights into the genesis of his later ideas.

The Practice of Deliberation

Schwab was deliberately provocative in his address "The Practical: A Language for Curriculum" at the annual meeting of the American Educational Research Association in 1969 (subsequently published in slightly different forms in 1969 and 1970) when he stated:

> The field of curriculum is moribund, unable by its present methods and principles to continue its work and desperately in search of new and more effective principles and methods. . . . [It] has reached this unhappy state by inveterate and unexamined reliance on theory in an area where theory is partly inappropriate in the first place and where the theories extant, even when appropriate, are inadequate to the tasks which the curriculum field sets for them. (1970, p. 26)

Schwab begins arguing the case for practical reasoning by explaining that the theories typically used in education are inappropriate because they are abstract, general, and have been borrowed from other fields. For him, participants in curriculum decisions must be familiar with a wide range of theories that they can draw upon eclectically to solve specific, practical problems. Such problems—"the practical"—are concrete but likely to change, whereas most theories are states of mind and universal. Yet the borrowing of parts of theories can be done appropriately. He uses the phrase "the eclectic" to describe the process by which parts of theories are identified as fitting with specific practical situations and therefore as potentially useful in solving problems. People making curriculum decisions use the eclectic in reflecting about practical curriculum problems. Doing so is the heart of the process of deliberation. According to Schwab,

> Deliberation is complex and arduous. It treats both ends and means and must treat them as mutually determining one another. It must try to identify, with respect to both, what facts may be relevant. It must try to ascertain the relevant facts in the concrete case. It must try to identify the desiderata in the case. It must generate alternative solutions. It must make every effort to trace the branching pathways of consequences which may flow from each alternative and affect desiderata. It must then weigh alternatives and their costs and consequences against one another and choose, not the right alternative, for there is no such thing, but the best one. (1969, p. 42)

In deliberation that leads to the best decisions about how to solve problems arising in the practical, Schwab (1969) suggests that groups must pass through three stages.

1. The first stage is discovery of what different members of the group want and how these wants may be affected by particular actions. (Walker's [1971] use of the term *platform* conveys the same idea—namely, that it is not until members of a group have declared and argued about their stands on a particular curriculum problem that they are able to appreciate the significance and implications of their own positions.)

2. Discovery of one's own wants and those of other people leads to the second stage, consensus. In this stage, the group sifts alternatives until it reaches some general conclusions about what should and can be done.

3. Finally, the group moves into the third stage, utilization. In this stage, the group again sifts alternatives, this time deciding on the best way to solve the specific problem (or problems) that spurred the deliberation.

Merely reaching the third stage is no assurance, however, that good decisions have been made. Schwab (1973) warns that some deliberations can be dominated by one point of view (for instance, by advocates of subject-centered, or society-centered, or individual-centered curricula). What appears to be consensus may actually be domination by those most experienced in deliberations. As Roby (1983) suggests, "Beginning deliberators generally will do it less well than experienced ones, with results that may lead them to abandon the process. If we acquire good habits and character by exercise, how can we exercise them when we don't yet have them?" (p. 3).

Commonplaces

Another term that Schwab introduced with considerable effect was *commonplaces*. He uses that term to identify four considerations that must be included in any practical curriculum decision. These four considerations are not at all like Tyler's four basic questions, which must be answered in sequential order. Schwab's four commonplaces are the concrete stuff of which a curriculum is composed: "subject matter," "learner," "teacher," and "milieu." Deliberation about practical curriculum problems deals with the mutual influences among them. According to Connelly and Clandinin (1988), these four commonplaces appear and reappear constantly in curricular statements and are particularly useful in tracking historical curriculum trends and analyzing controversial contemporary issues. St. Maurice (1991) is less supportive, arguing that Schwab's commonplaces are not congruent with contemporary circumstances, controversies, and consequences of schooling.

Curriculum deliberation, therefore, is always directed toward all four of these commonplaces simultaneously. Schwab himself has written extensively about subject matter, especially about the structure of the disciplines in general and about substantive and syntactical structures (content and principles of organization) of particular disciplines (1964). He suggests that subject matter should not be conceived too narrowly and that students should be encouraged to consider alternative ways of organizing subjects. Major emphasis needs to be directed toward how various conceptions of a discipline can aid the thinking of students (Fox, 1985).

Students, of course, are the group for whom curricula are intended. Ideally, students should engage in deliberations with other students and with the teacher, whom Schwab sees as a facilitator of deliberation and as a resource for students. Experienced teachers can draw upon various past experiences to respond to practical problems and to generate creative options, especially if they are familiar with the milieu of the school.

The milieu can facilitate learning and stimulate interests or it can constrict and repel. If the milieu adversely affects the other commonplaces, then it clearly must be altered. There is also the added complication that school milieus themselves change rapidly and are influenced by the broader milieu of society in general (Reid, 1988). Schwab argues that balance must be maintained among the four commonplaces. On some occasions, teachers may present knowledge from the disciplines, while on other occasions students may initiate inquiry that leads them to discover knowledge themselves or to acquire certain skills. Sometimes it is the teaching environment—the milieu—that provides the catalyst for action.

Curriculum Development

Schwab takes pains to point out that all four commonplaces must be considered in curriculum deliberation and that no single commonplace should be considered more important than the others, although he does admit that for particular practical problems all commonplaces may not be equally relevant. Still, curriculum deliberation is a group activity, and no individual can possibly have full knowledge of all four commonplaces.

Therefore, in his writings in the 1970s, Schwab advocates that groups should include scholars knowledgeable about curriculum development but also familiar with teaching and classrooms (Schwab, 1970, 1971, 1973). However, in the last of his seminal papers (Schwab, 1983), he argues that local school groups (for example, teachers, principals, parents, board members), rather than academic specialists, should be the major participants. This may be a contradiction in his ideas about curriculum development, or he may simply be making a distinction between curricula developed centrally (at the national or state level) and curricula developed by local school districts.

It is interesting to note that Schwab never defined *curriculum* until his 1983 paper, in which he states:

> Curriculum is what is successfully conveyed to differing degrees to different students, by committed teachers using appropriate materials and actions, of legitimated bodies of knowledge, skill, taste, and propensity to act and react, which are chosen for instruction after serious reflection and communal decision by representatives of those involved in the teaching of a specified group of students who are known to the decision makers. (1983, p. 240)

That is, Schwab conceptualizes curriculum as a practical activity in terms of what happens in classrooms, after careful deliberation by the committed stakeholders (especially teachers and students).

Evaluation of the Approach

Although some writers have indicated that Schwab's writings are pedantic and convoluted (Eisner, 1984) and that he obscures rather than clarifies major terms (Van Manen, 1977), Schwab has had a major impact on the curriculum field. His theory about practical reasoning and deliberation applied to curriculum development has been picked up and elaborated upon by a number of influential specialists in curriculum, such as Walker (1971), Reid (1978, 1993), and Connelly and Clandinin (1988). Numerous papers and articles have been produced by scholars on various ideas in his theory, such as deliberation, the practical, and commonplaces. For example, symposia on deliberation and the practical have reappeared frequently at the annual meetings of the American Educational Research Association.

Yet Schwab's approach has not been put to the test at the school level in any comprehensive way. Some writers, such as Elbaz (1981), have written case studies describing its use in specific schools. Others, such as Schubert (1986), have extended Schwab's concepts using matrix analyses. As we have noted, deliberation may already be used widely—if unconsciously and unintentionally—in hammering out curriculum decisions in many local school districts and schools. But there has been no widespread, organized move in American schools toward the use of practical inquiry and deliberation as the basis for curriculum development. Eisner (1984) suggests that American society may be unreceptive to curriculum deliberation: "Our schools are buffeted by demands for immediate remedies to preconceived educational ills. . . . [S]uch remedies are not the fruits of competent deliberative processes. Quite the opposite. . . . In the present climate the kind of deliberative style that Schwab advocates is unlikely to find a receptive audience" (p. 205).

Schwab's approach provides many useful insights into how curriculum decisions can be perceived and treated as practical problem solving. To be better problem solvers, Schwab suggests, we need continuing practice in deliberation within a community open to its use. That is, deliberation should lead toward consensus building and solving practical problems deemed important by the group; it should not degenerate into a competition to advance individual agendas. Whether Schwab's theory places too much reliance on an open community is debatable. Schwab, of course, argues for the widespread use of deliberation in curriculum development (Schwab, 1983), and his curriculum theory has been commended subsequently by various writers such as Tyler (1984) and Reid (1986, 1993). Wegener (1986) highlights and supports the view of community inherent in Schwab's work when he states that Schwab is advocating "responsible communal deliberation (a group) and an eclectic attitude and function" (p. 231).

Other writers, such as Van Manen (1977), argue that Schwab's philosophy of knowledge is rooted in the empirical-analytic tradition and thus is far more restrictive than it appears on the surface. Walker and Soltis (1986) believe that, although Schwab's approach is flexible and dialectical, he underemphasizes the personal basis for many important questions, such as what our purposes for teaching should be and why we should hold them. Such specific criticisms aside, most critics agree that Schwab's theorizing describes a flexible and workable approach to making curriculum decisions that emphasizes intelligent, cooperative participation in identifying and solving practical problems. It invites teachers and other educators who live closest to the results of these decisions to participate actively in making them. Schwab's theory takes little account of the experienced curriculum but leaves ample room for teachers to modify the planned curriculum when enacting it. Although it has not been widely used in curriculum planning and development in the United States, it may indeed present a highly accurate picture of how practical deliberation and consensus building does or should occur. Thus, its potential for enlightening curriculum decision makers and for guiding future curriculum projects remains very high. As noted by Reid (1999b) in his correspondence with Schwab over a five-year period, "What he offers, above all, is the example of a mind in action and concerned with action" (p. 396).

Critical-Exploratory Theorizers: Understanding Curriculum in Terms of What Has Been, Is, and Might Be

Theorizers in this category are particularly diverse. Nonetheless, there are just two general approaches to how they treat problems of schooling and curriculum. One general approach emphasizes the connections between schooling and the existing social order. This approach provides critical analysis of prevalent social structures and mainstream curriculum practices. These critiques are concerned with such issues as domination, exploitation, resistance, and what constitutes legitimate knowledge. Collectively, this approach tends to use similar technical terms, such as *cultural capital* (the ability of certain groups in society to transform culture into a commodity and to accumulate it) and *cultural reproduction* (the idea that the school's role is to pass on to succeeding generations the present culture without changing it). Many of these theorizers maintain—and with some justification—that a new technical language is needed to provide new insights and interpretations about existing social structures.

The second general approach within this group is an emphasis on the personal nature of learning and on people, rather than ideas, as the basis for action. In other words, these theorizers' primary concern is with individual experience itself and with how systematic education can contribute to high-quality experiencing. They locate the value of curriculum planning and development in the experienced curriculum, not in the planned curriculum. Although most recognize the importance of the preconscious realm of experience and emphasize that often knowledge is personally constructed by each individual, they believe that teachers, in planning and in enacting what is planned, play a key role in influencing the quality of their students' experiences.

Of course, despite the diversity of the critical-exploratory category, many of its theorizers find ways of linking their analyses of the external social context of curriculum and schooling with the personal experience of individual students and teachers. Figure 4.5 lists some of the many subheadings in this category and some of the major theorizers.

Before examining the subcategories listed in Figure 4.5, we need to consider the term *reconceptualist,* which has been used as an umbrella term since the 1970s and early 1980s to describe new forms of theorizing that were then emerging. It is still frequently used today, especially to capture the sense of exploration that we intend in titling our third category of theorizing, "critical-exploratory," but its use has created some avoidable confusion. As we pointed out earlier in introducing the third category, Macdonald (1971), in one of the most influential papers written on curriculum theorizing, reviewed the field in terms of the modes of inquiry being used and concluded that there were three groups of theorizers: (1) a large group who attempted to develop theories explicitly as guidelines for prescribing practice, (2) a smaller group who used empirical research to attempt to validate curriculum variables and the relationships among them, and (3) a third, very small group who perceived theorizing as a creative, intellectual task. These three groups closely parallel the three categories used in this chapter. He coined the term *reconceptualists* for the

Social and cultural control
  Young (1971, U.K.)
  Bernstein (1973, U.K.)

Social reproduction
  Althusser (1971, France)
  Bowles & Gintis (1976, U.S.)
  Lundgren (1976, Sweden)

Cultural reproduction
  Sharp & Green (1975, Australia)
  Bourdieu & Passeron (1977, France)
  Willis (1978, U.K.)
  Apple (1979, U.S.)
  Anyon (1980, U.S.)
  Lawn & Barton (1980, U.K.)
  Whitty (1980, U.K.)
  Connell et al. (1982, Australia)
  Giroux (1982, U.S.)
  Kemmis (1986, Australia)

Literary artist
  Eisner (1974, 1979, 1991, U.S.)
  Stenhouse (1975, U.K.)
  McCutcheon (1982, U.S.)
  Vallance (1983, U.S.)

Existential/psychoanalytic
  Macdonald (1971, U.S.)
  Huebner (1975, U.S.)
  Greene (1975, U.S.)
  Klohr (1980, U.S.)
  Pinar (1980, U.S.)
  Grumet (1981, U.S.)
  Brady (1984, Australia)
  Schubert, Willis, & Short (1984, U.S.)
  Haggerson (1988, U.S.)
  Willis & Schubert (1991, U.S.)
  Miller (1992, U.S.)

Phenomenological
  Willis (1979, U.S.)
  Van Manen (1980, 2000, Canada)

Autobiographical/biographical
  Pinar (1972, 1974, U.S.)
  Pinar & Grumet (1976, U.S.)
  Goodson (1981, U.K.)
  Butt (1983, Canada)
  Connelly & Clandinin(1988, Canada)
  Meath-Lang (1999, U.S.)
  Miller (1992, U.S.)

Gender analysis and feminist pedagogy
  Klein (1986, U.S.)
  Shakeshaft et al. (1991, U.S.)
  Pagano (1992, U.S.)
  Kenway & Modra (1992, Australia)
  Miller (1992, U.S.)
  Lather (1991a, U.S.)
  Britzman (1995, U.S.)
  Ellsworth (1997, U.S.)
  Grumet & Stone (2000, U.S.)

Gender analysis and male identity
  Sears (1992a, U.S.)
  Pinar (1997, U.S.)
  Leck (1999, U.S.)
  Sumara & Davis (1999, U.S.)
  Kendall (2000, U.S.)

Race
  Banks (1993, U.S.)
  McCarthy (1988, U.S.)
  Castenell & Pinar (1993, U.S.)
  Watkins (1993, U.S.)
  Berlak (1999, U.S.)
  Flecha (1999, U.S.)

Postmodern/poststructural
  Lather (1991b, U.S.)
  Giroux (1992, U.S.)
  Doll (1993, U.S.)
  Hargreaves (1994, Canada)
  Slattery (1995, U.S.)

FIGURE 4.5
Critical-Exploratory theorizers
Source: After Reid (1981).

third group because members criticized existing conceptual schema and provided new ways of viewing and exploring everything that the broadest conceptions of curriculum seem to entail. Macdonald noted that this last group was not only examining and critiquing political structures but also studying broad vistas of what it means to be human.

Initially, the term proved useful, for it seemed to suggest that whatever *reconceptualists* stood for was newer—and probably better—than what had gone before, and reconceptualists certainly were united in their opposition to the rationalistic and scientific approaches to theorizing that had prevailed in the 1960s, as exemplified by this statement by Lawn and Barton (1980):

> The dominance of a particularly powerful paradigm, which we may call "technological," has restricted theoretical analysis. . . . Firstly, it has a non-problematic view of scientific decision making in which alternatives are neither generated nor evaluated. . . . Secondly, the emphasis on quantification and predictability has led to an increasingly elaborate concern for tests, procedures and rules. . . . [T]hirdly, the question is raised whether its influence has been really concerned with the improvement of teaching and learning, or with the control, cost and content of education. (p. 48)

However, as theorizers interested in reconceptualizing the field grew in number and in influence, it became increasingly important to clarify what they did and did not have in common. For instance, some theorizers used philosophical analysis and methods drawn from mainstream social science, while others used case studies, biography, psychoanalytic techniques, and literary theory. Perhaps the most successful effort to map common characteristics of reconceptualists was undertaken by Klohr (1980), who identified nine foci of their efforts:

1. A holistic, organic view is taken of people and their relation to nature.
2. The individual becomes the chief agent in the construction of knowledge; that is, he/she is a culture creator as well as a culture bearer.
3. The curriculum theorists draw heavily on their own experiential base as method.
4. Curriculum theorizing recognizes as major resources the preconscious realms of experience.
5. The foundational roots of this theorizing lie in existential philosophy, phenomenology, and radical psychoanalysis; they [reconceptualists] also draw from humanistic reconceptualizations of such cognate fields as sociology, anthropology, and political science.
6. Personal liberty and the attainment of higher levels of consciousness become central values in the curriculum process.
7. Diversity and pluralism are characteristics both of the social ends and the means proposed to attain these ends.
8. A reconceptualization of supporting political-social operations is basic.
9. New language forms are generated to translate fresh meanings, for example, metaphors. (Klohr, 1980, p. 3)

However, a close examination of Klohr's foci reveals that some are clearly not appropriate to all reconceptualists. For example, a focus on the "preconscious realms of experience" applies to theorists such as Pinar and Grumet, who use psychoanalytic techniques in their theorizing, but it does not apply to Apple. Conversely, a focus on a "reconceptualization of supporting political-social operations" applies to Apple but far less to Pinar or Huebner.

Despite these difficulties with the term *reconceptualist*, readers should be aware of its history in carrying forward new forms of curriculum theorizing that emerged in the 1970s (see, for example, Pinar, Reynolds, Slattery, & Taubman, 1995).

Whether the endeavors over the decades since the 1970s represent a shift in basic thinking about curriculum sufficiently profound to be considered a paradigm shift in Kuhnian terms (Kuhn, 1962), is debatable. Pinar et al. (1995) suggest that there has been such a shift and, along with Rogan and Luckowski (1990), that the work of reconceptualists represents a paradigmatic advancement over the Tyler rationale. Brown (1988) concludes that a first approximation to a paradigm shift has been under way and that the new generation of curriculum scholars, as they gain a firm foothold in universities, will begin to challenge the received wisdom of traditional points of view.

There is certainly nothing finished or final about reconceptualism, for ideas and methods are constantly evolving. Rather, a "proliferation of schools" (Brown, 1988, p. 28) has developed with considerable differences among them.

Social and Cultural Control, Social Reproduction, and Cultural Reproduction.   We have listed these subcategories together because of the similarities in how their major theorizers analyze the relationship between society or culture and schooling. Early writers in all three subcategories were sociologists, such as Young (1971) and Bernstein (1973), who focused on forms of power and social control. Other writers who theorized about the role of schools in society developed an approach known as social reproduction. For example, Althusser (1971) argues that schools are important because they reproduce the work skills and attitudes needed for social relations in the wider society. Bowles and Gintis (1976) claim that their economic analysis shows that social relationships in schools (for example, relationships between administrators and teachers, teachers and students, and students and their work) directly correspond to hierarchical divisions of labor in society. Still other writers have broadened the focus from social reproduction to cultural reproduction. They identify and analyze the links among culture, class, domination, and education. Such theorizers about cultural reproduction—as exemplified by Bourdieu and Passeron (1977); Giroux (1982, 1990); Apple (1979); Connell, Ashenden, Kessler, and Dowsett (1982); and Kemmis (1986, 1989)—often point out how schools have served to oppress groups disadvantaged by class, race, and gender and how disadvantaged groups can work to change oppressive systems of education.

Although these theorizers often write from a neo-Marxist perspective, their critiques have attacked the problems of society and schooling in a variety of ways. Giroux (1982) described traditional educational theorizing as "dancing on the surface of reality . . . ignoring not only the latent principles that shape the deep grammar of the existing social order, but also those principles underlying the genesis and nature of its own logic" (p. 1). Apple suggests a number of political questions that should be asked about the legitimacy of the knowledge included in a curriculum. For example:

> Why and how are particular aspects of a collective culture represented in schools as objective factual knowledge?

> How, concretely, may official knowledge represent the ideological configurations of the dominant interests in a society?
>
> How do schools legitimate these limited and partial standards of knowing as unquestioned truths? (Apple, 1979, p. 7)

Some writers have conducted empirical studies using methods from anthropology, sociology, or economics. For example, Willis (1977) used ethnographic methods in studying how an English secondary school struggled with working-class ideology and conflict. Young (1971) and Bowles and Gintis (1976) included the examination of historical records in their studies of social control and social reproduction. In Australia, Connell et al. (1982) used a variety of methods to study fourteen-year-olds and their families in Sydney and Adelaide, concluding that schooling does reproduce the structures of inequality in society and that working-class families are especially disabled by ordinary systems of education.

There is no doubt that these curriculum theorizers have had a considerable impact on curriculum writings. They have alerted curriculum planners and developers to a number of ingrained problems in the usual—and usually unexamined—relationship between schools and the society in which they are embedded. Their approach has exposed classroom practices that have remained hidden when approached by prescriptive theorizers (Taylor, 1979). For example, Willis's (1977) vivid account of the culture of a working-class secondary school and the actions and motives of "the lads" can be contrasted with positivist accounts of schools, such as Goodlad's (1984) *A Place Called School*. Also, these critiques may be particularly timely in a period of disenchantment with big government and bureaucracies. In taking on the powers-that-be within society, the romantic critics of the 1960s (for example, Holt, 1964; Illich, 1971) found ready listeners because of their rhetoric. Arguments raised by writers such as Apple (1979), Giroux (1982, 1990), and Anyon (1980) are more persuasive, however, both because there is growing disenchantment with the powers they attack and because their assertions are backed by significant research.

Some critics of these theorizers have focused on their writing style (Raban, 1974). Others believe they collectively are intolerant of all but Marxian interpretations of society and schools (Taylor, 1979). But other critics of these theorizers have raised more serious questions about their substance. Goodson (1983, 1992) questions how theorizers such as Young (1971) have used (or, in his opinion, misused) historical data to support particular historical interpretations. He suggests that this "raiding" of history by using snapshots of certain eras is dangerous because even the major structural features of schooling change over time. He cites the history of professional organizations devoted to the teaching of specific academic subjects. When formed in the nineteenth-century, most were relatively powerless, yet historically most have been able to exert a powerful influence on maintaining a place for their subjects in school curricula. Therefore, Goodson suggests that sociologists who use nineteenth-century data to support their notion of "powerlessness" are oversimplifying events, if not being willfully misleading.

Even more important, Reid (1981) questions what the theorizing of this group leads to, observing that although they claim to know what should exist after society and schooling have been changed, they never seem to describe it in any detailed way. Some critics might suggest that a statement like the following is typical in describing only generalities.

> We need to recapture what a genuine socialist alternative would be: first, to help us think and work through the issues surrounding new models of curriculum and teaching, and, secondly, to place education again on the socialist agenda. (Apple, 1981, p. 154)

While it is true that these socially oriented theorizers have collectively written more fully and more eloquently about what is wrong with society and schools than about what a reconstructed system of education would entail, their basic message to curriculum developers is still very strong and very clear. They have insisted that curriculum decisions be made in light of the old truth that the purpose of schooling is not only to conserve the best features of society as it exists, but also to improve society. To fulfill this double purpose, curriculum developers must, therefore, constantly examine society and school practices for their underlying values and unintended consequences and then endeavor to keep values and consequences as close as possible to the surface of the planned curriculum, the enacted curriculum, and the experienced curriculum. Some of the theorizers in these subcategories have, in fact, offered specific suggestions on how to go about doing this, but no single way of describing precisely how to do so has emerged nor is one likely to emerge. Therefore, although this group of theorizers perhaps holds a common social vision, they have opened up numerous possibilities for planners and developers to use in making curriculum decisions without prescribing what those decisions should be.

Literary Artist.   Under this subcategory are scholars whose approach to curriculum theorizing can be exemplified by Eisner's approach to curriculum planning (see chapter 3). In some ways this approach is similar to the deliberative approach of the descriptive theorizers already discussed. The main difference is that the deliberations of curriculum development committees usually lead toward public meanings and group decisions, whereas literary artists are concerned with personal experience as well (Barone, 1982; Eisner, 1991; Eisner & Vallance, 1974). Indeed, all theorizers in this subcategory emphasize to one degree or another that learning is highly personal.

Since we have previously discussed Eisner's approach to curriculum planning, we will not repeat that discussion here. Essentially, members of this group see themselves, curriculum developers, teachers, students, and virtually every other person as involved in an ongoing process of making meaning in their own lives and conveying meaning to others. This process centers on personal perception and choice. In it, the curriculum is considered a medium through which individuals learn how to deepen their own perceptions, refine their own meanings, and make increasingly wise choices about how to portray meanings (Eisner, 1992). In so creating curricula, they encourage others to respond in kind. All of this happens within the ecological structure of schools (Eisner, 2000). Hence, this approach to curriculum theorizing particularly emphasizes the interaction between the enacted curriculum and the experienced curriculum.

Existential and Psychoanalytic Theorizing.   Writers who do existential and psycho-analytic theorizing begin with individual experience but point to the importance of how schooling influences experience. Schools represent nature (things that exist prior to human intervention, such as physical sites and space) and culture (things that are human creations, such as beliefs and objects), but the culture of schools tends to be taken for granted. Whenever people take culture for granted, they tend to become less aware—hence, less free. Therefore, we need to attend especially to those parts of culture that are not compelled directly by nature and about which we can make decisions. In particular, the task is to transform schooling that constrains human freedom (Grumet, 1981; Miller, 1992; Pinar, 1980). To be free, people need to be aware of how they as individuals experience the world around them and, thus, how their decisions about transforming the world are related to their decisions about how to define themselves as individual persons.

Macdonald (1981) goes about the task by considering the issue of human liber-ation and how this can be achieved through curriculum studies. According to Macdonald, each of us can become more liberated. He proposes a transcendental ideology of education under which curriculum decisions can be made. That ideology centers on the individual person and on the question of how all potential for each person can be realized. Pinar (1980) uses the metaphor of an educational journey for each individual and suggests that autobiographical accounts are extremely useful for attending to, and reflecting on, lived experiences of the world. Each person must elu-cidate his or her journey and cultivate an awareness of his or her existential freedom. In Pinar's (1980) words: "One experiences intellectual and biographic movement. . . . [S]uch a capacity to risk—intellectually, biographically—is a capacity we are obli-gated to develop" (p. 11). The curriculum should foster this journey.

These theorizers thus value techniques that put individuals in touch with their own experience yet permit them to move on. Some theorizers (for example, Grumet, 1981; Miller, 1992; Pinar, 1980) have published sensitive and insightful autobiograph-ical accounts of their educational experience. Also, collections of autobiographical ac-counts by members of the curriculum field (Goodson, 1992; Willis & Schubert, 1991) have appeared. In fact, during the 1990s, a growing number of insightful case studies and narratives that connect individual experience with the characteristics of schooling in increasingly sophisticated ways have been written by these theorists, often using rich and evocative imagery and metaphors and thus fulfilling Van Manen's (1978) earlier description of their work as a synthesis of poetic and novelistic approaches.

Phenomenological Theorizing.   Willis (1979) uses the term *phenomenology* to refer to the lived quality of the interior experience, or "life world," of the individual and suggests that each individual holds a personal and peculiarly human consciousness about each concrete situation experienced. Each experience includes a fusing of affective, cogni-tive, and physiological reactions to the situation. Phenomenology attempts to get at the experience itself, the curriculum each person lives. Both Willis (1991) and Van Manen (1980) cut through some of the highly technical language of phenomenological philosophers. For instance, Van Manen indicates that phenomenology is really asking one simple question: What is it like to have a certain experience—for example, an educational experience? Although it is possible to express a feeling about an experience (for example, "I feel bored"), it is very difficult to describe in detail the particulars or components of such a feeling. According to Van Manen (1980), curriculum specialists such as Tyler somehow assume that it is possible to know about and describe learning experiences because they use phrases such as "selecting, planning, and organizing learning experiences." But this is false confidence, for we do not know what it is really like when a child has an experience or when he or she comes to understand something.

Van Manen (1990, 2000) uses phenomenological theorizing to question people about the root character of their experience. For instance, teachers can be asked: What is it like to be a teacher? In what ways is a teacher different from, say, a parent? He suggests that phenomenology helps people to reflect on their actual consciousness of situations rather than on public expressions of them. It is a means by which they get to know themselves and can be achieved only by examining concrete situations, such as teaching. Phenomenological theorizing is not about testing hypotheses but getting individuals to reflect thoughtfully about what they see, feel, and believe; it involves teachers in constantly seeking out the essence of the experience of teaching.

Autobiographical/Biographical Theorizing. This approach to theorizing focuses on the centrality of personal experience in the curriculum. In 1972 Pinar first wrote about his interest in the autobiographical method. Subsequently he formulated the term *currere* to explain his emphasis. Currere refers to an existential experience of institutional structures. The method of currere is a strategy for self-reflection that enables the individual to encounter experience more fully and more clearly, as if creating a highly personal autobiography (Pinar & Grumet, 1976).

In the mid-1990s, Pinar et al. (1995) contended that autobiographical/biographical theorizing had become a major area of scholarship. They distinguished three streams of scholarship:

- Autobiography that focuses on such major concepts as currere, voice, place, and imagination (as developed by Connelly & Clandinin, 1988; Grumet, 1976; Kincheloe & Pinar, 1991; Meath-Lang, 1999; Miller, 1992; and Pinar, 1974).
- Feminist autobiography that focuses especially on community and the reclaiming of the self (as developed by Miller, 1992; Pagano, 1990; Britzman, 1992; and Luke, (1996).
- Biography that focuses on the lives of teachers using collaborative biography, autobiographical praxis, and personal practical knowledge (as developed by Butt, 1983; Connelly & Clandinin, 1988; Goodson, 1981; and Schubert, 1991).

Clearly, autobiographical/biographical theorizing has proliferated since the early 1970s, as witnessed by new journals that have emerged and numerous research studies that have been funded. Pinar et al. (1995) stress that this kind of theorizing is not just about accumulating personal knowledge, but also using personal knowledge to transform both personal and social worlds.

We discuss Pinar's method of currere in detail later in the chapter.

Gender Analysis and Feminist Pedagogy.   Pinar et al. (1995) describe a growing interest in theorizing about curriculum as "gender text." Doing so involves analyzing the unequal ways in which people are treated because of their gender and sexuality, and how knowledge and values develop under society's prevailing assumptions about gender. Many different terms may be used in examining how gender and curricula are related. For example, Kenway and Modra (1992) use the phrase *feminist pedagogy* to describe the social theory and politics of feminists, explaining several variations of feminism, including liberal feminism (working toward equality with males in access to education), socialist feminism (criticizing educational practices exploitative of females), and radical feminism (seeking a distinctively women's educational culture). Analysis of schooling in terms of gender points out how it has been organized around different socially perceived roles and status for men and women. The dominant and enduring trend until the 1960s was for education to be male-oriented (Anyon, 1994; Shakeshaft, Nowell, & Perry, 1991).

Various feminist theorizers have proposed curricula and school practices to assist teachers. Kenway et al. (1996) see these as superior to the typical "authoritarian" and "therapeutic" teaching practices. They believe typical practices ignore the emotional dimensions of teaching and learning. Both authoritarian and therapeutic practices often alienate students. However, practices in which female students enjoy themselves and feel good about feminism encourage girls to "become critical, informed, and skilled advocates for a better world" (p. 7). Nonetheless, they caution against the erroneous assumption that "all girls have similar needs, interests, pleasures, and anxieties, that what oppresses one, oppresses all, and that what 'empowers one' 'empowers all'" (p. 11).

Other feminist theorizers make additional points. Miller (1992) notes the unconscious ways that female teachers internalize patriarchal assumptions about learning and schooling. Noddings (1994) refers to "caring" in teaching and how such caring can help students grow as persons in all their fullness. Davies and Bank (1992) provide empirical data about how primary school children are constrained by the dominant discourses on gender.

Radical feminists have been vocal in criticizing the idea of traditional academic disciplines as representing unchanging reality. Rather, they argue, academic disciplines have been male interpretations of reality glazed over with claims of objectivity. As a result of these critiques, especially in higher education, academic disciplines are now widely viewed as far more malleable than before, and curricula have been altered as feminists have introduced "feminist critiques and theories within their various disciplines and departments as well as starting separate women's studies programs" (Middleton, 1992, p. 18). Klein (1986) suggests that women's studies curricula can be considered as the following:

- Re-action and re-vision, as women confront the androcentric world view
- Action and vision, as women assess women's experience from within a gynocentric perspective
- A combination of the two foregoing approaches that fuses critique and new vision

Numerous analyses of women's studies by feminist critics have emerged in recent decades; for example, Arnot and Dillabough (1999) and Grumet and Stone (2000). For some critics, creating women's studies has been their predominate concern. Other concerns have focused on: reconceptualizing curriculum theorizing from a feminist perspective; the ecological dimensions of feminist theory and knowledge; and identity and popular culture, gender, and postmodernism (Luke, 1996; Shore, 2000).

Like other emerging forms of reconceptualism, on a wide scale women's studies in (particular) and feminism (in general) are relatively new (as is gender theorizing itself), and it is debatable how much conceptual or political fusion has thus far occurred. A myriad of ununified advocacy movements in education may be the current state of affairs, and Pagano (1992) predicts that "the educational challenge in the foreseeable future will be to teach people to acknowledge and understand their own passions, their own advocacy positions, without being reduced to them" (p. 150). Nonetheless, some feminist critiques of education have offered the following ideas about gender as a basis for new ways of theorizing about curriculum:

- *Essentialism.* Males and females are different, and these differences are innate; the unique characteristics determined by female biology enable women to appropriate many societal functions previously done by males and to do them better (Belenky, Clinchy, Goldberg, & Tarule, 1988).
- *Social constructionism.* Gender is socially constructed by economic, cultural, and political forces in society that may be challenged (Chodorow, 1978; Slaughter, 1997).
- *Ecological feminist theory.* The relationship between humans and nature that maintains life will become increasingly important (DeMocker, 1986).
- *Poststructuralism.* Exploring the contradictions and injustices in society based on gender will promote feminist self-understanding and self-determination (Lather, 1991a, 1998).

Gender Analysis and Male Identity.   Feminist curriculum theorizers have not been the only scholars exploring the frontier of gender studies. Increasingly, a number of scholars have theorized about male identity. In particular, they have been challenging "heteronormativity."

Sears (1992a, 1992b, 1999) has been a major figure in highlighting homosexual issues and supporting the struggle for social justice for gays and lesbians. He uses the term *queer* to signify "those who have been defined or have chosen to define themselves as sexual outsiders" (1999, p. 4). He defines teaching queerly as "creating classrooms that challenge categorical thinking, promote interpersonal intelligence, and foster critical consciousness" (1999, p. 5), contending that such teaching requires a re-examination of taken-for-granted assumptions about diversity, identities, childhood, and prejudice. He elaborates his ideas by offering five basic propositions:

- Diversity is a human hallmark. Despite evidence supporting this idea, many educators attempt to "mold children into curriculum cookie-cutter identities" (p. 5), such as male or female, heterosexual or homosexual.

- Sexualities are constructed essences. Although the predisposition for sexual behavior is biologically based, sexual identity is constructed within a cultural context.
- Homophobia and heterosexism are acquired. "The belief in the superiority of heterosexuality . . . and the deep-seated hatred or fear of those who love the same gender (homophobia) are acquired early in life and serve a variety of functions" (p. 7).
- Childhood innocence is a fictive absolute. Believing that children are absolutely innocent "is a veneer that we as adults impress onto children, enabling us to deny desire comfortably and to silence sexuality" (p. 9).
- Families are first. As Stacey (1999) points out, the concepts of family and parenthood have become "unhinged" in this era of postmodernity.

Other theorizers within this group include Sumara and Davis (1999), Aitken (1999), Pinar (1983, 2000), and Leck (1999), who adds "many of the consequences we see in the lives of racialized, gendered, and sexualized minorities are the results of the dogmas that have disallowed teachers, parents, and schools from participating in an open dialogue about children, sexuality and diversity" (p. 257). Sumara and Davis (1999) take an even stronger line in asserting that curriculum theorizers must interrupt heteronormative thinking. Their suggestions for queer curriculum theorizing include:

- The need to work toward a deeper understanding of the forms that curriculum can take so that sexuality is understood as a necessary companion to all knowing.
- The need to call into question the very existence of heterosexuality as a stable category and to examine the unruly heterosexual closet.
- The need to understand and interpret differences among persons rather than noting differences among categories of persons.
- The need to interrupt common beliefs of what constitutes experiences of desire, of pleasure, and of sexuality.

The title of Aitken's (1999) editorial in *Curriculum Inquiry,* "Leaping Boundaries of Difference," seems to capture the purpose of current queer curriculum theorizing, and this purpose may be realized, he suggests, by successfully attacking flawed patriarchal notions of society and culturally sanctioned expressions of heterosexuality. Pinar (1983, 1994, 1997, 2000) has also written extensively about homosexual issues from an autobiographical perspective. He warns that theorizers must be aware of politically enforced heterosexuality, stating "as a feminist man it is clear to me I must confront my own manhood, understood of course not essentialistically, but historically, socially, racially, in terms of class and culture" (Pinar, 2000, p. 2).

Racial Theorizing.   Race is a "complex, dynamic, and changing construct" (Pinar et al., 1995, p. 316). Race has a powerful influence on schooling in general and the curriculum in particular, yet McCarthy (1988) contends that theorizing about race and racial inequality did not come into its own in curriculum until recent decades.

Past neglect has been supplanted, however, by recent theorizers such as Watkins (1993), McCarthy (1988), Villenas and Deyhle (1999), and Pinar (2000). Race can be a powerful, autonomous focal point for theorizers, yet it also intersects with other foci such as gender and postmodernism.

Watkins (1993) portrays issues concerning race in terms of six historical orientations, which he contends illustrate how "Black curriculum development is inextricably tied to Black America's experience of slavery and oppression in the United States" (p. 321). He describes six orientations to these issues as:

- *Functionalism.* Black education in the eighteenth century relied on self-help efforts and religious altruism.
- *Accommodationism.* In the late nineteenth century, the curriculum for Black education emphasized vocational training, physical/manual labor, and character building, all premised on racial subservice for Negroes.
- *Liberalism.* In the early decades of the twentieth century, liberal education was initiated at some Black colleges.
- *Black nationalism.* In the twentieth century, education that focused on political oppression and separation was promoted by Black nationalists such as Malcolm X and the Black Muslims.
- *Afrocentrism.* Especially recently, advocacy has increased for Africa-oriented education rather than the traditional Eurocentric curriculum of most American schools.
- *Social reconstructionism.* Throughout the twentieth century, progressives have argued for education promoting a reformed, egalitarian society.

Wright (2000) notes that a recent development in racial theorizing has been interdisciplinary work undertaken in "whiteness studies," as described by Fine, Weis, Powell, and Wong (1997); Kincheloe, Steinberg, Rodriguez, and Chennault (1998); and Young and Rosiek (2000).

Theorizing about race is likely to exert an increasingly strengthening force on the direction of curriculum theorizing in general. Pinar et al. (1995) contend "any comprehensive theory of curriculum must include race and its concepts—such as multiculturalism, identity, marginality, and difference—as fundamental" (p. 310). Yet, herein lies a problem: Multiculturalism is not attractive to everyone. A number of writers such as McCarthy (1988), Berlak (1999), Phillion (1999), and Richardson and Villenas (1999) argue that multiculturalism is a questionable solution to racial inequality in schooling since it does not deal directly with the underlying problem. Rather, in promoting pluralistic, culturally diverse curricula, it "disarticulates elements of black radical demands for restructuring of school knowledge" (McCarthy, 1993, p. 228).

Postmodern Theorizing.   Since the early 1980s the term *postmodern* has been applied to various pursuits or occupations, as in "postmodern art" and "postmodern architecture." Presumably, what is postmodern replaces what is modern as a defining characteristic. Postmodern curriculum theorizing—at least when it is sufficiently foresighted—should be, therefore, on the leading edge of future changes in education.

According to Hargreaves (1995), "modernity" was the defining social condition of many developed nations up to the 1960s. Its characteristics included:

- A major emphasis upon rational, scientific methods and the use of technology to control nature
- The division of production methods involving separation of family and work
- The development of specialized, hierarchical bureaucracies to control decision making
- Achievement of social progress by systematic development and rational applications
- Economic and social organizations focused upon capitalist production

Modernity has had the potential to bring about progress. To a certain extent it has been successful—as witnessed by efficiency, productivity, prosperity, the welfare state, and mass education. Yet there are also signs that modernity as a social condition has become exhausted and no longer relevant, in terms of:

- Economic markets having become saturated, with profitability declining
- Many Western economies experiencing fiscal crises
- Bureaucracies being blamed for inefficiencies and inflexible decision making

Of course, it may be the case that we are simply entering a new phase of modernity. Giddens (1990) uses the term *high modernity* to describe a social condition in which decisions and actions are more diffuse, radicalized, and universalized than before. He argues that it is not necessary to invent a new term such as *postmodernism;* rather, we should be examining the nature of modernity to understand the extension and intensification of conditions. Yet, many others argue that modernism is on the wane and must be replaced (Griffin et al., 1993; Jencks, 1992; Slattery, 1995). Doll (1993) contends that postmodernism, as characterized by open systems, indeterminacy, the discrediting of metanarratives, and a focus on process, will bring about megaparadigmatic changes in society and in education. McLaren and Farahmandpur (2000) argue that postmodernism has already made impressive advances in helping educators map the hidden trajectories of power and to peel away layers of ideological mystification.

Not only are there numerous interpretations of *postmodern,* but there are also distinctions that can be made between *postmodernism* and *postmodernity* and related terms such as *poststructuralism, deconstruction, postcolonialism,* and *postindustrialism.* Hargreaves (1995) uses *postmodernity* to refer to prevailing patterns of social conditions, whereas he perceives *postmodernism* as a set of styles and practices such as intellectual discourse or cultural forms. Others, such as Slattery (1995), use *postmodern* to refer to both patterns of social conditions and styles and practices; Griffin et al. (1993) understands it as a diffuse sentiment rather than any set of common doctrines; and Jencks (1986) sees it as continual growth and movement with no firm definition possible. Atkinson (2000) views postmodern as "a release from certainties" characterized by resistance towards certainty and resolution; rejection of fixed notions of reality, knowledge, or method; acceptance of complexity, of lack of clarity, and of multiplicity; and refusal to accept boundaries or hierarchies in ways of thinking.

Still another variation of postmodernism is *poststructuralism,* the rejection of modernity's structuralist view of the world. For example, structuralists believe in invariant forms of knowledge and of society that give meaning to the world, whereas Foucault (1972) argues that attempts to establish such a system of homogenous relationships—a network of causality—fail to take into account the underlying but changing social and political assumptions upon which such systems ultimately are built. Structuralists identify systems to create meaning, whereas poststructuralists endeavor to dismantle systems to expose their variable and contingent nature (Slattery, 1995).

Deconstructionism is another variation involved in exposing the contradictions and fallacies embedded within modernity. The idea of deconstruction does not imply a tearing down; rather, it is simply being alert to contradictions and fallacies in Western thought and rationality, "alert to the implications, to the historical sedimentation of the language we use" (Derrida, 1972). Here, again, the task is to avoid being trapped in the vested meanings of the modern and to seek out new meanings.

Postcolonialism is a third and more specific variation of the postmodern philosophy that, according to Giroux (1992), challenges the ideological and material legacies of imperialism and colonialism. Postcolonial adherents challenge imperial centers of power and contest dominant Eurocentric thinking and writing on politics, social theory, and history. Spivak (1985) argues that it is necessary to unlearn the sense of "privilege" fostered by colonialism; this legacy must be examined to make visible the various exclusions and repressions that permit specific forms of privilege to remain (for example, privilege that benefits males, whiteness, heterosexuality, and property holders).

While different postmodernists may disagree on specific details of their critiques of the hidden political, social, and cultural assumptions of the present, they (and related groups) collectively agree that schooling is far more complex and ambiguous than traditional curriculum writers describe it and, therefore, that modernist standardized curriculum packages are likely to be grossly inappropriate in the present, if they ever were appropriate. Thus, teachers need to enter into dialogue about the uncertainties, the concerns, the doubts, and the questions that pervade teaching, including those that surround selecting and enacting curricula. The challenge is to transcend traditional, positivist approaches to curriculum development. Teachers need to create methods to develop and incorporate various postmodern discourses into their daily teaching. Examples of how this challenge can be met include the following:

- Teachers and students need to become engaged in telling their life stories and especially to reflect upon ideas that appear to have been hidden or forgotten (Graham, 1991).
- Curriculum experience in schools must be open to reflection, because from a postmodern standpoint everything requires recursive interpretation. Thus the official syllabi and curriculum documents cannot be used in any passive way, as, for instance, in a teacherproof curriculum.
- Through dialogue and debate, teachers and students must deconstruct norms and values about race and gender, especially those that perpetuate religious bigotry, political repression, and cultural elitism.

- Teachers need to encourage students to undertake aesthetic reflections whereby they can gain some intrinsic coherence about the body, the spirit, and the cosmos.
- Teachers need to promote holistic inquiry with their students in terms of the classroom environment, the wider natural environment, and the inner personal environment (Slattery, 1995).
- Teachers and students must be encouraged to become ironic in reconciling the foundationless status of their beliefs and commitments—and the commitments of others—with the desire to create, develop and defend them". (Parker, 1997, p. 142)

Postmodern theorizing is diverse and eclectic. Perhaps this is both its strength and its weakness. It points to the future but rejects claims of certainty about what the future will be. For instance, Giroux (1992) points out that within society are constantly shifting configurations of culture, power, and knowledge. He uses the phrase *border pedagogy* to denote a recognition of the margins of these configurations, alerting teachers to help students become border crossers, free individuals capable of listening, thinking, writing, and speaking in ways that resist permanent closure on the search for meaning.

Hostile critics, however, contend that openness to the future is not enough. Barrow (1999) claims that proponents of postmodernism postulate a theory that seeks to deny the coherence of theory—a central contradiction—and concludes, "the label 'postmodern' is simply too confused to be useful" (p. 419). Green (1994) even more negatively argues that postmodernism "has so far contributed little that is distinctive or theoretically fruitful and it seems unlikely that it will" (p. 73), and that "postmodernism . . . taken to extremes, can only lead to moral nihilism, political apathy, and the abandonment of the intellect to the chaos of the contingent" (p. 74). Finally, Behar-Horenstein (2000) flatly dismisses postmodern theorizing as "a gross distortion of reality and a reductionist critique of the field" (p. 20).

Review of the Category.   Although the category of critical-exploratory curriculum theorizers can best be characterized by its diversity, virtually all writers within it question prevailing assumptions about society, schools, and personal experience. Virtually all are engaged in exploration of new ways of conceiving of education and of conducting school practice. What most sets them apart from the prescriptive and descriptive theorizers of our first two categories is, as we have suggested, their purpose, and that purpose precludes taken-for-granted acceptance of limiting beliefs. In this sense, virtually all such theorizers can be included under the umbrella term *reconceptualist*, described earlier in this chapter, even though some critics (Molnar, 1992, 2000) think the term too broad to be useful.

It is very clear that a number of these scholars began to grapple with new and varied understandings of curriculum in the 1970s. Pinar was a driving force in these beginnings. In 1979 he founded the *Journal of Curriculum Theorizing* (now renamed *JCT: An Interdisciplinary Journal of Curriculum Studies),* which provided an important early outlet, especially for existential/psychoanalytic and phenomenological theorizers, and which has achieved worldwide recognition. In 1983 Van Manen founded another new journal, *Phenomenology and Pedagogy*. Also beginning in the 1970s, edited collections of papers (for example, Pinar, 1974, 1975; Willis, 1978) started to appear, many of which provided new theoretical perspectives. Some of these publications were the product of annual conferences, the first being held at Rochester in 1973. These JCT conferences provided a meeting ground for curriculum theorizers to explore psychological, political, and cultural dimensions of curriculum. Academics who were very active in this first wave of new theorizing included Macdonald (1971), Huebner (1975), Klohr (1980), Greene (1975), and Pinar (1974, 1975). Others quickly joined in, such as Grumet (1981), Pagano (1983), and Miller (1992).

According to Pinar (1995), these early endeavors were undertaken to create an "intellectual breakthrough" (p. 366). Academics had been stifled by the 1960s national curriculum reform movement, and in the 1970s "[t]he field shifted from a preoccupation with the narrow proceduralism associated with the Tyler Rationale to theoretical understanding broadly conceived" (p. 366). Miller (1996) speculates that a second wave of theorizing may have begun in the 1990s, focusing on how to bring reconceptualist theorizing to elementary and secondary schools; however, Sears (1992b) dismisses the efficacy of any second wave comprised of protégés of the first wave of theorizers, saying of these protégés that "they are proving equally irrelevant and ineffectual" (p. 9).

Still, Wright (2000), writing more recently, contends that we are surfing a "third wave" of cutting edge curriculum theorizing. "This latest group of academics is pushing the theoretical limits of curriculum theorizing, stressing inter/post-disciplinarity and complexifying the struggle for social justice in theory and in praxis" (Wright, 2000, pp. 9–10). He contends that the principal focal points for this latest wave of theorizing are race, class, and gender. These are followed by multiculturalism, critical pedagogy, sexuality, sexual orientation, disability, and cultural studies. He highlights in particular the recent theorizing about popular culture (Gough, 2000). Many of these focal points, of course, are reflected in the subcategories we have used in this chapter to define and to illustrate critical-exploratory curriculum theorizing.

We believe the ideas and arguments of many of the academics in this category are compelling. Collectively, both their criticisms of the old and their explorations of the new contain many practical implications and applications for schools. However, hostile critics of these theorizers have disagreed on both counts.

On the count of compellingness, some critics have been put off by the enthusiasm and eloquence of these theorizers. For instance, the comprehensive volume on curriculum theorizing by Pinar et al. (1995) is a classic example of shared enthusiasm, of rallying cries of celebration coined in phrases such as "a paradigm shift" and "the future lies with the reconceptualist" (p. 238). Milburn (2000) objects to the tone of such remarks, criticizing what he considers the partisan advocacy used by many of these theorizers and their simplification and exaggeration of the historical development of curriculum and their depiction of the contemporary scene. Tanner and Tanner (1981) suggest that many of these approaches to theorizing are "remakes" of earlier theorizing and therefore their claims of a cataclysm are clearly overwrought.

On the count of practicality, Milburn (2000) argues that these theorizers are overly concerned with presentism, and he questions the validity of the claim that their theorizing has produced a paradigm shift. Feinberg (1985) contends that although reconceptualist theorizers have produced exciting ideas, they have not yet produced practical ideas, since there is still no school implementing a reconceptualized curriculum. While we find some truth in these criticisms, we also find a bit strange the notion that paradigm shifts or practicality are demonstrated only by the wholesale implementation in schools of something representing critical-exploratory theorizing in a pure form. In fact, educational change rarely works that way. In the twentieth century, the new practices of progressive education—despite some attending fanfare—gradually insinuated themselves into the schools over many decades, and then often in modified forms that coexisted with the older traditional education. Practices consistent with reconceptualized theorizing are the lineal descendants of progressive education, and they may prove to be the most powerful changes that insinuate themselves into schools during the twenty-first century.

Still, there are cautions to be taken very seriously. Apple (2000), himself a critical-exploratory theorizer, insists on the importance of the "gritty materialities" involved in making close connections between theoretical discourses and real transformations in educational practices, arguing that "while the construction of new theories and utopian visions is important, it is equally crucial to base these theories and visions in an unromantic appraisal of the material and discursive terrain that now exists" (p. 229). Hlebowitsh (1999) offers the following challenge: "To be the bearer of the field, the new curricularists have to have an answer. This means that they have to find a way to transcend their own proclivity toward criticism and protest, and frame a useful theory of conduct that could endure their own style of criticism" (p. 353).

AN EXAMPLE: WILLIAM PINAR'S APPROACH

William Pinar's autobiographical/biographical approach is by no means representative of the whole of the very large and very complex category of critical-exploratory curriculum theorizers. Other theorizers, for instance, may place more emphasis on direct action in the social world, whereas Pinar emphasizes the basis for action within personal experience. But this is mostly a question of which starting point—the outer social or the inner personal—any one theorizer prefers, not a rejection of the connections between outer and inner. Pinar's approach, therefore, offers one way in which curriculum developers can become increasingly sensitive to the centrality of personal experience in the curriculum.

Of the curriculum theorizing we discuss in this chapter and the approaches to curriculum planning discussed in chapter 3, Taba's theorizing is based on Tyler's approach, and Schwab's theorizing heavily influenced Walker's approach; Pinar's theorizing, however, parallels Eisner's approach. Although there are significant similarities between Pinar and Eisner, each seems to have developed his ideas independently, without any direct influence from the other. The main influences on Pinar appear to have been scholars such as Klohr, Macdonald, Greene, and

Huebner, whom he studied or worked with during his doctoral program in curriculum at Ohio State University in the late 1960s and early 1970s. Early in his own academic career, he made some major contributions to moving curriculum theorizing in new directions, including establishing annual reconceptualist conferences and a new journal. A prolific writer, Pinar has published numerous articles and authored and edited numerous books, including *Heightened Consciousness, Cultural Revolution, and Curriculum Theory* (1974), *Curriculum Theorizing: The Reconceptualists* (1975), and *Toward a Poor Curriculum* (with Madeleine Grumet, 1976), which provided the early outlines of his theory.

Basic Assumptions

Pinar takes basically an experimental attitude toward life. He emphasizes that all learners (teachers and students) need to cultivate an internal dialectic (Pinar, 1980). In simpler terms, this means we respond to an idea, to a text, to another person; the ways we respond can enable us to understand, build upon, and transform our thoughts and feelings. Through our lived experiences and our dialectic reflections, we can improve the quality of our own lives and those of others. Pinar criticizes the idea of curriculum design in terms of the temerity of designing educational experiences for others. He makes this argument:

> One cannot predict human response, except in trivial matters and in artificially circumscribed circumstances, as necessary for experiments. Classrooms, while certainly artificially limited, are not sufficiently limited for the teacher to know with much certainty the response his or her lesson will receive. (Pinar, 1980, p. 75)

Pinar, therefore, does not believe curricula should have predetermined goals toward which all decisions are directed. Planning should remain as personal, individual, and informal as possible. He does, however, espouse two general principles that teachers should keep in mind when deciding what to teach and how to teach it. These two principles are, first, that teachers must analyze and reflect upon their personal biases, values, and behavior before intervening in the lived worlds of students; and, second, that teachers must, through their conversations with each student, draw out qualities of clarity, self-honesty, and creativity, both in their students and in themselves (Feinberg, 1985).

Currere and the Teacher's Role

Because Pinar does not believe it is possible to design a curriculum for others, he does not advocate that curriculum planning proceed through specific steps or phases. However, he does suggest that individuals can reflect on their own experiences autobiographically, and there are some general steps they can take to become aware of the course of their experiences, a course that he describes by the word *currere*, derived from the same Latin root as *curriculum*. (Pinar et al., 1995). Thus, for Pinar the course of individual experience is the curriculum. He describes four steps that students can take to help them along this course:

STEP 1: One returns to the past, brackets one's past experience in schools, and brings that remembrance of the past to an understanding of the present.

STEP 2: One imagines the future, perhaps one's future intellectual interest or career.

STEP 3:   One considers the present—the ideas, interests, people, and setting that constitute the present.

STEP 4:   One attempts to integrate the self-knowledge that has been gathered. Mind, emotions, behavior, and body are integrated into a more meaningful whole. (Pinar & Grumet, 1976, pp. 51–63)

As one example of how a teacher can help a student discover *currere,* Pinar (1980) suggests that a student might begin reading passages from a book of interest. The initial purpose is to "give oneself to the text" and not to interpret. The student then records passages of interest. Next, the teacher and student go over these passages and discuss the themes the student finds in them. Sometime later, the student studies new pieces of writing that interpret or further develop these themes and then writes short descriptions of his or her own biographic situation at the present time. Finally, the teacher and the student compare the pieces of writing that interpret the text and the autobiographical pieces written by the student, discussing degrees of correspondence between the two. At this point, both the teacher and the student should be able to explore and analyze their own experiences reflexively, thus transforming the quality of their experiences.

To promote this kind of historical-biographical analysis in students, teachers must undertake the same journey. Therefore, teachers must reflect on the course of their own lived experiences, even though that journey may prove as painful as revelatory. Pinar suggests that both teachers and students should use the resources of their imaginations and their creativity in dealing with traumas and in enriching personal satisfactions (Feinberg, 1985; Graham, 1992).

Classroom Climate

In various papers Pinar notes the type of classroom climate that is antithetical to *currere.* He maintains that psychic deterioration occurs in many classrooms where there is:

- Hypertrophy of fantasy life, prompting a retreat into daydreaming as an escape from boredom
- Criticism by others, resulting in loss of self-esteem
- Estrangement from Self and self-knowledge, numbing children to their own experience
- Dreariness and over-rationalized reality of schooling, leading to atrophy of aesthetic and sensuous sensibility (Pinar, 1975, pp. 359–383)

In contrast, he suggests that "caring" is a critical part of the classroom climate (Pinar, 1992). He maintains that caring by a teacher involves "receiving the other." For instance, through the use of eye contact, teachers can demonstrate to students that they care about them, and through all their actions, teachers can communicate to students that they are far more important than the subject matter being taught. Caring is something unspecified but central in a desirable classroom climate. He takes an example of "caring" from Noddings (1982) to illustrate how he as a teacher might relate to students in a classroom. Suppose, he surmises, that a very bright boy achieved very poorly in mathematics. Most teachers might insist that the boy must work harder and not waste his talents, but, Pinar suggests (1992), these teachers probably have not grasped the reality of what it feels like to hate mathematics. Instead, they have projected their own realities upon the student in a manipulative way. A better way to help the boy learn mathematics is for his teacher to let him know that the teacher understands and sympathizes with his feelings.

Curriculum Development Exemplars

Pinar's theorizing has not been used to guide large-scale curriculum projects, which is not surprising, for his methods are based on the assumption that no one can actually create a curriculum for someone else. Since each individual ultimately determines the course of his or her own experience, other people, such as teachers and anyone else involved in making curriculum decisions, can only aid individual students in this task. Since the theory applies to individual situations and requires some commitment on the part of everyone involved in those situations, its collective use even in schoolwide projects is difficult to find. There are, however, numerous examples of the theory being used by individual teachers in their own classrooms, and some of the better-known examples have been reported in the professional curriculum literature by professors influenced by Pinar's ideas.

Pagano (1983) describes a course she taught to preservice teachers. The course was a methods course, but it was based on the humanities. Her purpose was to get preservice teachers to be producer-critics of their own moral fictions and to use these to reflect on their educational values and their teaching. During the semester, these student teachers were required to construct three texts: a "life text," a "work text," and a "response text." The life text was their educational autobiography; the work text was an account of each student teacher's teaching experiences; and the response text was their interpretations and reactions to books and materials they had used. Regular seminars were held to explore dominant themes and particular concerns about their three texts. At the end of the seminars, the student teachers were asked to write critical papers that united the various recurring themes and attitudes. They were to do their papers in the form of a short story that presented some problem associated with their own teaching. In doing this exercise, the student teachers became increasingly conscious of the choices they were making about both teaching methods and subject matter content.

Krall (1982) describes a unit entitled "Field Studies in Environmental Education," in which she and a group of seven university students undertook a four-week field study of Navajo culture. During this period, each student was asked to select a particular topic related to the Navajos and to complete an independent study. Data were collected in the form of journals. Brief papers were written and shared with others at the completion of the unit. Krall documented in considerable detail the profound changes that occurred in her students as a result of this experience, as revealed by the following statements from two of the journals:

> *Gordon:* But, as I look back over my emergence through the Navajo Way, it is their ability to read the land through mythological eyes which sings out to me.
> *Terry:* My immersion into the Navajo Way has led me to Sipapu... my place of emergence... I have found a metaphor to live by.... (Krall, 1982, pp. 202–203)

Evaluation of the Approach

Evaluating the contribution of Pinar's curriculum theorizing is difficult for two closely related reasons.

First, the system of categories does not apply well to Pinar. Pinar is classified as different from Dewey and Apple in some respects and different from Schwab and Eisner on others, yet there are striking similarities among all of these theorizers.

In fact, for reasons we discussed in chapter 2, Pinar, Apple, Schwab, and Eisner can be seen as carrying out lines of theorizing that Dewey set forth at the beginning of the twentieth-century. For instance, Schwab's notions of practical reasoning and deliberation flow directly from Dewey and apply to group situations, while Eisner's notions of artistry in curriculum planning and Pinar's notions of currere are similar forms of thinking (though less emphasized by Dewey) that apply to individual situations. Or, the critiques of Apple, which begin with analysis of society and lead to implications for individuals, and Pinar's critiques, which begin with analysis of individual experience and lead to implications for society, may be macro and micro versions of the kinds of critiques of society and education that Dewey began. The implications of Pinar's theory are greater than they seem at first glance.

Second, what we have described above as Pinar's theorizing is merely one early version (although certainly the best known and probably the most influential version) of a larger body of work. In fact, as Pinar has many times suggested, the methods of currere he described early in his career are only a few of the methods that can be devised for helping individual students become increasingly reflective about the course of their experience and its quality. Therefore, his theorizing is something that can evolve (and has evolved) and be built upon by other theorizers—more so than Schwab's theorizing and far more so than Taba's. Therefore, judging it only in the form we have described is not as appropriate as considering it in terms of what it has led to.

These points have often been overlooked by critics of Pinar's theorizing (and, for that matter, by critics of "reconceptualist" theorizers in general)—especially by early critics, but also by current ones. A visitor from the United Kingdom to a reconceptualist conference in the United States in the early 1980s was mildly perplexed about the lack of practical guidance he found there: "Reconceptualism is more concerned with questions of faith than with the practical, and unfortunately the eloquence of the medium is standing in the way of whatever message is being sent" (Rodger, 1984, p. 64). Other more impatient critics who seem to have missed substantive points have written hostilely about style. "Consciousness and transcendence is an enchanting prospect," but what does this mean for classroom teaching or teacher training practices? (Feinberg, 1985, p. 92). In an early and insightful assessment of reconceptualist thought and practice, Mazza (1982) contends that persons who make such criticisms of Pinar's work (and the work of other reconceptualists) do not see the larger issues at stake. She argues in particular that:

1. Their theorizing is a process in movement and not a completed project.
2. It will take a considerable length of time and amount of future research and dialogue.

3. New forms of inquiry have to be conceived prior to any recommendation for practice.
4. There has been an overemphasis on practice in the curriculum field in the past (Mazza, 1982, pp. 15–16).

Substantive criticisms of Pinar's theorizing can and have been raised, however. To some critics, the major weakness of Pinar's theorizing is that it provides auto-biographical accounts by individuals but no general principles that can explain their validity to a wider audience of scholars and teachers. Brady (1984) refers to the relative fragmentation of this type of theorizing. A related criticism is that auto-biographical reports can minimize the effects of ideology. In Pinar's theorizing, individual students are asked to reflect on their own experiences, and teachers participate by reading journals or through informal discussions with students. But individual students may remain unaware of their own underlying values and beliefs or of the overriding structures of society that shape their lived experiences. The efforts of teachers may mislead or simply fail to overcome naiveté or false conclusions.

According to Mazza (1982) and Sharp and Green (1975), too much trust can be placed in the power of reflexivity (i.e., self-analysis) to penetrate the powerful ideological influences on teachers' and students' beliefs and actions. However, this criticism has been addressed by Eisner (1979, 1985, 1991), who has written extensively about principles that can be used (such as structural corroboration and referential adequacy) in making generalizations from specific cases. Van Manen (1990) has also pointed out how phenomenology is "the science of examples" (p. 121).

These criticisms notwithstanding, there are a number of major advances that Pinar and similar theorizers have achieved. Without a doubt, Pinar has stimulated the imagination of educators. He has raised serious challenges about traditional approaches to curriculum. His criticism of ends-means rational planning, for instance, has been comprehensive and highly convincing (for example, Pinar, 1978). He has produced stimulating critiques and categorizations of the curriculum field (Pinar 1978, 1988; Pinar et al., 1995).

Pinar and other critical-exploratory theorizers have generated some new perspectives on curriculum and a new language for curriculum theorizing. Aside from Pinar's own term *currere* (the course of one's experience, made meaningful by remembering and reflecting on one's past and projecting one's hopes for the future), terms now commonly used in curriculum theorizing include *reflexivity* (self-analysis), *praxis* (posing and solving problems through reflexivity), *phenomenological* (theorizing about phenomena as consciously experienced), *hermeneutics* (the process of interpretation), and *critical theory* (analysis of society and its relationship to education). Pinar and colleagues have used such terms to develop alternative modes of curriculum inquiry and, in so doing, to advance new propositions.

Pinar's use of currere as a method, Grumet's (1979) use of self-report in teacher education, and Pagano's (1983) use of moral fictions are examples of new ways of investigating curriculum phenomena. Each relies on psychoanalytic approaches to raise one's consciousness about phenomena occurring in one's lived world— "We teachers are conceived by others, by the expectations and the fantasies of our students and the demands of parents, administrators, policymakers and politicians" (Pinar, 1992, p. 233). Short (1991) has edited a book elucidating seventeen different forms of curriculum inquiry now in use, many of them arising out of the work of the 1970s and 1980s critical-exploratory theorizers.

It also appears that Pinar and other theorizers who have explored new methods or challenged existing approaches to curriculum development have assisted greatly in supplanting quantitative methods of educational evaluation from their former position of preeminence. Much recent curriculum theorizing has highlighted the qualitative character of educational experience, "which emphasizes direct intuitive understanding through encounters with and portrayals of the experienced qualities of a situation and through linking such specifics with the external world" (Willis, 1981, p. 186). Along with other exponents of qualitative evaluation (most notably Eisner), Pinar has helped pave the way for the current widespread use of case studies and narratives in curriculum research and evaluation.

While these observations are not about Pinar's theorizing itself, but also about what it has led to, they do suggest the practical character of this work. Pinar's theorizing has been criticized for providing curriculum developers with few specific guidelines in making decisions; however, it outlines a general method for teachers to use in helping students identify and improve the course of their own experiences. In locating the source of all curriculum decisions in the experienced curriculum, it heightens the role of the teacher as the enactor of what is experienced and as a colleague in identifying and interpreting what is experienced. As Graham (1992) suggests, it may be one of the best hopes for keeping alive what is most human in education. In this way, Pinar's theorizing has placed the practice of curriculum planning and development in a new light.

4.4   CURRICULUM THEORY AND THEORIZING TODAY

We have argued in this chapter that curriculum is neither a scientific nor an academic discipline. It is a field of inquiry that touches on ethical choice and epistemology and is also concerned with explaining educational phenomena. It looks for general principles, but it also looks toward individual experience. In so doing, it links thought and practice. The issues with which it deals are so diverse and variable that creating a single theory of curriculum seems impossible. Many people have tried and failed. Although some ideas may have endured over the decades, other ideas have been prominent for a short time only, and all have been questioned and challenged.

In the 1960s, curriculum scholars began a concerted effort to achieve a unified approach to curriculum planning and development and to end competition among subject-centered, society-centered, and individual-centered conceptions of curriculum, which had become serious rivals early in the twentieth-century. Encouraged by the conceptual simplicity and the practical success that the Tyler rationale had achieved as a guide for curriculum planning and development, some scholars, no doubt, believed that their efforts would result in a single, comprehensive theory of curriculum. While this activity centered in the United States, scholars from other nations, especially Canada, Australia, the United Kingdom, and several other European countries, were involved. As early as 1969, Schwab described this attempt as moribund (Schwab, 1969). Now, at the beginning of the twenty-first century, it has not resulted in the single curriculum theory hoped for (and perhaps still deemed possible by a few scholars), but it has resulted in the many forms of curriculum theorizing described in this chapter. Curriculum theorizing is alive and well because theorizers are actively pursuing a range of problems from different perspectives and using a variety of methodologies.

Various attempts have been made to capture the scope of theorizing. Histories document how curriculum theorizing has affected school practices in the United States and explore the emergence and decline of major approaches; these histories include Gwynn and Chase (1969); Tanner and Tanner (1990, 1995); Schubert (1980, 1986); Kliebard (1982, 1986, 1992); Franklin (1986); and Willis, Schubert, Bullough, Kridel, and Holton (1993). A promising area within historical scholarship that came into prominence in the 1980s is the analysis of theorizing inherent in specific school subjects as they have developed over the decades (Cooper, 1984; Goodson, 1983, 1988, 1989; Popkewitz, 1987).

The examples of theorizing included in this chapter should be seen in the light of history. They illustrate the divergent approaches that have been taken and continue to be developed by curriculum specialists. Some approaches have been more dominant at some times than others. In the 1990s, approaches based on the analysis of social structures and/or personal experience became increasingly common. New classifications of theorizing continue to appear in the literature (Glatthorn, 1987; Huenecke, 1982; Pines, 1981; Short, 1987). These conceptions of curriculum add insights about diversity and directions in theorizing, but further studies of the effects of theorizing at the school level are needed.

What is needed more urgently, however, is increasing and continuing dialogue between theorizers at all levels, from teachers to academics, so that we can learn from our history and our diverse perspectives. Walker (1980) claimed that "a rich confusion is the right state for curriculum writing" (p. 81). We believe this is so, but writing is only one of many ways to contribute to the dialogue about the richness of curriculum theorizing in which this chapter has invited readers to participate.

■ QUESTIONS AND REFLECTIONS

1. Reflect on your own work as a teacher and on your experience as a student (in the past or the present). What theoretical principles do you follow in making curriculum decisions as a teacher? What principles did you (or do you now) as a student expect your teachers to follow? Do they differ? If so, give reasons.

2. Well-developed curriculum theories should function as directive forces for those practitioners in schools who must plan, use, and evaluate curricula. Do you agree or disagree with this statement? What are some questionable assumptions on which the statement seems based?

3. "Over the past twenty years the American curriculum field has attempted 'to take back' curriculum from the bureaucrats, to make the curriculum field itself a conversation, and in so doing, revitalize practice theoretically" (Pinar 1999, p. 367). In light of this statement, consider the point of view you hold about the relationship between curriculum theorizing and school practice.

4. Until we know a particular value we hold, it holds us—we are not in possession of it; it affects our work and thinking although we are unaware of it. Reflect upon the major explicit and implicit values that have guided your teaching. How do they relate to the values implicit in the theories described in this chapter? Try to describe your current value orientation and its influence on how you now theorize about curriculum.

5. "More radical and far-sweeping educational and political action is necessary if the goal of feminist education—the abolition of gender as an oppressive cultural reality—is to be achieved" (Sultana, 1990, p. 21). Discuss the implications of this statement for curriculum theorizing and curriculum practice.

6. "In the struggle between bureaucratic control and personal empowerment that marks the transition to postmodernity, collaborative relationships and the particular forms they take are central" (Hargreaves, 1994, p. 58). Do you think that teachers, either among themselves or with others, are building up collaborative relationships? How might doing so assist them in coping with the pressures of postmodernism?

7. "Postmodernism has little of value to offer educational theory but it has many dangers. The greatest of these is that the logic of the postmodern argument points towards an individualistic educational consumerism in many respects similar to that advocated by the free-marketeers of the new Right" (Green, 1994, p. 76). Discuss the implications of this statement for curriculum theorizing and curriculum practice.

8. "Curriculum theorizing has been overtly politicized. It has been variously institutionalized, . . . queered, raced, gendered, aestheticized, psychoanalyzed, moralized, modernized and postmodernized . . . [so] that it presently demands a high degree of flexibility and tolerance from all involved" (Wright, 2000, p. 10). Consider the implications of this point of view for the future of curriculum theorizing and school practice.

■ SUGGESTED READING

A useful series of articles on curriculum theorizing has been included in theme issues of curriculum journals:

Curriculum Inquiry, 29(3) 1999.

Theory into Practice, 21(1), 1982; and *31*(3), 1992.

Curriculum Perspectives, 4(1), 1984; *4*(2), 1984; and *11*(4), 1991.

Important books (see the chapter bibliography) include the following:

Apple (1982)

Beyer & Apple (1998)

Connell et al. (1982)

Eisner & Vallance (1974)

Lawn & Barton (1981)

Pinar (1975)

Pinar et al. (1995)

Reid (1978)

Schubert (1986)

Sears & Marshall (1990)

Slattery (1995)

Walker (1990)

▌ BIBLIOGRAPHY

Aitken, J. A. (1999). Leaping boundaries of difference. *Curriculum Inquiry, 29*(2), 149–157.

Althusser, L. (1971). Ideology and the ideological state apparatuses. In L. Althusser, *Lenin and philosophy and other essays.* New York: Monthly Review Press.

Anderson, R. (1981). *Self-instruction as a method of preparing elementary school social studies teacher trainees to apply an inductive teaching model.* Unpublished doctoral dissertation, Stanford University.

Anyon, J. (1980). Social class and the hidden curriculum of work. *Journal of Education, 162*(1), 67–92.

Anyon, J. (1994). The retreat of Marxism and socialist feminism: Postmodern and poststructural theories. *Curriculum Inquiry, 24*(2), 115–134.

Apple, M. W. (1979). *Ideology and curriculum.* London: Routledge & Kegan Paul.

Apple, M. W. (1981). Social structure, ideology and curriculum. In M. Lawn & L. Barton (Eds.), *Rethinking curriculum studies.* London: Croom Helm.

Apple, M. W. (1982). *Education and power.* Boston: Routledge & Kegan Paul.

Apple, M. W. (2000). Can critical pedagogies interrupt rights policies? *Educational Theory, 50*(2), 229–258.

Arnot, M., & Dillabough, J. (1999). Feminist politics and democratic values in education. *Curriculum Inquiry, 29*(2), 174–190.

Atkinson, E. (2000). *What can post-modern thinking do for educational research?* Paper presented at the annual meeting of the American Educational Research Association, New Orleans.

Banks, J. (1993). The canon debate, knowledge construction, and multicultural education. *Educational Researcher, 22*(5), 4–14.

Barone, T. (1982). Insinuated theory from curriculum-in-use. *Theory into Practice, 21*(1), 38–43.

Barrow, R. (1999). The need for philosophical analysis in a post-modern era. *Interchange, 30*(4), 415–432.

Beauchamp, G. A. (1975). *Curriculum theory* (3rd ed.). Wilmette, IL: Kagg.

Beauchamp, G. A. (1982). Curriculum theory: Meaning, development and use. *Theory into Practice, 21*(1), 23–27.

Behar-Horenstein, L. (2000). Can the modern view of curriculum be refined by post-modern criticism? In J. Glanz & L. Behar-Horenstein (Eds.), *Paradigm debates in curriculum and supervision.* Westport, CT: Bergin & Garvey.

Belenky, M., Clinchy, B., Goldberg, N., & Tarule, J. (1988). *Women's ways of knowing: The development of self, voice and mind.* New York: Basic Books.

Berlak, A. (1999). Teaching and testimony: Witnessing and bearing witness to racisms in culturally diverse classrooms. *Curriculum Inquiry, 29*(1), 99–128.

Bernstein, B. B. (1973). *Class, codes, and control: Vol. 1. Theoretical studies towards a sociology of language.* London: Routledge & Kegan Paul.

Beyer, L. E., & Apple, M. W. (Eds.). (1998). *The curriculum: Problems, politics, and possibilities* (2nd ed.). Albany: State University of New York Press.

Bobbitt, J. F. (1918). *The curriculum.* Boston: Houghton Mifflin.

Bobbitt, J. F. (1924). *How to make a curriculum.* Boston: Houghton Mifflin.

Boomer, G. (Ed.). (1982). *Negotiating the curriculum.* Sydney: Ashton Scholastic.

Bourdieu, P., & Passeron, J. (1977). *Reproduction in education, society and culture.* London: Sage.

Bowles, S., & Gintis, H. (1976). *Schooling in capitalist America.* New York: Basic Books.

Brady, P. (1984). Chasing ghosts out of the machine: A deconstruction of some curriculum theory. *Curriculum Perspectives, 4*(2), 64–66.

Brice, L. (2000). *Deliberative discourse enacted: Task, text, and talk.* Paper presented at the annual meeting of the American Educational Research Association, New Orleans.

Britzman, D. (1988). The question of belief: Writing post-structural studies in education. *Journal of Curriculum Theorizing, 8*(3), 229–238.

Britzman, D. (1992). The terrible problem of knowing thyself: Toward a post-structural account of teacher identity. *Journal of Curriculum Theorizing, 8*(3), 23–46.

Brown, T. M. (1988). How fields change: A critique of the "Kuhnian" view. In W. F. Pinar (Ed.), *Contemporary curriculum discourses* (pp. 16–30). Scottsdale, AZ: Gorsuch Scarisbrick.

Bruner, J. S. (1966). *Toward a theory of instruction.* Cambridge, MA: Belknap.

Butt, R. (1983). *The illucidatory potential of autobiography and biography in understanding teachers' thoughts and actions.* Paper presented at the Bergamo Conference, Dayton, Ohio.

Castenell, L., & Pinar, W. F. (Eds.). (1993). *Understanding curriculum as racial text: Representations of identity and difference in education.* Albany: State University of New York Press.

Caswell, H. L., & Campbell, D. S. (1935). *Curriculum development.* New York: American Book Company.

Charters, W. W. (1923). *Curriculum construction.* New York: Macmillan.

Cherryholmes, C. H. (1982). What is curriculum theory? A special problem in social theory. *Theory into Practice, 21*(1), 28–33.

Chodorow, N. (1978). *The reproduction of mothering.* Berkeley: University of California Press.

Chung, S., & Walsh, D. J. (2000). Unpacking child-centeredness: A history of meanings. *Journal of Curriculum Studies, 32*(2), 215–234.

Clune, W. H. (1998). The national standards in math and science: Developing consensus, unresolved issues, and unfinished business. *Teachers College Record, 100*(1), 6–7.

Connell, R. W., Ashenden, D. J., Kessler, S., & Dowsett, G. W. (1982). *Making the difference.* Sydney: Allen & Unwin.

Connelly, F. M. (1978). How shall we publish case studies of curriculum development? An essay review of Reid and Walker's *Case studies in curriculum change. Curriculum Inquiry, 8,* 73–82.

Connelly, F. M., & Clandinin, D. J. (1988). *Teachers as curriculum planners.* New York: Teachers College Press.

Cooper, B. (1984). On explaining change in school subjects. In I. F. Goodson & S. J. Ball (Eds.), *Defining the curriculum.* Lewes, England: Falmer.

Cornbleth, C. (1988). Curriculum in and out of context. *Journal of Curriculum and Supervision, 4*(1), 85–96.

Coulby, D. (2000). *Beyond the national curriculum.* London: Routledge/Falmer.

Davies, B., & Bank, C., (1992). The gender trap: A feminist Poststructural analysis of primary school children's talk about gender. *Journal of Curriculum Studies, 24*(1), 1–26.

Davies, I. K. (1971). *The management of learning.* London: McGraw-Hill.

DeMocker, S. (1986). *A trail of desire: Aspects of relationship with nature.* Unpublished doctoral dissertation, University of Rochester.

Derrida, J. (1972). Discussion: Structure, sign and play in the discourse of the human sciences. In R. Macksey & E. Donato (Eds.), *The structuralist controversy* (pp. 247–272). Baltimore: Johns Hopkins University Press.

Dewey, J. (1900). *The school and society.* Chicago: University of Chicago Press.

Dewey, J. (1902). *The child and the curriculum.* Chicago: University of Chicago Press.

Dev, P., & Walker, D. F. (1999). From virtual frog to frog island: Design studies in a development project. *Journal of Curriculum Studies, 31*(6), 635–660.

Doll, W. E., Jr. (1987). Foundations for a postmodern curriculum. Paper presented at the annual meeting of the American Educational Research Association, Washington, D.C.

Doll, W. E., Jr. (1993). *A post-modern perspective on curriculum.* New York: Teachers College Press.

Durkin, C., McNaughton, A., Myers, C., & Wallen, M. (1974). *Taba program in social science.* Menlo Park, CA: Addison-Wesley.

Eggen, P. D., Kauchak, D. P., & Harder, R. J. (1979). *Strategies for teachers: Information processing models in the classroom.* Englewood Cliffs, NJ: Prentice Hall.

Eggen, P. D., Kauchak, D. P., & Harder, R. J. (1988). *Strategies for teachers: Information processing models in the classroom.* Englewood Cliffs, NJ: Prentice Hall.

Eisner, E. W. (1974). Instructional and expressive objectives: Their formulation and use in curriculum. AERA Monograph Series in Curriculum Evaluation, No. 3. In M. Golby (Ed.), *Curriculum Design.* London: Open University Press.

Eisner, E. W. (1979). *The educational imagination.* New York: Macmillan.

Eisner, E. W. (1984). No easy answers: Joseph Schwab's contributions to curriculum. *Curriculum Inquiry, 14*(2), 201–210.

Eisner, E. W. (1985). *The educational imagination* (2nd ed.). New York: Macmillan.

Eisner, E. W. (1991). *The enlightened eye.* New York: Macmillan.

Eisner, E. W. (1992). Educational reform and the ecology of schooling. *Teachers College Record, 93*(4), 610–627.

Eisner, E. W. (1996). Objectivity in educational research. In M. Hammersley (Ed.), *Educational research: Current issues*. Buckingham: Open University.

Eisner, E. W. (2000). Those who ignore the past . . .? 12 easy lessons for the next millennium. *Journal of Curriculum Studies, 32*(2), 343–357.

Eisner, E. W., & Vallance, E. (1974). *Conflicting conceptions of curriculum*. Berkeley, CA: McCutchan.

Elbaz, F. (1981). The teacher's "practical knowledge": Report of a case study. *Curriculum Inquiry, 11*(1), 43–72.

Ellsworth, E. (1997). *The uses of the sublime in teaching difference*. Paper presented at the annual meeting of the American Educational Research Association, San Diego.

England, T. (2000). Rethinking democracy and education: Towards an education of deliberative citizens. *Journal of Curriculum Studies, 32*(2), 305–313.

Erickson, H. L. (1995). *Stirring the head, heart and soul*. Thousand Oaks, CA: Corwin.

Feinberg, P. R. (1985). Four curriculum theorists: A critique in the light of Martin Buber's philosophy of education. *Journal of Curriculum Theorizing, 6*(1), 5–164.

Fine, M., Weis, L., Powell, L., & Wong, L. M. (Eds.). (1997). *Off white: Readings on race, power, and society*. London: Routledge.

Fisher, B. A., & Ellis, D. G. (1990). *Small group discussion making: Communication and the group process* (3rd ed.). New York: McGraw-Hill.

Flecha, R. (1999). Modern and post-modern racism in Europe: Dialogic approach and anti-racist pedagogies. *Harvard Educational Review, 69*(2), 150–172.

Foucault, M. (1972). *The archaeology of knowledge and the discourse on language*. New York: Pantheon.

Fox, S. (1985). The vitality of theory in Schwab's conception of the practical. *Curriculum Inquiry, 15*(1), 63–90.

Fraenkel, J. R. (1992). Hilda Taba's contributions to social studies education. *Social Education, 56*(3), 172–178.

Franklin, B. (1986). *Building the American community: The school curriculum and the search for social control*. Lewes, England: Falmer.

Giddens, A. (1990). *The consequences of modernity*. Cambridge: Cambridge Press.

Giroux, H. A. (1982). Power and resistance in the new sociology of education: Beyond theories of social and cultural reproduction. *Curriculum Perspectives, 2*(3), 1–14.

Giroux, H. A. (1990). Curriculum theory, textual authority, and the role of teachers as public intellectuals. *Journal of Curriculum and Supervision, 5*(4), 361–383.

Giroux, H. A. (1991). *Postmodernism, feminism and cultural politics*. Albany: State University of New York Press.

Giroux, H. A. (1992). *Border crossings: Cultural workers and the politics of education*. New York: Routledge.

Glatthorn, A. A. (1987). *Curriculum leadership*. Glenview, IL: Scott Foresman.

Goodlad, J. I. (1984). *A place called school: Prospects for the future*. New York: McGraw-Hill.

Goodlad, J. I., & Richter, M. N. (1977). Decisions and levels of decision-making: Processes and data sources. In A. A. Bellack & H. M. Kliebard (Eds.), *Curriculum and evaluation*. Berkeley, CA: McCutchan.

Goodson, I. (1981). Life history and the study of schooling. *Interchange, 11*(4), 15–29.

Goodson, I. F. (1983). *School subjects and curriculum change*. London: Croom Helm.

Goodson, I. F. (1988). *The making of curriculum*. Lewes, England: Falmer.

Goodson, I. F. (1989). "Chariots of fire": Etymologies, epistemologies and the emergence of curriculum. In G. Milburn, I. F. Goodson, & R. J. Clark (Eds.), *Re-interpreting curriculum research: Images and arguments* (pp. 13–25). London: Falmer.

Goodson, I. F. (1992). On curriculum form: Notes toward a theory of curriculum. *Sociology of Education, 65,* 66–75.

Gordon, I. F. (Ed.). (1968). *Criteria for theories of instruction*. Washington, DC: Association for Supervision and Curriculum Development.

Gough, N. (1984). Practical curriculum theorizing. *Curriculum Perspectives, 4*(1), 65–68.

Gough, N. (2000). Locating curriculum studies in the global village. *Journal of Curriculum Studies, 32*(2), 329–342.

Graham, R. J. (1991). *Reading and writing the self: Autobiography in education and the curriculum*. New York: Teachers College Press.

Graham, R. J. (1992). Currere and reconceptualism: The progress of the pilgrimage, 1975–1990. *Journal of Curriculum Studies, 24*(1), 27–42.

Green, A. (1994). Postmodernism and state education. *Journal of Education Policy, 9*(1), 67–83.

Greene, M. (1975). Curriculum and consciousness. In W. Pinar (Ed.), *Curriculum theorizing: The reconceptualists* (pp. 299–317). Berkeley, CA: McCutchan.

Griffin, D. R., Cobb, J. B., Ford, M. P., Gunter, P., & Ochs, P. (1993). *Founders of constructive postmodern philosophy: Pierce, James, Bergson, Whitehead, and Hartshorne.* Albany: State University of New York Press.

Grumet, M. (1976). Existential and phenomenological foundations. In W. Pinar & M. Grumet, *Toward A Poor Curriculum.* Dubuque, IA: Kendall/Hunt.

Grumet, M. (1979). Supervision and situation: A methodology of self-report for teacher education. *Journal of Curriculum Theorizing, 1*(1), 191–257.

Grumet, M. (1981). Restitution and reconstruction of educational experience, an autobiographical method for curriculum theory. In M. Lawn & L. Barton (Eds.), *Rethinking curriculum studies.* London: Croom Helm.

Grumet, M., & Stone, L. (2000). Feminism and curriculum: Getting our act together. *Journal of Curriculum Studies, 32*(2), 183–197.

Gwynn, J. M., & Chase, J. G. (1969). *Curriculum principles and social trends* (4th ed.). New York: Macmillan.

Haggerson, N. L. (1988). Reconceptualizing inquiry in curriculum: Using multiple research paradigms to enhance the study of curriculum. *Journal of Curriculum Theorizing, 6*(1), 81–102.

Hall, W. C., & Myers, C. B. (1977). The effect of a training program in Taba teaching strategies on teaching methods and teacher perceptions of their teaching. *Peabody Journal of Education, 7,* 162–173.

Hargreaves, A. (1994). Restructuring, restructuring: Postmodernity and the prospects for educational change. *Journal of Education Policy, 9*(1), 47–65.

Hargreaves, A. (1995). *Changing teachers, changing times.* London: Cassell.

Helsby, G., & Saunders, M. (1993). Taylorism, Tylerism, and performance indicators: Defending the indefensible. *Educational Studies, 19*(1), 55–77.

Herrick, V. E., & Tyler, R. W. (Eds.). (1950). *Toward improved curriculum theory.* Chicago: University of Chicago Press.

Hirst, P. H. (1965). Liberal education and the nature of knowledge. In R. D. Archambault (Ed.), *Philosophical analysis in education.* London: Routledge & Kegan Paul.

Hlebowitsh, P. S. (1992). Amid behavioral and behavioristic objectives: Reappraising appraisals of the Tyler rationale. *Journal of Curriculum Studies, 24*(6), 533–547.

Hlebowitsh, P. S. (1999). The burdens of the new curricularist. *Curriculum Inquiry, 23*(3), 343–353.

Holt, J. (1964). *How children fail.* New York: Pitman.

Huebner, D. (1975). Curricular language and classroom meanings. In W. Pinar (Ed.), *Curriculum theorizing: The reconceptualists* (pp. 217–237). Berkeley, CA: McCutchan.

Huenecke, D. (1982). What is curriculum theorizing? What are its implications for practice? *Educational Leadership, 39*(4), 290–294.

Hughes, P. (1972). *The teacher's role in curriculum design.* Sydney: Angus & Robertson.

Hutchins, R. M. (1968). *The learning society.* New York: Praeger.

Illich, I. D. (1971). *De-schooling society.* London: Calder & Boyars.

Jackson, P. (Ed.). (1992). *Handbook of research on curriculum.* New York: Macmillan.

Jencks, C. (Ed.). (1992). *The post-modern reader.* New York: St. Martin's Press.

Jickling, B. (1988). Paradigms in curriculum development: Critical comments on the work of Tanner and Tanner. *Interchange, 19*(2), 41–49.

Johnson, B., & Reid, A. (Eds.). (1999). *Contesting the curriculum.* Sydney: Social Science Press.

Johnson, M., Jr. (1967). Definitions and models in curriculum theory. *Educational Theory, 17,* 127–140.

Joyce, B., Murphy, C., Showers, B., & Murphy, J. (1989). School renewal as cultural change. *Educational Leadership, 47*(3), 70–77.

Kemmis, S. (1986). *Curriculum theorizing: Beyond reproduction theory.* Geelong, Australia: Deakin University.

Kemmis, S. (1989). *Metatheory and metapractice in educational theorising and research.* Unpublished paper, Deakin University, Geelong, Australia.

Kendall, C. N. (2000). How does one promote homosexuality? A Western Australian legal analysis of possible high school education strategies aimed at combating lesbian and gay youth suicide and HIV/AIDS transmission rates. *Curriculum Perspectives, 20*(1), 9–18.

Kennedy, K. (1984). Lessons from a curriculum development project. *Curriculum Perspectives, 4*(1), 53–60.

Kenway, J., Blackmore, J., & Willis, S. (1996). Beyond feminist authoritarianism. *Curriculum Perspectives, 16*(1), 1–12.

Kenway, J., & Modra, H. (1992). Feminist pedagogy and emancipatory possibilities. In C. Luke & J. Gore (Eds.), *Feminisms and critical pedagogy.* New York: Routledge.

Kilpatrick, W. H. (1918). The project method. *Teachers College Record, 19*(4), 1–26.

Kincheloe, J., & Pinar, W. (Eds.). (1991). *Curriculum as social psychoanalysis: The significance of place.* Albany: State University of New York Press.

Kincheloe, J., Steinberg, S., Rodriguez, N., & Chennault, R. (Eds.). (1998). *White reign: Deploying whiteness in America.* New York: St. Martins Press.

Kirst, M. W., & Walker, D. F. (1971). An analysis of curriculum policy-making. *Review of Educational Research, 41*(5), 479–509.

Klein, M. F. (1992). A perspective on the gap between curriculum theory and practice. *Theory into Practice, 31*(3), 191–197.

Klein, R. (1986). *The dynamics of women's studies: An exploratory study of its international ideas and practices in higher education.* Unpublished doctoral thesis, University of London, Institute of Education.

Kliebard, H. M. (1974). The development of certain key curriculum issues in the United States. In P. H. Taylor & M. Johnson, Jr. (Eds.), *Curriculum development: A comparative study.* London: National Foundation for Educational Research.

Kliebard, H. M. (1977). Curriculum theory: Give me a "for instance." *Curriculum Inquiry, 6*(4), 257–268.

Kliebard, H. M. (1982). Curriculum theory as a metaphor. *Theory into Practice, 21*(1), 11–17.

Kliebard, H. M. (1986). *The struggle for the American curriculum, 1890–1958.* Boston: Routledge & Kegan Paul.

Kliebard, H. M. (1992). *Forging the American curriculum: Essays on curriculum history and theory* New York: Routledge.

Klohr, P. (1980). The curriculum theory field—Gritty and ragged. *Curriculum Perspectives, 1*(1), 1–8.

Krall, F. R. (1982). Navajo tapestry: A curriculum for ethno-ecological perspectives. *Journal of Curriculum Theorizing, 3*(2), 165–208.

Kuhn, T. (1962). *The structure of scientific revolutions.* Chicago: University of Chicago Press.

Lather, P. (1991a). *Getting smart: Feminist research and pedagogy with/in the postmodern.* London: Routledge.

Lather, P. (1991b). Deconstructing/deconstructive inquiry: The politics of knowing and being known. *Educational Theory, 41*(2), 153–173.

Lather, P. (1998). Against empathy, voice and authenticity. Paper presented at the annual meeting of the American Educational Research Association, San Diego.

Lawn, M., & Barton, L. (1980). Curriculum studies: Reconceptualism or reconstruction? *Journal of Curriculum Theorizing, 2*(1), 47–56.

Lawn, M., & Barton, L. (Eds.). (1981). *Rethinking curriculum studies.* London: Croom Helm.

Leck, G. M. (1999). Afterword. In W. J. Letts & J. T. Sears (Eds.), *Queering elementary education.* Lanham, MD: Rowman & Littlefield.

Luke, C. (Ed.). (1996). *Feminisms and pedagogies of everyday life.* Albany: State University of New York Press.

Lundgren, U.P. (1976). *Frame factors and the teaching process: A contribution to curriculum theory and theory of teaching.* Stockholm: Almqvist & Wiksell.

Macdonald, J. B. (1971). Curriculum development in relation to social and intellectual systems. Seventieth yearbook of the National Society for the study of Education. Chicago: University of Chicago.

Macdonald, J. B. (1981). Curriculum, consciousness and social change. *Journal of Curriculum Theorizing, 3*(1), 143–153.

Macdonald, J. B. (1982). How literal is curriculum theory? *Theory into Practice, 21*(1), 55–61.

Mann, J. S. (1968). A discipline of curriculum theory. *School Review, 76*(4), 359–378.

Marsh, C. J. (1987). Curriculum theorizing in Australia. *Journal of Curriculum Theorizing, 7*(2), 7–29.

Mazza, K. A. (1982). Reconceptual inquiry as an alternative mode of curriculum theory and practice: A critical study. *Journal of Curriculum Theorizing, 4*(2), 5–89.

McCarthy, C. (1988). Rethinking liberal and radical perspectives on racial inequality in schooling: Making the case for nonsynchrony. *Harvard Educational Review, 58*(3), 265–279.

McCutcheon, G. (1982). What in the world is curriculum theory? *Theory into Practice, 21*(1), 18–22.

McCutcheon, G. (1985). Curriculum theory/curriculum practice: A gap or the Grand Canyon? In A. Molnar (Ed.), *Current thought on curriculum.* Alexandria, VA: Association for Supervision and Curriculum Development.

McGaw, B., & Glass, G. (1980). Choice of metric for effect size in meta-analysis. *American Educational Research Journal, 17*(3), 325–338.

McKenzie, G. R. (1979). The fallacy of excluded instruction: A common but correctable error in process oriented teaching strategies. *Theory and Research in Social Education, 7*(2), 17–31.

McLaren, P., & Farahmandpur, R. (2000). Reconsidering Marx in post-Marxist times: A requiem for postmodernism. *Educational Researcher, 29*(3), 25–33.

McNeil, J. D. (1977). *Curriculum: A comprehensive introduction.* Boston: Little, Brown.

Meath-Lang, B. (1999). *Teachers responding to the voice of others.* Paper presented at the Bergamo Conference on Curriculum Practice, Dayton, Ohio.

Middleton, S. (1992). Developing a radical pedagogy: Autobiography of a New Zealand sociologist of women's education. In I. F. Goodson (Ed.), *Studying teachers' lives.* London: Routledge.

Milburn, G. (2000). Understanding curriculum. *Journal of Curriculum Studies, 32*(3), 445–452.

Miller, J. L. (1992). Shifting the boundaries: Teachers challenge contemporary curriculum thought. *Theory into Practice, 31*(3), 245–251.

Miller, J. L. (1996). Curriculum and the reconceptualization: Another brief history. *Journal of Curriculum Theorizing, 12*(1), 6–8.

Miller, J. L. (2000). What is left in the field: A curriculum memoir. *Journal of Curriculum Studies, 32*(2), 253–266.

Molnar, A. (1992). Contemporary curriculum discourse: Too much ado about too much nothing. *Theory into Practice, 31*(3), 198–203.

Molnar, A. (2000). Zap me! Linking schoolhouse and marketplace in a seamless web. *Phi Delta Kappan, 81*(8), 601–603.

Noddings, N. (1982). Caring. *Journal of Curriculum Theorizing, 3*(2), 139–148.

Noddings, N. (1994). Postmodern musings on pedagogical uses of the personal. *Journal of Curriculum Studies, 26*(4) 355–360.

O'Brien, M. (1986). Feminism and the politics of education. *Interchange, 17*(2), 91–105.

Olson, J. (1989). The persistence of technical rationality. In G. Milburn, I. F. Goodson, & R. J. Clark (Eds.), *Re-interpreting curriculum research: Images and arguments* (pp. 102–109). London: Falmer.

Ornstein, A. C., & Hunkins, F. P. (1993). *Curriculum: Foundations, principles and theory* (2nd ed.). Boston: Allyn & Bacon.

Pagano, J. A. (1983). *Moral fictions.* Paper presented at the annual meeting of the American Educational Research Association, Montreal.

Pagano, J. A. (1990). *Exiles and communities: Teaching in the patriarchal wilderness.* Albany: State University of New York Press.

Pagano, J. A. (1992). Women and education: In what ways does gender affect the educational process? In J. Kincheloe & S. Steinberg (Eds.), *Thirteen questions* (pp. 143–150). New York: Lang.

Parker, S. (1997). *Reflective teaching in the post-modern world.* Buckingham: Open University Press.

Perkinson, H. J. (1993). *Teachers without goals, students without purposes.* New York: McGraw Hill.

Peters, R. S. (1966). *Ethics and education.* London: Allen & Unwin.

Phenix, P. H. (1964). *Realms of meaning: A philosophy of the curriculum for general education.* New York: McGraw-Hill.

Phillion, J. (1999). Narrative and formalistic approaches to the study of multiculturalism. *Curriculum Inquiry, 29*(1), 129–148.

Pinar, W. F. (1972). Working from within. *Educational Leadership, 29*(4), 329–331.

Pinar, W. F. (Ed.). (1974). *Heightened consciousness, cultural revolution, and curriculum theory.* Berkeley, CA: McCutchan.

Pinar, W. F. (Ed.). (1975). *Curriculum theorizing: The reconceptualists.* Berkeley, CA: McCutchan.

Pinar, W. F. (1978). Notes on the curriculum field. *Educational Researcher, 7*(8), 5–11.

Pinar, W. F. (1980). The voyage out: Curriculum as the relationship between the knower and the known. *Journal of Curriculum Theorizing, 2*(1), 7–11.

Pinar, W. F. (1983). Curriculum as gender text: Notes on reproduction, resistance, and male-male relations. *Journal of Curriculum Theorizing, 5*(1), 26–52.

Pinar, W. F. (1988). The reconceptualization of curriculum studies, 1987: A personal retrospective. *Journal of Curriculum and Supervision, 3*(2), 157–167.

Pinar, W. F. (1992). "Dreamt into existence by others": Curriculum theory and school reform. *Theory into Practice, 31*(3), 228–235.

Pinar, W. F. (1994). *Autobiography, politics, and sexuality: Essays in curriculum theory, 1972–1992.* New York: Peter Lang.

Pinar, W. F. (1997). Regimes of reason and male narrative voice. In W. G. Gierney & Y. S. Lincoln (Eds.), *Representation and the text: Reframing the narrative voice.* Albany: State University of New York Press.

Pinar, W. F. (1999). Not burdens — breakthoughs. *Curriculum Inquiry, 23*(3), 365–367.

Pinar, W. F. (2000). Strange fruit: Race, sex and an autobiographics of alternity. Paper presented at the annual meeting of the American Educational Research Association, New Orleans.

Pinar, W. F., & Grumet, M. (1976). *Toward a poor curriculum.* Dubuque, IA: Kendall/Hunt.

Pinar, W. F., Reynolds, W. M., Slattery, P., & Taubman, P. M. (1995). *Understanding curriculum.* New York: Lang.

Pines, A. L. (1981). *Curriculum development and instructional planning within an epistemological-psychological framework: A theoretical synthesis.* Paper presented at the annual meeting of the American Educational Research Association, Los Angeles.

Popkewitz, T. S. (Ed.). (1987). *The formation of school subjects.* Lewes, England: Falmer.

Posner, G. F. (1998). Models of curriculum planning. In L. E. Beyer & M. W. Apple (Eds.), *The curriculum: Problems, politics, and possibilities.* Albany: State University of New York Press.

Prawat, R. S. (2000). The two faces of Deweyan pragmatism: Inductionism versus social constructivism. *Teachers College Record, 102*(4), 805–840.

Raban, J. (1974). *Soft city.* London: Hamilton.

Reid, W. A. (1978). *Thinking about curriculum.* London: Routledge & Kegan Paul.

Reid, W. A. (1979). Practical reasoning and curriculum theory: In search of a new paradigm. *Curriculum Inquiry, 9*(3), 187–208.

Reid, W. A. (1981). Core curriculum: Precept or process. *Curriculum Perspectives, 1*(2), 25–32.

Reid, W. A. (1986). Curriculum theory and curriculum change: What can we learn from history? *Journal of Curriculum Studies, 18*(2), 159–166.

Reid, W. A. (1988). The institutional context of curriculum deliberation. *Journal of Curriculum and Supervision, 4*(1), 3–16.

Reid, W. A. (1992). The state of curriculum inquiry. *Journal of Curriculum Studies, 24*(2), 165–178.

Reid, W. A. (1993). Does Schwab improve on Tyler? A response to Jackson. *Journal of Curriculum Studies, 25*(6), 499–510.

Reid, W. A. (1994). *Curriculum planning as deliberation.* Oslo: University of Oslo.

Reid, W. A. (1999a). *Curriculum as institution and practice.* Mahwah, NJ: Lawrence Erlbaum.

Reid, W. A. (1999b). The voice of the practical: Schwab as correspondent. *Journal of Curriculum Studies, 31*(4), 385–397.

Reid, W. A. (2000). *Why globalization will not cause fundamental curriculum change.* Paper presented at the annual meeting of the American Educational Research Association, New Orleans.

Richardson, T., & Villenas, S. (2000). Other encounters: Dances with whiteness in multicultural education. *Educational Theory, 50*(2), 255–273.

Roby, T. W. (1983). *Habits impeding deliberation.* Paper presented at the annual meeting of the American Educational Research Association, Montreal.

Rodger, I. A. (1984). A wet day in Ohio: A report on a reconceptualist conference. *Curriculum Perspectives, 4*(2), 63–64.

Rogan, J., & Luckowski, J. (1990). Curriculum tests: The portrayal of the field, Part 1. *Journal of Curriculum Studies, 22*(1), 17–39.

Ross, A. (2000). *Curriculum studies and critique.* London: Falmer.

Rugg, H. O. (Ed.). (1927). *The foundations of curriculum-making.* Twenty-sixth yearbook of the National Society for the Study of Education, Part II. Bloomington, IL: Public School Publishing Company.

Scheffler, I. (1973). *Reason and teaching.* London: Routledge & Kegan Paul.

Schubert, W. H. (1980). *Curriculum books: The first eighty years.* New York: University Press of America.

Schubert, W. H. (1986). *Curriculum: Perspective, paradigm, and possibility.* Upper Saddle River, NJ: Merrill/Prentice Hall.

Schubert, W. H. (1991). Teacher lore: A basis for understanding praxis. In C. Witherall & N. Noddings (Eds.), *Stories lives tell: Narrative and dialogue in education.* New York: Teachers College Press.

Schubert, W. H. (1992). Practitioners influence curriculum theory: Autobiographical reflections. *Theory into Practice, 31*(3), 236–244.

Schubert, W. H., Willis, G., & Short, E. (1984). Curriculum theorizing: An emergent form of curriculum studies in the United States. *Curriculum Perspectives, 4*(1), 69–73.

Schwab, J. J. (1950). Criteria for the evaluation of achievement tests: From the point of view of the subject-matter specialist. In *Proceedings of the Educational Testing Service Invitational Conference on Testing Problems.* Princeton, NJ: Educational Testing Service.

Schwab, J. J. (1954). Eros and education. *Journal of General Education, 8,* 54–71.

Schwab, J. J. (1960). The teaching of science as enquiry. In J. J. Schwab & P. F. Brandwein, *The teaching of science.* Cambridge, MA: Harvard University Press.

Schwab, J. J. (1964). Structure of the disciplines: Meanings and significances. In G. W. Ford & L. Pugno (Eds.), *The structure of knowledge and the curriculum* (pp. 1–30). Chicago: Rand McNally.

Schwab, J. J. (1969). The practical: A language for curriculum. *School Review, 78*(1), 1–23.

Schwab, J. J. (1970). *The practical: A language for curriculum.* Washington, DC: National Education Association.

Schwab, J. J. (1971). The practical: Arts of the eclectic. *School Review, 79,* 493–542.

Schwab, J. J. (1973). The practical 3: Translation into curriculum. *School Review, 81,* 501–522.

Schwab, J. J. (1983). The practical 4: Something for curriculum professors to do. *Curriculum Inquiry, 13*(3), 239–265.

Sears, J. (Ed.). (1992a). *Sexuality and the curriculum.* New York: Teachers College Press.

Sears, J. (1992b). The second wave of curriculum theorizing: Labyrinths, orthodoxies and other legacies of the glass bead game. *Theory into Practice 31*(3), 210–218.

Sears J. (1999). *Teaching queerly: Some elementary propositions.* In W. J. Letts & J. T. Sears (Eds.), *Queering elementary education.* Lanham, MD: Rowman and Littlefield.

Sears, J. T., & Marshall, J. D. (1990). *Teaching and thinking about curriculum: Critical inquiries.* New York: Teachers College Press.

Shakeshaft, C., Nowell, I., & Perry, A. (1991). Gender and supervision. *Theory into Practice, 30*(2), 134–139.

Sharp, R., & Green, A. (1975). *Education and social control: A study in progressive primary education.* London: Routledge & Kegan Paul.

Shore, Z. L. (2000). Girls learning, women teaching: Dancing to different drummers. *Education Studies, 31*(2), 132–141.

Short, E. C. (1987). *Curriculum research in retrospect.* Paper presented at the annual convention of the Society for the Study of Curriculum History, Washington, DC.

Short, E. C. (Ed.). (1991). *Forms of curriculum inquiry.* Albany: State University of New York Press.

Silberstein, M., & Ben-Peretz, M. (1979). *The process of curriculum development: Two levels of interpretation.* Paper presented at the annual meeting of the American Educational Research Association, San Francisco.

Skilbeck, M. (1976). School-based curriculum development. In J. Walton & J. Welton (Eds.), *Rational curriculum planning: Four case studies.* London: Ward Lock.

Slattery, P. (1995). *Curriculum development in the postmodern era.* New York: Garland.

Slaughter, S. (1997). Class, race, and gender and the construction of post-secondary curricula in the United States: Social movement, professionalization and political economic theories of curricula change. *Journal of Curriculum Studies, 29*(1), 1–30.

Smith, D. L. (1984). Curriculum theory revisited: A comment and direction. *Curriculum Perspectives, 4*(2), 67–72.

Spivak, G. C. (1985). Strategies of vigilance. *Block, 10*(9), 12–17.

Spivak, G. C. (1993). *Outside in the teaching machine.* New York: Routledge.

St. Maurice, H. (1991). A guide to common places: On the use of loci in educators' discourse. *Journal of Curriculum Studies, 23*(1), 41–53.

Stacey, J. (1999). Gay and lesbian families are here. In S. Coontz (Ed.), *American families: A multicultural reader.* New York: Routledge.

Stenhouse, L. (1975). *An introduction to curriculum research and development,* London, Hienemann Educational.

Sultana, R. G. (1990). Gender, schooling and transformation: Evaluating liberal feminist action in education. *New Zealand Journal of Educational Studies, 25*(1), 13–27.

Sumara, D., & Davis, B. (1999). Interrupting heteronormativity: Toward a queer curriculum theory. *Curriculum Inquiry, 29*(2), 191–206.

Taba, II. (1962). *Curriculum development: Theory and practice.* New York: Harcourt, Brace, & World.

Taba, H. (1966). *Teaching strategies and cognitive functioning in elementary school children.* San Francisco: San Francisco State College.

Taba, H. (1967). *Teachers' handbook for elementary social studies.* Reading, MA: Addison-Wesley.

Tanner, D., & Tanner, L. (1981). Emancipation from research: The reconceptualists' prescription. *Educational Researcher 8*(6), 8–12.

Tanner, D., & Tanner, L. N. (1990). *History of the school curriculum.* New York: Macmillan.

Tanner, D., & Tanner, L. N. (1995). *Curriculum development: Theory into practice* (3rd ed.). New York: Macmillan.

Taylor, W. (1979). Power and the curriculum. In C. Richards (Ed.), *Power and the curriculum: Issues in curriculum studies.* London: Nafferton.

Tripp, D. H. (1984). Life in a tenured (curriculum) position. *Curriculum Perspectives, 4*(2), 59–62.

Tyler, R. W. (1949). *Basic principles of curriculum and instruction.* Chicago: University of Chicago Press.

Tyler, R. W. (1984). Personal reflections of the practical 4. *Curriculum Inquiry, 14*(1), 97–102.

Vallance, E. (1982). The practical uses of curriculum theory. *Theory into Practice, 21*(1), 4–10.

Vallance, E. (1983). The critic's perspective: Some strengths and limitations of aesthetic criticism in education. *Curriculum Perspectives, 3*(2), 23–28.

Vallance, E. (1986). A second look at conflicting conceptions of curriculum. *Theory into Practice, 25*(1), 24–30.

Van Manen, M. (1977). Linking ways of knowing with ways of being practical. *Curriculum Inquiry, 6*(3), 205–228.

Van Manen, M. (1978). Reconceptualist curriculum thought: A review of recent literature. *Curriculum Inquiry, 8*(4), 365–374.

Van Manen, M. (1980). *Pedagogical theorizing.* Paper presented at the annual meeting of the American Educational Research Association, Boston.

Van Manen, M. (1990). *Researching lived experience.* Albany: State University of New York Press.

Van Manen, M. (2000). Moral language and pedagogical experience. *Journal of Curriculum Studies, 32*(2), 315–327.

Villenas, S., & Deyhlc, D. (1999). Critical race theory and ethnographics challenging the stereotypes: Latino families, schooling, resilience and resistance. *Curriculum Inquiry, 29*(4), 416–443.

Waks, L. J. (2000). Reid's theory of curriculum as institutionalized practice. *Journal of Curriculum Studies, 32*(4), 589–598.

Walker, D. F. (1971). A naturalistic model of curriculum development. *School Review, 80*(1), 51–65.

Walker, D. F. (1980). A barnstorming tour of writing on curriculum. In A. W. Foshay (Ed.), *Considered action for curriculum development.* Washington, DC: Association for Supervision and Curriculum Development.

Walker, D. F. (1990). *Fundamentals of curriculum.* New York: Harcourt Brace Jovanovich.

Walker, D. F., & Soltis, J. (1986). *Curriculum and aims.* New York: Teachers College Press.

Watkins, W. H. (1993). Black curriculum orientations: A preliminary inquiry. *Curriculum Inquiry, 63*(3), 321–338.

Wegener, C. (1986). Being practical with Schwab. *Curriculum Inquiry, 16*(2), 215–232.

Westbury, I. (1972). The character of a curriculum for a practical curriculum. *Curriculum Theory Network, 10*(4), 25–36.

Westbury, I. (1999). The burdens and excitement of the "new" curriculum research: A response to Hlebowitsh's "The burdens of the new curricularist". *Curriculum Inquiry, 29*(3), 355–363.

Wheeler, D. K. (1967). *Curriculum process.* London: University of London Press.

Whitty, G. (1980). Ideology, politics, and curriculum. In *Society, education, and the state* (Unit 8). Milton Keynes: Open University.

Willis, G. (Ed.). (1978). *Qualitative evaluation: Concepts and cases in curriculum criticism.* Berkeley, CA: McCutchan.

Willis, G. (1979). Phenomenological methodologies in curriculum. *Journal of Curriculum Theorizing, 1*(1), 65–79.

Willis, G. (1981). A reconceptualist perspective on curriculum theorizing. *Journal of Curriculum Theorizing, 3*(1), 185–192.

Willis, G. (1991). Phenomenological inquiry: Lifeworld perceptions. In E. C. Short (Ed.), *Forms of curriculum inquiry* (pp. 173–186). Albany: State University of New York Press.

Willis, G., & Schubert, W. H. (Eds.). (1991). *Reflections from the heart of educational inquiry: Understanding curriculum and teaching through the arts.* Albany: State University of New York Press.

Willis, G., Schubert, W. H., Bullough, R. V., Kridel, C., & Holton, J. T. (Eds.). (1993). *The American curriculum: A documentary history.* Westport, CT: Greenwood.

Willis, P. V. (1977). *Learning to labour.* London: Saxon House.

Wright, H. K. (2000). Nailing Jell-O to the wall: Pinpointing aspects of state-of-the-art curriculum theorizing. *Educational Researcher 29*(5), 4–13.

Young, M. F. D. (Ed.). (1971). *Knowledge and control.* London: Collier Macmillan.

Young, M. F. D., & Rosiek, J. (2000). Review of white right: Deploying whiteness in America. *Educational Researcher, 29*(2), 39–44.

Zais, R. S. (1976). *Curriculum: Principles and foundations.* New York: Crowell.

Curriculum Development and Change

ABOUT THIS CHAPTER

While many decisions about the curricula enacted in classrooms are made by individual teachers, most decisions that result in beneficial curriculum change at the level of the school or higher are made collectively over an extended period of time and often by a large number of individuals and groups with diverse ideas and diverse levels of expertise. Such change begins with careful planning, and careful planning requires cooperative action by those who may or may not agree.

This chapter examines collective curriculum development, identifying the major individuals and groups who ordinarily participate, considering how they participate, and discussing why and how change occurs in curricula in use in schools.

WHAT YOU SHOULD DO

1. Become familiar with the various individuals and groups who can be involved in curriculum development and why they become involved.
2. Consider how curriculum development includes planning, implementing, evaluating, and revising the curriculum.
3. Understand what is involved in planning and producing curricula for specific sites as well as for more general use.
4. Understand the reasons why schools become involved in curriculum change.
5. Critically appraise some models of curriculum change.
6. Relate the discussions in this chapter to the examples and ideas described in the three previous chapters.

■ SOME OPTIONAL APPROACHES

Depending on the school or school district in which you teach, there are several options available that will help you to make the best use of this chapter.

Option A

1. If you teach in a school or school district in which curriculum development projects have only occasionally been initiated in recent years, reflect upon and list the following:
   - ❑ Who was involved in each project?
   - ❑ What was the scale of the activity?
   - ❑ Have the curricula been implemented in schools?
   - ❑ Have the intended goals been achieved?
   - ❑ What were some problems for the personnel involved?
2. Compare your list with the details given in sections 5.3 and 5.4.
3. Consider how the specifics of your school or school district influenced the extent to which changes to curricula actually occurred. What specifically facilitated or limited change?
4. Read the discussion of change and change models (sections 5.5 and 5.6) and consider how it does or does not apply to your school or school district.

Option B

1. If you teach in a school or school district in which curriculum development projects have frequently been initiated in recent years, reflect upon and list the following:
   - ❑ Who initiated the projects?
   - ❑ What strategies did the initiators use?
   - ❑ Who subsequently became involved?
   - ❑ What were the eventual results of the projects?
   - ❑ Did any of the projects lead to long-term curriculum changes?
2. Compare your list with the details given about change and change models (sections 5.5 and 5.6).
3. How important is identifying the "felt needs" of a school in initiating and carrying out a curriculum development project? Who initiates such projects at your school? How successful have they been? What were some problems?
4. Reread and reconsider the discussions of curriculum development (sections 5.3 and 5.4), applying them to your school or school district.

5.1   INTRODUCTION

This chapter investigates two closely related topics: curriculum development and curriculum change. The two topics are often treated as if they are the same since the idea of development implies change over time and any form of curriculum change can be considered a development of some kind. In practice, however, many curriculum development projects lead to no curriculum changes whatsoever. Some such projects are abandoned; others continue over time, with participants becoming increasingly frustrated by the lack of hoped-for changes or increasingly satisfied with the changes they believe are occurring but in fact are not. Of course, some curriculum changes are not the result of intentional planning. Neither are all changes—planned or unplanned—beneficial.

The phrase *curriculum development* has itself come into widespread use because it encompasses much of the actual complexity involved as schools and school districts make decisions about what their curricula should be. The phrase implies not only that the curriculum ordinarily changes slowly but that beneficial changes can be planned. Furthermore, in modern curriculum development seldom does an authoritative individual or a small group make all decisions that other people, such as teachers, are slavishly bound to follow. Hence, *curriculum development* also now suggests the idea of cooperative planning by any number of interested individuals and groups. However, it may still leave room for the planned curriculum to develop further as it is enacted by individual teachers in their classrooms or experienced by individual students. For instance, our own definition of a curriculum as "an interrelated set of plans and experiences that a student undertakes under the guidance of the school" requires collective and intentional planning but still leaves room for individual variations in practice.

In light of these considerations, curriculum development can be defined as a collective and intentional process or activity directed at beneficial curriculum change. How it takes place is always at issue, for there is no one right way to go about it (as we have suggested in previous chapters of this book), and whether change resulting from intentional curriculum development is or is not beneficial is always an open question.

There are many different approaches to curriculum development and different value orientations that underlie them. Nonetheless, in this chapter, we investigate the general characteristics of curriculum development at both the generic (national, state, or district) level and the site-specific (school or classroom) level, especially considering how collective curriculum development takes place and how it can lead to change. In the first sections of the chapter, we identify some of the major participants and analyze the process of curriculum development. In latter sections of the chapter, we discuss curriculum change and how school personnel may become receptive to innovative curricula, and we introduce and analyze various models of curriculum change.

Still, for curriculum development to result in real change, that change must take place in individual classrooms. Thus, in subsequent chapters, we continue to investigate curriculum development but shift our focus toward the specific, considering the role of school personnel—particularly teachers—in planning curricula (chapter 6) and in translating written curricula into classroom practices (chapter 7). In chapter 8 we examine another characteristic of intentional curriculum development: curriculum evaluation.

5.2   SOME IMPORTANT TERMS

This section defines several important terms in curriculum development.

Curriculum Developers

There is no agreement about what people who make curriculum decisions should be called, and various terms have been used to describe them, such as *curriculum planners, curriculum designers, curriculum improvers,* and *curriculum developers.* The last term has been adopted here because it carries with it the broad implications described in section 5.1, it subsumes some of the other terms, and it is widely used in the literature.

Generally, curriculum developers are persons charged with the responsibility of planning, designing, and producing a curriculum, whether it be in the form of a brief document or an elaborate curriculum package. In their final product, the developers may provide specific guidelines for implementing the written curriculum (with or without having first tried it out in schools) and evaluating the effects on students and teachers. The range of activities of curriculum developers depends, of course, on things such as the scale of the curriculum they are producing, the time available, and the level of funding.

Curriculum Change

Curriculum change is a generic term that subsumes a whole family of concepts such as innovation, development, and adoption. It includes changes that can be either planned or unplanned (unintentional, spontaneous, or accidental). Fullan (1991) maintains teachers participating in a school curriculum development project face four core changes: (1) some form of regrouping or new grouping (restructuring) of the curriculum itself; (2) the use of new curriculum materials; (3) changes in teaching practices (that is, adoption of new activities, skills, or behaviors); and (4) changes in beliefs or understandings of how the curriculum affects learning. Also according to Fullan (2000), for planned curriculum change to be sustained within a school, the school needs to be connected to and nurtured by the external community.

Innovation

The term *innovation* may mean either a new object, idea, or practice or the process by which a new object, idea, or practice comes to be adopted by an individual group or organization. Early studies in the curriculum literature (for example, Havelock, 1969; Rogers & Shoemaker, 1971) tended to view innovations as objects or events, similar to a new piece of machinery for a manufacturer or a new advertising promotion by a retailer. Much more emphasis is now placed on innovation as a process, as evident in the following definition by Henderson (1985): "Innovation process is the planned application of ends or means, new to the adopting educational system, and intended to improve the effectiveness and/or efficiency of the system" (p. 3). This definition, with its emphasis on intention and application, indicates that the process of innovation includes not only an awareness of alternatives but a definite intention to implement one or more alternatives. Many early studies of innovations tended to focus on knowledge, awareness, and decisions about adopting alternatives (Mort, 1953; Rogers, 1962), but few explored the crucial area of implementation to find out how teachers were actually using a curriculum innovation.

Henderson's definition also directs attention to improving the effectiveness of a system. Educators do not always agree with the contention that a change has to be an improvement to qualify as an innovation. Whether an innovation is regarded as an improvement or not depends, of course, on the judgment of whoever makes the decision about adoption, with the judgment usually made in terms of aspirations and past experiences. If an innovation seems different from what existed before, then it may be perceived as likely to bring about improvement. Innovations are not objective and unchanging; they are constantly being changed and redefined as a result of experience (Bolam, 1974). In other words, the initial perception of an innovation by teachers and other individuals or agencies may be that it is new and an improvement on what they were doing, but a final judgment of its worth cannot be made until some later time when they have become fully conversant with the innovation and how it has applied to their situations (Poppleton, 2000).

The inclusion of the idea of improvement within the concept of innovation emphasizes the political nature of curriculum innovations. While other educational terms such as *child development* or *instructional level* tend to be regarded as referring to something intrinsic in the educational process, curriculum innovations are often initiated because certain authorities are not satisfied with what they believe is going on in schools and want to do something different (Scder, 1999). The tremendous explosion in the United States of studies on standards and school effectiveness is a sure sign of the political nature of innovations (Goodlad, 1999).

Diffusion and Dissemination

Diffusion and *dissemination* are two terms crucial to understanding how innovations spread. Rogers (1983) defines diffusion as "the spontaneous, unplanned spread of new ideas" (p. 5). Diffusion, therefore, involves the spread of information and ideas that were previously unfamiliar and that may result in the adoption of an innovation. Groups or individuals who know something about an innovation often seek out further information before making a decision about adoption. The transfer of information is rarely a one-way process. Rogers (1983) was right in his assessment that diffusion typically involves the two-way communication of information. Information about an innovation can, of course, be diffused by different communication channels, from mass media to face-to-face exchange. Both one-way and two-way forms of diffusion are means by which curriculum innovations are spread.

The term *dissemination* is often used synonymously with *diffusion,* but it really has a narrower focus and applies to intentional efforts to inform individuals or groups about an innovation and to gain their interest in it (Coulby, 2000). Emphasis falls on arousing interest in the innovation so that potential clients will adopt it. Some writers (for example, Rosenau, 1973; Zaltman, Florio, & Sikorski, 1977) see dissemination very much like marketing, and they provide detailed guidelines about how a range of tactics such as direct mailings, workshops, visits, or telephone calls can be used in certain situations. They analyze each of these tactics according to criteria such as relative cost, coverage, impact, and user convenience. For other writers (Sarason, 1990; Simpson, 1990), curriculum dissemination is not a matter of attempting to spread the same innovation everywhere. They see dissemination as occurring within a cultural framework. They maintain that change agents need to be aware of a school system's attitudes and administrative structure and should disseminate innovations only where they are well suited to prevailing norms.

5.3   THE CURRICULUM CONTINUUM

One way of depicting the process of curriculum development that incorporates many of the ideas and terms we have discussed is as a continuum, as shown in Figure 5.1.

Pressures for change and incentives to try out innovative practices might emanate from local perceptions (for example, the perceived need to improve student achievement in mathematics) or from newly proposed models (for example, a curriculum emphasizing vocational skills). The planning and development of a new curriculum, depending on the scale of the activity, might then occur over a period of a few months or extend over several years. Once the new curriculum package has been developed, the developers might next attempt to disseminate it directly to individual schools and teachers, although some schools might already have learned of the innovation indirectly, through diffusion. Evaluation studies might be used to provide evidence of the desirability of the curriculum and to further the likelihood of its adoption. Once a school has made a decision to adopt an innovative curriculum, actually implementing it can be extremely complicated, often taking a matter of years and requiring the support of external agencies as well as the persistence of those teachers acting as implementers. If these efforts continue successfully over a sufficient period of time, however, then the innovation will be translated from a planned curriculum to an enacted curriculum, hence becoming a permanent part of the total offerings of the school. Fullan (2000) estimates that the entire process of implementation takes about three years for an elementary school and about six years for a secondary school.

Figure 5.1 is based on the premise that the development of the innovative curriculum is undertaken by a team external to the school that eventually adopts and institutionalizes it. If the new curriculum is a local, school-based endeavor, then the activities of dissemination, evaluation, and implementation merge into a single, ongoing process of development.

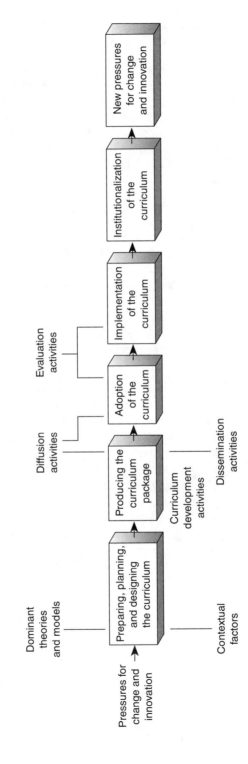

FIGURE 5.1
The curriculum continuum

161

5.4   CURRICULUM DEVELOPMENT AS A PLANNED ACTIVITY

For some schools or school districts, specific individuals and groups are charged with the responsibility of curriculum development (Young, 1990). Individuals such as the district superintendent, principals, and teachers may compose a district curriculum committee. How much each of these persons actually becomes active in making curriculum decisions for a school or district often depends on the scale of curriculum development undertaken (Watson, Fullan, & Kilcher, 2000).

Ideally, teams undertaking curriculum development should have members with expertise in six areas:

- *Subject matter.* Persons must know the substance of a particular discipline, its philosophy, and its limitations.
- *Pedagogy.* Persons must be skilled teachers and knowledgeable about students, the school environment, and the teaching process.
- *Curriculum design.* Persons must have skills in searching out needs, organizing purposes, and combining learning experiences in meaningful ways.
- *Evaluation.* Persons must be able to clearly identify and to appropriately weigh the value of ongoing activities as well as the overall impact of a package.
- *Organization.* Persons must have organizational and entrepreneurial skills.
- *Writing.* Persons must have skills in writing documents with clarity and conviction.

Ornstein and Hunkins (1993) and Senge, Cambron-McCabe, Lucas, Smith, Dutton, and Kleiner (2000) emphasize the need for curriculum development to be a cooperative activity, and, consequently, they are concerned about different groups (such as teachers, teacher organizations, students, parents, scholar-experts, and other professional educators) being adequately represented. Downs (2000) refers to schools as professional learning communities in which the collective capacity contributes to the growth of the school as a whole.

Who participates in actual curriculum development often depends on the attitudes and values that schools, districts, or states hold. Some states and school districts place minimal emphasis on the involvement of students and parents in curriculum development, and even the involvement of teachers is insignificant. In contrast, other states and school districts welcome the participation of students, parents, and other citizens alongside that of professional educators (King & Newmann, 2000).

Levels of Curriculum Development

Five levels at which curriculum development takes place can be readily identified:

1. At the national level, curriculum development is undertaken by teams, the composition of which may vary but which usually include both subject specialists and experts in curriculum design. Teachers may also be active members of these teams or be observers who provide advice at times. In the United States during the 1960s

and 1970s, many national teams funded by Title III grants produced innovative curricula in a wide variety of academic areas but particularly in mathematics, the sciences (physics, chemistry, biology), and the social sciences (history, geography, economics, political science, anthropology). In the 1990s, emphasis shifted to the development of uniform national standards for a variety of subjects (Resnick, Nolan, & Resnick, 1996).

2. At the state level, there was little interest in systematic curriculum development until the mid-1980s. As noted by Kirst (1987), previous state priorities were directed toward the setting of minimum standards and the financing of categorical programs. By the early 1990s, however, the focus of many states (led in particular by California) had shifted toward developing statewide curricular frameworks and aligning them with textbooks, testing, and accreditation (Holdzkom, 1992; Steffy, 1993). These efforts were accompanied by a rapid increase in states legislating curriculum standards, so that by the 2000s most states had some such standards in place. The vast majority of states have also linked these standards with formal assessments of schools, putting pressure on school districts to emphasize and to standardize curricular content, perhaps at the expense of other concerns such as multicultural education (Bohn & Sleeter, 2000). (For a discussion of these developments, see chapter 9.)

3. At the school district level, curriculum development projects have been conducted since the nineteenth century, but their frequency, range, and magnitude vary enormously. Major curriculum revision is continuously ongoing in some districts and is unheard of in others. In still others, it is limited by district budgets and competing priorities. Typical district curriculum development projects undertaken by teacher committees include writing the rationale and objectives for revised curricula or evaluating textbooks and related commercial materials. Curriculum revision and review seem to be more common than activities directed toward the development of new curricula.

4. At the school level, teachers often work cooperatively in deciding how to coordinate subject matter, both within academic areas (such as mathematics, reading, music, and art) and among years or grade levels (Fisher, Sax, & Grove, 2000). District curricula may provide numerous examples, guidelines, or constraints, or teachers in a particular school may collectively make most curriculum decisions for themselves.

5. At the classroom level, individual teachers may be relatively free to make numerous curricular decisions, both about what they teach and how they teach it. It is here that the planned curriculum becomes both the enacted curriculum and the experienced curriculum, of course. Though officially restricted by state laws and school district policies concerning what must be taught and what cannot be taught, almost all teachers can make enough curriculum decisions to give what they teach its own distinctive texture (Linne, 2001; Marzano, Pickering, & Pollock, 2001). For instance, usually classroom teachers, regardless of the subjects they are teaching, make those decisions that bring the three curricular focal points of subject matter, society, and the individual into the balance that they think most appropriate for their own students.

Examples of Curriculum Development at the National Level. Although the enacted curriculum and the experienced curriculum take place in the classroom, the planned curriculum may, of course, be planned at any or all levels: national, state, school district, school, and classroom. But since the 1990s in the United States and also in other countries, most curriculum reform projects of high visibility have been focused at the national level. The two examples that follow illustrate some of the political priorities and value orientations of their developers.

EXAMPLE 1: NATIONAL GOALS AND STANDARDS IN THE UNITED STATES

In the United States, various national groups have been involved in developing curriculum standards for academic subjects. For example, the National Council of Teachers of Mathematics (NCTM) organized four working groups comprised of teachers, supervisors, mathematics educators, and mathematicians to create standards for curricula for grades K–4, 5–8, and 9–12, including suggestions about how these curricula should be evaluated. NCTM widely distributed drafts of these standards to teachers, mathematicians, parents, and business leaders in an attempt to ensure rigorous and scholarly review of them and broad support for them. Additionally, NCTM used still other working groups to develop accompanying professional standards for teaching. An initial report by Romberg (1993) suggested that these standards for mathematics curricula were well received; a number of states, such as California and Texas, produced curriculum frameworks based on them. However, more recently they have proved controversial as local districts have attempted to develop specific materials and resources consistent with them for use in their own schools. Such efforts to create top-down national uniformity that are then followed by a mixed reception at the local level are reminiscent of the curriculum reform movement of the late 1950s and the 1960s (discussed in chapter 2).

In fact, many recent national curriculum projects in the United States, such as that of the NCTM, have been undertaken under the influence of the federal goal-setting initiative titled *America 2000* (U.S. Department of Education, 1991; discussed in chapter 9) and have involved a substantial commitment from political leaders, professional associations, and project teams around the nation (Cornbleth, 1996). Although highly political in origin and impact, most such projects have included substantial collaborative efforts between federal, state, and local agencies in developing curriculum standards in various subject matter areas. The personnel involved have been predominantly subject specialists and assessment experts, and federal funding has been provided for a National Education Standards and Improvement Council and for a National Skills Standards Board. Since the general educational goals of *America 2000* have been closely linked with efforts to establish national curriculum standards, such curriculum projects are more accurately seen as national rather than local (Resnick et al., 1995, 1996).

Although national educational goals and national curriculum standards have received wide publicity in the United States and bipartisan political support, the initial enthusiasm of most citizens seems to wane upon careful consideration of what such goals and standards actually mean for local schools. Goodlad (1999) describes the publicity as a "drumbeat for hard and rough standards rising to a crescendo" (p. 572), but the standards movement itself as a rain dance repeated again and again to distract citizens from "the paucity of promised outcomes" (p. 572). Labaree (2000) explains that although the current push for uniform standards is strong, Americans have in the past always vigorously resisted them because of three traditional commitments:

- To preserving local control of schools (standards being seen as "an infringement of individual liberty," p. 29)
- To expanding access to schooling rather than improving the quality of learning
- To using long-term markers of success (for example, acquiring a specific number of Carnegie Units, which represent time spent in class, to determine entry into college) rather than short-term measures of specific learnings

Other scholars are also critical of the use of standards. Orlich (2000) contends that they "are politically inspired and coerced by state governments" (p. 469) despite developmental limits on what some students may be able to learn. Sirotnik and Kimball (1999) contend that uniform standards must be used only with extreme caution in assessing schools, for such assessment must not be driven by a single indicator or simplistic formulas and each school must be seen in terms of its own context as well as in comparison to other schools. Selden, as reported in O'Neil (1995), argues that any attempt to link national standards with a national high-stakes, student exam system is unlikely to succeed. Hargreaves, Earl, Moore, and Manning (2001) question the use of uniform standards this way: "How is it possible to meet the ambitions of standards-based reform without getting down in its frequent, practical problems of overstandardization, underresourcing, deprofessionalization, and curricular narrowness?" (p. 9).

Given these difficulties with uniform curricula and standards, there seems to be little likelihood that the United States will develop a national curriculum short of all state governments mandating precisely the same things for all schools. Thus, standards-based curriculum documents may continue to be used in the future as many curriculum documents are used today, as resources selected or rejected by individual districts, schools, and teachers.

EXAMPLE 2: TECHNOLOGY AS A SCHOOL SUBJECT IN THE UNITED KINGDOM, AUSTRALIA, AND NEW ZEALAND

In the 1980s and 1990s, efforts in the United Kingdom, Australia, and New Zealand (countries with far more centrally controlled educational systems than the United States) to introduce a new school subject under the name "technology" provide another illustration of curriculum development at the national level. The introduction of new subjects into the school curriculum is always difficult for many reasons: there may be no recognized content, concepts, or techniques; there may be no corresponding university subjects or community of academic scholars; and interest groups of teachers may hold diverse values or have conflicting priorities. As the new and immature subject fights for a place with numerous established school subjects, there are many problems in defining what it is, in implementing it, and in finding appropriately qualified teachers. As a result, curriculum development activities intended to standardize a new subject almost always require political initiatives at the national level (Griffith, 2000).

In the United Kingdom, Australia, and New Zealand, arguments ran that technology epitomizes the need to prepare students for the twenty-first century—to ensure that the present generation of young students is not "technologically disadvantaged because of the limitations in their schooling experiences" (Morrow, 1994, p. 8). As noted by Medway (1992), technology as a new school subject invented by curriculum designers brings together "a set of activities which in the 'real world' are found to be widely scattered across a diverse spread of occupations and functions" (p. 79). Johnson (1989) identified technology as including the following set of technological areas to be studied in schools: materials, energy, manufacturing, agriculture and food, biotechnology and medical technology, environment, communications, electronics, computers, transportation, and space. According to McCormick (1990), the value of technology is not identical to the value of any other school subject since technology is the following:

- *Wide-ranging.* It is found in areas of human activity associated with, for example, food, health, energy, and work.
- *Multidimensional.* Problems and their solutions must be developed and judged according to a variety of criteria, including economic, social, and environmental considerations as well as technical criteria.
- *Integrative.* It demands a variety of kinds of knowledge, understanding, and skills that must be integrated when dealing with a problem. It is not sufficient to look at problems from the point of view of one discipline.
- *Value-judgmental.* Careful weighing of alternatives needs to be exercised in all technological activity.
- *Human-related.* The problems technologists tackle serve both to create and to satisfy human needs and wants.
- *Process-centered.* Processes central to technology include designing, creating systems, modeling, decision making, planning, producing, and manufacturing.
- *Concept-particular.* Technology introduces students to basic concepts such as control, quality, and information in ways unique to it and not to other subjects.

Based on such ideas promulgated from many sources, but especially the national government, the technology foundation subject eventually included in the National Curriculum in the United Kingdom comprises four major concepts:

- Developing and using systems
- Working with materials
- Developing and communicating ideas
- Satisfying human needs

It includes standard assessment tasks (SATs) and attainment targets intended to provide teachers with guidelines for learning activities, but in actuality, the targets are of little help to teachers in selecting specific curriculum content. Thus, even this nationally directed curriculum leaves teachers some room to select the enacted curriculum of their own classrooms.

In contrast, in the decentralized system of the United States, similar attention to including technological subjects in the school curriculum has necessarily remained far more diffuse. Nonetheless, in some districts magnet schools focused on science, technology, and mathematics have been created and have been able to recruit extremely able students (Manno, Finn, & Vanourek, 2000). In the best of these schools, facilities are typically comprehensive and well resourced due to major financial inputs by business and industry, not by the federal government (Gresham, Hess, Maranto, & Milliman, 2000). Interestingly, curricula tend to be similar since most learning activities are based on an engineering model that is high level but narrowly focused on applied science.

Activities of Curriculum Developers

It is worth reflecting on the major goals that curriculum developers might have in mind as they go about their tasks. These goals can be related to three broad kinds of activities, which Skilbeck (1982) describes as (1) activities that are designed to maintain and reinforce existing syllabi, resources, and practices; (2) activities that are designed to produce innovative curricula and concrete experimentation; and (3) activities that are predominantly speculative and "think-tank" approaches to possible future curricula.

The first kind of activities—those designed to maintain existing practices—involves developers making only minor modifications to an existing curriculum, perhaps because the curriculum has been found satisfactory and merely needs updating or perhaps because time constraints or the political climate are such that nothing more than slow, gradual change is likely to succeed. The third kind of activities—the speculative ones—involves developers in creative, lateral thinking, speculating on how and in what combination different learning activities might be organized. Very few, if any, actual curricula would be developed by speculative activities since they are directed toward conceptualizing new approaches to be applied in the future.

In contrast, the second kind of activities—ones promoting innovative curricula and concrete experimentation—covers the middle ground of innovation and change: new and different curricula are conceptualized, and actual concrete programs are produced, tried out, and made available for use in schools. As an example of this middle ground, Eisner (1990) argues that creative curriculum development takes place when teachers interact with curriculum materials in ways that amplify their own thinking skills and build on the individual interests and aptitudes of their students.

Some authors, such as Apple (1990), argue that little change comes out of most curriculum development activities. He asserts that typical activities simply secure compliance to elite agendas—a practice of conveying legitimate knowledge. In other words, although most such activities give the appearance of thoughtful reappraisal of existing values and practices, they actually reiterate them, thereby in effect contributing to their continuing unexamined acceptance. Kirst and Meister (1985) observe that few educational reforms involving curriculum development continue for more than a few years and that American secondary schools have remained remarkably stable. When supposedly innovative curricula are carefully examined, they usually seem little more than old curricula in new forms.

Since curriculum development varies tremendously in purpose, scope, and time, any list of basic activities undertaken by developers must be general. The following list applies primarily to large-scale curriculum development, but similar activities can be found in smaller projects:

- Determining what types of new curricula are needed
- Formulating purposes and goals of the curriculum development activity (and, in so doing, disagreeing about particular goals and emphases)
- Using research results on learning and psychological development to guide activities designed for students
- Accomplishing the work through coordinated, cooperative group actions
- Assessing market demands and implementation needs
- Supplying trial teachers with requisite understandings of the new material and providing training where needed
- Considering ways of evaluating curricula
- Arguing for prolonged development-revision cycles and continued funding

Usually underlying these activities are the intentions of developers to work together to produce a viable curriculum and their understanding that to do so they must find out what needs to be done and how it can be done. Then, one might ask, how do developers come to agree upon what is to be done? Or do they? The well-known fact is that the single activity that curriculum developers spend the most time on is arguing, since rarely do they agree entirely on purposes or directions, let alone procedures. The explanation for this state of affairs is that different positions cannot be understood until they have been clearly enunciated, explored, and subjected to criticisms. Then and only then can informed consensus be reached. What appears to be inefficiency in curriculum development is, therefore, actually another— and perhaps the most basic—task that needs to be undertaken: deliberation (Reid, 1999). Time spent debating, defending, and advocating particular points of view is not time wasted if it leads in the long run to beneficial change. Anyone contemplating involvement in curriculum development should be apprised of this fact. As Eisner (1975) commented in reference to his involvement as a curriculum developer in the Kettering Art Project, "It is paradoxical that 'inefficiency' in group deliberation can be more efficient than efficiency" (p. 37).

Expertise and Control of Curriculum Development

Another controversial question is whether curriculum development should be the province of specialists and experts or of classroom teachers. Seemingly a combination of specialists and practitioners is desirable; but without sufficient funding to release teachers from their normal workloads, many curriculum development projects have been dominated by specialists and experts.

Virtually all national and state curriculum development projects involve specialists of some kind, whether they are academics, administrators, or technical experts. They are typically persons who have a wealth of experience in education and usually have senior status in an educational system or institution. Although these individuals might bring considerable experience and ample qualifications to the tasks of curriculum development, the question still remains: Should they be given control? Hayes (1977) sees curriculum development as a moral enterprise in that developers make choices among activities according to some criteria of goodness. Should they have the power to make these choices, or should these choices be made by a broader spectrum of people? Carson (1984) also asks who should have control over curriculum development. He concedes that there may be political reasons for experts to have this control, but he argues that control should be in the hands of classroom teachers.

Rogers and Shoemaker (1971) argue that specialists tend to be members of superordinate groups. In their view, specialists have access to a range of knowledge and information that is not available to others; therefore, they are likely to use their own kind of specialized knowledge to emphasize particular approaches to curriculum development. Specialists can be expected to use their authority, their formal positions in educational institutions, and their specialized knowledge in this way simply because they have the power and the backing of a superordinate group. For all these reasons, they tend to gain political control of the process of curriculum development. The views of the superordinate group may then dominate decisions about the curricula developed, and these decisions are passed on to the subordinate group, the teachers, who are charged with the responsibility of implementing the curricula. For example, the Tyler rationale (see chapter 3) gives a prominent place to learning theorists in curriculum development, but are the decisions made by such theorists actually more likely—or even as likely—to lead to good and appropriate curricula than are the decisions of teachers who have an intuitive feel for what works well in their own classrooms and with their own students?

The alternative to the specialist is, therefore, the classroom practitioner. According to Paris (1990), only classroom teachers have sufficient competence to be curriculum developers since they understand the structure of schooling and have had that understanding refined by direct experience. Feiler, Heritage, and Gallimore (2000) contend that teacher-leaders in a school can be ideal for undertaking this role. Fullan and Hargreaves (1991) argue that teachers who are constructively critical of society and existing school practices negotiate what the curriculum will be with other interested parties such as students and the community. However, there is also the matter of availability of funds to allow classroom teachers to participate in curriculum development. Even when a district prefers homegrown curricula, the typical school board may remain reluctant to pay for their development (Odden, 2000).

There are no easy answers to all such questions or easy resolutions to the issues they raise. In general, evidence from the United States suggests that curriculum development at the national and state levels is dominated by specialists, and at the district, school, and classroom levels, teachers play a prominent role. Even so, the degree of specialization of those engaged in curriculum planning varies considerably. Specialists may include full-time academics and professional consultants, state and school district officials who have extensive experience in curriculum and who are engaged in the projects on a full-time or a part-time basis, and teachers who have undertaken academic studies in curriculum and are working on specific projects for limited periods.

Site of Activities

For purposes of discussion, it is useful to distinguish between large-scale curriculum development and small-scale, teacher-level curriculum development. Walker (1990) proposes the use of the terms *generic* and *site-specific* to represent this simple dichotomy. Thus, large-scale curriculum projects, which reached their zenith in the United States in the 1970s and reappeared in the late 1990s as national standards projects, might be termed generic because their locus is the nation, region, or state. Such projects can usually be identified by four general characteristics:

1. They are undertaken by large teams of curriculum workers, who are often hired because of their specific expertise and who are engaged in full-time work on a project for several years.
2. They make extensive use of surveys and questionnaires to assess what needs to be done.
3. Their development activities are assigned to teams of specialists, and the products of these activities are regularly and systematically reviewed and piloted.
4. They use elaborate procedures to communicate information, to advertise the availability of their products, and to train potential users; final products are made available to schools by the developing agencies or are published by commercial publishers.

In contrast, curriculum development activities that are confined to a single school or, in some cases, to a single school district might be called local, or site-specific. Site-specific curriculum development projects can usually be identified by these four characteristics:

1. They are undertaken by a small group of teachers, almost always working on the project part time.
2. Their assessments of what needs to be done are brief and informal.
3. Their activities tend to focus on the production of materials.
4. They may use generic materials as guides, sometimes even incorporating such materials into their final products.

Generic and site-specific curriculum development can be considered extreme opposites. Of course, between these two extremes fall many projects that blend the characteristics of both extremes in various ways (see, for example, Fox, 1992; Marsh & Bowman, 1987; Watson et al., 2000). In general, generic approaches, which minimize teacher involvement and which concentrate on the production of standard packages, appear not to have been very successful, based on the low adoption rates of national project materials produced in the 1960s and 1970s in the United States. It is too early yet to judge the adoption rates of the 2000s for projects based on national standards, such as those by the National Council of Teachers of Mathematics (see, for example, Crawford & Witte, 1999), and the National Association for Sports and Physical Education (see Lambert, 2000).

Other research studies (for example, Louis & Kruse, 1995; Newmann & Wehlage, 1995) reveal that projects that utilize the collaborative work of teachers have a high rate of success. Yet other studies, such as those associated with the Study of Dissemination Efforts Supporting School Improvement (DESSI), have noted that many centrally developed curricula were adopted by schools and implemented very faithfully.

Huberman and Crandall (1982) argue that the source of a curriculum development product is quickly blurred and that the ideal of a democratic, locally controlled and adopted project is a caricature of what usually happens, for almost always centralized controls emerge. Of more importance, they believe, is who manages and "owns" the process of implementation. Walker (1990) has also noted circumstances under which site-specific curriculum development projects meet with limited success. He suggests that site-specific activities often ignore important problems or needs because powerful lobby groups force a project to take certain directions and not others. Further, site-specific developers are often overly ambitious in their expectations of what they can accomplish and the time required. Modified site-specific approaches, which combine some generic characteristics (such as the use of consultants to assist with subject area problems), usually have a higher degree of success (Rogers & Babinski, 1999; Wasley, 1999).

Use of Products

Although some curriculum development activities lead only to statements of policy, most result in the production of specific, concrete curriculum packages. The question then becomes, What happens to these products?

Curriculum developers may hold very different views about how their products should be used. Curriculum packages that include texts and student workbooks as well as detailed teacher guides indicate that the developers have some very definite intentions for use. Such intentions may result from the scale of the project since curriculum projects that are amply funded tend to be the most prescriptive about how their products should be used. However, there are many exceptions. How prescriptive a project is about the use of its products is probably more closely related to the underlying value orientations of the developers. There are curriculum projects that are not prescriptive and in which the developers encourage users to adapt materials in new ways. In fact, they may discourage rigorous conformity by not providing specific details on how the materials should be used in classrooms. Issues concerning the adaptation and use of curriculum materials will be discussed in detail in chapter 6, which examines the process of curriculum implementation.

Typology

Various typologies of curriculum development occur in the literature. We have already made mention of the generic and site-specific categories advocated by Walker (1978, 1990). Walker's categories do not constitute a full typology in themselves, but Short (1983) incorporates them (along with the other basic categories we have just discussed, using slightly different names) into a full typology, which delineates the combinations of salient characteristics a curriculum development project can have:

1. Expertise required:
   - Scholar-dominated group
   - Curriculum specialist-dominated group
   - Milieus expert-dominated group
   - Balance-coordinated group
2. Seat of curriculum development:
   - Externally based (generic)
   - User based (site-specific)
3. Conceptions of use-setting realities:
   - Implementation as directed
   - Limited adaptation
   - Open adaptation

Placed in a three-dimensional matrix, as depicted in Figure 5.2, these categories represent twenty-four different combinations. Short (1983) contends that the most common combinations are the following:

Scholar-dominated/generic/implementation as directed (type I)
Milieus expert-dominated/generic/limited adaptation (type II)
Balance-coordinated pattern/site-specific/open adaptation (type III)

He asserts that types I and II have many deficiencies and that type III is the most desirable as long as the school personnel and other participants within it have access to outside resources (scholars, materials, finance). This assertion is, of course, consistent with the general direction of the research studies on curriculum development to which we have previously referred.

5.5 THE PROCESS OF EDUCATIONAL CHANGE

The discussion in the preceding section described some of the activities that can occur if a group decides that a new curriculum is needed and if the group has the resources and the determination to create it. However, most of the discussion has been based on the assumption that the personnel of a school want to change the old curriculum. This assumption is not always true. Often teachers wish to continue doing what they have been doing—sometimes for good reasons and sometimes for bad. In fact, teachers are in a key position to reject a new curriculum, whether through indifference, ignorance, fear, or a well-warranted belief that the new curriculum will prove inferior to the old one (Poppleton, 2000).

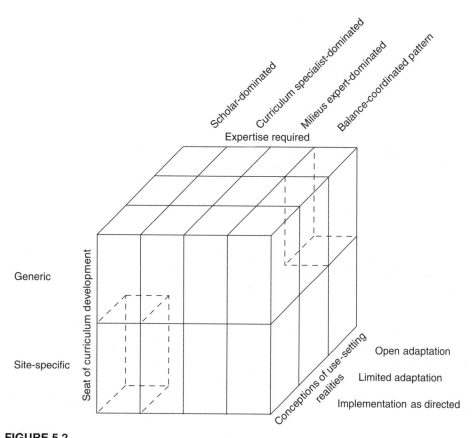

FIGURE 5.2
Matrix for identifying curriculum development strategies
Source: After Short (1983).

It is one thing to plan and then create a new curriculum, another thing to have that curriculum formally adopted by a school, and still another thing to see that curriculum actually come into widespread use. Building support for a new curriculum is often a sensitive matter. There is no reason to suppose that teachers should enthusiastically embrace a curriculum that has been decided for them by others (Farrell, 2000; Soder, 1999). Neither can it be assumed that, because a curriculum is new and has been extensively tested, it will still meet the needs of a specific school considering its adoption. Sometimes a new innovation should be rejected; at other times, its acceptance requires the efforts of people especially adept at facilitating change. Such people have become known as "change agents."

Research extending back to the 1940s has provided information about the evolutionary development of the concept of change agents. In studies in the 1940s, Lewin defined change agents as professionals who by their leadership and participation bring about change, and he analyzed their role in unfreezing and moving existing situations to enable innovations to be adopted and continued (refreezing). During the 1960s, Rogers and Shoemaker (1971) reviewed several hundred studies

FIGURE 5.3

Percentage of people in each category of adoption

Source: After Rogers (1983).

Innovators	2.5%
Early adopters	13.5%
Early majority	34.0%
Late majority	34.0%
Laggards	16.0%

concentrating on how innovations are adopted within an organization. They hypothesized that members of any organization can be categorized according to their degree of innovativeness as "innovators," "early adopters," "early majority," "late majority," or "laggards." Figure 5.3 lists Rogers's (1983) estimates of the percentage of people who fall within each of these categories.

During the 1970s and 1980s, attention turned to how individual educators promote change within particular contexts. A number of studies focused on how classroom teachers promote and react to change. Hall, Loucks, Rutherford, and Newlove (1975) and Leithwood and Montgomery (1982) developed a set of stages to explain how classroom teachers adjust to innovation over time and how their behaviors, in turn, influence other teachers. Huberman and Crandall (1982), Feld (1981), and Larkin (1984) conducted studies on superintendents and central office administrators as change agents. More recently there has been a surge of interest in how school principals can provide encouragement and incentives for curriculum change (Evans & Mohr, 1999; Fullan, 1988; Griffin, 1990; Heller & Firestone, 1994). There has also been considerable interest in studying the effectiveness of external experts who can provide on-site support for teachers and facilitate their efforts to implement new curricula (Goodman, 1994; Miles, Saxl, & Lieberman, 1988).

Attributes of an Innovation

The extent to which an innovation is favorably received depends both on the communication among participants and on the specific attributes of the innovation. Rogers and Shoemaker (1971) identify six attributes that in studies of adoption and implementation consistently stood out as most important:

1. *Relative advantage:* the degree to which an innovation is perceived to be better than the idea it supersedes
2. *Status:* the importance attached to a subject or program
3. *Relative reward:* the strength of the reward if the innovation is used
4. *Compatibility:* the degree to which an innovation is perceived as being consistent with existing values and practices
5. *Complexity:* the degree to which an innovation is perceived as relatively difficult to understand and use
6. *Triability:* the degree to which an innovation may be experimented with on a limited basis

Fullan and Pomfret (1977) suggest that explicitness and complexity are the two attributes that most greatly influence successful implementation. Drawing upon various research studies, they argue that an innovation is likely to be successful when it has clear specifications from the outset or when it incorporates procedures whereby developers and users cooperatively define specifications. In contrast, innovations that are very complex (for example, requiring new and difficult skills) tend to be less successful. However, other studies indicate that complexity can be a positive attribute. For example, Clark, Lotto, and Astuto (1984) conclude that innovations that are perceived to be complex may in fact have relative advantages because potential adopters see worthwhile change as requiring extra effort and are less inclined to be bothered with innovations that involve only trivial changes.

Contexts of Innovations

Schools in which curricular innovations can be successfully implemented vary enormously in terms of the interests and expertise of their staffs, their organizational structures, and their resources (Feiler et al., 2000; Fullan, 1991; Wideen, 1994). Each staff is unique, having its own informal and formal values and norms and its own leaders. Each school also has its own organizational climate. Students, too, represent a specific mix according to their socioeconomic status and the values, beliefs, and norms that they hold. Then, too, the local community can influence or be influenced by the school. Parents and community groups may make known their own ideas about the type of curriculum they want taught in the school. Conversely, teachers may try to influence students' attitudes on these issues and, indirectly, their parents' attitudes. Conflicting points of view represented by the numerous "cultures" of a school (parents, students, teachers, administrators) often result in tensions on particular curriculum issues.

Because of these differences, it is not possible to predict how participants at a specific school will react to a proposal to implement a curriculum innovation. Readiness for change is clearly of major importance, but readiness is influenced by numerous things, such as advocacy and support by the central administration; access to information; teachers' beliefs and expectations; community pressure, support, opposition, or apathy; availability of external funds; and new legislation or policy (Caldwell, 1993). Because of the complexity of any school and the complexity of the context in which it exists, each situation must be regarded as a unique and organic whole presenting new opportunities and new challenges (Williams & Williams, 1994). Any kind of educational innovation, including curriculum change, is never a simple matter. Just because one school has adopted a new curriculum does not mean that another school will do so or should do so. Curriculum change, therefore, is not simply a matter of replicating in a new situation a series of events or procedures that have proved successful in a previous situation. However, similar situations may appear on the surface.

5.6   CHANGE MODELS

All models of curriculum change posit similarities between situations and are necessarily general to some degree; therefore, they run the risk of taking an overly simple or even mechanistic approach to the process of developing a curriculum. Still, they are worthy of study because of the insights they can provide into why different approaches to curriculum planning and development run the gamut from highly successful to dismal failure. All such models attempt to elucidate what takes place during the process of curriculum development, but some are more flexible than others. For instance, all to one degree or another treat the curriculum as the planned curriculum, but some are sensitive to the enacted curriculum as well. Change models also provide descriptions of some basic educational structures, and some models, in fact, account broadly for the overall character of specific situations, including the climate of a particular school and the social context in which the school exists.

Some of the models we examine in this section attempt to describe the process of curriculum change (for example, the Center-Periphery Model). Others attempt to explain how the process of curriculum change works (for example, the Negotiation Model). The models we examine can be grouped under two headings: those that treat change as emanating primarily from influences external to the school and those that treat change as primarily emanating from within the school. In general, models in the former group refer to the planned curriculum only, whereas some models in the latter group are sensitive to the enacted curriculum. Each of these two groups can be divided into several subgroups, as shown in Figure 5.4.

External to the School		
Organizational change	*Diffusion of knowledge*	*Interactive*
Research, Development, and Diffusion (Clark & Guba, 1965)	Center-Periphery Model (Schon, 1971)	Negotiation Model (MacDonald & Walker, 1976)
Internal to the School		
Organizational change	*Interactive*	*Individual*
Proactive/Interactive Change Model (Zaltman et al., 1977)	Problem Solving (Lippitt et al., 1958)	CBAM Models Levels of Use (Hall et al., 1975)
Growth-System-Action Model (Leithwood & Montgomery, 1982)	Action Research (Elliott, 1980)	
Organizational Development Model (Schmuck & Runkel, 1972)	Conflict Model (Schelling, 1963)	

FIGURE 5.4
Change models relating to curriculum

Models External to the School

In this section, several important external models are described.

1. The RD&D (Research, Development, and Diffusion) Model was first proposed by Clark and Guba (1965) and later, in similar forms, by numerous other writers, such as Havelock (1971). It has become the classical model for large-scale curriculum development projects. The RD&D Model assumes that changing the curriculum is an orderly, planned sequence in which experts assist in identifying a problem, finding a solution, and then diffusing (or, more accurately in many cases, disseminating) that solution. The new curriculum, like a high-performance product, is planned, carefully designed and tested, and may be widely adopted, both nationally and internationally. Comprehensive surveys of potential users may be undertaken prior to the development of the curricular products. Hence, emphasis in this model falls on producing a uniform, high-quality innovation rather than on accommodating the interests and wishes of individual teachers or the characteristics of particular schools in which the innovation might be used. Figure 5.5 delineates the basic steps in the RD&D Model.

Although the RD&D Model has been widely used, it has been strongly criticized. House (1979) argues that the model overemphasizes technology and is unable to transform schools. Similarly, Fullan (1991) criticizes it for underestimating the innovative capacities of individual teachers and schools and for ignoring the micropolitical features of schools. Carter and O'Neill (1995) object to the userproof and passive consumer emphases of the RD&D Model and note that it concentrates almost entirely on the development and diffusion of standard products with little emphasis on helping users implement the innovation that has been delivered to them. These criticisms are sound, and there is no doubt that this model—however accurately it may portray the basic steps of large-scale projects—offers little help to teachers and other school personnel struggling to understand the realities of curriculum development at the school level.

2. The CP (Center-Periphery) Model was developed by Schon (1971). It is similar to the RD&D Model, but it emphasizes diffusion more than the development of standardized curriculum products. It, too, has been widely advocated by other

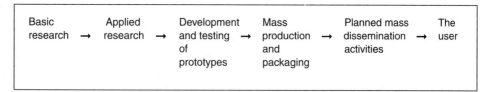

FIGURE 5.5
Research, Development, and Diffusion Model
Source: After Havelock (1971).

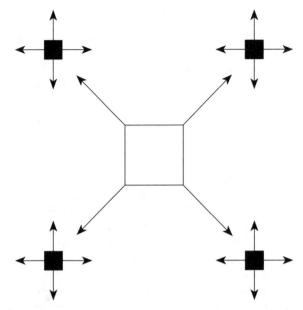

FIGURE 5.6
The Proliferation of Centers Model
Source: After Schon (1971).

writers. Schon's particular variation of the CP Model, the Proliferation of Centers Model, is diagrammed in Figure 5.6.

It incorporates two assumptions basic to the RD&D Model (the innovation must be produced prior to its diffusion, and diffusion is a centrally managed process). However, it overcomes some of the weaknesses of the RD&D Model by including both a primary center and secondary centers from which diffusion takes place. Whereas the primary center develops the curricular products, the secondary centers communicate directly with schools about these products and how they can be used. The secondary centers are managed by the primary center but serve to decentralize and broaden diffusion, and—sometimes—to destandardize the curricular products to make them appropriate for adoption by specific schools. The primary center usually selects the territories into which secondary centers will expand, trains the agents of diffusion, and monitors the decentralized operations of the secondary centers. This model emphasizes the importance of diffusion in curriculum change, directing the flow of change from central to peripheral areas. This emphasis is so strong that, in actuality, the model blurs the line between unintentional diffusion and intentional dissemination.

The CP Model, and especially Schon's Proliferation of Centers version, is an adequate description of the primary centers (the National Foundation for Educational Research, school boards, and project teams) and the secondary centers (local teachers centers) that have created some curriculum change in the United Kingdom. Barrow's (1984) and Nicholl's (1982) studies of the dissemination activities of eighty-two school council projects in the United Knigdom indicated that many of the successful project

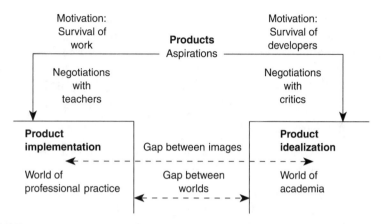

FIGURE 5.7
The Negotiation Model
Source: After MacDonald & Walker (1976).

teams developed links with secondary centers such as Local Educational Authorities (LEAs), Her Majesty's Inspectors (HMI), colleges, and teachers centers.

However, despite the reality that it portrays, one of the major problems with the CP Model is that it virtually ignores the developmental stages of producing an innovation and gives minimal consideration to how teachers and schools actually adopt and implement an innovation. Therefore, this model is subject to many of the same criticisms as is the RD&D Model.

3. The Negotiation Model proposed by MacDonald and Walker (1976) is directed at describing and explaining why the form in which an innovation is implemented often differs considerably from the form that its creators intended for use (see Figure 5.7). In this respect, it clearly acknowledges differences between the planned curriculum and the enacted curriculum. According to MacDonald and Walker, the differences arise not so much from inadequate communication between developers and practitioners in schools but because their respective motivations are not congruent. Attention to the process of developing and implementing a new curriculum can itself foster the false notion among participants that consensus is being reached and problems are yielding to the coordinated goodwill when, in fact, huge gaps exist between the rhetoric and the reality (Croll & Abbott, 1994). In actuality, developers and practitioners usually engage in a series of trade-offs about what the innovation is and how it will be used. Developers, who hold an idealized image of the innovation, may knowingly or unknowingly disguise differences between their own educational convictions and the convictions held by practitioners.

The Negotiation Model brings to the surface some of the persuasive strategies of manipulation that operate in the real world of curriculum projects and school-level implementation. Although developers may manipulate their rhetoric to ensure adoptions in schools, teachers behave in a similar manner because of their own problems in negotiating with students and school administrators (Apple, 1990). The

Negotiation Model, therefore, is particularly helpful in identifying and explaining basic tensions and stresses that exist beneath the surface of large-scale curriculum development projects initiated externally to those schools in which implementation takes place (Miller & Olsen, 1994), but it can also be used to identify similar tensions and stresses in small-scale projects within individual schools.

Models Internal to the School

In this section, several important internal models are described, and the issues they pose are analyzed.

1. The Proactive/Interactive Change Model was developed by Zaltman et al. (1977). It is rooted in the academic fields of systems analysis and organizational development; it is based on the premise that internal forces within a school can initiate and implement curriculum change but that such change requires rational planning and systematic communication over time. The model postulates that the activities of curriculum development proceed through the following nine stages, which occur in linear sequence, although participants may occasionally return to and repeat a previous stage:

STAGE 1: *Stating the organizational mission*—leading to the identification of problems within the organization

STAGE 2: *Awareness/diagnosis of performance gap*—perceiving problems, the necessary first step in unfreezing an organization

STAGE 3: *Problem-solving objectives*—generating statements of what the curriculum development team wants to accomplish

STAGE 4: *Resources and constraints*—identifying available resources and possible sources of resistance to what the team wants to accomplish

STAGE 5: *Alternative solutions*—building an inventory of possible solutions

STAGE 6: *Testing/trial: demonstration*—communicating the team's plans to the rest of the staff

STAGE 7: *Decision making: the adoption or rejection of alternative solutions*—inviting the rest of the staff to participate in making subsequent decisions

STAGE 8: *Implementation and control*—implementing the innovation, the refreezing of new practices

STAGE 9: *Evaluation*—evaluating the impact of the innovation

The Proactive/Interactive Change Model is especially applicable to schools in which planning groups of teachers are encouraged to work on curriculum development projects by having resources made available to them and by being released from some of their regular classroom duties. For instance, several teams might be at work simultaneously in the same school and their plans coordinated at stage 6 or stage 7. The model provides numerous and useful checklists of what ideally should be done to facilitate this kind of coordination.

However, the Proactive/Interactive Change Model has been criticized on the grounds that the realities of school-initiated curriculum change rarely seem to be as rational (Fullan & Hargreaves, 1991), convivial (Carter & O'Neill, 1995), or productive (Ellis & Fouts, 1993) as the systems approach portrays them. The claim of Zaltman et al. (1977) that they have produced a normative model does not mitigate such criticisms. Again, in the case of the Proactive/Interactive Change Model, there seems to be a gap between the idealized version of reality portrayed by change models and the reality of what goes on in schools themselves.

2. Various change models based on the idea of problem solving have been proposed by numerous writers. The one we describe here is based on the assumption that, if a group of teachers becomes aware of a problem or a deficiency with the existing curriculum, then the group will typically go through a series of steps or processes necessary to solve the problem. These processes are (a) analysis of needs, (b) diagnosis of problems, (c) search and retrieval of ideas, (d) fabrication of a solution (selection of a curricular innovation), and (e) evaluation of the effectiveness of the solution in satisfying the original needs.

Of particular interest is the emphasis this model places on the needs of users. Teachers in schools determine their problems and then make decisions about what kind of curriculum innovation to make and how to implement it. Outside change agents, if used at all, only assist with the processes involved; they do not provide direction about the problems to be solved, nor do they offer possible solutions. The problem-solving activities are perceived as localized, internal school matters. The local school relies on its own resources, not on external resources. Most important, the model stresses that all activities are self-initiated and self-applied.

The Problem-Solving Model has often proved useful in analyzing curriculum development activities that have been initiated by individual schools, such as many of the new charter schools that began to spring up in the late 1990s (Manno et al., 2000). Groups of schools also have based cooperative approaches to curriculum on this model; for example, groups in the United States include the Coalition of Essential Schools (Diamond, 1994) and groups in Canada include the Learning Consortium in Ontario (Fullan, 1993) and the Critical Thinking Cooperative in British Columbia (Werner, 1995).

The Coalition of Essential Schools was established at Brown University in 1984 by Theodore Sizer, a noted educational reformer. Schools that joined the coalition subscribed to a set of common principles, including collective planning, personalizing teaching and learning, and developing a school climate that supports trust and a commitment to learning. By 1988, fifty schools had joined, and in the 2000s there are approximately 1,000. Commitment to the common principles by itself was not enough, however, without sufficient time set aside for planning (and, hence, problem solving). Sizer (1989) points out that "the planning for a restructured program takes substantial committing of effort and emotional energy. Much planning by a significant number of the staff during summer months and during the academic year is necessary, and both time and arrangements for daily or at least weekly meetings of the key faculty are essential" (p. 4).

Wasley (1994) undertook case studies of coalition teachers over a four-year period, during which time she made frequent visits to classrooms and involved teachers in reflecting upon their work. She noted that these collaborating teachers shared some distinct characteristics that were quite different from practitioners working in conventional schools.

Despite the general usefulness of the Problem-Solving Model in accounting for the curriculum development activities that take place within specific schools, practical constraints on schools often make its use highly problematic. In fact, the ideal four steps of analysis of needs, diagnosis of problems, search for solutions, and selection and implementation of a solution may actually occur only infrequently. When time for planning remains short, few of the four problem-solving steps may be fully carried out, and solutions are often proposed before all options are known.

3. The Action Research Model (Elliott, 1980; Foshay, 1994; Kemmis & McTaggart, 1988) is another model based on problem solving and applicable to school-level curriculum change. It has been the principal basis for the "teacher as researcher" movements in the United Kingdom and the United States since the 1980s (McKernan, 1993). The processes involved in doing action research are similar to those described by the Problem-Solving Model:

- Teachers come together as a group to consider ways of improving a program or practice.
- A field of action is identified by the group, and a specific plan is developed and implemented.
- During the implementation phase, participants reflect, rethink, and again discuss the issues; if necessary, they replan.
- After the period of implementation and reflection, revisions are made to the original plan.
- A revised version is implemented, and the cycle begins again.

The Action Research Model places heavy emphasis on individual teachers, collective deliberations, and networking (Lieberman & McLaughlin, 1992; Lucas, 1999; McKernan, 1993). It has proved beneficial to groups of teachers in schools working on such priorities as constructivism (Perkins, 1999), Internet studies (Schofield & Davidson, 2000), and inclusiveness (Fisher et al., 2000). As a form of curriculum planning and development, it is subject to the same kinds of advantages and disadvantages we have noted about models and methods that emphasize the role of teachers. We discuss action research in detail in chapter 7.

4. The Organizational Development (OD) Model, described by Schmuck and Runkel (1972), is still another model based on problem solving, but within it emphasis falls more on the process of solving problems than on specific solutions themselves. Miles (1993) contends that its two basic elements are provision of feedback and emphasis on normative change. This model assumes that persons who self-consciously and systematically attempt to solve problems will improve themselves in many different ways, and this kind of individual improvement will lead directly to the improvement of the organization as a whole. According to Schmuck and Miles (1971), "Organizational development is a planned and sustained effort to apply behavioral science for system improvement, using reflexive, self-analytic methods" (p. 1). The term *system* may refer to any group ranging in size from an entire school

district, to a single school, to a secondary school department (such as English, social studies, or mathematics), to a small team of teachers.

The phrase "reflexive, self-analytic methods" refers to ways in which teachers themselves assess, diagnose, and transform their own organization. To do this, teachers often need help, usually from an external consultant whose task is to assist them in going through the following steps, which the OD Model describes:

- Establishing specific tasks
- Working out guiding principles for the type of data to be collected about the whole organization, its subsystems, and its processes
- Examining and reflecting upon the data in a nonthreatening environment
- Putting forward difficulties, problems, and possible solutions
- Devising plans to resolve problems in which strategies used by participants are mutually supportive and reinforcing
- Obtaining feedback on performances, reflecting upon results, and establishing new directions

When used as a model of curriculum development, the OD Model usually places more emphasis on participants than on the curriculum innovation that they are developing (Arends, 2000; Snyder, Acker-Hocevar, & Snyder, 1994). Hence, this model has a mixed history of use in curriculum development projects. Much depends on the users' ability not to lose sight of people, process, or product.

5. Conflict models have been applied to virtually every social activity imaginable. The Conflict Model, described by Schelling (1963), applies to curriculum development. In general, conflict models stress the exercise of power and how individuals and groups use power to achieve their ends. The formal positions that individuals and groups hold in society do not necessarily determine the distribution of power since many individuals can exert power without any formal status in an organization. (For example, successfully running for major political office in the United States now requires spending large amounts of money on political campaigns but not necessarily on having acquired the experience that would qualify the candidate for that office in the first place; therefore, those who supply campaign funds may be more powerful than those who hold office.) Further, the distribution of power is never stable; it oscillates with the actions and inactions of individuals over specific issues.

Proponents of conflict models emphasize the bargaining that takes place between individuals and groups because of different preferences and resources (Margolis, 1991). Bargaining can be explicit in terms of specific proposals or implicit in terms of strategies used by individuals to predict likely behaviors by others. Above all, conflict requires individuals to adapt to those with whom they are in conflict. Every adversary must take account of each opponent's moves. The ability of one person to gain his or her ends depends in part on the choices other participants make. Bargaining as a process has to be maintained; otherwise, no one can gain anything.

Lieberman and McLaughlin (1992) emphasize that, in all forms of bargaining and negotiation, teachers will network with one another without someone coordinating them. This observation seems to capture a pattern common in many schools in which teachers are largely in charge of their own domain and the opportunities for direction by the principal or the school district are very limited indeed. Weick (1976) refers to this dispersal of responsibilities and directions in schools as a "loosely coupled system." Such a system enables all kinds of political bargaining to occur; for example, individual teachers or small groups can mobilize their efforts to win support for small schedule changes or, sometimes, for major changes in the curriculum. Although a loosely coupled system may be based on cooperation rather than conflict (or some combination of the two), various curriculum writers have pointed to conflict (or political) models as useful ways of describing most interactions within schools. Apple (1990), for instance, describes the coalitions that are built up at the school level among educators, parents, and community members in fighting for particular programs. Connell (1983) perceives curriculum as "a vehicle of social relations. It is one of the ways in which social privilege, power and disadvantage are transmitted" (p. 8). Fullan (1999) maintains that it is crucial to "establish alliances among diverse parties inside and outside the school" (p. 81).

Teachers and other educators need to consider carefully the specifics of their own situations in deciding whether a conflict model or a model stressing cooperation or personal development best applies to the curriculum development activities that take place there.

6. Concerns-Based Adoption Model (CBAM) is a curriculum development model proposed by Hall, Wallace, and Dossett (1973). It takes a different approach than do other problem-solving models in that its focus is on the individual teacher and not on the group. CBAM does not address the issue of how or by whom change is generated. Its focus is on the point at which a decision is made to adopt an innovation (whether it is developed externally or internally). Hall et al. maintain that individual teachers make decisions about the degrees of acceptance or rejection of a specific innovation, and they do so not because of the public reasons usually given but because of the specific concerns that they develop as they become involved with the innovation. CBAM postulates what these concerns might be and how they might change as teachers become increasingly familiar with the innovation (Van den Berg, 1993). It therefore is a model perhaps more useful than any other we have discussed in this chapter in assessing the point at which the planned curriculum becomes the enacted curriculum.

We discuss CBAM in detail in chapter 7.

A Model Spanning External, Internal, and Personal Influences

Goodson (2000) has proposed a model that spans external, internal, and personal influences on curriculum change. He argues that in postmodern times it is simplistic to examine only external or internal models without connecting them to the interests and projects of those people most heavily invested in a particular change. Goodson's model identifies four issues that must be sufficiently addressed to create the connections between the external, the internal, and the personal necessary to maximize the possibility of success for the project.

1. *Mission: Institutionalize new purposes.* Although the mission of a particular curriculum change may arise externally, "the delivery of change is in the hands of internal change agents and closely linked to their personal projects and concerns. To succeed, change must be part of their mission" (p. 18).

2. *Micro-politics: Re-negotiate school practices.* There must be an internal re-negotiation of professional practices for those people—primarily teachers—who will live most closely with the curriculum change. This re-negotiation must be handled delicately, since "each school has its own instinctive micro-politics" (p. 19).

3. *Memory work: Engage the community.* Goodson contends that engagement with the local community is neglected by most change models. Therefore, it is necessary to consider local opinion and "to develop community awareness of new reforms" (p. 19).

4. *Movement: Generalize to other schools.* Usually, for a curriculum change to be successful a school must form coalitions with other like-minded schools. Goodson characterizes these coalitions as small-scale social movements providing chains of support for the new curriculum.

Goodson's model clearly casts attention on how external mission, internal politics, and personal identity are connected within the process of curriculum change. The considerations he identifies may become increasingly important in describing this process within the current context of postmodernity (discussed in chapter 4).

5.7   PRINCIPLES AND GUIDELINES

Finally, we note that, despite the usefulness of considering the process of curriculum development and change in terms of the models we have described, models are no substitute for a deep intuitive understanding of the process itself. Some recent writers have suggested that deep understanding of the process can best be encouraged by each individual's attempting to identify directly the most basic principles and guidelines involved in educational change, not through attempting to identify models, which necessarily rarefy the process to some degree. For example, Figure 5.8 summarizes Fullan's (1993) eight basic lessons about change.

These basic lessons (or principles and guidelines) exemplify Fullan's own value orientation and are consistent with what can be considered a process-oriented model of curriculum development with emphasis on both the individual and the organization. We think, however, that they come closer to capturing the essentially paradoxical nature of the process of curriculum development and change than do any of the change models described in the research literature, and thus we encourage readers to develop their own ways of understanding this process.

Lesson one:	You can't mandate what matters. (The more complex the change, the less you can force it.)
Lesson two:	Change is a journey, not a blueprint. (Change is nonlinear, loaded with uncertainty and excitement and sometimes perverse.)
Lesson three:	Problems are our friends. (Problems are inevitable, and you can't learn without them.)
Lesson four:	Vision and strategic planning come later. (Premature visions and planning are blind.)
Lesson five:	Individualism and collectivism must have equal power. (There are no one-sided solutions to isolation and group think.)
Lesson six:	Neither centralization nor decentralization works. (Both top-down and bottom-up strategies are necessary.)
Lesson seven:	Connection with the wider environment is critical for success. (The best organizations learn externally as well as internally.)
Lesson eight:	Every person is a change agent. (Change is too important to leave to the experts; personal mindset and mastery are the ultimate protection.)

FIGURE 5.8
Eight basic lessons about educational change
Source: After Fullan (1993).

5.8   CONCLUDING COMMENT

In this chapter, we have not advocated one particular approach to curriculum development and change. As we have done in previous chapters and will do throughout the book, we have described alternative approaches to certain curriculum matters and basic issues that must be faced in selecting among alternatives. Although in our discussions we have occasionally interjected our professional opinions, we encourage readers to select their own alternatives, just as teachers must often make such selections in their own professional lives.

In this chapter, we have attempted to point out why the terms *curriculum development* and *change* are inextricably related. Often the creation and adoption of a new curriculum is considered a nonproblematic process achievable by a single education official or perhaps a small group in authority making all decisions about what the curriculum should be and where it should be taught. However, numerous studies in recent decades have unequivocally demonstrated the complexities of curriculum development and the equally complex problems associated with bringing about curriculum change in schools (Rosenshine, 1995). This chapter has introduced some basic but general topics in curriculum development. These topics will be elaborated in more detail in the following three chapters, which focus on the teacher as planner, implementer, and evaluator of curriculum development and change.

▮ QUESTIONS AND REFLECTIONS

1. Which of the following considerations most influence generic curriculum development? Which most influence site-specific curriculum development?
   a. Limited resources (time and money)
   b. Official policies and priorities
   c. Community expectations
2. To what extent do you see curriculum development as a moral activity? Give examples from your teaching experience.
3. It is often argued that the role of the teacher is fundamental to curriculum development. Do you agree? How can a teacher best fulfill this role? What are some potential constraints?
4. Of the models of curriculum change discussed in this chapter, which seems to best describe your own school or school district? Why? What seem to be the principal discrepancies between this model and the specifics of curriculum development and change with which you are familiar?
5. Examine a curriculum developed recently and with which you are familiar. Who initiated it? What steps were taken to implement it? How were impediments overcome? Is it likely to be used for a considerable length of time? If not, why?
6. "Most innovations that have lasted began with teachers involved in the planning" (Vanterpool, 1990, p. 39). "Teachers are not willing to explore innovations because they guard jealously the privacy of their own classroom and their established procedures." Compare and contrast these statements using examples from schools with which you are familiar.
7. What do you understand by the terms *educational reform* and *educational renewal*? Are the priorities for "reform" different from those of "renewal"? How would you classify your concerns about change in terms of "reform" and "renewal"? Explain.
8. Is cost the major impediment to comprehensive school change? What are other major impediments? Explain.
9. The rationale for standards-based educational reform rests on the premise that such reform will increase student learning. Is this rationale sound? What evidence supports or refutes it? Comment on the strengths and weaknesses of a standards-based curriculum.

▮ SUGGESTED READING

There are a number of insightful articles on curriculum development and change (see the chapter bibliography), including the following:

Farrell (2000)

Fullan (2000)

Goodlad (1999)

Labaree (2000)

Short (1983)

Some important books (see the chapter bibliography) include the following:

Beyer & Apple (1998)

Fullan (1993, 1999)

Glatthorn (1987)

Louis & Kruse (1995)

Newmann & Wehlage (1995)

▉ BIBLIOGRAPHY

Apple, M. W. (1983). Raising the issues. In I. J. Hutchins (Ed.), *Shaping the curriculum* (Vol. 2, pp. 9–17). Adelaide: Australian Curriculum Studies Association.

Apple, M. W. (1990). *Ideology and curriculum.* New York: Routledge.

Arends, R. I. (2000). *Learning to teach* (5th ed.). Boston: McGraw Hill.

Barrow, R. (1984). *Giving teaching back to teachers.* London: Wheat Sheaf Books.

Bell, T. H. (1993). Reflections one decade after *A Nation at Risk. Phi Delta Kappan, 74*(8), 593–597.

Beyer, L. E., & Apple, M. W. (1998). *The curriculum: Problems, politics, and possibilities* (2nd ed.). Albany: State University of New York Press.

Bohn, A. P., & Sleeter, C. E. (2000). Multicultural education and the standards movement. *Phi Delta Kappan, 82*(2), 156–159.

Bolam, R. (1974). *Planned educational change: Theory and practice.* Bristol, England: University of Bristol.

Bolam, R. (1982). *Strategies for school improvement.* Paris: Organisation for Economic Cooperation and Development.

Caldwell, R. (1993). Paradox and uncertainty in the governance of education. In H. Beare & W. L. Boyd (Eds.), *Restructuring schools.* London: Falmer.

Carson, A. S. (1984). Control of the curriculum: A case for teachers. *Journal of Curriculum Studies, 16*(1), 19–28.

Carter, D. S. G., & O'Neill, M. H. (1995). *Case studies in educational change: An international perspective.* London: Falmer.

Clark, D. L., & Guba, E. G. (1965). *An examination of potential change roles in education.* Paper presented at the Symposium of Innovation and Planning School Curricula, Airlie, VA.

Clark, D. L., Lotto, L. S., & Astuto, T. A. (1984). Effective schools and school improvement: A comparative analysis of two lines of inquiry. *Educational Administration Quarterly, 20*(3), 103–118.

Connell, R. W. (1983). Raising the issues, II. In J. Hutchins (Ed.), *Shaping the curriculum* (Vol. 2, pp. 1–8). Adelaide: Australian Curriculum Studies Association.

Cornbleth, C. (1996). *An America curriculum?* Paper presented at the annual meeting of the American Educational Research Association, New York.

Coulby, D. (2000). *Beyond the national curriculum.* London: Routledge/Falmer.

Crandall, D. P. (1988). *Implementation aspects of dissemination: Reflections toward an immodest proposal.* Paper presented at the annual meeting of the American Educational Research Association, New Orleans.

Crawford, M., & Witte, M. (1999). Strategies for mathematics: Teaching in context. *Educational Leadership, 57*(3), 34–39.

Croll, P., & Abbott, D. (1994). *Coercion or compromise: How schools react to imposed change.* Paper presented at the annual meeting of the American Educational Research Association, New Orleans.

Datta, L. E. (1980). Changing times: The study of federal programs supporting educational change in the case for local problem solving. *Teachers College Record, 82*(1), 101–116.

Diamond, L. (1994). A progress report on California's charter schools. *Educational Leadership, 52*(1), 41–45.

Downs, A. (2000). Successful school reform efforts share common features. *Harvard Education Letter: Research Online,* March/April.

Eisner, E. W. (1975). Curriculum development in Stanford's Kettering Project: Recollections and ruminations. In J. Schaffarzick & D. H. Hampson (Eds.), *Strategies for curriculum development.* Berkeley, CA: McCutchan.

Eisner, E. W. (1990). Creative curriculum development and practice. *Journal of Curriculum and Supervision, 6*(1), 62–73.

Eisner, E. W. (2000). Those who ignore the past . . . : 12 "easy" lessons for the next millennium. *Journal of Curriculum Studies, 32*(2), 343–357.

Elliott, J. (1980). The implications of classroom research for the professional development of teachers. *World Yearbook in Education.* London.

Ellis, A. K., & Fouts, J. T. (1993). *Research on educational innovations.* Princeton Junction, NJ: Eye on Education.

Evans, P. M., & Mohr, N. (1999). Professional development for principals. *Phi Delta Kappan, 80*(7), 530–532.

Farrell, J. P. (2000). Means, ends and dead-ends in thinking about school change. *Curriculum Inquiry, 30*(3), 265–270.

Feiler, R., Heritage, M., & Gallimore, R. (2000). Teachers leading teachers. *Educational Leadership, 57*(7), 66–69.

Feld, M. M. (1981). The bureaucracy, the superintendent, and change. *Education and Urban Society, 13*(4), 38–49.

Fisher, D., Sax, C., & Grove, K. (2000). The resilience of changes promoting inclusiveness in an urban elementary school. *Elementary School Journal, 100*(3), 213–226.

Foshay, A. W. (1994). Action research: An early history in the United States. *Journal of Curriculum and Supervision, 9*(4), 317–325.

Fox, C. A. F. (1992). The critical ingredients of making change happen. *NASSP Bulletin, 76*(541), 71–77.

Frey, K., Frei, A., & Langeheine, R. (1989). Do curriculum development models really influence the curriculum? *Journal of Curriculum, 21*(6), 553–559.

Fullan, M. G. (1982). *The meaning of educational change.* New York: Teachers College Press.

Fullan, M. G. (1988). *What's worth fighting for in the principalship?* Toronto: Ontario Teachers Federation.

Fullan, M. G. (1991). *The new meaning of educational change.* London: Cassell.

Fullan, M. G. (1993). *Change forces.* London: Falmer.

Fullan, M. G. (1999). *Change forces: The sequel.* London: Falmer.

Fullan, M. G. (2000). The three stories of education reform. *Phi Delta Kappan, 81*(8), 581–584.

Fullan, M. G., & Hargreaves, A. (1991). *Working together for your school.* Melbourne: Australian Council for Educational Research.

Fullan, M. G., & Pomfret, A. (1977). Research on curriculum and instruction implementation. *Review of Educational Research, 47*(2), 335–397.

Glatthorn, A. A. (1987). *Curriculum leadership.* Glenview, IL: Scott, Foresman.

Goodlad, J. I. (1999). Flow, eros, and ethos in educational renewal. *Phi Delta Kappan, 80*(8), 571–578.

Goodman, J. (1994). External change agents and grassroots school reform: Reflections from the field. *Journal of Curriculum and Supervision, 9*(2), 113–135.

Goodson, I. F. (2000). Social histories of educational change. *Journal of Educational Change, 2*(1), 2–15.

Gresham, A., Hess, F., Maranto, R., & Milliman, S. (2000). Desert bloom: Arizona's free market in education. *Phi Delta Kappan, 81*(10), 751–757.

Griffin, G. A. (1990). Leadership for curriculum improvement: The school administrator's role. In A. Lieberman (Ed.), *Schools as collaborative cultures: Creating the future now.* London: Falmer.

Griffith, R. (2000). *National curriculum: National disaster?* London: Routledge/Falmer.

Hall, G. E., & Hord, S. M. (1984). *Change in schools.* Albany: State University of New York Press.

Hall, G. E., Loucks, S. F., Rutherford, W. L., & Newlove, B. W. (1975). Levels of use of the innovation: A framework for analyzing innovation adoption. *Journal of Teacher Education, 26*(1), 5–9.

Hall, G. E., Wallace, R. C., & Dossett, W. A. (1973). *A developmental conceptualization of the adoption process within educational institutions.* Unpublished paper. Austin: University of Texas, Research and Development Center for Teacher Education.

Hargreaves, A., Earl, L., Moore, S., & Manning, S. (2001). *Learning to change: Teaching beyond subjects and standards.* San Francisco: Jossey-Bass.

Havelock, R. G. (1969). *A guide to innovation in education.* Ann Arbor, MI: Center for Research and Utilization of Knowledge.

Havelock, R. G. (1971). *Planning for innovation through the dissemination and utilization of knowledge.* Ann Arbor, MI: Center for Research and Utilization of Knowledge.

Hayes, H. E. (1977). Curriculum development as a moral enterprise. *Curriculum Inquiry, 6*(3), 229–236.

Heller, M. F., & Firestone, W. A. (1994). *Heroes, teams and teachers: A study of leadership for change.* Paper presented at the annual meeting of the American Educational Research Association, New Orleans.

Henderson, J. C. (1985). *Organisation development and the implementation of planned change.* Unpublished doctoral dissertation, Murdoch University, Perth, Western Australia.

Holdzkom, D. (1992). The influence of state agencies on curriculum. *NASSP Bulletin, 76*(11), 12–23.

House, E. R. (1979). Technology versus craft: A ten-year perspective on innovation. *Journal of Curriculum Studies, 11*(1), 1–16.

Huberman, A. M., & Crandall, D. P. (1982). A study of dissemination efforts supporting school improvements. In *People, policies, and practices: Examining the chain of school improvement.* Andover, MA: The Network.

Johnson, J. R. (1989). *Technology: Report of the Project 2061, Phase 1 Technology Panel*. Washington, DC: American Association for the Advancement of Science.

Kemmis, S., & McTaggart, R. (1988). *The action research planner* (3rd ed.). Geelong, Australia: Deakin University Press.

King, B. M., & Newmann, F. M. (2000). Will teacher learning advance school goals? *Phi Delta Kappan, 81*(8), 576–580.

Kirst, M. W. (1987). Curricular leadership at the state level: What is the new focus? *NASSP Bulletin, 71*(498), 34–38.

Kirst, M. W., & Meister, G. R. (1985). Turbulence in American secondary schools: What reforms last? *Curriculum Inquiry, 15*(2), 169–186.

Labaree, D. F. (2000). Resisting educational standards. *Phi Delta Kappan, 81*(1), 28–33.

Lambert, L. T. (2000). The new physical education. *Educational Leadership, 57*(6), 34–39.

Larkin, R. F. (1984). *Achievement directed leadership: A superintendent's perspective*. Paper presented at the annual meeting of the American Educational Research Association, New Orleans.

Leithwood, K. A., & Montgomery, D. A. (1982). The role of the elementary school principal in program improvement. *Review of Educational Research, 52*(3), 309–339.

Lieberman, A. (Ed.). (1986). *Rethinking school improvement*. New York: Teachers College Press.

Lieberman, A., & McLaughlin, M. W. (1992). Networks for educational change: Powerful and problematic. *Phi Delta Kappan, 73*(9), 673–677.

Linne, A. (2001). The lesson as a pedagogical text: A case study of lesson designs. *Journal of Curriculum Studies, 33*(2), 129–156.

Lippitt, R. O., Watson, Y., & Westly, K. (1958). *The dynamics of planned change*. New York: Harcourt, Brace, & Jovanovich.

Louis, K. S. (1980). *Products and processes: Some preliminary findings from the R & D Utilization Program and their implications for federal dissemination policies*. Paper presented at the annual meeting of the American Educational Research Association, Boston.

Louis, K., & Kruse, S. (Eds.). (1995). *Professionalism and community*. San Francisco: Corwin Press.

Lucas, C. A. (1999). Developing competent practitioners. *Educational Leadership, 56*(8), 45–48.

MacDonald, B., & Walker, R. (1976). *Changing the curriculum*. London: Open Books.

Manno, B. V., Finn, C. E., & Vanourek, G. (2000). Beyond the schoolhouse door: How charter schools are transforming U.S. public education. *Phi Delta Kappan, 81*(10), 736–744.

Margolis, H. (1991). Understanding, facing resistance to change. *NASSP Bulletin, 75*(537), 1–8.

Marsh, D. D., & Bowman, G. A. (1987). *Top-down versus bottom-up reform in secondary schools*. Unpublished paper, University of Wisconsin, Madison.

Martin, D. S., Saif, P. S., & Thiel, L. (1987). Curriculum development: Who is involved and how? *Educational Leadership, 44*(4), 40–48.

Marzano, R. J., Pickering, D. J., & Pollock, J. E. (2001). *Classroom instruction that works*. Alexandria, VA: Association for Supervision and Curriculum Development.

McCormick, R. (1990). Technology and the national curriculum: The creation of a subject by committee. *Curriculum Journal, 1*(1), 39–52.

McKernan, J. (1993). Varieties of curriculum action research: Constraints and typologies in American, British and Irish projects. *Journal of Curriculum Studies, 25*(5), 445–457.

Medway, P. (1992). Constructions of technology: Reflections on a new subject. In J. Benyon & H. Mackay (Eds.), *Technological literacy and the curriculum*. London: Falmer.

Miles, M. B. (1993). Forty years of change in schools: Some personal reflections. *Educational Administration Quarterly, 29*(2), 213–248.

Miles, M. B., Saxl, E. R., & Lieberman, A. (1988). What skills do educational "change agents" need? An empirical view. *Curriculum Inquiry, 18*(2), 157–193.

Miller, L., & Olsen, J. (1994). Putting the computer in its place: A study of teaching with technology. *Journal of Curriculum Studies, 26*(2), 121–141.

Morrow, A. (1994). *Straggling down the highway: Technology, schools, and equity*. Paper presented at the Learning Environment Technology Conference, Sydney.

Mort, P. R. (1953). Educational adaptability. *School Executive, 71*, 1–23.

Newmann, F., & Wehlage, G. (1995). *School restructuring*. Madison: University of Wisconsin Press.

Nicholl, J. (1982). *Patterns of project dissemination*. London: Schools Council.

Odden, A. (2000). The cost of sustaining educational change through comprehensive school reform. *Phi Delta Kappan, 81*(6), 433–438.

O'Neil, J. (1995). On using the standards: A conversation with Ramsey Selden. *Educational Leadership, 52*(6), 12–14.

Orlich, D. C. (2000). Education reform and limits to student achievement. *Phi Delta Kappan, 81*(6), 468–472.

Ornstein, A. C., & Hunkins, F. (1993). *Curriculum foundations: Principles and theory* (2nd ed.). Boston: Allyn & Bacon.

Paris, C. L. (1990). *Teacher initiative and curriculum change: Altered processes, altered paradigms.* Paper presented at the annual meeting of the American Educational Research Association, Boston.

Perkins, D. (1999). The many faces of constructivism. *Educational Leadership, 57*(3), 6–11.

Popkewitz, T. S. (1985). *Educational reform rhetoric, ritual, and social interest.* Unpublished paper presented at the University of Salamanca, Spain.

Poppleton, P. (2000). *Receptiveness and resistance to educational change: Experiences of English teachers in the 1990s.* Paper presented at the annual meeting of the American Educational Research Association, New Orleans.

Reid, W. A. (1999). *Curriculum as institution and practice.* Mahwah, NJ: Lawrence Erlbaum.

Resnick, L. B., Nolan, K. J., & Resnick, D. P. (1995). Benchmarking education standards. *Education, Evaluation and Policy Analysis, 17*(4), 438–461.

Resnick, L. B., Nolan, K. J., & Resnick, D. P. (1996). Caution heeded—a response to "High standards and cultural diversity: Cautionary tales of comparative research." *Education Evaluation and Policy Analysis, 18*(3), 262–264.

Rogers, D. L., & Babinski, L. (1999). Breaking through isolation with new teacher groups. *Educational Leadership, 56*(8), 38–40.

Rogers, E. M. (1962). *Diffusion of innovations.* New York: Free Press.

Rogers, E. M. (1983). *Diffusion of innovations* (3rd ed.). New York: Free Press.

Rogers, E. M., & Shoemaker, F. F. (1971). *Communication of innovations.* New York: Free Press.

Romberg, T. A. (1993). NCTM's standards: A rallying flag for mathematics teachers. *Educational Leadership, 50*(5), 36–41.

Rosenau, F. S. (1973). *Tactics for the educational change agent.* San Francisco: Far West Laboratory.

Rosenshine, B. (1995). *Why do innovations come and go, and come back?* Paper presented at the annual meeting of the American Educational Research Association, San Francisco.

Sarason, S. B. (1990). *The predictable failure of educational reform.* San Francisco: Jossey-Bass.

Schelling, T. (1963). *The strategy of conflict.* London: Oxford University Press.

Schmuck, R. A., & Miles, M. B. (Eds.). (1971). *Organizational development in schools.* La Jolla, CA: University Associates.

Schmuck, R. A., & Runkel, P. (1972). *Handbook of organizational development in schools.* Palo Alto, CA: National Press Books.

Schofield, J. W., & Davidson, A. L. (2000). *Internet use and teacher change.* Paper presented at the annual meeting of the American Educational Research Association, New Orleans.

Schon, D. A. (1971). *Beyond the stable state.* London: Penguin.

Senge, P., Cambron-McCabe, N., Lucas, T., Smith, B., Dutton, J., & Kleiner, A. (2000). *Schools that learn: A fifth discipline.* London: Nicholas Brealey.

Short, E. C. (1983). The forms and use of alternative curriculum development strategies: Policy implications. *Curriculum Inquiry, 13*(1), 43–64.

Simpson, G. W. (1990). Keeping it alive: Elements of school culture that sustain innovation. *Educational Leadership, 47*(8), 34–37.

Sirotnik, K. A., & Kimball, K. (1999). Standards for standards-based accountability systems. *Phi Delta Kappan, 81*(3), 209–214.

Sizer, T. (1989). Diverse practices, shared ideas: The essential school. In H. Walberg & J. Lane (Eds.), *Organizing for learning: Toward the 21st century.* Reston, VA: National Association of Secondary School Principals.

Skilbeck, M. (1982). *Curriculum development* (Occasional Papers No. 9). Bangkok: Asian Program of Educational Innovation for Development.

Snyder, K. J., Acker-Hocevar, M., & Snyder, K. (1994). *Organizational development in transition: The schooling perspective.* Paper presented at the annual meeting of the American Educational Research Association, New Orleans.

Soder, R. (1999). When words find their meaning: Renewal versus reform. *Phi Delta Kappan, 80*(8), 568–570.

Steffy, B. E. (1993). Top-down-bottom-up: Systemic change in Kentucky. *Educational Leadership, 51*(1), 42–44.

U.S. Department of Education. (1991). *America 2000: An education strategy.* Sourcebook. Washington, DC: U.S. Department of Education.

Van den Berg, R. (1993). The concerns-based adoption model in the Netherlands, Flanders and the United Kingdom: State of the art and perspective. *Studies in Educational Evaluation, 19,* 51–63.

Vanterpool, M. (1990). Innovations aren't for everyone. *Principal, 69*(4), 38–43.

Walker, D. F. (1978). *An approach to curriculum development.* Unpublished paper, Stanford University.

Walker, D. F. (1990). *Fundamentals of Curriculum.* New York: Harcourt, Brace & Jovanovich.

Wasley, P. A. (1994). *Stirring the chalkdust.* New York: Teachers College Press.

Wasley, P. A. (1999). Teaching worth celebrating. *Educational Leadership, 56*(8), 8–13.

Watson, N., Fullan, M., & Kilcher, A. (2000). *The Role of the district: Professional learning and district reform.* Paper presented at the annual meeting of the American Educational Research Association, New Orleans.

Weick, K. (1976). Educational organizations as loosely coupled systems. *Administrative Science Quarterly, 21,* 35–47.

Werner, W. (1995). Reforming the Canadian curriculum. *Curriculum Journal, 6*(2), 225–233.

Wideen, M. F. (1994). *The struggle for change.* London: Falmer.

Williams, J. C., & Williams, J. B. (1994). Change at the chalk face: A case study of the factors affecting the adoption of curriculum innovation. *Journal of Curriculum Studies, 26*(2), 201–216.

Young, J. H. (1990). Teacher participation in curriculum development: A study of societal and institutional levels. *Alberta Journal of Educational Research, 36*(2), 141–156.

Zaltman, G., Florio, D. H., & Sikorski, L. A. (1977). *Dynamic educational change.* New York: Free Press.

6

Curriculum Planning: Levels and Participants

ABOUT THIS CHAPTER

This chapter distinguishes three levels of curriculum planning: the planning of policies, the planning of programs, and the planning of lessons. It focuses on how planning by teachers actually proceeds in individual schools, and in so doing, it examines in detail the contributions made to curriculum planning by people often referred to as "key stakeholders." Key stakeholders include teachers, principals, parents, students, and external facilitators—all people who for personal or professional reasons ordinarily have the strongest interests in planning. Either their lives are touched directly by the curriculum (as in the case of teachers, parents, and students), or their professional roles include some direct responsibility for the curriculum (as in the case of teachers, principals, and external facilitators).

WHAT YOU SHOULD DO

1. Differentiate among three levels at which curriculum planning occurs in schools: policy, programs, and lessons.
2. Reflect on the backgrounds, priorities, and skills ordinarily brought to curriculum planning by key stakeholders, especially teachers, principals, parents, students, and external facilitators.

SOME OPTIONAL APPROACHES

The following three options for reading this chapter are among those you may want to consider.

Option A

1. Based on your own preferred approach to planning (review chapters 3 and 4, if necessary), devise a very simple curriculum project that you could introduce in

your local school or school district. In particular, try to establish answers to these questions:

- ❏ Who would be involved in the planning?
- ❏ What would be the rationale for the project, and how could that rationale best be explained?
- ❏ What human and material resources would be needed?
- ❏ What might be the outcomes for students if the plan were implemented?
- ❏ What expectations would you have about possible resistance to the plan and conflicts over it?

2. Read sections 6.3 through 6.7, which deal with major stakeholders, and then reconsider your plan, making any revisions you consider necessary.

Option B

1. Read sections 6.3 through 6.7, which deal with major stakeholders and school settings.
2. Reflect upon a curriculum project that you were involved in recently. Analyze the following questions:
   - ❏ Was the project a success?
   - ❏ How should the success of the project have been judged (for instance, in terms of student achievement, quality of the curriculum itself, breadth of implementation, satisfaction among teachers, or in other ways)?
   - ❏ How was it judged? By whom?
   - ❏ What do you think should have been done differently and why?

Option C

1. Read sections 6.1 and 6.2 on levels of curriculum planning. Then answer the following questions:
   - ❏ What do you consider to be some important curriculum needs or priorities at your school?
   - ❏ What steps would you take to find out whether your judgments are soundly based or not? (Examples would be interviewing people or collecting other information.)
   - ❏ Which needs would you list as deserving the highest priority? How did you arrive at this list? How would you justify your list of priorities to others?
2. Read sections 6.3 through 6.7 on major stakeholders. In the light of this information, reconsider the priorities you listed.

6.1 INTRODUCTION

If the program of a school is to be coordinated, systematic, or unified in any way, then curriculum planning is indispensable. How, then, can a coherent curriculum be planned that still leaves room for flexibility in implementation by individual teachers? This question is at the heart of the distinction among the planned curriculum, the enacted curriculum, and the experienced curriculum, which this book attempts to take into account. The question is one for which we have thus far provided only partial answers. In this chapter and the following chapter, we attempt a more complete answer. This chapter focuses on organized curriculum planning in individual schools, identifying the key stakeholders involved and how they contribute to the process. The following chapter focuses on flexible curriculum implementation. The answer that the chapters collectively provide is not prescriptive, however. In keeping with the general approach to curriculum that we have been following, we describe alternative possibilities, and we ask readers to choose wisely among these alternatives, depending on their own specific situations and their own value orientations.

Although nearly everyone who is a teacher or who is in training to become a teacher has at one time or another considered what the curriculum should be, most find careful study of the major stakeholders involved in curriculum planning and of their motivations, priorities, and expectations to be quite illuminating. Such study offers an invitation to place oneself inside the process of curriculum planning and to experience it from other people's perspectives. This is something that even persons experienced in curriculum planning and development may not have done before.

Some participants in curriculum planning are interested primarily in general policies, some in programs, and others in specific lessons. Not only do the interests and motives of different individuals and groups influence the process but so, too, does the specific school setting in which curriculum planning takes place. Some settings are conducive to positive relationships among participants, fruitful deliberations, and constructive decisions, while other settings are constraining and full of conflict.

6.2 PLANNING AT DIFFERENT LEVELS

Teachers are among the key stakeholders (persons with strong personal or professional interests) in curriculum planning. Undoubtedly, they are the major participants in curriculum planning in individual schools and school districts. Even in situations in which the curriculum to be taught is specified, each classroom teacher can still make important planning decisions. The teacher is the filter through which the mandated curriculum passes (McCutcheon, 1988). Teachers filter general policies and objectives that may have originated with federal, state, and district officials and conceive of ways of enacting them, taking account of the specific contexts of the teachers' own communities and schools and making necessary adjustments. Teachers may also be involved in identifying planning issues, seeking ways to define them, and finding resolutions. They may critically inquire into all such matters in order to reflect on and to improve their own practice. Their inquiries and reflections occur proactively in mentally planning possible lessons, interactively in considering actual lessons in progress, and postactively in weighing the value of lessons they have

taught. Teachers may undertake all these activities either individually or collaboratively with other teachers.

In addition, as they go about their planning, individual teachers have to be
mindful of various reforms. Little (1993) and Galton, Hargreaves, Comber, and Wall
(1999) state that elementary teachers must take note of major changes in content
and method associated with the entire spectrum of the elementary curriculum.
Secondary teachers, usually more directly, have to consider reforms such as new state
curriculum frameworks, standardized test protocols, national standards, and initiatives intended to improve basic skills.

However, despite the ultimate importance of teachers, curriculum planning
may take place on several different levels, ranging from the macro to the micro, and
these levels should be clearly differentiated.

Policies and Programs: The Macro and Intermediate Levels

The macro level of curriculum planning is concerned with general policy. Teachers
may or may not have been participants in the deliberations that led to such policy
statements. At this level, official documents produced by the federal government, by
state departments of education, or by school districts may contain policy statements
about the curriculum that either limit the ability of schools to make their own policies or encourage them to do so. These documents can include policy statements
pertaining to the curriculum as a whole, or they can be master plans for specific subjects or groups of subjects (Arends, 2000). In general, the intent of planners who
create policy statements is to set the direction of specific programs that will follow
from such statements.

The planning of programs is the intermediate level of curriculum planning; and
while programs may be created at the level of individual schools, usually they arise
from planning done by the state or the school district. Again, teachers may or may
not have been participants in the planning of statewide programs, but they are usually participants in the curriculum planning of school districts (Watson, Fullan, &
Kilcher, 2000). Plans by state departments and school districts that are highly prescriptive usually include details about the following:

- The range of subjects and electives to be taught
- The amount of time to be given to each subject
- The syllabi to be used, specifying objectives, content of courses, and forms
  of assessment for individual subjects
- The procedures (such as testing programs) to be followed for monitoring
  standards in schools and methods of teaching

In contrast, some state departments and school districts provide only minimal guidelines (analogous to the advisory, nonbinding suggestions made by various branches
of the U.S. federal government), essentially providing only general statements of
goals for particular subjects. Under these circumstances, individual schools may establish their own general policies about curricular matters such as the use of time
and testing.

Since state departments and school districts are concerned with planning programs, they may make centrally developed curriculum documents or packages available from which local schools may select specific units. In many school districts, curriculum guides for each subject are produced by committees of teachers and distributed to all schools. These guides may reflect the packages prescribed or simply made available by a state department. Also, numerous commercial publishers attempt to create attractive curriculum packages for entire subjects or grade levels, which they hope individual schools or districts will adopt. For instance, textbooks are often designed to complement curriculum guides and, in some cases, are used almost exclusively by teachers in preference to the conventional curriculum guides (English, 1987). Curriculum guides (and corresponding textbooks, which themselves may contain additional guidelines and recommended activities for teachers) can be comprehensive documents of 100 or more pages and contain the following:

- Detailed lists of goals and objectives
- A complete structure and sequence for the content to be taught
- Specific, highly detailed teaching units, including examples of content, questions, and tests and quizzes
- Background information for teachers about the subjects to be taught, including follow-up references

When guides are this elaborate, they are, in effect, programs. Much depends, of course, on whether such guides are actually requirements or options for individual schools and whether they have been made by teachers themselves or by outside agencies or commercial groups.

Lessons: The Micro Level

Whenever policies and programs have originated from above, teachers must plan their activities around them for periods of time, ranging from a full-year course to a daily lesson of a few minutes. Therefore, in individual schools and classrooms, teachers typically consult the program guides provided and then draw up their own specific curricular plans in the form of lesson plans. A lesson plan may be a document summarizing things such as objectives, contents of the curriculum, activities for students, methods of instruction, and forms of evaluating students; and it may be drawn up to cover not only daily lessons but the entire flow of classroom activities for a week, a month, or even an entire year. The connotations of the phrase "lesson plan" usually suggest a brief period of time.

However, whatever the time frame a lesson plan encompasses, it represents curriculum planning at the micro level. It is here that the general macro-level policies adopted by the state or district and the intermediate-level programs agreed upon collectively by the district or the school are transformed into the specific practices of individual teachers (King & Newmann, 2000). Not only may a lesson plan combine the macro, intermediate, and micro levels of curriculum planning, but it may lead directly from the planned curriculum to the enacted curriculum and even to the experienced curriculum, depending on the degree of flexibility that it permits.

6.3   TEACHERS

Teachers are, of course, the final planners, and, in practice, many daily lesson plans are not written out but remain in the heads of experienced teachers. In fact, many of the numerous decisions made daily by classroom teachers are the result of their long experience, not of self-conscious planning. The best of these decisions, no matter how spontaneous they may appear to be, are at least partially the indirect result of conscious planning that an experienced teacher has undertaken over a period of years. In this sense, because of their previous experience in planning flexible practices, good teachers are able to take advantage of the unforeseen opportunities that arise in their classrooms. Despite these complexities, curriculum planning in individual schools can, in general, be summarized as involving the use of statements of policy to guide the planning of collective programs that, in turn, lead to specific lessons.

Green (1988) highlights some of the contradictions associated with curriculum planning that bridges the gaps between policies, programs, and lessons. Creating programs is widely acknowledged as a critical, professional-practical activity; yet when such plans are seen as blueprints that must be followed in all details by individual teachers, programming becomes valued for the wrong reasons, "namely as a means of surveillance, assessment and hence control of teachers and teaching" (p. 2). Green suggests that the technical approaches to programming (which focus on efficiently reaching specified outcomes) should be de-emphasized in favor of the idea of programming as composing—that is, as an activity by each teacher that involves imagining, thinking, making meaning, and creating forms (curricula) that embody that meaning. This view of curriculum planning is in line with the considerable amount of slippage that seems inevitably to take place between the formal curriculum, as envisaged by policy documents, and the actual curriculum carried out in individual classrooms.

Numerous studies (Huberman, 1980, 1992; Jackson, 1968; Lortie, 1975; Young, 1990) provide striking pictures of the slippages that can occur. Some of these pictures are very positive and indicate the high level of professionalism exhibited by teachers as they make their own decisions, but these studies contain other pictures that reveal the enormity of teachers' tasks and the frustrations teachers often experience. Teachers rely on the content and methods outlined in textbooks, syllabi, and teachers' guides for their planning, but what they actually teach is a unique blend based on their own preferences. They put together their own syntheses based on their intuitive feelings and in keeping with their own artistic flairs. Stenhouse (1988), in a paper published posthumously, is just one of many authors to argue that teaching is an art. In contrast, Zahorik (1987) suggests that teaching can be viewed as a science and an art simultaneously, but that the metaphor of science is a more useful and powerful one. Often teachers experience frustration because they feel pressured publicly to describe teaching as primarily a science, even when privately and personally they view it as primarily an art.

Teacher Beliefs and Constructivism

The belief systems of teachers strongly affect how they teach, and many neophyte teachers begin their careers with beliefs that date back to early contact with their own teachers. The beliefs of teachers may change, however, dependent upon the professional situations they encounter. In some cases, such change may strengthen their confidence; in other cases, it can lead to self-doubt about their adequacy as teachers.

Various writers, such as Tillema (2000), contend that all teachers need opportunities to explicitly discuss, elaborate, and construct their own beliefs. This is especially true in schools that hope to encourage students to emulate their teachers in constructing their own knowledge instead of receiving it from others (Holt-Reynolds, 2000; Rainer, Guyton, & Bowen, 2000). Scherer (2001) considers constructivist teaching to include the following practices:

- Teachers seek and value students' points of view.
- Lessons are structured to challenge students' suppositions.
- Students are encouraged to recognize relevance in the curriculum.
- Teachers plan lessons around ideas.
- Students are assessed on the ability they demonstrate in daily classroom investigations.

Windschitl (1999) suggests that constructivism can't be grafted onto traditional teaching techniques. "Rather, it is a culture—a set of beliefs, norms, and practices that constitute the fabric of school life" (p. 752).

This approach to teaching has been widely advocated under the "constructivist" label for several decades (Perkins, 1999), although it is clearly an outgrowth of many of the practices of progressive education developed throughout the twentieth century. As such, it has a long history of helping students to learn curriculum materials in conventional ways but also to understand them in deeper ways. However, constructivist teaching can be very time consuming, and some students, expecting authoritative, clear-cut answers to all questions, may be confused by it. Some constructivist teachers may have their beliefs shattered by negative classroom experiences or by external forces such as high-stakes testing (Brooks & Brooks, 1999).

Nonetheless, in reality many teachers also take a constructivist approach to curriculum planning, even though they may not consciously apply that label to it.

How Teachers Plan

Numerous research studies undertaken over the years shed light on how teachers actually go about curriculum planning. These studies demonstrate that the process is too complicated to be reducible to a simple formula or to a series of determinant steps. For example, studies by Zahorik (1975), Clark and Yinger (1977), McCutcheon (1980), Ben-Peretz and Tamir (1981), Sardo-Brown (1990), and Martin-Kniep and Uhrmacher (1992) reveal that specifying objectives is seldom important to teachers, although the necessity for teachers to do so is increasingly becoming the conventional wisdom among politicians and educational bureaucrats (Ormell, 1992). Teachers may be making greater use of prespecified objectives in their planning of lessons, but, as Spady (1993) and Fitzpatrick (1991) suggest, this may be due to pressures to conform with new national standards. Marsh (1997) reports that advocates of the use of objectives claim that such planning leads to programs that maximize learning by enabling teachers to focus on the capabilities of students and to teach flexibly. Despite such claims, Ellis and Fouts (1993) indicate that the empirical evidence available at present is inconclusive.

Clark and Yinger (1977) note that teachers often make plans around students and activities and seldom use objectives as a starting point. Zahorik (1975) reports that teachers' most frequent decisions in planning curricula are choosing content and activities. Such studies suggest that teachers commonly use a sequence of steps in planning, but this sequence is itself flexible and more appropriately viewed as a kind of mental checklist and planning cycle than construed as a rigid, end-means model. Zahorik (p. 11) describes four steps that teachers in his research sample used:

1. They endeavor to understand the activity selected.
2. They imagine using the activity.
3. They think of ways to modify the activity.
4. They create a mental image of the revised activity.

McCutcheon (1980) similarly describes the complex internal dialogue that teachers engage in. This dialogue involves teachers in rehearsal of the lesson to be taught and reflection upon how they taught similar lessons on previous occasions. Deliberation, in the formal sense described by Walker (see chapter 3) and Schwab (see chapter 4), is not practiced fully by teachers as they plan, for instead of weighing many alternative courses of action, they tend to dwell on what they have done in the past that has worked out well. Formal deliberation, therefore, may be more appropriate in collective curriculum planning than in individual curriculum enactment.

In planning curricula, teachers are involved in making various judgments, but it is far from clear whether their decisions are based on some explicit value-orientation or on some combination of intuition and previous experience. For example, teachers make judgments about appropriate activities, materials to be used, satisfactory levels of student achievement, necessary follow-up activities (including homework and grading), and many other matters throughout the entire day. During instruction itself, they make numerous on-the-spot judgments about how students are reacting, about topics that need to be recapitulated or retaught, and about activities that can be omitted. However, teachers may base these on-the-spot judgments on incomplete conceptualizations of the complex situations with which they are faced. This is not to suggest that teachers' planning is predominantly subjective or haphazard. Like all educators, teachers have implicit, if not explicit, ideas about what good teaching is all about. They have their theories about what works in the classrooms and what does not. It is likely, however, that their theories or plans are concerned primarily with the instrumental goal of transferring knowledge to their students (Olson, 1989). Under the pressure of getting this job done well, teachers seem little concerned about the deeper question of what knowledge should be taught in schools. Thus, teachers' planning typically is about "how" far more than "what."

A new influence on curriculum planning is the Internet. Certainly, the Internet has become available in schools in the United States extremely rapidly and has been accompanied by high expectations about its potential usefulness (Schofield & Davidson, 2000). Parents want their children to learn how to access information on computers and, generally, students are eager to do so, with many attaining high levels of competency. Thus, teachers may plan their lessons so that students are encouraged to access various Internet sites, obtaining information from government departments, research centers, community organizations, businesses, and individuals. This information often is available in different formats such as text, video, audio, and graphics. Of course, the Internet can also be used to publish information created by students. Students can prepare reports and add them to the school's website, thereby making information available to students in other schools (Pearson, 2000).

While most teachers focus their attention on planning at the micro level of the classroom, attention also needs to be given to the macro and intermediate levels. Many contemporary writers (Apple, 2000; Beyer & Apple, 1998; Giroux, 1992) exhort teachers to break away from the shackles of domination by powerful groups in society. These writers argue that school knowledge is controlled not by teachers but by major groups that hold vested interests in using the curriculum to maintain their privileged positions in society. Therefore, teachers need to generate their own theories about what to teach—especially, to exploring inequalities and injustices—and to transform the oppression that currently occurs in society and is reflected in schools (Smyth, Dow, Hattam, Reid, & Shacklock, 2000). Some teachers may respond to this rhetoric, and there are published examples of groups of teachers actively developing new approaches to teaching and proposing atypical ideas about what knowledge is of most worth (Behar & George, 1994). However, there have been such examples in previous eras, and major changes in how teachers think as they do their jobs are not likely to come about rapidly. Classroom teachers are inundated with pressing day-to-day problems that require immediate solutions. Their hectic timetable means that teachers rarely have an opportunity for reflection or a chance to share ideas with colleagues. Nonetheless, Giroux (1991) argues that the ability of teachers to reflect on their deepest concerns is a basis for their professional empowerment.

Not only the nature of the job itself but the working conditions on the job force most teachers to make decisions on the run (Wise, 2000). The reactions of students to a lesson may cause a teacher to make hasty alterations to a plan or an ongoing activity. The demands generated by a roomful of students tax a teacher's resourcefulness and ingenuity to the full, and the teacher may consequently relegate to the "too hard" pile many ideals and theories about what teaching should or could be about. Furthermore, much of the planning done by individual teachers is done in isolation. A teacher seldom has adult observers, so there is little opportunity to obtain feedback about particular classroom actions, apart from student reactions. Because of time constraints, a teacher may have no opportunity—and perhaps not even the inclination—to discuss planning with colleagues. Recently, massive intensifications of teachers' workloads have occurred in many Western countries (Easthope & Easthope, 2000), further compounding the problem. McMahon (2000) identifies the drives to micro-manage schools and to raise standards as counterproductively placing new strains on how teachers use their time.

If problems arise in choosing what to teach and how to teach it, teachers tend to draw on their previous teaching experiences (Lortie, 1995). It is only in cases of emergency that teachers may seek help from others. After all, teachers gain considerable satisfaction from honing their craft of teaching (Dembo & Gison, 1985; Smylie, 1988); and when they seek assistance, that can easily be construed as a sign of confusion or incompetence. When teachers seek help, they tend to seek it from members of the same craft, namely fellow teachers at the same school, and not from specialists external to the school or from school administrators.

The process of fine-tuning and adjusting is a continuous activity. The dilemma for teachers is that this fine-tuning is done without any real knowledge of how successful they are actually being in helping their students learn what is most important in the long run. In other occupations, it is possible to point to tangible, concrete outcomes, but in teaching that is seldom the case. Teachers have to work on hunches and intuitions, trying to keep long-term goals in sight while endeavoring to solve the numerous major and minor problems that constantly crop up along the way.

Interacting with Other Faculty

The plans of individual teachers can be influenced by subtle and not-so-subtle pressures from other faculty members. Teachers newly appointed to a school quickly learn the acceptable routines and the expected standards of teaching. A hierarchy based on seniority tends to operate at both elementary and secondary schools (Feiler, Heritage, & Gallimore, 2000). Newly appointed faculty are not expected to be too innovative. They will certainly not be given the "best" classes, which are usually reserved for senior faculty.

Faculty members only rarely share ideas about planning with others, and for compelling reasons. Teaching is their craft, and there are matters of territory to maintain. If teachers start to share their teaching experiences, they run the risk of exposing their failures, and they could face ridicule and censure. But some swapping of ideas can occur without much risk during informal discussions, such as those that take place during the lunchtime break. Huberman (1980) uses the phrase "a collection of recipes" to describe the sharing of ideas that ordinarily takes place among teachers. But teachers do not simply take recipes from other teachers and use them without modification. A process of adaptation occurs in which teachers reassemble new ideas collected from others in a form that suits the special needs of a particular classroom. Sometimes in elementary schools, but more often in secondary schools and especially high schools with subject departments, two or more teachers may develop strong professional bonds through team planning and teaching (Siskin, 1994). Unfortunately the pressures of tight schedules and various administrative chores often dampen enthusiasm for such cooperative planning.

Given these conditions, the influence of other faculty members on a teacher's curriculum planning is, more often than not, predominantly negative. Teachers' room conversations will provide cues to a teacher about the acceptability or nonacceptability of something new in the school, and it is unlikely that a teacher will get direct assistance from others who are indifferent or hostile to any new ideas or ventures. As a consequence, the planning that most teachers undertake is confined to activities that will not incur the wrath of other teachers; that is, it is confined primarily to their own classrooms. Holmes (1991) notes that teaching in isolation is not necessarily less effective than teaching based on planning with other teachers, but for the innovative teacher intent on doing something new that might change the curriculum or even the organizational procedures of a school, even individual plans may be heavily censured by the staff and ultimately vetoed by the administration.

Site-Based Management

All in all, schools themselves may suffer from external shocks, work overload, too few resources, and poor morale (Kirst, 1993), and teachers have to maintain stability in what is potentially a very unstable environment. One way of attempting to do so is through what has now become widely known as site-based management (SBM), which emphasizes participatory decision making by the entire staff of a school and even members of the community. The process can be considered one of collaborative curriculum development. Smylie, Lazarus, and Brownlee-Conyers (1996) suggest that SBM can be effective and fulfilling, but David (1996) warns that it can also have destabilizing effects. One intent is, of course, to improve student achievement within a particular community, but SBM can itself raise issues about who makes decisions—teachers, students, parents, or community members (Conway & Calzi, 1996; Guskey & Petersen, 1996).

There is nothing new about SBM. In fact, most of the principles and practices of SBM, like those of constructivist teaching, were worked out by progressive educators during the first half of the twentieth century, and, in general, SBM includes the kind of deliberation explicated by Schwab (see chapter 4). For example, in the 1930s, each of the thirty experimental schools or school districts that participated in the Eight-Year Study (see chapter 2) were freed from most external requirements and, therefore, made their own on-site decisions about what their curricula would be. SBM depends, of course, on individual schools actually having real freedom to make decisions. While some guidelines may be handed down from above, if these become too restrictive, then SBM exists in name only. Hence, SBM tends to merge all three levels of curriculum planning as teachers make their own decisions about policies, programs, and lessons.

For SBM to work in practice, people in legal authority over a school must exercise restraint in exerting their control over the curriculum and must demonstrate leadership in promoting harmonious curriculum deliberations among those who work within the school (Price & Vallie, 2000). This mixture of restraint and leadership applies to the federal government, to state governments, to school boards, to superintendents, and to principals. It is a form of administration that is basically antithetical to the familiar staff-and-line arrangement, in which all members of an organization are ranked within a hierarchy in which people of higher rank give directives to those of lower rank. Instead of giving directives and otherwise attempting to control what other members of the organization do, administrators have three functions:

1. They help discern the purposes of the organization.
2. They create conditions under which members of the organization who do its substantive work can best carry out their tasks.
3. They attempt to create external support for the organization.

Seen in this light, an administrator is a facilitator of an organization's work, just as a teacher can be a facilitator of student learning.

Applied to a school, this form of administration acknowledges teachers as the people who do the substantive work. The school principal, however, may help teachers consider what the curriculum should be and how it might fit with the curricula of other schools. In addition, the principal should provide both material and psychological support to the teachers in their deliberations and should be prepared to explain to the community what they are doing while deliberations are in progress and what they have accomplished when any new curriculum has been developed. In this sense, the principal is not the instructional leader of the school (as much recent professional literature insists) but the leader of instructors.

The superintendent and school board members may play similar roles. Board members, for instance, have the duty to understand the issues that led to deliberations and to carry on a dialogue with the community about those issues. While outside consultants, other school personnel, members of the community, and even students may participate in curriculum deliberations, deliberations under SBM center on teachers, the classroom problems they encounter, and the curricular solutions they propose. Basic decisions about curriculum and instruction (most obviously, how to enact the planned curriculum) remain foremost among the professional tasks of teachers, for they are the people closest to the specific circumstances within which decisions must be made.

In SBM, each school plans and implements its own curriculum; however, these curricula are not necessarily out of touch with each other. The idea behind SBM is not individualism for the sake of individualism. States or school districts may provide general guidelines, the understanding of subject matter of the teachers of one school may parallel that of teachers in another school, consultants may offer similar advice, teachers may face common classroom problems, and the characteristics of the community in which a school exists may be similar to those of other communities (Watson et al., 2000). The idea behind SBM is that students benefit because the curricula they are taught are developed for them specifically, based on a close assessment of their individual characteristics and needs and on an assessment of the available resources in the school and the community, and that teachers benefit because they do most of the assessing and develop specific curricula that they believe will lead to the greatest benefit for students. Hence, teachers exercise professional judgments and develop some sense of personal commitment to the curricula they create. Differences among the planned curriculum, the enacted curriculum, and the experienced curriculum tend to be minimized, and teachers are allowed flexibility in implementation. Furthermore, when curricula are developed and implemented in this way, they can be constantly monitored by the teachers of a school, and future changes in light of changing circumstances are usually easier to make than when curricula have been externally imposed on the school.

SBM is not a panacea. Many on-site conflicts and problems can and do arise. Some scholars, such as Davies and Ellison (2000), argue that a rigorous theoretical framework for understanding how SBM can be optimized is still lacking. Nonetheless, SBM clearly encourages the development of a professional culture within a school in which teachers, other personnel, and members of the community work collaboratively in ongoing cycles of curriculum development and improvement.

Educational Policies and Priorities of School Districts

Clearly, school districts vary enormously in the degree to which they prescribe what planning teachers can and cannot do; the policies on planning and the practices of any district may change because of changes in the policies of the state (Tyree, 1993). Some districts provide only very brief guidelines in the expectation that teachers will do almost all curriculum planning in their respective schools, including the planning of policies and programs. In contrast, other districts provide detailed curricula to be followed by all teachers in the expectation that teachers will plan only a few details of their daily lessons (Olebe, Jackson, & Danielson, 1999).

Teachers who desire a lot of assistance usually prefer the latter kind of district since the tasks of planning are greatly simplified for them, even though what they teach is regimented. Other teachers, especially more experienced ones, who desire to follow their own initiatives usually prefer the former kind of district, particularly if that district also provides direct support for their efforts, such as small-scale grants for experiments with new curricula and released time from ordinary duties to participate on curriculum committees, to visit other schools, and to consult with curriculum specialists from outside the district (Shkedi, 1995). The priorities of a particular school district may vary over time as different circumstances arise. For example, a shortage of math and science teachers may necessitate the creation of additional curriculum resource materials in those subjects, with funding being made available for this purpose.

Regardless of their preferences, teachers have to work within the existing priorities of their districts. Certainly, any curriculum that they collectively plan and develop will have to fit within the general guidelines established by the district if it is actually to come into widespread use. Still, most districts are tolerant of a certain amount of slippage. In general, there is more freedom to deviate from curriculum guidelines in elementary schools than in senior high schools, where curricula are circumscribed by graduation requirements and tests such as the SAT.

Organizational Policies of Individual Schools

The curriculum planning undertaken by teachers also has to conform to the various rhythms and rituals of daily school life (Lucas, 1999). Elementary teachers are not as confined by bells and short instructional periods as secondary teachers are, but there are other restrictions. In planning their curricula, elementary teachers must ensure that their proposals will not cause undue noise in corridors or in adjacent classrooms. Field trips or special instruction that pulls students out of their regular classrooms can disrupt the plans of other teachers if good communications and agreed-upon schedules are not maintained. Also, all kinds of daily administrative procedures, such as taking attendance, listening to the principal's announcements on the public address system, and distributing notices for parents, can severely limit any attempts to develop innovative curricula.

The routines of schooling in both elementary and secondary schools encourage teachers to develop and maintain teaching practices that are predominantly traditional and that do not affect (positively or negatively) other teachers (Young, 1989). In practice, this means that a teacher may have little scope to vary the usual arrangement of furniture or the usual teaching venue, to use materials not previously approved by district officials, or to engage students in activities that will unsettle them for subsequent lessons with other teachers.

Societal Pressures

Schools and districts are subject to curricular pressures from special interest groups both within the community and from further afield, especially over controversial issues that arise. Such issues might concern the inclusion of a particular book in a course or in the school library; the adoption of a new teaching method; or the introduction of curricular units dealing with sexuality, race, politics, or religion. Teachers involved in planning curricula in potentially controversial areas have to be extremely sensitive to the feelings of parents and the community, and they may need to take special steps to obtain the support of the school's or the district's administration. Special-interest groups have their own agendas that they may wish to see followed by schools, although often the pressures they are prepared to exert on schools lie dormant until awakened by a specific incident. Such groups can, therefore, have very restrictive influences on curricula being developed (Thornton, 1988). In extreme cases, curricula already being taught in schools can be vetoed by powerful groups (Marsh & Stafford, 1988). In still other cases, such groups may successfully impose their own curricula on the schools.

Usually the influence of special-interest groups is less conspicuous and more indirect. In some cases, a group's influence may be viewed positively by the educational community—for example, when it is in line with what most people would consider better-quality schooling (such as the National Geographic Society's efforts to strengthen the teaching of geography). In other cases, a group's influence may be perceived as negative—for example, when a group is grinding a particular ideological ax, intent on imposing its own brand of orthodoxy on everyone else. In this context, the news media tend to dwell on whatever seems controversial, thereby magnifying the importance of some of the least benign pressures on schools, if not actually heightening them. Frequently special-interest groups lobby influential figures in the government or the community to support their agendas. Occasionally such groups are able to influence the passage of legislation that affects the schools.

These pressures may be keenly felt by a teacher engaged in curriculum planning, especially pressures to limit what the curriculum might otherwise be. Under these circumstances, teachers need to call upon their most creative skills in planning and enacting the best curriculum possible.

6.4   PRINCIPALS

If most schoolwide attempts at curriculum planning are to be successful, they require some form of involvement and commitment by the school principal. Numerous research studies point to the leadership of the principal as critical to constructive curriculum change in individual schools. Yet the principal must often walk a fine line between encouraging collaborative curriculum planning and attempting to dominate the process (Wildy, Louden, & Robertson, 2000). For instance, in site-based management the principal provides both material and psychological support to the teachers in their deliberations and can be a spokesperson to explain to the community what they are doing while deliberations are in progress and what they have accomplished when any new curriculum has been developed. At the same time, it is also important that teachers have opportunities to solve their own planning problems. In the words of an elementary school principal, "This process of 'letting go' can be likened to a tightly wound watch spring. As we moved toward site-based management, I had to let it unwind incrementally; with each release of the spring, new potential and energy was realized. The rewards for all of us soon became apparent" (Bergman, 1992, p. 48).

Studies by Leithwood and Montgomery (1982), Leithwood and Stager (1989), Fullan (1988), and Heller and Firestone (1994) suggest the goals that elementary school principals should pursue include the following:

- Principals should have a vision of what they want for their school in the years ahead.
- Principals should make their goals public to all concerned parties. They should ensure that their expectations are made known, particularly to teachers and to students.
- Principals should take action, directly or indirectly, to see that their goals are acted on and accomplished.
- Principals should develop and maintain good working relationships and a keen understanding of the work and progress of each teacher on their staff.

School principals may vary the methods they use to reach these goals (such as encouraging collaborative efforts versus supporting the initiatives of individual teachers), but these four goals seem essential for principals who are able to lead successful curriculum projects.

Studies examining the role of high school principals—such as those by Hall, Rutherford, and Griffin (1982); Fullan and Hargreaves (1991); Glatthorn (1993); and Wildy et al. (2000)—reach similar conclusions but also point out the busy and complex role of the typical secondary school principal, who usually shoulders responsibility for all programs. These researchers maintain that effective high school principals are those who have developed skills in the following areas:

- Developing interpersonal relations and organizational management
- Initiating innovations (and being unwilling merely to maintain a smooth-running organization)
- Finding out about and monitoring the degree to which the school is attaining its goals
- Obtaining resources and support for projects they believe in and are willing to fight for

Numerous systems exist for categorizing the daily tasks of principals. For example, a very simple system of categories might divide daily activities into administrative activities and pedagogical activities. This way of categorizing would seem to suggest that school principals should spend as much time concentrating on pedagogical tasks (providing leadership, support, instruction) as they do on administrative tasks (answering inquiries from the public, writing letters, filling out forms, making financial decisions). However, various studies indicate that school principals do not spend equal time on these two areas; instead, they spend far more time on administrative tasks. Evans and Mohr (1999) contend that principals, in fact, fail to spend enough time on focused reflection, preferring instead to do numerous routine tasks.

Figure 6.1 is a more detailed system of categories classifying a principal's tasks, as proposed by Rutherford and Huling-Austin (1984). This system of categories can help principals track how they use their time and energy and, hence, help them balance their time between tasks aimed at improving curriculum and instruction and time devoted to other tasks. This system also reminds principals that their tasks are all interrelated. For instance, the introduction of a new curriculum may cause some teachers (and students) to react differently than anticipated, thus necessitating changes in the scheduling of the school day or in the use of facilities. Changes in one category or subcategory are almost certain to cause changes in others.

Leadership Styles of School Principals

Principals seem to develop their own particular coping strategies, a style of behavior that enables them to achieve valued ends; however, the same style may interfere with the achievement of other ends valued less highly (Starratt, 1993). For instance, some principals tend to resist changes suggested by teachers. Of course, not all suggestions should be put into practice, but some principals are resistant to changes for defensive reasons: to thwart challenges to their leadership, to prevent having their weaknesses exposed, or to avoid the additional work a new curriculum would require. If, however, principals favor curriculum change, then they are likely to adopt a much different style.

Curriculum and instruction
- Reviewing or revising existing subjects
- Influencing specific teaching methods
- Introducing new subjects and units

Academic performance of students
- Influencing achievement in all subjects
- Encouraging students to achieve in accordance with their abilities
- Monitoring tests and examinations in specific subjects

Nonacademic development of students
- Managing or controlling students' behavior
- Influencing students' welfare and attitudes
- Influencing students' extracurricular activities

Professional and personal performance of staff
- Influencing the performance of teachers
- Influencing the performance of administrators
- Easing the transition of new teachers
- Influencing the performance of student teachers
- Supporting the welfare of teachers and their personal development

Administration and school organization
- Scheduling classes and other school programs
- Influencing students' choices of classes
- Influencing other student decisions
- Influencing the operational efficiency of the school

School facilities
- Managing the use of buildings and grounds for school activities
- Initiating changes to improve instruction
- Initiating changes to improve aesthetics

External relations
- Managing the use of buildings and grounds for community activities
- Providing positive public relations with the local community
- Maintaining regular communication with district and state education department officials

FIGURE 6.1

The principal's domains of control and supervision

Source: After Rutherford & Huling-Austin (1984).

It is also worth noting that leadership styles can be influenced by highly questionable stereotypes. For example, some people believe that the most effective school principals are males; and as a result, females may have fewer opportunities to become principals even though a majority of teachers are female (Porter, 1994). At the same time, a study by Lee, Smith, and Cioci (1993) revealed that male teachers rated the leadership of female principals they work for as relatively ineffective, even though on measures of self-efficacy and staff influence the female principals exceeded male principals in their effectiveness with both male and female teachers. Enomoto (2000) contends that educational management must be largely reconceived to expose questionable assumptions about gender.

Hall and Rutherford (1983), Leithwood and Stager (1989), Foster (1989), and Grace, G. (1999) have conducted research on the styles of elementary and secondary principals. Figure 6.2 outlines the three major styles reported by Hall and

Responders
- See their role as mainly administrative
- Allow teachers and others to take the lead in decision making
- Perceive teachers as professionals and so do not interfere with their instructional role
- Strive for strong personal relationships with their staffs
- Make decisions in terms of immediate issues
- Do not speak about long-term goals and plans
- Are flexible and willing to make changes at short notice to solve immediate problems

Managers
- Provide basic support for all members of their staffs
- Keep teachers informed about decisions
- Are sensitive to needs of teachers
- Protect teachers from unreasonable external pressures
- Do not typically initiate change but will follow through on changes given high priority by others, especially on changes initiated higher up in the school district

Initiators
- Have clear, decisive, long-range policies and goals for their schools
- Work hard to translate their goals into practice
- Make decisions in terms of what is best for students, not necessarily what is easiest or whether it makes their teachers happy
- Have strong expectations for students, teachers, and themselves
- Seize the lead in making things happen that they believe are in the best interests of their schools
- Are willing to reinterpret district and state policies and programs to suit the needs of their schools

FIGURE 6.2
Three different styles of principals
Source: Hall & Rutherford (1983).

Rutherford (1983), based on their study of twenty-five elementary school principals. They term principals who adopt these styles as responders, managers, and initiators, depending on the characteristic clusters of values and coping strategies through which they approach their work.

Responders value maintaining good relations with their staffs. They tend to listen to others rather than initiate ideas, to delegate responsibilities, and to be generally low-key and undemanding. They help teachers when they request assistance, but they do not hold many long-term goals, nor do they anticipate crises before they happen. Managers value getting tasks achieved far more than maintaining good personal relationships. They are orderly, well organized, and have established procedures for all routine tasks. Managers also may put in long hours before and after school to complete their own routine administrative tasks so that they can be available to teachers during school hours. They may prefer face-to-face contact with teachers, but they frequently use written memoranda to provide directives. They intervene directly with teachers about curriculum matters. Initiators value constructive change and take steps to stimulate it. They tend to be secure and confident. They make their expectations clear, typically couching them in terms of what is good for students.

In addition to identifying these styles, Hall and Rutherford (1983) also considered their influence on the planning, development, and implementation of new curricula in the twenty-five elementary schools. They found that managers and initiators intervened far more often than responders in getting staffs involved in curriculum projects and that, by far, initiators intervened directly in classrooms the most often. All three styles of principals were successful in initiating new programs, but the highest levels of implementation were achieved by initiators. However, the researchers also found a more positive psychological climate in schools led by managers than by initiators. Presumably, initiators are able to stimulate more curriculum change, but their demands and expectations also create greater strains among teachers.

Some of these findings about leadership may no longer hold true in light of recent pressures principals have come under. Southworth (2000) contends that in the United Kingdom, principals are predominantly managerial. Woods (2000) concurs, pointing out that principals increasingly are subject to "performativity," the expectation that they perform like enterprising, competitive entrepreneurs. Soder (1999) argues that "school renewal" is now widely seen as secondary to "school reform," with its emphasis on standards, high-stakes testing, and immediate results.

Finally, although these three styles illustrate different ways in which school principals approach curriculum planning, there is no conclusive evidence to indicate that any one of the three is better than either of the others (Murphy & Rodi, 2000).

6.5 PARENTS

There are enthusiastic—and vivid—accounts in the professional literature about the benefits of the participation of parents in local schools (Fullan, 1991; Halford, 1996; Maclure & Walker, 2000; West, 1993); still other accounts place parent participation in a negative light (Fine, 1993; McLaughlin, 1992; Woods, 1988). For example, Bryk, Lee, and Smith (1990) suggest that parents possess a variety of skills, talents, and interests that can enrich the curriculum, no matter how talented their children's teachers happen to be. In contrast, Fine (1993) contends that "parents enter the contested public sphere of public education typically with neither resources nor power. They are usually not welcomed, by schools, to the critical and serious work of rethinking educational structures and practices, and they typically represent a small percent of local taxpayers" (pp. 682–683).

Different value orientations on the part of educators lead to very different views about what are desirable and undesirable forms of parental participation. Figure 6.3 identifies seven levels of parental participation, ranging from the most passive (receiving reports about children's progress) to the most active (making decisions). The levels are based on works by writers such as Cervon and O'Leary (1982), Fitzgerald and Pettit (1978), and Beacham and Hoadley (1985). Generally, these writers assume that the desirability of parental participation increases as its level moves from passive to active.

1. **Receiving reports about their children's progress**
   - Take-home announcements
   - Report cards
   - Telephone calls
   - Home visits
   - Parent-teacher conferences
2. **Attending special events for parents**
   - Picnics
   - Work days (devoted to cleaning up and fixing up buildings and grounds)
   - Art shows, plays, concerts, science fairs
   - Assemblies
   - Open-house days
   - Parents' evenings
3. **Raising funds**
   - Bake sales, rummage sales
   - Walkathons
4. **Passively participating in educational activities**
   - In-service days for parents
   - Seminars on special topics
   - Classroom observation
5. **Assisting in noninstructional activities**
   - Organizing sports days, quiz nights
   - Supervising students on field trips
   - Contacting local businesses about opportunities for work experience for students
   - Researching library topics
   - Preparing supplies, noninstructional materials
6. **Assisting teachers in instruction**
   - Teaching skills (such as pottery making, basketball)
   - Guest speaking
   - Leading school trips
   - Preparing teaching materials
   - Maintaining student records
7. **Making decisions**
   - Screening applicants for teaching positions
   - Advising or sitting on curriculum committees

FIGURE 6.3
Parental participation in local schools

The first and most passive level of parental participation typifies the attitude of "teacher knows best." Parents are notified of school events and their child's progress. Conversations between parents and teachers provide opportunities for parents to raise questions. Face-to-face meetings can be highly satisfying to parents and teachers, but few parents take full advantage of such opportunities because of their busy daily schedules or their hesitance about appearing personally at the school (Coldron & Bolton, 1991). Teachers often complain that the parents they need to meet most do not come to parent-teacher conferences.

At the second level of participation, parents do come to the school for special events designed for them. Such events enable parents to observe special skills (dance routines, artwork) that students have achieved, but they also provide an opportunity for teachers and parents to interact socially. These occasions can help establish a positive rapport between parents and teachers.

The third level of participation involves parents in raising funds for the school, a traditional and significant task often taken on by parent-teacher associations or organizations. Resources always seem scarce. Funds are always needed to purchase additional library books, sports equipment, or microcomputers. Parents are usually very willing to be involved in fund-raising activities such as school bazaars and bake sales if they can see that the funds generated provide additional resources that benefit their children. However, most parents probably do not get involved beyond this level of participation in schools.

The next level requires parents to participate in educational activities, often specifically intended for them. Parents may participate in seminars and workshops dealing with topics such as values analysis, sex education, and math skills. These activities can provide a useful way for parents to learn not only about the topics covered but about the teachers' points of view (Epstein, 1995). Also, most schools permit parents to observe classes informally. Here parents can observe their own children learning and experience firsthand some of the everyday problems of teaching and the various managerial tasks involved.

The fifth and sixth levels of participation involve parents in actively assisting teachers in curriculum planning. In effect, a parent with sufficient time and inclination could function in most schools very much as a teacher aide does. In the beginning grades of elementary school, parents are often sought after to read stories to small groups of children and also to assist with arts and crafts. A variation on this is Kemp's (1985) home parent-tutor plan, which involves training parents of children with reading difficulties how to tutor them at home in ways that directly support the teaching done at school. In fact, the idea behind many programs intended to get preschool children ready for school is to educate their parents in how to provide a stimulating home environment. In any case, in schools themselves, parents may begin by assisting teachers in noninstructional activities (the fifth level) and then move on to assisting in instruction (the sixth level). Collectively, parents possess a wide range of special skills that can be a welcome and varied addition to the school curriculum. Furthermore, changes in employment patterns in the 1990s enabled a number of parents to take on some of these tasks (Fege, 2000; Halstead, 1994). For example, Love (1986) describes a high school in which eighteen parents each devoted a half-day per week to teaching the following subjects: math, art, library, knitting and crocheting, job interviews, tennis, social studies, fitting and turning (metalwork), and choir. Several states, including California (Solomon, 1991), have undertaken formal programs to involve parents at this level.

The seventh and most active form of parental participation is in making decisions for schools. In some districts, parents can be involved on school committees that screen candidates for teaching positions or that make selections of curricula (Fried, 1999). The only more influential way for parents to participate directly in making decisions for schools is to become members of the school boards or school committees that exercise the legal responsibility for the operation of local school districts (Zlotkin, 1993).

Desirable versus Actual Practices

Little hard evidence is available about the percentage of parents who are found at each level listed in Figure 6.3, but it seems a certainty that far more parents are passive rather than active participants in the activities of local schools (for example, Becker, 1981; Rosenholtz, 1989). Given that active participation seems to have the positive effects of providing substantial psychological benefits to parents, helping parents help their children learn, and making the schools more fully integrated into the life of the community, parents should be encouraged to participate more fully and more actively in curriculum planning than is now the case.

However, assuming that a high degree of active parental participation will occur simply because it should occur and the opportunities for it to occur are available is far too optimistic, even simplistic. Parents have themselves spent many years in school as students, yet when they venture into their children's schools, they may do so with various anxieties, feeling overwhelmed and poorly informed about typical school activities. McTaggart (1984) notes that "parents' knowledge of what goes on in schools tends to be restricted to the treatment of educational problems given by the media. . . . The images are both incomplete and confrontationist" (p. 12).

This situation is especially severe for parents of low socioeconomic status and for parents of minority ethnic groups (Cornbleth, 1996; Jackson & Cooper, 1989; MacLure & Walker, 2000), who often need special encouragement, guidance, and support before they are willing to become involved with school personnel. Their willingness seems to depend on their feeling safe, especially on feeling that there are not too many risks involved (Crozier, 1997). Andrews (1985) maintains that the typical response from such parents tends to be: "Every other time I've complained or spoken out too much, my kid has been picked on" or "It doesn't affect my kid, she/he is doing OK" (p. 30).

Many parents find the language of educators—and of teachers in particular—obscure, if not incomprehensible. As a necessary part of their training, teachers become involved in academic disciplines and may come increasingly to speak the language of the specialist, not appreciating why the layperson cannot understand the particular jargon of their profession. Thus, the only common ground of communication between teachers and parents is often reduced to mundane comments about how well individual children are coping with specific subjects and whether they like school. In this way, teachers make their subject matter and methods of teaching seem inaccessible to parents; however, parents can also build up barriers around their family life, their interests, and their ambitions (Fowler & Corley, 1996; Kenway, Alderson, & Grundy, 1987). The barriers between teacher and parents may require a considerable amount of time and goodwill to break down. Boomer (1985) refers to parents' building up these barriers as a form of self-imposed "educational apartheid. . . . [Parents] develop their own special forms of protection; an array equivalent of moats, barricades, deflection and passwords" (p. 1).

Very few parents readily volunteer to be involved in school activities (Aronson, 1996), yet most parents have various expectations (sometimes unrealistic ones) about what teachers should and could do for their children. Nor are teachers free from blame, for they are sometimes unwilling to discuss the specifics of their teaching with parents, yet they still expect parents to support them by seeing to it that children complete homework assignments and treat teachers as figures of authority deserving the highest respect (Hartley & Owen, 1986; Lareau, 1986). Then, too, the training of teachers tends to focus narrowly on the craft of teaching itself. Many preservice courses are devoted to how to teach, but few contain any units on how to communicate with parents or how to understand their points of view, motivations, and frustrations. Therefore, many teachers enter the profession a bit naïvely, not having carefully considered how they can encourage parents to participate actively in the school or assist in the education of their children. Lareau (1986) suggests that teachers and parents look at schooling in fundamentally different ways: teachers hold a universalistic perspective as they attempt to impose uniform standards on all children, whereas parents hold a particularistic perspective as they consider the well-being of their own children (Lasky, 2000). However, Hoover-Dempsey, Bassler, and Brissie (1987) suggest that such differences tend to break down if both teachers and parents consider how they mutually contribute to the education of children.

In 1993 California passed legislation placing a high priority on beginning teachers working actively with parents. Teacher training institutions now devote portions of their programs to (1) developing the communication skills of beginning teachers so they can enter into dialogue with families, (2) teaching them how to involve parents in educational activities with children in the home, and (3) familiarizing them with methods of connecting home culture to school learning (Hiatt-Michael, 2000). Teacher training throughout the United States is likely to increasingly follow this pattern.

6.6 STUDENTS

Students often express interest in a number of school-related issues and, given the opportunity, can be active participants in dealing with them (Allen, 1995). This is the case of the curriculum and how it is taught, where there is considerable potential for student participation in decision making. Many different people may create the planned curriculum, and teachers may enact variations of it, but students experience it in their own ways. Furthermore, many professional educators—ourselves among them—assume that the more broadly based the group that considers curriculum matters, the more likely it is to make informed decisions. However, because students can participate in curriculum planning and implementation does not necessarily mean that they should participate. Arguments can be advanced both ways.

Reasons for Student Participation

Figure 6.4 lists some basic reasons for including students in curriculum planning.

1. To learn fully, students must be given the opportunity to be active, responsible, and engaged with what they are learning (Skilbeck, 1984, p. 244).
2. Students most immediately experience the lived-in qualities of schooling (Vallance, 1981, p. 10).
3. Students are involved in out-of-class activities that are part of the broad environment (or curriculum) of the school (Skilbeck, 1984, p. 244).
4. Students, as clients of schools, have certain expectations and rights, including the right to evaluate the quality of the services they receive (Dynan, 1980, p. 4) and the right to negotiate what they learn (Hargreaves, 1992).
5. Student participation leads to positive and collegial relationships between students and teachers (Dunn, 1986, p. 3).

FIGURE 6.4
Some arguments for student participation in curriculum planning

Argument 1: Students Should Be Engaged in What They Learn.   Allen (1995) argues that if we are serious about empowerment in education, then students should be encouraged to voice their concerns and opinions about curricula, to participate in decisions, and to talk and act like citizens in a democracy. Furthermore, if students become active participants in decision making, then more positive collegial relationships will develop between teachers and students (Grace, G.; 1999; Johnson & Johnson, 1994). Fullan (1991) suggests that "we must start treating students as people—we should stop thinking of students just in terms of learning outcomes and start thinking of them as people who are being asked to become involved in new activities" (p. 189).

Reid (1982) gives a practical example in describing how a ninth-grade English class blossomed when students were given the opportunity to negotiate their curriculum with the teacher. The students were asked to compile a list of things that they didn't know about their school. The ensuing small-group discussions led the students to compile their own list of priorities and to work out the sources they would need for finding the necessary information. Reid concludes, "Students are responsible and trustworthy people who, if allowed to use their sense of responsibility in a meaningful way, do become independent learners, capable of generating and following through a quest for knowledge and understanding that will prove intrinsically rewarding" (p. 22).

Argument 2: Students Experience the Lived-In Quality of Schooling.   Vallance (1981) emphasizes what she calls the "lived-in" experiences of schooling. The experiences of students are primarily what education is about; hence, firsthand accounts of these experiences—and especially the experiences of ethnic minorities—are extremely valuable sources of information for those involved in planning and then enacting curricula (Banks, 1994; Goodlad & Oakes, 1988; Sapon-Shevin, 2001). Students could simply fill out anonymous surveys of their preferences and reactions, or they might provide detailed explanations of particular experiences, conveying them directly to other participants in curriculum planning.

Argument 3: Students Are Involved in Out-of-Class Activities.   Skilbeck (1984) suggests that students participate in a wide variety of out-of-class (or extracurricular) activities, and, especially at the high school level, they often occupy positions of leadership in these activities. These activities are an integral part of the life of a school, and the "extracurricular" is extra only in the sense that it is not part of the central academic curriculum. It, too, may be planned with care and enacted flexibly. Students who lead student councils, athletic teams, debate clubs, and numerous other groups often have much to say that is pertinent to the academic curriculum, and they can be effective contributors to the process of planning both curricular and extracurricular activities.

Argument 4: Students Have the Right to Negotiate and Evaluate What They Learn. Another reason often advanced for student participation is that students are, in effect, clients of the school. In business dealings, clients have specific expectations and rights; in virtually every profession, clients decide what services they want and whether these services have been performed satisfactorily. In schools, although most students are minors and their attendance is required by law, they are still clients since the school exists to serve their needs. Typically, of course, students are not afforded the rights of clients; there is an unequal distribution of status and authority between teachers and students. A number of writers such as King (1990) suggest that many students are alienated from schools because of these inequalities. They feel that they are powerless to influence what the curriculum will be and tend to see school as "a chore to be got through and finished with as soon as possible" (Dynan, 1980, p. 42). Their participation in planning and evaluating what they do in school is one way of ending their alienation and establishing some of their rights as clients of the school.

A variation on this argument focuses on rights themselves. A number of writers (Andrews, 1985; Maguire, 2000) assert that students have legal rights that include curriculum decision making. Some of these legal rights have in fact been tested in the courts since the 1960s, and court decisions have upheld student rights such as the following (Blakers, 1980; Fitzgerald & Pettit, 1978):

- The right to an effective education, as measured by the outcomes of schooling
- The right to have access to schools that effectively respond to different needs and cultures
- The right to be educated in an environment that is comfortable and conducive to learning
- The right to equality of educational opportunity
- The right of access to and instruction in all things that affect social development

Compelling reasons for including students in curriculum planning may, therefore, be found in the concept of rights itself and in how courts are now applying this concept to schools.

Argument 5: Students Establish Positive Relationships with Teachers.   Positive collegial relationships between students and teachers may be fostered when students are active participants in curriculum decision making (Grace, M., 1999; Martin, Saif, & Thiel, 1987). Dunn (1986) cites examples of students collecting data about ongoing teaching practices and how their role as participant-evaluators led to better relationships with their teachers. Both students and teachers shared in solving problems of mutual concern. Similarly, Savage and McCord (1986) suggest that students as young as fourth graders can collect data about what goes on in classrooms—information that can become the basis for subsequent shared decisions between students and teachers.

Reasons against Student Participation

The basic reasons usually given against students participating in curriculum planning begin with the traditions of education in Western societies. The traditions of schooling and teaching place heavy emphasis on the authority of teachers and on their professional training, with the result that teachers are entrusted with most, if not all, classroom decisions. These traditions leave little opportunity for the participation of nonprofessionals—whether students, parents, or members of the community. In other clinical professions, such as medicine and dentistry, members of the profession take responsibility and are held accountable for their decisions; therefore, tradition holds, the same must be the case in teaching. After all, teachers receive intensive training in areas such as child development, learning styles, philosophical studies, educational measurement, and subject-specific methodology. They have professional knowledge and expertise that the community at large does not have. Students, certainly, do not have sufficient background or breadth of experience to make useful contributions to curriculum planning. Indeed, a traditional view of education holds that students are students precisely because they lack something that the teacher has (and, they hope, is willing to pass on to them); therefore, they must trust the teacher's judgment about what is most worthwhile to learn.

A related reason shifts focus from the intellectual authority of teachers to their social authority. In order to create a particular classroom climate, teachers spend inordinate amounts of time bringing order and stability out of chaos. The task is extremely difficult, and they do it because only certain climates provide the optimal conditions for learning to take place. For the good of all students, therefore, this task is not one that can be constantly disrupted or constantly subjected to revision and redirection. The creation and maintenance of a productive working environment requires mutual respect between teacher and students and harmonious interactions between them. Traditionalists argue that, when students participate in decision making, the teacher's authority to make decisions for the good of everyone may suffer. Discipline and the very ability of a classroom to function may break down. Abraham (1995) argues that sex-based harassment and disruptive behavior can increase in these circumstances. Thus, the teacher must be regarded by students as the decision maker.

A less convincing reason, but nevertheless of some importance, is that external constraints, such as standardized testing, leave little room for teachers to deviate from established and relatively narrow curricula, particularly in some academic areas. There is little point, therefore, in encouraging students to participate in curriculum planning if, in fact, there is no viable alternative to the existing curriculum, which may be time-honored, textbook-bound, and examination-oriented. The argument can be extended to include the influence of powerful groups from outside the school, such as business associations, that may be unwavering in their support for traditional subjects. In the eyes of these groups, students participating in curriculum planning may be regarded with suspicion. Teachers would be seen as caving in to their demands for watered-down courses and opting to use nonprofessionals instead of exercising their own professional judgment.

At present, it is not at all clear whether there is a definitive worldwide trend toward greater student participation in curriculum decision making. Forms of education that encourage student participation (such as constructivism and others derived from progressive education) appear to be on the rise (for example, Brooks & Brooks, 1999; Perkins, 1999), but this trend may be balanced by trends that exist in many Western nations toward the bureaucratization of education and the centralization of control over school curricula.

6.7 EXTERNAL FACILITATORS

When teachers become involved with curriculum planning in their schools, they may overflow with enthusiasm yet lack knowledge and experience. Questions arise. Who should serve on the curriculum committee? Should the committee attempt to define highly specific objectives? How can certain topics be integrated across the various subject areas in the curriculum or at different grade levels? What form should the curriculum take? Seldom do such questions have definitely right and wrong answers, and even people with considerable experience in curriculum planning and development are often puzzled about how to answer them for the specific circumstances that exist in each school. Principals, too, are often frustrated about managing curriculum change in their schools and dealing with the myriad tasks that must be attended to, such as maintaining close links with parents, community groups, and local industries. This is especially the case with site-based management (Bergman, 1992).

To keep the process of curriculum planning and development running smoothly, schools may call on external facilitators. The name "external facilitator" is deliberately general. It applies to anyone from outside the school who has special knowledge, skill, or experience helpful in guiding curriculum planning on the many rough issues that the planners inevitably have to deal with. External facilitators may have various titles, such as "linker," "trainer," or "consultant," but their basic function is the same. They may be experienced teachers from other schools within a district, but usually larger districts employ their own full-time specialists. State departments of education also employ full-time specialists in curricula of various kinds (such as reading or secondary school science) or in the general process of curriculum planning and development; these specialists are available to local districts or schools (Slavin, 2000). Some external facilitators enjoy national or international reputations and may be hired as consultants on a contractual basis by federal and state agencies.

Perhaps even more important than the abilities of external facilitators is how they are perceived by those whom they are intended to help (Fullan, 1999). Reputations count, but so do the reasons why an external facilitator may have been brought into a particular school in the first place. Much depends on who is giving assistance, when, and why. Few teachers are reluctant to accept assistance when it is offered in a cooperative spirit, without threats (implied or explicit), and if matters of privacy and confidentiality are observed. Often, however, teachers perceive external facilitators as outsiders who enter the school in order to obtain inside information about how well the teachers are performing their jobs. Mulford (1981) describes this problem as the "assess/assist dilemma." When assistance seems linked with decisions about tenure, teaching assignments, or the allocation of resources, then assessment will predominate over assistance in the minds of most teachers. Therefore, external facilitators who are the most successful in assisting curriculum projects are usually those who are most successful at alleviating teachers' fears (or potential fears) about assessment.

Good external facilitators walk a fine line between being overly directive and insufficiently directive. Problems are pressing, and answers are uncertain. Too much advice offered at the wrong time can be less helpful than no advice at all. Various research studies (Fullan, 1991; Goodman, 1994; Miles, Saxl, & Lieberman, 1988) suggest that it takes a special type of person to be a good external facilitator. Figure 6.5 lists some of the personal attributes of external facilitators that research studies commonly list as desirable. Notwithstanding that few external facilitators, in all probability, possess all of these attributes, the list captures much of the ability to deal with complexity, the innovativeness, and the tenacity and drive that seem characteristic of many persons who take on the role of external facilitator.

---

1. They have a tolerance for ambiguity.
2. They are entrepreneurial.
3. They like the freedom to organize their own work.
4. They are loners.
5. They cope well with performing multiple roles.
6. They cope well when overloaded with work.
7. They receive intrinsic satisfaction from assisting others.
8. They are candid and straightforward.
9. They are aware of the personal and emotional risks involved.
10. They have motivation and drive.
11. They can be enthusiastic without being overly enthusiastic.
12. They cope well with frustrations.

FIGURE 6.5
Desirable attributes of external facilitators

Not only do external facilitators face the difficult problems of curriculum planning, but they also have to withstand conflicting pressures and sometimes unrealistic demands from school principals and teachers (Scott, 1999). Principals often view external facilitators as threats to their own authority within their schools. Teachers tend to be skeptical, respecting them only if they can demonstrate a wide repertoire of practical skills. Highly competent external facilitators may be keenly sought after by teachers, however. The reputation of successful external facilitators seems to spread widely among teachers, who may seek out particular individuals to help them. Thus, success can lead to impossible workloads for those external facilitators who are best known and most highly respected.

6.8   CONCLUDING COMMENT

The various stakeholders we have described in previous sections of this chapter most usually interact in a single setting: the local school, the place where curriculum planning and curriculum enactment meet. We stress that good curriculum planning in schools often requires overcoming many obstacles. With very few exceptions, even small-scale curriculum planning requires that participants engage in extensive deliberations. Therefore, finding appropriate times for participants to meet is often crucial to the success of a project. With proper incentives to teachers (including, perhaps, their temporary release from some duties), time may be found outside of the ordinary school day. Usually, however, a better solution is to rearrange the school schedule so that teachers may meet regularly during school hours. Aside from teaching itself, curriculum planning is the most important professional activity teachers engage in; the point is to find sufficient time for it rather than appending it to a long list of agenda items at a hectic and obligatory faculty meeting.

Another difficulty is that participants may not be aware that curriculum planning rarely proceeds smoothly along the lines originally envisaged for it, arriving at the one inevitable proposal for curriculum change. In the process of curriculum planning, new ideas surface and new directions are explored. The leader of a school curriculum project, whether the principal, a teacher, or an external facilitator, should understand that the unforeseen is potentially a source of frustration for participants and should help participants to live with the ambiguity that the unforeseen creates. The task of the leader is to facilitate collaboration between colleagues, not to insist that certain conclusions must be reached (Lieberman & McLaughlin, 1992).

As a school-based group begins to plan a curriculum, it may encounter still another difficulty: realizing that it needs help but not knowing where to turn. How can it obtain needed expertise, information, or finances? We have already described in general terms the external facilitators who can be called upon in such circumstances. However, there is a wide variety not only of individuals but of both public and private agencies that can be of assistance in curriculum planning. Some valuable resource persons may be available from within the school, but many more are available from without. By calling on the services of external resource persons and agencies, a curriculum planning group may be able to overcome many of its problems (Ornstein & Hunkins, 1988). For instance, such an agency might be able to provide a planning group with a curriculum document produced in another state or even another country that is relevant to the group's task and that is easily adaptable to the particular local situation. Seldom does a group need to rely solely on its own resources. The number of resource persons and agencies that might be contacted is vast. Figure 6.6 lists some of the most important resources available (both external and internal to the school) and possible reasons for contacting them.

Title	Possible Reasons for Seeking Contact
Education officials	
Superintendent, assistant superintendent	Formality, regulation requirements
Curriculum director	Formality, regulation requirements
Curriculum/research officers	Advice, expertise in deficient areas
Technology/media officers	Technical advice
Liason/advisory specialists	Advice, expertise in deficient areas, invitations, to visit schools
In-service officers	Advice, enrollment in courses
Teacher's center officers	Advice, expertise in deficient areas
Professional agencies/specialists	
Professors	Informal discussions, enrollment in courses
Curriculum project members (from other schools)	Informal discussions
Authors of educational books and journals	Informal discussions
Professional associations	Liaison, advice
Teacher's unions	Advice, funding
National agencies	Advice, funding
State departments of education	Materials, consultations
Testing agencies	Technical services
Educational laboratories	Advice, technical services
Community agencies	
Service organizations	Materials, guest speakers, funding
News media	Disseminating information
Special-interest groups	Guest speakers
Commercial organizations	Materials, guest speakers, funding
Internal personnel	
Principal	Support and approval, leadership
Deputy principal	Support with administrative details
Librarian	Provision of materials
Curriculum specialists	Advice, consultations, leadership
Other teachers	Informal discussions, support
Students	Support and collaboration
Parents	Support, liaison

FIGURE 6.6
Some resource persons and agencies

Each curriculum planning group must consider its own circumstances in deciding what help it needs and who can best provide it. Each group should also be prepared to make its own decisions about what advice from external resources it should act upon and what advice it should reject. That is an issue only the group itself—and not the external resource persons and agencies—can resolve.

Finally, although we have just stressed difficulties to be overcome by any group planning a school curriculum, we suggest there are numerous intrinsic satisfactions to be found simply in participating in curriculum planning. We reject the technical approach to curriculum planning and development, which attempts to identify all components of the process, fitting them together in assembly line fashion until the best possible curriculum emerges. Rather than a technical metaphor to represent the process of curriculum planning, we prefer a different one.

Purves (1975) uses the metaphor of a game to portray how curriculum planners might go about their task. Assuming that planners have a particular approach or model in mind, they should go about their task in the spirit of playing a board game. The board game is serious and challenging. In it the number of pieces on the board is relatively fixed and there are a number of rules that have to be followed, but the strategies used by any one player or group can vary. Some pieces of the curriculum game are depicted in Figure 6.7.

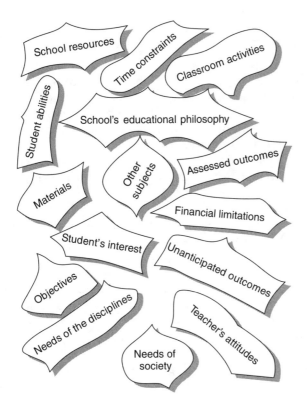

FIGURE 6.7
Pieces of the curriculum game

According to Purves, the rules of the curriculum game are simple:

1. Players can start with any piece, but all pieces must be picked up.
2. All pieces must be considered in terms of their relationship with other pieces.
3. Players win the game if all pieces can be placed in some relation to each other. (1975, pp. 120–121)

Since the pieces can always be placed in some relation to each other, everyone who plays wins! That is the biggest surprise in playing the curriculum game. Playing is fun. There is literally an infinite number of winning strategies, moves, and solutions, even though they all cannot be consciously considered. But, each winning player can still be asked, "Why have you chosen to place the pieces in that particular pattern?" We expect each player to answer differently, but, we hope, each answer will, in its own way, be equally thoughtful. The metaphor of the game thus highlights yet again how curriculum planning is artistic and creative, not technical. In actuality, of course, the process of curriculum planning is far more complex than playing a game—and far more fun and rewarding, with more far-reaching consequences.

We ask our readers to recall this metaphor when they are hard at work seeking out and meticulously considering all the information and ideas that go into curriculum planning.

■ QUESTIONS AND REFLECTIONS

1. What are the advantages of team curriculum planning versus individual curriculum planning? Give reasons.
2. How can principals balance the needs of teachers with the needs of students in curriculum planning? How do principals promote a democratic ethos at their respective schools?
3. "All curriculum making is essentially a political process." Do you agree or disagree with this statement? What light has this chapter shed on the issues that this statement raises?
4. "School leaders can no longer view parents as appendages to schooling or meddlers in their work" (Fege, 2000). Describe how parents can be directly involved in planning the curriculum. Explain why few parents are active participants.
5. "Providing opportunities for students to generate their own curriculum requires risks and courage" (Grace, M., 1999). Why is it important for students to be involved in curriculum planning? Give and then discuss an example of student involvement that you have observed.
6. Constructivist theory is difficult to translate into practice despite its many advantages. To what extent can teachers incorporate constructivism into their classroom planning? What are some likely advantages and disadvantages?
7. Is site-based management (SBM) more likely than centralized planning to bring about school improvement? Are SBM planners more empowered and more autonomous than central planners? Discuss.
8. How can the Internet be used to help teachers in curriculum planning? What impact might it have on curriculum planning over the next several decades?

■ SUGGESTED READING

The following are insightful articles on curriculum planning (see chapter bibliography):

Conway & Calzi (1996)

English (1987)

Hatch (2000)

Martin et al. (1987)

Smylie et al. (1996)

Young (1989)

Zahorik (1987)

Books useful in curriculum planning (see the chapter bibliography) include the following:

Apple (1986)

Fullan (1999)

Fullan & Hargreaves (1991)

Glatthorn (1987)

Lieberman & McLaughlin (1992)

Lortie (1975)

Scott (1999)

■ BIBLIOGRAPHY

Abraham, J. (1995). *Divide and school.* London: Falmer.

Allen, J. B. (1995). Friends, fairness, fun and the freedom to choose: Hearing student voices. *Journal of Curriculum and Supervision, 10*(4), 286–301.

Andrews, G. (1985). *The parent action manual.* Melbourne: Schools Community Interaction Trust.

Apple, M. W. (1986). *Teachers and texts.* New York: Routledge & Kegan Paul.

Apple, M. W. (2000). Can critical pedagogies interrupt rightist policies? *Educational Theory, 50*(2), 229–258.

Arends, R. I. (2000). *Learning to teach* (5th ed.). Boston: McGraw Hill.

Aronson, J. Z. (1996). How schools can recruit hard-to-reach parents. *Educational Leadership, 53*(7), 58–60.

Banks, J. A. (1994). Transforming the mainstream curriculum. *Educational Leadership, 51*(8), 4–8.

Beacham, J., & Hoadley, R. (1985). *Techniques for participation in decision making: For previously uninvolved groups.* Canberra: School and Community Project, Canberra College of Advanced Education.

Becker, H. (1981). Teacher practices of parent involvement at home—a statewide survey. Paper presented at the annual meeting of the American Educational Research Association, Washington, DC.

Behar, L. S., & George, P. S. (1994). Teachers as change agents: Implications for how teachers use curriculum knowledge. Paper presented at the annual meeting of the American Educational Research Association, New Orleans.

Ben-Peretz, M., & Tamir, P. (1981). What teachers want to know about curriculum materials. *Journal of Curriculum Studies, 13*(1), 45–53.

Bergman, A. A. (1992). Lessons for principals from site-based management. *Educational Leadership, 50*(1), 48–51.

Beyer, L. E., & Apple, M. W. (1998). *The curriculum: Problems, politics, and possibilities* (2nd ed.). Albany: State University of New York Press.

Blakers, C. (1980). *Principle seven.* Australian Council for State School Organisations Discussion Paper. Canberra: Australian Capital Territory.

Boomer, G. (1985). Long division: A consideration of participation, equality and brain power in Australian education. Paper presented at the Australian Council for State School Organisations annual conference, Launceston, Tasmania.

Brooks, M. G., & Brooks, J. G. (1999). The courage to be constructivist. *Educational Leadership, 57*(3), 18.

Bryk, A., Lee, V., & Smith, J. (1990). High school organisation and its effects on teachers and students. In W. Y. Cloune & J. F. White (Eds.), *Choice and control in American education: Vol. 1. The theory of choice and control in education.* London: Falmer.

Caldwell, B. J. (1994). The principal's role in radical decentralisation in Victoria's schools of the future. Paper presented at the annual meeting of the American Educational Research Association, New Orleans.

Cervon, B., & O'Leary, K. (1982). A conceptual framework for parent involvement. *Educational Leadership, 40*(2), 48–49.

Clark, C. M., & Yinger, J. (1977). Research on teacher thinking. *Curriculum Inquiry, 7*(4), 279–304.

Coldron, J., & Bolton, P. (1991). "Happiness" as criterion of parents' choice of school. *Journal of Education Policy, 6*(2), 169–178.

Conway, J. A., & Calzi, F. (1996). The dark side of shared decision making. *Educational Leadership, 53*(4), 45–49.

Cornbleth, C. (1996). *An American curriculum?* Paper presented at the annual meeting of the American Educational Research Association, New York.

Crozier, G. (1997). Empowering the powerful: A discussion of the interrelation of government policies and consumerism with social class factors and the impact of this upon parent interventions in their children's schooling. *British Journal of Sociology, 18*(2), 187–200.

David, J. L. (1996). The who, what and why of site-based management. *Educational Leadership, 53*(4), 4–9.

Davies, R., & Ellison, T. (2000). *Site-based management, myths and realities.* Paper presented at the annual meeting of the American Educational Research Association, New Orleans.

Dembo, M. H., & Gison, S. (1985). Teachers' sense of efficacy: An important factor in school improvement. *Elementary School Journal, 86*(2), 173–184.

Dunn, J. G. (1986). Realizing a classroom asset. *Curriculum Perspectives, 7*(2), 37–40.

Dynan, M. P. (1980). *Do schools care? The student view.* Perth: Education Department of Western Australia.

Easthope, C., & Easthope, G. (2000). Intensification, extension and complexity of teachers' workload. *British Journal of Sociology of Education, 21*(1), 43–56.

Ellis, A. K., & Fouts, J. T. (1993). *Research on educational innovations: Eye on education.* Princeton, NJ: Princeton Junction.

English, F. W. (1987). It's time to abolish conventional curriculum studies. *Educational Leadership, 44*(4), 50–53.

Enomoto, J. (2000). Probing educational management as gendered: An examination through model and metaphor. *Teachers College Record, 102*(4), 375–393.

Epstein, J. L. (1995). School-family-community partnerships: Caring for the children we share. *Phi Delta Kappan, 76*(9), 701–712.

Evans, P. M., & Mohr, N. (1999). Professional development for principals. *Phi Delta Kappan, 80*(7), 530–532.

Fege, A. F. (2000). From fund raising to hell raising: New roles for students. *Educational Leadership, 57*(7), 39–43.

Feiler, R., Heritage, M., & Gallimore, R. (2000). Teachers leading teachers. *Educational Leadership, 57*(7), 66–69.

Fine, M. (1993). (Ap)parent involvement: Reflections on parents, power, and urban public schools. *Teachers College Record, 94*(4), 682–710.

Fitzgerald, R. T., & Pettit, D. W. (1978). *Schools and the community: A growing relationship.* Schools Commission Special Report, Burwood State College, Melbourne, Victoria.

Fitzpatrick, K. A. (1991). Restructuring to achieve outcomes of significance for all students. *Educational Leadership, 48*(8), 18–22.

Foster, W. (1989). Toward a critical practice of leadership. In J. Smyth (Ed.), *Critical perspectives of educational leadership.* London: Falmer.

Fowler, R. C., & Corley, K. K. (1996). Linking families, building community. *Educational Leadership, 53*(7), 24–26.

Fried, R. L. (1999). Parent anxiety and school reform. *Phi Delta Kappan, 80*(4), 264–271.

Fullan, M. G. (1988). *What's worth fighting for in the principalship?* Toronto: Ontario Teachers Federation.

Fullan, M. G. (1991). *The new meaning of educational change.* London: Cassell.

Fullan, M. G. (1999). *Change Forces: The Sequel.* London, Falmer.

Fullan, M. G., & Hargreaves, A. (1991). *Working together for your school.* Melbourne: Australian Council for Educational Research.

Galton, M., Hargreaves, L., Comber, C., & Wall, D. (1999). *Inside the primary classroom: 20 years on.* London: Routledge.

Giroux, H. A. (1980). Critical theory and rationality in citizenship education. *Curriculum Inquiry, 10*(4), 329–366.

Giroux, H. A. (1991). Curriculum planning, public schooling, and democratic struggle. *NASSP Bulletin, 75*(532), 12–25.

Giroux, H. A. (1992). *Border crossings: Cultural workers and the politics of education.* New York: Routledge.

Glatthorn, A. A. (1987). *Curriculum leadership.* Glenview, IL: Scott, Foresman.

Glatthorn, A. A. (1993). Teacher planning: A foundation for effective instruction. *NASSP Bulletin, 77*(551), 1–7.

Goodlad, J. I., & Oakes, J. (1988). We must offer equal access to knowledge. *Educational Leadership, 45*(5), 16–19.

Goodman, J. (1994). External change agents and grassroots school reform: Reflections from the field. *Journal of Curriculum and Supervision, 9*(2), 113–135.

Grace, G. (1999). *School leadership.* London: Falmer.

Grace, M. (1999). When students create curriculum. *Educational Leadership, 57*(3), 49–53.

Green, B. (1988). *Imagining the curriculum: Programming for meaning in subject English.* Unpublished paper, Murdoch University, Perth, Western Australia.

Guskey, T. R., & Petersen, K. D. (1996). The road to classroom change. *Educational Leadership, 53*(4), 10–15.

Halford, J. M. (1996). How parent liaisons connect families to school. *Educational Leadership, 53*(7), 34–37.

Hall, G. E., & Rutherford, W. L. (1983). *Three change facilitator styles: How principals affect improvement efforts.* Austin: University of Texas, Research and Development Center for Teacher Education.

Hall, G. E., Rutherford, W. L., & Griffin, T. H. (1982). *Three change facilitator styles: Some indicators in a proposed framework.* Paper presented at the annual meeting of the American Educational Research Association, Los Angeles.

Halstead, J. M. (Ed.). (1994). *Parental choice and education.* London: Kogan Page.

Hargreaves, A. (1992). Time and teachers' work: Teacher preparation time and the internification thesis. *Teachers College Record, 94,* 87–108.

Hartley, R., & Owen, J. M. (1986). *National evaluation of the participation and equity program.* Melbourne: Melbourne College of Advanced Education.

Hatch, T. (2000). What does it take to break the mold? Rhetoric and reality in new American schools. *Teachers College Record, 102*(3), 561–589.

Heller, M. F., & Firestone, W. A. (1994). *Heroes, teams and teachers: A study of leadership for change.* Paper presented at the annual meeting of the American Educational Research Association, New Orleans.

Hiatt-Michael, D. (2000). *Parent involvement as a component of teacher education programs in California.* Paper presented at the annual meeting of the American Educational Research Association, New Orleans.

Holmes, M. (1991). The classroom: Solitude, isolation and rules. *Curriculum Inquiry, 21*(2), 135–140.

Holt-Reynolds, D. (2000). What does the teacher do? Constructivist pedagogies and prospective teachers' beliefs about the role of a teacher. *Teaching and Teacher Education, 16,* 21–32.

Hoover-Dempsey, K. V., Bassler, O. C., & Brissie, J. S. (1987). Parent involvement: Contributions of teacher efficacy, school socio-economic status, and other school characteristics. *American Educational Research Journal, 24*(3), 417–435.

Huberman, M. (1980). *Finding and using recipes for busy kitchens: A situational analysis of routine knowledge use in schools.* Washington, DC: National Institute of Education.

Huberman, M. (1992). The role of the classroom teacher as a curriculum leader. *NASSP Bulletin, 76*(547), 11–19.

Hunter, B. (1992). Linking for learning: Computer and communications network support for nationwide innovation in education. *Journal of Science Education and Technology, 1*(1), 23–34.

Jackson, B. L., & Cooper, B. S. (1989). Parent choice and empowerment: New roles for parents. *Urban Education, 24*(3), 263–286.

Jackson, P. (1968). *Life in classrooms.* New York: Holt, Rinehart, & Winston.

Johnson, D. W., & Johnson, R. T. (1994). *Teaching students to be peacemakers: Results of five years of research.* Unpublished paper, University of Minnesota.

Kemp, M. (1985). Parents as teachers of literacy: What are we learning from them? *Australian Journal of Reading, 8*(3), 17–29.

Kenway, M., Alderson, A., & Grundy, S. (1987). *A process approach to community participation in schooling: The Hamilton Project.* Perth: Queen

Elizabeth Silver Jubilee Trust Fund Project, Murdoch University.

King, B. B. (1990). *Creating curriculum together: Teachers, students, and collaborative investigation.* Paper presented at the annual meeting of the American Educational Research Association, Boston.

King, M. B., & Newmann, F. M. (2000). Will teacher learning advance school goals? *Phi Delta Kappan, 81*(8), 576–580.

Kirst, M. W. (1993). Strengths and weaknesses of American education. *Phi Delta Kappan, 74*(8), 613–618.

Lareau, A. P. (1986). *Perspectives on parents: A view from the classroom.* Paper presented at the annual meeting of the American Educational Research Association, San Francisco.

Lasky, S. (2000). The cultural and emotional politics of teacher parent interactions. *Teaching and Teacher Education, 16,* 843–860.

Lee, V. E., Smith, J. B., & Cioci, M. (1993). Teachers and principals: Gender-related perceptions of leadership and power in secondary schools. *Educational Evaluation and Policy Analysis, 15*(2), 153–180.

Leithwood, K. A., & Montgomery, D. J. (1982). A framework for planned educational change: Application to the assessment of program implementation. *Educational Evaluation and Policy Analysis, 4*(2), 157–167.

Leithwood, K. A., & Stager, M. (1989). Experts in principals' problem solving. *Educational Administration Quarterly, 25*(2), 126–161.

Lieberman, A., & McLaughlin, M. W. (1992). Networks for educational change: Powerful and problematic. *Phi Delta Kappan, 73*(9), 673–677.

Little, J. W. (1993). Teachers' professional development in a climate of educational reform. *Educational Evaluation and Policy Analysis, 15*(2), 129–151.

Lortie, D. E. (1975). *School teacher: A sociological study.* Chicago: University of Chicago Press.

Lortie, D. (1995). Dan Lortie's "School Teacher": A 20 year perspective. Paper presented at the annual meeting of the American Educational Research Association, San Francisco.

Loucks, S. F., Cox, P. L., Miles, M. B., Huberman, A. M., & Eiseman, J. W. (1982). *Portraits of the changes, the players, and the context: A study of dissemination supporting school improvement.* Andover, MA: The Network.

Louis, K. (1981). External agents and knowledge utilization. In R. Lehming & M. Kane (Eds.), *Improving schools: Using what we know.* Beverly Hills, CA: Sage.

Love, D. (1986). Community involvement. *West Australian High School Principals Association Newsletter, 10*(1), 2–4.

Lucas, C. A. (1999). Developing competent practitioners. *Educational Leadership, 56*(8), 45–48.

Maclure, M., & Walker, B. M. (2000). Disenchanted evenings: The social organization of talk in parent-teacher consultations in U.K. secondary schools. *British Journal of Sociology of Education, 21*(1), 18–22.

Maguire, S. (2000). A community school. *Educational Leadership, 57*(3), 49–53.

Marsh, C. J. (1997). *Key concepts for understanding curriculum.* London: Falmer.

Marsh, C. J., & Stafford, K. (1988). *Curriculum practices and issues* (2nd ed.). Sydney: McGraw-Hill.

Martin, D. S., Saif, P. S., & Thiel, L. (1987). Curriculum development: Who is involved and how? *Educational Leadership, 44*(4), 40–45.

Martin-Kniep, J. O., & Uhrmacher, P. B. (1992). Teachers as curriculum developers. *Journal of Curriculum Studies, 24*(3), 261–271.

McCutcheon, G. (1980). How do elementary school teachers plan? The nature of planning and influences on it. *Elementary School Journal, 81*(1), 4–23.

McCutcheon, G. (1988). Curriculum and the work of teachers. In L. E. Beyer & M. W. Apple (Eds.), *The curriculum: Problems, politics, and possibilities* (pp. 191–203). Albany: State University of New York Press.

McDonald, J. P. (1989). When outsiders try to change schools from the inside. *Phi Delta Kappan, 71*(3), 206–211.

McLaughlin, M. W. (1992). How district communities do and do not foster teacher pride. *Educational Leadership, 50*(1), 33–35.

McMahon, A. (2000). Managing teacher stress to enhance pupil learning. Paper presented at the annual meeting of the American Educational Research Association, New Orleans.

McTaggart, R. (1984). Action research and parent participation: Contradictions, concerns, and consequences. *Curriculum Perspectives, 4*(2), 7–14.

Miles, M. B., Saxl, E. R., & Lieberman, A. (1988). What skills do educational "change agents" need? An empirical view. *Curriculum Inquiry, 18*(2), 157–194.

Mulford, W. (1981). Consulting with an education system is about the facilitation of coordinated effort. In H. Gray (Ed.), *The management of educational institutions: Practice, consultancy, research.* London: Falmer.

Murphy, J., & Rodi, M. (2000). *Principal evaluation: A review.* Paper presented at the annual meeting of the American Educational Research Association, New Orleans.

Olebe, M., Jackson, A., & Danielson, C. (1999). Investing in beginning teachers: The California model. *Educational Leadership, 56*(8), 41–44.

Olson, J. (1989). Surviving innovation: Reflection on the pitfalls of practice. *Journal of Curriculum Studies, 21*(6), 503–508.

Ormell, C. (1992). Behavioral objectives revisited. *Educational Research, 34*(1), 23–33.

Ornstein, A. C., & Hunkins, F. P. (1988). *Curriculum: Foundations, principles and issues.* Upper Saddle River, NJ: Prentice Hall.

Pearson, J. (2000). Personal computers. In C. J. Marsh (Ed.), *Teaching studies of society and environment.* Sydney: Prentice Hall.

Perkins, D. (1999). The many faces of constructivism. *Educational Leadership, 57*(3), 6–11.

Porter, P. (1994). *Women and leadership in education.* (Occasional Paper, No. 23). Canberra: Australian College of Education.

Price, J. N., & Vallie, L. (2000). *Becoming agents of change: Cases from preservice teacher education.* Paper presented at the annual meeting of the American Educational Research Association, New Orleans.

Purves, A. (1975). The thought fox and curriculum building. In J. Schafferzick & D. Hampson (Eds.), *Strategies for curriculum development.* Berkeley, CA: McCutchan.

Rainer, J., Guyton, E., & Bowen, C. (2000). *Constructivist pedagogy in the classroom.* Paper presented at the annual meeting of the American Educational Research Association, New Orleans.

Reid, J. A. (1982). Negotiating education. In G. Boomer (Ed.), *Negotiating the curriculum.* Sydney: Ashton Scholastic.

Rosenholtz, S. (1989). *Teachers' workplace: The social organization of schools.* New York: Longman.

Rutherford, W. L., & Huling-Austin, L. (1984). *Changes in high schools: What is happening, what is wanted.* Paper presented at the annual meeting of the American Educational Research Association, New Orleans.

Sapon-Shevin M. (2001). Schools fit for all. *Educational Leadership, 58*(4), 34–39.

Sardo-Brown, D. (1990). Experienced teachers' planning practices: A USA survey. *Journal of Education for Teaching, 16*(1), 57–71.

Savage, T. V., & McCord, M. K. (1986). *The use of student evaluation in the assessment of teacher competence.* Paper presented at the annual meeting of the American Educational Research Association, San Francisco.

Scherer, M. (1999). Perspectives: the C word. *Educational Leadership, 57*(3), 5.

Scherer, M. (2001). Improving the quality of the teaching force: A conversation with David C. Berliner. *Educational Leadership, 58*(8), 6–11.

Schofield, J. W., & Davidson, A. L. (2000). *Internet use and teacher change.* Paper presented at the annual meeting of the American Educational Research Association, New Orleans.

Scott, G. (1999). *Change matters.* Sydney: Allen & Unwin.

Shkedi, A. (1995). Teachers' attitudes toward a teachers' guide: Implications for the roles of planners and teachers. *Journal of Curriculum and Supervision, 10*(2), 155–170.

Siskin, L. (1994). *Realms of knowledge: Academic departments in secondary school.* London: Falmer.

Skilbeck, M. (1984). *School-based curriculum development.* London: Harper & Row.

Slavin, R. E. (1987). Mastery learning reconsidered. *Review of Educational Research, 57*(2), 175–213.

Slavin, R. E. (2000). Putting the school back in school reform. *Educational Leadership, 58*(4), 22–27.

Smylie, M. A. (1988). The enhancement function of staff development: Organizational and psychological antecedents to individual teacher change. *American Educational Research Journal, 25*(1), 1–30.

Smylie, M. A., Lazarus, V., & Brownlee-Conyers, J. (1996). Instructional outcomes of school-based participative decision making. *Educational Evaluation and Policy Analysis, 18*(3), 181–198.

Smyth, J., Dow, A., Hattam, R., Reid, A., & Shacklock, G. (2000). *Teachers' work in a globalizing economy.* London: Falmer.

Smyth, W. J. (1986). *Leadership and pedagogy*. Geelong, Victoria: Deakin University Press.

Soder, R. (1999). When words find their meaning: Renewal versus reform. *Phi Delta Kappan, 80*(8), 568–570.

Solomon, Z. P. (1991). California's policy on parent involvement. *Phi Delta Kappan, 72*(5), 359–362.

Southworth, G. (2000). *School leadership in English schools at the close of the twentieth century: Puzzles, problems and cultural insights*. Paper presented at the annual meeting of the American Educational Research Association, New Orleans.

Spady, W. (1993). *Outcome-based education* (Workshop Report No. 5). Canberra: ACSA.

Starratt, R. J. (1993). *The drama of leadership*. London: Falmer.

Stenhouse, L. (1988). Artistry and teaching: The teacher as focus of research and development. *Journal of Curriculum and Supervision, 4*(1), 43–51.

Thornton, S. J. (1988). Curriculum consonance in United States history classrooms. *Journal of Curriculum and Supervision, 3*(4), 308–320.

Tillema, H. H. (2000). Belief change towards self-directed learning in student teachers: Immersion in practice or reflection on action. *Teaching and Teacher Education, 16*, 575–591.

Tyree, A. K. (1993). Examining the evidence: Have states reduced local control of curriculum? *Education Evaluation and Policy Analysis, 15*(1), 34–50.

Vallance, E. (1981). *Focus on students in curriculum knowledge: A critique of curriculum criticism*. Paper presented at the annual meeting of the American Educational Research Association, Los Angeles.

Wasley, P. A. (1994). *Stirring the chalkdust*. New York: Teachers College Press.

Watson, N., Fullan, M., & Kilcher, A. (2000). *The role of the district: Professional learning and district reform*. Paper presented at the annual meeting of the American Educational Research Association, New Orleans.

West, S. (1993). *Educational values for school leadership*. London: Kogan Page.

Wildy, H., Louden, W., & Robertson, J. (2000). *Using cases for school principal performance standards: Australian and New Zealand experiences*. Paper presented at the Annual Meeting of the American Educational Research Association, New Orleans.

Wiles, J., & Bondi, J. (1989). *Curriculum development: A guide to practice*. Upper Saddle River, NJ: Merrill/Prentice Hall.

Windschitl, M. (1999). The challenges of sustaining a constructivist classroom culture. *Phi Delta Kappan, 80*(10), 751–755.

Wise, A. E. (2000). Creating a high-quality teaching force. *Educational Leadership, 58*(4), 18–21.

Woods, P. (1988). A strategic view of parent participation. *Journal of Education Policy, 3*(4), 323–334.

Woods, P. A. (2000). *Redefining professionality and leadership: Reflexive responses to competitive and regulatory pressures*. Paper presented at the annual meeting of the American Educational Research Association, New Orleans.

Young, J. H. (1989). Teacher interest in curriculum committees: What factors are involved? *Journal of Curriculum Studies, 21*(4), 363–376.

Young, J. H. (1990). Teacher participation in curriculum development: A study of society and institutional levels. *Alberta Journal of Educational Research, 36*(2), 141–156.

Zahorik, J. A. (1975). *Curriculum theory and classroom realities*. Paper presented at the annual meeting of the Association for Supervision in Curriculum Development, Washington, DC.

Zahorik, J. A. (1987). Teaching: Rules, research, beauty, and creation. *Journal of Curriculum and Supervision, 2*(3), 275–284.

Zlotkin, J. (1993). Rethinking the school board's role. *Educational Leadership, 51*(2), 22–25.

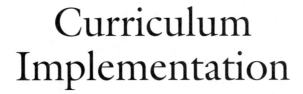

Curriculum
Implementation

▐ ABOUT THIS CHAPTER

This chapter examines what happens when a planned or written curriculum is enacted in a classroom. It especially considers why the enacted curriculum may differ considerably from the planned curriculum and under what circumstances the differences that occur are desirable or undesirable. In addition, it critically reviews recent thinking on the process of curriculum implementation, describing both strategies and tactics that seem to work well and what about the process of implementation remains problematic and puzzling to researchers.

▐ WHAT YOU SHOULD DO

1. Become familiar with the major problems involved in curriculum implementation.
2. Understand the implications of the ideas of fidelity of curriculum implementation (that is, that the enacted curriculum should remain identical to the planned curriculum) and adaptation in curriculum implementation (that the teacher should appropriately modify the planned curriculum in enacting it).
3. Critically reflect on the basic ideas that underlie research on curriculum implementation.
4. Critically reflect on some common approaches that have been used in schools to support the process of curriculum implementation.

▐ SOME OPTIONAL APPROACHES

The options described here differ according to the circumstances that prevail in individual schools or school districts. You may wish to consider all options or only the one option closest to the circumstances of the schools with which you are most familiar.

Option A

1. If you are teaching in a state or a school district that has recently introduced a new curriculum, reflect on the following:
   a. The incentives provided for teachers to implement curricula in accordance with specific guidelines
   b. The extent to which you and other faculty members accepted these guidelines
   c. The improvements (if any) that occurred in student achievement
2. Read section 7.5 on the fidelity versus adaptation debate and consider how you stand on this matter.
3. Read section 7.6 on four approaches to curriculum implementation, especially the subsection on curriculum alignment.
4. Reconsider your attitude about the new curriculum in light of the basic ideas about implementation presented in this chapter.

Option B

1. When you have been faced with implementing a new curriculum, which of the following changes did you consider the most difficult to make?
   ❑ Changes in materials (such as textbooks and videotapes)
   ❑ Changes in teaching practices
   ❑ Changes in the organization of course content
   ❑ Changes in beliefs or understandings
2. In your experience, how high a priority were each of these changes given by your school or district? How did these priorities affect the relative success of implementation of new curricula? Now read the chapter in its entirety and consider if your ideas about what affects the success of an implementation have changed.

Option C

1. Read section 7.6 on four approaches to curriculum implementation. Have you had experience with any of these approaches: Action Research, Concerns-Based Adoption Model (CBAM), Curriculum Alignment, or Comprehensive School Reform Programs? Who initiated these approaches in your school and to what extent was faculty involved? What impact did any of these approaches have on curriculum implementation?
2. Read section 7.5 on the fidelity versus adaptation debate. If you have a professional development policy at your school, is study or practice in curriculum implementation ever considered within it? What kinds of training would you recommend?

7.1   INTRODUCTION

A curriculum starts as a plan. It becomes a reality only when teachers implement it with real students in real classrooms. Careful planning and development are obviously important to a good curriculum, but they count for nothing unless teachers are aware of what a plan calls for and how they can implement it in their own classrooms. Curriculum implementation, therefore, can be considered the process of enacting the planned curriculum. Put another way, curriculum implementation is the translation of a written curriculum into classroom practices. Doing so can be very complex and problematic (Fullan, 1999).

Many people (including many educators) believe that the enacted curriculum should be identical to the planned curriculum. However, strictly speaking, this is an impossibility since the planned curriculum is an abstract document and the enacted curriculum is a flesh-and-blood creation. Furthermore, this belief is contrary to the maxim "precision in planning, flexibility in execution," which, as we have pointed out several times, underlies all our own arguments throughout this book.

Therefore, we suggest that a far more realistic and fruitful way of looking at the relationship between the planned curriculum and the enacted curriculum is to see it as analogous to the text of a play and an actual production of that play put on the stage by living actors. Even when a single, authentic text of a play exists (as is not the case with the plays of Shakespeare, for instance), there is still room for interpretation of that text by the director of the play and still further room for interpretation of the director's interpretation by the actors. In this sense, there is no such thing as the single authentic production of *Hamlet* nor of any other play. There are, however, many interesting, engaging, and insightful interpretations of *Hamlet* filled with nuances that Shakespeare may or may not have intended. Likewise, in implementation of curriculum, there is room for different interpretations. Furthermore, as members of the audience react in different ways to the production of a play, so, too, do students experience the enacted curriculum in different ways.

The analogy we suggest honors both the distinctions and the connections among the planned curriculum, the enacted curriculum, and the experienced curriculum that we have proposed throughout this book. A technical approach to curriculum implementation, which treats the planned curriculum and the enacted curriculum as identical, does not. Even though some subject areas admit to greater degrees of interpretation than others (for instance, drama more so than mathematics) and all interpretations are not equally defensible, it can be argued that the analogy still holds.

With this analogy in the background, this chapter examines some approaches to curriculum implementation and basic issues that arise out of them. Underlying the chapter is the assumption that teachers are very much like directors and actors of a play; the text (planned curriculum) is there for them, but they must still interpret (enact) it. Teachers may act alone when they enact a curriculum, even one planned for use throughout a school or an entire district; but sometimes they seek out fellow teachers and external resource persons to assist them. In either case, they monitor what occurs, especially the specifics of the curriculum, the specifics of their teaching, and the specific reactions of their students. By observing these specifics carefully and by conversing about them with their colleagues, teachers often are able both to assess how well they are implementing a new curriculum and to make beneficial changes in that curriculum and in their teaching. Among teachers, the object of implementing a new curriculum is seldom to maintain that curriculum in the form in which it has been planned but to use it appropriately—modifying it if necessary—so that students will obtain the maximum benefits from its use.

7.2   SOME DEFINITIONS AND ISSUES

As noted by Fullan (1999) and Scott (1999), a curriculum, however well designed, must be implemented if it is to have any impact on students. Although this is obvious, there are thousands of curriculum documents now gathering dust on storeroom shelves because they were never implemented or because they were implemented unintelligently. The obvious importance of curriculum implementation has not necessarily led to widespread understanding of what it entails or of what is problematic about it.

The term *implementation* is used frequently in educational circles but rather loosely. For example, Fullan and Pomfret (1977) consider it as what an innovation consists of in practice. However, this idea gives little hint of what implementation involves or what attitudes educators might hold about it. In school districts where teachers and principals have the opportunity to choose among competing curriculum packages, attitudes are clearly important. For example, according to Leithwood (1981), only when a teacher perceives the current curriculum as in some way dysfunctional is that teacher likely to pursue an alternative. But in many districts, teachers and principals do not have the freedom to choose among alternatives, especially when a revised or new curriculum has been produced for use in all schools. Then their task is to find out how to use the new curriculum as beneficially as possible. In these circumstances, the dominant questions for each teacher usually become these:

How do I do it?
Will I ever get it to work smoothly?
To whom can I turn for assistance?
Is what I am doing consistent with the plan?
What is the effect on my students?

This "how to" of using a new curriculum is a major concern for teachers because, as craft specialists, they gain most of their intrinsic satisfaction from being successful in using a particular approach and materials with their students. However, implementing any new curriculum effectively may take a considerable period of time since individual teachers need to become competent and confident in how to use it. A new curriculum can be said to have been institutionalized only when it is completely accepted by the teachers of a school and the teaching of it has become a matter of routine. Nonetheless, some writers (for example, Snyder, Bolin, & Zumwalt, 1992) argue that the idea of institutionalization unduly implies that the curriculum is something concrete and static. These writers suggest that "curriculum enactment" is a more useful way of describing the ongoing process of implementation because it emphasizes the educational experiences that students and teachers jointly undergo as they determine what the curriculum will be like in each classroom.

There is also the matter of commitment to change (Cuban, 1992). Not all teachers will automatically accept the notion that a newly proposed curriculum is what they should use, nor will all want to use it with their students (Fullan & Hargreaves, 1991). Most would no doubt welcome the opportunity to choose among several alternatives. In fact, some teachers might be perfectly satisfied with their existing curriculum. In situations where teachers have no choice about whether or not to use a new curriculum, they may embrace the new curriculum with enthusiasm, becoming what is known as "consonant" users (willing to conform to the new curriculum), or they may be reluctant, making considerable alterations in the curriculum, thus becoming what is known as "dissonant" users (unwilling to conform). In extreme cases, a dissonant user may erect a facade of compliance while adopting Machiavellian tactics to resist or even to undermine the new curriculum. Again, the attitudes of individual teachers are extremely important in implementation.

There are two extreme views about curriculum implementation that often appear in academic writing and in the media but that rarely, if ever, occur in practice. One view is that teachers have absolute power over what will or will not be implemented in their classrooms. In reality, it is not possible for any individual teacher to possess such broad power; hence, this first extreme view is inaccurate because it assumes that a teacher:

- Has the authority to introduce any new course or topics at any time without restrictions from the system, parents, or the community
- Knows about and has access to the full range of knowledge, skills, and resources that make up a particular topic or unit
- Is able to spend the long periods of time needed to prepare instructional materials
- Has access to finances adequate to provide instructional materials needed or can enlist others to prepare or supply them
- Has a thorough and full command of knowledge about the interests, skills, and developmental needs of students and is able to incorporate this knowledge into the courses or units being developed

Such a teacher would be involved in all curriculum activities from design to institutionalization. Site-based management (SBM) is sometimes described in the literature in this way, with teachers engaged without restriction in all phases of planning, development, and implementation. Such descriptions often characterize total and exclusive teacher involvement in all phases as entirely positive and desirable. However, because it is unrealistic to expect any one teacher to undertake all necessary tasks, there are very real restrictions on what an individual teacher can do in SBM.

The other extreme view is that an external authority exercises complete control over what teachers do in their classrooms, directing teachers to select and use particular topics or units in specified ways. The system is stereotyped as centrally planned and may be characterized as being dictatorial, authoritarian, and traditional. Some writers have used extreme and dramatic examples to comment negatively about officious authorities or district administrators who visit individual schools or classrooms to ensure that the official curricula are being taught as intended. Such writers direct their criticism at the bureaucratic obsession for uniformity, which sometimes may require that all schools teach the same curricula at the same time in the same way.

It is doubtful that complete prescription of, and control over, everything teachers do has ever occurred. Although guidelines about curriculum and teaching may be prescribed in detail, there are countless ways in which teachers can responsibly and professionally get around both the spirit and the substance of such prescriptions (Fullan, 1991). For example, teachers can easily vary the content of a course or the sequence in which it is taught. They can emphasize particular values or issues or dismiss them entirely. Unless a superior is observing a teacher constantly, little can be known about what really goes on behind the classroom door (Goodlad & Klein, 1970).

A realistic view of curriculum implementation lies, therefore, between these two extremes. Some subjects in a school may be considered the essential core of the curriculum and be spelled out in detail in a curriculum guide. Especially for such subjects, teachers usually are expected to cover certain topics in a certain sequence. The most commonly used term in the professional literature for adherence to prescribed details in implementing a curriculum is *fidelity* of use. Alternatively, for some subjects, teachers are expected to exercise their creative flair and to implement their own individual versions of the curriculum. Doing so is commonly referred to as *adaptation*.

7.3   INFLUENCES ON IMPLEMENTATION

Researchers have investigated the process of curriculum implementation and what makes it successful. In the early 1980s, Fullan (1982) produced a list of what he called "factors affecting implementation," and this list has been widely cited in the professional literature ever since. He suggested that the process could be analyzed in terms of characteristics of the curriculum innovation or change, characteristics of the school, characteristics of the school district, and characteristics external to the school system. Figure 7.1 is a listing of the specific characteristics Fullan identified.

Later, Fullan and some colleagues (Fullan, Bennett, & Rolheiser-Bennett, 1989) reviewed the professional literature on curriculum implementation since the 1950s and suggested that it emphasized four themes, which they labeled (1) adoption, (2) implementation, (3) standardization, and (4) restructuring.

In the 1960s, the first theme—adoption—was prominent. A common but naïve assumption of the time was that a formal decision by a district or a school to adopt a curricular innovation was sufficient to ensure its use in all classrooms. A vast number of failed innovations were recorded during this decade.

During the 1970s, the attention of researchers shifted toward the second theme—implementation—and numerous studies of the implementation of individual innovations were undertaken. Some of these were large-scale, such as the Rand Study (Berman & McLaughlin, 1975) and the Study of Dissemination Efforts Supporting School Improvement (DESSI) (Crandall and associates, 1983). Fullan et al. (1989) argued that these studies were of little value in understanding imple-

A. **Characteristics of the change**
    1. Need for and relevance of the change
    2. Clarity
    3. Complexity
    4. Quality and practicality of the program

B. **Characteristics of the school district**
    5. The history of attempts at innovation
    6. The adoption process
    7. Central administrative support and involvement
    8. Staff development and participation
    9. The intended time line and the information system
    10. The school board and the community

C. **Characteristics of the school**
    11. The principal
    12. Teacher-teacher relations
    13. Teacher orientations

D. **Characteristics external to the local system**
    14. The role of government
    15. External assistance

FIGURE 7.1
Some influences on implementation
Source: After Fullan (1982).

mentation because they focused on single innovations: "Schools are not in the business of implementing innovations one at a time, they are in the business of managing multiple innovations simultaneously" (p. 3).

Fullan et al. (1989) found the third theme—standardization and testing of students and teachers—to be ongoing during the four decades they considered. However, they concluded that, despite enormous investments of resources, energies, and expectations, this approach to curriculum implementation is doomed to failure because it trivializes the teaching profession.

Finally, the fourth theme—restructuring—has emerged (see Fullan, 1993, 1999) and may be typical of contemporary approaches to implementation. Fullan and his colleagues found that such approaches focus on changing the characteristics of schools to include practices such as partnerships, career ladders, coaching, and mentoring. While such practices may seem to some researchers to be promising ways of promoting successful curriculum implementation, other researchers have their doubts. Hargreaves (1989), for example, suggested that these attempts at contrived collegiality are superficial, failing to truly restructure schools.

House, another prominent researcher, identified three perspectives (the technical, the political, and the cultural) as useful in explaining how and why certain approaches to implementation have persisted over the decades (House, 1979, 1996). The technical perspective (see the discussion of the Proactive/Interactive Change Model in chapter 5) assumes that systematic planning and a rational approach to implementation can overcome the typical problems teachers face, such as lack of time and expertise. In a later paper, House (1996) refers to this perspective in terms of transaction-cost economics. The political perspective (see the discussion of the Negotiation Model in chapter 5) recognizes that, in practice, people do not behave entirely rationally. This perspective emphasizes the balance of power among stakeholders as what determines the success or failure of an innovation. The cultural perspective suggests that the deeply ingrained beliefs and values of stakeholders, which are socially shared and shaped, are what ultimately affect what happens in classrooms. This perspective suggests that successful implementation usually depends on transforming the culture that stakeholders share. In practice, it is likely that all three perspectives can be used to explain what happens in any school. Indeed, Corbett and Rossman (1989) have argued that the three perspectives depict processes that actually operate in schools, that they are closely intertwined, and that they often occur simultaneously.

McLaughlin (1987) found that efforts by federal or state officials to promote successful curriculum implementation in local schools depend on what she described as "local capacity," "motivation and commitment," "internal institutional conditions," and "balance between pressure and support." The local capacity to implement an innovation can be improved by increasing financial support and the training of teachers as long as these increases are significant and continue over a period of years. The motivation and commitment of teachers and administrators are more difficult to improve. Doing so depends on the values of local leaders and their assessment of the relative worth of a particular innovation. However, on some occasions, the involvement of local leaders in a project leads directly to greater commitment (Fullan, 1986). McLaughlin (1987) and Cuban (1992) also report that the structures and policies within schools and the relative stability and support for teachers can have a major effect upon their willingness to implement new curricula. That is, the internal institutional conditions have to be conducive to change. Furthermore, some balance between pressure and support is essential. Pressure is required to focus attention on a specific innovation, and it provides the necessary legitimacy to embark on a new project. But support, whether financial or in the form of expert assistance, is also required to get the project started.

McLaughlin (1987) further argues that implementation is not about transmitting what has previously been agreed to, but about bargaining and transformation. Implementation must be framed in terms of individual actors' incentives, beliefs, and capacities—a point also confirmed by Werner (1987), Crandall (1988), and Lewis (1988). Nonetheless, since the 1990s terms such as *educational standards* and *school indicators* have appeared with increasing frequency in the professional literature, perhaps heralding a return to a more rigid view of curriculum implementation among some researchers. Examples are Porter (1993), who argues for school standards for the delivery of the enacted curriculum and cites the professional standards for teaching mathematics developed by the National Council of Teachers of Mathematics; Blank (1993), who describes indicators based on student outcomes, instructional time, curriculum content, teacher quality, and school conditions and resources; and Schmidt, Valverde, Houang, Wiley, Wolfe, and Bianchi (1996), who urge the adoption of a multicategory curriculum framework for measuring the alignment of various elements of implementation.

7.4 DISCOVERING AND DESCRIBING WHAT HAPPENS IN IMPLEMENTATION

Curriculum development can involve substantial investments of resources, time, and expertise (Fullan, 1999). For commercial ventures, it is crucial that developers obtain feedback about how their product is being used. Future efforts clearly require building on past successes and avoiding past failures. For noncommercial curriculum development projects that are funded from within the school district, there is less urgency to obtain feedback about the success of implementation. Even so, districts must undertake new initiatives from time to time, and they are expected to be able to account reasonably for how money and time are being invested in curriculum development. As a result, feedback on how a curriculum has been used provides valuable information.

Attempts to describe the implementation of new curricula are fraught with all kinds of difficulties. For example, do you focus on the curriculum materials, or what the teacher is doing, or what the students are doing? If you intend to describe all three, what criteria do you use to select instances of each since all exist continuously and simultaneously in the classroom? Are there optimal times to examine how a curriculum is being implemented, such as after six months of operation, or a year, or even longer? Attempts to discover degrees of implementation are even more difficult. Decisions have to be made about what kinds of data to collect. Should such data be obtained through observations of classrooms, through interviews, through analyses of documents, or from questionnaires and self-reports? Also, data that could be used to evaluate the personnel involved in a project almost inevitably have a punitive air about them and so can lead to considerable uneasiness about who is assessing whom and for what purposes.

Implementation: Student Activities and Achievements

A major reason for producing a new curriculum is to provide better opportunities for students to learn. Rarely, however, is it possible to measure what students learn with sufficient accuracy to lead to unequivocal conclusions about the effectiveness of a new curriculum. The test scores of students depend on much more than the curriculum itself, and there are also numerous unanticipated consequences and unknown side effects of any curriculum, which test scores do not begin to get at. Therefore, attempts to discover the full effects of a new curriculum on students cannot be limited to measuring what is most easily measurable. The issue of discovering and then forming some judgments about what happens to students must be approached in broad terms and with considerable caution.

The prolonged periods of time needed and the costs involved in developing control and experimental groups from which to obtain comparative data about curricula make such analyses of curriculum effectiveness very expensive—with little prospect of getting conclusive results. In theory, it might seem desirable to construct a test to demonstrate the superiority of a particular curriculum over another, but results have been very limited. For example, Walker and Schaffarzick (1974) analyzed twenty-six evaluations of major national projects in the United States that compared high school classes using innovative curricula with those using traditional curricula in the same subject areas, as measured by an objective, paper-and-pencil test. They found no substantial advantages for the innovative curricula and concluded:

> All that these results permit us to say is that innovative curricula almost always led to higher achievement scores on tests whose content more closely resembled that of the innovative curriculum, while traditional curricula occasionally led to higher scores on tests whose content more closely resembled that of the traditional curriculum. (p. 421)

Despite the lack of empirical evidence linking testing with student achievement, high stakes testing of students became a political priority in many states during the 1990s (Nave, Miech, & Mosteller, 2000), and there is pressure from some quarters for a single national test for all students (Porter, 1993). A differing point of view holds that a more promising development is authentic assessment of student learning, such as through the use of portfolios of student work or through increasingly sophisticated ways of measuring problem solving, reasoning, and critical thinking (Resnick & Tucker, 1992).

Implementation: Use of Curriculum Materials

Curriculum materials figure prominently in the day-to-day activities of teachers and students. In fact, surveys have revealed that students spend up to 80 percent of their time engaged with particular curriculum materials (Cornbleth, 1990). Clearly, any comprehensive study of implementation must include information about how curriculum materials are used. In the 1970s, several writers offered their own schemes for how to analyze curriculum materials, but none of these schemes proved particularly useful, primarily because they were extremely time consuming and tended to analyze materials apart from their actual use in classrooms (Anderson & Tomkins, 1983). During the 1980s, more attention was paid to developing checklists that provide ratings of curriculum materials in use. A checklist that has been widely used is the Innovations Configuration (IC), developed at the University of Texas at Austin by Hall and Loucks (1978). (The IC is described in some detail in section 7.6 of this chapter.) For the DESSI study, Loucks and Crandall (1982) developed the Practice Profile, which also provides a standardized, systematic way of collecting information about the characteristics of curriculum materials and how they are actually used in classrooms. The rapid growth in the use of the Internet by teachers and students has also spread numerous new ideas about what can be included in checklists of curriculum materials and how they can be used (Means, 2001). In particular, the Internet has become a huge new resource for teachers and students (Molnar, 2000; Schofield & Davidson, 2000).

Teachers, principals, and other stakeholders involved in implementing a curriculum may wish to use existing inventories and checklists or devise their own approach for discovering how materials are being used.

Implementation: Teacher Activities

Various methods have been used over the decades to attempt to discover how teachers implement curricula. These methods range from interviews and formal observations of classrooms to checklists, questionnaires, and self-reports. Efforts by local districts to understand what their teachers do while implementing new curricula are usually casual and sporadic.

Methodological difficulties in using checklists and rating scales include the problem of achieving interrater reliability (Blank, 1993; Smithson, 1992) and the potential problem of ignoring many of the complexities of classrooms that influence what teachers do (Kimpston, 1983). Questionnaires have been used in a number of studies, although they rely on self-report data, so doubts can arise over the authenticity of the responses. Portfolios have been used in some school districts.

Again, participants in the study of an implementation can rely on existing means of finding out what teachers are actually doing with the new curriculum, or they can devise their own methods appropriate to the specific situations they are investigating.

7.5   RESEARCH ON IMPLEMENTATION

As we have pointed out, Fullan and Pomfret's (1977) review of research on implementation has been widely cited in the professional literature on curriculum. Not only did the authors bring into prominence implementation as a distinct step in curriculum planning and development, they also helped define and shape much subsequent research on implementation. Among their greatest influences on researchers was their use of the terms *fidelity perspective* and *process perspective*.

Fidelity of Implementation

The fidelity perspective on implementation is now well established in the literature. Proponents emphasize the importance of the planned curriculum and assume that when the planned curriculum is exemplary and demonstrably effective, it will be readily and completely accepted by teachers. House (1979) referred to the "firm faith in the technological process" (p. 10) held by proponents of fidelity in curriculum implementation. Roitman and Mayer (1982) noted that hard-line proponents insist that curriculum innovations enacted in the classroom should closely—if not completely—correspond to what is planned. Why else devote considerable resources, time, and energy to planning the best possible curriculum for use in schools if teachers do not actually use it? And if teachers use it in only partial or modified form, won't its effectiveness be likely to suffer from dilution?

Ariav (1988) used the phrase "curriculum literacy" to suggest that many teachers lack understanding of what the curriculum should be and lack skill in how best to teach it. The fidelity perspective assumes that because teachers have a low level of curriculum literacy, the planned curriculum must be highly structured and teachers must be given explicit instructions about how to teach it. Since both the curriculum and instructions to teachers are specified, the fidelity perspective leaves little room for a curriculum to be tailored for any particular or changing circumstances of the specific schools or classrooms in which it is intended to be taught. The underlying assumptions are:

> Central planning and definition are necessary to eliminate the inefficiency that occurs when locals or users are left with leeway to define an innovation and to participate in decisions about how to implement a policy or program. The less ambiguity and authority left to implementers, the greater the fidelity. Evaluation is conducted to assess how closely implementation resembles the plan for program execution and to provide information for retooling implementation toward the ideal. (Heck, 1980, p. 5)

This approach treats teachers as passive recipients of the wisdom of the curriculum developers; teachers must be thoroughly trained to use the new curriculum, but, once trained, they will be able to teach it at a high level of technical proficiency.

Fidelity of curriculum implementation seems to lend itself more readily to some situations than to others, particularly those where the content of the curriculum is unusually complex and difficult to master, where it requires definite sequencing, or where students' understanding of it depends on their being appropriately matched with specific curricular strands. Many of the national curriculum projects undertaken in the United States in the 1960s and 1970s (some federally sponsored, some privately sponsored) were developed from the fidelity perspective on implementation. For example, in the Biological Sciences Curriculum Study Project (BSCS), the teacher's role was tightly prescribed:

> A programmed discussion is provided via a series of single topic films. At certain points in the presentation, there is teacher intervention with specified questions, which are provided for his/her use. The teacher is also provided with prototypes of the kinds of answers he/she may receive, and with suggested ways of handling these answers so that he/she does not cut off discussion or discourage inquiry. (Grobman, 1970, p. 117)

Many of these national projects undermined whatever chance they had at success by taking the idea of fidelity of implementation to the extreme of attempting to design teacherproof curriculum packages. In such packages, not only were both the curriculum and the directions to teachers spelled out in extreme detail, but the teacher's role as mediator between the curriculum and the student was reduced to the barest possible minimum in order not to dilute the work of the developers of the curriculum. Naturally, for both good reasons and bad, such packages were viewed extremely negatively by many teachers. In districts and schools where teacherproof curricula were adopted, often they were never implemented or implementation was quickly abandoned; and in the relatively few schools where they were implemented, teachers almost always found ways to modify them in practice to fit specific classroom realities that developers had been unable to foresee. (For a discussion of these issues within the curriculum reform movement of the 1960s, see chapter 2.)

The major trend of the 1990s toward centralized curricula developed around uniform standards (for instance, the "New Standards" of Tucker and Codding, 1998) has also required strict adherence (fidelity) by teachers.

Adaptation in Implementation

The alternative approach to curriculum implementation was termed the *process perspective* by Fullan and Pomfret (1977), but it has also become known as *adaptation* or *mutual adaptation*. Proponents of this approach maintain that the differing circumstances facing schools and teachers require on-site modifications in the curriculum (Berman & McLaughlin, 1975). They suggest that in reality all planned curricula become modified during the process of implementation and that such modification to suit the specific and changing situations faced by the teachers who enact them is essential if the curricula are to have the greatest possible benefits for students. In their own work, Fullan and Pomfret seemed to favor this approach, particularly in their analysis of the Rand Study, which, at the time, was possibly the most comprehensive research study on implementation ever undertaken, encompassing 293 projects in school districts in different regions of the United States. The researchers in the Rand Study concluded that successful innovations occurred when planned curricula were not highly specified or packaged in advance but were mutually adapted by users within specific institutional settings (Berman & McLaughlin, 1975). Yet it should also be noted that different projects were based on rather different assumptions about students, teachers, and learning as well as how the curricula would be implemented in different institutional settings (Snyder et al., 1992).

Mutual Adaptation. The term *mutual adaptation* was first used by Dalin and McLaughlin (1975) to describe implementation in which adjustments are made to both the innovative curriculum and to the institutional setting. In mutual adaptation, the process is a two-way street between developers and users. Since the 1970s, many researchers have argued that mutual adaptation consists of agreed-on modifications arranged between developers and users and, as such, represents the most effective way of ensuring successful implementation of a new curriculum. House (1979) maintained that implementation is really a political decision and emphasized personal, face-to-face interaction as a key part of it. MacDonald and Walker (1976) maintained that implementation really involves negotiation and that there are trade-offs to be made between curriculum developers and teachers. Farrar, Desanctis, and Cohen (1979) and Rudduck and Kelly (1976) interpreted curriculum implementation in terms of the culture of the school. For example, mutual adaptation can be characterized as evolution, in which what at first appears to be a precise blueprint is increasingly perceived by teachers as something malleable: "the needs and values of those within the organization add, subtract, modify and invent. . . . Some variations are less discordant than others, but virtually none is a single composition with everyone playing from the same score" (Farrar et al., 1979, p. 96).

The Continuing Debate: Fidelity of Use versus Mutual Adaptation

Since the issue of fidelity of use versus mutual adaptation came into prominence in the 1970s, debate over it has continued. During the late 1970s, mutual adaptation was widely recommended in the professional literature in the curriculum field. Reports based on the Rand Study were widely published and supported by still other studies (Goodlad, 1975; Greenwood, Mann, & McLaughlin, 1975; McLaughlin, 1978). As a result, federal grants, which earlier had gone to large-scale national projects, were largely channeled to local districts and schools to enable them to plan and implement their own curricula. Nonetheless, other researchers who addressed the problems of implementation supported fidelity of use but in more moderate versions than had first been proposed.

Some researchers maintained that implementation can be measured. Hall and Loucks (1977) developed a series of instruments for measuring the implementation of the Concerns-Based Adoption Model (CBAM, discussed in detail in section 7.6). Leithwood and Montgomery (1982) developed profiles of curriculum innovations, maintaining that each innovation is unique and teachers can be tracked as they progress gradually from non-use to full use. Their profiles have also been used to distinguish between what some researchers consider acceptable levels of fidelity of use and unacceptable levels characterized by drastic mutation in which an innovation loses its integrity (Roitman & Mayer, 1982). Another perspective on fidelity of use was introduced by Eveland, Rogers, and Klepper (1977), with their introduction of the term *reinvention*. Studies by Blakely, Mayer, Roitman, and Gottschalk (1983) have demonstrated that reinvention, defined as "adding to existing components of an innovation, or a modification of existing components (within the bounds of existing components but beyond the specified variations)" (p. 9), typically occurs as teachers implement a curriculum. They suggested that moderate levels of fidelity of use can still occur when teachers reinvent additions that make the innovation more appropriate for their own classrooms. Of course, it is difficult to say when reinvention crosses the line between fidelity of use and mutual adaptation.

Studies that supported some limited adaptation came under increased criticism in the early 1980s. For example, Datta's (1980) analysis of the Rand methodology led her to conclude that the programs studied were largely locally developed and were not examples of programs dependent on federal funding. She argued that the authors of the Rand reports were not justified in using mutual adaptation as the single way of explaining successful implementation. Loucks (1983) noted that there were contradictory findings in the Rand reports and that, although mutual adaptation was strongly evident in the field studies, survey data of the sites revealed moderate levels of fidelity of use at the same time. Roitman and Mayer (1982) questioned the lack of any specific measure of fidelity of use in the Rand reports, arguing that to measure implementation in terms of "the extent to which projects met their own goals, different as they might be for each project" (Berman & McLaughlin, 1975, p. 50) was biased in favor of adaptation and missed the point of fidelity of use.

Another major study of implementation in the United States titled Dissemination Efforts Supporting School Improvement (DESSI) took place from

1978 to 1982. Researchers surveyed 146 different schools and undertook case studies of twelve sites. Using checklists based on Hall and Loucks (1978), the DESSI researchers obtained data that indicated high levels of fidelity of use. For example, Crandall et al. (1983) noted that teachers in the sample averaged 0.8 on a 0 to 1 scale of fidelity of use. In a related report, two of these researchers reached the following conclusions (Huberman & Crandall, 1982, pp. 80–81; italics in original):

1. Faithfulness [fidelity] in implementing an innovation is higher than one had expected.
2. "Locally adaptive," democratic enterprise is a caricature. The *source* of innovations is quickly blurred once local implementation begins.
3. Levels of commitment and local "ownership" were no higher in locally developed than in disseminated, state-administered, projects. Nor was there less commitment in faithfully implemented innovations.

In the 1990s, both fidelity of use and mutual adaptation continued as influences on curriculum implementation, especially as a follow-up to some of the major curriculum trends of the 1980s. For example, in the United States, the Bush administration sponsored a well-publicized national conference in 1989 that recommended seven national goals for schools, ranging from improving literacy to decreasing dropout rates. While such general goals are not a curriculum (and the federal government lacks the constitutional authority to enforce a national curriculum on the states and local school districts), the goals themselves were clearly promoted in order to create uniformity, thus also promoting the idea of fidelity of use among both citizens and educators alike. In contrast, although in the 1990s the Clinton administration supported the setting of national performance standards for schools to meet, it suggested that schools could meet them in a variety of ways, thus promoting the idea of mutual adaptation.

The numerous reports by national commissions in the 1980s (Boyer, 1982; National Commission on Excellence in Education, 1983; Peters & Waterman, 1982; Task Force on Education for Economic Growth, 1983) have also been interpreted in a variety of ways. Ginsberg and Wimpelberg (1987) suggested that these reports created a lot of dialogue and publicity but had very limited actual impact on schools, perhaps just enough to be characterized as trickle-down reform. Yet when foundations, state governors, and state legislatures have taken recommendations of these reports seriously, the result has been changes for schools, such as longer school days, more time devoted to certain subjects, and more formal graduation requirements. State mandates may not have affected day-to-day teaching very much, but the overall emphasis on efficiency and setting standards of minimal achievement—all within an ethos of a technical-rational outlook—has had an impact on many schools (Cornbleth, 1986; Werner, 1991).

Thus, in the 1990s, policies promoted by the federal government as well as by state mandates influenced curriculum development and, in general, pushed in the direction of fidelity of use. In contrast, increased professionalization among teachers and grassroots demands for local curriculum development (such as SBM) pushed in the direction of mutual adaptation (Fullan, 2000). As early as the 1980s, some school districts began to attempt to outmaneuver state officials by anticipating state actions, thereby defusing the need for state mandates (Firestone & Bader, 1989). Writers such as Silberstein and Ben-Peretz (1987) have suggested that education officials are gradually becoming increasingly aware of both sides of the fidelity–adaptation debate and are more inclined to recommend different approaches for different circumstances, such as for different subjects, different localities, and different cultural groups. Nonetheless, despite the recent trend in the United States in the direction of fidelity, there is no clear trend internationally. Whereas Silberstein and Ben-Peretz concluded that Israel is moving from a centralized approach to curriculum planning and development to greater teacher autonomy and opportunities for adaptation of materials, Van den Akker (1988) and Knip and Van der Vegt (1991) concluded that research studies in the Netherlands have demonstrated that initial efforts for curriculum implementation are more effective when fidelity of use prevails.

Attention has also been directed to how the professional careers and personal lives of teachers influence how they participate in curriculum implementation (Hargreaves & Fink, 2000; Wise, 2000). Curriculum projects that require protracted periods of time for the completion of implementation can provide many new professional opportunities for teachers. Some teachers seek out these opportunities, while others—especially those in different phases of their careers—find these opportunities threatening (Huberman, 1993). Goodson (1992) has emphasized the importance of teachers' life histories and has been highly critical of curriculum implementation that depersonalizes teachers. Noddings (1986, 2000) holds a similar view, arguing for an ethic of caring and suggesting that such an ethic is what fidelity is really about.

Lest the fidelity-adaptation debate itself obscure the issues, consider once again the analogy of the planned curriculum as the text of a play and the enacted curriculum as the performance of the play. Clearly, some fidelity is necessary, for without any the performance of a play would bear no relationship whatsoever to what the author had written or even to his or her general intentions. The director and the actors could, of course, improvise an entirely new play, but that play would be a different play, and in doing so, they would be receiving little or no help from the text they had abandoned. However, recall, as well, that actually performing a play necessitates some interpretation of the text, for no text can spell out everything that must be done to make the performance of a play a practical reality. In this sense, adaptation is inevitable.

In light of this analogy, Noddings's (1986, 2000) ethic of caring applies to curriculum implementation in many ways. The developers of a curriculum must care about both the integrity of the subject matter that they are recommending and how it influences the lives of students. Fidelity, therefore, is not merely pertinent to the curriculum, it is also pertinent to the purposes—to the people—for which the curriculum is intended. Any sense of fidelity of use that obliterates the possibility of adaptation in practice to better serve these larger purposes distorts what caring is about and, therefore, is ethically indefensible. However, teachers must care not only about improving their students' lives but also about how the curriculum can best do so. Adaptation, therefore, cannot be merely a way of avoiding fidelity to a curriculum that scrupulously and rigorously reveals to students the actuality of the larger world in which they live. Any play worth writing, worth performing, and worth attending is based on this kind of ethic of caring, just as is any curriculum worth planning, worth enacting, and worth experiencing. Curriculum implementation and the performance of a play share the same educational purpose: mediating between the lived, existential reality of individual people and the broader reality of the world that the curriculum demonstrates to them. In this sense, the real debate is not about fidelity versus adaptation but about how to honor both fidelity and adaptation simultaneously.

7.6 SUPPORTING CURRICULUM IMPLEMENTATION

However curriculum implementation is conceived, it is rarely fully successful on a large scale unless it receives support. Numerous research studies have been conducted on how curriculum implementation can best be supported and why. While the body of this research is far from definitive (and is likely to remain so), it nonetheless holds some interesting and worthwhile lessons.

Federal and State Actions

At the federal and state levels, various programs have assisted schools with implementing curricula. In some cases, federal agencies have provided incentives for school districts to adopt and implement externally developed programs, while in other cases they have provided funds for external facilitators to assist with the implementation of locally developed curricula. In an analysis of federal support for curriculum implementation since the 1950s, Crandall (1988) suggested that there have been three distinct eras, which he labeled "demonstration," "evaluation," and "dissemination."

The Elementary and Secondary Education Act (ESEA) of 1965 was the beginning of a period of unprecedented federal activism in education (Crandall, 1988). New federal programs such as Follow Through, Right-to-Read, and Bilingual Education quickly followed, channeling funds to local schools for use with children with special needs.

Initially, during the late 1960s, the idea behind these programs was not only to help such children but to identify new, locally developed programs that could be used as models for other schools to emulate. This was the era of demonstration. Presumably local educators would want to use—and could use equally well—effective programs developed by other local educators. However, the assumption that a program that worked well in the local setting in which it was developed would work equally well in other settings proved naïve, for often what is most critical to the effectiveness of a program is the local setting itself. In retrospective observations on the Rand reports, McLaughlin (1989) noted:

> The common idea behind these substantively distinct federal programs was that more money or better ideas—enhanced "inputs"—would enable local educators to improve school practice. A cynical, retrospective description of that era of federal education policy might dub it the "missing input model of education policy." (p. 3)

Given the disappointments of this first era, the early 1970s ushered in a second, more cautious era, one in which programs were carefully scrutinized and formally evaluated, especially in terms of how much they improved students' academic achievement. Numerous research studies were initiated that attempted to answer two fundamental questions: is the program working? and is it cost-effective? Examples include studies by Glass (1970); Wargo (1972); Sieber, Louis, and Metzger (1972); and Berman and McLaughlin (1975). During this era, the basic assumption underlying the federal strategy was that, if an elaborate evaluation study showed that a program improved student achievement at minimal cost, then the program could be widely used. Not only did this assumption overlook the lessons of the previous era, it overestimated the ability of educational research to provide clear answers to the two fundamental questions about specific programs. Ironically, much money was wasted on futile efforts to demonstrate cost-effectiveness.

A third era soon followed, dating from the mid-1970s. The federal government began to promote dissemination. However, dissemination had over the years become focused more and more on the sharing of ideas, information, and expertise and less and less on whole programs intended as models to be followed without adaptation. In the 1970s, the National Diffusion Network (NDN) was funded by the U.S. Office of Education, and various programs devoted to dissemination were funded by the National Institute of Education, such as the State Capacity Building Program and the Research and Development Exchange. The NDN, in particular, used a number of approaches to dissemination, such as using developer-demonstrators (usually practicing teachers) and other dissemination agents within each state as state facilitators (SFs). As Crandall (1988) has noted, "The strategy was for SFs to help school people define their improvement needs, make them aware of . . . projects that could meet those needs, and arrange for . . . training and implementation assistance in the practice of their choice" (p. 30).

During the 1980s and the 1990s, massive federal budget cuts for education occurred. At the same time, states assumed greater control over the curricula of local schools, resulting in no small measure from pressures arising from various reports and commissions. For example, many states increased their requirements for high school graduation and even in times of financial austerity devoted more funds to improving curricula at both the secondary and elementary levels (Kirst, 1993). Throughout this period, however, the general trends in the United States were mixed, and the underlying tensions between fidelity of use and mutual adaptation remain unresolved (O'Neil, 2000).

The most recent federal development has been the Comprehensive School Reform Programs (CSRP) created by the United States Congress in 1998.

Thousands of schools across the nation have received awards of at least $50,000 each to implement whole-school models. In many cases the models are quite prescriptive, indicating that fidelity of use is a priority. (A detailed analysis of CSRP is provided later in this chapter.)

Approaches to Implementation

Several major approaches to supporting curriculum implementation have emerged over the decades. These approaches focus either on the group involved in implementation or on individual teachers. The four most prominent of these approaches are known as (1) Action Research, (2) Concerns-Based Adoption Model (CBAM), (3) Curriculum Alignment, and (4) Comprehensive School Reform Programs (CSRP).

Action Research. According to Wallace (1987), Action Research originated in the United States and its name was coined by Collier in 1945. It can be traced to Lewin's (1948) studies of the impact of change on community workers, originally referred to as action-training-research. Subsequently, other educators such as Corey (1953) used Action Research with groups of teachers to improve their schools through democratic means. Although Action Research was largely forgotten by educators in the 1960s, it was revived in the 1970s as a result of the efforts of Stenhouse (1973) and Elliott (1975) in the United Kingdom and Clark (1976) and Tikunoff, Ward, and Stacey (1978) in the United States. This revival continued in Australia in the 1980s because of the work of Grundy and Kemmis (1982) and Carr and Kemmis (1983).

Action Research is a particular type of problem solving. Christenson, Slutsky, Bendau, Covert, Dyer, and Risko (2000) describe it as "a type of inquiry that is fluid, emergent and cyclical." It involves groups of teachers in systematically analyzing educational problems of concern to them, planning programs, enacting them, evaluating what they have done, and then repeating the cycle if necessary. As such, Action Research is very much central to the approaches to curriculum planning and development taken by progressive educators throughout the twentieth century (see chapter 2). Typically, Action Research requires the services of an external consultant or facilitator to assist teachers (Grundy, 1987). Figure 7.2 depicts the stages of Action Research as a spiral. In the Action Research spiral, teachers first come together as a group to consider ways of improving a program or practice. They identify a field of action. (The implementation of an innovative curriculum might fall within this field.) Next they develop and then enact a specific plan. Throughout the steps of development and enactment the teachers continuously monitor what they are thinking and doing: observing, reflecting, discussing, learning, and replanning. Eventually they evaluate what they have enacted in some kind of formal sense, using what they have discovered as the basis for revising plans and actions as they repeat the spiral.

Hawkins (1998) and Haltrup and Bickel (1993) emphasize that Action Research is not a closed system; it is open-ended, and the spiral may be repeated indefinitely. Kemmis (1991) emphasizes the idea that Action Research is predominantly participatory rather than technical; teachers are involved in all stages, and through self-reflection, they initiate their own plans for improvements. As such, Action

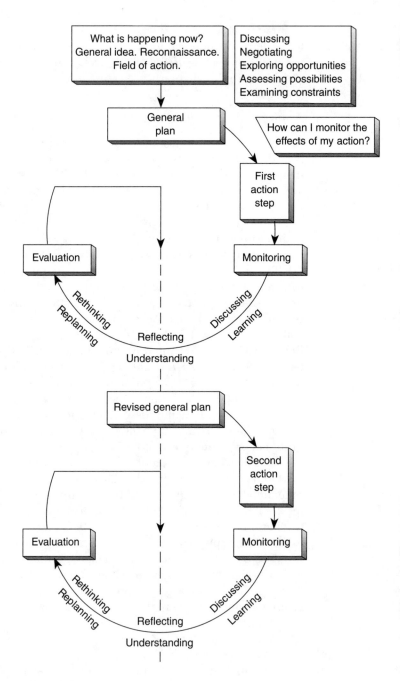

FIGURE 7.2
The Action Research spiral

Source: After Kemmis & McTaggart (1988).

What is happening now? General idea. Reconnaissance. Field of action.

Discussing
Negotiating
Exploring opportunities
Assessing possibilities
Examining constraints

General plan

How can I monitor the effects of my action?

First action step

Evaluation

Monitoring

Rethinking
Replanning

Reflecting

Understanding

Discussing
Learning

Revised general plan

Second action step

Evaluation

Monitoring

Rethinking
Replanning

Reflecting

Understanding

Discussing
Learning

Research lends itself to adaptation in curriculum implementation, not to fidelity of use. Other studies (for example, Burnaford, Brodhagen, & Beane, 1994; McTaggart & Singh, 1986) note that teachers involved in Action Research tend to assert emancipatory values rather than using the content to produce a curriculum as if it were a finished product. They are inclined to break free from restrictive routines and to take an overtly political stand on educational issues, such as overcoming inequity and discrimination.

Thus, Action Research cannot be adequately characterized as simply following the basic steps of the spiral; the intentions of the participants must be considered as well. At one level, participants may take a technical approach, expecting the group to be directed by one or more persons who possess special expertise or knowledge, aiming to create more efficient practices or products as determined by those who provide direction, and operating within a framework of existing values and constraints. At a more advanced level, participants may take a collaborative approach, expecting to participate fully in collectively directing themselves as a group, aiming to develop new practices or products, and using personal wisdom (in addition to technical knowledge) to guide action. At the most advanced level, participants may take an emancipatory approach in which they extend the intentions and actions of the collaborative approach to include sharing a radical consciousness and acting to remove constraints to still more fruitful participatory problem solving.

Feldman, Redrick, & Weiss (1999) contend that Action Research has three dimensions, which can be labeled as "personal," "professional," and "political." The personal dimension relates to individual development, the professional dimension is about control over teaching knowledge, and the political dimension focuses on social change, particularly change in the direction of justice and democracy. Zeichner's (1993) review of the research literature on Action Research suggests that it has often been successful in facilitating personal development (for example, self-confidence), but that it has had more limited success in promoting professional and social change. McKernan (1993) uses the terms *scientific, practical-collaborative,* and *critical* to describe what he sees as three levels or subtypes of Action Research based on his survey of project leaders in the United States, the United Kingdom, and Ireland. Redrick and Feldman (2000) sees Action Research as having three dimensions clustered around the understandings and intentions of participants. These dimensions are the theoretical orientations of participants, their purposes, and the types of reflection they engage in. Each of these dimensions is subdivided as follows:

1. Theoretical orientations to Action Research
   - Technical: uncovering action that follows rules, with emphasis on control
   - Practical: understanding the environment through interaction and consensus
   - Emancipatory: engaging in autonomous action leading to empowerment
2. Purposes of Action Research
   - Personal: understanding self and others; developing personal knowledge
   - Professional: sharing knowledge, especially for staff development
   - Political: becoming aware of socioeconomic, racial, gender, and other kinds of inequalities

3. Types of reflection in Action Research
   - Autobiographical: examining the meanings of one's personal stories
   - Collaborative: sharing personal stories and asking questions about how they relate to the stories of others
   - Communal: interacting with others in cultural, historical, and institutional contexts

Action Research, therefore, may serve to focus the attention of individual teachers on how they perceive and function within their own classrooms, or it may expose resistance, suspicion, and alienation within bureaucratic organizations and lead to corrective steps. Especially in this latter sense, Action Research is related to some politically oriented forms of curriculum theorizing (discussed in chapter 4), and it can lead to greater school-staff collegiality and feelings of empowerment. Since it is also a basis for teachers conducting research into their own classrooms, it helps teachers to solve their own problems and to improve practice. For all these reasons, it is a growing form of professional development for reflective practitioners (Beyer, 1996; Christenson et al., 2000). For example, it is being used increasingly in preservice teacher-training programs to encourage participants to reflect on and to challenge conventional views of education. Cochran-Smith (1994) and Price and Valli (2000) suggest that it enables preservice teachers to reflect on how knowledge is socially constructed and how teachers gain knowledge. Hollingsworth (1996) has used feminist models of Action Research to study collaborative conversations among preservice teachers.

Despite these benefits, there can be problems in using Action Research with preservice teachers or experienced teachers. Christenson et al. (2000) contend that principals often feel threatened by activities that can lead to teacher empowerment. Hursh (1995) notes that teachers may be loathe to embark upon Action Research if doing so places them under pressure to comply with high-stakes testing and the standardization of the curriculum. Beattie (1989) and Lubeck and Post (1999) assert that Action Research has limited impact when teachers are allocated insufficient time and resources to engage in it or are not free to make the changes in their teaching patterns that they come to feel are educationally worthwhile. Clandinin and Connelly (1992) warn that some people who are overzealous about Action Research may become involved "in a power struggle to replace one hegemony with another, to gain control of the messages within the conduit" (p. 378).

Concerns-Based Adoption Model.   The Concerns-Based Adoption Model (CBAM) "is arguably the most robust and empirically grounded theoretical model for the implementation of educational innovations to come out of educational change research in the 1970s and 1980s" (Anderson, 1997, p. 331). It emphasizes that collective change results from changes in individuals and how they relate to each other. It is widely used, especially in Europe, to monitor large-scale changes in schools involving multiple innovations.

According to Hall and Hord (1987) and Rutherford, Hord, Huling, and Hall (1983), assumptions that underlie CBAM include the following:

- Change is a process, not an event, requiring time, energy, and resources to support it.
- Change is achieved incrementally and developmentally and entails developmental growth in feelings about the skills in using new programs.
- Change is accomplished by individuals first. Institutions cannot change until the individuals within them change.
- Change is a highly personal experience.
- Change can be facilitated by change agents providing diagnostic, client-centered support to individual teachers.

CBAM begins with the assumption that there is a specific curriculum that should be adopted by a district or a school. The question then becomes how to assist teachers in adopting this curriculum as their own. To do so, CBAM centers on the concerns of the teachers, not the school or the district. It attempts to provide data that will help teachers successfully implement a new curriculum. Ordinarily, these data are not sufficient by themselves, and an external facilitator or change agent is also necessary. Expressed another way, CBAM assumes the existence of a resource system (the agency or the institution seeking adoption of the new curriculum) and a user system (the teachers working in a school). The major task is for members of the resource system to help members of the user system develop their own diagnostic data so that they can become independent. Independence is fully achieved when the user system (the teachers) have fully assimilated the new curriculum and are capable of maintaining it on their own.

The conceptual basis for CBAM derives from work by Fuller (1969). Fuller identified a developmental sequence through which preservice teachers passed as they became more experienced. She found that all preservice teachers experienced the same sequence of concerns, moving from concerns about self, to concerns about teaching, to concerns about students. Hall, Wallace, and Dossett (1973) examined how this sequence applied to educational change, refining Fuller's sequence of concerns into their own sequence as well as creating a sequence of how teachers used innovations. They named these two sequences Stages of Concern (SoC) and Levels of Use (LoU). SoC can be used to track the concerns of teachers as they implement a new curriculum, and LoU can be used to track what teachers actually do during implementation.

Hall and Loucks (1978) subsequently added the Innovations Configuration (IC), which can be used to track the different adaptations curriculum innovations take as they are implemented by different schools and different teachers. Over the last decade the IC has also been used to help groups reach consensus about what ideal teaching practices look like.

Stages of Concern.   Stages of Concern (SoC) focus on teachers' feelings as they become involved in implementation. Hall, George, and Rutherford (1979) used the term *concern* to refer to a state of being mentally aroused about something. Teachers' concerns vary both in type and intensity. At any particular time, teachers might be concerned about several issues, but some concerns will be more immediate and more intense than others. Hall et al. argued that, as teachers become increasingly involved in implementation, they tend to move through seven developmental stages. These stages have been confirmed by a number of studies, including those reviewed by Marsh (1990), Rutherford (1990), and Van den Berg (1993).

The seven stages are listed in Figure 7.3. Movement is from an initial stage, in which teachers are mostly uninvolved with the innovation, to other stages, in which their concerns change from personal, to the tasks of implementation, to the immediate impact on students, to universal benefits. Individual teachers progress through these stages at their own rates and do not necessarily reach all of them. The SoC can be used to create a profile of the intensity of a teacher's concerns at each of these stages. Data for compiling a SoC profile can be obtained from questionnaires and rating scales for open-ended statements designed and refined by Hall and Loucks (1977).

Stages of Concern		Definitions
0	Awareness	Little concern about or involvement with the innovation is indicated.
1	Informational	A general awareness of the innovation and interest in learning more detail about it are indicated. The person seems to be unworried about himself or herself in relation to the innovation. She or he is interested in substantive aspects of the innovation in a selfless manner, such as general characteristics, effects, and requirements for use.
2	Personal	Individual is uncertain about the demands of the innovation, his or her adequacy to meet those demands, and his or her role in the innovation. This includes analysis of his or her role in relation to the reward structure of the organization, decision making, and consideration of potential conflicts with existing structures or personal commitments. Financial or status implications of the program for self and colleagues may also be reflected.
3	Management	Attention is focused on the processes and tasks of using the innovation and the best use of information and resources. Issues related to efficiency, organizing, managing, scheduling, and time demands are utmost.
4	Consequence	Attention focuses on impact of the innovation on students within teacher's immediate sphere of influence. The focus is on relevance of the innovation for students; evaluation of student outcomes, including performance and competencies; and changes needed to increase student outcomes.
5	Collaboration	The focus is on coordination and cooperation with others regarding use of the innovation.
6	Refocusing	The focus is on exploration of more universal benefits from the innovation, including the possibility of major changes or replacement with a more powerful alternative. Individual has definite ideas about alternatives to the proposed or existing form of the innovation.

FIGURE 7.3

Stages of concern about an innovation

Source: After Hall et al. (1973).

SoC profiles of teachers involved in implementing a new curriculum can be useful to a school, a school district, or external facilitators, particularly in devising in-service activities that target major concerns. For example, in-service activities for teachers with intense concerns about how the new curriculum should be used (stage 3, management) could emphasize techniques for efficiently organizing materials and time. For teachers with intense concerns about working with other teachers (stage 5, collaboration), in-service activities could focus on interpersonal communications and techniques for fostering group deliberations.

The SoC has been widely used in a number of countries, as noted in studies by Wells and Anderson (1997), Bailey and Palsha (1992), and Guan (2000). Of special interest is a confirmatory study by Marsh and Penn (1988), who found that the concerns of students engaged in a remedial reading program progressed in a sequence similar to SoC.

Second-generation research in Belgium and the Netherlands (Van den Berg, 1993; Van der Vegt and Vandenberghe, 1992; Vandenberghe, 1983) has produced an alternative version of SoC that includes an increased number of self-oriented concerns.

Levels of Use. Levels of Use (LoU) can be used to track what teachers actually do during the implementation of a new curriculum. The eight levels of use proposed by Hall et al. (1973) are described in Figure 7.4. They have been corroborated by various follow-up studies (for example, James & Hall, 1981; Loucks & Melle, 1980; and Rutherford, 1978). These studies suggest that teachers progress through these levels as their familiarity and expertise with an innovation increase.

The levels are measured through a focused interview developed by Loucks, Newlove, and Hall (1975). Rather than asking a specific list of predetermined and presequenced questions, the interviewer uses a branching technique whereby certain decision points during the interview provide cues to initiate a particular set of questions. As with the SoC questionnaire, the LoU interview is generic and can be used to analyze the implementation of any kind of new curriculum simply by changing the focus. Usually each LoU interview is tape-recorded so that the teacher's responses can later be carefully coded and, if necessary, verified by independent coders.

Knowing what levels individual teachers are on can aid in implementing a new curriculum. For example, a teacher on LoU III (mechanical use) is probably teaching the curriculum in a superficial, step-by-step fashion without reflecting much on students' needs and attitudes. Giving this teacher more information about the curriculum, more encouragement, or more help with how to teach it may be necessary to help the teacher toward implementing it fully. In contrast, a teacher on LoU IVB (refinement) is probably already experimenting with different teaching methods to help students make optimal progress with the curriculum.

Innovation Configuration (IC). SoC and LoU are parts of CBAM that provide information about the feelings and actions of individual teachers as they become involved in implementing a new curriculum. However, it is also important to identify major components or characteristics of the new curriculum itself in order to assess whether

Levels of Use	Definition of Use
O Non-use	State in which the user has little or no knowledge of the innovation, no involvement with the innovation, and is doing nothing toward becoming involved.
	Decision Point A The user takes action to learn more detailed information about the innovation.
I Orientation	State in which the user has recently acquired or is acquiring information about the innovation and/or has recently explored or is exploring its value orientation and its demands on user and user system.
	Decision Point B The user makes a decision to use the innovation by establishing a time to begin.
II Preparation	State in which the user is preparing for first use of the innovation.
	Decision Point C Changes, if any, and use are dominated by user needs.
III Mechanical use	State in which the user focuses most effort on the short-term, day-to-day use of the innovation with little time for reflection. Changes in use are made more to meet user needs than client needs. The user is primarily engaged in a stepwise attempt to master the tasks required to use the innovation, often resulting in disjointed and superficial use.
	Decision Point D-1 A routine pattern of use is established.
IVA Routine	Use of the innovation is stabilized. Few, if any, changes are being made in ongoing use. Little preparation or thought is being given to improving innovation use or its consequences.
	Decision Point D-2 The user changes use of the innovation based on formal or informal evaluation in order to increase client outcomes.
IVB Refinement	State in which the user varies the use of the innovation to increase the impact on clients within the immediate sphere of influence. Variations are based on knowledge of both short- and long-term consequences for clients.
	Decision Point E The user initiates changes in use of innovation based on input of and in coordination with what colleagues are doing.
V Integration	State in which the user is combining own efforts to use the innovation with related activities of colleagues to achieve a collective impact on clients within their common sphere of influence.
	Decision Point F The user begins exploring alternatives to or major modifications of the innovation presently in use.
VI Renewal	State in which the user reevaluates the quality of use of the innovation, seeks major modifications of, or alternatives, to the present innovation to achieve increased impact on clients, examines new developments in the field, and explores new goals for self and the system.

FIGURE 7.4

Levels of use of an innovation

Source: After Hall and Hord (1987).

its operational use is consistent with its intended use. When the most essential characteristics of a new curriculum are not made explicit, teachers may also be unable to determine if how they are implementing it is consistent with how other teachers are doing so (Hall & George, 2000).

Any new curriculum (innovation) includes its own distinctive cluster of operational forms or configurations, such as how teaching materials are supposed to be used and the kinds of activities suggested for students. Some of these configurations might be acceptable to all teachers involved in implementation, but some might not. There is always some slippage between the configurations intended by developers and those enacted by teachers. The Innovation Configuration (IC), developed by Hall and Loucks (1981), creates an inventory of essential characteristics of the curriculum from the points of view of both developers and teachers. The IC does not ensure that everyone will agree on what is essential, but it helps everyone clearly identify differences between the planned curriculum and the enacted curriculum, and, when disputes arise (about, for instance, fidelity of use versus mutual adaptation), it provides a basis for informed discussion about differences and for possible adjustments in the curriculum.

Hall and Loucks (1981) have suggested that creating an IC for a new curriculum includes the following steps:

STEP 1:   Ask the developer about intended components and emphases.
STEP 2:   Interview and observe a small number of users.
STEP 3:   Refine interview questions; interview a large number of users.
STEP 4:   Construct an IC checklist and use it with a number of users.
STEP 5:   Analyze the checklist data to identify dominant configurations.
STEP 6:   Use the data to provide appropriate staff development or in-service activities.

The major thrust of interviews with developers and teachers is to obtain concrete descriptions of what the innovation looks like in classrooms. Helpful questions include the following:

Would you describe your innovation to me?
What does the innovation look like when implemented?
What do teachers do?
What do students do?
What would I see in a classroom where the innovation was in use?
What are the most essential components of the innovation?
Which of these are the most important?
Which are the least important?

Figure 7.5 is an example of an IC for a social studies curriculum. In this particular IC, seven components have been deemed essential and are listed vertically; each component has up to four variations, which are listed horizontally. The IC is written from the point of view of the developer insofar as the variations to the left of the dotted line are what the developer considers ideal; those between the dotted and the solid line are acceptable, and those to the right of the solid line are unacceptable. However, the point of view of any particular teacher might be that the developer has been entirely too prescriptive and the labels should be reversed. In this case, there would be great differences between developer and teacher about the ideal and the unacceptable but still room for compromise in the middle on what acceptable characteristics of the curriculum might be. An IC is useful not only for these purposes but also to help track how a new curriculum is actually being used.

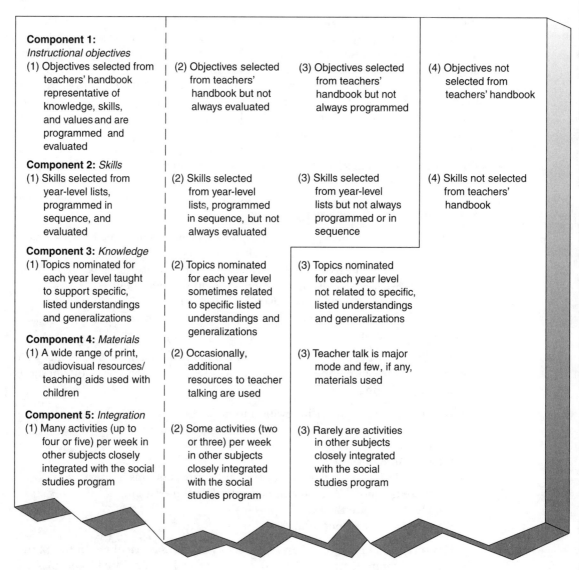

FIGURE 7.5
Innovation configuration: Social studies K-10 syllabus

Research Studies Using CBAM. Since the development of CBAM in the 1970s, numerous studies using it have been undertaken (for example, in the United States, by Alquist & Hendrickson, 1999; George, Hall, & Uchiyama, 2000; Hall, 1992, 1999; Hall & George, 2000; and Wheeler, 1996; in Canada, by Anderson, 1993, 1997; and Anderson & Stiegelbauer, 1994); in the United Kingdom, by Peers, 1990; in Belgium, by Vandenberghe, 1983; in the Netherlands, by Van den Berg, 1983, 1993; and in Australia, by Kember & Mezger, 1990; Kennedy, 1983; and Marsh, 1987, 1990). Such

Component 6: *Values awareness*

| (1) Many learning activities (four or five) used each week to encourage children to reflect upon different values and what it means to be committed to particular ones | (2) Some learning activities (two or three) used each week to encourage children to reflect upon different values and what it means to be committed to particular ones | (3) Rarely learning activities used to encourage children to reflect upon different values and what it means to be committed to particular ones | |

Component 7: *Testing*

| (1) A balance between informal and formal procedures is used to assess children, derived from the programmed instructional objectives | (2) Some informal but mostly formal procedures used to assess children, derived from the programmed instructional objectives | (3) Formal procedures only used to assess children, derived from the programmed instructional objectives | (4) No informal or formal procedures used to assess children |

Code: _____ variations to the right are unacceptable
variations to the left are acceptable

_ _ _ _ _ _ variations to the left are ideal
as prescribed by the developer

FIGURE 7.5 *continued*
Source: After Marsh (1984).

studies have pointed out how the specific context of an innovation influences how it is implemented, but they have also confirmed the value of CBAM (including SoC and LoU) in promoting full implementation and in guiding staff development. Rutherford (1990) contends that the numerous research studies on CBAM confirm that preservice and in-service teachers do have concerns about themselves, the tasks of teaching, and the impact on student learning, as SoC reveals. Van den Berg (1993) concludes that the CBAM instruments have been used in diverse fields and have demonstrated their value for individuals coping with organizational change. Snyder et al. (1992) state:

> CBAM has provided researchers, policymakers, and users with a common language to talk about the implementation of innovations. It lends support to the notion that the implementation of curriculum itself is worthy of study and has consequences for staff development and program evaluation. (p. 408)

Anderson (1997) supports these ideas, contending that CBAM is primarily descriptive and predictive, not prescriptive, and that it is as relevant now to understanding curriculum implementation as it was when first developed. Now it is being applied to such innovations as cooperative learning, portfolio assessment, constructivist approaches to science and math education (George et al., 2000), and the use of computers and the Internet (Ang & Lim, 1999; Guan, 2000; Wheeler, 1996).

Nonetheless, weaknesses in CBAM have also been uncovered. One major weakness is that LoU and SoC consist of fixed stages that do not discriminate completely between how different teachers in different schools might implement a new curriculum. Hall and Hord (2001) concede that contextual influences are not considered by CBAM, and studies by Fennell (1992) and Anderson (1997) indicate that contextual influences such as organizational linkages play a large part in teacher progress on SoC and LoU. According to Leithwood and Montgomery (1982), SoC and LoU underestimate the real complexity of any innovation and so create an incomplete picture of how implementation occurs. It is evident that the SoC stages are not as universal as first thought. The comprehensive validation studies undertaken by Belgian and Dutch researchers have produced a revised set of stages of concern. As Anderson notes, the SoC framework "presents a possible, not a necessary progression of teacher concerns about a change" (p. 334) and "despite its intuitive and empirical attraction, CBAM in its present state does not fully explain teacher change in response to innovations in curriculum and instruction" (p. 363).

Curriculum Alignment.   The phrase "curriculum alignment" covers a number of related practices that were adopted increasingly by states and school districts during the 1980s and 1990s as part of the push for effective schools. This push continues strongly in the first decade of the twenty-first century, focused on the use of uniform curriculum standards.

Basically, Curriculum Alignment attempts to ensure maximum congruency between the planned curriculum and the enacted curriculum through extensive testing of what is taught. As Soder (1999) observes, it is a modern descendant of the efficiency movement in curriculum of the early twentieth century (see chapter 2). Its proponents, however, claim it to be "a sea change in thinking about learning" (Tucker & Codding, 1998, p. 74). It adheres to a strict interpretation of fidelity of use, which permits little or no room for adaptation in curriculum implementation. Teachers themselves are evaluated in terms of how well their students meet prescribed standards, as measured by tests that have also been standardized. In fact, many states have applied similar notions of standardization to the initial preparation and the licensing of teachers (Sowell & Zambo, 1997; Wise & Leibrand, 2000).

Most of the arguments for so-called "effective schools" that surfaced in the 1980s and 1990s were based on the belief that the academic achievement of students has been steadily declining. In response, the idea of effectiveness has been defined in terms of increasing academic achievement, particularly as measured by standardized tests, the most convenient—though certainly not the most refined or the most accurate—way of determining what goes on in schools. A further belief is that a major reason for the decline of academic achievement is a decline in the quality of the curriculum, if not its outright fragmentation at the hands of many teachers. Given these beliefs, the arguments for aligning the enacted curriculum with the planned curriculum may seem very convincing. If the planned curriculum has been developed by a number of knowledgeable, well-trained specialists and represents an informed consensus at the district level (or at the state level or even at the national level), then it should be followed closely by all teachers. Actually creating this kind of uniformity depends, of course, on many things but particularly written curriculum frameworks or curriculum guides for all teachers to follow, committees to screen textbooks, and especially testing.

Curriculum frameworks are official documents that describe what is to be taught. Some descriptions may be general only, but others may spell out the curriculum in considerable detail, as in the mathematics curriculum published by the National Council of Teachers of Mathematics (NCTM) (Bay, Reys, & Reys, 1999). Textbook committees, especially at the state level, have enormous leverage (Brandt, 1989). Often they, too, are under pressure to accept a standardized curriculum as defined by the textbooks of major commercial publishers. Standardized tests place teachers under still other pressures for uniformity, particularly when teachers are formally evaluated or rewarded on the basis of the test scores of their students. Although Curriculum Alignment has its supporters among educators, it has numerous detractors. Some critics suggest that it is an invidious device to reduce the autonomy and creativity of teachers. Others note that it gives far too much power to tests and leads to teachers teaching the test only (Sirotnik & Kimball, 1999).

Curriculum Alignment has been adopted more fully and more enthusiastically in some states than others. It is not surprising that in the 1980s California began to use Curriculum Alignment extensively in attempting to create uniformity in curriculum implementation, beginning with legislation passed in 1983 (Marsh, 1988). The California Department of Education produced and published curriculum frameworks for all major subjects. These frameworks, together with published model curriculum standards, prescribed things such as general content, specific lessons, materials and activities, skills and attitudes, and measures of accomplishment to be taught or aimed at by California's teachers (Kierstead & Mentor, 1988). The Department of Education also developed new criteria for the selection of textbooks. These criteria emphasized thinking, problem solving, and attention to controversial and ethical issues (Marsh, 1988). Finally, California also refined its statewide testing program so that it more closely matched the new curriculum frameworks and model curriculum standards. These changes clearly created greater uniformity in curricula implemented in California schools; however, the state still left some latitude for school districts to develop their own scope and sequence charts for each subject and to produce course guides and achievement standards.

Early research reports on these changes in California pronounced Curriculum Alignment a success (Kirst, 1987; Marsh & Bowman, 1988), with one suggesting that top-down, content-oriented Curriculum Alignment was effective in California high schools under the following circumstances (Marsh & Bowman, p. 19):

  a. The content of the reform is targeted at all students and constitutes a toughening of existing academic programs.

b. The local implementation process is stimulated by external pressure, especially in the form of testing.

c. The content of the reform extends across the school and includes alignment of curriculum, textbooks, teaching strategies, and testing.

d. The roles of state, district, and school are complementary.

e. The local decision-making process complements rather than competes with the existing structures.

f. The reform fits within the school and district.

g. Key players are able to institutionalize their efforts within the regular program of the school.

These reports were focused, of course, on the effectiveness of California's efforts to create uniformity through curriculum alignment, not on the effectiveness of the uniformity on increasing academic achievement among students (which, in any case, could not be determined except over a much more extended period of time) or even on the desirability of uniformity in the first place. In general, these reports ran contrary to the vast majority of research on curriculum implementation, particularly those studies that support mutual adaptation over fidelity of use. More recent reports on California's efforts with Curriculum Alignment are far less optimistic and paint a far more complicated picture, pointing out how the social, economic, political, and educational climates in California (or any other state) influence each other. Given the complexities of disentangling these mutual influences, attempts to deem large-scale experiments with Curriculum Alignment as unqualified successes or failures are unwise (Orlich, 2000).

Comprehensive School Reform Programs (CSRP).   A series of approaches to curriculum implementation begun in the 1990s and likely to be tried out increasingly in the 2000s is known collectively as Comprehensive School Reform Programs (CSRP). These approaches are all very similar to one another and have been made possible on a wide scale by the Comprehensive School Reform Demonstration (CSRD) passed by the United States Congress in 1998. The idea behind CSRP is that previous efforts to reform or even to improve schools have been unsuccessful because they were piecemeal, failing to focus comprehensively on the "whole school" and to design fully what were to be the new innovations.

To qualify for funding from CSRD, schools must commit themselves to the following (Education Commission of the States, 1998):

- Promoting high standards for all children
- Addressing all academic subject areas and grade levels
- Selecting a model program that is research-based and research-tested
- Being goal-oriented
- Making provision for professional development of teachers
- Aligning available resources across all grades and subject areas
- Facilitating parent and community involvement

Thousands of schools across the United States have received awards of at least $50,000 to implement CSRP (McChesney & Hertling, 2000); however, a participating school must select the particular reform program it will use from a catalog of thirty-three approved, research-based models. Interestingly, some of these models are more fully developed than others. CSRP has been promoted since 1991 by the New American Schools Development Corporation (now the New American Schools) and backed by substantial corporate and foundation funding, but this expenditure of time and money has enabled the authors of only nine of the thirty-three models to develop fully the curriculum materials needed and to undertake follow-up research studies. Some of the models available focus on school processes, such as Sizer's (1992) "Coalition of Essential Schools"; others focus on the curriculum itself, such as Slavin & Madden's (2001) "Success for All."

Although principals are seen as playing a critical role in providing the leadership for successfully implementing a reform model, the majority of programs have external design teams to assist schools in the process of implementation. According to McChesney and Hertling (2000), the tasks of the design teams are to:

- Integrate all aspects of reform
- Provide a strong vision that sustains schools
- Maintain a strong focus on results
- Use research and development skills

Some external design teams have proved to be highly prescriptive (thus supporting fidelity of curriculum implementation), while others have been more flexible (thus permitting considerable adaptation).

Many schools are now involved in trying out CSRP, but as yet there are no definitive, long-range studies of its overall usefulness. Proponents such as Slavin (2001) contend that the approach has enormous potential for creating programs and models that are strongly research-based and that will lead to great improvement in student achievement in a variety of schools. Other educators are more cautious. Hatch (2000) reports that even schools receiving large amounts of CSRD funding have great difficulty in "breaking the mold" and finding "the right balance between exploiting current practices and exploring new ideas that may lead to success in the future" (p. 565). McChesney and Hertling (2000) consider as problematic whether CSRP will be sustained. It does provide a variety of programs, but taken collectively these programs may focus too narrowly on the planned curriculum while ignoring the realities of the enacted curriculum and the experienced curriculum.

Other approaches to curriculum implementation, such as those we have described in this chapter, may, of course, be preferable to CSRP for at least some schools at least some of the time. Therefore, also likely to be particularly troublesome in the long run are unresolved issues arising from the involvement of courts in forcing all schools within a state to adopt CSRP. For instance, for an account of the New Jersey Supreme Court's requiring 319 elementary schools in the state to implement comprehensive, whole-school programs, see Hendrie (1999).

7.7   CONCLUDING COMMENT

How a planned curriculum is implemented as the enacted curriculum in any school is a complex process that can vary enormously from school to school. The personnel of some schools may prefer to make few changes in the original plan (as in fidelity of use), the personnel of other schools may choose to make many changes (as in mutual adaptation), or—as is often the case—there may be considerable differences of opinion among the personnel of any school. The only certainty about curriculum implementation is that there is no one right way of going about it for all teachers in all schools. The ongoing issues concerning curriculum implementation are not likely to be resolved, but in recent years there has been growing awareness of the complexity of the process, hence more reason for both caution and guarded optimism. Educators may be ready to understand the process more and to prescribe it less.

■ QUESTIONS AND REFLECTIONS

1. When is it appropriate to monitor curriculum implementation? How? Should implementation be monitored in terms of what teachers do, in terms of effects on students, or in some other way?

2. Pressure and support are both needed to ensure that implementation occurs. Do you agree? How might pressure and support occur simultaneously within your school or school district?

3. "Sustaining school-wide reform programs past the initial stage of enthusiasm is one of the biggest problems that schools face" (McChesney & Hertling, 2000, p. 14). How might a principal sustain a high level of enthusiasm? What would be the incentives for teachers?

4. What kind of Action Research project would you care to be involved in? Describe it in both theoretical and practical terms.

5. According to Fullan et al. (1989), for a new curriculum to be fully implemented there are four core changes required of teachers: (a) in class groupings and organization, (b) in materials, (c) in practices and behaviors, and (d) in beliefs and understand-

ings. If you agree with these four core changes, give examples to illustrate their importance. If you do not agree, put forward other, more important ways in which teachers must change.

6. "Because implementation takes place in a fluid setting, implementation problems are never 'solved.' Rather they evolve. . . . New issues, new requirements, new considerations emerge as the process unfolds" (McLaughlin, 1987, p. 174). What are the implications of this statement for implementing new curricula? What parts of implementation can or cannot be planned in advance? What contingency plans should be developed?

7. Do you believe that curriculum implementation should be considered as fundamentally closed-ended or open-ended? Carefully weigh both the advantages and the disadvantages of considering curriculum implementation in each way.

8. "The essential nature of an innovation can be eroded: with small, almost imperceptible alterations the school 'tames' it" (Jansen & Van der Vegt, 1991, p. 33). To what extent

should adaptation be permitted in school settings? Is it necessary for all of a planned innovation to be maintained? Can strict fidelity of use be maintained without violating the autonomy of teachers and students?

9. "Testing certain content in certain ways will result in an alignment of classroom practices with the official view of what and how subjects should be taught" (Matheison,

1991, p. 201). Does testing ensure that fidelity of use will occur? What are some problems associated with curriculum controlled by testing?

10. Reflect upon the growing popularity of Comprehensive School Reform Programs. How crucial are external design teams in helping schools to achieve satisfactory levels of implementation? What are the problems in relying upon external teams?

■ SUGGESTED READING

Some useful articles on curriculum implementation (see the chapter bibliography) include the following:

Fullan & Miles (1992)

Hargreaves & Fink (2000)

Huberman (1988)

Kirst (1993)

Marsh (1988)

McChesney & Hertling (2000)

McLaughlin (1989)

Van den Berg (1993)

Books containing extended discussions of curriculum implementation (see the chapter bibliography) include the following:

Crandall et al. (1983)

Fullan (1991)

Fullan (1993)

Fullan (1999)

Hall & Hord (1987)

Loucks-Horsley & Hergert (1985)

Marsh (1996)

■ BIBLIOGRAPHY

Alquist, A., & Hendrickson, M. (1999). Mapping the configurations of mathematics teaching. *Journal of Classroom Teaching, 34*(1), 18–26.

Anderson, B. L. (1993). The states of systemic change. *Educational Leadership, 51*(1), 14–18.

Anderson, R. M., & Tomkins, G. S. (1983). *Understanding materials: Their role in curriculum development.* Vancouver: University of British Columbia.

Anderson, S. E. (1993). *Revisiting the concerns based adoption model.* Unpublished paper. University of Toronto.

Anderson, S. E. (1997). Understanding teacher change: Revisiting the concerns based adoption model. *Curriculum Inquiry, 27*(3), 331–367.

Anderson, S. E., & Stiegelbauer, S. (1994). Institutionalization and renewal in a restructured secondary school. *School Organisation, 14*(3), 279–293.

Ang, W. H., & Lim, B. (1999). Integrating IT. *Thinking and Teaching Review, 8*(3), 25–31.

Ariav, T. (1988). *Growth in teachers' curriculum knowledge through the process of curriculum analysis.* Paper presented at the annual meeting of the American Educational Research Association, New Orleans.

Bailey, D. B., & Palsha, S. A. (1992). Qualities of the stages of concern questionnaire and implications for educational innovations. *Journal of Educational Research, 85*(4), 226–232.

Barrows, L. K., & Klenke, W. H. (1980). *Documenting change: Procedures, problems and possibilities.* Paper presented at the annual meeting of the American Educational Research Association, Boston.

Bay, J. M., Reys, B. J., & Reys, R. E. (1999). The top 10 elements that must be in place to implement standards-based mathematics curricula. *Phi Delta Kappan, 80*(7), 503–506.

Beattie, C. (1989). Action research: A practice in need of theory? In G. Milburn, I. F. Goodson, & R. J. Clark (Eds.), *Re-interpreting curriculum research: Images and arguments.* London, Ontario: Althouse.

Berg, G. (1982). Changes in the steering of Swedish schools: A step towards "societification of the state." *Journal of Curriculum Studies, 24*(4), 327–344.

Berman, P., & McLaughlin, M. W. (1975). *Federal programs supporting educational change: Vol. 4. The findings in review.* Santa Monica, CA: Rand Corporation.

Beyer, L. (1996). *Creating democratic classrooms: The struggle to integrate theory and practice.* New York: Teachers College Press.

Blakely, C., Mayer, J., Roitman, D., & Gottschalk, R. (1983). *The implementation of disseminated educational innovations: Is the modified RD&D model viable?* Paper presented at the annual meeting of the American Educational Research Association, Montreal.

Blank, R. K. (1993). Developing a system of education indicators: Selecting, implementing and reporting indicators. *Educational Evaluation and Policy Analysis, 15*(1), 65–80.

Boyer, E. L. (1982). *High school: A report on secondary education in America.* New York: Harper & Row.

Brandt, R. (1989). On curriculum in California: A conversation with Bill Honig. *Educational Leadership, 47*(3), 10–13.

Burnaford, G., Brodhagen, B., & Beane, J. (1994). *Teacher action research at the middle level: Inside an integrative curriculum.* Paper presented at the annual meeting of the American Educational Research Association, New Orleans.

Carr, W., & Kemmis, S. (1983). *Becoming critical: Knowing through action research.* Geelong, Australia: Deakin University.

Christenson, M., Slutsky, R., Bendau, S., Covert, J., Dyer, J., & Risko, G. (2000). *The rocky road of teachers becoming action researchers.* Paper pre-sented at the annual meeting of the American Educational Research Association, New Orleans.

Clandinin, D. J., & Connelly, F. M. (1992). Teacher as curriculum maker. In P. W. Jackson (Ed.), *Handbook of research on curriculum.* New York: Macmillan.

Clark, A. F. (Ed.). (1976). *Experimenting with organizational life: The action research approach.* New York: Plenum.

Clough, E., Aspinwall, K., & Gibbs, B. (Eds.). (1989). *Learning to change: An LEA school-focused initiative.* London: Falmer.

Cochran-Smith, M. (1994). The power of teacher research in teacher education. In S. Hollingsworth & H. Sockett (Eds.), *Teacher Research and Educational Reform: Ninety-third year book of the National Society for the Study of Education.* Chicago: University of Chicago.

Corbett, H. D., & Rossman, J. B. (1989). Three paths to implementing change: A research note. *Curriculum Inquiry, 19*(2), 163–190.

Corey, S. (1953). *Action research to improve school practices.* New York: Teachers College Press.

Cornbleth, C. (1986). Ritual and rationality in teacher education reform. *Educational Researcher, 15*(4), 5–14.

Cornbleth, C. (1990). *Curriculum in context.* London: Falmer.

Crandall, D. P. (1988). *Implementation aspects of dissemination: Reflections toward an immodest proposal.* Paper presented at the annual meeting of the American Educational Research Association, New Orleans.

Crandall, D. P., and associates (1983). *The study of dissemination efforts supporting school improvement (DESSI).* Andover, MA: The Network.

Cuban, L. (1992). Curriculum stability and change. In P. W. Jackson (Ed.), *Handbook of research on curriculum.* New York: Macmillan.

Dalin, P., & McLaughlin, M. W. (1975). *Strategies for innovation in higher education.* Stockholm: Educational Research Symposium on Strategies for Research and Development in Higher Education.

Datta, L. E. (1980). Changing times: A study of federal programs supporting educational change and the case of local problem-solving. *Teachers College Record, 82*(1), 101–115.

Day, C., Pope, M., & Denicols, P. (Eds.). (1990). *Insight into teachers' thinking and practice.* London: Falmer.

Education Commission of the States. (1998). *Comprehensive school reform: Allocating federal funds.* Denver: Education Commission of the States.

Elliott, J. (1975). Initiation into classroom discussion. In J. Elliott & B. MacDonald (Eds.), *People in classrooms.* Norwich, UK: Centre for Applied Research in Education, University of East Anglia.

Eveland, J. D., Rogers, E., & Klepper, C. (1977). *The innovation process in public organizations: Some elements of a preliminary model.* Springfield, VA: American Society for Public Education.

Farrar, E., Desanctis, J. E., & Cohen, D. K. (1979). *Views from below: Implementation research in education.* Cambridge, MA: Huron Institute.

Feldman, A., Redrick, M., & Weiss, T. (1999). *Teacher development and action research: Findings from five years of action research in schools.* Paper presented at the annual meeting of the American Educational Research Association, Montreal.

Fennell, W. (1992). An investigation of the relationships between organizational-cultural linkages and teachers' stages of concern toward a policy of implementation. *Alberta Journal of Educational Research, 38*(1), 9–26.

Firestone, W. A., & Bader, B. D. (1989). *District coalitions for reform: A preliminary report on the application of coalition theory to district operations.* Paper presented at the annual meeting of the American Educational Research Association, San Francisco.

Fullan, M. G. (1982). *The meaning of educational change.* New York: Teachers College Press.

Fullan, M. G. (1986). *School improvement efforts in Canada.* Toronto: Council of Ministers of Education.

Fullan, M. G. (1991). *The new meaning of educational change.* London: Cassell.

Fullan, M. G. (1993). *Change forces.* London: Falmer.

Fullan, M. G. (1999). *Change forces: The sequel.* London: Falmer.

Fullan, M. G. (2000). The three stories of education reform. *Phi Delta Kappan, 81*(8), 581–584.

Fullan, M. G., Bennett, B., & Rolheiser-Bennett, C. (1989). *Linking classroom and school improvement.* Paper presented at the annual meeting of the American Educational Research Association, San Francisco.

Fullan, M. G., & Hargreaves, A. (1991). *Working together for your school.* Melbourne: Australian Council for Educational Administration.

Fullan, M. G., & Miles, M. B. (1992). Getting reform right: What works and what doesn't. *Phi Delta Kappan, 73,* 745–752.

Fullan, M. G., Miles, M. B., & Taylor, G. (1980). Organization development in schools: The state of the art. *Review of Educational Research, 50*(1), 121–184.

Fullan, M. G., & Pomfret, A. (1977). Research on curriculum and instruction implementation. *Review of Educational Research, 47*(2), 335–397.

Fuller, F. F. (1969). Concerns of teachers: A developmental conceptualization. *American Educational Research Journal, 6*(2), 207–226.

George, A. A., Hall, G. E., & Uchiyama, K. (2000). Extent of implementation of a standards-based approach to teaching mathematics and student outcomes. *Journal of Classroom Interaction, 35*(1), 8–25.

Ginsberg, R., & Wimpelberg, R. K. (1987). Educational change by commission: Attempting "trickle down" reform. *Educational Evaluation and Policy Analysis, 9*(4), 344–360.

Glass, G. V. (1970). *Data analysis of the 1968–69 Survey of Compensatory Education (Title 1), final report.* Boulder: Laboratory of Educational Research, University of Colorado.

Goodlad, J. I. (1975). *The dynamics of educational change.* New York: McGraw-Hill.

Goodlad, J. I., & Klein, M. F. (1970). *Behind the classroom door.* Worthington, OH: Jones.

Goodson, I. F. (1992). (Ed.). *Studying teachers' lives.* London: Routledge.

Gottfredson, D. C. (1987). An evaluation of an organization development approach to reducing school disorder. *Evaluation Review, 11*(6), 23–47.

Greenwood, P. W., Mann, D., & McLaughlin, M. W. (1975). *Federal programs supporting educational change: Vol. 3. The process of change.* Santa Monica, CA: Rand Corporation.

Grobman, H. (1970). *Developmental curriculum projects: Decision points and processes.* New York: Peacock.

Grundy, S. (1987). *Curriculum: Product or praxis.* London: Falmer.

Grundy, S., & Kemmis, S. (1982). *Three modes of action research.* Geelong, Australia: Deakin University.

Guan, H. K. (2000). *The implementation of an innovative computer course in Singapore: Perception and practice.* Unpublished doctoral dissertation, University of Western Australia.

Hall, G. E. (1992). The local educational change process and policy implementation. *Journal of Research in Science Teaching, 29*(8), 877–904.

Hall, G. E. (1999). Using constructs and techniques from research to facilitate and access implementation of an innovative mathematics curriculum. *Journal of Classroom Interaction, 34*(1), 1–8.

Hall, G. E., & George, A. A. (2000). *The use of innovation configuration maps in assessing implementation: The bridge between development and student outcomes.* Paper presented at the annual meeting of the American Educational Research Association, New Orleans.

Hall, G. E., George, A. A., & Rutherford, W. L. (1979). *Measuring stages of concern about the innovation: A manual for use of the SoC questionnaire* (2nd ed.). Austin: University of Texas, Research and Development Center for Teacher Education.

Hall, G. E., & Hord, S. M. (1987). *Change in schools: Facilitating the process.* Albany: State University of New York Press.

Hall, G. E., & Hord, S. M. (2001). *Implementing change: Patterns, principles, and potholes.* Boston: Allyn and Bacon.

Hall, G. E., & Loucks, S. F. (1977). A developmental model for determining whether the treatment is actually implemented. *American Educational Research Journal, 14*(3), 263–276.

Hall, G. E., & Loucks, S. F. (1978). Innovation configurations: Analyzing the adaptations of innovations. In *Procedures for adopting educational innovations program.* Austin: University of Texas, Research and Development Center for Teacher Education.

Hall, G. E., & Loucks, S. F. (1981). Program definition and adaptation: Implementation for inservice. *Journal of Research and Development in Education, 14*(2), 46–58.

Hall, G. E., Wallace, R. C., & Dossett, W. A. (1973). *A developmental conceptualization of the adoption process within educational institutions.* Unpublished paper. Austin: University of Texas, Research and Development Center for Teacher Education.

Haltrup, R. A., & Bickel, W. E. (1993). Teacher-researcher collaborations: Resolving the tensions. *Educational Leadership, 50*(6), 38–40.

Hargreaves, A. (1989). *Curriculum and assessment reform.* Milton Keynes, UK: Open University Press.

Hargreaves, A., & Fink, D. (2000). The three dimensions of reform. *Educational Leadership, 57*(7), 30–34.

Hatch, T. (2000). What does it take to break the mold?: Rhetoric and reality in new American schools. *Teachers College Record, 102*(3), 561–589.

Hawkins, K. H. (1998). Cacophony to symphony: Memoirs in teacher research. *Harvard Educational Review, 68*(1) 80–95.

Heck, S. (1980). *Structured and unstructured approaches to implementation: Whom does the shoe fit?* Paper presented at the annual meeting of the American Educational Research Association, Boston.

Henderson, J. C. (1985). *Organisation development and the implementation of planned change.* Unpublished doctoral dissertation, Murdoch University, Perth, Western Australia.

Hendrie, C. (1999). N.J. schools put reform to the test. *Education Week*, April 21, 13–14.

Hollingsworth, S. (1996). Repositioning the teacher in US schools and society: Feminist readings of action research. In C. O'Hanlon (Ed.), *Professional development through action research in education settings.* London: Falmer Press.

House, E. R. (1979). Technology versus craft: A ten-year perspective on innovation. *Journal of Curriculum Studies, 11*(1), 1–16.

House, E. R. (1996). A framework for appraising educational reforms. *Educational Researcher, 25*(7), 6–14.

Huberman, A. M. (1993). *The lives of teachers.* New York: Teachers College Press.

Huberman, A. M., & Crandall, D. P. (1982). *A study of Dissemination Efforts Supporting School Improvement (DESSI): Vol. 9. People, policies, and practices: Examining the chain of school improvement.* Andover, MA: The Network.

Huberman, M. (1988). Teacher careers and school improvement. *Journal of Curriculum Studies, 20*(2), 119–132.

Hursh, D. (1995). Developing discourses and structures to support action research for educational reform. In S. Noffke & R. Stevenson (Eds.), *Educational action research: Becoming practically critical.* New York: Teachers College Press.

James, R. K., & Hall, G. E. (1981). A study of the concerns of science teachers regarding an implementation of ISCS. *Journal of Research and Science Teaching, 18*(6), 27–33.

Jansen, T., & Van der Vegt, R. (1991). On lasting innovation in schools: Beyond institutionalisation. *Journal of Educational Policy, 6*(1), 33–46.

Kember, D., & Mezger, R. (1990). The instructional designer as a staff developer: A course team approach consistent with the concerns-based adoption model. *Distance Education, 11*(1), 50–70.

Kemmis, S. (1991). Emancipatory action research and postmodernisms. *Curriculum Perspectives, 11*(4), 59–66.

Kemmis, S., & McTaggart, R. (1988). *The action research planner* (3rd ed.). Geelong, Australia: Deakin University Press.

Kennedy, K. J. (1983). *Assessing the implementation characteristics of educational innovation and practice.* Unpublished paper, Macquarie University, Sydney, Australia.

Kierstead, J., & Mentor, S. (1988). Translating the vision into reality in California schools. *Educational Leadership, 46*(2), 35–40.

Kimpston, R. D. (1983). *Curriculum fidelity and implementation tasks employed by teachers.* Paper presented at the annual meeting of the American Educational Research Association, Montreal.

Kimpston, R. D., & Anderson, D. H. (1988). Factors affecting teachers' and principals' stages of concern over carrying out benchmark testing. *Journal of Curriculum and Supervision, 3*(4), 321–334.

Kirst, M. W. (1987). Curricular leadership at the state level: What is the new focus? *NASSP Bulletin, 71*(498), 8–12.

Kirst, M. W. (1993). Strengths and weaknesses of American education. *Phi Delta Kappan, 74*(8), 613–618.

Knip, H., & Van der Vegt, R. (1991). Differentiated responses to a central renewal policy: School management of implementation. *Journal of Education Policy, 6*(2), 123–131.

Leithwood, K. A. (1981). Managing the implementation of curriculum innovations. *Knowledge: Creation, Diffusion, Utilization, 2*(3), 341–360.

Leithwood, K. A., & Montgomery, D. J. (1982). A framework for planned educational change: Application to the assessment of program implementation. *Educational Evaluation and Policy Analysis, 4*(2), 157–167.

Lewin, K. (1948). *Resolving social conflicts.* New York: Harper & Row.

Lewis, M. E. (1988). Continuation of a curriculum innovation: Salient and alterable viables. *Journal of Curriculum and Supervision, 4*(1), 52–64.

Loucks, S. F. (1983). *Defining fidelity: A cross-study analysis.* Paper presented at the annual meeting

of the American Educational Research Association, Montreal.

Loucks, S. F., & Crandall, D. P. (1982). *The practice profile: An all-purpose tool for program communication, staff development, evaluation, and improvement.* Andover, MA: The Network.

Loucks, S. F., & Melle, M. (1980). *Implementation of a district-wide science curriculum: The effects of a three-year effort.* Paper presented at the annual meeting of the American Educational Research Association, Boston.

Loucks, S. F., Newlove, D. W., & Hall, G. E. (1975). *Measuring levels of use of the innovation: A manual for trainers, interviewers, and raters.* Austin: University of Texas, Research and Development Center for Teacher Education.

Loucks-Horsley, S., & Hergert, L. F. (1985). *An action guide to school improvement.* Alexandria, VA: Association for Supervision and Curriculum Development.

Lubeck, S., & Post, J. (1999). The creation of a Head Start community of practice. In L. Soto (Ed.), *The politics of early childhood education.* Albany, NY: State University of New York Press.

MacDonald, B., & Walker, R. (1976). *Changing the curriculum.* London: Open Books.

Marsh, C. J. (1984). *Curriculum development and the social studies K–10 syllabus.* Unpublished paper, Murdoch University, Perth, Western Australia.

Marsh, C. J. (1987). Curriculum theorizing in Australia. *Journal of Curriculum Theorizing, 7*(2), 7–29.

Marsh, C. J. (1990). *Curriculum implementation: An analysis of the use of the concerns-based adoption model (CBAM) in Australia, 1981–1987.* Paper presented at the annual meeting of the American Educational Research Association, Boston.

Marsh, C. J. (1996). *Handbook for beginning teachers.* Sydney: Longman.

Marsh, D. D. (1988). *Key factors associated with the effective implementation and impact of California's educational reform.* Paper presented at the annual meeting of the American Educational Research Association, New Orleans.

Marsh, D. D., & Bowman, G. A. (1988). *Building better secondary schools: A comparison of school improvement and school reform strategies in California.* Paper presented at the annual meeting of the American Educational Research Association, New Orleans.

Marsh, D. D., & Penn, J. (1988). Engaging students in innovative instruction: An application of the stages of concern framework to studying student engagement. *Journal of Classroom Interaction, 23*(1), 8–14.

Matheison, S. (1991). Implementing curricular change through state-mandated testing: Ethical issues. *Journal of Curriculum and Supervision, 6*(3), 201–212.

McChesney, J., & Hertling, E. (2000). The path to comprehensive school reform. *Educational Leadership, 57*(7) 10–15.

McKernan, J. (1993). Varieties of curriculum action research: Constraints and typologies in American, British, and Irish projects. *Journal of Curriculum Studies, 25*(5), 445–457.

McLaughlin, M. W. (1978). Implementation as mutual adaptation: Change in classroom organization. In D. Mann (Ed.), *Making change happen.* New York: Teachers College Press.

McLaughlin, M. W. (1987). Learning from experience: Lessons from policy implementation. *Educational Evaluation and Policy Analysis, 9*(2), 171–178.

McLaughlin, M. W. (1989). The Rand change agent study ten years later: Macro perspectives and micro realities. Unpublished paper. Stanford University, Center for Research on the Context of Secondary Teaching.

McLaughlin, M. W., & Marsh, D. D. (1978). Staff development and school change. *Teachers College Record, 80*(1), 69–94.

McTaggart, R., & Singh, M. G. (1986). New directions in action research. *Curriculum Perspectives, 6*(2), 7–14.

Means, R. (2001). Technology use in tomorrow's schools. *Educational Leadership, 58*(4), 57–61.

Miles, M. (1979). *Symposium reactor report.* Paper presented at the annual meeting of the American Educational Research Association, San Francisco.

Miles, M. B. (1993). Forty years of change in schools: Some personal reflections. *Educational Administration Quarterly, 29*(2), 213–248.

Mitchell, S. (1988). *Applications of the concerns-based model in program evaluation.* Paper presented at the annual meeting of the American Educational Research Association, New Orleans.

Molnar, A. (2000). Zap me! Linking schoolhouse and marketplace in a seamless web. *Phi Delta Kappan, 81*(8), 601–603.

National Commission on Excellence in Education. (1983). *A nation at risk: The imperative for educational reform.* Washington, DC: U.S. Government Printing Office.

Nave, B., Miech, E., & Mosteller, F. (2000). A lapse in standards. *Phi Delta Kappan, 82*(2), 128–132.

Noddings, N. (1986). Fidelity in teaching, teacher education, and research for teaching. *Harvard Educational Review, 56*(4), 496–510.

Noddings, N. (2000). *Care and coercion in school reform.* Paper presented at the annual meeting of the American Educational Research Association, New Orleans.

Olson, J. K. (1982). Three approaches to curriculum change: Balancing the accounts. *Journal of Curriculum Theorizing, 4*(2), 90–96.

Olson, L. (1999). Following the plan. *Education Week,* April 14, 29–32.

O'Neil, J. (2000). Fads and fireflies: The difficulties of sustaining change. *Educational Leadership, 57*(7), 6–9.

Orlich, D. C. (2000). Education reform and limits to student achievement. *Phi Delta Kappan, 81*(6), 468–472.

Peers, I. S. (1990). Utility of concerns-based staff development in facilitating education and training about HIV/AIDS in schools and colleges. *British Educational Research Journal, 16*(2), 179–189.

Peters, T. L., & Waterman, R. H. (1982). *In search of excellence.* New York: Harper & Row.

Popkewitz, T. S. (1982). *Motion as education change: The misuse and irrelevancy of two research paradigms.* Unpublished paper, University of Wisconsin-Madison.

Porter, A. C. (1993). School delivery standards. *Educational Researcher, 22*(5), 24–30.

Pratt, H., Thurber, J. C., Hall, G. E., & Hord, S. M. (1982). *Case studies of school improvement: A concerns based approach.* Paper prepared for the International School Improvement Project, Leuven, Belgium.

Price, J. N., & Vallie, L. (2000). *Becoming agents of change: Cases from preservice teacher education.* Paper presented at the annual meeting of the American Educational Research Association, New Orleans.

Redrick, M., & Feldman, A. (2000). Orientations, product, reflections: A framework for understanding action research. *Teaching and Teacher Education, 14*(3), 27–37.

Resnick, L., & Tucker, M. (1992). *The new standards project.* Pittsburgh: University of Pittsburgh Press.

Roitman, D. B., & Mayer, J. P. (1982). *Fidelity and reinvention in the implementation of innovations.* Paper presented at the annual conference of the American Psychological Association, Washington, DC.

Rudduck, J., & Kelly, P. (1976). *The dissemination of curriculum development.* Windsor, UK: National Foundation for Educational Research.

Rutherford, W. L. (1978). *A personal interview: A tool for investigating and understanding change in schools.* Paper presented at the annual meeting of the American Educational Research Association, Toronto.

Rutherford, W. L. (1990). *Concerns of teachers: Revisiting the original theory after twenty years.* Paper presented at the annual meeting of the American Educational Research Association, Boston.

Rutherford, W. L., Hord, L. L., Huling, L., & Hall, G. E. (1983). *Change facilitators: In search of understanding their role.* Unpublished paper. University of Texas, Research and Development Center for Teacher Education.

Schmidt, W. H., Valverde, G. A., Houang, R. T., Wiley, D. E., Wolfe, R. G., & Bianchi, L. J. (1996). *Studying the intended, implemented and attained curriculum: Strategies for measurement and analysis in large-scale international research.* Paper presented at the annual meeting of the American Educational Research Association, New York.

Schmuck, R. A., & Miles, M. B. (Eds.). (1971). *Organizational development in schools.* La Jolla, CA: University Associates.

Schofield, J. W., & Davidson, A. L. (2000). *Internet use and teacher change.* Paper presented at the annual meeting of the American Educational Research Association, New Orleans.

Scott, G. (1999). *Change matters.* Sydney: Allen and Unwin.

Sharman, R. G. (1987). Organisational supports for implementing an instructional innovation. *Alberta Journal of Educational Research, 33*(4), 236–246.

Sieber, S. D., Louis, K. S., & Metzger, L. (1972). *The use of educational knowledge: Evaluation of the pilot state dissemination program.* New York: Bureau of Applied Social Research, Columbia University.

Silberstein, M., & Ben-Peretz, M. (1987). The concept of teacher autonomy in curriculum materials: An operative interpretation. *Journal of Curriculum and Supervision, 3*(1), 29–44.

Sirotnik, K. A., & Kimball, K. (1999). Standards for standards-based accountability systems. *Phi Delta Kappan, 81,*(3), 209–214.

Sizer, T. (1992). *Horace's School.* New York: Houghton Mifflin.

Slavin, R. E. (2001). Putting the school back in school reform. *Educational Leadership, 58*(4), 22–27.

Slavin, R. E., & Madden N. A. (Eds.). (2001). *One million children: Success for all.* Mahwah, NJ: Lawrence Erlbaum.

Smithson, J. (1992). *Content, pedagogy, and conceptual aim: Findings from a two-year study of teacher practice.* Madison, WI: Wisconsin Center for Educational Research.

Snyder, J., Bolin, F., & Zumwalt, K. (1992). Curriculum implementation. In P. W. Jackson (Ed.), *Handbook of research on curriculum.* New York: Macmillan.

Snyder, K., Acker-Hocevar, M. A., & Snyder, K. (1994). *Organizational development in transition: The schooling perspective.* Paper presented at the annual meeting of the American Educational Research Association, New Orleans.

Soder, R. (1999). When words find their meaning: Renewal versus reform. *Phi Delta Kappan, 80*(8), 568–570.

Sowell, E., & Zambo, R. (1997). Alignment between standards and practices in mathematics education: Experiences in Arizona. *Journal of Curriculum and Supervision, 12*(4), 356–366.

Stenhouse, L. (1973). The Humanities Curriculum Project. In H. Butcher & H. Pont (Eds.), *Educational research in Britain* (Vol. 3). London: University of London Press.

Task Force on Education for Economic Growth. (1983). *Action for excellence: A comprehensive plan to improve our nation's schools.* Denver: Education Commission of the States.

Tikunoff, W. J., Ward, B. A., & Stacey, F. (1978). Toward an ecology based curriculum: Professional growth through participatory research and development. In American Association of Teacher Educators (Eds.), *Breakaway to multidimensional approaches: Integrating curriculum development and in-service education.* Washington, DC: American Association of Teacher Educators.

Tripp, D. H. (1985). *Action research and professional development.* Professional Development Project. Melbourne: Australian College of Education.

Tucker, M. S., & Codding, J. B. (1998). *Standards for our schools*. San Francisco: Jossey Bass.

Van den Akker, J. (1988). The teacher as learner in curriculum implementation. *Journal of Curriculum Studies, 20*(1), 47–56.

Van den Berg, R. (1983). *The functioning of school principals in relation to large scale change efforts in the Netherlands*. Paper presented at the annual meeting of the American Educational Research Association, Montreal.

Van den Berg, R. (1993). The concerns-based adoption model in the Netherlands, Flanders, and the United Kingdom: State of the art and perspective. *Studies in Educational Evaluation, 19,* 51–63.

Vandenberghe, R. (1983). *Studying change in the primary and secondary schools of Belgium and the Netherlands*. Paper presented at the annual meeting of the American Educational Research Association, Montreal.

Van der Vegt, S., & Vandenberghe, H. (1992). *Schools implementing a central reform policy: Findings from two national educational contexts*. Paper presented at the annual meeting of the American Educational Research Association, San Francisco.

Walker, D. F., & Schaffarzick, J. (1974). Comparing curricula. *Review of Educational Research, 44*(1), 83–111.

Wallace, M. (1987). A historical review of action research: Some implications for the education of teachers in their managerial role. *Journal of Education for Teaching, 13*(2), 97–116.

Wargo, M. J. (1972). *ESEA Title 1: A reanalysis and synthesis of evaluation data from fiscal year 1965 through 1970, final report*. Palo Alto, CA: American Institute for Research.

Wells, J. G., & Anderson, D. K. (1997). Learners in a telecommunication course: Adoption, diffusion, and stages of concern. *Journal of Research on Computing in Education, 30*(1), 83–105.

Werner, W. (1987). Training for curriculum implementation. *Pacific Education, 1*(1), 40–53.

Werner, W. (1991). Defining curriculum policy through slogans. *Journal of Education Policy, 6*(2), 225–238.

Wheeler, J. R. (1996). *A descriptive study of small enrollment, northeast Kansas schools: Local area networks, Internet, and teacher's levels of concern towards Internet as a tool for teaching and learning*. Unpublished doctoral dissertation, University of Kansas.

Wise, A. E. (2000). Creating a high quality teaching force. *Educational Leadership, 58*(4), 18–21.

Wise, A. E., & Leibrand, J. A. (2000). Standards and teacher quality. *Phi Delta Kappan, 81*(7), 612–621.

Woodworth, W., Meyer, G., & Smallwood, N. (1982). Organization development: A closer scrutiny. *Human Relations, 35*(4), 307–320.

Zeichner, K. M. (1993). Action research: Personal renewal and social reconstruction. *Educational Action Research 1,* 199–219.

8

Curriculum Evaluation and Student Assessment

■ ABOUT THIS CHAPTER

This chapter examines the closely related ideas of curriculum evaluation and student assessment. In doing so, it differentiates these ideas, identifies the persons ordinarily involved in evaluation and assessment, gives examples of techniques that can be used, discusses the appropriateness of different standards, and describes some of the key questions and issues that must be addressed. The chapter concludes by describing and critically commenting on four different models of curriculum evaluation and presenting a short case study of each model in use.

■ WHAT YOU SHOULD DO

1. Differentiate between the ideas of curriculum evaluation and student assessment, understanding when and under what circumstances student assessment is or is not an appropriate part of curriculum evaluation.
2. Develop a personal appreciation of what is at stake in evaluating a curriculum.
3. Understand the basic differences between formal and informal approaches to evaluation and assessment.
4. Become conversant with techniques, criteria, and questions involved in conducting evaluations and assessments.
5. Critically examine the four models and associated case studies of curriculum evaluation, relating these to the broader issues of curriculum planning and development and, especially, heightening insight about how these do or do not fit with your own preferred approaches to curriculum.

▮ SOME OPTIONAL APPROACHES

You may wish to consider the following options in terms of how evaluation is related to your personal theories of teaching.

Option A

1. Evaluation is heavily value laden. Choices about evaluation reflect personal priorities and biases. In this light, reflect upon recent lessons you have taught. Make note of what concrete data you focused on in formulating your ideas about how well those lessons went. Compare how you used these data informally with the formal assessment techniques described in section 8.3. Consider techniques you did not use and why.
2. Attempt to reconcile how you have informally evaluated your lessons with your own theory of curriculum, which you have been developing and refining as you have been reading this book. (If necessary, review chapter 4 and other parts of the book.) Is there congruence? Proceed to read section 8.7 of this chapter on the four models of evaluation. Does any one of these models closely approximate your approach to evaluating your lessons?
3. Read about some of the basic issues involved in curriculum evaluation (section 8.2). How do ideas such as accountability and peer reviews among teachers complicate these issues?

Option B

1. Refer back to the approaches to curriculum theorizing described in chapter 4. Try to identify techniques of evaluation that might be central to each one. Select one of these approaches and more closely consider techniques consistent with it, especially in terms of the issues about persons, responsibilities, and standards described in sections 8.4, 8.5, and 8.6.
2. Consider the relevance of the approach you have selected to the four models of evaluation described in section 8.7. Do you now wish to make major changes in your preferred approach to curriculum theorizing?
3. Next, draw up a list of techniques of assessment that seem consistent with your preferred approach and appropriate to the circumstances in which you teach. Compare your list with the techniques described in section 8.3. Are there differences between the techniques you would use to evaluate your own classroom and those that have been commonly used in formal curriculum evaluations? If so, how do you account for the differences? Were the techniques that you used primarily examples of curriculum evaluation or of student assessment? Which techniques should you use?
4. Consider how you would use or modify your techniques to conduct evaluations of your own classroom over an extended period in order to improve your teaching and your decisions about how to enact curricula.
5. Carefully consider how different techniques of evaluation influence the experienced curriculum of your students.

8.1 INTRODUCTION

Evaluation is an activity that permeates virtually everything human beings do. To be human is, in fact, to be constantly engaged in asking questions and formulating judgments about whatever touches your life. Is something worth doing? How well is it being done? Do I like it? Should I spend my time doing something else? Of course, most of the moment-to-moment decisions people make about how to lead their lives are made informally and without much conscious thought.

However, when decisions are on significant matters or when what one decides directly influences someone else (especially when done as part of one's professional duties, as in teaching), reflective thought is called for, and the informality with which evaluation begins may give way to formal steps and techniques, even if such formality narrows the basis on which decisions are made. For instance, teachers are constantly scanning their own classrooms, sizing up everything they can about what is happening there. They make many decisions intuitively on the basis of such informal observations, their past professional experience, and their general beliefs about good practice. Only less frequently do they find it necessary (or even possible) to formally evaluate some of the many things happening in their classrooms.

Current ideas of curriculum development, which evolved during the twentieth century, assume that evaluation is ongoing during the entire process of planning and implementing a curriculum and that it may lead directly to a further cycle of beneficial change. However, given the practical difficulties entailed in formally evaluating a curriculum at every step along the way, from its initial planning to its being experienced by each student, and given the narrowness with which educational evaluation in general has historically been conceived in the United States, curricula have ordinarily been formally evaluated only after they have been put into practice—and then usually only in terms of their presumed influence on student learnings. The narrowness of ordinary approaches to curriculum evaluation has often obscured the most pressing problems encountered by teachers concerning the slippages that occur between the planned curriculum and the enacted curriculum and, then, the experienced curriculum. In addition to its intended effect on what students learn, a curriculum can be evaluated in myriad other ways, including the accuracy with which it represents reality, its internal consistency, its appropriateness, its teachability, its pleasurableness, and its many possible unintended consequences (Donmoyer, 1990; Haney & Madaus, 1989). In this chapter, we focus on formal approaches to curriculum evaluation, but we attempt to do so in ways that expose the underlying issues.

The terms *evaluation* and *assessment* are often used synonymously in education, yet there are significant differences in what they imply. Essentially, the process of evaluation, whether formal or informal, is philosophical; that is, it is an attempt to weigh and appropriately to value something (such as a person, an action, a process, or an object). The professional literature points out that evaluations can be made in terms of merit and worth. Merit refers to how well something is done. It applies, for instance, to the workmanship that goes into an object or the skillfulness with which an activity is carried out. *Worth* refers to the importance of doing something. It applies to the intrinsic value of the object or activity. It is possible for something to have more merit than something else yet to have less worth, and vice versa. For example, consider the relative values an experienced literary critic might assign to a nearly perfect limerick on a trivial theme and to a flawed epic poem on a theme central to human existence. Curricula, too, can be evaluated in terms of merit and worth, and curriculum evaluation can apply to small-scale projects (such as a single teacher and that teacher's class) or to massive, large-scale projects (such as a statewide or even national curriculum involving thousands of schools and teachers).

In contrast to the broad philosophic process implied by the term *evaluation,* the term *assessment* now implies to many educators a much more narrow and technical process of determining how much a student has learned. Therefore, measurement of student learning—usually through formal, paper-and-pencil testing—is often seen as the hallmark of assessment, and curriculum evaluation itself has sometimes been reduced to little more than an attempt to measure as precisely as possible the degree to which the learnings specified as desirable in the planned curriculum have been reached. Thus, much more complex ways of determining the merit and worth of a curriculum by looking as fully as possible at many things (including what may have happened to students beyond prespecified learning) have been subsumed under a single way of looking at few things.

Almost as if to challenge such undue narrowness, a broader view of student assessment and its place in curriculum evaluation grew up during the 1980s and 1990s. Known widely as authentic assessment, this view attempts to consider all the many things that happen to students and all the many ways students can demonstrate what they have learned, such as through portfolios of their work. In general, authentic assessment considers qualitative techniques (such as careful observation of classrooms and use of anecdotal records) more important than quantitative techniques (such as standardized tests) in exploring "new routes to excellence" (Eisner, 1999, 2000) and in examining the purposes and effects of teaching and learning (Broadfoot, 1996; Wiggins, 1998). (We discuss in detail authentic assessment and the use of student portfolios in section 8.3.)

For closely related reasons, Skilbeck (1982) suggests that curriculum evaluations should themselves remain small-scale rather than becoming large, managerial, and objectified. When small, they remain "intelligent forms of reflection on experience, self-appraisal and forward thinking" (p. 20). In his opinion, educators often amass vast amounts of unmanageable quantitative data, but this mistake can be avoided by being quite clear about such questions as these:

What do I need to know about this activity?
How can I most economically find out?
How can I use what I know?
What do I need to make known to others?

In large-scale curriculum evaluations questions tend to be more impersonal and divorced from the concerns of teachers themselves. Such evaluations can accumulate immense quantities of data. For example, the Virginia Beach (Virginia) School District (1984) employed a team of five full-time professional staff members over a two-year period to collect, analyze, and synthesize data from "meetings with teachers, students, parents, community representatives, supervisors and administrators; suggestion forms, public hearings, visitations to school systems, colleges and universities; conference attendance; consultant suggestions; and review of literature and existing documents" (p. 6). Of course, both the merit and worth of any evaluation depend not on the amount of data collected but on the intelligence with which data are used. Those people who conduct formal evaluations and the techniques they use are also subject to evaluation.

Rogers and Badham (1992) suggest that, because of such constraints as lack of time, expertise, and resources, curriculum evaluation should be highly focused. They support the following principles:

- The evaluation should be limited to a few specific foci.
- Only essential information should be collected.
- Maximum use should be made of information already available.
- The evaluation should seem worthwhile and credible to the staff involved.

However, a problem with these suggestions is that when an evaluation becomes too highly focused, it may avoid real but underlying complexities of the situation. Curriculum evaluation includes studying how teachers and students interact with each other and with a curriculum or syllabus in a particular setting. It is not confined to investigating only what students have learned or to analyzing lesson plans. Rather, curriculum evaluation can involve examination of the goals, rationale, and structure of both the planned curriculum and the enacted curriculum; a study of the context in which the enacted curriculum occurs (including inputs from parents and the community); and an analysis of the interests, motivations, reactions, and achievements of the students experiencing the curriculum.

Various authors note the need for curriculum evaluation to be wide-ranging and responsive to specific situations (Carr & Harris, 2001; Norris, 1990; Ornstein & Hunkins, 1993). A curriculum usually represents a plurality of interests, and in many cases obtaining consensus about what it should be is extremely difficult. Different individuals and groups within a school (such as administrators, teachers, students, and parents) may have very different views of what the curriculum should contain and how it should be taught, and these perspectives need to be included in formal curriculum evaluations.

8.2 PURPOSES OF CURRICULUM EVALUATION

During most of the twentieth century, educational evaluation in the United States was dominated by the scientific testing and measurement movement. Specificity of learning and efficiency of learning were seen as the major goals of schooling. This was true of curriculum evaluation as well. Although the Eight-Year Study (discussed in chapter 2) in basic ways ran contrary to this trend, it also illustrates the underlying tensions and issues in curriculum evaluation that have emerged more fully in recent decades.

With Ralph W. Tyler as head of its evaluation committee, the Eight-Year Study followed students through their eight secondary school and college years (from 1933 to 1941) and compared students from secondary schools that implemented experimental, often individual-centered, curricula with students from traditional secondary schools. Using then novel means of student assessment, it found that students from the experimental schools did slightly better academically in college but were decidedly better off in terms of their personal lives. For instance, the Eight-Year Study collected data about all phases of students' lives, thus suggesting that curricula were concerned with far more than teaching students factual information. In demonstrating the worth of individual-centered curricula, it also demonstrated the viability of one of the hallmarks of progressive education: Dewey's notion that the curriculum is the experience of the individual. Perhaps its greatest contribution was in the many new techniques it developed for examining individual experience. It investigated the experienced curriculum, not just the planned curriculum or the enacted curriculum, and in this way, it was well ahead of its time. Despite the novelty of its approach, it did not abandon one assumption that it shared with the scientific testing and measurement movement: that the curriculum could be evaluated in terms of its effects.

The fact that the Eight-Year Study did not represent a complete break from what preceded it is not surprising, for Tyler was himself a major exponent of scientific testing, which was still gaining strength in the 1920s and 1930s. In his early writings (Tyler, 1930), he was primarily concerned with designing tests that measured knowledge and that eliminated unreliability and subjectivity, and he emphasized the use of objectives (conceived in terms of student behaviors) in testing. For him, tests should be designed to indicate whether students had achieved the particular objectives of a course, and validation of tests should be in terms of whether they contained items that directly measured specific course objectives. At the time, Tyler's approach was different from that of most other advocates of testing, who were chiefly concerned about devising instruments to test the presence or absence of particular content (knowledge) and skills.

Under Tyler's direction, the Eight-Year Study used a variety of tests, scales, inventories, questionnaires, checklists, and logs to gather data about students. To the extent that these data were interpreted consistently with the overall experience and personal development of students, the Eight-Year Study was consistent with Dewey's basic ideas about individual experience and ran contrary to the scientific testing movement. However, to the extent that data were interpreted consistently with Tyler's notions about objectives, the study represented something incompatible with Dewey. Willis (1998) suggests that it often ran contrary to Dewey by treating generalized results as more important than the immediate and specific qualities of students' experiences. He states:

> In creating new techniques for collecting information about developmental growth, the study also seemed to suggest that desirable experiencing could be inferred directly from evidence of growth and that all useful evidence could be somehow discerned objectively, without painstakingly sifting the divergent—and perhaps equally valuable—perspectives of different participants for their own insights. In so

embodying a less than full notion of experiencing and a utilitarian means-ends rationale implicit in the search for objective results, the Eight-Year Study was thereby also consistent with the technical approach to curriculum evaluation. (p. 322)

In any case, Tyler's emphasis on the use of objectives was to prove influential after World War II, especially through the popularization of his rational-linear approach to curriculum planning and development (see chapter 3), and that approach was itself compatible with the taxonomies of educational objectives that began to appear in the 1950s and with the national curriculum projects sponsored by the federal government of the United States in the 1960s. Was it desirable or even possible to move beyond where the Eight-Year Study had left off?

Against this historical background, it has become clear, however, that the scope and focus of educational evaluation generally, and of curriculum evaluation particularly, have changed markedly over the last two or three decades. Practices inherited from the scientific testing and measurement movement and from Tyler's emphasis on objectives and student behaviors have, in fact, given way to broader concerns about the need to collect information and to make judgments about all phases of curriculum development from planning to implementation (Longstreet & Shane, 1993). Numerous forms of qualitative research and evaluation have been developed and now exist side-by-side with traditional quantitative forms. Kemmis (1982) summarizes such trends when he defines evaluation as "the process of marshaling information and arguments which enable interested individuals and groups to participate in the critical debate about a specific programme" (p. 23).

Although this definition refers to evaluation in general, it is quite relevant to curriculum evaluation, since, as we have stated, curriculum evaluation is about teachers, students, and their interactions with a curriculum or syllabus within a particular setting. These ideas encompass what Schwab (1969) has called the commonplaces of curriculum: teacher, learner, subject matter, and milieu (see chapter 4). Any curriculum evaluation must necessarily consider the mutual influences among these commonplaces. In the past, not all commonplaces have been considered equally. For example, milieu has often been entirely left out of evaluations that focus on objectives and student behaviors. Also important in curriculum evaluations are accounts (sometimes as descriptive case studies) of what teachers think and do, for such studies can assist teachers in analyzing their teaching, especially if the studies are not undertaken for purposes of certification or accountability.

Clearly, evaluation studies can serve many different purposes; therefore, three basic questions to ask before undertaking a curriculum evaluation are: Why evaluate? What to evaluate? and, On what basis to evaluate?

Why Evaluate?

Answers to this question deal with both policies and motives. When a curriculum is being implemented or has been implemented on a large scale (across a school, school district, state, or nation), the obvious purposes for a formal evaluation are closely related to confirming the policies that led to the creation of the curriculum in the first place. However, especially within a particular school, an evaluation may be undertaken for a multitude of highly individual reasons. As an example, teachers undertake evaluations for a variety of reasons, including the following:

- To improve teaching and to better meet the needs of students
- To examine any effects of introducing a new curriculum
- To justify school practices to the public
- To respond to dissatisfaction with school procedures
- To settle conflicts within the school about power, roles, or personalities

Because evaluations within individual schools rely on conviviality and cooperation, it is essential that disparate motivations, such as those listed, be discussed by the staff who, in a series of informal and formal meetings, may come to a consensus about what the most important purposes of the evaluation are for them.

Since teaching always has unintended side effects, it is also important to examine the multitude of things that are going on and that affect the planned or written curriculum, the ostensive target of most formal evaluations. Scriven (1973) emphasizes the importance of "goal free" evaluation, in which the purposes of the evaluation are not confined to attempting to determine whether the publicly stated goals of the curriculum are reached. The public or official goals, of course, may not match the personal purposes held by individual teachers or other members of the school staff in undertaking the evaluation. In a subsequent paper, Scriven (1983) argues that the purposes of evaluation must allow consideration not only of side effects, but of whether the official goals of the curriculum and the personal purposes of the school staff are soundly based.

What to Evaluate?

Schwab's four curriculum commonplaces provide the answer to the question of what to evaluate: teacher, learner, subject matter, and milieu. Although all four are needed, each of the commonplaces may receive different degrees of emphasis within any given evaluation. Sources of information about the commonplaces vary greatly. For example, information about the social milieu of a school itself might be obtained by interviewing students, teachers, and administrators; whereas information about the social milieu within which the school exists might be obtained by interviewing parents, employers, and other members of the community. Information about the subjects taught in a school might come from school administrators, external subject matter specialists, publishers, superintendents, and parents. The range and choice of sources of data relate back to the purposes of the evaluation, its scale, and the time and funding available.

Only when the purpose and the focus of the evaluation have been agreed on is it possible to plan how to obtain the kinds of information needed.

On What Basis to Evaluate?

Before beginning the evaluation, participants should also consider the value-orientations upon which they wish to base their determinations of merit and worth.

Diagnostic and formative _____ Summative

Informal _____ Formal

Criterion-referenced _____ Norm-referenced

Process _____ Product

Learner-judged _____ Teacher-judged

Internal _____ External

Inclusive _____ Exclusive

Liberal _____ Technicist

FIGURE 8.1
Some bipolar value positions implicit in educational evaluation

Short of fully examining every philosophic assumption held by each person involved in an evaluation, the evaluators should at least be aware of the differing values implicit in how they might collect and analyze data. Harris and Bell (1990) suggest that analysis of data can be done in terms of bipolar constructs. Emphasizing one end of a continuum on which a particular construct exists may lead to different conclusions about merit and worth than does emphasizing the other end of the continuum. Figure 8.1 lists some bipolar constructs on which an evaluation may be based.

Diagnostic and Formative versus Summative. Students come into classrooms with varying backgrounds and interests, so beginning a new unit without checking their knowledge and understandings may be inappropriate. Some students may lack prerequisite skills, or their interests may lie with topics other than the ones to be taught. However, if the students already possess the skills or knowledge to be taught, their interest and enthusiasm might be dampened because of needless repetition of lessons. What is more, teachers need to be continually aware of changes in students as they progress through the curriculum. Diagnostic data about students come before a unit has begun; formative data come while the unit is in progress. Both kinds of data remind teachers that they must maintain instruction at levels appropriate to their students. In fact, the curriculum can then be modified in light of differing students and how they change. In this sense, teachers constantly undertake diagnostic and formative evaluation through all stages of instruction. Such data about instructional units permit a curriculum to be revised in "mid-stream" (Blubaugh, 1999).

In contrast, summative evaluation strives for data that indicate the degree to which students have reached the final goal of the curriculum. The curriculum is considered a given, and students are expected to change in accordance with it. Figures 8.2, 8.3, and 8.4 list some techniques that can be used to obtain diagnostic, formative, and summative data and indicate optimal times for using these techniques. Research on whether curriculum evaluations should be primarily diagnostic and formative or primarily summative is inconclusive. Pryor and Torrance (1996)

Techniques	Diagnostic	Formative	Summative
Informal observing and recording of student behavior	Anecdotal records	*Anecdotal records*	Anecdotal records
	Case histories	Case histories	Case histories
	Checklists	*Checklists*	Checklists
	Rating scales by teachers	*Rating scales by teachers*	Rating scales by teachers
	Unobtrusive techniques	Unobtrusive techniques	*Unobtrusive techniques*
Informal collecting of information from students	*Interest inventories*	Interest inventories	Interest inventories
	Rating scales by students	*Rating scales by students*	Rating scales by students
	Questionnaires	Questionnaires	Questionnaires
	Interviews	Interviews	*Interviews*
	Sociograms	Sociograms	Sociograms
	Self-reports	Self-reports	*Self-reports*
Analysis of examples of student work	Individual and group projects	Individual and group projects	*Individual and group projects*
	Content analysis of workbooks	*Content analysis of workbooks*	Content analysis of workbooks
	Logbooks and journals	Logbooks and journals	*Logbooks and journals*
	Portfolios	Portfolios	*Portfolios*
Testing of students	Objective tests	Objective tests	*Objective tests*
	Standardized tests	Standardized tests	*Standardized tests*
	Essay tests	Essay tests	*Essay tests*
	Semantic differentials	Semantic differentials	*Semantic differentials*
	Attitude scales	Attitude scales	Attitude scales
	Simulation and role playing	*Simulation and role playing*	*Simulation and role playing*
	Assessment tasks	Assessment tasks	*Assessment tasks*

FIGURE 8.2
Techniques that can be used to obtain data about students
Note: Italics refer to optimal occasions to use particular techniques.

note that many arguments for formative approaches are not based on empirical evidence, and Sadler (1989) and Gipps (1996) found that even when teachers gave students valid and reliable judgments about their work, improvement did not necessarily follow.

Informal versus Formal.   The purpose of informal assessment of students is similar to that of diagnostic and formative assessment, but the use of informal assessment is usually more continuous and less obtrusive. Informal observations of natural situations are especially valuable for gaining information about what is happening to students (Filer, 1993). The less obvious it is to students that they are being evaluated, the more natural will be their behavior. Gipps, McCallum, and Hargeaves (2000) suggest that some typical informal methods include:

- Questioning, especially "delving"
- Using other teachers' records
- Observing
- Listening
- Making mental notes
- Eavesdropping

Typically, elementary school teachers rely on informal evidence, while secondary teachers tend to use paper and pencil tests and other written evidence (McMillan, Workman, & Myran, 1999).

Formal assessments are planned and, usually, quite obtrusive. Weekly tests or any planned assignments could be categorized as formal assessments. Often parents request the results of formal testing of their children (Orlich, Harder, Callahan, & Gibson, 1998). The techniques for obtaining data about students shown in Figure 8.2 include both informal and formal assessments.

Criterion-Referenced versus Norm-Referenced. Criterion-referenced measures of students avoid pitting students against each other; norm-referenced measures do not. Criterion-referenced measures show how students compare to an external standard by specifically defining a level (or criterion) the student is supposed to reach. The presumption is that the student will persevere until reaching it. The difficulty lies in defining learning in terms of tasks to be mastered. Certain subjects, such as mathematics and mechanical drawing, are particularly amenable to this kind of specificity, but other subjects, such as creative writing and art, are not.

Norm-referenced measures compare students with other, usually similar students. These measures simply provide comparative age-based data on how well certain students perform on a test (for example, math or reading) compared with other students of the same age. Norm-referenced measures may provide useful data about the performance of students on specific tasks but do not provide information about an individual's potential or attitude.

Process versus Product. Most student assessments have traditionally involved judgments about what students produce, such as reports, projects, or objects. Products are often perceived to be the major priority of a course. Yet processes such as developing thinking skills, solving problems, and working cooperatively in groups may be more important (Silver, Strong, & Perini, 2000; Withers & McCurry, 1990). The phrase "performance assessment" emphasizes process rather than product and looks at how students plan and carry out new work, especially whether they use good judgment in choosing content (Wiggins, 1998).

Learner-Judged versus Teacher-Judged.   At most levels of schooling, the teacher does the judging about standards and how well students have met them; however, students may also be consulted or even given responsibility for self-assessment. The presumed value of students' judging themselves lies in heightening their abilities to see clearly their own strengths and weaknesses and in developing their motivation and capability to improve on both their strengths and weaknesses.

Internal versus External.   Internal assessments and evaluations are those created and carried out by the persons being evaluated (usually students but also teachers and others). They usually take place at the local level, within individual schools. External evaluations involve the importing of high-status assessments (such as statewide or nationwide standardized tests) into the local site. Harnisch and Mabry (1993), writing in the 1990s, pointed out that the predominant means of evaluating public education has been standardized testing; they observed that "each year elementary and secondary school students take 127 million standardized tests mandated by states and districts. About three standardized tests per year per student and 20 million school days are devoted to such testing" (p. 179). No doubt these figures are now much higher due to the major new national and state initiatives for standardized testing undertaken in the 2000s. Mehrens (1998) suggests that high-status assessments can influence teaching practices, but not always for the better.

Inclusive versus Exclusive.   Whatever form student assessment takes, clearly it should be inclusive in the sense that it fairly and accurately applies to all students independently of gender, ethnicity, handicap, or any other characteristic that has nothing to do with the worth of the individual. In other words, no assessment should be biased, yet numerous studies have shown that many forms of assessment are exclusive of certain students. For example, some multiple-choice tests tend to be biased against females (Gipps & Murphy, 1994; Salvia & Ysseldyke, 1998), and teachers must be constantly alert for subtle biases they may hold against students of ethnic groups other than their own.

Liberal versus Technicist.   A number of writers charge that traditional forms of student assessment are technicist in the negative sense that they are used to perpetuate the prevailing social hierarchy (Broadfoot, 1996; Hargreaves, Earl, Moore, & Manning, 2001). For instance, many forms of assessment, especially traditional written examinations, narrowly represent academic learning as superior to other kinds. In contrast, a liberal orientation to assessment provides a wider framework, looking at the social, economic, and political considerations that form the overall cultural milieu in which the school exists (Filer, 2000).

Figure 8.3 lists techniques for collecting data on student-teacher interactions; Figure 8.4, on teaching practices. Whether using such data in student assessments or in more general evaluations, evaluators should remain vigilant about implicit value assumptions they may hold that influence how they collect or analyze data.

Informal observing and recording	Audiotaping and videotaping Observation Category systems Unobtrusive techniques Colleague observation	
Informal collection of information from students	Interviews Questionnaires Rating scales Group discussions	
Formal visits by supervisors (superintendents, principals)	Combination of observation, checklists	

FIGURE 8.3
Techniques that can be used to obtain data about student-teacher interactions

Techniques	Diagnostic	Formative	Summative
Informal observing and recording of teacher and student behavior		*Audiotaping and videotaping*	
		Colleague observation	
		Rating scales by colleagues	
		Observation	
		Category systems	
		Self-ratings by teachers	Self-ratings by teachers
Informal collection of information by students	*Questionnaires*	Questionnaires	Questionnaires
		Postlesson reaction sheets	
	Interviews	Interviews	Interviews
	Group discussions	Rating scales	*Rating scales*
		Group discussions	*Group discussions*
		Semantic differential	*Semantic differential*
Analysis of materials used by teachers and students		*Annotation of materials used by students*	Annotation of materials used by students
		Observing materials in use	
		Sample of student workbooks	
		Rating of syllabus by teachers	Rating of syllabus by teachers
		Rating of materials by teachers	Rating of materials by teachers
Formal observing of teachers		External rating	External rating
		Peer rating	Peer rating

FIGURE 8.4
Techniques that can be used to obtain data about teaching practices
Note: Italics refer to optimal occasions to use particular techniques.

8.3   EXAMPLES OF STUDENT ASSESSMENT

As we have pointed out, student assessment is only part of curriculum evaluation. Comprehensive curriculum evaluation requires collecting and carefully weighing many different types of information about the many different topics and issues on which curriculum planning, implementation, and change all hinge. Nonetheless, what happens to students—particularly their academic progress—remains at the heart of curriculum evaluation. In this section, we discuss a few of the many techniques for gathering information about students that curriculum evaluators have at their disposal. The examples are taken from Figure 8.2 and hence deal mostly with student achievement. The techniques illustrated include those which are traditional and modern, quantitative and qualitative. In view of the most important recent developments, we begin with an extended discussion of authentic assessment.

Authentic Assessment

Authentic assessment or, sometimes, the assessment of authentic learning are two names that were popularized in the 1990s and continue to be widely described in the assessment literature of the 2000s. Authentic assessment encompasses far more than what students learn as measured by standardized tests or even by ordinary teacher-made tests. Authenticity arises from assessing what is most important, not from assessing what is most convenient. Fundamentally, then, there is nothing new about authentic assessment as a reaction against narrowness in education and a return toward the kind of education that connects feeling, thinking, and doing as advocated by John Dewey and other progressives early in the twentieth century. Applied to the curriculum, authentic assessment suggests that the curriculum must be directed at learning in the broadest possible sense; hence, the curriculum itself should be evaluated in terms of how well it contributes to students' deep understandings not only of subject matter but also of their own lives. In this sense, the popularization of authentic assessment represents another manifestation of grassroots, bottom-up approaches to curriculum planning. For instance, it suggests that the kind of standardized, subject-centered curriculum recommended in *A Nation at Risk* (see chapter 2) is insufficient by itself and must be balanced by considerations drawn from students as individuals and from the many problems of society.

Eisner's connoisseurship model of curriculum evaluation (discussed in section 8.7) has been an important influence on authentic assessment. Acting in accordance with this model, teachers become increasingly self-reflective connoisseurs and critics of their own classrooms, and students become increasingly self-reflective connoisseurs and critics of their own work. Both teacher and student can best do so by entering into an ongoing dialogue about the educational value of what transpires. This kind of dialogue can take many forms, but it is inherently educational in itself as a mutual search for meaning (Eisner, 1999).

Links with Constructivism.   A number of scholars link authentic assessment with constructivism, a theory that views knowledge as something constructed by individual human beings, not merely discovered, and that draws heavily upon recent work by cognitive psychologists (Phillips, 1995; von Glaserfield, 1995). According to Brooks and Brooks (1993), constructivist pedagogy involves teachers and students in a "self-regulated process of resolving inner cognitive conflicts that often become apparent through concrete experience, collaborative discourse, and reflection" (p. vii). Constructivist teachers are those who assist their students in resolving these cognitive conflicts and in exploring ideas and concepts in order to create knowledge. Torrance and Pryor (2000) use a slightly different term, *divergent assessment,* to emphasize the discovery of what students know or can do beyond what the teacher may have anticipated. They endorse open questioning as facilitating constructivist learning. Some typical characteristics of constructivist teachers are listed in Figure 8.5.

Fundamentally, authentic assessment is a way of capturing and somewhat formalizing the myriad things that perceptive teachers have always considered—although often intuitively—about what is happening to their students (Gipps et al., 2000). The advantages of formalizing the process are in making it increasingly accessible to more and more teachers and in keeping it viable as an integral part of flexible curriculum planning and development against the inroads of centralized curriculum control. The basic danger in formalizing the process is that the more widely it is used, the more likely it is to be reduced to a formula co-opted by centralizing influences and thus to lose much of its flexibility and value. Basically, however, constructivist teachers are engaging in the planning and development of individual-centered curricula in which the authenticity of learning is determined by the curriculum as experienced by the student.

In authentic assessment, therefore, the tasks students undertake are more practical, realistic, and challenging than traditional paper-and-pencil tests are (Pryor & Torrance, 1996). Students are engaged in more meaningful, context-bound activities, focusing their energies on "challenging, performance-oriented tasks that require

---

1. They encourage and accept student autonomy and initiative.

2. They use raw data and primary sources.

3. They use cognitive terminology such as *analyze, predict,* and *create* when framing tasks.

4. They allow student responses to drive lessons, to shift instructional strategies, and to alter content.

5. They inquire about students' understandings of concepts before sharing their own understandings of those concepts.

6. They encourage students to engage in dialogue, both with the teacher and with one another.

7. They ask open-ended questions and encourage students to ask questions of each other.

8. They seek elaboration of students' initial responses.

9. They allow wait time after posing questions.

10. They provide time for students to construct relationships, patterns, and theories.

FIGURE 8.5

Characteristics of constructivist teachers

Source: After Brooks & Brooks (1993).

1.   Teachers collect evidence from multiple activities.

2.   Assessments reflect the tasks that students will encounter in the world outside schools.

3.   Assessments reveal how students go about solving problems as well as the solutions they formulate.

4.   Procedures for assessments and the contents of assessments are derived from students' everyday learning in schools.

5.   Assessments reflect local values, standards, and control; they are not imposed externally.

6.   The tasks students are assessed upon include more than one acceptable solution to each problem and more than one acceptable answer to each question.

FIGURE 8.6
Some characteristics of authentic assessment
Source: After Eisner (1993), McTighe (1997), and Paris & Ayres (1994).

analysis, integration of knowledge, and invention" (Darling-Hammond, Ancess, & Falk, 1995, p. 2). Eisner (1993) states that the tasks of authentic assessment are "more complex, more closely aligned with life than with individual performance measured in an antiseptic context using sanitized instruments that were untouched by human hands" (p. 224). Some general characteristics of authentic assessment are listed in Figure 8.6.

To exemplify authentic assessment in practice, we discuss two techniques of student assessment that can be used consistently with the principles of authentic assessment: performance tasks and portfolios of student work.

Performance Tasks.   According to Wiggins (1998), "We must anchor our assessments in worthy, authentic performance problems, tasks, and projects" (p. 139). In this sense, performance tasks can be considered as planned parts of regular classroom instruction. They are specific, concrete tasks students perform as part of the typical school day. Much depends, of course, on how they are used, and when used aptly by a teacher with a light hand and consistently with constructivism, they can help students fully engage themselves in what they are learning and help the teacher better understand how students are reacting to what has been planned for them. Performance tasks, therefore, can be used to provide evidence about how the experienced curriculum is being influenced by the planned curriculum and the enacted curriculum. Although performance tasks can be considered forms of testing, what sets them apart as authentic is that they are more natural ways of discovering what is going on than are external or standardized tests. Judgments based on the ongoing activities of students are more likely to be realistic and meaningful to both teachers and students than are those based on contrived situations.

Performance tasks may vary considerably in the length of time needed to complete them. Some can easily be accommodated in a single lesson or period, but others might extend over several weeks, depending on what needs to be considered. Some tasks may be comprised of brief, intense activities (for example, role playing),

1. Portfolios	13. Individual and group projects
2. Journals	14. Field trips
3. Role playing	15. Problem-solving tasks
4. Imaginative writing	16. Concept mapping
5. Designing/presenting community projects	17. Induction/deduction tasks
	18. Panel discussions
6. Team interviewing	19. Dramatic enactments
7. Model building	20. Computer simulations
8. Surveys involving parents	21. Flowcharts
9. Keeping dialogue diaries	22. Songs
10. Mini-investigations	23. Collages
11. Position papers	24. Dances
12. Reports based on reflective/critical thinking	25. Plays

FIGURE 8.7
Some classroom activities that can be used as performance tasks

whereas others may require extended time for exploratory investigation, analysis, and presentation. Performance tasks are likely to be created mainly by individual teachers; but as students become familiar with the activities, they are likely to become willing and important planners and developers. For some tasks, students may have the opportunity for self-assessment. By reflecting on their performance or on something concrete they have created, students are likely to understand what they need to know and do in order to learn still more. The opportunities for using such ongoing activities for student assessment are many and varied (Wiggins & McTighe, 1998). Figure 8.7 lists twenty-five classroom activities that can be used consistently with the principles of authentic assessment.

Yet creating authentic performance tasks is no easy matter since such tasks should be natural parts of the school day, should be meaningful to students, and should help teachers discover how students are experiencing these activities in a deep sense, not just how they are performing them (Darling-Hammond & Falk, 1997). In addition, teachers must almost always sift through multiple and potentially changing criteria for judging the worth of what is happening to individual students, choosing those criteria that are most appropriate for each specific situation (Andrade, 2000). The following questions form a useful checklist for teachers in creating assessment tasks:

- What knowledge, skills, or attitudes will the students demonstrate?
- How will this activity enhance the curriculum taught in my class?
- What criteria will I use for assessing students on the task?
- Will I design the task myself, collaborate with other teachers, or collaborate with my students?
- What length of time will be available to complete the task?

- What individual or group activities will be included?
- What materials and equipment will be needed?
- Will I alone assess the students on this task, will other teachers be involved, or will students assess themselves?
- How will what I learn be used to improve further teaching and learning?

Students should find an authentic performance task to be inviting, the format should be easy to follow, directions should be clear, and, especially, the task should be achievable by a large majority of students (Marzano, 2000). Those students who do not successfully complete the task the first time around should be given other opportunities and any needed help, with the clear expectation that they will be successful in the near future. If an assessment task is indeed based on ongoing classroom learning and the interests of the students, there should be no difficulty in creating ones that are appealing and highly motivating. As noted by Brookhart and De Voge (1998), authentic performance tasks involve students in mental effort (persistence, analysis), not just in completing the overt tasks themselves.

The reality check comes when considering the criteria to be used to judge the students. The criteria may be difficult to spell out, and doing so in advance may narrow the basis for assessment, making the task less authentic and more like a standardized test. Nonetheless, stating explicit criteria in advance will give most students clear notice of what is expected of them, usually motivating some to exceed those criteria (Wiggins, 1998). In either case, the criteria used should relate to process (for example, evidence of investigative skills) as well as product (for example, presentation of models, charts, written materials) and, when possible, provide opportunities for students to assess themselves and their peers.

Here are some of the advantages and disadvantages of authentic performance tasks:

Advantages
- They are a powerful means of linking curriculum and assessment (Ross, 1996; Sperling, 1994).
- They are a more natural and less contrived way of providing realistic data about students than are more traditional forms of evaluation.
- They provide a meaningful context for students (Meyerson, 1995).
- They can be a tangible way to display and celebrate students' achievements (McTighe, 1997).
- They can provide credible evidence of student achievement to parents and the community (Hebert, 1998).
- Students can reflect upon what they have learned (Means, 2001).

Disadvantages
- They can be very time-consuming to prepare.
- Justifying their use to others may be difficult since there is little empirical evidence to demonstrate their validity and reliability (Linn, Baker, & Dunbar, 1991; Torrance, 1993).
- Making judgments based on multiple criteria can be difficult (McGaw, 1996).

Portfolios. The use of portfolios of student work has been central to the movement for authentic assessment. Their use has been based on the belief that what is most significant in any educational situation arises from the student's perception of that situation. Thus, authentic assessment emphasizes individual-centered curricula, in which the teacher helps the student identify interests and makes suggestions about how the student can deepen and broaden those interests in ways that lead to a wide variety of worthwhile and concomitant learnings. Despite the teacher's help, however, authenticity requires the student to take responsibility for what is learned. Only in this way does learning become integrated with the rest of the student's life rather than remaining something apart, as an isolated lesson selected by someone else. Given the responsibility that students must take for their own learning, it becomes incumbent upon them to demonstrate what they have learned and not simply to wait for their teachers to make these discoveries. Therefore, such use of student-initiated projects is an integral part of authentic assessment, and portfolios of student work are perhaps the most telling form of demonstration.

The idea of a portfolio is derived from the world of art. Artists create collections of their work that display much about themselves both professionally and personally, ranging from their skills and abilities to their aesthetic and ethical sensibilities. Applied to education, the creation of portfolios suggests that what the student has learned is most authentically demonstrated by what the student creates over a period of time, not by tests given at specific times. The teacher may initially suggest a topic or set a problem for the student to investigate as the beginning of a project, but the student makes the basic decisions about what to do and how. In carrying out their projects, students can also learn how to assess themselves. They may become increasingly reflective about both their work and themselves as they ponder over what to include in their portfolios and how it will demonstrate growth in their skills and understandings as their projects unfold. In assessing the portfolios of their students, teachers can consider what the portfolios demonstrate about learnings in the broadest and deepest possible senses. For instance, teachers can consider the depth of students' understandings and their abilities to use evidence appropriately, to make connections among different ideas coherently, and to develop their own points of view defensibly.

Portfolios can include any number of things—not only finished work but also notes, drafts, preliminary models and plans, logs, and other records; not only written work but also audiotapes, videotapes, photographs, three-dimensional creations, and other artifacts. Students decide what to create and what to include in their portfolios; hence, the portfolios reveal not only what individual students have done but also the strategies they have used in making their decisions. Teachers, therefore, can assess not only the finished products portfolios contain but also the processes students have followed in carrying out their projects. What kind of decisions have been made? How wise have they been? Where have they led? What are the alternatives? There may be numerous opportunities as projects unfold for teachers to discuss these questions with students and thus to offer advice and constructive criticism. Much of the authenticity of assessing portfolios is in the opportunities they provide to both teachers and students for considering the development of interests, attitudes, and values as well as skills and conventional academic learnings (Lyons, 1999).

For all these reasons, the use of portfolios is consistent with constructivism. Schwager and Carlson (1995) suggest:

> As a child grows he/she integrates information from the environment which results in the construction of personal theories or schema about how the world works. As additional experiences and information are encountered, children "fine-tune" and restructure their theories by elaboration and reorganization of the cognitive structures they have created. (p. 11)

Advocacy of portfolios by cognitive psychologists and their use in well-known projects have also helped to build acceptance for them (Resnick & Klopfer, 1989; Simmons & Resnick, 1993), and teachers using portfolios have found that they provide both sensitive and credible evidence of student achievement to parents and the community.

Computer-assisted instruction is becoming more prevalent and more sophisticated year-by-year. It now enables students to do a variety of projects (individually or in groups), and these are useful inclusions in portfolios because they provide tangible evidence of a range of problem-solving skills. For example, Lifter and Adams (1997) report that many of the eight levels of multiple intelligence are incorporated into computer software CD-ROMs. Eisner (1997) points out that computers can now create multimedia displays that capture meanings from alternative forms of data.

Figure 8.8 lists some examples of what can be included in a portfolio, although in practice there is virtually no limit on what a portfolio might contain.

Precisely how portfolios are used in any class is an open matter. Often the teacher provides some directions for students and may require samples of certain kinds of work. The teacher, too, may discuss with students how their portfolios will be evaluated and undertake individual interviews with them before awarding final grades. All such points about the use of portfolios may become matters of negotiation between teacher and students. As one example, Case (1994) reports that an elementary teacher and her class negotiated the following requirements for portfolios:

---

1. Essays
2. Journals
3. Summaries
4. Records, such as daily logs
5. Self-assessments, such as checklists and rating forms
6. Experiments
7. Demonstrations of skills
8. Rough drafts and finished products

9. Research notes
10. Team or group activities
11. Creative works
12. Major projects or products, such as dioramas, oral history collections, audio- and videotapes, photographs, charts, cards, and timelines
13. Tests
14. Teacher comments

FIGURE 8.8
Examples of what a student portfolio might contain

- A cover letter explaining the choices students made and describing themselves as learners
- A table of contents
- At least two samples related to their writing
- At least two samples related to their reading
- Another piece of their own choosing

They negotiated the following basis for grading:

- How well the students compare the samples and explain why they were included
- The actual content (Is there enough? Is there too much?)
- Neatness and organization
- Effort expended
- Clarity and completeness of the cover letter

Other teachers, of course, might have required or negotiated far different things. Still other teachers might have placed no requirements whatsoever on the portfolios of their students (other than urging students to demonstrate as fully as possible what they have learned) and might have decided on specific criteria for assessment only after having received the completed portfolios.

Many states are moving toward mandating that school systems use portfolios as a part of student assessment (Hebert, 1998). Once mandated, however, portfolios and their use are almost always subject to external controls far removed from individual classrooms, thereby potentially undermining the very authenticity for which student portfolios are valued in the first place. External controls may be deemed necessary to demonstrate the credibility of portfolios to the general public, but some educators have questioned whether state-level control can be justified (Salvia & Ysseldyke, 1998), especially in terms of the added expense of time, energy, and money that may be involved. Similarly, Torrance and Pryor (1995) note that overenthusiasm about the use of portfolios may blind educators to the enormous new responsibilities entailed.

Here are some of the advantages and disadvantages of portfolios:

Advantages
- They enable students to be actively involved in constructing their own knowledge.
- They encourage students to assess themselves (Supovitz, 1994).
- They encourage teachers to allow students to create a broad range and wide variety of items for assessment (Paris & Ayres, 1994).
- They require students to demonstrate thinking and expressive skills (Wiggins, 1992).
- They can provide an equitable and sensitive portrayal of what students know and are able to do (Darling-Hammond et al., 1995).
- They can provide credible evidence of student achievement to parents and the community.

Disadvantages
- Teachers need large amounts of time to help students select tasks, to provide support, and to assess portfolios.
- The grades students receive on portfolios correlate only moderately with other grades, and inter-rater agreement on grades for portfolios is low (Herman & Winters, 1994; Linn, 1993).
- Displaying and storing large numbers of bulky portfolios is difficult.
- A portfolio may not represent an individual student's work as much as it actually represents the aid that the student has received from parents, teachers, or other students.

Other Forms of Assessment

In this section we discuss four commonly used techniques for obtaining information useful in student assessments. These techniques are only a few that can be used to obtain such information (see Figure 8.2), but they have stood the test of time. The techniques we discuss here are not ordinarily considered part of authentic assessment as we have described it in the preceding section; but used sensitively and nonobtrusively, they may be consistent with at least some of the principles of authentic assessment. In other words, how a particular technique is used is sometimes more important to good assessment and evaluation than the specific procedures that the technique entails.

Objective Tests.   Teachers commonly use objective tests. Such tests contain items that can be marked quickly by hand or by machine (Clarke, Madaus, Horn, & Ramos, 2000). Such tests are deemed objective because all answers can be definitely classified as correct or incorrect and, therefore, no subjective judgments go into the scoring. Of course, many subjective decisions about what items to include and how items are stated go into the creation of such a test. Well-constructed items are thus a necessity for test results to be valuable, and it is important that the items cover all portions of the curriculum being evaluated. Sometimes a scatter diagram (shown in Figure 8.9) of the topics and objectives to be tested is a useful way of ensuring that what the test covers matches what the curriculum covers.

The most common types of objective tests are the following:

1. Matching
   For example:
   Match items in column A with those in column B.

A. Plants	**B. Life cycle**	
1. strawberry	(a) annual	_____
2. black raspberry	(b) biennial	_____
3. celery	(c) perennial	_____
4. fern	(d) biennial	_____
5. carrot	(e) perennial	_____
	(f) perennial	_____

TOPIC: Plants	Recall	Comprehension	Analysis	Synthesis	Evaluation	Total
1. Leaves	4	3	2	-	1	10
2. Edible plants	2	5	1	1	1	10
3. Plant classification	2	2	4	1	1	10
4. Pollination, fertilization, and seeds	2	2	3	2	1	10
5. Photosynthesis	2	4	2	1	1	10
TOTAL	12	16	12	5	5	50

FIGURE 8.9
A scatter diagram of objective questions within a science unit on plants

2. Alternative choice (true-false, yes-no)
   For example:
   Since fungi must depend on other living things for food, they cannot make their own food. True or false?

3. Multiple choice
   For example:

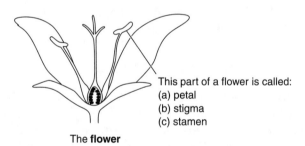

This part of a flower is called:
(a) petal
(b) stigma
(c) stamen

The **flower**

4. Completion
   For example:
   Five things necessary to carry out photosynthesis in plants are

   1. _____
   2. _____
   3. _____
   4. _____
   5. _____

   Virtually all teachers undergo training that makes them aware of the principal advantages and disadvantages of objective tests.

Advantages
- They can measure a wide range of specific topics included within the curriculum.
- They are quick, efficient, and—when well constructed—reliable.

Disadvantages
- They require considerable skill and time to construct.
- They do not measure things such as creativity and divergent thinking.

Essay Tests.   Essay tests, whether in the form of short paragraphs written by elementary students or full-fledged essays by older students, are also commonly used by teachers. They provide students with the opportunity to demonstrate that they have synthesized diverse topics and created a defensible point of view of their own. Essay tests are particularly useful in helping teachers determine whether students understand the meaning and significance of what the curriculum covers (Filer, 1993). Such tests are not, however, good indicators of whether students have learned or can recall specific pieces of knowledge since the questions or problems permit students to respond in individual ways. The quality of students' responses can also vary because of stress, health, and even changes in the weather. Also, teachers may have very different notions of what constitutes a good essay.

For teachers who are especially concerned about reliability, Cangelosi (1990) makes the following suggestions:

1. Select essay questions that cover major topics in the curriculum.
2. Carefully define the task presented in each question.
3. Use questions requiring brief answers and include as many questions as practicable.
4. Do not use optional questions.

Of course, the more specifically the students' tasks are defined, the less opportunity they have to demonstrate original or creative thinking (Salvia & Ysseldyke, 1998). Since essay tests by nature deal with meaning and significance, efforts to make them into highly reliable indicators of specific factual knowledge may defeat their basic purpose and should thus be undertaken only with considerable caution (Harris & Bell, 1990).

Here are some of the advantages and disadvantages of essay tests:

Advantages
- They are easily and quickly prepared.
- They provide students with the opportunity to demonstrate understanding, organization, and expression of ideas.

Disadvantages
- They are time-consuming to grade.
- They do not systematically measure factual knowledge.

1. Which things in science are the most exciting to learn about?

2. Place a circle around any of the following if you learned about them last year.

   plants   seeds   frogs   fish   birds

3. Are you still interested in finding out more about any of these topics? Which ones?

4. Have you tried out any scientific experiments? Which ones do you remember?

5. What are some scientific problems you would like to solve?

FIGURE 8.10
A student interest inventory

Interest Inventories.   Knowledge of the interests of students in different academic subjects can often be obtained through the use of questionnaires known as student interest inventories, as shown in Figure 8.10. With such knowledge, a teacher can call on individual students to provide the entire class with detailed information about their special interests. Such students might bring collections or other samples of their interests from home, or they might act as expert judges of the work produced by groups of students. Elementary school students are usually especially eager to share their special interests with other members of the class, and, in so doing, they help increase the enthusiasm of everyone.

Knowledge of students' interests helps the teacher plan lessons and other activities, particularly in making choices about what topics to add, modify, or omit. The information obtained from interest inventories may have considerable diagnostic value to a teacher, but it can also be useful in formative or summative evaluations.

Here is a summary of the advantages and disadvantages of interest inventories:

Advantages
- They enable the teacher to build on activities that are already of considerable interest to individuals in the class.
- They permit the teacher to keep track of changing interests.

Disadvantages
- Some students may try to impress the teacher by talking about topics they do not really understand or even have an interest in.
- Some students may be reluctant to divulge their interests.

Rating Scales.   Rating scales have a wide range of uses during the teaching of a curriculum. It is possible for a teacher to rate the level of skill of an entire class, a small group, or individual students. Figure 8.11 depicts a rating scale.

It is important to bear in mind that use of a rating scale may not create new knowledge for the teacher; it may merely make explicit those judgments that a teacher already holds. However, students' skills may change over time or be demonstrated in

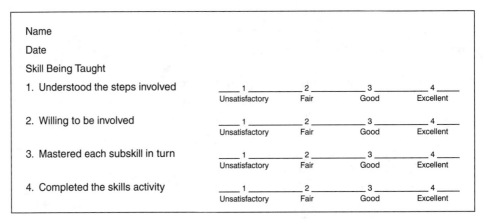

FIGURE 8.11
A rating scale

new ways, so making explicit judgments may clarify for the teacher how well students are mastering general skills, specific topics, or a whole curriculum. Because the teacher rates students on a numerical scale, this approach seems to some people more appropriate for rating specific skills than general understandings or even more nebulous items such as values and attitudes. Therefore, a teacher may wish to confine the use of rating scales to only what is specific and concrete. For instance, a rating scale might be used to diagnose why a certain student is having trouble learning a particular topic. Information from the scale might also help the teacher focus discussions with a student over a period of time.

An interesting variation is to have a small group of students carry out a task or demonstrate a skill and ask the remainder of the class to rate the group's performance. Comments by peers are often helpful to students and may be accepted more readily than if they were made by the teacher. The problem with such activities is that the purpose is sometimes lost in the activity, which becomes an end in itself. Rating scales are helpful to students and teachers only if they provide useful feedback about present behaviors concisely and expeditiously; if they become time-consuming and complicated, then their purpose is lost (Cangelosi, 1991).

Here is a summary of the advantages and disadvantages of rating scales:

Advantages
- They crystallize teachers' judgments about individual students or groups of students.
- They can be done quickly and easily.

Disadvantages
- They provide teachers with no new information.
- They are difficult to compile and to use other than for specific skills and competencies.

8.4   PERSONS INVOLVED IN EVALUATIONS

Depending on the size and scope of a curriculum and the purposes for evaluating it, evaluation can be done by a few people (even a single teacher in a classroom) or by a large number of persons. In the United States, educational evaluation has moved in the direction of small and informal assessments by teachers involving broad samples of students' work (Eisner, 1993; Wiggins, 1998). This kind of evaluation is now described by commonly used phrases such as "authentic assessment" and "portfolio assessment" as described earlier in this chapter; and, in general, it is consistent with the kind of evaluation that Dewey recommended early in the twentieth century. Nevertheless, counter-pressures for accountability and effective expenditures of public dollars have kept large-scale, formal evaluations conducted by experts very much in vogue as well.

Curriculum evaluation today is still heavily influenced by many of the same assumptions and practices that characterized it during the 1960s and 1970s, when it became formalized and bureaucratized under the impact of federal funding. Thus, many curriculum evaluations are directed by experts and specialists who may be hired by states or school districts expressly for these tasks, or they may be designed by university professors on leave as paid consultants to private agencies. The literature on curriculum evaluation still contains numerous references to the characteristics of "good" evaluators, such as technical competence, personal integrity, and objectivity, just as it has for the last several decades (Nevo, 1983; Stufflebeam, Foley, Gephart, Guba, Hammond, Merriman, & Provus, 1971).

Even when the evaluation of a curriculum remains relatively small and informal, as when undertaken by a few teachers in a single school, experts are usually available to supply help as needed. For instance, a specialist in evaluation from the school district or from the state department of education may be able to aid teachers in developing a plan for gathering appropriate data. On some occasions, school staff may be able to obtain small grants (for example, from their school district) to employ external consultants for particular tasks, such as organizing and coordinating the evaluation or interpreting the data that it collects.

8.5   ARE THERE UNIFORM STANDARDS?

Whether there are specific standards that should be used in all educational evaluations is a matter of some debate. Obviously the smaller and less formal the evaluation, the less likely participants are to be concerned with standardized procedures. But informality does not prevent an evaluation from being done well. Many fine curriculum evaluations have, in fact, been based solely on the informal, naturalistic observations of teachers. However, the collective evaluation community in the United States has moved in the direction of adopting uniform standards, even if these standards may apply mostly to formal, large-scale evaluations, especially those that take a technical approach to evaluation.

Still, the best-known and perhaps most influential move in this direction was also an effort to adopt standards specific enough to be useful but general enough not to become unduly prescriptive. This move was the set of standards adopted in 1981 by the Joint Committee on Standards for Educational Evaluation. This committee (chaired by Daniel Stufflebeam and including members of major professional associations such as the American Educational Research Association and the American Psychological Association) was able to reach consensus on thirty standards, divided into four general areas designated "utility," "feasibility," "propriety," and "accuracy."

Utility includes eight standards for obtaining data that are informative, timely, and influential. Stufflebeam (1981) notes that these standards require evaluators to acquaint themselves with their audiences, to work out with them what information they need, and to plan evaluations responsive to these needs. In general, the standards under utility are concerned with how to conduct high-quality evaluations that serve practical purposes.

Feasibility includes three standards for making decisions that are realistic in terms of costs and benefits, prudence, and diplomacy. The techniques and procedures used in an evaluation should not only be workable in an immediately practical sense; they also should fit appropriately with the particular context in which the evaluation occurs. For instance, the evaluator needs to anticipate and plan for the different positions and reactions of interest groups and other stakeholders in the curriculum.

Propriety includes eight standards intended to alert evaluators to actions that might be construed as unlawful, unscrupulous, or unethical. Stufflebeam (p. 187) concludes that "these standards require that evaluations be conducted legally, ethically, and with due regard for the welfare of those involved in the evaluation as well as those affected by the results."

Accuracy includes eleven standards aimed at conveying accurate information. They deal with the use of reliable sources of information, acceptable forms of measurement, unbiased analysis of data, and objective reporting of results.

House (1980) contends that utility standards are of limited value because they serve the status quo and embody existing inequalities. He believes that there are key values upon which all evaluation standards should be based, namely moral equality, moral autonomy, impartiality, and reciprocity. These values should provide the foundation for fair agreement and conduct in an evaluation. Norris (1990) supports House on these points.

Of course, biases are built into any set of standards, and collectively the joint committee's standards assume that evaluations should be formal and evaluators should remain strictly objective and neutral. Therefore, the standards are not entirely applicable to the kind of informal assessing that we suggest teachers continuously do in their classrooms (and which, in fact, often becomes the most telling data used in formal, large-scale studies). Nor are they entirely applicable to other well-established forms of research, such as "participant observation," in which the researcher-evaluators deliberately immerse themselves within a situation in order to experience it as other participants do. The standards also do not face the critical issue of whether evaluators should strive to be completely unbiased (which, in reality, they cannot achieve) or whether they should strive to clearly identify the biases they do hold so that others can better understand the basis for their judgments.

Nonetheless, given these limitations, the standards do not seem to have prevented the development in the 1980s and 1990s of creative approaches to evaluation in which techniques and methods are fitted to the purposes and the circumstances of the evaluation, and not the other way around. The creation of the standards may also have helped those people intent on doing only objective evaluations to do them more flexibly than was the case previously. In general, outside specialists or expert consultants helping a school or school district to conduct a formal curriculum evaluation should be familiar with or act in accordance with standards like those of the Joint Committee on Standards for Educational Evaluation.

8.6 PREPARING FOR A FORMAL EVALUATION

When a school is in the process of preparing to evaluate its curriculum formally, there are a number of steps it can take to ensure that the evaluation will be thorough and fair and lead to constructive outcomes. It is essential for the school staff to show commitment and to create a working climate conducive to cooperation. Unless staff members are willing to explore ideas and alternatives with one another and to try out some specific form of evaluation, the evaluation as a whole is not likely to run smoothly or to lead to beneficial change. Both physical and psychological space are needed. A separate office from which the evaluation can be coordinated may be sufficient physical space, and a supportive, frank atmosphere and scheduled times to discuss issues may provide the psychological space.

Guba and Lincoln (1981) suggest that evaluation teams are far preferable to an individual evaluator, regardless of the scale of the evaluation. A team usually includes pluralistic values. It can provide multiple roles, multiple perspectives, and multiple strategies. Thus, a team is likely to develop more creative, comprehensive, and viable plans and procedures for a formal evaluation than if the task is left to a single member of the school staff.

A team need not conduct its work without outside help, however. Even if external consultants are unavailable or unwanted, checklists of questions that proved useful to other schools in planning previous evaluations may give needed focus to the team's deliberations. Ornstein and Hunkins (1993) identify six steps that should carry a school through the entire process of evaluation (pp. 342–343):

1. Focus on what is to be evaluated
2. Collect information about it
3. Organize the information
4. Analyze the information
5. Report the information
6. Recycle the information

Figure 8.12 is a much more detailed checklist recommended by Hughes, Russell, and McConachy (1979). It was first used in the 1970s but variations of it are still in use in the 2000s. It contains thirteen steps. The questions relating to purposes and motivations are perhaps the most critical; they need to be thought through very

1. **Purposes**

   What are the purposes of the evaluation?

   Are they expressed in specific terms—for example, improving school morale?

   Are the purposes understood by and acceptable to all those concerned?

   Who is likely to oppose the evaluation?

2. **Motivations**

   Why is the evaluation being undertaken now?

   Will the evaluation meet a felt need of those involved with the school?

   Who wants to be involved in the evaluation?

   Who should be involved—

       Principal?

       Senior staff?

       Teachers?

       Those with a vested interest, such as parents, students, and members of the school board?

       Others?

3. **Participants**

   Who will carry out the evaluation?

       Principal and/or senior staff?

       Classroom teachers?

       Students?

       Parents?

       Representatives of an outside body, such as a consultant, school board members, the principal, or teachers from another school?

       A combination of the above, such as a group consisting of teachers, a parent, and a consultant?

   What will be the nature of the involvement of various participants?

   Will there be a representative planning team or steering committee?

   Is the evaluation likely to be seen as threatening to any of the participants?

   How can any perceived threat be minimized?

4. **Evaluation roles**

   There are a number of possible roles (not necessarily separate people):

       Evaluator (one involved in information collection and judgment)

       Facilitator (one involved in assisting an evaluation but not in judgment)

       Consultant (a person called on for special contribution to one or more aspects, such as assisting with interviewing only)

   To what extent are such roles used in the evaluation?

   Is the evaluation organized in a realistic fashion for the people involved, particularly with respect to—

       Time (to obtain valid results, to maintain interest, time for organization)?

       Personnel (is the central figure organizing or coordinating the evaluation being given released time for the activity)? Finance?

   What is the time span of the evaluation?

5. **Intended audiences**

   Are the audiences of the evaluation clearly defined?

   What access to information will the various audiences have?

6. **Area/issue to be evaluated**

   What will be evaluated?

       Appropriateness of school goals?

       Extent to which school goals have been achieved?

       Process, such as teacher/student interaction, parent/teacher interaction, principal/teacher interaction, etc.?

       Teaching strategies?

       Reporting?

FIGURE 8.12

Questions to ask when planning an evaluation

Source: After Hughes et al. (1979).

7. **Collection of information**
   Available methods include—
   Observation—structured or unstructured
   Interviews—structured or unstructured
   Questionnaires
   Documentary analysis of reports, records, minutes, etc.
   Content analysis of curriculum materials
   Reports of informal discussions and conversations
   Achievement tests—criterion- and norm-referenced
   Diaries and self-reports
   Audio-and videotape recordings
   Are there appropriate safeguards to ensure that the information is valid and reliable?

8. **Feasibility of methods used to collect information**
   In terms of:
   Time available
   Availability of personnel with the necessary expertise
   Acceptability of those whose views and activities will be documented

9. **Judgments**
   What are the procedures for the analysis of information?
   How will the information be categorized?
   Are there appropriate safeguards to validate the information?

10. **Release of information**
    Who will have control over what is collected and reported?
    What procedures will govern the collection and release of this information?
    Who will have the right to reply to, correct, and validate reports of the views and activities of individuals and groups?
    Will all, or only part, of the information be released?

11. **Reports**
    Is the evaluation going to be reported in a form (content, style, and format) that is readily available to those for whom it is designed?
    Will negative aspects of the school be reported and to whom?
    Has the release date for reporting been identified?
    Are different reports for different groups necessary, such as parents, school staff, education departments?

12. **Outcomes**
    Is it possible to see or to predict positive outcomes from the evaluation?
    Have these outcomes been identified clearly?
    What steps have been taken for ensuring that the evaluation feeds into the appropriate decision-making process?
    Are the participants aware from the beginning of the possible outcomes?
    Have follow-up procedures been established to make participants aware of the actual effects of the evaluation?

13. **Resources**
    Are particular resources needed to make the evaluation more effective?
    Specialized personnel?
    Secretarial assistance?
    Administrative personnel?
    Equipment, paper, postage?
    Working space?
    Time available for those staff conducting the evaluation?
    Printing and media production?
    Time given by parents and/or students?
    Example of evaluation undertaken by the other schools?
    Planning guidelines for teachers?

carefully before the evaluation is undertaken. Other questions (such as those under "intended audiences" and "feasibility of methods used to collect information"), which can be answered only tentatively in the early stages of an evaluation, may need to be reassessed at later stages. The checklist itself provides no answers for these questions, nor does it reveal when and how often to pose them. This is something that each evaluation team must work out for itself.

This checklist is just one example of how the steps involved in curriculum evaluation can be organized. Variations can and do occur, often beneficially when they fit the particular needs and circumstances of an individual school. The answers that a school collectively arrives at for the basic questions on a checklist may depend, of course, on the value orientations of the staff and the community as well as a host of practical considerations. These answers may lead the school to adopt a specific model of curriculum evaluation.

8.7   EVALUATION MODELS

Evaluation models are useful as general outlines of how a specific evaluation can be conducted. Like checklists of questions, they should not be regarded as invariant steps to be followed rigidly regardless of the particular circumstances a school finds itself in. Above all, a school should adopt a model only if the staff as a whole feels reasonably comfortable with it and if it is congruent with the school's general value orientations. And the school should be prepared to modify the model or abandon it altogether if circumstances warrant. Doing so may lead the evaluation team into a new round of deliberations, but, in actuality, ongoing deliberation is often the key to a good curriculum project, including specific deliberations about planning, development, and evaluation. The maxim "precision in planning, flexibility in execution" applies to curriculum evaluation as well as to all else in curriculum planning and development.

According to Stufflebeam (1981), at the beginning of the 1980s, more than forty models had been developed to describe or prescribe how evaluations might be planned and undertaken. More recently, many other models have been advocated, although, in general, these are variations on older ideas. The four examples that we have chosen to describe here have been extremely influential over an extended period of time and are still widely followed, both in their original and in modified forms. We have selected them because of both their historical influence and their present use. The first, Ralph W. Tyler's objectives model, follows from his rational-linear approach to curriculum planning (discussed in detail in chapter 3). The second, Robert Stake's countenance model, emphasizes the use of both formal and informal data in describing the context of curriculum and instruction. The third, Malcolm Parlett and David Hamilton's illuminative model, uses techniques from social anthropology and related fields to ascribe meanings to a situation. The fourth, Elliot W. Eisner's connoisseurship model, similarly ascribes meaning but relies on artistic and other qualitative techniques; it follows from Eisner's approach to curriculum planning (also described in detail in chapter 3). Each of these four models is followed by a brief case study to illustrate how it has been used in actual practice.

Objectives Model

Tyler's evaluation model follows directly from the curriculum model he put forward in *Basic Principles of Curriculum and Instruction* (Tyler, 1949). The following quotation from this book clearly outlines Tyler's views about evaluation:

> [Evaluation] is essentially the process of determining to what extent the educational objectives are actually being realized by the program of curriculum and instruction. However, since education objectives are essentially changes in human beings, that is, that the objectives aimed at are to produce certain desirable changes in the behavior patterns of the students, then evaluation is the process for determining the degree to which these changes in behavior actually take place. (p. 111)

This model is based on a strict ends-means rationale. It begins by determining and then stating objectives in terms of student behaviors. Tyler insists that objectives be derived from students, contemporary society, and subject specialists and that they pass through the screens of educational philosophy and the psychology of learning. The task of the evaluator is not to inquire into the merits of such curriculum objectives but to determine the extent to which the student behaviors stipulated in the objectives are realized in practice.

To do so, Tyler originally proposed the use of formal instruments such as tests, although he did not restrict tests to paper-and-pencil versions only. He included less formal means of identifying changes in students, including the use of many of the same kinds of inventories, questionnaires, and logs used in the Eight-Year Study (see chapter 2). However, in *Basic Principles of Curriculum and Instruction,* he insists that an ends-means rationale be strictly observed and that evaluators strive for precision and objectivity. Therefore, this model of evaluation stresses that tests selected by the evaluator should meet conventional standards of objectivity, reliability, and validity. He also insists that they be used on a pre/post basis in order to measure changes in student behaviors that presumably have resulted because of the curriculum. Information derived from tests and other instruments then enables developers to make adjustments in the curriculum that—in principle, at least—on future occasions can lead to the stipulated objectives being more completely realized. Figure 8.13 is a schematic breakdown of the objectives model.

Although less flexible than Tyler's approach in the Eight-Year Study, the objectives model of curriculum evaluation was a major advance over the ordinary practices of the 1940s, which were confined to measuring only the academic achievement of students and then only through standardized, norm-referenced tests (Fraser, 1983). Even today, its logic and practical simplicity make it attractive to curriculum planners and developers and to some teachers, for it requires neither teachers nor evaluators to consider the complexities of classrooms beyond asking whether stated objectives are being reached.

FIGURE 8.13
Tyler's objectives model of curriculum
evaluation

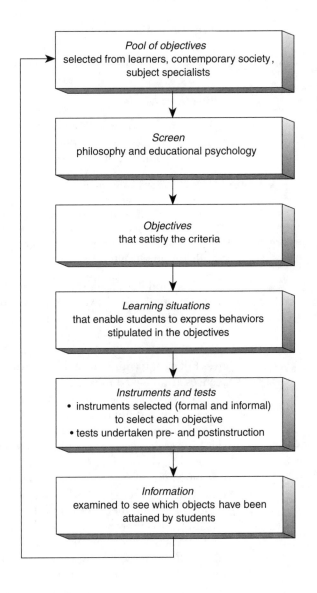

Another feature that has contributed to its longevity is its blend of new concepts within an existing scientific tradition (Shane, 1980). Concepts that were new at the time included the stating of objectives in terms of student behaviors, the derivation of appropriate learning experiences (and not just content) from objectives, the use of vertical and horizontal integration in organizing learning experiences, and the use of feedback and recycling so that the curriculum is continuously revised and updated. However, Tyler's model blended these concepts with older ideas from the scientific testing movement, which emphasized measurement, objectivity, validity, and reliability and which had become familiar to most American educators during the first half of the century (Rubin, 1991). Although the objectives model differentiates measurement and evaluation, it strongly suggests that evaluation cannot be done soundly unless based on scientific measurements that precede it. Much of its simplicity is that once objectives have been determined (which, according to the model, is not the province of the evaluator), there is little left to do but take measurements.

Despite its simplicity, there are some serious problems with the objectives model, the most obvious one being that the model does not enable an evaluator (whether the classroom teacher or an external evaluator) to make judgments about the objectives of a curriculum. For example, what happens if an evaluator is not confident that the selected objectives are the appropriate ones for a given program? What values are implicit in the philosophical and psychological screens used in selecting objectives? Is it always desirable to begin an evaluation study by examining whether particular objectives have been achieved or not? The model does not address such questions.

An evaluator is also likely to run into problems interpreting data. As noted by Guba and Lincoln (1981), it may be possible to make positive judgments when the data clearly show that particular objectives have been achieved, but how large must the discrepancy be between what an objective specifies and how well students perform before the curriculum is judged negatively? Also, what if the discrepancy is positive, with students outpacing the objectives? How can an evaluator then decide whether particular objectives are appropriate or whether they should be revised? Finally, the objectives model of curriculum evaluation assumes that discrepancies between objectives and what students actually learn can be attributed to the curriculum, yet it is clear that many other things both inside and outside of school strongly influence student learning. Therefore, use of the model can lead to sound curricula being altered and unsound curricula being left unchanged.

Guba and Lincoln (1981) capture the major problems of the objectives model in the following statement:

> In practice, the Tyler model is convergent in its effects, particularly in creative situations such as curriculum development. Premature insistence on the *a priori* stipulation of objectives can lead to a premature closure. Once objectives are formally stated and the evaluation process has begun, it becomes enormously difficult to break out from the original list, to delete useless objectives, and to add others that may have emerged. (p. 7)

■ CASE STUDY

National Assessment of Educational Progress (NAEP)

Tyler's prominence in evaluation led to his appointment as director of the National Assessment of Educational Progress (NAEP), an organization that was established in 1966 to collect data on a large scale from students and adults in an effort to develop sound public policy about education in the United States. It was funded initially from private sources but later the federal government took over its funding. The general purposes of NAEP, as first stated in 1966, were to assess the educational progress of large populations in order to provide the public with dependable information to help in understanding educational problems and needs (Merwin & Womer, 1974). Specifically, NAEP had the following goals:

- To illustrate specific knowledge, skills, and attitudes that young people have and have not attained
- To measure changes in knowledge, skills, and attitudes over time
- To provide information to teachers to assist them in planning learning experiences, so that knowledge already acquired is avoided and knowledge not yet acquired can be targeted

Throughout most of its existence NAEP has obtained data about knowledge, skills, and attitudes of students at ages nine, thirteen, and seventeen, and from adults. Considering the presence of Tyler, that NAEP from its inception emphasized objectives is not surprising. Its first major activity was to produce a pool of objectives that could be used as a basis for developing appropriate test items. Although in its initial years NAEP considered only certain core subjects, it later expanded into measuring attainment in almost all standard subjects. Its normal procedure has been to create tentative pools of objectives and then invite a wide cross-section of people from across the nation to attend regional conferences at which the pools are examined. Participants are asked to judge each objective in terms of two questions:

Is this something important for people to learn today?
Is it something I would like to have my children learn?

Once objectives have passed through this screen, specialized testing agencies produce specific test items that match these objectives (Merwin & Womer, 1974).

The actual collection of data for NAEP has been based on an item-sampling technique. Rather than requiring all students and adults who are tested to complete a totally comprehensive test of each subject, subsets of items are administered to different groups. The number of individuals sampled each year is large (75,000 to 100,000). Test items for each of the four age groups overlap, so it is possible to make comparisons among groups. Results are presented in terms of the percentage of each group making the correct response to each item. No results are available for individual students or school systems, and there are no norms or group scores. Figure 8.14 shows several related items from the Citizenship Test and the results from each age group. While only 49 percent of nine-year-olds had correct knowledge about the powers of the president of the United States, 89 percent of adults did so. It is impossible to conclude that the increased knowledge of each age group is attributable to formal schooling alone; however, in cases in which the knowledge of one age group does not substantially exceed that of younger groups or in which the knowledge of all groups seems low, it is possible for schools to teach materials intended to rectify this lack of progress.

A. Does the President have the right to do anything affecting the United States that he wants to do? (Yes, No, I don't know)

B. (If yes) Why? (Part B was not scored; it was asked to ensure that respondents understood Part A and to give them a chance to explain their position.)

C. (If no) Why not?

(If answer to C is vague) Who or what would stop him from doing what he wants?

Acceptable reasons to C (examples): People could stop him; elected officials could stop him; checks and balances system of government; laws stop him; country would be a dictatorship; not the democratic way.

Unacceptable reasons to C (examples): Police or Vice-President would stop him; he wouldn't be doing his job; he might do something that could hurt the country; he would be doing what is right; people vote for him not to; he can't do it; everybody, even the President, has some limitations; he just advises us; he can't do everything since he is only one person.

Results

		Age		
	9	13	17	Adult
Stated that the President does *not* have the right to do anything affecting the United States that he wants (No to A)	49%	73%	78%	89%
Stated that the President does not have the right and gave an acceptable reason (acceptable reason to C as well as No to A)	18%	53%	68%	80%

FIGURE 8.14

Sample questions from the NAEP Citizenship Test

Source: Merwin & Womer (1974, p. 318). Reprinted with permission.

It is clear that the NAEP does not evaluate specific curricula. Rather, it provides a general yardstick against which knowledge that is usually a part of most curricula can be measured over extended periods of time. Nor does the measurement of such objectives address the issue of whether these objectives are desirable in the first place or whether other objectives would be more desirable. Still, in the decades in which NAEP has been in existence, the data that it collects have been widely used by teachers, curriculum specialists, and educational policymakers. These data suggest, in general, that levels of basic knowledge attained by different age groups have remained reasonably constant over many years, substantial evidence that runs contrary to the popular belief of the 1990s and 2000s that American schools have been in steep decline since the 1960s.

The NAEP illustrates the logic, simplicity, and utility of Tyler's objectives model. It does not overcome the problems in the model itself, particularly problems in using the model to evaluate specific curricula or classroom practices, but it does exemplify circumstances in which the model can be used appropriately to arrive at generalizations potentially useful in maintaining or modifying curricula.

Countenance Model

Both historically and conceptually, Stake's countenance model represents an advance over Tyler's model. In a seminal paper, Stake (1967) criticized what he saw as the deficiencies of educational evaluation in the 1960s. He considered informal methods of evaluation to be incomplete because they usually depended too much on casual observations, implicit goals, and subjective judgments, but he also argued that formal methods then in use failed to consider most of what actually happened to a curriculum in a given school.

He called for expanding the "countenance" (face) of evaluation through greater use of formal methods to obtain data about what was happening in a school over and above whether objectives were being realized, such as "the match between what an educator intends to do and what he does do" (in effect, the slippage between the planned curriculum and the enacted curriculum) and "the antecedent conditions and classroom transactions" (the influence of the social context and the school climate on teaching). More specifically, Stake argued that evaluation should consider antecedents (general goals, materials, student aptitudes), transactions (classroom interactions between teachers and students), and outcomes (formal learnings, attitudes, appreciations). Each of these three should be considered in terms of intents of the program, observations of both intended and unintended effects, standards or values held by affected individuals and groups, and judgments about the worth of different standards.

Evaluators, he contended, should distinguish between describing and judging, but they must do both. They can consider the congruence between the intents of a curriculum and all that they observe (not just the student behaviors specified by the objectives, as suggested by Tyler), but they can also identify the logical contingencies that characterize how antecedents, transactions, and outcomes are related in the curriculum. The countenance model of evaluation substantially broadened the focus of curriculum evaluation beyond objectives only. However, as Guba and Lincoln (1981) point out, it was still an objectives-oriented approach, and not until the 1970s did Stake move away from objectives, advocating more naturalistic and informal techniques and developing "responsive evaluation," intended to provide curriculum decision makers with what they need to know, not necessarily with only what they think they need to know.

As pictured in Figure 8.15, the countenance model is essentially an organizational framework for undertaking curriculum evaluation. Within it, the evaluator's task is to collect data for two matrices, the description matrix and the judgment matrix, and each matrix is subdivided into antecedents, transactions, and outcomes.

The first step is to determine the intents of a particular curriculum. Stake used the term *intents* to avoid controversies about goals and behavioral versus nonbehavioral objectives. According to Stake, intents should be listed in terms of antecedents, transactions, and outcomes. Antecedent intents relate to any conditions prior to the implementation of a curriculum and might include students' interests and motivations, community beliefs, and teacher backgrounds and interests. Transaction intents are the purposes expressed by the participants in a curriculum, including students, teachers, administrators, and parents. These intents tend to be dynamic and

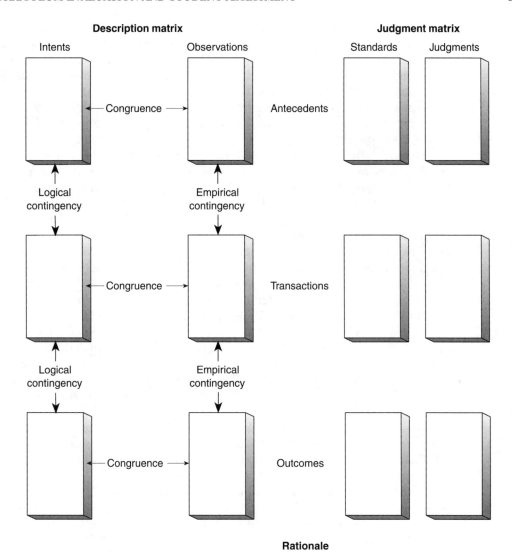

FIGURE 8.15
Stake's countenance model of evaluation
Source: After Stake (1967).

changeable because of the countless encounters each day between participants. Outcome intents include intended student learnings and also anticipated effects on teachers, administrators, parents, and other members of the community.

The second step is to collect observational data about the use of a particular curriculum. Stake permits data collected through informal observations, but he also insists on the use of formal methods, such as questionnaires and psychometric tests. He points out that observations must include the ongoing transactions within a curriculum in order to note discrepancies between intents originally specified and intents that actually occur.

The third step is to analyze discrepancies in terms of contingency and congruence. *Contingency* refers to the relationships between antecedents, transactions, and outcomes. For example, a teacher's intended interactions (transactions) with students might be based on a sound understanding of students' abilities and interests, and observational data could confirm whether such intents had been realized. Congruence refers to whether intents actually occurred: "to be fully congruent the intended antecedents, transactions, and outcomes would have to come to pass" (Stake, 1967, p. 533).

The fourth step is to analyze the overall rationale of the curriculum. Stake maintains that it is important to collect data about both the explicit and the implicit rationale. Both formal statements and incidental comments by curriculum developers and teachers become sources of data.

The fifth step is to collect data for the judgment matrix. The standards column of the matrix refers to both absolute standards, such as ideal specifications that might be established by subject matter experts, and relative standards, such as those based on comparisons with other curricula. Stake notes that discrepancies between intents and observations are analyzed in terms of these standards.

The final step is to make judgments based on the evaluator's interpretations of how the discrepancies can be explained in terms of the standards.

Stake's countenance model clearly represented a significant advance over Tyler's objectives model, first, because it attends to other relevant data (antecedents and transactions), and, second, because it distinguishes between description and judgment. But therein lies a difficulty. The scale and range of activities suggested by Stake for collecting data for the twelve cells of the matrix represent a mammoth task, even for an experienced, full-time evaluator. For all practical purposes, this model removes the evaluation of a curriculum from teachers, those persons who enact it. In some ways, the countenance model provides a useful framework, but, as with Tyler's model, it does not provide specific guidelines about how standards are to be derived or how competing values between different participants can be analyzed. It is certainly more than a "mnemonic device for planning an evaluation study" (Worthen & Sanders, 1973, p. 125), but it falls short in explaining the criteria for judgments that Stake believes should be made public and explicit (Guba & Lincoln, 1981). Nonetheless, it had considerable influence in the late 1960s and early 1970s in warning educational evaluators to broaden their focus. It is still particularly useful in helping evaluators (including individual teachers) consider what kind of observations can go into a curriculum evaluation.

■ CASE STUDY

Twin City Institute of Talented Youth

Stake and Gjerde (1977) undertook an evaluation of the Twin City Institute of Talented Youth (T-City) summer program in Minneapolis, Minnesota, in 1971. By this time, Stake had moved away somewhat from his 1967 countenance model in the direction of an informal, responsive model of evaluation, which more carefully considered the interests of participants in a curriculum and which he later developed in detail (Stake, 1975). Therefore, the T-City evaluation does not represent a completely pure type, although it does incorporate most of the ideas and procedures of the countenance model.

The rationale behind T-City was that a high-quality academic summer program for secondary school students who might become future leaders would help them not only develop their skills in art, language, and science but strengthen their commitment to, and appreciation of, the most universal concerns of humankind. The intent of T-City was characterized in terms of antecedents, transactions, and outcomes. The 800 students selected for the program were high achievers from secondary schools in the Minneapolis School District and likely to be highly motivated to excel in an elite summer program.

The intended transactions between students and teachers revolved around "problem-centered courses which encourage thought, inquiry and creativity" (Stake & Gjerde, 1977, p. 207). Intended outcomes focused on students becoming increasingly willing and able to share ideas with peers and thus increasing personal awareness of themselves and others. There was little emphasis on the acquisition of knowledge and skills. Stake and Gjerde used various techniques for collecting data, including questionnaires given to students during the final week of the program, teacher interviews and questionnaires, and informal classroom observations. Although these techniques yielded little data on antecedents, they yielded ample data on student-teacher interactions:

> The quality of the learning also was high. The students were tuned in. They were busy. They responded to the moves of their teachers. They improvised, they carried ideas and arguments, indignations and admirations to the volleyball court, to the Commons, to the shade of campus elms and Cannon River Oaks. (Stake & Gjerde, 1977, p. 272)

To identify standards appropriate for making judgments about T-City, Stake and Gjerde sought out the views of curriculum specialists and teachers. They concluded that T-City's emphasis on humanization, personal awareness, and problem solving were relative standards worthy of attainment. Data about the perspectives of students, teachers, and outside observers indicated that there were logical contingencies between the plans (antecedents) of teachers and their practices. The evaluators were also convinced that there was a high degree of congruence between the explicit intents of the program and what actually took place. Stake and Gjerde's (1977) judgments of T-City were highly positive:

> T-City 71 has succeeded. It is even a best buy. It satisfies a social obligation to specially educate some of those who will lead—in the arts, in business, in government, in life. The teachers of T-City 71 have blended a summer of caring, caprice, openness and intellectual struggle to give potential leaders a summer of challenge. (p. 272)

Although these judgments are stated in terms of the general objectives of the project having been reached, they are based primarily on Stake and Gjerde's comprehensive analysis of the internal coherence of the project as defined by the countenance model and their observations of many concrete specifics of the project in action. The T-City evaluation thus demonstrates both the utility and the flexibility of the countenance model and points in the direction of the still more flexible responsive model Stake was then in the process of developing.

Illuminative Model

The development of the illuminative model by Parlett and Hamilton (1972) represents a still more dramatic loosening of the hold of Tyler's objectives model on curriculum evaluators. The illuminative model makes ample use of informal, observational means of collecting data and is perhaps the best-known example of the nonconventional approaches to evaluation that emerged in the 1970s. Stake's countenance model of the 1960s had already broadened the concept of curriculum evaluation by including consideration of interactions between teachers and students and of the social context in which the curriculum to be evaluated existed, even though it did not break sharply from Tyler's ideas about objectives. The illuminative model, however, like other nonconventional approaches then emerging, broadened the concept of evaluation much further, sufficiently so that it represented a direct confrontation with the traditional approach of Tyler.

Proponents of the new approaches were extremely critical of the traditional approach. Parlett and Hamilton (1972, p. 2), for example, called it "the agricultural-botany paradigm whereby the effectiveness of an innovation was evaluated in terms of whether it had reached required standards on pre-specified criteria, like seeds in specially controlled seed beds." Hamilton, Jenkins, King, MacDonald, and Parlett (1977) noted that conventional approaches had followed the experimental and psychometric traditions dominant in educational research, and the unfulfilled aim of these traditions of achieving fully objective methods had led to studies that were artificial and restricted in scope. In contrast, the new, nonconventional approaches of the 1970s used methods derived from such fields as social anthropology, psychiatry, and ethnography.

They differed from the traditional approach to curriculum evaluation by focusing on how the curriculum actually worked in action, rather than on its objectives only; by adapting methods to suit specific situations, rather than being bound by experimental or preordinate designs; and by providing ideas and information to all participants in the curriculum, rather than to remote decision makers only. Hamilton et al. (1977) summed up these new approaches as collectively being "more naturalistic and more adaptable. . . . [They] endorse empirical methods which incorporate ethnographic fieldwork, to develop feedback materials which are couched in the natural language of the recipients, and to shift the locale of formal judgment from the evaluator to the participants" (p. 339).

The illuminative model clearly involved some new assumptions, concepts, and methodologies. Parlett and Hamilton (1972) singled out two concepts for special attention: the instructional system and the learning milieu. In their opinion, the formalized plans that make up an instructional system should not be the source from which an evaluator extracts goals or objectives. Because each educational situation and the context in which it exists are unique, it is neither desirable nor even possible to evaluate as if each concrete situation should be an abstract ideal. A curriculum is never implemented exactly as planned; hence, it is essential to examine the learning milieu itself. They argue that the learning milieu represents a complicated pattern of interactions between teachers and students and that the evaluator must examine this pattern closely to understand what the curriculum really is. An evaluator's primary task is to search out the particular configuration of each learning milieu by identifying such things as the constraints that exist within it, its pervasive operating assumptions, and the practices, perspectives, and preoccupations of teachers and students. Parlett and Hamilton stress that

> Illuminative evaluation is not a standard methodological package, but a general research strategy. It aims to be both adaptable and eclectic. The choice of research tactics follows not from research doctrine, but from decisions in each case as to the best available techniques: the problem defines the methods used, not "vice versa." (p. 8)

Figure 8.16 depicts the three overlapping stages of the illuminative model. The first stage is designated "observing." In it, evaluators take on the role of social anthropologists and observe the complex learning milieu. No attempt is made to control or manipulate this milieu. Rather, the task is to make meaning out of the complex interactions that take place there and to build up a continuous record of the major patterns of practices and activities. At this stage, evaluators depend chiefly on observations, but to corroborate their findings they may also interview teachers and students. The second stage is designated "inquiring." In it, evaluators focus

	Observing	Methods
Stage 1	**Observing** Familiarization with day-to-day reality of the setting: to build up a continuous record of ongoing events, transactions, and informal remarks and to isolate significant features	**Methods** Social anthropological. Major use of observation in classrooms and interviewing teachers and students. Also use of primary sources such as committee minutes. The attempt is to use unstructured methods to unravel patterns and relationships.
Stage 2	**Inquiring** Selection of a number of occurrences for more sustained and intensive inquiry	**Methods** Observations directed toward specific activities. Interviews with teachers and students and more focused. Use of survey-type questionnaires and attitude tests.
Stage 3	**Seeking general principles** Placing of individual findings within a broader explanatory context. Seeking cause-and-effect patterns	**Methods** Continued use of observations, interviews, and questionnaires.

FIGURE 8.16
Parlett and Hamilton's model of evaluation
Source: After Parlett & Hamilton (1972).

more precisely on the specifics that seem to be of greatest importance within the milieu. The questioning of teachers and students becomes narrower and data from earlier observations are reexamined to identify particular influences. Questionnaires and surveys might be used to derive specific information about the attitudes and opinions of teachers. The third stage is designated "seeking general principles." In it, evaluators should at last be able to discern patterns of causes and effects and be able to derive some general statements explaining how well the curriculum is working out in practice. Doing so usually requires sifting through data to find corroborating evidence from several sources (triangulation), and it may be necessary to seek new data in order to explain gaps in the total pattern.

Parlett and Hamilton stress that these stages overlap as the evaluators' focus becomes more precise. There are vast amounts of data, but gradually what is most important emerges and evaluators are able to understand and to explain the major patterns of influence working within a particular milieu. Throughout these stages, specific data derived directly from within the entire milieu gradually illuminate evaluators' understanding of the curriculum, and it then becomes their duty to similarly illuminate the understandings of other persons.

The illuminative model completely overturns the idea promulgated by the objectives model that evaluation can be done only in terms of the fit (or lack thereof) between prespecified objectives and what actually happens (Norris, 1990). It also represents an advance over the countenance model in encouraging the collection of a wider variety of data and their use in a wider variety of ways. Nonetheless, its use is not without problems. Parlett and Hamilton (1972) acknowledged that without careful cross-checking of findings, the approach can become completely subjective. Furthermore, evaluators using this model must be highly competent in many ways. For instance, they need good interpersonal skills, since unobtrusively obtaining many kinds of information from teachers and students requires considerable tact and diplomacy. Critics of the illuminative model also have raised cautions about the subjectivity of qualitative data. Parsons (1976) and Norris (1990) note that the methods of social anthropology should be used with great care. Scientists working in social anthropology adopt rigorous standards, and the same levels of rigor may apply to curriculum evaluation.

■ CASE STUDY

The Humanities Curriculum Project

The Humanities Curriculum Project (HCP) was conducted in the United Kingdom from 1967 to 1972. It was designed to help adolescents of average and below-average ability develop their understanding of social situations and the controversial value issues that human actions raise. Among the premises on which HCP was based were that class sessions should be open discussions of controversial issues and that such discussions should protect the divergent views of participants rather than attempt to achieve consensus. Barry MacDonald was commissioned in 1968 to evaluate HCP.

According to Stenhouse (1975), the holistic approach to evaluation that MacDonald took was very similar to—and perhaps helped shape—the illuminative model then being developed by Parlett and Hamilton.

In a later reflection on HCP, MacDonald (1978) makes clear his ideas about the role of the evaluator. He maintains that evaluators must understand before attempting to quantify, and in the case of HCP "one must appreciate the complexity of HCP's impact in the trial schools. . . . [T]he situation is so complex that it's incumbent upon evaluators to move up closer . . . to the phenomena of the teacher's world . . . and to the phenomena of the pupil's world also" (p. 24). In more recent reflections on HCP, MacDonald (1995) concludes, "It is also hardly surprising that such close up studies of social action . . . should lead to the establishment of participant rights on a scale not previously contemplated by the research community" (p. 48).

From 1968 to 1972, materials used in HCP were tried out in thirty-six schools. MacDonald soon found that it was not feasible to study all schools and settled for an in-depth study of eight representative schools. Staffs at these schools were encouraged to be "experimental colleagues" (Aston, 1980), meaning that the evaluation team and the teachers jointly explored issues and developed approaches to teaching HCP. MacDonald and his team spent much of their time observing classrooms and talking with teachers and students, much as stage 1 of the illuminative model (see Figure 8.16) indicates. While some schools welcomed the team's presence, others objected to the desire of the team to "question pupils freely about their experience both of the school and of HCP without obligation to report the content of such interviews back to the school" (MacDonald, 1978). In addition to observations and conversations, the team also collected data from questionnaires, interviews, reading comprehension tests, personality scales, projective scales, motivation-attitude scales, and self-concept tests (Verma, 1980).

The evaluation team was able to use data from all these sources to gradually identify major patterns within HCP. For example, the team was able to establish that HCP was being implemented successfully in a variety of schools, but only when the social context was favorable. The team then provided specific advice about the social context to decision-making groups involved with HCP (examination boards, the funding agency, local education authorities, and schools themselves). MacDonald (1978) emphasized the uniqueness of individual schools and their ways of implementing HCP, especially emphasizing that decision makers should avoid common prescriptions for implementation in all schools. He noted that the impact of HCP in each school "is not a set of discrete effects but an organically related pattern of acts and consequences" (p. 34).

MacDonald's evaluation of HCP indicated that curriculum evaluation could illuminate the complexity of individual schools and yet develop some general understandings about basic patterns of practice among them and the specific beliefs on which practice was based. The evaluation of HCP did, in effect, demonstrate the workability of the illuminative model even before Parlett and Hamilton introduced it under that name.

Educational Connoisseurship Model

Eisner introduced his educational connoisseurship model in several papers in the 1970s (Eisner, 1975, 1976, 1977). Although its basics have remained the same, he has continued to refine and elaborate it, especially in later books (Eisner, 1979, 1985, 1991). It bears some similarity to the illuminative model, especially in that both permit evaluators to become participants within the situation (or participants to become evaluators), doing precisely what Ross and Cronbach (1976) suggested in their statement: "It is of little use if the evaluator just runs alongside the train and makes notes through the windows. He/she must board the train and influence (interact) with the engineer, the conductor and the passengers" (p. 25). Nonetheless, the educational connoisseurship model represents a significant step beyond the illuminative model in abandoning explanations in terms of cause-and-effect relationships. In doing so, it became the first model of educational evaluation to deal fully with issues of objectivity versus subjectivity, and its importance in clarifying these issues and in opening up new modes of evaluation is difficult to overstate. Influential when introduced, the educational connoisseurship model has grown more so in the 1990s and the 2000s, and its principles underlie trends in the evaluation of students such as authentic assessment and portfolio evaluation (discussed above; see also, Eisner, 1993).

The educational connoisseurship model grew out of Eisner's background in art and art criticism. Other writers have argued that a curriculum can be considered as a work of art and that aesthetic criticism can be used to capture some of the ineffable and particular qualities that a curriculum presents to each participant (Vallance, 1977). Eisner (1979) took this argument further in suggesting, "The sources of knowledge are at least as diverse as the range of information provided by the senses. Each of the senses provides a unique content that is not replicable by other sense modalities" (p. 176). Perhaps the greatest power of Eisner's model is that it makes this way of apprehending reality available to evaluators. In a paper comparing scientific and artistic approaches, Eisner (1980) made his views quite clear: "What artistic approaches seek is to exploit the power of form to inform. . . . In short, form is regarded as a part of the content of what is expressed and bears significantly on the kinds of meanings people are likely to secure from the work" (p. 3).

The model is based on the closely related ideas of educational connoisseurship and educational criticism, as briefly outlined in Figure 8.17. Connoisseurship is the art of appreciation, especially the ability to make fine discriminations between different qualities. An educational connoisseur is, therefore, a person particularly adept at discerning and judging what goes on in classrooms. Criticism is the art of disclosure, especially the ability to make clear the reasons for judgments. An educational critic is, therefore, a person particularly adept at explaining the quality of what goes on in classrooms.

Educational connoisseurship requires that an evaluator knows how to look, to see, and to appreciate (Eisner, 1979). There are three basic questions that an evaluator must address. The first question is, What do I see in this classroom? The evaluator needs to develop an intimate appreciation of the particular classroom and at

Educational connoisseurship	Educational criticism
Private: Art of appreciation	Public: Art of disclosure
What do I see in this classroom?	Description
What reflections can I make about what I have experienced?	Interpretation and appraisal by the use of
How can I render my reflections to others?	metaphor and simile
	theme

FIGURE 8.17
Eisner's educational connoisseurship model
Source: After Eisner (1979).

the same time to compare it with others. The evaluator's first entrance into the classroom is important because it is at this time that what is unique is likely to become evident and comparisons with other classrooms readily come to mind. Once the evaluator has become familiar with the classroom (perhaps by observing teacher and students, by talking with them, by examining their work, or in many other ways), the second question must be pondered: What reflections can I make about what I have experienced? At this stage, the evaluator needs to think about the particular qualities of the classroom that seemed to be most noteworthy. McCutcheon (1979) describes the essence of this stage as "to puzzle over what was encountered and to engage in a dynamic reverie about the classroom. This phase—reflection—is particularly important, for during this phase points of focus for the criticism are developed and interpretations are formed" (p. 8). The third question, How can I render my reflections to others? involves evaluators thinking about how they can re-create in words the various qualities and meanings that they have encountered in the classroom. Doing so may seem difficult, for the evaluator must somehow engage other people in what the evaluator has personally encountered. Considering how this can best be done leads directly into educational criticism.

Eisner (1979) defines educational criticism as "the art of disclosing the qualities of events or objects that connoisseurship perceives." It consists of three interrelated processes: description, interpretation, and appraisal. *Description* is usually written. It is the characterizing of the classroom in ways that help readers approximate the same perceptions that the evaluator experienced there. *Interpretation* is the attributing of meanings to the classroom and the specifics within it. (This part of Eisner's model is both a forerunner of and an example of what is now often referred to as constructivist research or simply deconstructionism, basically research that moves beyond accepting facts as givens to consider how meaning is formed within the contexts of problematical situations.) Appraisal is the judging of the quality of what led to the evaluator's experience. In appraising, evaluators ordinarily attempt to answer the two key questions about the worth and merit of what transpires in classrooms: Was it worth doing? and, Was it done well?

Educational critics may use figurative language, such as metaphor and simile, to enhance their descriptions, since metaphorical language can heighten vividness and concreteness and thus help readers experience what the critic has perceived. A description of a third-grade classroom by Donmoyer (1980) illustrates the use of metaphorical language:

> Throughout the room books and papers form unplanned collages on desk tops and shelves. In the back of the room, partially hidden from view by a permanent room divider, large sheets of insulation fall haphazardly against the wall. Nearby commercially prepared ecological activity cards spill out of their package onto countertop and floor, while large cardboard boxes covered with dog-eared black construction paper and white construction paper stripes lay exhausted atop one another like victims of a knockdown, drag-out bar room brawl. (p. 14)

Still another way in which evaluators may increase the effectiveness of their descriptions is by identifying pervasive themes within the classroom. A theme is an important or repeated activity or idea that captures the essence of what is going on. Identifying themes may not only provide focus, but also give a piece of educational criticism a sense of unity.

Initially, the educational connoisseurship model struck many researchers and evaluators as lacking the objectivity and rigor of scientific approaches. However, Eisner has explained not only how subjective techniques uncover salient qualities of situations that may be missed altogether by researchers who attempt to objectify the classroom, but also how subjectivity has equally appropriate standards of rigor. Eisner (1979) points out that instead of talking about validity and reliability, the educational critic can talk of structural corroboration and referential adequacy. *Structural corroboration* is how observations can be used collectively to verify their truth or falsity. Essentially it is a process of triangulation in which different observations (possibly taken at different times by different observers holding different assumptions and using different techniques) are compared in terms of their consistency or inconsistency. *Referential adequacy* is how fitting observations are (and the descriptions, interpretations, and appraisals based on them). If a piece of educational criticism enables readers to experience a classroom in new, more adequate ways, then it represents a more accurate view of that classroom than did previous views, regardless of whether they were based on data obtained objectively or subjectively. For instance, any educational criticism contains cues that enable readers to arrive at new insights. If the total experience is such that readers are able to form a more comprehensive view of what the critic has observed, then the criticism has been more fitting (in the sense of referring more adequately) than any previous basis for the readers' views has been.

Eisner also points out that the trustworthiness of a piece of criticism may depend on the amount of time a critic has spent observing. First observations may be accurate and complete, but ordinarily even connoisseurs are able to perceive more fully and more precisely when given ample time. Eisner argues that educational evaluation studies do not typically provide enough time for evaluators to observe carefully.

The educational connoisseurship model represents a major break from all other models that were widely used for curriculum evaluations in the 1970s. Although the countenance model and the illuminative model were then known, the predominate influence on both large-scale and small-scale curriculum evaluations was, of course, Tyler's objectives model. Although Tyler had pushed curriculum evaluation considerably beyond the use of paper-and-pencil tests of students' academic achievement only, Tyler's model was itself premised on the rationality of science and objectivity. Therefore, in considering the significance of the educational connoisseurship model, Guba and Lincoln (1981) concluded that it "demonstrates that the scientific paradigm is not essential to the development of a powerful and useful evaluation approach. . . . Further, the model provides a fresh new perspective about how to make evaluations . . ." (p. 22). And Vallance (1983) regarded the model as one that "can help us to see the qualities and value of the lived-in experience offered by the curriculum, much as the art critic attempts to help us see the experience offered by the work of art" (p. 24). Thus, the model is able to focus powerfully on what actually happens in specific classrooms as a planned curriculum is transformed into an enacted curriculum and then as it is experienced by students and teachers alike.

Nonetheless, the model cannot be used casually. On one hand, all observations of a classroom are not equal, nor are all opinions. On the other hand, there are no definite credentials nor any specific training required for the educational connoisseur-critic. Experience is obviously helpful, but in many modern societies, most adults have had years of experience in classrooms and their children are engaged in obtaining that experience firsthand. Everyone in a particular school or community may be at least potentially a connoisseur-critic, but everybody is not necessarily a good one. Although similar problems arise in many other fields of human endeavor, criteria for deciding on whom to listen to and why remain unusually nebulous in education. Related problems also arise. For example, a piece of criticism may brilliantly express certain specific and nearly ineffable qualities of a classroom yet remain incomplete and misleading because it ignores something obvious about the backgrounds of students or teachers or the political context of the school. Or the connoisseur-critic's words describing a classroom may communicate effectively with most readers yet remain inaccessible to the children who are the students in that classroom.

In reality, many criteria apply to decisions about the appropriateness and fittingness of a piece of educational criticism. On this matter, Donmoyer (1990) suggests that structural corroboration and referential adequacy are not sufficient criteria in themselves and that verification-as-persuasion (whereby evaluators adjust their criticisms to the perspectives and purposes of their readers) should also be considered. The use of Eisner's educational connoisseurship model, therefore, does not lead to particular steps or methodology nor to any particular form for resulting evaluations. This kind of flexibility may seem troubling to some evaluators yet exhilarating to others.

■ CASE STUDY

The City Building Basic Skills Curriculum

Numerous case studies based on the educational connoisseurship model now exist, many of considerable breadth, sophistication, and utility. However, at the time Eisner introduced the model and in the years immediately following, there were few examples of educational criticism (Barone, 1979; McCutcheon, 1979; Vallance, 1975, 1977; Willis, 1978). The case study reported by Donmoyer (1980), which appears here in abbreviated form, is an early example of the use of the educational connoisseurship model in a curriculum evaluation. Donmoyer and a colleague undertook a qualitative evaluation of "The City Building Basic Skills Curriculum," an activity-based, elementary school program being implemented in a California school district. In this curriculum, students constructed a city of the future. Five teachers agreed to teach the curriculum after a brief in-service training program.

Each evaluator spent a short but concentrated period of time observing the five teachers in their classrooms. Evaluators also undertook an extensive analysis of the curriculum guide and related documentary materials. They then wrote criticisms of individual classrooms based on all these data. The criticisms were addressed to the five teachers and to the administrators of their school. The intent was to provide formative evaluation data to assist the teachers in implementing the curriculum and to help the administrators decide whether the curriculum should be continued in subsequent years. In these criticisms, the evaluators attempted to portray the salient features of each classroom. They used metaphors extensively to capture the idiosyncratic qualities of the teachers. As an example:

> Energizing the activities of all the groups and particularly the activities of the planning commission is the electric personality of the teacher, Mr. Diemo. With his wire-rim glasses, his dark blue corduroy pants, and a blue and white gingham shirt that could easily feel at home on the cover of a John Denver album, Mr. Diemo . . . projects a contemporary image. . . . Mr. Diemo is a consummate theatrical performer. His voice sings with a velvet intensity; his movements seem almost dance-like. Even when standing still, talking to students about their various activities, his hips mirror the emotion of his voice, springing or sliding or oozing from side to side, as though under the influence of Bob Fosse's choreography. His arms and shoulders move, too, often in broad, intense, expressively flowing gestures not unlike the gestures of a French cabaret singer. (Donmoyer, 1980, p. 14)

These pieces of educational criticism were generally well received by the teachers and the administrators. Administrators commented favorably on the accuracy of the descriptions, and most of the teachers were receptive to the comments made about them. Some teachers expressed reservations, however. For instance, they raised the issue of whether evaluators had spent sufficient time in discussions with them. The evaluators agreed that time had not been sufficient for them fully to build up mutual trust and respect with the five teachers. Some of the teachers were troubled by the evaluators' use of metaphorical language, especially when it focused on such personal matters as their appearance and lifestyles. The evaluators themselves had similar reservations, but they thought that as long as ethical standards about disclosure of reports were maintained, the metaphorical language helped the teachers to see new perspectives and to come to new realizations about the curriculum.

In reflecting on the evaluators' roles in this project as educational connoisseurs and critics, Donmoyer (1980) concluded that the use of the educational connoisseurship model had helped the five teachers and the administrators to step outside themselves and to view through the eyes of other human beings how the teachers personalized the curriculum. The evaluation uncovered no definitely right or wrong ways to do this, but it was deemed successful in helping everyone understand the complexity of what was going on. In that way, especially, it seemed likely to help the teachers improve their practices in the future, and Donmoyer suggested that ample time be included in future projects for teachers and evaluators to give each other feedback and support.

8.8 CONCLUDING COMMENT

Curriculum evaluation and student assessment are an integral part of beneficial curriculum change, whether undertaken informally or formally. Curriculum evaluation can serve many purposes and be done in many different ways. Some forms of evaluation (such as Tyler's objectives model) deal only with the planned curriculum, other forms with broader focus (such as Stake's countenance model and Parlett and Hamilton's illuminative model) also consider the enacted curriculum, and still other forms with the broadest focus (such as Eisner's educational connoisseurship model) include the experienced curriculum. Decisions about the purposes and forms of curriculum evaluation to be used in any school should be made consistently with the specific circumstances that exist within that school and the social context within which the school itself exists. This chapter has presented alternative ideas and forms of curriculum evaluation and student assessment that decision makers can choose among. Making such decisions as soundly as possible requires a carefully thought-out general theory of curriculum that includes understanding of curriculum planning, development, and evaluation and how they are intertwined.

■ QUESTIONS AND REFLECTIONS

1. One of Dewey's ideas on which progressive education is based is that the curriculum is found within the experience of the individual. Consider what teachers must then look for in evaluating the experience of their students. What techniques seem most appropriate for this kind of evaluation?

2. If you are a teacher, how often do you informally evaluate your own teaching (including how you enact curricula)? How often do you do so formally? How often does your school do so? What pressures and tensions are you under because of these three kinds of evaluation?

3. Select four or five techniques of student assessment that you have used in your classroom. Write a short critique of the strengths and weaknesses that you have found in each, especially considering the degree of compatibility or incompatibility of each technique with the principles of authentic assessment.

4. According to Madaus (1989), high-stakes tests are those in which results are directly linked to important rewards or sanctions, therefore powerfully influencing how teachers teach and how students learn. Carefully consider the long-term effects of high-stakes testing on curriculum evaluation and student assessment, developing your own point of view.

5. "Evaluating student achievement plays an unavoidable major role in teaching: How do you manage to incorporate sound evaluation and assessment practices into an already overloaded schedule of complex teaching responsibilities?" (Cangelosi, 1990, p. 215). Discuss.

6. With reference to a specific group of students, reflect upon the assessment techniques you typically use. Why do you use these? Which others might you use in the future? Which ones would you not use? Give reasons.

7. What are the advantages of portfolios over checklists and rating scales? Under what circumstances would portfolios be especially valuable for learners?

8. "Assessments should reflect on tasks students will encounter in the world outside schools and not merely those limited to the schools themselves" (Eisner, 1993, p. 226). How might this be done? Give details of techniques you would use to achieve this end.

9. Consider a recent round of informal curriculum evaluation at a school with which you are familiar. What techniques and models of evaluation were used? Were these particularly suited or unsuited to the specific circumstances of the school in question? What seemed to be the most positive result of this evaluation? What seemed to be its most negative result?

10. How has this chapter changed your own general theory of curriculum that you have been developing while reading this book?

■ SUGGESTED READING

Some influential articles on curriculum evaluation (see the chapter bibliography) include the following:

Donmoyer (1990)

Eisner (1993)

Herman & Winters (1994)

Linn et al. (1991)

Mortimore (1992)

Wiggins (1992)

Important books on curriculum evaluation (see the chapter bibliography) include the following:

Eisner (1979, 1985, 1991)

Hamilton et al. (1977).

Harris & Bell (1990)

House (1986)

Marzano et al. (1993)

Norris (1990)

▮ BIBLIOGRAPHY

Andrade, H. G. (2000). Using rubrics to promote thinking and learning. *Educational Leadership, 57*(5), 13–18.

Aston, A. (1980). The Humanities Curriculum Project. In L. Stenhouse (Ed.), *Curriculum research and development in action.* London: Heinemann.

Azzara, J. R. (2001). The heart of school leadership. *Educational Leadership, 58*(4), 62–68.

Barone, T. (1979). Of Scott and Lisa and other friends. In E. W. Eisner, *The educational imagination.* New York: Macmillan.

Blackmore, J. (1988). *Assessment and accountability.* Geelong, Australia: Deakin University Press.

Blubaugh, D. (1999). Bringing cable into the classroom. *Educational Leadership, 56*(5), 61–65.

Broadfoot, P. (1979). *Assessment, schools and society.* London: Methuen.

Broadfoot, P. (1996). *Education, assessment, and society.* Bristol, UK: Open University Press.

Brookhart, S., & De Voge, J. G. (1998). *Testing a theory about the role of classroom assessment in student motivation and achievement.* Paper presented at the annual meeting of the American Educational Research Association, San Diego.

Brooks, J. G., & Brooks, M. G. (1993). *The case for constructivist classrooms.* Alexandria, VA: Association for Supervision and Curriculum Development.

Cangelosi, J. S. (1990). *Designing tests for evaluating student achievement.* New York: Longman.

Cangelosi, J. S. (1991). *Evaluating classroom instruction.* New York: Longman.

Cangelosi, J. S. (1992). *Systematic teaching strategies.* Melbourne: Longman.

Carr, J. F., & Harris, D. E. (2001). *Succeeding with standards.* Albany: State University of New York Press.

Case, S. H. (1994). Will mandating portfolios undermine their value? *Educational Leadership, 52*(2), 46–47.

Clarke, M. M., Madaus, G. F., Horn, C., & Ramos, M. A. (2000). Retrospective on educational testing and assessment in the twentieth century. *Journal of Curriculum Studies, 32*(2), 159–182.

Cunningham, G. K. (1998). *Assessment in the classroom.* London: Falmer.

Darling-Hammond, L., Ancess, J., & Falk, B. (1995). *Authentic assessment in action.* New York: Teachers College Press.

Darling-Hammond, L., & Falk, B. (1997). Using standards and assessments to support student learning. *Phi Delta Kappan, 79*(3), 190–199.

Donmoyer, R. (1980). The evaluator as artist. *Journal of Curriculum Theorizing, 2*(2), 12–26.

Donmoyer, R. (1990). Curriculum evaluation and the negotiation of meaning. *Language Arts, 67*(3), 274–286.

Donmoyer, R. (1996). A focus on educational reform and the role of research in the reform process. *Educational Researcher, 25*(7), 4–5.

Eisner, E. W. (1975). *Applying educational connoisseurship and criticism to educational settings.* Unpublished paper, Stanford University.

Eisner, E. W. (1976). Educational connoisseurship and educational criticism: Their forms and functions in educational evaluation. *Journal of Aesthetic Education, 10*(3–4), 135–150.

Eisner, E. W. (1977). On the use of educational connoisseurship and criticism for evaluating classroom life. *Teachers College Record, 78,* 345–358.

Eisner, E. W. (1979). *The educational imagination.* New York: Macmillan.

Eisner, E. W. (1980). *On the differences between scientific and artistic approaches to qualitative research.* Paper presented at the annual meeting of the American Educational Research Association, Boston.

Eisner, E. W. (1985). *The educational imagination* (2nd ed.). New York: Macmillan.

Eisner, E. W. (1991). *The enlightened eye.* New York: Macmillan.

Eisner, E. W. (1993). Reshaping assessment in education: Some criteria in search of practice. *Journal of Curriculum Studies, 25*(3), 219–234.

Eisner, E. W. (1997). The promise and perils of alternative forms of data representation. *Educational Researcher, 26*(6), 4–9.

Eisner, E. W. (1999). The uses and limits of performance assessment. *Phi Delta Kappan, 80*(9), 658–661.

Eisner, E. W. (2000). Those who ignore the past. . .: 12 "easy" lessons for the next millennium. *Journal of Curriculum Studies, 32*(2), 343–357.

Filer, A. (1993). Context of assessment in a primary classroom. *British Educational Research Journal, 19*(1), 95–107.

Filer, A. (Ed.). (2000). *Assessment: Social practice and social product.* London: Routledge/Falmer.

Fraser, B. J. (1983). *An historical look at curriculum evaluation.* Paper presented at the annual meeting of the Society for the Study of Curriculum History, Montreal.

Gipps, C. V. (1996). *Quality assurance in teachers' assessment.* Paper presented at the annual conference of the British Educational Research Association, London.

Gipps, C., McCallum, B., & Hargeaves, E. (2000). *Classroom assessment and feedback strategies of "expert" elementary teachers.* Paper presented at the annual meeting of the American Educational Research Association, New Orleans.

Gipps, C., & Murphy, P. (1994). *A fair test?: Assessment, achievement, and equity.* Buckingham, UK: Open University Press.

Guba, E. G., & Lincoln, Y. S. (1981). *Effective evaluation.* San Francisco: Jossey-Bass.

Hamilton, D., Jenkins, D., King, C., MacDonald, B., & Parlett, M. (Eds.). (1977). *Beyond the numbers game.* London: Macmillan.

Haney, W., & Madaus, G. (1989). Searching for alternatives to standardized tests: Whys, whats, and withers. *Phi Delta Kappan, 70*(9), 683–687.

Hargreaves, A., Earl, L., Moore, S., & Manning, S. (2001). *Learning to change.* San Francisco: Jossey-Bass.

Harnisch, D. L., & Mabry, L. (1993). Issues in the development and evaluation of alternative assessments. *Journal of Curriculum Studies, 25*(2), 179–187.

Harrington-Lueker, D. (1991). Beyond multiple choice: The push to assess performance. *Executive Educator, 13*(4), 20–32.

Harris, D., & Bell, C. (1990). *Evaluating and assessing for learning.* London: Kogan Page.

Hebert, E. A. (1998). Lessons learned about student portfolios. *Phi Delta Kappan, 79*(8), 583–585.

Herman, J. L., & Winters, L. (1994). Portfolio research: A slim collection. *Educational Leadership, 52*(2) 48–55.

House, E. R. (1980) *Evaluating with validity.* Beverly Hills: Sage.

House, E. R. (Ed.). (1986). *New directions in educational evaluation.* Lewes, England: Falmer.

Hughes, P., Russell, N., & McConachy, D. (1979). *A guide to evaluation.* Canberra: Curriculum Development Corporation.

Jenkins, J. A. (1994). *Statewide assessment: Alternative approaches and alternative needs.* Paper presented at the annual meeting of the American Educational Research Association, New Orleans.

Kemmis, S. (1982). Seven principles for program evaluation in curriculum development and innovation. *Journal of Curriculum Studies, 14*(3), 221–240.

Lifter, M., & Adams, M. E. (1997). *Integrating technology into the curriculum.* Melbourne: Hawker Brownlow.

Linn, R. L. (1993). Educational assessment: Expanded expectations and challenges. *Educational Evaluation and Policy Analysis, 15*(1), 1–16.

Linn, R. L., Baker, E. L., & Dunbar, S. B. (1991). Complex, performance-based assessment: Expectations and validation criteria. *Educational Researcher, 20*(8), 15–21.

Longstreet, W. S., & Shane, H. G. (1993). *Curriculum for a new millenium.* Boston: Allyn & Bacon.

Lyons, N. (1999). How portfolios can shape emerging practice. *Educational Leadership, 56*(8), 35–38.

MacDonald, B. (1978). *The experience of curriculum innovation* (Occasional Publications No. 6). Norwich, UK: Centre for Applied Research in Education, University of East Anglia.

MacDonald, B. (1995). The evaluation of the Humanities Curriculum Project. *JCT, 10*(4), 43–49, 64–65.

Madaus, G. F. (1989). *The distortion of teaching and testing: High-stakes testing and instruction.* Unpublished paper, Boston College.

Marsh, C. J., & Stafford, K. (1988). *Curriculum: Practices and issues* (2nd ed.). Sydney: McGraw-Hill.

Marzano, R. J. (2000). *Transforming classroom grading.* Alexandria, VA: Association for Supervision and Curriculum Development.

Marzano, R. J., Pickering, D., & McTighe, J. (1993). *Assessing student outcomes.* Alexandria, VA: Association for Supervision and Curriculum Development.

McChesney, J., & Hertling, E. (2000). The path to comprehensive school reform. *Educational Leadership, 57*(7), 10–15.

McCutcheon, G. (1979). Educational criticism: Methods and application. *Journal of Curriculum Theorizing, 1*(2), 5–25.

McGaw, B. (1996). *Technical issues in assessments.* Paper presented at the annual meeting of the American Educational Research Association, New York.

McMillan, J. H., Workman, D., & Myran, S. (1999). *Elementary teachers' classroom assessment and grading practices.* Paper presented at the annual meeting of the American Educational Research Association, Montreal.

McTighe, J. (1997). What happens between assessments? *Educational Leadership, 54*(4), 6–13.

Means, R. (2001). Technology use in tomorrow's schools. *Educational Leadership, 58*(4), 57–61.

Mehrens, W. A. (1998). *Consequences of assessment: What is the evidence?* Paper presented at the annual meeting of the American Educational Research Association, San Diego.

Merwin, J. C., & Womer, F. B. (1974). Toward national assessment: History and results. In D. A. Payne (Ed.), *Curriculum evaluation.* Lexington, MA: Heath.

Meyerson, M. J. (1995). *Naturalistic assessment: Teachers' concerns and confidence.* Paper presented at the annual meeting of the American Educational Research Association, San Francisco.

Ministry of Education. (1994). *British Columbia performance assessment.* Victoria, BC: Author.

Mortimore, P. (1992). Quality control in education and schools. *British Journal of Educational Studies, 40*(1), 23–37.

Nevo, D. (1983). The conceptualization of educational evaluation: An analytical review of literature. *Review of Educational Research, 53*(1), 117–128.

Norris, N. (1990). *Understanding educational evaluation.* London: Kogan Page.

Orlich, D. C., Harder, R. L., Callahan, R. C., & Gibson, H. W. (1998). *Teaching strategies* (5th ed.). Boston: Houghton Mifflin.

Ornstein, A. C., & Hunkins, F. (1993). *Curriculum: Foundations, principles, and issues* (2nd ed.). Engelwood Cliffs, NJ: Prentice Hall.

Paris, S. G., & Ayres, L. R. (1994). *Becoming reflective students and teachers with portfolios and authentic assessment.* Washington, DC: American Psychological Association.

Parlett, M., & Hamilton, D. (1972). *Evaluation as illumination: A new approach to the study of innovatory programs* (Occasional Paper No. 9). Edinburgh: Centre for Research in the Educational Sciences, University of Edinburgh.

Parsons, C. (1976). The new evaluation: A cautionary note. *Journal of Curriculum Studies, 8*(2), 125–138.

Phillips, D. C. (1995). The good, the bad, and the ugly: The many faces of constructivism. *Educational Researcher, 24*(7), 5–12.

Pryor, J., & Torrance, H. (1996). Teacher-pupil interaction in formative assessment: Assessing the work or protecting the child? *Curriculum Journal, 7*(2), 205–226.

Resnick, L. B., & Klopfer, L. E. (Eds.). (1989). *Toward the thinking curriculum: Current cognitive research.* Alexandria, VA: Association for Supervision and Curriculum Development.

Rogers, G., & Badham, L. (1992). *Evaluation and schools.* London: Routledge.

Ross, E. W. (1996). The role of portfolio evaluation in social studies teacher education. *Social Education, 60*(3), 162–166.

Ross, L., & Cronbach, L. J. (1976). "Handbook of Evaluation Research": Essay review. *Educational Researcher, 5*(8), 9–19.

Rossi, P. H., & Freeman, H. E. (1993). *Evaluation: A systematic approach* (5th ed.). Newbury Park, CA: Sage.

Rubin, L. (1991). Educational evaluation: Classic works of Ralph W. Tyler. *Journal of Curriculum Studies, 23*(2), 193–198.

Sadler, R. (1989). Formative assessment and the design of instructional systems. *Instructional Science, 18,* 119–144.

Salvia, J., & Ysseldyke, J. E. (1998). *Assessment* (7th ed.). Boston: Houghton Mifflin.

Schwab, J. J. (1969). The practical: A language for curriculum. *School Review, 78,* 1–23.

Schwager, M. T., & Carlson, J. S. (1995). *Teacher perceptions in learning and assessment and their interrelationships.* Unpublished paper, University of California, Riverside.

Scriven, M. (1973). Pros and cons about goal-free evaluation. *Evaluation Comment, 3*(4), 1–4.

Scriven, M. (1983). Evaluation as a paradigm for educational research. *Australian Educational Research, 10*(3), 5–18.

Shane, H. G. (1980). Significant writings that have influenced the curriculum: 1906–81. *Phi Delta Kappan, 62*(5), 311–314.

Silver, H., Strong, R. W., & Perini, M. J. (2000). *So each may learn.* Alexandria, VA: Association for Supervision and Curriculum Development.

Simmons, W., & Resnick, L. (1993). Assessment as the catalyst of school reform. *Educational Leadership, 50*(5), 11–15.

Skilbeck, M. (1982). The role of evaluation in curriculum development at the school level. In N. Russell, P. Hughes, & D. McConachy (Eds.), *Curriculum evaluation: Selected readings.* Canberra: Curriculum Development Centre.

Sperling, D. H. (1994). Assessment and reporting: A natural pair. *Educational Leadership, 52*(2), 10–13.

Stake, R. E. (1967). The countenance of educational evaluation. *Teachers College Record, 68*(7), 523–540.

Stake, R. E. (Ed.). (1975). *Evaluating the arts in education: A responsive approach.* Columbus, OH: Merrill.

Stake, R.E., & Gjerde, C. (1977). An evaluation of T-city. In D. Hamilton, D. Jenkins, C. King, B. MacDonald, & M. Parlett (Eds.), *Beyond the numbers game.* London: Macmillan.

Stenhouse, L. (1975). *Introduction to curriculum research and development.* London: Heinemann.

Stufflebeam, D. L. (Chairman, Joint Committee on Standards for Educational Evaluation). (1981). *Standards for evaluations of educational programs, projects, and materials.* New York: McGraw-Hill.

Stufflebeam, D. L., Foley, W. J., Gephart, W. J., Guba, E. G., Hammond, R. L., Merriman, H. O., & Provus, M. M. (1971). *Educational evaluation and decision-making in education.* Itasca, IL: Peacock.

Supovitz, J. (1994). *Encouraging learning through portfolio assessment.* Paper presented at the annual meeting of the American Educational Research Association, New Orleans.

Torrance, H. (1993). Combining measurement-driven instruction with authentic assessment: Some initial observations of national assessment in England and Wales. *Educational Evaluation and Policy Analysis, 15*(1), 81–90.

Torrance, H., & Pryor, J. (1995). *Making sense of formative assessment: Investigating the integration of assessment with teaching and learning.* Paper presented at the annual meeting of the American Educational Research Association, San Francisco.

Torrance, H., & Pryor, J. (2000). *Developing formative assessment in the classroom.* Paper presented at the annual meeting of the American Educational Research Association, New Orleans.

Tyler, R. W. (1930). Measuring the ability to infer. *Educational Research Bulletin, 9*, 5–7.

Tyler, R. W. (1949). *Basic principles of curriculum and instruction.* Chicago: University of Chicago Press.

Vallance, E. (1975). *Aesthetic criticism and curriculum description.* Unpublished doctoral dissertation, Stanford University.

Vallance, E. (1977). The landscape of "The Great Plains Experience." *Curriculum Inquiry, 7*(2), 87–106.

Vallance, E. (1983). The critic's perspective: Some strengths and limitations of aesthetic criticism in education. *Curriculum Perspectives, 3*(2), 23–28.

Verma, G. K. (Ed.). (1980). *The impact of innovation* (Occasional Paper No. 19). Norwich, UK: Centre for Applied Research and Education, University of East Anglia.

Virginia Beach School District. (1984). *Evaluation plan for Virginia Beach School District, Virginia.* Virginia Beach: Virginia Beach School District.

von Glaserfield, T. (1995). *Radical constructivism: A way of knowing and learning.* London: Falmer.

Wiggins, G. (1989). A true test: Toward more authentic and equitable assessment. *Phi Delta Kappan, 70*(9), 703–713.

Wiggins, G. (1992). Creating tests worth taking. *Educational Leadership, 49*(8), 26–33.

Wiggins, G. (1998). *Educative assessment.* San Francisco: Jossey-Bass.

Wiggins, G., & McTighe, J. (1998). *Understanding by design.* Alexandria, VA: Association for Supervision and Curriculum Development.

Willis, G. (Ed.). (1978). *Qualitative evaluation: Concepts and cases in curriculum criticism.* Berkeley, CA: McCutchan.

Willis, G. (1998). The human problems and possibilities of curriculum evaluation. In L. E. Beyer & M. W. Apple (Eds.), *The curriculum: Problems, politics, and possibilities* (2nd ed., pp. 339–357). Albany: State University of New York Press.

Withers, G., & McCurry, D. (1990). Student participation in assessment in a cooperative climate. In B. Low & G. Withers (Eds.), *Developments in school and public assessment.* Melbourne: Australian Council for Educational Research.

Worthen, B. R., & Sanders, J. R. (1973). *Educational evaluation: Theory and practice.* Worthington, OH: Jones.

Wright, C. (1989). Black students-white teachers. In B. Troyna (Ed.), *Racial inequality in education.* London: Tavistock.

9

Politics and Curriculum Decision Making

◾ ABOUT THIS CHAPTER

When curriculum planning and implementation are done by more than one or two persons, disagreements almost inevitably arise over not only what the curriculum should be but how decision making itself should take place. Some disagreements are easily resolved, but others take on distinctly political tones. This chapter considers what happens when curriculum decision making becomes politicized. It describes some of the principal decision makers and influences on them, examining questions concerning who actually makes what decisions, when, and on what basis. The chapter places the recent trend toward centralized decision making in historical and social context and describes some implications of this trend for teachers.

◾ WHAT YOU SHOULD DO

1. Become familiar with the principal individuals and groups who participate in curriculum decision making.
2. Reflect on how these individuals and groups ordinarily influence decisions and whether their influence has a positive or negative impact on curricula.
3. Understand how the historical and social context for decisions influences the individuals and groups who make them.
4. Become familiar with the underlying conflicts concerning who initiates the curriculum, who sets curriculum priorities, who implements the curriculum, and who is responsible for what happens with the curriculum. Consider current development such as the growth of charter schools.
5. Identify and then carefully weigh the basic assumptions on which centralized and decentralized control of curricula are based.
6. Consider whether the trend toward centralized decision making has in fact led to the deprofessionalization of teachers as curriculum planners and implementers.

■ SOME OPTIONAL APPROACHES

Readers may find that any of the following options (among many other possible options) provides a useful perspective from which to consider this chapter.

Option A

1. Consider the control of curriculum in the United States in terms of shared responsibility at the local, state, and federal levels of government. Reflect on what actually is controlled at each level. Identify the major conflicts that occur among these levels of government. Use current developments such as charter school reform to illustrate your argument.
2. What are the reasons these conflicts occur? Are these conflicts endemic to the situation, or do they occur from time to time because of specifics of the situation?
3. Is there a long-term resolution for these conflicts—a paradigm for optimizing shared control of curriculum decision making? How would the powers and prerogatives of each level of government be modified within this paradigm?

Option B

1. Consider what role local educators (particularly teachers) should play in wide-scale curriculum planning and development. Should they or "experts" make most of the decisions?
2. Consider the evidence included in this chapter on the major influences of different decision makers. Does this evidence indicate that any particular decision makers will be more or less susceptible to influences that might lead to poor decisions?
3. Does the trend toward centralized decision making also lead toward the deprofessionalization of teachers? Carefully weigh the ideas and evidence presented in section 9.8.

Option C

1. Do recent historical and social trends in the United States lead toward a centralized national curriculum, toward strengthening traditionally decentralized curricula, or toward something else entirely? Is the growth of charter schools strengthening decentralization?
2. Consider possible future scenarios in the United States (or in any other country with which you are familiar) that might drastically change the kind or relative degrees of control that different curriculum decision makers now hold. Which scenarios would include the most beneficial changes? Which would include the least beneficial changes?
3. What is the most likely future scenario and its impact on the control of curricula? To what extent is charter school reform a current, viable change?

9.1 INTRODUCTION

The issues that surround curriculum planning and development are not just theoretical and practical but also political and social. As we have pointed out throughout this book, many approaches to curriculum theorizing and curriculum practice have been worked out during the last century as curriculum (as a field of systematic study and work) has moved from infancy toward maturity. In the future, still other approaches will surely emerge, but the basic problem for teachers and curriculum specialists then—as now—will remain the same: choosing appropriately among competing alternatives.

Thus far, we have presented readers with major theoretical and practical alternatives and attempted to provide some perspective on how sound choices can be made among them. However, such choices are seldom completely free choices. The problem is not simply one of *what* the choices are; issues arise about *how* the choices are made. Much depends not only on the expectations and beliefs of educators but on the expectations and beliefs of society at large. In this chapter, we examine the politics of making curriculum choices within the context of society and consider many of the individuals and groups influencing curriculum decision making and how they are influential, drawing examples from recent history. The social context, history, and examples we describe are from the United States, but the general ideas they illustrate may also be applied to other countries.

Political issues are inherent in the basic nature of curriculum decision making. Theoretically, a curriculum could be created by a single person, usually a teacher. Such a curriculum might be an ad hoc creation intended only for a single student on a single occasion. Ordinarily, however, curricula are intended for more than one student and for repeated use, and careful coordination becomes increasingly important as a curriculum extends beyond the purview of a single teacher to be shared across classrooms, schools, school districts, states, or an entire nation. Recent ideas about curriculum planning and development attempt to take into account the complexity that results when the people involved in making decisions about planning, implementing, evaluating, and changing a curriculum pursue these tasks jointly. Cooperation is necessary, but often frictions occur, no matter how well defined the roles of each participant seem to be. In reality, questions always arise about who should make what decisions, when, and on what basis. There is no one right answer for these questions, but different answers have different consequences, which may not be equally acceptable to participants in the process. By its very nature, therefore, curriculum planning and development is as much a political process as it is a theoretical or practical process.

Klein (1991) describes the situation this way:

> The question of who makes curriculum decisions is a fundamental and timeless issue which has received continuing discussion and debate throughout the history of the curriculum field. The answers to this question have changed over time and are certain to change in the future, given the increasing rate and complexity of change in the world. It is one of those fundamental questions which will always need to be

reconsidered as new social contexts, pressures, and knowledge come to bear upon it. The array of participants who are officially designated or who function through default to make curriculum decisions is complex enough, but the question centers around not only who makes them, but also what type of curriculum decision is under discussion. Thus, the question is very complex and multifaceted, but the complexity is not often recognized when debates about curriculum are held in public and educational forums and when operational answers are to be formulated. (p. 1)

How, then, do participants in curriculum planning and development actually participate in making decisions? And what are the implications, especially for teachers?

The politics of curriculum decision making is not a well-defined area within the general study of curriculum, and researchers have described what happens in different ways. Donmoyer (1990), for example, portrays participants as being involved in building coalitions with other self-interested actors, engaging in deliberation using practical reasoning, or using traditional operating procedures as a basis for resolving specific problems and conflicts. Similarly, Elmore and Sykes (1992) contend that participants either use rational means and goal-directed behavior to achieve mutually agreeable ends or else political bargaining occurs with actors advocating their own political interests. However, Lawton (1980) and Fullan (2000) both point to some of the least-desirable characteristics of the politics of curriculum decision making. Lawton suggests that control is the key concern of most participants. He contends that case studies reveal comparatively little partnership among participants and more emphasis on accountability as a means of dealing with their dissatisfaction and distrust. Fullan (1991) describes "negative politics—power most often used not to do things" (p. 582), which leads inevitably to resistance, self-protection, and avoidance.

Clearly, some people enter into curriculum deliberations openly and cooperatively, while those who see the process as largely hostile and competitive may participate primarily to protect their own interests (Smyth, Dow, Hattam, Reid, & Shacklock, 2000; Whitty, 2000). The best interests of students may be one motivation behind curriculum decisions, but it is seldom the only one.

9.2   DECISION MAKERS AND INFLUENCES ON THEM

In a formal sense, curriculum decision makers can be defined as those individuals or groups who, because of their professional status or positions of authority, wield influence and have some degree of power to determine courses of action to be followed in schools. Their influence on curricula is not casual or incidental. Teachers always make decisions about how curricula are enacted in their classrooms. Principals can and do make decisions that affect the planned and the enacted curricula in their schools. Superintendents often make decisions that affect the curricula in use in a number of schools and the activities of hundreds of teachers and students.

Although such decisions are part of their professional roles, teachers may themselves be influenced by their students, principals by parents, and superintendents by prominent members of the community. In general the influence of students, parents, and members of the community remains indirect, and such individuals or groups cannot be considered curriculum decision makers unless they have some kind of official status within the curriculum deliberations of a school or district, such as being voting members of a curriculum committee.

The Decision Makers

Figure 9.1 lists some individuals and groups ordinarily considered curriculum decision makers. Their decisions may range from creating highly detailed and individualized plans for specific classrooms to adopting externally created programs for use throughout a school district or an entire state.

At the school level, teachers and principals are mainly concerned with decisions that are directly related to day-to-day teaching. Teachers tend to focus on the curricula of their own classrooms and the classrooms of other teachers with whom they work most closely. Principals tend to be more concerned with coordination within curricula or across grade levels (Ornstein & Hunkins, 1993; Wildy, Louden, & Robertson, 2000). At the district level, superintendents are mainly concerned with decisions about general programs. Usually they work closely with their school boards or school committees (ordinarily not educational professionals but groups of citizens charged by law with making many administrative decisions for their districts).

Decision makers	Predominant Level of Involvement	Example of a Goal/Demand	Influence on Policies	Influence on Specific Curricula	Influence on Teaching Methods
Teachers	School	Daily physical education classes	Low	Medium	High
Principals	School	Sequential math and English curricula	High	Medium	Medium
Superintendents	District	Emphasis on specific skills	High	High	Medium
School boards	District	School improvement program	High	High	Medium
State heads of education	State	Programs for intellectually talented students	High	Low	Low

FIGURE 9.1
Curriculum decision makers

At the state (or sometimes even the federal) level, commissioners of education or officers of educational agencies make policy decisions about establishing or terminating total programs, such as programs for intellectually talented students.

Curriculum decision makers—teachers, principals, and administrators—do not operate in a vacuum since they are indirectly influenced by many other individuals and groups. This influence may be great and may arise in many ways, ranging from informal conversations to meetings with special interest organizations or to information passed on by the media. Sometimes influential individuals and groups may simply make their own views known in a general way. At other times, they may have a specific agenda, such as including certain kinds of topics within a curriculum or ensuring that a curriculum is taught from what they consider to be the proper point of view. Some groups may be satisfied if the language in which a curriculum is written includes key terms or slogans that they wish to promote. Others may wish to influence the processes or procedures under which decisions about the curriculum are made. Still others may wish to influence the content of the curriculum itself.

Groups that are concerned about language, procedures, and substance and that deliberately set out to promote their own agendas are commonly termed *pressure groups*. They have specific goals in mind and have devised appropriate methods to achieve these goals. Even when they do not have official status within curriculum deliberations, pressure groups often exert powerful influences on participants and on their decisions. (See, for example, Zahorchak and Boyd's [1994] account of different pressure groups debating outcomes-based education in Pennsylvania.)

Some Influential Groups

So many different groups influence curriculum decision makers in so many different ways that it is impossible to plot out with precision the various interactions and points of leverage they have at the various levels of educational systems (Fullan, 1999; Scott, 1999). However, it is possible to list some of the most influential groups and to describe in general ways how their influence works. Figure 9.2 lists such groups along with some tentative judgments about their levels of involvement and influence. The list includes both professional and nonprofessional organizations. Some of the groups listed ordinarily have benign motives, such as improving the quality of education in general. Other groups listed usually have more narrow interests.

School Boards. School boards are examples of groups that ordinarily have benign motives, but this generalization is not always true. At the district level, school boards occupy an ambiguous position since their members are both decision makers and influencers of other decision makers. Although school boards are legally charged with administering local school districts, they are nonprofessionals and may feel that the curriculum decisions are best left to the professional educators of the district. However, they are involved in a number of matters that impinge on curriculum decisions, including providing resources and hiring teachers and support staff. How much direct influence a school board exercises over curriculum decisions appears to vary greatly from district to district. Studies reported by Lasky (2000) and Maclure

Influences	Predominant Level of Involvement	Example of a Goal/Demand	Influence on Policies	Influence on Specific Curricula	Influence on Teaching Methods
Local community	School	Local history for bicentennial celebration	Low	Low	Low
Students	School	New class in music	Low	Low	Medium
Parents	School	Audiovisual equipment for school library	Low	Low	Low
School boards	School	Local work-experience programs	Medium	Medium	Low
Teachers unions	State	Reduced class sizes	Medium	Medium	Low
Professional associations	State/national	Professional development opportunities	Medium	High	High
Colleges/universities	State/national	Stimulate interest in new reading approaches	Medium	Low	Low
News media	State/national	Literacy and numeracy	Medium	Low	Low
State/national education agencies	State/national	Core curriculum	Low	Low	Low
Textbook publishers	State/national	Standard delineations of topics	Low	High	Medium
Testing agencies	State/national	Literacy levels	Medium	High	Low
Employers	State/national	Basic skills	Medium	Medium	Low
State government	State/national	Driver education	Medium	Low	Low
Federal government	National	Transition to work program	Low	Low	Low

FIGURE 9.2

Influences on curriculum decision making

and Walker (2000) indicate that it is difficult to determine whether school boards are typically involved in actual decision making. These studies suggest that some school boards do share in decision making, along with principals and other staff members of particular schools. However, the majority of school boards appeared only to be *near* to curriculum decisions made by principals and teachers. That is, most boards did not participate fully in decision making yet still exercised some influence over decisions.

Although the motives of a school board may be benign, the board may be substantially influenced by the power structures within the community. Thus, whatever influence a board has on curriculum decisions may reflect the motives of other people. McCarty and Ramsey (1971) identified four different types of power structures that exist between a community and the school board and superintendent:

1. In a *dominated* community, a small group within the community actually controls who becomes members of the board and, consequently, the board's policies. The superintendent either follows the wishes of this small, behind-the-scenes group or is removed from office. Hence, this group may for all practical purposes control curriculum decisions through both the board and the superintendent.

2. In a *factional* community, the school board is made up of representatives of several competing groups within the community, and one such group ordinarily maintains control of the board and its policies. Whenever substantive decisions are to be made about the curriculum, the controlling faction may insist on controlling these decisions, and the superintendent then comes under pressure to comply with the wishes of this faction.

3. In a *pluralistic* community, the board is also made up of members of different groups within the community, but no one group is able to control the board. Often the board's policies are the result of shifting and temporary alliances. In this kind of community, the board may exert little influence on the curriculum decisions of the superintendent and teachers, who nonetheless must exercise some caution about what decisions the community is willing to accept lest a controversial decision unite a majority of the board against them.

4. Finally, in an *inert* community, the school board is largely indifferent to any decisions about the curriculum and exerts little or no influence whatsoever. Under these circumstances, the superintendent and the teachers of the district have considerable freedom to make decisions on their own.

News Media.   Although seldom organized in any unified way, another group that influences curriculum decision making is the news media (both print and electronic). On the surface, the principal function of the news media appears to be reporting notable events to the public. In the case of education, the news media might therefore report that a school district had adopted a new curriculum. Beneath the surface, however, the function of the news media is more complicated. For instance, the news media might report that a new curriculum adopted in one district was achieving outstanding results since the scores of students on standardized reading tests had risen dramatically. Such a report might create considerable public pressure in another district to adopt the same curriculum. Yet there might be considerable differences between the two districts in, say, the socioeconomic compositions of their populations or in the experience and expectations of their teachers. These differences may be critical; and because of them, what worked well in one district may not work well in another. Furthermore, the news report has said directly or at least strongly implied that the reading scores in the first district rose *as a result of* the new curriculum (something that not even the best educational experts could be entirely certain of). Finally, the report has assumed (and indirectly conveyed this assumption to some members of the public) that standardized test scores are a good indicator of the overall quality of a curriculum when, in fact, all they may indicate is that teaching has been narrowed to only those things measured by the test.

The news media rarely deal fully with complex issues involved in education, yet the complexity is precisely what curriculum decision makers must deal with if their decisions are to be soundly based. Often, therefore, news media create unrealistic expectations in the public about education, while at other times picking up and heightening unrealistic expectations that the public already holds. In either case, the news media indirectly exert influence on curriculum decision makers because of what they have chosen to report about education and how they have chosen to report it. New sources of news via the Internet also include these biases (Futoran, Schofield, & Eurich-Fulmeret, 1995).

Unfortunately the news media are not above suspicion about their own motives. In the United States, the lines that traditionally separated factual reporting, investigative reporting, entertainment, and outright commercialism have become increasingly blurred. The more this blurring has occurred, the less the news media have been able to perform their traditional educative function for the whole society and the less society can rely on the news media to help it obtain sufficient facts and details from which to make informed judgments.

Textbook Publishers. Examples of groups listed in Figure 9.2 that ordinarily have narrow interests in curriculum decision making are textbook publishers. Although publishers may portray their only interest as creating the finest textbooks available for use within the curriculum chosen by a school or district, their interests obviously extend to capturing the largest possible share of the textbook market. Hence, publishers are constantly concerned that the specific topics included in their texts match the topics that decision makers include in school curricula. They also attempt to influence educators' selection of textbooks by providing free sample copies of texts to teachers, by including supplementary materials (such as teachers' guides, coordinated videotapes and audiotapes, CD-ROMS, and sample tests), or by engaging in other promotions. Occasionally, educators defer curriculum decisions to a publisher by adopting a textbook and letting it be their curriculum. Thus, some decisions about content and organization are actually made by publishers, not educators. In these cases, educators usually point to the convenience of standardizing the curriculum through the widespread use of the same textbooks and suggest that teachers like the books and find them highly usable with their students. In states where textbooks must be approved by a state board before they can be used in any of the public schools within the state, publishers may mount intensive lobbying campaigns to ensure that their books are on the approved lists. To increase the likelihood of widespread approval and use, textbooks often omit controversial topics altogether or approach them only extremely cautiously. Frequently, too, textbooks are deliberately written down to the lowest reading levels of all students with whom they might be used.

For all these reasons, textbooks are usually highly standardized and often have much of their potentially educative value drained from them. Since textbooks sell to a national market and teachers spend a considerable portion of their time teaching from them (estimates range up to 90 percent of teaching time), they have led to a great deal of curriculum standardization and vapidness.

Employers.   Employers, even more than textbook publishers, are a group motivated by business interests. In some cases, business interests may fit well with school curricula, which may have been shaped with the goal of training students for employment in the occupations prevalent in society. Historically, however, the curriculum has been a battleground for different business groups seeking to use the schools for their own economic purposes. Spring (1993) characterizes what this history has led to:

> During the 1980s and 1990s, business interests assumed ever-greater control of state educational policies; local school districts signed compacts with private industry councils; and corporations participated in adopt-a-school programs. This pattern represents a continuation of the human capital theories that fostered the rise of vocational education in the early part of the 20th century. Since then, the educational goal of preparing citizens for participatory democracy has been replaced by that of preparing them for employment. (p. 220)

Spring suggests that business groups such as employers are often preoccupied with short-range goals, with reducing the costs of employment, and with increasing profits. Changes in short-range business goals have led to constant changes in educational policies, such as the national push in the United States in the 1970s for more career and vocational education in the public schools, followed in the 1980s by the demand from business interests for more scientists and engineers. Therefore, making curriculum decisions in order to meet the immediate needs or future projections of businesses for employees is dangerous at best. Doing so might not be in the best interests of students; for in seeking to maximize profits, employers may pressure schools to create an abundant pool of labor trained strictly for the employers' benefit. Students may find the job market glutted with persons with similar training, and wages may be driven down. These narrowly trained students may be handicapped in the future if they seek different kinds of employment.

The influence of business groups and employers on curriculum decision making is often strong since taking into account relevant characteristics of society (such as economic characteristics) is something that decision makers should do (Caldwell, 1998). Nonetheless, decision makers must balance the focal point of the society and its associated economic concerns against the focal points of subject matter and the individual.

State Governments.   In the United States, legal control of schools rests in the hands of state governments, so many of the groups listed in Figure 9.2 may choose to focus their influence on state governments themselves (even when, as in the case of parents, their usual involvement is with the schools). At the state level of decision making, various interest groups attempt to influence curriculum by persuading governors, legislators, and senior state educational officials to champion their causes (Beyer & Apple, 1998). They may try to influence political and education officials through informal personal contacts, by making presentations at public hearings or to state committees, or by obtaining representation on such committees. These groups may be seeking things such as the introduction of new courses into public schools, the introduction of new materials into existing courses, or the removal of controversial books from school libraries. They may hope that the state will accede to their requests by passing new educational laws or by drafting new or reinterpreting old educational regulations. While many of the efforts of such groups at the state level may not appear to have much influence on curriculum decision making in school districts or individual schools, most groups can substantially alter the social and the legal context within which local decisions are made (Walker, 1990).

State governments may also influence curriculum decisions through their own actions that are more or less independent of the pressures of different interest groups. Each state maintains a state department of education (in some states under other names), which is made up of professionals, many of whom are specialists in education in the specific subjects that make up the general curriculum. One function of such a department is to provide educational leadership throughout the state. Specialists from the department may therefore be made available to provide advice or to suggest new directions to local educators struggling with how to improve an existing curriculum or with how to develop a new one. Additionally, the state department of education is in an ideal position to maintain close contact with local school districts and thus to assess changes in social and educational conditions throughout the state. On the basis of these assessments, the department of education can make recommendations for changes in policies and laws directly to top educational officials or to the governor and the state legislature.

Because a state department of education is a group of professionals who are knowledgeable about the latest thinking and developments in education, its suggestions to the state often parallel those of teacher unions, professional associations, colleges and universities, and testing agencies. However, because it is also a branch of the state government, its suggestions may be more readily accepted by state officials because those suggestions lack the taint of self-interest often associated with suggestions from private groups.

Levels of Influence

Most of the groups we have just discussed influence curriculum decisions predominantly at the state and national levels. However, their influence (like the influence of students, parents, and the local community, which we have discussed in detail in earlier chapters) can be profoundly felt by local educators. Further complicating the picture in recent years has been the growing influence of the federal government. Constitutionally, the federal government of the United States has no authority over local schools, and historically it has exerted little influence on curriculum. However, in recent decades, it has sponsored or created entire programs and provided incentives for schools to adopt them (for example, bipartisan support and funding support for charter schools). It has also shaped curricula by providing disincentives (usually in the form of withholding or not granting funds) when its rules and regulations have not been complied with. Finally, it has come more and more to be both a collector and a formulator of public opinion about education (roles that historically it left to the states and local communities), which can be both positive and negative (for example, see Good, 1996; Natriello, 1996).

Considering the complicated influences of different groups and the different levels on which they can work, remembering that the influence of various groups waxes and wanes over time and in different contexts, and understanding that political bargaining has no sacrosanct rules, let us now look at four highly political questions commonly asked about curriculum decision making:

Who initiates the curriculum?
Who determines priorities?
Who implements the curriculum?
Who is responsible for what happens?

9.3   WHO INITIATES THE CURRICULUM?

The answer to the question of who initiates the curriculum was once very simple and definite. During the first half of the twentieth century, the persons who made decisions about particular curricula were the senior officials in state departments of education and in school districts—usually superintendents and curriculum directors. Franklin (1986) recounts that major curriculum writers in the 1920s such as Franklin Bobbitt, W. W. Charters, and Hollis Caswell were actively involved in school positions. Bobbitt was assistant superintendent of schools in Los Angeles when he developed his approaches to curriculum planning, Charters was involved in a number of curriculum projects on vocational studies, and Caswell developed his planning principles while serving as a curriculum consultant. State laws required certain subjects to be taught in schools, but those laws were usually sufficiently nonspecific so that superintendents and curriculum directors could define for the teachers of their districts the particular topics those subjects would include. Superintendents and curriculum directors, too, could usually gain the approval of their school boards about what supplementary subjects would be taught in addition to those required by state law.

In the latter half of the century, answering the question became more complicated. For example, during the late 1950s and the 1960s, university academics working in high-powered teams sponsored by the federal government attempted to initiate curriculum change via subject-centered projects. Their brief was to produce the best curricula possible within their respective subject disciplines (Tanner & Tanner, 1995). Kliebard (1986) notes that the entry of the federal government into curriculum through its massive funding of projects altered the relative strength of the various groups that previously had influenced local curriculum development. Local efforts at curriculum revision and change were often superseded by centrally controlled endeavors.

During the 1980s, this trend continued. Many national curriculum reform proposals were issued that were directly and unmistakably political (Carlson, 1988). Various "blue-ribbon" committees and commissions advocated a variety of directions and principles for elementary and secondary education, but very few concerned themselves with how their recommendations would be implemented. These reform reports tended to be long on rhetoric but short on analysis. Many of them emphasized excellence and economic productivity as general goals and traditional subject-centered curricula as the means of reaching these goals, as did the best known and most influential of these reports, *A Nation at Risk: The Imperative for Educational Reform* (National Commission on Excellence in Education, 1983). Other well-known reports of this era, such as those issued by the Task Force on Education for Economic Growth (1983), Boyer (1982), and Peters and Waterman (1982), made similar suggestions, including recommending national standardized tests, a longer school day, and merit pay for teachers. (For a detailed discussion of *A Nation at Risk*, see chapter 2.) By the 1990s, however, most states (California being the most notable exception) had not produced detailed plans for implementing such curriculum reforms.

As discussed in chapter 7, such phrases as "comprehensive reform" and "whole-school reform" became powerful educational slogans during the late 1990s, and the thinking behind these slogans likely will increasingly influence school curricula well into the twenty-first century. Politicians at national, state, and local levels seem to compete in calling for high standards for schools, and the public increasingly demands that all students be successful in meeting them. These goals can be reached, many believe, by adopting research-based models that have been proved successful in increasing student achievement—despite only slender proof to date for the models and despite the formidable obstacles to finding a few sure paths to success in a highly diverse and heterogeneous society. In general, some models focus on the process of schooling (Sizer, 1992), while others are curriculum-based (Slavin & Madden, 2001). Schools adopting these models are attracted by the funding they can receive from such sources as the Comprehensive School Reform Demonstration Program or from other programs based on similar assumptions. In return, however, schools must follow a model's procedures for addressing all academic subjects and grade levels and for involving parents and the community. Perhaps the most important underlying questions concern how well all this will actually be done in practice and how much variation will be permitted.

Of course, it remains to be seen whether this kind of broad reform will prove to be a good thing or a bad thing in the long run. Proponents such as Slavin (2001) consider that this push toward national curriculum reform has enormous potential; others such as Hatch (2000) and McChesney and Hertling (2000) raise concerns about whether the reform can be sustained.

Whereas in the first half of the twentieth century curricula seem to have been initiated largely by educators themselves and often at the local level, in the second half of the century and into the twenty-first century the balance shifted in the direction of centralized control of curricula by senior school administrators, academics from subject-matter disciplines, political leaders, and senior public servants. Although centralized control is control of the planned curriculum, not necessarily the enacted curriculum, there has been a corresponding shift toward the attitude that curricula should be enacted precisely as planned. Apple (1990b) notes that, when the public holds this attitude, the ability of educators themselves to initiate the curriculum is limited: "This attitude bespeaks a profound mistrust of teachers, administrators, and curriculum scholars. They are decidedly not part of the solution; they are part of the problem" (p. 527). In a similar vein, McNeil (1990) suggests that the work of curriculum scholars has been marginalized. Politicians at all levels have become increasingly conspicuous in their role as initiators of the curricula now being implemented in American schools. This observation leads directly to the possibility that efforts to reform curricula on a national basis—particularly to create uniformity and to invest centralized control in the hands of politicians and other noneducators—have been a cause of the problems in education that politicians and some noneducators most loudly lament (Hatch, 2000). If so, then investing politicians with still greater authority to initiate the curriculum may exacerbate problems, not alleviate them.

9.4   WHO DETERMINES PRIORITIES?

The question of who determines priorities is similarly controversial. Again, on the surface of things, the persons who initiate a curriculum might seem to be the ones who also determine priorities. On the whole, this surmise is probably true, but there are numerous exceptions that should be considered.

Over the decades, different organizations and agencies with responsibilities for education at the local, state, and federal levels have attempted to set their own priorities. The visibility and powers of local school departments, state departments of education, and the U.S. Department of Education have and will continue to vary over the years; but each organization maintains certain responsibilities for disseminating policy statements about curriculum, for emphasizing particular curriculum priorities, and for encouraging these priorities through direct funding or via special-purpose grants. Checks and balances also exist so that the activities of an organization at one level do not unduly interfere with organizations operating at different levels. Given these circumstances and the tradition of decentralized control of American schools in general, it would also seem unlikely that national curriculum priorities can be set in the United States; nonetheless, efforts to establish national curriculum priorities emerged in the 1990s as well as talk of actually going beyond the priorities to establish a unified curriculum for the nation as a whole (Koretz, 1994). Furthermore, the American public seems to be increasingly receptive to such ideas.

Perhaps reacting to the public mood, President George H. W. Bush convened an education summit conference with the state governors in September 1989, and several months later, as a follow-up to this conference, he announced a new national education initiative titled *America 2000*. At the center of this initiative were six national goals to be attained by the year 2000:

1. All children in America will start school ready to learn.
2. The high school graduation rate will increase to at least 90 percent.
3. American students will leave grades four, eight, and twelve having demonstrated competency in challenging subject matter including English, mathematics, science, history, and geography. . . .
4. U.S. students will be first in the world in science and mathematics achievement.
5. Every adult American will be literate and will possess the knowledge and skills necessary to compete in a global economy and exercise the rights and responsibilities of citizenship.
6. Every school in America will be free of drugs and violence and will offer a disciplined environment conducive to learning. (U.S. Department of Education, 1991, p. 19)

That these goals were both lofty and unreachable did not deter Bush from following up in April 1991 with the related announcement that new world-class standards in the five core subjects of history, mathematics, science, geography, and English and a voluntary national testing program in these subjects would commence in September 1993. In May 1991, the National Assessment of Educational Progress (NAEP), an organization appointed by Congress, endorsed the setting of basic, proficient, and advanced national levels of achievement in basic academic subjects (Glaser, 1991). Although such actions may have been more political than substantive, some educators have interpreted them as indicators of a growing federal resolve to set curriculum priorities that local schools will eventually be obliged to accept—whether the priorities are realistic or not. Within this scenario, local school districts or states might still initiate their own curricula, but priorities for these curricula would be set perhaps by the federal government itself or perhaps by some other nationally central group, such as a coalition of business leaders.

Changes in federal administrations or the political parties in control of Congress may make little difference in this strategy of politicizing curriculum priorities while providing little or no real support to schools. It is one way in which presidents can be seen as education presidents without taking any political risks. Furthermore, in 1989, Republican George H. W. Bush's eventual successor, Democrat William Clinton, was then one of the state governors who helped develop the goals of *America 2000*. Assuming the presidency in 1993, Clinton continued to push for national goals and standards. Yet without considerable fiscal support that the federal government was then highly unlikely to provide, there seemed little possibility that uniform national curriculum priorities would be accepted throughout the United States. In the meantime, calls for national testing periodically waxed and waned, virtually disappearing in the early 1990s (Koretz, 1994), while increasing in the late 1990s due in part to support from the Clinton administration.

Emphasis on national testing increased to its highest level ever in 2001, when George W. Bush, the former President Bush's son and also a Republican, became president. Immediately after his inauguration, the new president proposed federal legislation that would substantially increase federal funding for public schools, especially in economically depressed areas. In return for federal aid, schools would be required to test all students for mathematical and reading proficiency at prescribed intervals. Schools that were deemed not to have made sufficient improvement in students' test scores in two years would be classified as "failing" and subject to being reorganized by state education officials or to being closed down altogether. Furthermore, children from poor families who attended "failing" schools would be given the option of transferring to nonfailing public schools or of leaving school to receive extensive tutoring. This provision for students to transfer or to be tutored seemed a fallback position from Bush's campaign promise to push for school vouchers, the highly controversial (and perhaps unconstitutional) use of public funds to pay for eligible students to attend private schools. In the 2000 election, referenda on school vouchers had been on the ballots in two states, Michigan and California, and had been overwhelmingly rejected by voters.

Interestingly, Bush's proposal did not require all testing for mathematical and reading proficiency to be identical. Rather, it would permit individual states to design their own testing programs. Nor did the proposal require all students to learn the same curricula or meet the same standards. Therefore, the educational policy pursued by the Bush administration in 2001 was clearly a step in the direction of uniform testing of students, of uniform standards, and of a uniform national curriculum for the United States, but it still left much of the journey untaken. Although the Bush proposal was debated by Congress throughout most of 2001, it was eventually enacted into legislation (with only minor changes) by large majorities in both the House of Representatives and the Senate. Whether it would be a precursor of future directions remained to be seen.

Regardless of what federal influence may have been during the 1990s and early 2000s, virtually every state has taken its own initiatives to improve the quality of education through methods that have tended to erode the ability of local school districts and teachers to make their own decisions about what their curricula will be. As early as the 1980s, California began to align textbooks, tests, examinations, and standards with state-initiated curriculum programs in order to promote greater student achievement in academic subjects. New curriculum content and methodologies were mandated by the California Department of Education and disseminated to school districts. Textbooks were reviewed by state textbook committees to ensure that they conformed to the new curricula. Standardized tests were also scrutinized and, where necessary, revised so that they, too, conformed. The process of alignment used in California is based on the assumption that student achievement will be maximized when variations from the curriculum priorities set by the state for all schools have been minimized. Critics, of course, have pointed out that this assumption and the efforts at alignment that follow from it reduce teacher autonomy and creativity. Despite mixed and controversial results in California, other states have undertaken similar initiatives.

Textbook publishers have also supported curriculum alignment for the simple reason that they are concerned with standardizing topics in order to sell their books as widely as possible. As we have described, textbook publishers often go to considerable lengths to avoid controversial topics (for example, evolution) and complex issues (for example, issues surrounding social class, race, or gender). Because textbooks are widely used in many school subjects (Driscoll, Dick, Johnson, & Flynn, 1990; Sosniak & Perlman, 1990), publishers have a strong influence on curriculum priorities, even if it is usually exercised quietly and indirectly. As Sosniak and Perlman note, "Textbooks provide the data with which students and teachers work, and pose the questions that define how the data should be understood. They define the content of instruction and the tasks students are expected to accomplish in the service of acquiring and demonstrating mastery of that content" (p. 436). Of course the growth of e-publishing and resources now available on the Internet may introduce a new dimension to the role of textbooks. It is possible that the Internet, with its instantaneous access to information and various media (Anderson & Alagurnalai, 1997) may largely replace traditional textbooks.

For similar reasons, organizations that create standardized examinations and tests (such as the Educational Testing Service) also set curriculum priorities that local educators live with since teachers can be placed under a great deal of pressure to prepare their students for standardized tests. Such tests may heavily influence students' placements in school, whether they graduate, or whether they gain admission to the colleges and universities they wish to attend. Standardized tests, too, are widely perceived by the American public as being scientific and thus providing an unbiased assessment of students' educational achievements. They are also perceived to provide information on U.S. schools compared with schools in other nations (Third International Mathematics and Science Study, 1996). Nationally, by far the best-known standardized test is the SAT (renamed the Scholastic Assessment Test in 1996 but still sometimes referred to by its original name, the Scholastic Aptitude Test). Created and administered by the Educational Testing Service, the SAT has been treated by the news media and the public since the 1950s as a highly reliable barometer of the quality of American education. Since many members of the public also believe that standardized measures of student achievement are good measures of how well teachers have taught, teachers are under all the more pressure to align the curricula that they enact in their classrooms with the curriculum priorities set by the creators of standardized tests.

Traditionally, members of the public, such as parents, who have been most interested and active in schools at the local level have not suggested that teachers be evaluated directly by the scores their students obtain on standardized tests. In general, these citizens have been supportive of curriculum priorities set by teachers themselves and of how teachers flexibly enact curricula. This tradition may be on the wane, however, because in recent decades the public has been barraged by a steady stream of criticism of the schools. For instance, reports of widespread declines in SAT scores have received broad publicity, even though the accuracy of such reports is highly questionable (Bracey, 1996). (In fact, Berliner and Biddle [1995] point out that close analysis of SAT scores indicates long-term national *increases,* a highly positive result for schools in the United States and for local curriculum development, especially in light of the steadily increasing proportion of the overall population taking the test.)

Thus, the freedom of local educators and even school boards themselves to set their own curriculum priorities may be eroding. This results both from tendencies for the state and federal levels to set curriculum priorities and from lack of public confidence in the ability of local educators to do so wisely. Parents and the community at large may wish to maintain their own role in curriculum decision making, but the powers of those decision makers to which the community is closest—teachers and school boards—may be declining because of declining community confidence and support.

Aside from these general tendencies, predicting future trends in the relative strength of local, state, and federal levels in setting curriculum priorities is difficult. Much depends on the mood of the nation as a whole. Currently, many national concerns are economic and social, and in recent years, individuals and groups playing on these concerns have been able to influence curriculum priorities disproportionately. Such individuals and groups will likely continue to attempt to do so in the future.

9.5   WHO IMPLEMENTS THE CURRICULUM?

The question of who implements the curriculum is by far the easiest of the four questions to answer. Although much can be made of the curriculum priorities set by the pronouncements of political leaders and official memoranda distributed by senior education officers, the actual impact of curricula on students depends on the persons responsible for curriculum implementation—teachers primarily, but also principals and other support personnel in individual schools. Priorities determined at remote levels remain priorities for the planned curriculum, but it is still teachers who ultimately enact curricula and create the conditions under which curricula are experienced by students. In other words, despite the pressures teachers may be under to comply with someone else's curriculum priorities, they almost always have sufficient wiggle room in their own classrooms so that they are the real enactors or implementers of the curriculum.

Various writers such as Connell (1983) have noted the increasing sophistication and expertise of classroom teachers in planning and managing the school curriculum. He cites their awareness of trends like action research as a means by which they can reflect and act upon the curriculum problems they encounter in their classrooms. McCutcheon (1988) is also highly positive about the abilities of most teachers as curriculum implementers. Based on the research she has conducted, she agrees that teachers are subject to constraints such as teacher competency tests and student achievement tests, yet most teachers can and do make highly sophisticated and intelligent decisions about what they teach and how. Teachers are the filters through which externally planned and mandated curricula pass, but teachers make necessary adjustments as they filter things such as the stated objectives of the curriculum in order to implement what they believe will be the most appropriate curricula for their individual students.

Apple (1990a) is also optimistic about teachers themselves, but he is pessimistic about the erosion of their freedom to make decisions about implementation. He argues that teachers face the prospect of becoming increasingly deskilled because of the encroachment of a technical rationale into education and concomitant efforts to standardize and control everything that teachers do in the name of raising standards and promoting efficiency. As examples, he cites behaviorally based curricula, prespecified competencies for teachers and students, and standardized testing. House (1996) makes similar points, particularly deploring extreme characterizations of teachers that tend either to idealize them or to demonize them.

Perhaps most readers would concur with Eisner (1990a) that in the future teachers should act in ways similar to a musical conductor—creatively and with imagination. He considers that curriculum practice in the classroom should cultivate productive idiosyncrasy and that it should increase rather than suppress individual differences. Yet it is also likely that teachers in the future will be subjected to further pressures toward uniformity and standardization. Thus, the question of who actually implements the curriculum is likely to become more difficult to answer in the future, particularly if there is less room for creative enactment by teachers.

9.6 WHO IS RESPONSIBLE FOR WHAT HAPPENS?

Since teachers are still the real implementers of the curriculum, they are often held responsible for everything that happens in the classroom. This is hardly fair, however—whether what happens is largely positive, largely negative, or some combination of the two. Teachers—like all other professionals, no matter how well trained—lack sufficient knowledge of how to create only desirable results, nor do they have complete control over the many conditions that influence results. For instance, it is unethical for a medical doctor to promise to cure a patient; for medical knowledge of sure, no-risk cures for all patients has never existed (nor will it), and a doctor never has complete control over everything that may happen to a patient. Therefore, it is both fair and realistic to hold medical doctors responsible only for what they should be able to do: provide reasonable treatment within the flexible boundaries of what the profession accepts as good practice. Similarly, teachers, too, should be held to high professional standards.

One reason, among many, why teachers cannot control everything that happens to students is that the curricula that they implement have usually been planned in part by others. Various individuals and groups, therefore, ordinarily share responsibility for the intended and actual curricula. In schools, individual teachers are required to teach planned specifics and to aim their teaching at certain standards of achievement for their students, but the conditions that they work under are influenced by other teachers, by principals, by superintendents, by school boards, by parents, and by the community at large (Hargreaves, Earl, Moore, & Manning, 2001). Some teachers receive ample psychological and material support; other teachers receive very little support of any kind. While teachers should always be held responsible for sound practice, there is always the temptation, nonetheless, to hold them responsible for what their students do or do not learn. In their professional capacities, teachers are, after all, the principal mediators between the planned curriculum (which may be stated in terms of intended learning outcomes) and their students, those for whom the curriculum is meant. And of course, no matter how good or bad the average teacher is, it is always the case that some teachers will teach more effectively than others.

Efforts to require responsibility for what happens in education have been growing steadily over recent decades under the name of *accountability*. The basic rationale for accountability is that when people are held responsible for their performance, their weaknesses can be identified and eliminated. Accountability does not work, however, if responsibility cannot be fixed (Caldwell & Spinks, 1998). Applied specifically to curriculum, accountability often means that the teacher is held responsible for what happens to students when the planned curriculum is implemented—whether or not the planned curriculum is defective, whether it has been properly matched with the students, and regardless of the level of support the teacher receives. Increasingly, whole schools have been reviewed partly for reasons of accountability but also as a means of coordinating programs across schools. For example, all Kentucky schools are assessed on an accountability index (Steffy, 1993). Data are now routinely obtained not only from school personnel but also from students and parents. There are, obviously, caveats to be observed, especially about whose interests are being served when responsibility that should be shared is placed on the shoulders of only one of the individuals or groups involved.

Most accountability reviews are still based on standardized tests of student achievement. For example, data from the NAEP have been used to identify groups of students at different age levels who presumably are underachieving. Other tests have provided data about the extent to which certain state mandates have been met. Glaser (1991) expresses these reservations about the narrowness of traditional accountability testing: "Assessment of the outcomes of schooling must be designed and employed in ways that take account of modern knowledge of human cognition, and allow us to develop educational environments in which levels of effectively useful knowledge are achieved for all students, and high-levels of competence are attained by many" (p. 22). Glaser notes there are indications that improved forms of accountability testing may be developed in the near future. He argues that, since American society is becoming more pluralistic and diverse, conventional testing is no longer appropriate and many practices of yesteryear are dysfunctional in American education today. For the future, he advocates integrated instruction and evaluation, with more emphasis on socially sensitive assessment of what happens in schools.

9.7   HOW POWER IS APPLIED: SOME EXAMPLES

In this book we have examined in some detail how various individuals and groups participate in the general process of curriculum development, including planning, implementing, evaluating, and changing the curriculum. For the most part, we assumed that participation was cooperative or at least not necessarily antagonistic. In this chapter, however, we have treated curriculum decision making as an arena in which participants may hold direct conflicts of interest. In this light, we now consider some of the basic ways in which participants may seek to exert control over curriculum decisions.

At the national level, the federal government actively influences the curriculum of American schools, even though control and administration of schools is constitutionally a responsibility of individual states. In recent decades, the federal government has been increasingly active because of a growing national belief that the quality of public education is a key to national well-being. As we have noted in this chapter, politicians have in recent decades proclaimed a number of national crises and then initiated new programs purportedly designed to resolve these respective crises (see the following section, Charter Schools as a Counter-Example). Many of these proposed solutions have been curricular.

Various strategies are used by the federal government to wield influence over the curriculum. Walker (1990, pp. 313–314) suggests that four policy tools have been the most prominent: law enforcement, categorical aid programs, curriculum development projects, and prestige of office.

- Law enforcement is a potent but limited influence. It applies to the enforcement of constitutional rights and federal laws that apply to schools. Examples include requiring instruction in the native languages (other than English) of students and prohibiting the treatment in prejudicial or stereotypical ways of socially and culturally sensitive differences in age, sex, race, or handicap.
- Categorical aid programs provide funds for purposes specified by the federal government. These funds have often been administered through national agencies or state departments of education. Local schools are under no obligation to apply for or to accept such funds, but, once accepted, the funds must be used only for the purposes specified. Examples include funds for bilingual programs, programs for the handicapped, programs for the early education of poor and minority children, and comprehensive reform programs.
- Curriculum development projects create new (presumably exemplary) curricula that can be adopted by local schools. Examples include the national curriculum reform projects funded through the National Science Foundation in the late 1950s and the 1960s (see chapter 2) and the New Standards Project in the 1990s (Simmons & Resnick, 1993).
- Prestige of office permits federal educational officials, particularly the president, to set the character of national discourse and debate about education. This debate may be focused directly on what the curriculum should be.

Examples include *A Nation at Risk: The Imperative for Educational Reform* (National Commission on Excellence in Education, 1983) and *America 2000: An Education Strategy* (U.S. Department of Education, 1991).

The federal government has also created special agencies to disseminate ideas and information about education, and these agencies have acted as resources for state and local curriculum development projects. Most prominent among them are the Regional Educational Laboratories and the National Research and Development Centers established in 1972. These agencies have undergone numerous reorganizations over the years in terms of both their geographical locations and the scope of their activities, but they have continued to provide comprehensive accounts of current trends in educational research and practice, and they have been a catalyst for the dissemination of ideas and strategies about curriculum that the federal government favors.

At the state level, governors and legislatures control the schools. For instance, local school districts exist only as a matter of state laws. Therefore, state governments have the authority to dictate curricula to all public schools (and, to a lesser extent, to private schools), but historically most states have delegated considerable authority to local school districts to determine the specific details of their curricula, if not the general outlines. This situation has changed quite drastically, however, as recent flurries of reform activities have to a large extent been initiated by states. Fullan (1991) suggests that in approximately twenty states in which the control of schools is most highly centralized, state governments have undertaken initiatives such as establishing minimum competencies, approving textbooks, establishing state syllabi and courses of study, requiring statewide examinations, and developing outcomes-based standards. The remaining states are more decentralized and tend to favor local discretion in curriculum decision making, although even these states may be moving gradually toward greater state controls. Pipho (1991) provides a detailed, state-by-state breakdown of legal actions having a bearing on how much centralized state control is exerted over the curriculum. Figure 9.3 is a categorization derived from Pipho of the relative amounts of control exercised by each state in curriculum matters. Recent developments, of course, may have changed how any particular state should now be categorized.

It is important to note that the initiatives that have occurred recently at the state level have often been led by governors and legislators rather than by state departments of education (Manno, Finn, & Vanourek, 2000). This is another sign of how curriculum decision making in the United States is becoming increasingly politicized. State departments of education are made up of professional educators and are relatively free of direct political pressures. Presumably, they can undertake initiatives primarily for educational reasons. Governors and legislators are professional politicians, however, and are directly influenced by their constituents and by organized lobby groups. Furthermore, education is an extremely large item in the budgets of all states; as a consequence, there is considerable interest in expenditures for education and in cost-benefit equations for new programs. In short, fiscal concerns may dominate over educational concerns.

Decentralized States

Alaska	Maryland	Ohio
Colorado	Massachusetts	Pennsylvania
Connecticut	Michigan	Rhode Island
Delaware	Minnesota	Vermont
Idaho	Montana	Washington
Illinois	Missouri	Wisconsin
Iowa	Nebraska	Wyoming
Kansas	New Hampshire	

Moderately Decentralized States

Maine	New York	Oregon
New Jersey	North Dakota	South Dakota

Centralized States

Alabama	Indiana	Oklahoma
Arizona	Kentucky	South Carolina
Arkansas	Louisiana	Tennessee
California	Mississippi	Texas
Florida	Nevada	Utah
Georgia	New Mexico	Virginia
Hawaii	North Carolina	West Virginia

FIGURE 9.3
Categorization of states by amount of state control

Walker (1990, pp. 318) suggests that states use all four of the policy tools used by the federal government to influence curriculum decisions but that states have an additional six at their disposal: mandates, regulation, program support, assistance, examinations, and curricular alignment.

- Mandates are orders that schools are legally bound to follow. For example, a state may require that schools use minimum competencies.
- Regulation is similar to mandates but less restrictive; it is the specification of limits within which schools must operate. For example, states may specify certain topics for inclusion in a curriculum.
- Program supports are financial resources offered to schools to establish, maintain, or improve specific programs—for example, in-service education for teachers.
- Assistance is also support for programs but in the form of advice, service, or consultation. For example, state departments of education often provide expert advice to schools on how to implement a new curriculum.
- Examinations are tests of student learning. They become policy tools when they are used to emphasize certain curricular specifics. For example, subjects in which there are statewide examinations almost always are given higher priority by schools than are other subjects.

- Curriculum alignment requires schools to create consistency in the goals, guides, textbooks, and tests that make up the curriculum of specific subjects. For example, topics covered in a textbook should also be covered by tests, and vice versa.

Walker also notes that, despite these controls over school curricula, states "do not require local schools to submit courses for approval and they do not police compliance with syllabi in any formal way" (p. 319). Nonetheless, states clearly have the authority and the ability to monitor school curricula this closely, if and when they care to do so.

Writers such as Lewis (1990) and Darling-Hammond (1990) have identified California as the state that pushed top-down curriculum reform the farthest in the 1990s. Darling-Hammond describes California's revised mathematics framework (along with other curriculum frameworks) as "the most ambitious curriculum reforms of any state in the nation" (p. 233). These frameworks emphasize ways of thinking (such as thinking critically, solving problems, and synthesizing information) rather than subject matter itself, thereby attempting to provide some student-centered focus for California curricula.

However, other changes California made pushed in far different directions. Uniformity and curriculum alignment were high priorities. The state specified goals, objectives, and content to be taught. It listed recommended textbooks for elementary schools but provided money only for those books listed. It developed testing programs for students and evaluation programs for districts. It mandated that teachers be evaluated on their instructional skills but recognized as skills only those teaching practices that conformed with the newly aligned curricula. It evaluated highly orderly, "time on task" classrooms as better than student-centered ones. In general, therefore, it created many mechanical and time-consuming procedures to assure compliance with its notions of what both curriculum and instruction should be. Even more important, it deliberately fostered a climate in which educators who deviated from its norms—especially by adopting individual-centered curricula— would pay a high professional price. This in itself seems to be a high price for an entire state to pay for centralized curriculum decision making. Klein (1991) concludes that the whole process California followed in exerting complete control over school curricula stifled creativity among both teachers and students, left out what is most significant about curricula (such as making decisions and experiencing consequences), and left local districts with little to do except comply with state mandates.

At the local level, there is much more opportunity for face-to-face communication but, Fuhrman and Elmore (1990) argue, no great reduction in the level of politicization. Local districts develop finely differentiated policies based on local needs and the wishes of local people. Local districts tend to focus on issues such as how the curriculum is organized, what specific courses of study should include, what supplementary materials should be selected, and what policies and actions are needed to comply with state mandates and federal regulations. Bargaining on such issues tends to take on a personal tone, even though a district may include many competing and well-organized interest groups. Implementation is also an important issue at the local level. The greater intimacy between a local district and its schools brings about a very demanding reality check for educators who wish to ensure that the curricula implemented seem appropriate to local students and their parents.

Well-documented case studies of curriculum decision making within individual schools are scarce, but the account of a Canadian school by Hannay (1990) illustrates what may be typical. The study focused on the deliberations of two committees at a high school in a district in the province of Ontario. The principal had decided that the provincial policy on school-based curriculum development would be used to develop new curricula for each of two subject-area departments. Hannay documented the deliberations of the two committees: the history committee and the geography committee. She discovered that, in attempting to follow the same policy, both committees encountered many of the same difficulties (such as philosophical mismatches among teachers, successful and unsuccessful leadership styles, problems with the availability and use of resources). However, largely because of the face-to-face character of the deliberations themselves, the geography committee was able to overcome these difficulties and create a curriculum, whereas the history committee failed to complete its task.

Future studies of this kind will no doubt shed further light on the character of curriculum deliberation within local schools and on how the bottom-up approach to curriculum decision making that it represents differs radically from the top-down approaches increasingly taken by state and federal governments.

Charter Schools as a Counter-Example

We have suggested that national trends in curriculum are away from bottom-up approaches (with decision making largely in the hands of local school districts and teachers) and toward top-down approaches (with centralized decision making largely in the hands of state education officials). Perhaps the most promising educational reform of the last decade, charter schools, reverses these trends, at least in part. Essentially, charter schools are public schools specifically designated by a state as exempt from some state regulations that apply to ordinary public schools. The idea is to provide considerable latitude to a charter school and the people within it to pursue their own views about what education should be. Thus, charter schools are schools of choice for the parents, students, and teachers involved in them and are conducive to on-site curriculum decision making. Although laws differ from state to state, in general charters for such schools may be granted to local school districts, to groups of parents or teachers, even to business organizations. In 1998, California had the highest number of students in the nation enrolled in its 130 charter schools (Wells, 1999). By 2000 charter laws were in place in thirty-six states, and national enrollment had swelled to some 350,000 students (Manno et al., 2000).

The boards that govern charter schools usually are small and composed of persons directly involved in running the schools. The schools themselves are typically small, with only 150 to 250 students, and encourage parents and teachers to work together to provide their own unique educational programs. To the extent that ordinary public schools cannot provide this degree of flexibility, charter schools may offer viable alternatives that attract and are specifically appropriate for many different types of students. For instance, a charter school may be governed by a group of like-minded parents who have a common view about the teaching of "at risk" students or children with learning disabilities. These governing boards are usually very different from most local school boards in composition and mode of operation.

Manno et al. (2000) describe charter schools as independent public schools of choice, open to all who wish to attend, freed from some regulations and pursuing their own programs (and in this respect similar to private schools), but paid for with tax dollars and responsible to the public. Charter schools have emerged with strong bipartisan support at the federal level as well as at state level. Good and Braden (2000) contend that they have been created because there is a widespread belief that a market-driven organization will outperform a traditional bureaucratic model. This view assumes that teachers in public schools neither work hard enough nor are sufficiently sensitive to the needs of students and that competition from charter schools will increase innovation and improve learning in ordinary public schools. Despite the negative image of teachers that this view entails, teachers' organizations have been cautiously supportive of charter schools, but with the proviso that charter schools, as public schools, should be staffed by licensed teachers.

Some studies suggest that in a number of cases charter schools have been extremely popular. Wells (1999) reports that she met hundreds of satisfied charter school educators and parents and concludes, "People who work in and send their children to charter schools are incredibly committed to these schools and their purposes" (p. 312). According to Gresham, Hess, Maranto, and Milliman (2000), teachers in Arizona's charter elementary schools experienced a sense of empowerment, and Wells, Lopez, Scott, and Holme (1999) enthuse that "in a post-modern manner, charter schools provide liberation from the constraints of the bureaucratic and modern public education system." Good and Braden (2000) describe charter schools as "the liveliest reform in American education."

Yet, in practice charter schools have not lived up to all the glowing rhetoric. Good and Braden (2000) contend that charter schools have not:

- Served as locations for experimentation and innovation, many having taken a traditional approach to classroom instruction
- Spent an increased proportion of their budgets on direct classroom instruction
- Improved access and equity for students, having instead further segregated students by ethnicity, income level, and special needs
- Provided reasonable physical environments for students, many charter schools occupying unstimulating, unattractive, and—in some cases—unsafe buildings

Wells (1999) considers that there is little evidence to indicate that students actually learn more in charter schools than in ordinary public schools. Mickelson (1999) notes that one of the most serious problems about business interventions into charter schools is that the strategic self-interest that guides business practices can often predominate over the altruism that the public expects schools to instill. A few charter schools have been closed because of financial mismanagement.

Despite such concerns and problems, the charter school movement has made an impact. Although the numbers of charter schools are still relatively small, they are rapidly growing. Disgruntled parents are transferring their children to charter schools, much like parents who transferred their children from public schools to the "free" or "open" schools that sprang up in the late 1960s and early 1970s. Such schools decided their own curricula in their own ways. Still, most alternative schools of that era were short-lived, and it is far from clear that a revolution is occurring now. It seems unlikely that there will be a great deal of support for Senator John Kerry's assertion, as quoted in Manno et al. (2000), "Let's make every public school in this country essentially a charter school . . . with decentralized control, site-based management, parental engagement, and high levels of volunteerism" (p. 743).

Yet, to the extent that charter schools do offer liberation and autonomy for parents, students, and teachers, they are places that run against the national current toward top-down curriculum decision making. Turner (1990) contends that charter schools are the consummate postmodern education reform.

9.8   IMPLICATIONS FOR TEACHERS

This chapter has briefly sketched a picture of some of the people and the influences involved in curriculum decision making. It is an incomplete picture, of course, for it does not capture the full complexity that such decisions always entail. Entire books are necessary for that. In general, however, it shows the individuals, interest groups, and governments involved and portrays the gradual movement in recent decades of the locus of such decisions from local schools and districts to the states and to the federal government. But it is also incomplete for another reason. Thus far it has not fully described the direct impact of increasingly centralized curriculum decisions on the ultimate decision makers—teachers, those people who decide how to enact what they may or may not have had much say in planning. The chapter concludes, therefore, by more fully considering the implications of the trend toward centralized decision making on local educators generally and on teachers specifically.

Some Messages

Brooks (1991), writing in the 1990s, suggests that the principal result of educational reforms has been more state-mandated curricula. His statement is equally applicable in the first decade of the twenty-first century. The typical rationale has been that, because some schools in a state were not of sufficient quality, the state could improve them by setting standards for student performance, which it required all schools to meet. This, in turn, could be done by mandating curricula and statewide testing programs. The underlying contradiction in this rationale is that, although the mandates are meant to improve weak schools, they apply to all schools. The general message of this rationale is that what is most important about education is its results in terms of measured student performance. Brooks believes that this strategy has improved a small number of local districts that historically had been deficient, but it also sends seven specific and unfortunate messages to local educators and teachers.

1. *"Curriculum development is not your responsibility"* (p. 153). Traditionally, states have mandated only general subjects that schools must teach but have left decisions about particular topics and appropriate materials, activities, and forms of instruction to local educators. Thus, teachers have traditionally been the decision makers about the texture and much of the substance of the curricula that they have enacted. The recent state strategy, however, tells teachers that their only responsibility is delivering the curriculum precisely as it has been planned for them. This strategy narrows the role of teachers in curriculum development, saps their initiative, and leaves them feeling less professional.

2. *"Testing drives instruction"* (p. 153). In the past, most school districts gave students only a few nationally normed achievement tests; but with the proliferation of more and more highly specific tests mandated by states, teachers have been all but forced to teach directly to the tests. Although many state departments of education claim that their tests are flexible and accommodate many styles of teaching and learning, Brooks believes that, in practice, such tests are not only used to define everything students should know, but they encourage students to seek only one simple and "correct" answer for every question asked—however complicated—thereby discouraging higher-order thinking.

3. *"It is more important to cover material than to learn it"* (p. 156). Similarly, state-mandated curricula and testing place teachers under considerable pressure to teach about each topic specified in the state syllabi and course guides. Teaching about a topic, however, does not necessarily lead students to understand it, especially when the pressures on teachers cause them to fall back more and more on the basic method of didactic, chalk-and-talk teaching. Falling by the wayside are other methods of teaching (such as the use of hands-on experiences, discovery activities, simulations, and student-developed goals) in which teachers mediate school experiences so that students can construct their own knowledge and thereby potentially enhance learning.

4. *"Minimum competence is the desired outcome"* (p. 156). Most state tests are scored against a state reference point, a raw score on a test (say, twenty-eight correct answers on a fifty-item test) selected by the state as that score that a student must equal or exceed to be deemed competent in the subject. Again teachers are under pressure, this time to help each student reach the state reference point, and students who do not reach this point ordinarily must receive remedial instruction. But since reference points are low enough so that many—perhaps most—students can reach them easily, more and more of the time and attention of teachers goes into getting weaker students up to minimal competency or goes directly into remedial instruction itself. In this way, both strong and weak students are encouraged to achieve minimum standards but nothing more.

5. *"We don't trust you!"* (p. 158). Brooks considers state-mandated curricula to be an "imposition" that has occurred "through a militarylike, hierarchical system of accountability" (p. 158). Top-down control indicates to teachers that they are not

trusted and is particularly disheartening because academic freedom and autonomy are two of the most basic job satisfactions for teachers, offsetting a multitude of dissatisfactions ranging from lack of support to unruly students. Top-down control with bottom-up responsibility is even worse, for it indicates a state is not willing to treat teachers as professionals even though it may claim that it does so.

6. *"Past effectiveness does not matter"* (p. 159). Most school districts have offered sound and comprehensive programs, as evidenced by general support from parents and students and by tangible data such as attendance and dropout rates. Despite past successes, however, good school districts are treated by state departments of education precisely like those districts that historically have been the worst. Local programs, innovations, and even cultural variations are devalued as the state pushes all districts toward curriculum uniformity.

7. *"More and sooner and quicker and tougher is better"* (p. 159). The recent curriculum reforms of most states have focused on early childhood education and on high school dropout rates, yet they seem based on the highly dubious assumption that what is good for some students is good for all students. Many state-mandated early childhood curricula ask young students to learn concepts for which they may not be developmentally ready, and many state-mandated secondary curricula increase the requirements for high school graduation in ways that encourage weak students to leave school because they see less chance of meeting the new requirements. Despite whatever good intentions state reformers may hold, attempting to improve education qualitatively by demanding more of students quantitatively may produce effects quite the opposite of what reformers intend.

Brooks laments the diminishment of education that these messages signify, especially the virtually complete exclusion of local educators from curriculum planning and the severe restrictions placed on their freedom to enact curricula in their own ways in their own schools and classrooms. He is not optimistic about reversing this trend in the foreseeable future, especially if state decision makers remain unwilling to examine the basic assumptions on which their strategy for curriculum reform rests.

Professionalization

Griffin (1991) also identifies the basic problem as the conflict between the actions of central curriculum decision makers that reduce the teacher's ability to make professional decisions and the need to treat teaching as the complex intellectual activity that it is. In analyzing the problem, Griffin focuses on the issue of professionalization.

He indicates the depth of the problem through this simple observation: "For many teachers in today's schools, it is hard to imagine that teachers in other times had primary, ongoing, and comprehensive control over curriculum decisions in their own classroom settings" (p. 123). In some states and school districts, he suggests, persons in central authority have so completely usurped the professional curriculum decisions made by teachers that the work of teachers has been reduced to paraprofessionalism—that is, to practice that is sufficiently standardized so that it can be easily learned, efficiently observed, and readily remediated. Unlike professional teachers, paraprofessionals do *not* use reflective and analytic skills and past experience to make complicated decisions about appropriate practices in constantly changing situations. Among the results of teaching being reduced to paraprofessionalism are that all classrooms are treated as if they are alike, the sense of efficacy of teachers is diminished, students have limited options for learning, and resources for problem solving are decreased.

In contrast, if the highest-quality individuals are to be attracted into teaching in sufficient numbers to make a real difference in the quality of education on a broad scale, then teaching must be a professional career. Griffin (pp. 131–139) identifies the following characteristics of a profession:

- Members of a profession possess specialized knowledge and skill.
- Professional work is carried forward in a collegium.
- Members of a profession contribute to the knowledge bases that guide their work and that of other colleagues.
- A profession is characterized by a career orientation.
- Members of a profession have considerable autonomy regarding the exercise of their professional knowledge and skill.

Griffin explains that, contrary to the popular belief that anyone who cares deeply about children will teach well, in actuality good teachers develop over an extended period of time a significant range of knowledge combined with many extremely complicated skills. This combination of knowledge and skill applies to decisions not only about instruction but also about curriculum:

> Certainly, curriculum theory and development constitute a specialized body of knowledge that should be a part of every professional teacher's repertoire. Knowledge of theoretical perspectives about curriculum and the various conceptions of curriculum planning is of extraordinary value to the enterprise of providing educational opportunity. (p. 132)

Centralized curriculum planning limits the opportunities teachers have to develop and exercise such professional knowledge and skills, hence diminishing the likelihood of high-quality teaching.

In precisely the same ways, centralized curriculum planning works against the other characteristics that make teaching a profession. For instance, it tends to exacerbate the long-standing professional problem of teachers being isolated in their own classrooms. When teachers are merely implementing the plans of others, there are few reasons for them to take the initiative to work with colleagues to identify and to ameliorate the specific problems of a particular school. There are few opportunities for them to create well-crafted solutions to problems and to communicate their approaches to still other teachers as part of a growing body of knowledge and lore useful to other professionals. There are few opportunities for teachers to change their career patterns (for instance, by moving into leadership roles, such as mentoring less-experienced teachers or even by making their own decisions about how to use time and materials) as their professional knowledge and skills deepen.

And there is little relief from the increasingly restrictive rules and regulations meant to standardize what they do.

Griffin is neither optimistic nor pessimistic about reversing the trend toward centralized curriculum planning and its debilitating effects on teachers as decision makers. He suggests a number of changes in teacher education to integrate intellectual knowledge and practical skills and thereby strengthen the basis for teaching as a profession, although he does not believe that such changes will be widely adopted quickly or easily. Among his recommendations are that programs of teacher education include: long-term curriculum planning; teaching as a collegial activity; inquiry into the knowledge base for teaching and the reflective, analytic character of teaching; and preparation for professional leadership.

Empowerment

In contrast to the pessimism of Brooks (1991) and the balance between optimism and pessimism of Griffin (1991), Schwartz (1991) is decidedly optimistic about reversing the trend toward centralized curriculum planning. She argues that education in general and curriculum in particular are often seen in terms of two organizational metaphors—the machine metaphor and the organic metaphor—and that the predominant view in society as a whole tends to swing back and forth between these two metaphors. When the machine metaphor predominates, centralized curriculum decision making increases. Emphasis falls on standardization and efficiency. When the organic metaphor predominates, local curriculum decision making increases. Emphasis falls on individual differences and creativity. Schwartz observes that, at the beginning of the 1990s, both metaphors vied for the attention of American society but that many of the most recent proposals for change are based on a growing recognition of the differences between the rationality of bureaucratic organizations such as central educational agencies and the socialization of educational organizations such as local schools and classrooms. Based on these recent proposals, she suggests the following:

> The next wave of educational reforms is expected to alter the structure of local school districts. Their bureaucratic form will be flattened by administrative decentralization as school-based management takes effect, and the central office will be shorn of important curriculum functions as newly empowered professionally oriented teachers help to fashion curriculum in local schools. (p. 194)

Certainly decentralization of curriculum decision making will lead to more autonomy for individual teachers. They will be able to participate more fully in planning the curriculum of their own schools, but they will also be freer to make their own decisions about how to enact the curriculum in their own classrooms in order to maximize the quality of the experienced curriculum of individual students. This kind of autonomy for teachers to participate fully in the management of schools and to make curriculum decisions is now often referred to as the *empowerment* of teachers. The idea of teacher empowerment, however, does not imply only that autonomy is gained when restrictions on the professional freedoms of teachers are removed. To be empowered fully, teachers must also know how to use their professional freedoms wisely.

9.9   A FINAL COMMENT ON CURRICULUM APPROACHES AND ISSUES

Throughout this book, we have attempted to point out that, while the curriculum is no one thing, there are many reasonable ways to understand it, to make decisions about it, and to enact it. Hence, we have described some of the most basic alternative approaches to curriculum planning and development that have been taken in the past or are being taken in the present. However, all approaches are not equally reasonable, wise, or appropriate. We have raised some of the ongoing issues entailed by choosing among these alternatives, and we have described some alternative approaches to curriculum that might be taken in the future.

Of course, we do not know what that future will be. Hence, in this final chapter, we have described some of the most basic pressures within American society on curriculum decision making. In the future, will centralizing pressures prevail, or will society recognize the decentralizing tendencies of traditional beliefs about autonomy and independence, of modern curriculum theorizing, and of the character of a pluralistic, multicultural society itself? The answer to this question is also something we do not know. What we can be reasonably certain of, however, is that those people who plan and enact curricula—particularly teachers and other curriculum specialists—will continue to weigh alternative approaches and the issues that choosing among alternatives entails. They will need to consider how curricula can be planned with precision yet enacted flexibly in order to meet the changing circumstances of schools and the specific needs of students. They will need to appropriately balance the focal points of subject matter, society, and the individual in making their decisions. And, perhaps above all else, they will need to be fully aware of what they are doing and why.

We hope this book contributes to the fullness of their understanding, to the wisdom of their decisions, and to the appropriateness of their actions.

■ QUESTIONS AND REFLECTIONS

1. Centralized control of curricula can be defended in terms of efficiency and equity. What assumptions are such defenses based on? What ideas, arguments, or evidence most undermine these defenses?

2. What weaknesses in public education can charter schools improve upon? What are the dangers of making all public schools into charter schools?

3. Who should ultimately control the curriculum? In answering, consider the rights of parents, the interests of the state and national governments, the needs of individual students, and the desirability of academic freedom for teachers.

4. "The drumbeat of critics' assertions about what happened in schools in earlier decades and policymakers' assumptions about

the past become a handy formula for taking action to reform schooling" (Cuban, 1992, p. 242). How has historical evidence been misused by curriculum reformers? What erroneous conclusions have been drawn? What more appropriate conclusions should have been drawn by reformers? What conclusions can be drawn about the history of curriculum reform?

5. "Schools in the future might well become 'cyber learning organizations for the techno generation' but that is only part of what they can be. If policy makers so wish, schools might also be constructed as 'social anchors' to locate young people in a civil society that is at once moral and purposeful" (Kennedy, 2000). Can schools actually be both of these things? If so, what obstacles must be surmounted first?

6. "We are certain of one thing. We will never move within the bureaucratic structure of new schools, to free schools. That structure was invented to assure domination and control. It will never produce freedom and self-actualisation. The bureaucratic structure is failing in a manner so critical that adaptations will not forestall its collapse. It is impractical. It does not fit the psychological and personal needs of the workforce" (Clark & Meloy, 1990, p. 21). To what extent do you agree with this point of view? If the bureaucratic structure of schooling is failing, why has it survived so long? Are there potential pitfalls in a democratic alternative?

7. To what extent do you believe that charter schools represent a fundamental change in the assumptions and the power structures of public education in the United States? Why do you believe as you do?

8. Explain how charter schools provide a viable option to the "one-size-fits-all" model of traditional public schools.

9. "We must preserve and protect those teachers (and materials) who without fear examine the problems of our society realistically" (Littleford, 1983). Do the ways in which curriculum decisions are made inhibit teachers from openly discussing societal issues? What are the specific reasons on which your opinion is based?

10. "Do schools exist to increase the nation's productivity or for other equally important personal and social goals?" (Passow, 1988, p. 254). What is your point of view about this matter? Why? What does it have to do with curriculum decision making?

■ SUGGESTED READING

Some useful articles (see the chapter bibliography) include the following:

Apple (1991)

Bracey (1996)

Eisner (1990a, 1990b)

Fuhrman & Elmore (1990)

Fullan (2000)

House (1996)

Whitty (2000)

Some useful books (see the chapter bibliography) include the following:

Beyer & Apple (1998)

Fullan (1991)

Jackson (1992)

Klein (1991)

Kliebard (1986)

Walker (1990)

■ BIBLIOGRAPHY

Anderson, J., & Alagurnalai, S. (1997). HTML: The next language of communication for information technology in open learning. *Unicorn, 23*(3), 11–20.

Apple, M. W. (1986). *Teachers and texts.* New York: Routledge & Kegan Paul.

Apple, M. W. (1990a). *Ideology and curriculum* (2nd ed.). New York: Routledge.

Apple, M. W. (1990b). Is there a curriculum voice to reclaim? *Phi Delta Kappan, 71*(7), 526–530.

Apple, M. W. (1991). The politics of curriculum and teaching. *NASSP Bulletin, 75*(532), 39–50.

Berliner, D. C., & Biddle, B. J. (1995). *The manufactured crisis: Myths, fraud, and the attack on America's public schools.* Reading, MA: Addison-Wesley.

Beyer, L. E., & Apple, M. W. (Eds.). (1998). *The curriculum: Problems, politics, and possiblilities* (2nd ed.). Albany: State University of New York Press.

Boyd, W. L. (1994). *National school reform and restructuring: Parallels between Britain and the United States.* Paper presented at the annual conference of the British Educational Management and Administration Society, Manchester.

Boyer, E. L. (1982). *High school: A report on secondary education in America.* New York: Harper & Row.

Bracey, G. W. (1996). International comparisons and the condition of American education. *Educational Researcher, 25*(1), 5–11.

Brooks, M. G. (1991). Centralized curriculum: Effects on the local school level. In M. F. Klein (Ed.), *The politics of curriculum decision-making: Issues in centralizing the curriculum* (pp. 151–166). Albany: State University of New York Press.

Caldwell, B. J. (1998). *Strategic leadership, resource management and effective school reform.* Paper presented at the annual meeting of the American Educational Research Association, San Diego.

Caldwell, B. J., & Spinks, J. M. (1998). *Beyond the self-managing school.* London: Falmer.

Carlson, D. L. (1988). Curriculum planning in the state: The dynamics of control in education. In L. E. Beyer & M. W. Apple (Eds.), *The curriculum: Problems, politics, and possibilities* (pp. 98–118). Albany: State University of New York Press.

Clark, D. L., & Meloy, J. M. (1990). Recanting bureaucracy: A democratic structure for leadership in schools. In A. Lieberman (Ed.), *Schools as collaborative cultures: Creating the future now.* London: Falmer.

Connell, W. F. (1983). Interview. In R. Bates & E. Kynaston (Eds.), *Thinking aloud: Interviews with Australian educators* (p. 306). Melbourne: Deakin University Press.

Cuban, L. (1992). Curriculum stability and change. In P. W. Jackson (Ed.), *Handbook of research on curriculum* (pp. 216–247). New York: Macmillan.

Darling-Hammond, L. (1990). Instructional policy into practice: The power of the bottom over the top. *Education Evaluation and Policy Analysis, 12*(3), 233–241.

Donmoyer, R. (1990). Curriculum, community, and culture: Reflections and pedagogical possibilities. In J. T. Sears & J. D. Marshall (Eds.), *Teaching and thinking about the curriculum* (pp. 154–171). New York: Teachers College Press.

Driscoll, M. P., Dick, W., Johnson, M., & Flynn, J. (1990). *Textbooks in schools: What part do they play in effective instruction?* Paper presented at the annual meeting of the American Educational Research Association, Boston.

Eisner, E. W. (1990a). Creative curriculum development and practice. *Journal of Curriculum and Supervision, 6*(1), 62–73.

Eisner, E. W. (1990b). Who decides what schools teach? *Phi Delta Kappan, 71*(7), 523–525.

Elmore, R., & Sykes, G. (1992). Curriculum policy. In P. W. Jackson (Ed.), *Handbook of research on curriculum* (pp. 185–215). New York: Macmillan.

Franklin, B. M. (1986). *Building the American community.* Lewes, UK: Falmer.

Fuhrman, S., & Elmore, R. (1990). Understanding local control in the wake of state education reform. *Educational Evaluation and Policy Analysis, 12*(1), 82–96.

Fullan, M. G. (1991). *The new meaning of educational change* (2nd ed.). London: Cassell.

Fullan, M. G. (1999). *Change forces: The sequel.* London: Falmer.

Fullan, M. G. (2000). The three stories of education reform. *Phi Delta Kappan, 81*(8), 581–584.

Futoran, G. C., Schofield, J. W., & Eurich-Fulmeret, R. (1995). The Internet as a K-12 educational resource: Emerging issues of information access and freedom. *Computers in Education, 24*(3), 229–236.

Glaser, R. (1991). *Testing and assessment: Past, present, and future.* Unpublished paper, University of Pittsburgh.

Good, T. L. (1996). Educational researchers comment on the education summit and other policy proclamations from 1983–1996. *Educational Researcher, 25*(8), 4–6.

Good, T. L., & Braden, J. S. (2000). Charter schools: Another reform failure or a worthwhile investment? *Phi Delta Kappan, 81*(10), 745–750.

Gresham, A., Hess, F., Maranto, R., & Milliman, S. (2000). Desert bloom: Arizona's free market in education. *Phi Delta Kappan, 81*(10), 751–757.

Griffin, G. A. (1991). Teacher education and curriculum decision making: The issue of teacher professionalism. In M. F. Klein (Ed.), *The politics of curriculum decision-making: Issues in centralizing the curriculum* (pp. 121–150). Albany: State University of New York Press.

Hannay, L. (1990). Canada: School-based curriculum deliberation case study. In C. Marsh, C. Day, L. Hannay, & G. McCutcheon, *Reconceptualizing school-based curriculum development* (pp. 98–121). London: Falmer.

Hargreaves, A., Earl, L., Moore, S., & Manning, S. (2001). *Learning to change: Teaching beyond subjects and standards.* San Francisco: Jossey-Bass.

Hatch, T. (2000). What does it take to break the mould? Rhetoric and reality in new American schools. *Teachers College Record, 102*(3), 561–589.

House, E. R. (1996). A framework for appraising educational reforms. *Educational Researcher, 25*(7), 6–14.

Jackson, P. W. (Ed.). (1992). *Handbook of research on curriculum.* New York: Macmillan.

James, T. (1991). State authority and the politics of educational change. *Review of Educational Research, 17,* 169–223.

Kennedy, K. J. (2000). *Schools for tomorrow.* Paris: OECD/CERI.

Kirst, M. W., & Walker, D. F. (1971). An analysis of curriculum policy-making. *Review of Educational Research, 41*(5), 479–509.

Klein, M. F. (Ed.). (1991). *The politics of curriculum decision-making: Issues in centralizing the curriculum.* Albany: State University of New York Press.

Kliebard, H. M. (1986). *The struggle for the American curriculum, 1893–1958.* Boston: Routledge & Kegan Paul.

Koretz, D. (1994). *National testing: The political process has prevailed.* Paper presented at the annual meeting of the American Educational Research Association, New Orleans.

Lasky, S. (2000). The cultural and emotional politics of teacher-parent interactions. *Teaching and Teacher Education 16,* 843–860.

Lawton, D. (1980). *The politics of the school curriculum.* London: Routledge & Kegan Paul.

Lewis, A. C. (1990). Getting unstuck: Curriculum as a tool of reform. *Phi Delta Kappan, 71*(7), 534–538.

Littleford, M. S. (1983). Censorship, academic freedom, and the public school teacher. *Journal of Curriculum Theorizing, 5,* 3.

Maclure, M., & Walker, B. M. (2000). Disenchanted evenings: The social organization of talk in parent-teacher consultations in UK secondary schools. *British Journal of Sociology of Education, 21*(1), 18–22.

Manning, J. (1982). School boards and the curriculum: A case study. *Curriculum Perspectives, 2*(2), 63–68.

Manno, R. V., Finn, C. E., & Vanourek, G. (2000). Beyond the schoolhouse door. *Phi Delta Kappan, 81*(10), 736–744.

McCarty, D., & Ramsey, C. (1971). *The school managers: Power and conflict in American public education.* Westport, CT: Greenwood.

McChesney, J., & Hertling, E. (2000). The path to comprehensive school reform. *Educational Leadership, 57*(7), 10–15.

McCutcheon, G. (1988). Curriculum and the work of teachers. In L. E. Beyer & M. W. Apple (Eds.), *The curriculum: Problems, politics, and possibilities* (pp. 191–203). Albany: State University of New York Press.

McNeil, L. M. (1990). Reclaiming a voice: American curriculum scholars and the politics of what is taught in schools. *Phi Delta Kappan, 71*(7), 517–518.

Mickelson, R. A. (1999). International business machinations: A case study of corporate involvement in local educational reform. *Teachers College Record, 100*(3), 476–512.

National Commission on Excellence in Education. (1983). *A nation at risk: The imperative for educational reform.* Washington, DC: U.S. Government Printing Office.

Natriello, G. (1996). Diverting attention from conditions in American schools. *Educational Researcher, 25*(8), 7–9.

Ornstein, A. C., & Hunkins, F. (1993). *Curriculum foundations: Principles and theory* (2nd ed.). Boston: Allyn & Bacon.

Passow, A. H. (1988). Whither (or wither)? school reform. *Educational Administration Quarterly, 24*(3), 246–256.

Peters, T. L., & Waterman, R. H. (1982). *In search of excellence.* New York: Harper & Row.

Pipho, C. (1991). Centralized curriculum at the state level. In M. F. Klein (Ed.), *The politics of curriculum decision-making: Issues in centralizing the curriculum* (pp. 67–97). Albany: State University of New York Press.

Schwartz, A. J. (1991). Organizational metaphors, curriculum reform, and local school and district change. In M. F. Klein (Ed.), *The politics of curriculum decision-making: Issues in centralizing the curriculum* (pp. 167–197). Albany: State University of New York Press.

Scott, G. (1999). *Change matters.* Sydney: Allen & Unwin.

Simmons, W., & Resnick, L. (1993). Assessment as the catalyst of school reform. *Educational Leadership, 50*(5), 11–15.

Sizer, T. (1992). *Horace's school.* New York: Houghton Mifflin.

Slavin, R. E. (2001). Putting the school back in school reform. *Educational Leadership, 58*(4), 22–27.

Slavin, R. E., & Madden, N. A. (Eds.). (2001). *One million children: Success for all.* Mahwah, NJ: Lawrence Erlbaum.

Smyth, J., Dow, A., Hattam, R., Reid, A., & Shacklock, G. (2000). *Teachers' work in a globalizing economy.* London: Falmer.

Sosniak, L. A., & Perlman, C. L. (1990). Secondary education by the book. *Journal of Curriculum Studies, 22*(5), 427–442.

Spring, J. (1993). *Conflict of interests: The politics of American education* (2nd ed.). New York: Longman.

Steffy, B. E. (1993). Top-down-bottom-up: Systemic change in Kentucky. *Educational Leadership, 51*(1), 42–44.

Tanner, D., & Tanner, L. N. (1995). *Curriculum development* (3rd ed.). New York: Macmillan.

Task Force on Education for Economic Growth. (1983). *Action for excellence: A comprehensive plan to improve our nation's schools.* Denver: Education Commission of the States.

Third International Mathematics and Science Study. (1996). U.S. National Research Center, Report No. 7. East Lansing, MI: U.S. National Research Center.

Turner, B. S. (1990). Periodization and politics in the postmodern. In B. S. Turner (Ed.), *Theories of modernity and postmodernity.* London: Sage.

U.S. Department of Education. (1991). *America 2000: An education strategy.* (Sourcebook.) Washington, DC: Author.

Walker, D. F. (1990). *Fundamentals of curriculum.* New York: Harcourt Brace Jovanovich.

Wells, A. S. (1999). Charter school reform in California: Does it meet expectations? *Phi Delta Kappan, 80*(4), 305–312.

Wells, A. S., Grutzik, C., Camochan, S., Slayton, J., & Vasudeva, A. (1999). Underlying policy assumptions of charter school reform: The multiple meanings of a movement. *Teachers College Record, 100*(3), 513–535.

Wells, A. S., Lopez, A., Scott, J., & Holme, J. J. (1999). Charter schools as postmodern paradox: Rethinking social stratifications in an age of deregulated choice. *Harvard Educational Review, 69*(2), 172–190.

Whitty, G. (2000). *Schooling and the reproduction of the English middle classes.* Paper presented at the annual meeting of the American Educational Research Association, New Orleans.

Wildy, H., Louden, W., & Robertson, J. (2000). *Using cases for school principal performance standards: Australian and New Zealand experiences.* Paper presented at the annual meeting of the American Educational Research Association, New Orleans.

Zahorchak, G. L., & Boyd, W. L. (1994). *The politics of outcome-based education in Pennsylvania.* Paper presented at the annual conference of the University Council for Educational Administration, Philadelphia.

Glossary

Action research involves teachers as individuals or in groups in investigating and improving their own classrooms, usually through ongoing cycles of planning, implementation, reflection, and revision.

Adaptation refers to teachers modifying a planned curriculum as they implement it.

Artistic approach is a form of curriculum planning introduced by Elliot W. Eisner in which teachers attempt to engage students in perceiving and interpreting meanings as fully as possible.

Assessment is a form of evaluation usually focused on students; it may be based on conventional test scores or include other ways of attempting to discover what students have learned.

Authentic assessment examines student learning in the broadest sense, eliciting multiple data on both what the student has learned and what the student can do.

Autobiographical/biographical theorizing is an approach to creating curricula that focuses on the personal experience of teachers and students.

Change models are descriptions of the process of curriculum development intended to explain and to aid in the implementation of new curricula.

Charter schools are independent public schools of choice, exempt from many state and local regulations, but responsible to the public through a governing body or board.

Commonplaces (in curriculum) are the four major considerations that go into any curriculum decision, namely: teacher, student, subject matter, and milieu.

Comprehensive reform (or whole-school reform) attempts to effect constructive change by considering the school as a cohesive unit and accounting as fully as possible for the relationships among its parts.

Concerns-based adoption model is a description of curriculum development proposed by Hall, Wallace, and Dossett that postulates the concerns of individual teachers as central to the process and predicts how these concerns might change as teachers become increasingly familiar with an innovation.

Conflict models of change use the concept of power and how individuals and groups use power to achieve their ends as the central explanation of curriculum change.

Constructivism is the belief that individuals construct their own meanings; in education, it is consistent with curricula and instruction that encourage students to make decisions about what to study and how.

Criterion-referenced measures in education are indicators of what students have learned interpreted in terms of comparisons with prespecified external standards.

Cultural reproduction is the belief that schools serve mainly to reproduce the inequities that exist in the society at large.

Currere is a term coined by William Pinar to describe the autobiographical process of individuals reflexively examining the course of their own experience.

Curriculum is derived from the Latin term for "the course to be run" and is commonly considered as the course of study of a school; however, it has many other meanings, such as, "An interrelated set of plans and experiences that a student undertakes under the guidance of the school."

Curriculum alignment is the process of matching the content of a curriculum with the tests used in assessing student learning.

Curriculum change is a generic term that can include planned or unplanned changes. It usually refers to changes in written curriculum documents, but it may also refer to changes in teachers' practices or even beliefs.

Curriculum developers are persons with the responsibility for planning, designing, and producing a curriculum, whether it be in the form of a brief document or an elaborate curriculum package.

Curriculum frameworks are official curriculum documents that describe in some detail what is to be taught.

Curriculum models are generic descriptions of curricula used to identify the basic considerations involved in curriculum decisions.

Curriculum packages are coordinated sets of curriculum materials, such as texts, workbooks, teachers guides, laboratory equipment, and reference sources.

Curriculum theories are sets of principles and methods sufficiently worked out and rationalized to provide a guide for creating curricula.

Curriculum theorizing is the ongoing process involved in creating curriculum theories.

Deconstructionism is the effort to expose the contradictions and fallacies embedded within modernity.

Deliberative approach (to curriculum planning) was introduced by Joseph Schwab. It describes the types of reasoning involved, the evidence used, and the interactions among people engaged in planning curricula.

Diagnostic evaluation is the attempt to discover the strengths and weaknesses of students so that increasingly appropriate educational activities can be provided for them.

Diffusion is the unplanned spread of a curriculum to new locales or schools.

Dissemination is the planned spread of a curriculum to new locales or schools, usually through the distribution of information about it.

Educational standards are specific criteria set to determine the relative degrees of success or failure of schools, lessons, curricula, or the like.

Eight-Year Study was a major research project that followed 1,475 matched pairs of students through their high school and college years (from 1933 to 1941) and indicated that students from experimental, progressive secondary schools did as well academically in higher education as students from traditional secondary schools, but were decidedly better off in terms of their personal development. It seemingly demonstrated the value of individual-centered curricula.

Evaluation is the attribution of merit and worth.

Existential and psychoanalytic theorizing is an approach to curriculum that contends people need to be aware of how they as individuals experience the world around them and, thus, of how their decisions about transforming the world are related to their decisions about how to define themselves as individual persons.

External facilitators are persons from outside a school who are called upon because of their special knowledge, skill, experience, or helpfulness in guiding curriculum development. Other titles include "linker," "trainer," and "consultant."

Fidelity of use refers to the adherence by teachers to the details of a planned curriculum as they are implementing it.

Formal assessments are planned, obtrusive activities that gather information, usually about student learning.

Formative evaluation is the collection and the weighing of the merit and worth of appropriate information during the planning and implementation stages of curriculum development.

Gender analysis and feminist pedagogy is an approach to curriculum theorizing that examines and attempts to correct inequities for females that arise in education due to the prevailing assumptions of society about gender and sexuality.

Gender analysis and male identity is an approach to curriculum theorizing that challenges heteronormativity in education by re-examining the taken-for-granted assumptions of society about diversity, sexual identity, childhood, and prejudice.

Generic curriculum development is large-scale curriculum development spanning many states and using large teams of curriculum workers.

Implementation is the process of incorporating a new curriculum into a school or classroom.

Informal assessments are typically continuous and minimally obtrusive activities that gather information, usually about student learning.

Innovation is a generic term used to describe something new and usually intended to be better than what it replaces, as, for instance, a curriculum innovation.

Internet connects a vast number of computers around the world providing easy communication and quick access to virtually unlimited amounts of information.

Merit (in evaluation) is how well done something is, regardless of the worth of doing it in the first place.

Modernity is the social condition characteristic of most developed countries up to the 1960s. In recent decades it has been at least partially supplanted by new, postmodern ways of viewing society.

Mutual adaptation refers to modifications made both to a new, innovative curriculum and to the institutional setting in which it is being implemented.

National curriculum development refers to the creation of new curricula through funding by a federal agency and the involvement of a large team of curriculum specialists and experts.

National goals and standards are aims and expectations for how they should be reached advocated by national groups, such as the federal government or professional associations. Usually, curriculum materials and resources are developed based on these standards.

Norm-referenced measures in education are indicators of what students have learned, interpreted in terms of comparisons among students. Usually students' test scores are compared with scores of other students of the same age or grade level.

Outcome statements are specifications of the levels of achievement students are supposed to reach as the result of a lesson, a curriculum, or some other educational activity.

Performance tasks are work students are assigned to complete, usually in accordance with specific criteria.

Phenomenological theorizing is a process of creating curricula by capturing the lived experience of individuals reflecting on their immediate consciousness of situations.

Portfolios are systematic collections of work created by students; they demonstrate what students have accomplished or learned.

Postcolonialism is an approach to curriculum theorizing that challenges the ideological and material legacies of imperialism and colonialism.

Postmodernism is a social consciousness characterized by a desire to challenge dated modernist assumptions, to question claims to truth, and to develop new ways of thinking.

Poststructuralism is an approach to curriculum theorizing that challenges the view that determinate structures underlie all reality. Thus, a poststructuralist curriculum invites each individual to encounter the indeterminate qualities of living.

Progressive education was a worldwide movement in the early twentieth century. It was strongly influenced by the ideas of John Dewey and emphasized the connections between school and society, the development of intellect through problem-solving, and the qualitative improvement of personal experience. It is the forerunner of many current ideas and methods of education.

Racial theorizing is an emerging approach to curriculum theorizing that brings to bear an interdisciplinary focus on racial inequality in schools and society.

Rational-linear approach is a method of curriculum planning introduced by Ralph W. Tyler. It involves four invariant steps: selecting objectives, selecting learning experiences, organizing learning experiences, and evaluating.

Reconceptualists are, in general, the major group of theorizers who have taken a critical and exploratory approach to curriculum issues and problems since the 1970s.

Reliability (in measurement) refers to how consistently any form of measurement actually measures that which it is supposed to measure.

School-based curriculum development includes the planning, design, implementation, and evaluation of a program for student learning by the educational institution of which those students are members.

School boards are groups of local citizens who are legally charged with administering local school districts.

School indicators are measures used to judge the quality of school programs. They include considerations such as student learning, instructional time, curriculum content, teacher performance, and school conditions and resources.

Self-assessment is the process of individuals (usually students) weighing and valuing the merit and worth of what they have done or accomplished.

Site-based management involves participatory decision making by the entire staff of a school and even members of the community.

Site-specific curriculum development is ordinarily small-scale curriculum development confined to a single school or single school district and undertaken by a small group of curriculum workers.

Social efficiency is the belief that the purpose of education is to fit the individual efficiently into the society as it is.

Social needs (in education) is the belief that the most important task for schools is to discover and to teach those abilities that students most need in order to get along successfully in society.

Social reconstructionists believe the primary role of the school is to change society for the better. The idea of reconstructing implies that change should be planned, not incidental.

Social reproduction is an approach to curriculum theorizing that contends that schools reproduce the work skills and attitudes needed for social relations in the wider society but that this process often reinforces social and economic stratification rather than promoting social mobility.

Standardized tests are uniform assessments of ability or achievement, ideally given under identical conditions in order to measure performance relative to specific criteria or to other people. Their usual form is paper-and-pencil.

Subject matter is the content of the curriculum. Since schools have neither the time nor the resources to teach everything, the basic question about subject matter is what to include and what to exclude.

Summative evaluation is the collection and weighing of the merit and worth of appropriate information following the completion of a program or curriculum. Often the information is valued in terms of the degree to which the program or curriculum has realized its stated objectives; in practice, only rarely are stated objectives themselves questioned.

Validity (in measurement) is the degree to which a test or instrument measures what it is supposed to measure.

Worth (in evaluation) is the attribution of value (either intrinsic value or market value) to something. This attribution may be based on considerations about merit (How well was it done ?) and significance (Was it worth doing in the first place?).

Name Index

Subject Index

Note: Italicized page numbers indicate illustrations.

ISBN 0-13-094512-9